THE ROUGH GUIDE TO

Iceland

written and researched by

David Leffman and James Proctor

**ROUGH
GUIDES**

roughguides.com

Contents

Introduction to
Iceland

Resting on the edge of the Arctic Circle and sitting atop one of the world's most volcanically active hot spots, Iceland is an inspiring mix of magisterial glaciers, bubbling hot springs and rugged fjords, where activities such as hiking under the Midnight Sun are complemented by healthy doses of history and literature.

Iceland is a place where nature reigns supreme. Aside from the modern and cosmopolitan capital, **Reykjavík**, population centres are small, with diminutive towns, fishing villages, farms and minute hamlets clustered along the coastal fringes. The **Interior**, meanwhile, remains totally uninhabited and unmarked by humanity: a starkly beautiful wilderness of ice fields, windswept upland plateaux, infertile lava and ash deserts and the frigid vastness of Vatnajökull, Europe's largest glacier. Iceland's location on the Mid-Atlantic ridge also gives it one of the most volcanically active landscapes on Earth, peppered with everything from naturally occurring hot springs, scaldingly hot bubbling mud pools and noisy steam vents to a string of unpredictably violent **volcanoes**, which have regularly devastated huge parts of the country. The latest events came in 2010, when Eyjafjallajökull erupted and caused havoc across Europe; and in 2015, when the eruption at Holuhraun created a huge new lavafield.

Historically, the **Icelanders** have a mix of Nordic and Celtic blood, a heritage often held responsible for their characteristically laidback approach to life. The battle for survival against the elements over the centuries has also made them a highly self-reliant nation, whose former dependence on the sea and fishing for their economy was virtually total. Having spent years being dismissed as an insignificant outpost in the North Atlantic (Icelanders gave up counting how many times their country was left off maps of Europe), the eruption under Eyjafjallajökull in 2010 saw the tourist industry, at least, wake up to Iceland's potential. Now close on a million foreigners visit annually – three times the national population – and Iceland is on a steep learning curve as it struggles to cope with tourist-driven inflation and sagging infrastructure at popular sights.

ABOVE GULLFOSS **OPPOSITE** HIKERS, GREATER REYKJAVÍK

HIKES AND HOT SPRINGS

In a country whose scenery is so iconic, and whose historical events are inextricably wrapped up with its landscape, the only real way to get to grips with Iceland is to get **outdoors**. It's where many Icelanders choose to spend their free time, too, though they often seem to have a fearless disregard for the weather, geological events and other natural hazards that foreigners take sensible precautions against.

Iceland's **hiking** trails are easy to get to, yet feel wonderfully remote and wild: on some of them it's possible to walk for days and not see anyone. The country is also small enough that it's feasible to simply pick two points on a map and walk between them – assuming, of course, that you're suitably equipped for any natural hazards along the way – though there are also many well-marked trails heading off across the landscape. After a hike, take the plunge in one of Iceland's many naturally heated outdoor "**hot pots**", often in stunningly scenic locations, where you can peel off your clothes and soak any aches away while admiring the surrounding mountains, volcanoes and seascapes. The top three spots for an outdoor soak are Landmannalaugar in southwestern Iceland (see p.119), Grettislaug in the northwest (see p.234) and Krossneslaug in the West Fjords (see p.221). And if you prefer more formal arrangements, just about every settlement across the country has its own geothermally heated swimming pool, too.

ICELANDIC HIKES: SIX OF THE BEST

Laugavegur An epic four-day hike over snowfields, moorland and desert between hot springs at Landmannalaugar and the highland valley of Þórsmörk: see p.120.
Jökulsárgljúfur Straightforward though lengthy trails follow a glacier river canyon down to Europe's largest waterfall: see p.275.
Hornstrandir You can spend days hiking across this totally unpopulated peninsula, which is probably the wildest, most remote corner of Iceland that is still accessible: see p.200.

Þórsmörk Isolated glacier valley in the southwest, covered in dwarf birch and wildflowers, with almost limitless hiking potential: see p.129.
Skaftafell Easily reached moorland plateau between two glaciers, with plenty of well-marked trails of up to a day's duration: see p.315.
Skógar to Þórsmörk Relatively straightforward 25km hike over mountains and snowfields, passing solidified lava from the 2010 eruption: see p.134.

Arctic Circle

Hornbjarg

Hornstrandir

Jökulfirðir

Ísafjarðardjúp

Drangajökull

Bolungarvík
Suðureyri
Flateyri
Ísafjörður
Jökulbunga

Norðurfjörður

Siglufjörður

Skagafjörður

Dýrafjörður

Gjögur

Skagi

Þingeyri
Gláma

Djúpavík

Hofsós

Arnarfjörður

Húnaflói

Tálknafjörður
Bíldudalur
Patreksfjörður

Hólmavík

Skagaströnd

Sauðárkókur

H

Brjánslækur
Látrabjarg

Vatnsfjörður

Reykhólar

Þingeyrar

Blönduós

Flatey

Hrútafjörður

Breiðafjörður

Hvammsfjörður

Hvammstangi

Blanda

Stykkishólmur

Búðardalur

Brú

Hellissandur
Rif
Ólafsvík
Búðir
Grundarfjörður
Snæfellsjökull
Arnarstapi

Hítarvatn

Arnarvatnsheiði

Hveravellir

KJÖLUR

Hofsjö

Bifröst

Langjökull

Kerlingarfjöll

Húsafell

Borgarnes
Reykholt
Skorradals-
vatn

Hvítárvatn

Faxaflói

Borgarfjörður

Akranes

Skjald-
breiður

Geysir

Gullfoss

Þórisva

Hvalfjörður

Þingvellir
Mosfellsbær

Laugarvatn

Hvítá

REYKJAVÍK

Garður
Garðabær
Kópavogur
Sandgerði
Hafnarfjörður
Hafnir
Keflavík
Reykjanestá

Hveragerði

Selfoss
Eyrarbakki
Stokkseyri

Þingvalla-
vatn

Flúðir

Skálholt

Landmanna-
laugar

Hekla

Þjórsá

Grindavík

Þorlákshöfn

Ölfusá

Hella

Hvolsvöllur

Þórsmörk

Eldey

Landeyjarhöfn

Eyjafjallajökull

Mýrdals-
jökull

ATLANTIC OCEAN

Surtsey

Westman Islands
Heimaey

Dyrhólaey

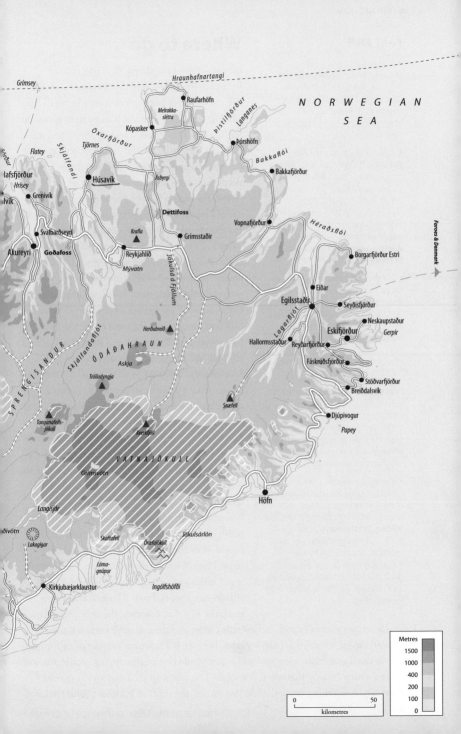

Grímsey

Hraunhafnartangi

NORWEGIAN
SEA

Melrakka-
slétta

Raufarhöfn

Kópasker

Þistilfjörður

Langanes

Þórshöfn

Flatey

Tjörnes

Öxarfjörður

Skjálfandi

Bakkaflói

Húsavík

Ásbyrgi

Bakkafjörður

lafsfjörður

Hrísey

Grenivík

Dettifoss

Ívík

Svalbarðseyri

Krafla

Grímsstaðir

Vopnafjörður

Héraðsflói

Akureyri

Goðafoss

Reykjahlíð

Borgarfjörður Estri

Mývatn

Faroes & Denmark

Jökulsá á Fjöllum

Eiðar

Egilsstaðir

Seyðisfjörður

Herðubreið

Neskaupstaður

ÓDÁÐAHRAUN

Eskifjörður

Gerpir

Skjálfandafljót

Askja

Hallormsstaður

Lagarfljót

Reyðarfjörður

SPRENGISANDUR

Trölladyngja

Fáskrúðsfjörður

Snæfell

Stöðvarfjörður

Tunganafells-
jökull

Breiðdalsvík

Kverkfjöll

Djúpivogur

VATNAJÖKULL

Papey

Grímsvötn

Langisjór

Höfn

öivötn

Lakagígar

Skaftafell

Jökulsárlón

Lómagnúpur

Öræfajökull

Kirkjubæjarklaustur

Ingólfshöfði

Metres	
	1500
	1000
	400
	200
	100
	0

0   50
kilometres

Where to go

Inevitably, most people get their first taste of Iceland in **Reykjavík**, rubbing shoulders with over half the country's population. It may be small, but what Reykjavík lacks in size it more than makes up for in stylish bars, restaurants and shops, and the nightlife is every bit as wild as it's cracked up to be: during the light summer nights, the city barely sleeps. Reykjavík also makes a good base for visiting **Geysir**, the original geyser, the ancient parliament site of **Þingvellir**, spectacular waterfalls at **Gullfoss** and the famous and sublime **Blue Lagoon**.

Beyond Reykjavík, Route 1, the **Ringroad**, runs out to encircle the island, and the wilder side of Iceland soon shows itself – open spaces of vivid green edged by unspoiled coastlines of red and black sands, all set against a backdrop of brooding hills and mountains. The **west coast** is dominated by the towns of **Borgarnes** and **Reykholt**, both strongly associated with the sagas, while the **Snæfellsnes Peninsula**, with views of the monster glacier at its tip, is one of the country's most accessible hiking destinations. Arguably Iceland's most dramatic scenery is found in the far **northwest** of the country, the **West Fjords**, where tiny fishing villages nestle at the foot of table-top mountains. **Ísafjörður** is the only settlement of any size here and makes a good base from which to strike out on foot into the wilderness of the **Hornstrandir Peninsula**. Beautifully located on the north coast, **Akureyri** is rightfully known as the capital of the north and functions as Iceland's second city. With a string of bars and restaurants, it can make a refreshing change from the small villages hereabouts. From Akureyri it's easy to reach the island of **Grímsey**, the only part of

Icelandic territory actually within the **Arctic Circle**; and the country's biggest tourist attraction outside the capital, **Lake Mývatn**. The lake is a favourite nesting place for many species of duck and other waterfowl and is surrounded by an electrifying proliferation of volcanic activity. Nearby **Húsavík** is one of the best places in the country to organize summer whale-watching cruises, while just inland, the wilds of **Jökulsárgljúfur National**

FROM TOP EYJAFJALLAJÖKULL ERUPTING; SEALS AT JÖKULSÁRLÓN

superlative hiking along deep river gorges to the spectacular **Dettifoss**, Europe's most powerful waterfall. Then there are the East Fjords which, despite easy access, remain the least touristed part of Iceland, perhaps because there are no major sights – just plenty of calm, quiet, grand scenery.

South of here, **Höfn** is a good base from which to visit Europe's biggest glacier, the mighty Vatnajökull, either on a skidoo trip or on foot through Skaftafell National Park, while the Jökulsárlón glacial lagoon offers the surreal chance to cruise alongside floating icebergs.

The south coast is marked by vast stretches of black, volcanic coastal sands punctuated by charming villages such as Vík, Iceland's southernmost settlement. Inland are more mighty waterfalls, including Skógarfoss and Seljalandsfoss; the wilderness surrounding Hekla, a highly active volcano which last erupted in 2000; at least one thermal outdoor pool to soak in; and a landscape central to *Njál's Saga*, one of the nation's great, visceral Viking romances. Iceland's most rewarding hiking route can also be found here: the five-day Laugavegur trail between extraordinary hot-springs scenery at Landmannalaugar and the beautiful highland valley of Þórsmörk, worth a visit in its own right. Just a quick ferry ride offshore from all this lies Heimaey, at the heart of the Westman Islands, which

TO WHALE OR NOT TO WHALE

The Icelandic government's decision to resume **commercial whaling** in late 2006 drove a wedge through Icelandic public opinion. Most of the population views whaling as a virtual birthright and is only too keen to turn a nationalistic blind eye to international protest, but it is also true that the nation's burgeoning **tourism industry** has led to a decline in its near-total dependence on the fishing industry. Consequently, promoters of tourism lost no time in pointing out that foreigners have flocked to Iceland in recent years to **watch whales** in their natural habitat, not to see them unceremoniously sliced up for the dinner table – and despite a seeming nonchalance, Icelanders are painfully aware that their tiny country on the very edge of Europe can ill afford any kind of international boycott.

ABOVE WHALE WATCHERS SPOTTING A MINKE WHALE **OPPOSITE CLOCKWISE FROM TOP** FISHERMAN IN TRADITIONAL SEAL-SKIN SUIT; REPLICA VIKING LONGSHIP; SEYÐISFJÖRÐUR

SEXUAL EQUALITY IN ICELAND

Regardless of the tongue-twisting name, Vigdís Finnbogadóttir put Iceland on the map when she became the world's first female president in 1980, high-profile proof of Iceland's approach to **sexual equality**. However, treating women as equals was nothing new in Iceland. Ever since Viking times, when every pair of working hands was required to farm, fish and simply exist in such a harsh climate, the nation's small population base has catapulted women into positions that for centuries were seen solely as a man's preserve in many other countries. Today, things are no different: both women and men often work long hours, fulfilling several roles, to keep the Icelandic economy ticking over. Generous childcare facilities provided by the Icelandic welfare state have also enabled women to re-enter the labour market shortly after having children, and work their way up the career ladder, often to the very top. Even the **Icelandic language** reflects the equal nature of society; there's often no specifically male or female word for a profession – just one term applied to both men and women.

hosts one of the world's largest puffin colonies and carries evidence of a catastrophic eruption during the 1970s which almost saw the island abandoned.

Iceland's barren Interior is best tackled as part of a guided tour – it's much easier to let experienced drivers of all-terrain buses pick their way across lavafields and cross unbridged rivers than to try it yourself. Pick of the options includes a traverse of Sprengisandur, an eye-numbing desert of black sand; Askja, a huge caldera close to the recent Holuhraun eruption site; and Herðubreið, a stark, awe-inspiringly beautiful table-top mountain crowned with ice.

When to go

Icelandic **weather** is notoriously unpredictable. In **summer** there's a fair chance of bright and sunny days, and temperatures can reach 17°C, but good weather is interspersed with wet and misty spells when the temperature can plummet to a chilly 10°C. Most museums and attractions are only open from late May to early September, and it's at these times, too, that buses run their fullest schedules. Although almost all of Iceland lies south of the Arctic Circle and therefore doesn't experience a true **Midnight Sun**, nights are light from mid-May to early August across the country; in the north, the sun never fully sets during June. Between September and January the Aurora Borealis or **Northern Lights** can often be seen throughout the country. In winter temperatures fluctuate at 7–8°C either side of freezing point and daylight is limited to a few hours – in Reykjavík, sunrise isn't until almost 11am in December; the sun is already sinking slowly back towards the horizon after 1pm.

TEMPERATURES AND RAINFALL

The table below shows the average maximum and minimum **temperatures** in Reykjavík, and average **monthly** rainfall.

	Jan	Feb	Mar	Apr	May	Jun	Jul	Aug	Sep	Oct	Nov	Dec
Max/min (°C)	2/-2	3/-2	4/-1	6/1	10/4	12/7	14/9	14/8	11/6	7/3	4/0	2/-2
Rainfall (mm)	89	64	62	56	42	42	50	56	67	94	78	79

OPPOSITE FROM TOP NORTHERN LIGHTS; PUFFIN, FLATEY

Author picks

Our hard-travelling authors visited every corner of Iceland, from the sandy beaches of the south coast to the remote villages of the West Fjords, to bring you some unique travel experiences. These are some of their own personal favourites.

Classic journeys Walking the four-day Laugavegur trail is a great way to see the wilds of Iceland, and for the less adventurous, the views unfolding from high-clearance bus tours across the Interior are just as unmissable. **See p.120 & p.325**

Best beaches The empty, golden strands at Breiðavík in the West Fjords are sublime on a sunny day, and the black volcanic sands near Vík on the south coast are equally compelling. See p.213 & p.136

Look for leviathans Whale watching from Reykjavík, or from Húsavík on the north coast, is a great way to get up close to the giants of the sea. See p.74 & p.274

Northern Lights Thanks to its northerly location, Iceland is a great place from which to see the Aurora Borealis. Take one of the special tours which operate from Reykjavík and prepare to be amazed. **See p.75**

Island idyll Off-the-beaten-track Flatey on the west coast, and Heimaey on the south coast, offer splendid rural scenery aplenty and a rich birdlife to boot. **See p.176 & p.139**

Amazing views There's mountain scenery to blow your mind along any road in the West Fjords, and on the devastated lava plains surrounding the flooded Askja caldera. See p.188 & p.328

Greatest landscapes For mountain backdrops and ready access to real wilderness, Ísafjörður is Iceland at its most alluring, while the highland valley of Þórsmörk offers trees, wildflowers and rugged, glacier-capped hilltops. See p.191 & p.129

Our author recommendations don't end here. We've flagged up our favourite places – a perfectly sited hotel, an atmospheric café, a special restaurant – throughout the Guide, highlighted with the ★ symbol.

21

things not to miss

It's not possible to see everything that Iceland has to offer on a short trip – and we don't suggest you try. What follows is a selective taste of the country's highlights: fantastic scenery, fascinating museums, spectacular buildings and a few ways to simply indulge yourself. All highlights are colour-coded by chapter and have a page reference to take you straight into the Guide, where you can find out more.

6

7

8

11

9 LAKE MÝVATN
Page 260

Mývatn's placid spread of water is a haven for wildfowl, while the lake's surrounds abound in volcanic formations, both extinct and highly active.

10 THE INTERIOR
Page 322

A trip into the desolate, uninhabited Interior is an unmissable opportunity to see the raw side of Iceland.

11 ÞÓRSMÖRK NATIONAL PARK
Page 129

Hike 25km over the mountains between Þórsmörk and Skógar, right past the steaming site of the 2010 volcanic eruption at Eyjafjallajökull.

12 BREIÐAVÍK
Page 213

This sweeping stretch of golden sand and turquoise water is Iceland's most beautiful beach.

12

13 THE SETTLEMENT EXHIBITION
Page 58
Travel back in time to the year 871 and see the remarkable remains of one of Reykjavík's earliest houses.

14 GEYSIR
Page 108
See Strokkur erupting at Geysir, after which all geysers are named.

15 ÞINGVELLIR NATIONAL PARK
Page 101
The dramatic site of Iceland's first parliament, set in a mighty rift valley where the Eurasian and American continental plates are slowly tearing apart.

16 WEST FJORDS
Page 188
Remote, forbidding yet totally compelling, the West Fjords are Iceland at its most scenically amazing.

14

15

16

17 THE PHALLOLOGICAL MUSEUM, REYKJAVÍK
Page 68
A chance to size up Iceland's most offbeat museum, containing the penises of both Icelandic man and beast.

18 WHALE WATCHING
Pages 74 & 274
Get up close to minke and humpback whales on a whale-watching tour from Reykjavík or Húsavík.

19 SKAFTAFELL NATIONAL PARK
Page 315
Skaftafell's blend of highland plateau, summer meadows and ice-blue glaciers is best explored by hiking, biking or climbing.

20 HALLGRÍMSKIRKJA
Page 67
Reykjavík's best-known landmark, the striking Hallgrímskirkja offers unsurpassed views of the capital from its tower.

21 DETTIFOSS
Page 278
Deep inside Jökulsárgljúfur National Park, encounter nature in the raw at Europe's most powerful waterfall.

17

18

19

Itineraries

Iceland's difficult terrain takes time to negotiate, and you can't cover the country in a single trip. Our Grand Tour concentrates on Iceland's main sights, while our other suggested routes focus on two fascinating regions, the island's west and north, and the south and east.

GRAND TOUR OF ICELAND

Two weeks in Iceland and no idea where to start? Our Grand Tour puts you on the right track.

❶ **Reykjavík** Though one of Europe's smaller capitals, the vibrant heart of Iceland offers everything from style-conscious bars and restaurants to great museums and galleries. **See p.50**

❷ **Blue Lagoon** Take a dip in the sublime waters of this famous open-air swimming pool, fed by geothermal water and set in the middle of a lavafield. **See p.95**

❸ **Golden Circle** See Þingvellir, site of Iceland's original open-air parliament, hot waterspouts at Geysir, and a stunning two-tier waterfall at Gullfoss. **See p.101**

❹ **Akureyri** Chill on the north coast in Iceland's second-largest town, renowned for its sunny summer days and thriving bar and restaurant scene. **See p.244**

❺ **Húsavík** Whale watching is on everybody's list of must-dos in Iceland, and the expertly run tours from Húsavík offer virtually guaranteed sightings. **See p.274**

❻ **Lake Mývatn** A proliferation of geological oddities, from bubbling mud pools to steam vents, clustered around a beautiful lake teeming with birdlife. **See p.260**

❼ **Dettifoss** Europe's largest waterfall plunges over bare granite into a deep, sunless chasm on the edge of the Interior. **See p.278**

❽ **The Interior** Venture into Iceland's uninhabited Interior to witness some truly awe-inspiring scenery: from glaciers to lava deserts, the views are jaw-dropping. **See p.322**

❾ **Heimaey** A steaming volcano cone, grassy clifftop walks and abundant wildlife make this small, self-contained island community an essential overnight stopover. **See p.139**

THE BEST OF THE WEST AND NORTH

This one-week tour guides you through the best destinations between Reykjavík and Akureyri, including a detour into the West Fjords.

❶ **Borgarnes** Step into Iceland's stirring past at the Settlement Centre and learn more about the country's Saga heroes. **See p.154**

❷ **Stykkishólmur** Skim across the waters of Breiðafjörður in a rigid inflatable, checking out the myriad islands and rich birdlife in this part of the west. **See p.170**

❸ **Flatey** A night on this idyllic island provides a taste of rural Iceland: stroll through flower meadows down to the shore to watch the thousands of birds that call Flatey home. **See p.176**

❹ Ísafjörður Explore the West Fjords' most agreeable town, and try a spot of sea kayaking too. **See p.191**

❺ Ósar The place to get up close to entire colonies of seals, lolling on the black volcanic sands. **See p.229**

❻ Hofsós Take a restorative swim in the new oceanside pool and drink in the extraordinary coastal vistas. **See p.236**

❼ Akureyri Iceland's second town offers a profusion of bars and restaurants, and the beautiful surroundings in Eyjafjörður are perfect for exploring on horseback. **See p.244**

THE SOUTH AND EAST

A one-week tour from Reykjavík to Mývatn via the south and east coasts, with an excursion into the fringes of the Interior.

❶ Borgarfjöður Eystri This tiny, isolated community has plenty of puffins, hiking trails and spiky mountains to investigate – you might even spot a Greenland shark being landed at the harbour. **See p.297**

❷ Papey Spot seals, razorbills and puffins on this half-day outing to a tiny islet, once home to reclusive monks. **See p.308**

❸ Jökulsárlón Glacial lagoon just above a black-sand beach, where you can cruise between powder-blue icebergs as they shear off the front of the ice sheet. **See p.314**

❹ Skaftafell Waterfalls, glaciers, peaks, moorland and almost unlimited hiking potential at this popular national park. **See p.315**

❺ Vík Pleasant village near Iceland's southernmost point, with bracing sea breezes, black-sand beaches and some easy scenic walking trails. **See p.136**

❻ Þórsmörk Camp and hike at this isolated highland valley, thick with summer wildflowers and hemmed in by spectacular peaks and glaciers. **See p.129**

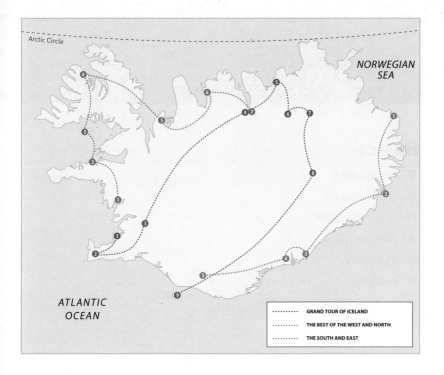

Arctic Circle

NORWEGIAN SEA

ATLANTIC OCEAN

.... GRAND TOUR OF ICELAND
.... THE BEST OF THE WEST AND NORTH
.... THE SOUTH AND EAST

THE ROAD TO SKAFTAFELL NATIONAL PARK

Basics

Getting there

Iceland's Keflavík International Airport, about 40km west of Reykjavík, is connected by an ever-increasing quantity of flights to Europe, the UK, Scandinavia, the US and Canada. It's also possible to reach Iceland year-round by sea via the Faroese superferry Norröna, which performs a regular crossing of the North Atlantic.

Airfares always depend on the **season**, with the highest being around June to August, when the weather is best; fares drop during the "shoulder" seasons – September to November and April to June – and you'll get the best prices during the low season, November to March (excluding Christmas and New Year).

An all-inclusive **package tour** can sometimes turn out to be the cheapest way of doing things. Deals range from a weekend city-break to Reykjavík and its surrounds to all-singing, all-dancing adventure holidays involving snowmobiling across Vatnajökull and whale watching in Húsavík. Check the specialist tour operator websites (p.28).

The cheapest **airfare deals** are always available online, either direct through the airline website or via a discount travel website.

Flights from the UK and Ireland

The cheapest deals from the UK are with **WOW** from London Gatwick (from £100 return) and easyJet from London (£120), Bristol (£120), Manchester (£70) and Edinburgh (£160).

Icelandair flies daily to Keflavík from London Heathrow, Birmingham, Manchester and Glasgow. Return fares from London Heathrow start at £200, whereas from Birmingham, Glasgow and Manchester they cost from £150.

The only direct flights between **Ireland** and Iceland are from Dublin with WOW (from €200); otherwise you'll need to travel via mainland Britain with Aer Lingus or discount masters Ryanair, and then pick up a connecting flight to Keflavík.

Flights from the US and Canada

Icelandair flies out of many cities across the US and Canada. The **frequency** – and cost – is reduced during the winter months; schedules change each year, depending on demand, and some routes are suspended altogether. Broadly speaking, you're looking at fares upwards of US$1500 return from the western US, or US$500 return from the eastern US or Canada. Budget airline WOW also fly from Boston or Washington DC from US$500 return.

Flights from Australia, New Zealand and South Africa

There are **no direct flights** to Iceland from Australia, New Zealand or South Africa, so you'll need to find a discounted airfare to somewhere that does – such as London – and arrange a flight to Reykjavík from there.

All return airfares to London **from Australian East-Coast gateways** are similarly priced, with the cheapest deals via Asia costing around AU$2000/2400/2800 (low, medium or high season). From Perth or Darwin, scheduled flights via Asia cost AU$110–220 less than if departing from eastern gateways, while flights via the US cost around AU$400 more. **From New Zealand** you can fly from Auckland to London via mainland US or Asia for NZ$2600/2900/3200. From Wellington and Christchurch all options cost NZ$200–300 more. To get to London **from South Africa**, count on around 6000/6400/6800 ZAR for a Cape Town–London return.

Airlines, agents and operators

AIRLINES

Aer Lingus Ⓦ aerlingus.com
Air China Ⓦ airchina.com
Air France Ⓦ airfrance.com
Air New Zealand Ⓦ airnz.co.nz
British Airways Ⓦ ba.com
Cathay Pacific Ⓦ cathaypacific.com
China Eastern Ⓦ flychinaeastern.com
easyJet Ⓦ easyjet.com

A BETTER KIND OF TRAVEL

At Rough Guides we are passionately committed to travel. We believe it helps us understand the world we live in and the people we share it with – and of course tourism is vital to many developing economies. But the scale of modern tourism has also damaged some places irreparably, and climate change is accelerated by most forms of transport, especially flying. All Rough Guides' flights are carbon-offset, and every year we donate money to a variety of environmental charities.

Emirates W emirates.com
Icelandair W icelandair.com
KLM W klm.com
Lufthansa W lufthansa.com
Malaysia Airlines W malaysiaairlines.com
Norwegian W norwegian.com
Qantas W qantas.com.au
Ryanair W ryanair.com
SAS W flysas.com
Singapore Airlines W singaporeair.com
Thai Airways W thaiairways.com
Virgin Atlantic Airways W virginatlantic.com
WOW W wowair.com

SPECIALIST AGENTS AND TOUR OPERATORS

50°N Australia W fiftydegreesnorth.com. Nordic specialist offering trekking, cycling and Northern Lights tours.

Activity Iceland W activityiceland.is, W buggy.is. Interior adventures by 4WD or ATV quad bikes.

Bentours Australia W bentours.com.au. Handles Icelandair ticket sales; also offers fly/drive and seven-day Iceland packages.

Borton Overseas US W bortonoverseas.com. Adventure-vacation specialists, offering a variety of Iceland tours with biking, hiking and rafting activities, plus farm and cabin stays.

Cave.is W cave.is. Lava tubes and cave tours around Reykjavík.

Discover the World UK W discover-the-world.co.uk. Well-established Nordic holiday specialist, with groups led by naturalists to Iceland, plus city breaks, fly/drive holidays and independent travel.

Explore UK W explore.co.uk. Cruises, small-group tours and super-jeep expeditions.

Extreme Iceland W extremeiceland.is. Hiking, caving and glacier-climbing packages.

Gray Line W grayline.is. Golden Circle, Blue Lagoon and other tours around southern Iceland.

Iceland Adventure US W icelandadventure.com. Small escorted tours to Iceland, including rafting and horseriding holidays.

Iceland Saga Tours US W reykjaviktours.com. Specializes in short breaks to the Icelandic capital including trips out to the Golden Circle attractions and the Blue Lagoon.

Macs Adventure UK & US W macsadventure.com. Self-guided walking and cycling holidays, including the classic Laugavegur trek.

Nordic Experience UK W nordicexperience.co.uk. Good deals on city breaks and fly/drive holidays.

Nordic Travel Australia W nordictravel.com.au. This long-established operator can book you onto pre-existing tours within Iceland or tailor special-interest packages – from driving, hiking or cycling around the highlights to snowmobiling across Vatnajökull.

Nordic Visitor W nordicvisitor.com. Reykjavík-based operator able to organize self-drive packages, guided hikes, and all manner of specialist and personalized tours.

North South Travel UK W northsouthtravel.co.uk. Competitive travel agency, whose profits are used to support projects in the developing world, especially in sustainable tourism.

Regent Holidays UK W regent-holidays.co.uk. Good package operator specializing in Iceland and Greenland.

Scanam World Tours US W scanamtours.com. Group and individual tours and cruises, plus cheap weekend breaks.

STA Travel US W statravel.com, UK W statravel.co.uk, Australia W statravel.com.au, New Zealand W statravel.co.nz, South Africa W statravel.co.za. Worldwide specialists in independent travel; also student IDs, travel insurance, car rental and more.

Taber Holidays UK W taberhols.co.uk. With over forty years' experience, this company specializes in regional tours of Iceland as well as city breaks to Reykjavík.

Trailfinders UK, Ireland and Australia W trailfinders.com. One of the best-informed and most efficient agents for independent travellers.

Travel CUTS Canada W travelcuts.com. Canadian youth and student travel firm.

TREX W trex.is. Coach charters and tours for sightseeing and trekking around Iceland. Also operates summer bus to Landmannalaugar and Þórsmörk.

USIT Ireland W usit.ie. Ireland's main student and youth travel specialists.

Getting around

Iceland's small scale makes getting around fairly straightforward – at least during the warmer months. From Reykjavík, it's possible to fly or catch a

THE NORRÖNA FERRY

It's possible to travel by sea to Iceland aboard the luxurious **Norröna ferry** (W smyril-line.com), but you'll need a cast-iron stomach – the gales, storms and colossal swell of the North Atlantic will quash any romantic images of following the Vikings' sea-road. One huge advantage, however, is that you can bring your own vehicle into Iceland this way (see p.30).

The ferry departs once a week, year-round, from **Hirtshals** in Denmark, travelling via **Tórshavn** in the Faroe Islands to Seyðisfjörður, in Iceland's East Fjords. Facilities include en-suite cabins, a swimming pool, a shopping arcade and even a fitness centre.

High season (mid-June through to late August) one-way fares from Denmark to Seyðisfjörður are €427 per person for one vehicle and two people sleeping in a couchette; a private cabin costs €574 per person.

bus to all major centres, and in summer there are even scheduled buses through the Interior. In winter, however, reduced bus services and difficult road conditions might make flying the only practical way to travel. It's also easy enough to rent cars, camper vans or four-wheel-drives, though those on a budget will find cycling a cheaper alternative.

On the ground, you'll probably spend a good deal of time on Route 1, or the **Ringroad** (known in Icelandic as the *Hringbraut*), which largely follows the coast in a 1500km circuit of the country via Reykjavík, Akureyri, Egilsstaðir and Höfn. Virtually the entire Ringroad is sealed, and in winter snowploughs do their best to keep the route open to all vehicles.

Elsewhere, while stretches around towns might be surfaced, the majority of Icelandic roads are **gravel**. While many of these are accessible to all vehicles, some – such as most **roads through the Interior** – are only negotiable in high-clearance four-wheel-drives.

By air

Flying in Iceland is good value: the cheapest single **airfare** from Reykjavík to Egilsstaðir, for instance, is 10,500kr, far less than the cheapest bus fare for the same journey – and takes just one hour instead of two days. As an added bonus, you'll get a different take on Iceland's unique landscape from above – flying over Vatnajökull's vast expanse of ice is about the only way to get a grasp of its scale.

The main **domestic airline** is **Flugfélag Íslands** (W airiceland.is), which flies all year from Reykjavík to Akureyri (from 13,500kr), Egilsstaðir (15,500kr), the Westman Islands (15,500kr) and Ísafjörður (10,500kr), with connections between April and October to Grímsey (9700kr), Vopnafjörður (19,200kr) and Þórshöfn (19,200kr). Their various **ticket types** are Full Flex, which are the most expensive; Semi Flex, which are twenty percent cheaper; and various Net fares, which are cheaper again but can't be altered.

Their competition is **Eagle Air** (W eagleair.is), flying from Reykjavík to the Westman Islands (from 13,000kr), Höfn/Hornafjörður (16,500kr) and Húsavík (16,000kr); again, there's a three-tier pricing system depending on how much flexibility you need.

Note that bad weather can cause cancellations at short notice and that it's best to book well ahead for summer weekends and holidays. **Luggage allowance** is 20kg, and you need to **check in** thirty minutes before departure.

By bus

Four **bus companies** provide regular long-distance services around Iceland. Three are based in Reykjavík: **Reykjavík Excursions** (W re.is), at the BSÍ terminal; **Sterna** (W sternatravel.com), at the Harpa Concert Hall; and the long-distance arm of Reykjavík's city bus operator, **Strætó** (W straeto.is), whose terminal is 5km south of the city centre at Mjódd. **SBA-Norðurleið** (W sba.is), which shares some routes with Sterna, is based in Akureyri. Between them, these companies cover the entire Ringroad, the West Fjords, local routes in the northeast and summer-only tracks across the Interior – including many places you could otherwise only reach in your own four-wheel-drive. A fifth operator, **Trex** (W trex.is), runs summer-only transfers between Reykjavík and Þórsmörk.

Bus travel is convenient but expensive: one-way **fares from Reykjavík** are 15,500kr to Akureyri; 11,000kr to Höfn; and around 25,000kr to Egilsstaðir. In purely point-to-point terms it costs less to fly, and if you can get a group together, car rental might work out cheaper, depending on how far you're going and for how long. Between October and June, the range of buses is also greatly reduced: Interior roads close, local services dry up, and even along the Ringroad there is no single bus service between Egilsstaðir and Höfn.

Bookings for main-road services can be made online or at the various terminals, though they're not really necessary as you can always pay on board, and extra buses are laid on if more than one busload of passengers turns up. Buses into the Interior, or local tours, will require advance booking, however.

Bus tours and buses through the Interior

Many of the bus companies also run **tours**, from year-round excursions along the Golden Circle to explorations of the Interior in summer. Though most tours only last a single day, you can get off along the way to camp or make use of mountain huts, and pick up a later bus – let the company know your plans in advance so a space can be

> ### BUS SCHEDULES
> Unless otherwise stated, **bus schedules** given throughout the Guide are for summer only, approximately June to mid-September. Winter timetables can vary considerably, so always check with the relevant bus company websites outside these months.

reserved for you. Make sure, too, that you know when the next bus is due.

Interior routes covered by bus tours include the **Fjallabak route from Landmannalaugar to Skafatafell** via Eldgjá's wild gorge system; and trips across the country to Mývatn either via the impressively barren **Sprengisandur route** or the easier and slightly more scenic **Kjölur route**. Local tours tackle the trip to the mighty **Askja** caldera south of Mývatn; and **Lakagígar**, site of a massive eighteenth-century eruption in the south of the country.

By car

Driving around Iceland allows far greater flexibility than taking the bus. **Car rental** is expensive for solo travellers but can work out a reasonable deal in a group, and it's also possible to **bring your own vehicle** into the country by ferry from Denmark (see p.31). UK, US, Canadian, Australian and New Zealand **driving licences** are all valid for short-term visits.

In summer you don't necessarily need a **four-wheel-drive** to experience the heart of the country, when both the Kjölur (Route 35) and the Kaldidalur (Route 550) open up to carefully driven conventional vehicles; these roads, however, are still very rough, and rental agencies do not allow their cars to be driven along them. Four-wheel-drive is essential for other Interior routes, most often because of sticky sand and numerous rivers (again, note that rental agencies – and their insurance companies – will not cover you for accidents at river crossings). Whatever you're driving, and wherever you are, note that you must not pull off the road or track, apart from at designated passing places or car parks: aside from the often unstable verges, you can cause serious erosion damage.

Fuel pumps are almost always automated: you pay at the pump using your credit/debit card with PIN. If you don't have a credit/debit card, buy a **dedicated card** for a particular brand of station (N1 is probably the most widespread). Fuel currently **costs** 225kr per litre for standard unleaded petrol (95 Octane, or *blýlaust*).

Car rental

Car-rental agencies, offering everything from small economical runarounds to camper vans, motor homes and gas-guzzling four-wheel-drives, are found in settlements across Iceland, though in smaller places the selection will be limited. Rental rates are highest June–August; book ahead and online for the best deals.

Rental options boil down to two types: a **daily rate** which covers the first 100km, after which you pay per additional kilometre; or an **all-inclusive rate** with unlimited mileage. **Add-on fees** insure against windscreen damage, gravel damage, and how much of the **CDW** (Collision Damage Waiver) you'll be liable for; altogether, these can sometimes double the daily rental cost. **One-way rental** (picking up the car in Reykjavík and leaving it in Akureyri, for instance) attracts an additional relocation fee. Also note that many agencies will lean on you to take out cover for **windscreen damage** (worth considering) and ash protection (which you really shouldn't need). Beware of washing a dirty car down before returning it, as grit and gravel can scratch the paintwork as you scrub away – better let the agency handle things.

Including CDW and unlimited kilometres, peak season (June–August) **prices** for a small sedan such as a Toyota Yaris start around 9,000kr per day. For a four-wheel-drive, you're looking at upwards of 20,000kr per day, plus heavy fuel consumption. **Camper vans** – while 25,000kr and up per day – do at least help you save money on accommodation. Expect thirty percent discounts if renting outside the peak season (Sept–May).

BUS PASSPORTS

Bus Passports – open tickets allowing you unrestricted travel on certain routes – are currently offered by Reykjavík Excursions (🅦 re.is) and Sterna (🅦 sterna.is), and are a lot cheaper than paying for the same fares as you go. They're only available through the summer and are subject to roads being open.

   Reykjavík Excursions' seven options range from their Hiking Passport (12,500kr), covering a return trip to Landmannalaugar and Skógar, to the Circle (42,000kr), which lets you orbit the country in either direction along the Ringroad, though you're not allowed to double back on your route; and the Combo, which covers the Ringroad and Interior routes but is valid between 7 days (58,000kr) and 15 days (91,500kr). **Sterna's** offerings cover a similar Hiking option (12,300kr), the Full Circle around the country via the Ringroad (35,100kr), and an East Circle via Kjölur (41,600kr).

CAR-RENTAL AGENCIES IN ICELAND

Avis Ⓦ avis.is
Budget Ⓦ budget.is
Caravan Ⓦ caravan.is
Car Rental Iceland Ⓦ carrentaliceland.is
Europcar Ⓦ europcar.is
Geysir Ⓦ geysir.is
Hasso Ⓦ hasso.is
Happy Campers Ⓦ happycampers.is
Hertz Ⓦ hertz.is
Kúkú Campers Ⓦ kukucampers.is
National Ⓦ nationalcar.is
Saga Ⓦ sagacarrental.is
Sixt Ⓦ sixt.is

Bringing your own vehicle

The *Norröna* vehicle ferry from Denmark to Seyðisfjörður in the East Fjords (see p.28) makes **bringing your own vehicle** into Iceland fairly straightforward, though obviously you have to get it to Denmark first. Assuming you have been living outside Iceland for the previous twelve months, you're allowed to import the vehicle and 200 litres of fuel (in fuel tanks, not jerry cans) duty free for up to one year starting from the date of entry. You'll need to produce proof that the vehicle is registered or rented by you, and has third-party insurance. Overstay and you'll be liable to full import duties on the vehicle.

Driving regulations and road conditions

Icelanders have a cavalier attitude to **driving** in conditions that most other people would baulk at – they have to, or would probably never get behind the wheel – and take dirt tracks and frozen twisting mountain roads very much in their stride. There's a national tendency not to use indicators, and to gravitate towards the road's centre. Low-volume traffic makes for few problems, though an increasing number of visitors have been involved in accidents caused by poor weather and road conditions – know your own abilities and the limits of your vehicle.

Cars are left-hand drives and you **drive on the right**. The **speed limit** is 50km an hour in built-up areas, 90km an hour on surfaced roads, and 80km an hour on gravel. **Seat belts** are compulsory for all passengers, and **headlights** must be on at least half-beam all the time.

Roadsigns you'll soon become familiar with – even if you stick to the Ringroad – are "Einbreið bru", indicating a single-lane bridge sometimes also marked by flashing yellow beacons; and "Malbik endar", marking the end of a surfaced road. **Bright orange signs** marked "Varuð" or "Hætta" (warning or

hazard) alert you to temporary local problems, such as roadworks, ground-nesting birds on the road ("fuglar á vegi") or **sandstorms**.

Other common problems include having other vehicles spray you with windscreen-cracking **gravel** as they pass – slow down and pull over as far as possible to minimize this, especially on unsurfaced roads. Most fields are unfenced so always beware of **livestock** wandering about. When there's snow – though you'd be unlucky to come across much around the Ringroad during the summer – you'll find that the road's edges are marked by evenly spaced yellow poles; stay within their boundaries. **Avoid skidding** on gravel or snow by applying the brakes slowly and as little as possible; use gears instead. **In winter**, everyone fits studded snow tyres to their cars to increase traction, so make sure any vehicle you rent has them too. Pack a good blanket or sleeping bag in case your car gets stuck in snow, and always carry food and water.

Rough roads and four-wheel-driving

Iceland's Interior routes, plus some shorter gravel tracks off the Ringroad, can be really rough, even if not requiring four-wheel-drive. **Four-wheel-drive-only roads** – on which you may encounter stretches of sand, boulders, ice or river crossings – are designated with an "F" on road maps (for instance, the Sprengisandur route is F26), and it's illegal to drive conventional vehicles along them.

Precautions for four-wheel-drivers include never tackling roads alone; being properly equipped with all rescue gear and tools (and knowing in advance how to use them); and always carrying more than enough fuel, food and water. Leave your details with **Safe Travel** (see box, p.32) or tell someone reliable where you're going and when you'll be back, so that a rescue can be mounted if you don't show – but don't forget to contact them when you do get back safely. You'll also need **advance information** on road and weather conditions (see box, p.33).

INTERIOR ROAD DATES

Interior roads only open between June and September each year. But the exact dates depend on weather conditions; after the long winter of 2014/15, many opened a month later than usual. Be aware that, as bus travel through the Interior is entirely dependent on the **roads being open**, advertised services can be cancelled in bad weather.

Vehicles easily **bog down** in snow, mud or soft sand, and if that happens it is vital to maintain **forward momentum**: while you're still moving forward, resist the temptation to change gear, as you'll lose your impetus by doing so. If you do stop moving forward, spinning wheels will quickly dig the vehicle in, so take your foot off the accelerator immediately. Hopefully you'll be able to reverse out – otherwise, start digging. Reducing tyre pressure to around 10psi increases traction on soft surfaces, but you'll need to pump tyres up again once you're back on harder surfaces.

Rivers are potentially very dangerous – many people have drowned in their cars in the Interior. They come in two types: **spring-fed rivers** have a constant flow, while **glacial rivers** fluctuate considerably depending on the time of day and prevailing weather conditions. These are at their lowest during the early morning and after a dry spell of weather; conversely, they can be much deeper in the afternoon once the sun has melted the glacial ice that feeds them, or when it's raining. Some rivers are bridged but many are not; **fords** are marked with a "V" on maps. You need to assess the depth and speed of the river first to find the best crossing point – never blindly follow other vehicle tracks, in case the crossing conditions have changed – and to wear a **lifejacket** and tie yourself to a lifeline when entering the river to check its depth. If the water is going to come more than halfway up the wheels, slacken off the fan belt, block the engine's air intake and waterproof electrics before crossing. Be sure to engage a low gear and four-wheel-drive before entering the water at a slow, steady pace; once in, don't stop (you'll either start sinking into the riverbed or get swept away), or change gear (which

lets water into the clutch). If you stall mid-stream in deep water, turn off the ignition immediately and disconnect the battery, use a winch to pull the vehicle out, and don't restart until you've ensured that water hasn't entered the engine through the air filter – which will destroy the engine.

Cycling

Bad roads, steep gradients and unpredictable weather don't make Iceland an obvious choice for a **cycling** holiday, but there are plenty of people who come here each summer just to pedal around. If you're properly equipped, it's a great way to see the country close-up – you'll also save plenty of money over other forms of transport.

You'll need a solid, 18- or 24-speed **mountain bike** with chunky tyres. You can **rent** these from various agents in Iceland for around 4000kr a day. If you're **bringing your own bike** to Iceland by plane, or getting it from one end of the country to the other by air, you'll need to have the handlebars and pedals turned in, the front wheel removed and strapped to the back, and the tyres deflated.

There are bike shops in Reykjavík, Akureyri and a couple of the larger towns, but otherwise you'll have to provide all **spares** and carry out **repairs** yourself, or find a garage to help. Remember that there are plenty of areas, even on the Ringroad, where assistance may be several days' walk away, and that dust, sand, mud and water will place abnormal strains on your bike. You'll definitely suffer a few **punctures**, so bring a repair kit, spare tyre and tubes, along with the relevant tools, spare brake pads, spokes, chain links and cables.

Around the coast you shouldn't need excessively warm **clothing** – a sweater and waterproof in addition to your normal gear should be fine – but make sure it's all quick-drying. If travelling through the Interior, weatherproof jackets, leggings, gloves and headwear, plus ample warm clothing, are essential. Thick-soled neoprene **surf boots** will save cutting your feet on rocks during river crossings.

It's not unfeasible to cover around 90km a day on paved stretches of the Ringroad, but elsewhere the same distance might take three days and conditions may be so bad that you walk more than you ride. Give yourself four weeks to circuit the Ringroad at an easy pace – this would average around 50km a day. Make sure you've worked out how far it is to the next store before passing up the chance to buy **food**, and don't get caught out by supermarkets' short weekend hours (see p.45). **Off-road cycling** is prohibited in order to protect the landscape, so stick to the tracks.

SAFE TRAVEL

If you're planning to hike, cycle or drive into Iceland's remoter corners, sign up first with ⓦ **safetravel.is**. The website provides alerts for hiking trail and highland road conditions, plus advice on how to prepare for your trip, and allows you to leave a travel plan and contact information with them, which will be followed up if you fail to report back at the appointed time.

Call 112 in case of an **emergency**. For those with smartphones, there's also a free **112 Iceland app** available which, when activated, transmits your location and nominated contact information to the Rescue Services.

If it all gets too much, put your bike on a **bus** for 3500kr. If there's space, bikes go in the luggage compartment; otherwise they are tied to the roof or back. Either way, protect your bike by wrapping and padding it if possible.

For help in planning your trip – but not bike rental – contact the **Icelandic Mountain Bike Club** (Íslenski Fjallahjólaklúbburinn, or ÍFHK; Ⓦ fjallahjolaklubburinn .is), which organizes club weekends and has heaps of advice for cyclists. You can download most of the latter and contact members through the website, which has English text.

Hitching

Hitching around Iceland is possible if you have plenty of time. Expect less traffic the further you go from Reykjavík, though you're unlikely to have to wait too long for the next vehicle if you stick to the Ringroad. In the past, hitchers were rare and often the first car would stop; nowadays, Icelanders have become hardened to the sight of foreigners thumbing lifts, and you certainly shouldn't take rides for granted.

Though Iceland is probably a safer place to hitch than elsewhere in Europe, Australia or the US, it still carries **inherent risks**. If you must hitch, never do so alone and remember that you don't have to get in just because someone stops. Given the wide gaps between settlements, it will probably be obvious where you are heading for, but always ask the driver where they are going rather than saying where it is you want to go.

The best places to **line up lifts** are at campsites or hostels; many hostels advertise available car space on their noticeboards. It's also worth checking out the **national car-sharing website**, Ⓦ samferda.net, to see if anyone in the town you're in is going your way.

Tours

Everywhere you go in Iceland you'll find **tours** on offer, ranging from whale-watching cruises, hikes, pony treks and snowmobile trips across southern glaciers to bus safaris covering historic sites, Interior deserts, hot springs and volcanoes or even sightseeing flights over lakes and islands. Some routes – like the popular Golden Circle via Þingvellir, Geysir and Gullfoss – you can also do independently easily enough, but in other cases you'll find that tours are the only practical way to reach somewhere.

Tours can last anything from a couple of hours to several days, with the widest range offered

---

WEATHER AND ROAD WEBSITES

English-language weather forecasts can be found at Ⓦ en.vedur.is, which predicts conditions over the forthcoming week. Ⓦ vegag.is shows continually updated road maps, with routes colour-coded according to their condition, along with views from roadside web-cams and information on safe driving in Iceland.

---

between June and September. **Booking in advance** is always a good idea; **details of tours** and operators are given throughout the Guide. In winter – which as far as tourism is concerned lasts from October to May – many operators close completely, and those that remain open concentrate on Northern Lights, four-wheel-driving and glacier exploration along the fringes of the southern ice caps, as the Interior itself is definitely off-limits by then. While bigger agents in Reykjavík offer trips almost daily in winter, don't expect to be able to just turn up at a small town off-season and get onto a tour – most will require a few days' advance warning in order to arrange everything.

Accommodation

Every settlement in Iceland has somewhere to stay in the shape of a hotel, guesthouse, hostel or campsite, with farms and some rural schools providing accommodation in between. Almost all formal lodgings are found around the settled coastal band; if you're heading into the wilds at any stage, you'll need to camp or make use of hiking huts.

Always **book accommodation in advance**. Tourism to Iceland has rocketed in recent years – in 2015 the country clocked up an incredible million visitors, three times the national population – and during the peak season (June–Aug) the industry is struggling to cope with demand. The only exceptions here are campsites which – aside from Reykjavík's – don't usually require advance reservations.

City hotels tend to stay open year-round, and though the habit is spreading to smaller settlements, many places still **shut down** in winter, or at least through December. Where accommodation does stay open, winter rates are around 25 percent cheaper than summer ones.

Budget accommodation options in Iceland include **made-up beds** (with linen supplied) and cheaper **sleeping-bag accommodation** (where you bring your own bag). In both cases you're paying for a bed in a dorm or shared room for less than the price of a single room. So, even if you don't intend to camp, consider bringing a sleeping bag to Iceland.

It's worth picking up the **Áning** and **Icelandic Farm Holiday** (🕸farmholidays.is) booklets from tourist information outlets, which between them cover the majority of accommodation and campsite options across the country.

ACCOMMODATION ORGANIZATIONS

Contact details for specific places to stay are given throughout the guide, some of which are run by the following organizations:

Edda 🕸hoteledda.is. Twelve schools around the country open as hotels during the summer holidays (see below).

Fosshótel 🕸fosshotel.is. Ten strategically located hotels, including at Reykjavík and Akureyri.

Hostelling International Iceland 🕸hostel.is. Thirty-three youth hostels, most of them within range of the Ringroad (see opposite).

Icelandair 🕸icelandairhotels.com. Nine upmarket hotels, mostly in southern Iceland.

Icelandic Farm Holidays 🕸farmholidays.is. Agent for 170 farms offering accommodation around Iceland.

Kea Hotels 🕸keahotels.is. Eight top-notch hotels in Akureyri, Mývatn and Reykjavík.

Hotels

Icelandic **hotels** are typically bland, modern, business-oriented blocks, though rooms are comfortable and well furnished as a rule. Bigger establishments might have their own pool, gym or sauna, and there will always be a restaurant, with breakfast included in the cost of a room. **Rates** begin around 30,000kr for an en-suite double; rooms with shared facilities are about 10,000kr cheaper.

A few country schools open up during the summer holidays as **hotels**, twelve of which come under the **Edda** banner (🕸hoteledda.is). They're aimed at the mid-range end of things, though a few also provide sleeping-bag accommodation with shared facilities. Most have a thermally heated pool in the grounds and there's always a restaurant. **Prices** start at 23,000kr for a double and, where available, 10,000kr for a made-up bed and 5000kr for sleeping bags.

Guesthouses

Guesthouses (*gistiheimilið*) tend to have more character than hotels, and they're often family-run. Rooms range from the barely furnished to the very comfortable, though facilities are usually shared, and you'll often find some budget accommodation available too. A breakfast of cereal, toast, cheese and coffee is included, or offered for an extra 1750kr; some places can provide all meals with advance notice. Doubles cost upwards of 18,000kr; made-up beds are around 9000kr per person and sleeping-bag accommodation will be about 6500kr.

Farms

You'll find plenty of **farms** in Iceland (some with histories going back to Saga times) which offer accommodation of some kind, ranging from a room in the farmhouse to hostel-style dormitories or fully furnished, self-contained cabins. Many also encourage guests to take part in the daily routine, or offer horseriding, fishing, guided tours or even four-wheel-drive safaris.

For the most part, farm **prices** are the same as for guesthouses; cabins sleeping four or more can work out a good deal for a group at around 25,000kr. Come prepared to cook for yourself, though meals are usually available if booked in advance.

Hostels

Hostelling International Iceland (🕸hostel.is) runs 33 hostels, ranging from big affairs in Reykjavík to old farmhouses sleeping four out in the wilds. All are owner-operated, have self-catering kitchens and either offer bookings for local tours or organize them themselves. Some provide meals with advance notice and have laundry facilities. Many open all year too, though you'd be hard-pushed to reach remoter ones until winter is well and truly over – turn up out of season, however, and you'll often receive a warm welcome.

Dormitory sleeping-bag accommodation is the norm (at around 4500kr), though doubles are sometimes offered (around 12,500kr).

Youth hostel associations

Holders of a Hostelling International card get a 25 percent discount – you can buy cards at Icelandic hostels or from hostelling associations in your own country.

US AND CANADA

Hostelling International–American Youth Hostels
Ⓦ hiusa.org.
Hostelling International Canada Ⓦ hihostels.ca.

UK AND IRELAND

Youth Hostels Association (YHA) UK Ⓦ yha.org.uk.
Scottish Youth Hostels Association UK Ⓦ syha.org.uk.
Irish Youth Hostel Association Ireland Ⓦ anoige.ie.
Hostelling International Northern Ireland Northern Ireland
Ⓦ hini.org.uk.

AUSTRALIA, NEW ZEALAND AND SOUTH AFRICA

Australia Youth Hostels Association Australia Ⓦ yha.com.au.
Youth Hostelling Association New Zealand New Zealand
Ⓦ yha.co.nz.

Camping

Camping is a great way to experience Iceland, especially during the light summer nights, when it's bright enough in your tent at midnight to feel like it's time to get up. You'll also minimize expenditure, whether you make use of the country's 150 or so campsites or set up for free in the nearest field.

Official campsites are only **open** between June and some point in September – though you're welcome to use them out of season if you can live without their facilities (just shower at the nearest pool). They vary from no-frills affairs with level ground, a toilet and cold running water to those sporting windbreaks, hot showers (always 500kr extra), laundry and sheltered kitchen areas. Electricity for motorhomes costs 600kr a night. On-site shops or cafés are unusual, so stock up in advance. Campsites in the Interior are very barely furnished, usually with just a pit toilet.

While a few campsites are free, **prices** are usually around 1200kr **per person** per day. If you plan to spend every night in a tent, a **Camping Card** (Ⓦ campingcard.is; €105) might save a lot of money: valid for 28 nights at **selected campsites** around the country, the one card covers up to two adults and four children.

If you're doing extensive hiking or cycling there will be times that you'll have to **camp in the wild**. The main challenge here is to find a flat, rock-free

> ### ACCOMMODATION ALTERNATIVES
>
> Useful websites that provide alternatives to standard hotel and hostel accommodation.
> **Airbnb** Ⓦ airbnb.com.
> **CouchSurfing** Ⓦ couchsurfing.org.
> **Vacation Rentals by Owner** Ⓦ vrbo.com.

space to pitch a tent. Where possible, always **seek permission** for this at the nearest farmhouse before setting up; farmers often don't mind – and might direct you to a good site – but may need to keep you away from pregnant stock or the like.

Note, however, that after years of having to repair damaged verges and tidy up campers' garbage, toilet paper and raw sewage, some understandably irate landowners have erected "No Camping" signs on their properties. When camping wild, you must bury anything biodegradable and carry all other rubbish out with you. It's also forbidden to camp in reserves and at many popular tourist destinations, except at designated areas.

Camping equipment

Your **tent** is going to be severely tested, so needs to be in a good state of repair and built to withstand strong winds and heavy rain – bring along a good-quality dome or tunnel design, with a space between the flysheet and the tent entrance where you can store your backpack and boots out of the weather. Whatever the conditions are when you set up, always use guy ropes, the maximum number of pegs and a flysheet, as the weather can change rapidly; in some places, especially in the Interior, it's also advisable to weight the pegs down with rocks.

Also invest in a decent **sleeping bag** – even in summer, you might have to cope with sub-zero conditions – and a **sleeping mat** for insulation and comfort. A waterproof sheet to put underneath your tent is also a good idea. Unless you find supplies of driftwood you'll need a **fuel stove** too, as Iceland's few trees are all protected. Butane gas canisters are sold in Reykjavík and at many fuel stations around the country, but you're possibly better off with a pressure stove capable of taking a variety of fuels such as unleaded petrol (*býlaust*) or kerosene (*steinolía*). White gas/Coleman Fuel, a naptha-based product recommended by several pressure stove manufacturers, is increasingly available; don't confuse it with the widely available thinner, white spirit/shellite.

As for **food**, never buy purpose-made freeze-dried stuff from specialist camping stores – most brands are expensive and barely palatable even when you're too exhausted to care after a hard day's hike. Normal boil/microwave-in-the-bag meals from the nearest supermarket are far cheaper and can't taste any worse.

Mountain huts

At popular hiking areas and throughout Interior Iceland you'll encounter **mountain huts**, which are maintained by Iceland's hiking organizations (see box, p.41). These can be lavish, multistorey lodges with kitchen areas and dormitories overseen by wardens, or very basic wooden bunkhouses that simply offer a dry retreat from the weather, and **cost 3500–7000kr** accordingly. You'll always have to supply bedding and food and should **book well in advance** through the relevant organization, particularly at popular sites such as Þórsmörk and Landmannalaugar. If you haven't booked – or can't produce a **receipt** to prove it – you may get in if there's room, but otherwise you'll have to pitch a tent; wardens are very strict about this, so if you don't have a tent to fall back on, you might find yourself having to hike to the next available hut late in the day.

Emergency huts, painted bright orange to show up against snow, are sometimes not so remote – you'll see them at a few places around the Ringroad where drivers might get stranded by sudden heavy snowfalls. Stocked with food and fuel, and run by the SVFÍ (Iceland's national life-saving association), these huts are for emergency use only; if you have to use one, fill out the guestbook stating what you used and where you were heading, so that stocks can be maintained and rescue crews will know to track you down if you don't arrive at your destination.

Food and drink

Although Iceland's food is unlikely to be the highlight of your trip, things have improved from the early 1980s, when beer was illegal and canned soup supplemented dreary daily doses of plain-cooked lamb or fish. The country's low industrial output and high environmental consciousness means that its meat, fish and seafood are some of the healthiest in Europe, with hothouses providing a fair range of vegetables.

While in Reykjavík and Akureyri the variety of food is pretty well what you'd find at home, menus elsewhere are far more monotonous and prone to fads; one year they all offer lobster, the next it'll be lamb or fish and chips. At least there's usually some alternative to fast-food grills or pizzas, however, even if salads have yet to really catch on; otherwise cooking for yourself will have to see you through.

Traditional foods

Iceland's cold climate and long winters meant that the settlers' original diet was low in vegetables and high in cereals, fish and meat, with **preserved foods** playing a big role. Some of the following traditional foods are still eaten every day; others crop up mainly at special occasions such as the midwinter Þorramatur feasts, though restaurants may serve them year-round.

Harðfiskur, wind-dried haddock or cod, is a popular snack, eaten by tearing off a piece and chewing away, though some people like to spread butter on it first. Most Icelandic **seafood** is superb, and even everyday things like a breakfast of **sild** (pickled herrings) are worth trying. **Hákarl** (Greenland shark) is a more doubtful delicacy, as it is first buried for up to six months in sand to break down the high levels of toxins contained in its flesh. Different parts of the rotted shark yield either white or dark meat, and the advice for beginners is to start on the milder-tasting dark (gler hákarl), which is translucent – rather like smoked glass. Either way, the flavour is likely to make your eyes water, even if connoisseurs compare the taste and texture favourably to a strong cheese. Don't worry if you can't stomach the stuff, because neither can many Icelanders.

As for meat, there's ordinary **hangikjöt**, which is hung, smoked lamb, popular in sandwiches and as part of a traditional Christmas spread; **svið**, boiled and singed sheep's heads; haggis-like varieties of **slátur** ("slaughter"), of which blood pudding (blóðmör) is a favourite; and a whole range of scraps pressed into cakes and pickled in whey, collectively known as **súrmatur** – leftover svið is often prepared like this, as is súrsaðir hrútspungar, or pickled rams' testicles.

Game dishes include the grouse-like ptarmigan (rjúpa), which takes the place of turkey at Icelandic Christmas dinners; an occasional reindeer (hreindýr) in the east of the country; and puffin (lundi) in the south, which is usually smoked before being cooked. In a few places you'll also come across whale or seal meat, as both are still hunted in limited numbers. Rather more appealing to non-Icelandic palates, lobster (humar), **salmon** (lax), **trout** (silingur) and **char** (bleikja) are all superb and relatively inexpensive. In addition to smoked salmon or trout, try the similar-looking *gravað*, whereby the fish is marinated with herbs until it's soft and quite delicious.

About the only endemic **vegetable** is *fjallagrös*, Iceland moss, a starch-rich lichen that's dried into almost tasteless, resilient black curls and snacked on raw or cooked with milk. Home-produced **cheese** and dairy products are very good, and it's worth trying yoghurt-like **skyr**, sold all over the country plain or flavoured with fruit. **Pancakes** known as *flatbrauð* or *laufabrauð* are traditionally eaten at Christmas, and a few places – notably at Hveragerði and Mývatn – bake a delicious **rye bread** called *hverabrauð* in underground ovens (see p.269).

Drinks

It's been said with some justification that Iceland runs on **coffee**, with just about everyone in the country firmly hooked. There's a definite café culture in the cities – including a national generic café chain, *Kaffitar* – and decent quality brews are offered even at rural cafés. In some supermarkets, hot thermoses of free coffee are laid on for customers to help themselves, and wherever you pay for a cup, the price usually includes a refill or two. **Tea** is also pretty popular, though not consumed with such enthusiasm. **Bottled water** and familiar brands of **soft drinks** are available everywhere. **Milk** comes in a bewildering range of styles, making a trip to the supermarket fridge quite a challenge if you can't read Icelandic. *Mjolk* is normal full-fat milk, *Lettmjolk* is skimmed, *AB Mjolk* is plain runny skyr, and *G-Mjolk* is UHT milk.

Alcohol

Alcohol is expensive – pick up a bottle on arrival (Keflavík airport's duty-free is the cheapest place to buy alcohol in the country) – and, with the exception of beer, only sold in bars, clubs, restaurants and state-owned liquor stores known as **vinbúð**. These are often tucked out of sight in

distant corners of towns and cities, and always have ludicrously restricted opening hours – sometimes just an hour, five days a week. Most Icelanders drink very hard when they put their minds to it, most often at parties or on camping trips – the August bank holiday weekend is notorious. It's surprising, then, to find that full-strength **beer** was actually illegal until March 1989, when the 75-year-old prohibition laws were revoked. In Reykjavík, March 1 is still celebrated as **Bjórdagurinn**, or Beer Day, with predictably riotous celebrations organized at bars throughout the capital. Beer is available in many supermarkets, and comes as relatively inexpensive, low-alcohol pilsner, and more expensive, stronger lagers. Some bars also serve domestically-brewed **boutique beers**: brands to look out for include Gæðingur, who produce a range of ales; and Steðji, known for its lagers.

All wine and most spirits are imported, though hard-liquor enthusiasts should try **brennivín**, a local spirit distilled from potatoes and flavoured with caraway seeds. It's powerful stuff, affectionately known as *svarti dauði* or "black death", and certainly warms you up in winter – you'll also welcome its traditional use to clean the palate after eating fermented shark.

Restaurants, cafés and bars

Just about every settlement in Iceland has a **restaurant** of some sort. In Reykjavík, and to a lesser extent Akureyri and the larger towns, you can get everything from traditional Icelandic fare to Mexican, Thai, Chinese, and Italian- and French-inspired dishes, and there are even a couple of vegetarian places. This is the most expensive way to dine – expect to pay upwards of 3000kr for a main dish – though keep your eyes peeled for lunchtime **specials**, or inexpensive fixed-price meals of soup, bread and stew. All-you-can-eat **smorgasbords** or buffets also crop up, especially around Christmas, when restaurants seem to compete with each other over the calorie contents of their spreads of cold meats and **cakes**.

GETTING LEGLESS FOR AN ARM AND A LEG

It's one of Iceland's greatest paradoxes: how can a country that charges some of the **highest prices for alcohol in Europe** also support such an eclectic scene of bars and clubs? Put simply, spending vast amounts of money on everyday items is a fact of life in Iceland, a country where import taxes and inflation have caused prices to soar; and even though alcohol prices in real terms have fallen in recent years, a half-litre of beer in Reykjavík will still cost at least double what you're used to paying at home. Icelanders get round the astronomical cost of booze by drinking at home before hitting the town. Buying beer and wine in the state-run alcohol store, the *vínbúð*, is the home-grown way of cutting costs.

In the country, pickings are slimmer. Some **hotel restaurants** have fine food, though it's more often filling than particularly memorable; prices can be as high as in any restaurant, but are generally lower. Otherwise, the only place offering cooked food might be the nearest **fuel station roadhouse**, which will whip up fast fodder such as **pylsur** (hot dogs), burgers, grills, sandwiches and **pizzas** – virtually Iceland's national dish – for a few hundred krónur.

Found all over the country, **bars**, besides being somewhere to have a drink, also usually sell meals and are frequently decorated along particular themes – decked out 1950s-style, for example, or hung with fishing memorabilia. **Cafés** are increasingly common even in small villages, offering light meals, coffee and cakes.

Self-catering

Self-catering will save a lot over eating out, though ingredients still cost more than they do at home – again, you might want to bring some supplies (especially camping rations) with you to save money. There are very few specialist food shops besides bakeries, but at least one **supermarket** in all villages, towns and cities. Don't expect to find them attached to campsites, however, and when travelling about, buy supplies when you can: don't get caught short by weekend shop hours, and know where the next supermarket is (they are listed throughout the Guide). There are no shops in the Interior.

Larger supermarkets are well stocked with all manner of groceries, plus fresh fruit, vegetables, fish and meat. Supermarkets also sell single-use barbecue packs (with aluminium tray, charcoal and firelighter) if you fancy eating alfresco. Iceland grows its own capsicums, mushrooms, tomatoes and cucumbers, but most other things are imported and therefore fairly expensive. **Bónus** and **Krónan** are the cheapest supermarket chains.

Rural stores – often incorporated into the local roadhouse – sell essential groceries and hardware, snacks, hot drinks and fast food; there's often a microwave for you to heat up pre-cooked meals. At worst, they'll be nothing more than a shelf or two of canned and dried food.

The media

Iceland's main daily papers are the right-wing Morgunblaðið and the right-of-centre Fréttablaðið, available all over the country and giving thorough coverage of national and international news.

If your Icelandic isn't up to it, there are roundups of the domestic news on Morgunblaðið's English-language website (Ⓦicelandmonitor.mbl.is) and the **Iceland Review** (Ⓦicelandreview.com). Reykjavík's bookshops – and libraries around the country – also have copies of **British and US newspapers**, plus international magazines such as *Time* and *National Geographic*.

Iceland's **radio stations** play a mind-numbingly repetitive menu of commercial pop, classical music and talk-back shows. The three **television channels** show a familiar mix of soaps, dramas, films and documentaries. All these media are predominantly Icelandic-language only, though films and TV shows are screened in their original language with subtitles.

Festivals

Though Iceland's calendar is essentially Christian, many official holidays and festivals have a secular theme, and at least one dates from pagan times. Some are already familiar: Christmas and Easter Monday are both holidays in Iceland and are celebrated as elsewhere in the Western world, as is New Year.

Harking back to the Viking era, however, Þorrablót is a midwinter celebration that originally honoured the weather god Þorri, and became something to look forward to during the bleakest time of the year. It is held throughout February, when people throw parties centred around the consumption of traditional foods such as *svið* and *hákarl* (see p.36), with some restaurants also laying on special menus.

Sjomannadagur, or Seamen's Day (June 4), is, unsurprisingly, one of the biggest holidays of the year, with communities organizing mock sea-rescue demonstrations, swimming races and tug-of-war events. This is followed by another break for **Independence Day** (June 17), the day that the Icelandic state separated from Denmark in 1944.

Although not an official holiday, **Jónsmessa**, on June 24, is the day that elves and other magical creatures are said to be out in force, playing tricks on the unwary; some people celebrate with a big bonfire, and it's also meant to be good for your health to run around naked.

Verslunnarmannahelgi, the Labour Day Weekend, takes place around the country on the first weekend in August. Traditionally, everybody heads into the countryside, sets up camp, and spends the rest of the holiday drinking and partying themselves into oblivion. On Heimaey in the Westman Islands, Þjóðhátíð is held on the same day and celebrated in the same way – there's live music, too, and a huge bonfire – though it nominally commemorates Iceland's achieving partial political autonomy in 1874.

One event to look out for, though it's not a single festival, is the annual stock round-up, or **rettir**, which takes place in rural areas throughout September. This is when horses and sheep are herded by riders on horseback down from the higher summer pastures to be penned and sorted; some farms offering accommodation allow guests to watch or even participate.

Sports and outdoor activities

Iceland has its own wrestling style, called glíma – a former Olympic sport where opponents try to throw each other by grabbing one another's belts – and there's a serious football (soccer) following; the Reykjavík Football Club was founded in 1899, and an Icelandic consortium owned the English-league club Stoke City between 1999 and 2006. Otherwise, there's not a great obsession with sport, and most people here go outside not to play games but to work or enjoy the Great Outdoors.

The lava plains, black-sand deserts, glacier-capped plateaus, alpine meadows, convoluted fjords and capricious volcanoes that make Iceland such an extraordinary place scenery-wise also offer tremendous potential for **outdoor activities**, whether you've come for wildlife or to hike, ride, ski, snowmobile or four-wheel-drive your way across the horizon. Further information on these activities is always at hand in local tourist offices, while you can find out more about the few **national parks and reserves** from the Department of Forestry or various Icelandic hiking organizations (see box, p.41). Many activities can be undertaken as part of an organized tour, sometimes with the necessary gear supplied or available for rent. Before you set out to do anything too adventurous, however, check your insurance cover.

HAZARDS

Awareness of Iceland's **natural hazards** – including the weather and geology – is taken very much for granted; don't expect to find warning signs, safety barriers or guide ropes at even patently dangerous locations on the edge of waterfalls, volcanoes or boiling mud pits. Always exercise **caution**, especially at heavily touristed locations – where you'll often see locals (and uninformed tourists) taking insane risks.

Swimming and hot pots

You probably won't be coming to Iceland to **swim**, but in fact this is a major year-round social activity with Icelanders. Just about every settlement has a swimming pool, usually an outdoor affair and heated by the nearest hot spring to around 28°C. There are also almost always one or two spa baths or **hot pots**, providing much hotter soaks at 35–40°C – another great Icelandic institution, and particularly fun in winter, when you can sit up to your neck in near-scalding water while the snow falls thickly around you. Out in the wilds, hot pots are replaced by **natural hot springs** – a welcome way to relax trail-weary muscles.

Icelandic swimming pools have their own **etiquette** that you need to follow. Remove your shoes before entering the changing rooms (there will be a rack in the pool lobby); leave your towel in the shower area between the changing rooms and the pool, not in your locker (this is so you can towel off before returning to the changing rooms, keeping them dry); and shower fully, with soap and without swimwear, before getting in the pool. Note that though there are always separate male and female changing rooms, very few pools have private cubicles.

Fishing

As Iceland is surrounded by the richest fishing grounds in the North Atlantic, **sea fishing** has always been seen as more of a career than a sport. The country's rivers and lakes, however, are also well stocked with **salmon** and **trout**, pulling in hordes of fly fishers during the **fishing season** (April 1 to September 20 for trout; June 20 to mid-September for salmon). Both fish are plentiful in all the country's bigger waterways, though the finest salmon are said to come from the Laxá in northeast

Iceland, and the Rangá in the south. During the winter, people cut holes in the ice and fish for **arctic char**; the best spots for this are at Þingvallavatn and Mývatn (see p.105 & p.260).

You always need a **permit** to fish. Those for char or trout are fairly cheap and easy to obtain on the spot from local tourist offices and some accommodation, but permits for salmon are extremely expensive and often need to be reserved a year in advance, as there is a limit per river. For further information, contact the **Federation of Icelandic River Owners** (Ⓦangling.is), whose website has a huge amount of English-language information.

Hiking

Hiking gets you closer to the scenery than anything else in Iceland. In reserves and the couple of national parks you'll find a few **marked trails**, though even here guideposts tend to be erratic and you'll always need to be competent at using navigational aids, especially in poor weather.

However long you're hiking for, always carry warm, weatherproof **clothing**, food and **water** (there are plenty of places where porous soil makes finding surface water unlikely), as well as a torch, lighter, penknife, **first aid kit**, a foil insulation blanket and a whistle or mirror for attracting attention. The country is carpeted in sharp rocks and rough ground, so tough, good-quality **hiking boots** are essential – though a pair of neoprene surf boots with thick soles are useful to ford rivers.

On lava, watch out for **volcanic fissures**, cracks in the ground ranging from a few centimetres to several metres across. These are easy enough to avoid when you can see them, but blanketed by snow they'll be invisible, so use a hiking pole to test

GRADING HIKES

Hiking trails in Iceland are not formally **graded**, though local organizations sometimes use a boot icon to indicate difficulty (one boot easy, five boots tough). It's always prudent to seek **local advice** about routes, but note that Icelanders, hardened since birth to the country's conditions, tend to make light of difficulties: a "straightforward" trail often means anything that doesn't actually involve technical skills and climbing gear, but might well include traversing knife-edge ridges or dangerously loose scree slopes.

the path ahead. Another hazard is **river crossings**, which you'll have to make on various trails all over the country. Glacier-fed rivers are at their lowest first thing in the morning, and rise through the day as the sun melts the ice and snow that feed into them. When looking for a crossing point, remember the river will be shallowest at its widest point; before crossing, make sure that your backpack straps are loose so that you can ditch it in a hurry if necessary. Face into the current as you cross and be prepared to give up if the water gets above your thighs. Never attempt a crossing alone, and remember that some rivers have no safe fords at all if you're on foot – you'll have to hitch across in a vehicle.

When and where to hike

The **best months** for hiking are June through to August, when the weather is relatively warm, flowers are in bloom, and the wildlife is out and about – though even then the Interior and higher ground elsewhere can get snowbound at short notice. Outside the prime time, weather is very problematic and you might not be able to reach the area you want to explore, let alone hike around it.

One of the beauties of Iceland is that you can walk just about anywhere, assuming you can cope with local conditions, though there are, of course, highlights. Close to Reykjavík, the **Reykjanes Peninsula** offers extended treks across imposingly desolate lava rubble; there are some short, easy hikes along steaming valleys near **Hveragerði**, while trails at **Þingvellir** include historic sites and an introduction to rift valley geology. Further east, **Laugavegur** is an exceptional four-day trail; and **Þórsmörk** is one of the most popular hiking spots in the country, a wooded, elevated valley surrounded by glaciers and mountain peaks with a well-trodden network of paths.

Along the west coast, the **Snæfellsnes Peninsula** is notoriously damp but peaks with the ice-bound summit of Snæfellsjökull, the dormant volcano used as a fictional gateway into the centre of the earth by writer Jules Verne. Further north there's **Hornstrandir**, the wildest and most isolated extremity of the West Fjords, a region of twisted coastlines, sheer cliffs and rugged hill walks. Those after an easier time should head to **Mývatn**, the shallow northeastern lake where you can make simple day-hikes to extinct craters, billowing mud pits, and still steaming lava flows; longer but also relatively easy are the well-marked riverside trails around nearby **Jökulsárgljúfur National Park**, which features some awesome canyon scenery. Over in the east, the best of the hikes take in the

---

ICELANDIC HIKING ORGANIZATIONS

For advance information on popular hiking areas such as Þórsmörk or Landmannalaugar, or simply if you want to sign up for an organized hike, Iceland has two **hiking organizations**. Both run guided treks of a couple of days' duration to a week or longer – though groups can be very large – and maintain various mountain huts in reserves and the Interior where you can book a bunk.

Ferðafélag Íslands (Touring Club of Iceland) Mörkin 6, IS-108 Reykjavík ☎ 568 2533, ⓦ fi.is
Útivist Hallaveigarstigur 1, IS-101 Reykjavík ☎ 561 4330, ⓦ utivist.is

---

highland moors and glaciated fringes of the massive Vatnajökull ice cap: at **Snæfell**, a peak inland from Egilsstaðir; **Lónsöræfi reserve** near Höfn; and **Skaftafell National Park**, another popular camping spot on Vatnajökull's southern edge.

Horseriding

Horses came to Iceland with the first settlers, and, due to a tenth-century ban on their further import, have remained true to their original stocky Scandinavian breed. Always used for **riding**, horses also had a religious place in Viking times and were often dedicated or sacrificed to the pagan gods; with the advent of Christianity, eating horse meat was banned, being seen as a sign of paganism. Nowadays, horses are used for the autumn livestock round-up, and for recreational purposes.

Icelandic horses are sturdy, even-tempered creatures which, in addition to the usual walk, trot, gallop and canter, can move smoothly across rough ground using the gliding **tölt** gait. The biggest breeding centres are in the country's south, but horses are available for **hire** from farms all over Iceland, for anything from an hour in the saddle to two-week-long treks across the Interior. **Places to hire horses** are given throughout the Guide, but to organize something in advance, contact Íshestar (ⓦ ishestar.is) or Eldhestar (ⓦ eldhestar.is), which run treks of all lengths and experience levels right across the country.

Snow and action sports

Snow sports – which in Iceland are not just practised in winter – have, surprisingly, only recently begun to catch on. Partly this is because the bulk of Iceland's population lives in the mild southwestern corner of the country, but also because snow was seen as just something you had to put up with; cross-country skiing, for instance, is such a fact of life in the northeastern winters that locals refer to it simply as "walking", and were baffled when foreign tour operators first brought in groups to do it for fun.

The possibilities for **cross-country skiing** are pretty limitless in winter, though you'll have to bring in your own gear. **Downhill skiing and snowboarding** are the most popular snow sports, with winter slopes at Bláfjöll (ⓦ skidasvaedi.is) only 20km from Reykjavík.

Plenty of tour operators offer glacier trips on **snowmobiles** or **skidoos**, which are like jet-skis for snow – the only way for the inexperienced to get a taste of Iceland's massive ice fields, and huge fun. Several of southwestern Iceland's larger rivers have caught the attention of **whitewater rafting** enthusiasts (contact ⓦ arcticrafting.is for more information), while Iceland also has surprisingly good **scuba diving** potential, the prime sites being in Þingvallavatn's cool but amazingly clear waters, at various shipwrecks, and at seal colonies around the coast: Dive Iceland (ⓦ dive.is) can sort out the details, though you'll need dry-suit skills.

Travel essentials

Children

Iceland presents few difficulties for **travelling with children**. Icelanders are very child-friendly people; cities and towns are relatively safe, low-crime places with familiar amenities; and supermarkets and pharmacies are well stocked with **nappies**, **formula** and anything else you might need (though do keep in mind where the next shops might be in the countryside). **Boredom** might be a problem on long car journeys between sights, though the many **swimming pools** – some sporting waterslides – make great places to let off steam once you arrive somewhere.

However, given the lack of **warning signs** or barriers at waterfalls, hot springs, cliffs, crevasses and the like, children must be closely supervised at

TAX REFUNDS

If you spend more than 4000kr in any single transaction on goods to take out of the country, you are entitled to a **tax refund** of fifteen percent of the total price, as long as you leave Iceland within ninety days. Ask for a **Refund Tax Free form** when you make your purchases, which needs to be filled out by the shop. Money can be refunded in full back onto your credit/debit card at **refund points** located in the departure halls at Keflavík, Reykjavík and Akureyri airports; the bank inside the Seyðisfjörður ferry terminal; and either on board all international cruise ships two hours before departure, or at Reykjavík port's Visitor Centre. The same places, plus refund points at Kringlan Shopping Mall and Reykjavík's Tourist Information centres, can make the refund in cash, but this incurs a commission.

all times in the countryside. Along with everyone else, children also need to come prepared for the **weather**, with plenty of warm, waterproof clothing and tough shoes for use outdoors.

Costs

Due to its small consumer base and dependency on imports, Iceland is an **expensive** country. To minimize costs, you need to be as **self-sufficient** as possible: bring food and a sleeping bag if you're intending to use self-catering budget accommodation, along with a tent and all camping gear if camping. **Bus passes** (see box, p.30) will minimize transport costs, and a **Hostelling International Card** (see p.35) will get you a few hundred krónur a night off Youth Hostel rates. **Seasons** also affect costs: places to stay and car-rental agencies drop their prices between October and June, though at that time inexpensive summer-only accommodation will be shut, campsites will probably be under snow, and bus services are infrequent or suspended.

Budget travellers who camp out every night, use a bus pass and cook for themselves can keep average **daily costs** down to around 10,000kr (though cyclists can cut this in half). Throw in a few nights in hostel-style accommodation and the occasional pizza and you're looking at 15,000kr. Mid-range travel still means using a bus pass to get around, but favouring hostels and eating out cheaply most of the time will set you back about 18,000kr a day. Staying only in guesthouses or hotels and eating in restaurants for every meal means that you're looking at daily expenses of upwards of 30,000kr.

None of the above takes into account **additional costs** for entertainment such as tours, entry fees, drinking or alternative transport such as flights and ferries, for which we've given prices in the Guide. **Car rental** will add a minimum 9,000kr a day, plus fuel, to daily expenses (see p.30).

Crime and personal safety

Iceland is a peaceful country, and it's unlikely that you'll encounter much trouble here. Most public places are well lit and secure, people are helpful, if somewhat reserved, and street crime and hassles are rare. Needless to say, hitching alone, or wandering around central Reykjavík late at night, is unwise.

Most incidents involve **petty crime** and are largely confined to Reykjavík. Many criminals are drug addicts or alcoholics after easy money; keep tabs on your cash and passport (and don't leave anything visible in your car when you park it) and you should have little reason to visit the **police** (*lögreglan*). If you do seek them out, you'll find them unarmed, concerned and usually able to speak English – remember to get an insurance report from them if you have anything stolen.

As for **offences** you might commit, **drink-driving** is taken extremely seriously, so don't do it: catch a taxi. Being incoherently **drunk** in public in Reykjavík might also get you into trouble, but in a country campsite you probably won't be the only one, and (within reason) nobody is going to care. **Drugs**, however, are treated as harshly here as in much of the rest of Europe.

Sexual harassment is less of a problem in Iceland than elsewhere in Europe. Although you might receive occasional unwelcome attentions in Reykjavík clubs, there's very rarely any kind of violent intent. If you do have any problems, the fact that almost everyone understands English makes it easy to get across an unambiguous response.

Culture and etiquette

Iceland is an egalitarian, outgoing country, and public behaviour is much the same as wherever you've come in from. Icelanders are proud of their country's modernity, its written culture and the fact that many people can trace their family histories right back to Saga times: they are thin-skinned about depictions of Iceland as a nation of backward, axe-wielding Beserkers in horned helmets.

Discussing the **environment** can lead to heated arguments; over-grazing of sheep has caused widespread erosion over the centuries, countered by the importation of arctic lupins to help stabilize and revitalize the soil – which are themselves now spreading out of control. The right to continue whaling is also pursued as a cultural issue. Pride in Iceland's Nordic heritage occasionally surfaces as low-level **racism**, though with noticeable popula-tions of Chinese, Thai and Filipino migrants settled in Reykjavík, not to mention tourists of all nationalities passing through, this is not a major issue.

The major **social blunders** made by visitors are usually at swimming pools (see p.39); forget to follow the rules about shoes, towels and showering and you can expect to be soundly rebuked by locals.

Electricity

Electricity is 240v, 50Hz AC. Plugs are round-pin with either two or three prongs; appliances fitted with overseas plugs need an adaptor.

Entry requirements

Citizens from Schengen countries, the European Economic Area, the US, Canada, Australia, New Zealand and many other nations require **no visa** to visit Iceland for up to ninety days providing that their passport is valid for at least ninety days after the date of arrival. For the full list, and information on how to apply for a visa if you do require one, contact the Icelandic Directorate of Immigration (🌐utl.is).

As regards customs regulations, all visitors to Iceland can bring in the following: camping gear and other travelling equipment for their own use in Iceland (including foodstuffs and other supplies, but no uncooked meat of any sort); and either 1 litre of spirits and 1 litre of wine, or 1 litre of spirits and 6 litres of beer, or 1.5 litres of wine and 6 litres of beer or 3 litres of wine. In addition to this, 200 cigarettes, or 250g of other tobacco products, are also permitted.

ICELANDIC EMBASSIES ABROAD

There are no Icelandic embassies or consulates in Australia, Republic of Ireland, New Zealand or South Africa. For the full list worldwide, check 🌐 iceland.is/iceland-abroad.
Canada Constitution Square, 360 Albert St, Suite 710, Ottawa, Ontario K1R 7X7 ☎ 613 482 1944, 🌐 iceland.is/ca; Consulate General Wellington Crescent, Suite 100, Winnipeg, Manitoba R3M 3Z2 ☎ 204 284 1535, 🌐 iceland.is/ca/win.

UK 2A Hans St, London SW1X 0JE ☎ 020 7259 3999, 🌐 iceland.is/uk.
US House of Sweden, 2900 K Street N.W. #509, Washington DC 20005-1704 ☎ 202 265 6653, 🌐 iceland.is/us; Consulate General 800 3rd Ave, 36th Floor, New York, NY ☎ 646 282 9360, 🌐 iceland.is/us/nyc.

Gay and lesbian travellers

Iceland is a very small and close-knit society, where it's generally said that two Icelanders meeting for the first time can usually find people they know in common – not exactly ideal condi-tions for a thriving **gay scene** to develop. Indeed, for years many gay people upped and left for the other Nordic capitals, most notably Copenhagen, where attitudes were more liberal and it was easier to be anonymous.

The **Icelandic gay and lesbian association**, Samtökin 78, at Laugavegur 3 in Reykjavík (🌐samtokin78.is), promotes awareness of homosexuality and gay rights at a political level and also offers a support network in the capital and out in rural communities, where attitudes towards homosexuality are not nearly as enlightened. In line with other cities where the gay scene has moved online, there are no longer any specifically gay bars in Reykjavík or the rest of Iceland.

Samtökin's efforts have certainly paid off at the political level – after much lobbying, Iceland's politi-cians not only agreed to allow **gay marriage** in 1996 (in effect the right to register legally a partner-ship between two same-sex partners, thus granting legal parity with straight couples), but also to allow gay men and lesbians to adopt children, making Iceland the first country in the world to pass such progressive legislation.

Health

Iceland's healthcare system is excellent and available in most communities. Tourist offices or accommodation can recommend doctors and hospitals – all of whom will be English-speaking. There's at least one **pharmacy**, or apotek, in every town, as well stocked as any you'll find at home. Most open during normal business hours, though some in Reykjavík and Akureyri stay open longer. **No vaccinations** are required for visitors to Iceland.

To avoid being charged for **emergency health-care** in Iceland, Scandinavian citizens must show medical insurance and a valid passport, while citizens of the European Economic Area can simply show their European Health Insurance Card and passport at a health centre or hospital for free treatment. Citizens of other countries need to contact the nearest Icelandic Embassy or representative for information on whether they qualify; if not, you'll have to pay at the time and then claim back the money from your travel insurance.

If you're spending much time outdoors, be aware that the weather and distance might cause difficulties if you need medical attention in a hurry, and it's wise to carry a **first-aid kit**. Two important items to include are a roll of elasticated sticking plaster (band aids) and crepe bandages – both vital for supporting and splinting sprained muscles or broken bones.

Most problems you'll encounter, however, are minor. Though you might not think the northern **sun** would be much trouble, it's still strong enough to cause sunburn and eye strain – especially when reflected off ice or snow – so use sunscreen and sunglasses. Hand cream or moisturizer and lip balm are a good idea too, as the **cold dry air**, wind and dust can painfully crack exposed skin. Eye drops will also relieve irritation caused by dust. **Flies** are not the problem in Iceland that they can be in Scandinavia; Mývatn (see p.260) is the only place you'll encounter them in plague proportions, though very few bite. **Water** is safe to drink throughout Iceland.

The most serious thing to worry about is **hypothermia**, wherein your core body temperature drops to a point that can be fatal. It's likely to occur if you get exhausted, wet and cold while out hiking or cycling; symptoms include a weak pulse, disorientation, numbness, and slurred speech. If you suspect hypothermia, seek shelter from the weather, get the patient as dry as possible, and prevent further heat loss – aside from clothing, a foil "space blanket" available from camping stores will help. Sugary drinks can also help (alcohol definitely doesn't), but serious cases need immediate hospital treatment. The best advice is to avoid hypothermia in the first place: while hiking, ensure you eat enough carbohydrates, drink plenty of water and wear sufficient warm and weatherproof clothing, including a woollen hat and gloves. During the colder parts of the year, **motorists** should always carry a blanket and warm gear too, in case they get stranded by snow.

Insurance

Travel insurance policies provide a level of cover for medical treatment and loss of personal items, as well as unforeseen cancellation or curtailment of your journey. Cover for **adventure activities** such as whitewater rafting, snow sports and trekking, usually incurs an extra premium. Read the small print of prospective policies carefully; cover can vary wildly for roughly similar premiums. Also make sure you check the level of **excess**, the amount of each claim that you have to pay. Note that no vehicle of any kind is insured against damage incurred while crossing a river.

With **medical coverage**, ascertain whether benefits will be paid as treatment proceeds or only after return home, and whether there is a 24-hour medical emergency number. When securing **baggage cover**, make sure that the per-article limit – typically under £500 equivalent – will cover your most valuable possession. If you need to **make a claim**, you should keep receipts for medicines and medical treatment, and in the event you have anything stolen, you must obtain an official statement from the police.

Internet

Iceland is one of the highest per-capita users of the **internet**, with most homes and businesses connected. Many Reykjavík cafés and most accommodation around the country provide free wi-fi for customers, while public libraries and tourist offices often have terminals with access at around 500–1000kr an hour.

ROUGH GUIDES TRAVEL INSURANCE

Rough Guides has teamed up with WorldNomads.com to offer great travel insurance deals. Policies are available to residents of over 150 countries, with cover for a wide range of adventure sports, 24hr emergency assistance, high levels of medical and evacuation cover and a stream of travel safety information. Roughguides.com users can take advantage of their policies online 24/7, from anywhere in the world – even if you're already travelling. And since plans often change when you're on the road, you can extend your policy and even claim online. Roughguides.com users who buy travel insurance with WorldNomads.com can also leave a positive footprint and donate to a community development project. For more information, go to ⓦ roughguides.com/travel-insurance.

Living in Iceland

European Economic Area nationals may stay in Iceland longer than three months on condition that they secure **work** for a further period of at least three months. Once in employment, there is no time limit on the length of stay in Iceland but **residence and work permits** are required; check with the Directorate of Immigration (Ⓦutl.is) and the Directorate of Labour (Ⓦvinnumalastofnun.is) for information. Non-EU nationals must apply for residence permits before leaving home, and must be able to prove they can support themselves without working.

Mail

Post offices are located in all major communities and are open from 9am until 4.30pm Monday to Friday, though a few in Reykjavík have longer hours. **Domestic mail** will generally get to the nearest post office within two working days, though a recipient living out on a farm might not collect it so quickly. For **international post** count on three to five days for mail to reach the UK or US, and a week to ten days to reach Australia and New Zealand. Anything up to 50g costs 153kr within Iceland, 180kr to Europe, and 240kr to anywhere else; up to 100g costs 185/310/490kr. International parcels aren't outrageously expensive – check Ⓦpostur.is for rates – but not particularly fast; ask at any post office about Express Mail if you're in a hurry, though you'll pay far more than for the normal service.

Maps

A range of excellent **maps** of the country, costing upwards of 2100kr, is available for all types of use – if you can't find what you want overseas, you'll be able to pick it up in Reykjavík and Akureyri, or sometimes from local tourist offices and fuel stations. In addition to the maps detailed below, Iceland's hiking clubs (see box, p.41) and national parks put out a few maps of varying quality for popular nature reserves and national parks (available from park offices).

Maps are published by **Mál og menning** (Ⓦforlagid.is) and **Ferðakort/lðnú** (Ⓦferdakort.is). Both produce single-sheet road maps of the entire country, along with four or five separate regional sheets at around 1:250,000. Ferðakort's speciality is detailed maps, suitable for hiking, of specific areas such as Westman Islands, Hornstrandir, Skaftafell and so on at 1:25,000–1:200,000; Mál og menning has a similar 1:100,000 series with 1:50,000 inserts. The best available **road atlas** is Mál og menning's 1:300,000

Kortabók, which breaks the country down into sixty pages as well as including plans of larger towns.

Money

Iceland's **currency** is the **króna** (krónur in the plural), abbreviated to either Isk, Ikr or kr. Notes are issued in 5000kr, 2000kr, 1000kr and 500kr denominations, and there are 100kr, 50kr, 10kr, 5kr and 1kr coins. At the time of writing the exchange rate was approximately 210kr to £1; 147kr to €1; 135kr to US$1; 104kr to CAN$1; 100kr to AU$1; and 88kr to NZ$1. Check **current exchange rates** at Ⓦxe.com.

Banks with ATMs are found around the country, including in many single-street villages. Normal **banking hours** are Monday to Friday 9.15am to 4pm, though a few branches in Reykjavík open for longer. All banks change **foreign currency** (not Australian and New Zealand dollars, however); some stores and accommodation in Reykjavík also accept US dollar, euro or UK sterling.

You can get around Iceland without ever touching cash: almost everywhere takes **credit cards** (Visa and MasterCard are the most widely accepted), and many businesses' tills – and all ATMs – are wired into the Cirrus/Maestro/Electron network, which allows you to pay, or draw cash from ATMs, direct from your home bank account using a **debit** or **bank card**. Cash withdrawals will be charged a fee per transaction; check with your bank for their rates.

Alternatively, you can use **travellers' cheques** to carry your funds around. Take only euro, UK sterling or US dollar cheques; Australian and New Zealand cheques are not cashable in Iceland. Some banks issue **Travel Money Cards**, basically an ATM card which has been precharged to a certain value, and which you can draw on until the funds are exhausted. Again, check with your bank for details, especially regarding compatibility with Icelandic machines.

Opening hours and public holidays

Shops are generally **open** Monday to Friday 10am–6pm and Saturday 10am to mid-afternoon; if they open on Sunday, it will probably be after noon. In cities and larger towns, supermarkets are open daily from 10am until late afternoon; in smaller communities, however, some places don't open at all at weekends.

Out in the country, **fuel stations** provide some services for travellers, and larger ones tend to open daily from around 9am to 10pm. **Office hours** everywhere are Monday to Friday 9am to 5pm; **tourist offices** often extend these through the weekends, at least in popular spots. Most businesses close on the public holidays listed below.

PUBLIC HOLIDAY DATES

Jan 1 New Year's Day
March/April Maundy Thursday, Good Friday, Easter Sunday, Easter Monday
April, first Thursday after April 18 First day of summer
May 1 May Day
May/June Ascension Day, Whit Sunday, Whit Monday
June 17 National Day
August Bank Holiday (first Monday)
Dec 24–26 Christmas Eve, Christmas Day, Boxing Day
Dec 31 New Year's Eve

Phones

All **phone numbers** in Iceland are seven digits long, with no regional codes. **Phone book** listings are arranged in order of Christian name – Gunnar Jakobsson, for instance, is listed under "G", not "J". Normal landline **rates** are reduced on domestic calls at weekends and Monday to Friday 7pm to 8am; on calls to Europe daily at 7pm to 8am; and to everywhere else daily at 11pm to 8am.

Iceland uses both GSM and NMT **mobile phone** networks. GSM covers most coastal regions, including all communities with over 200 inhabitants. Coming from the UK or EU, your own country's pay-as-you-go Sim cards might work in Iceland with

varying roaming rates. Alternatively, buy a new Sim from fuel stations or newsagents in Iceland. You'll only need NMT coverage if you're spending a lot of time in Iceland's Interior; contact Icelandic car rental companies or hiking organizations (see box, p.41) for more information.

Photography

Iceland is staggeringly scenic, as well as being packed with birds and enjoying weird atmospheric effects such as the **Northern Lights** (in winter) and the **Midnight Sun** (seen in late June only in the extreme north of the country). Prime **landscapes** to catch on camera include icebergs at Jökulsárlón; Strokkur erupting at Geysir; the rift valley at Þingvellir; desert along the Sprengisandur route; one of Vatnajökull's glaciers; the West Fjord's flat mountain tops; and Dettifoss, Europe's largest waterfall. As for **birds**, you simply must go home with a snap of a puffin (easiest on Heimaey or at Ingólfshöfði), while Mývatn's ducks, teeming seabird colonies anywhere around the coast (though best perhaps at Látrabjarg in the West Fjords) and white-tailed eagles (try on Snæfellsnes) are all worthy targets.

Shopping

Icelandic **woollen sweaters** are a practical memento of your trip, and cost upwards of 20,000kr. Many are now machine-made overseas (causing much indignation in Iceland), though it's still possible to find sweaters made by hand in cottage industries, where consistent patterns, colours, sizes, shapes and fittings are nonexistent – shop around until you find the right one. Other good clothing buys include woollen hats and mittens, and stylish – but extremely expensive – weatherproof outdoor gear made by local brands **66°N**, **Icewear** and **Cintamani**.

Stores in Reykjavík also stock a range of silver and lava **jewellery**, in some intriguing designs. And Iceland's wild-caught **smoked salmon** is probably the best you'll ever eat, firm-textured and robustly scented without being too oily – it costs much the same as you pay at home for farmed versions.

Time

Iceland is on **Greenwich Mean Time** (GMT) throughout the year. GMT is 5 hours ahead of US Eastern Standard Time and 10 hours behind Australian Eastern Standard Time.

OPERATOR SERVICES AND INTERNATIONAL CALLS

OPERATOR SERVICES IN ICELAND

Emergencies Fire, ambulance or police
☎112
International directory enquiries ☎114
International operator ☎115
National directory enquiries ☎118

CALLING HOME FROM ICELAND

Note that the initial zero is omitted from the area code when dialling the UK, Ireland, Australia and New Zealand from abroad.
US and Canada 00 + 1 + area code
Australia 00 + 61 + area code
New Zealand 00 + 64 + area code
UK 00 + 44 + area code
Republic of Ireland 00 + 353 + area code
South Africa 00 + 27 + area code

PHOTOGRAPHING THE NORTHERN LIGHTS

The **Northern Lights** are only visible in the darkness of winter, and from places with clear skies, away from light pollution. Probably the most magical place to view them is at Jökulsárlón in the southeast, especially from the nearby black-sand beach with its crystal-clear ice boulders which pick up the Lights' red and green glow. The colours are not always as intense as you'd expect, however, and to get good shots you'll need a camera capable of making exposures of a minute or more.

Tourist information

In addition to the websites listed below, Reykjavík's **tourist information offices** (see p.73) have brochures for the whole country, with independent tourist offices in almost every other town, often housed in the bus station. Your accommodation can be another good source of local details, as families may have lived in the region for generations, and have very thorough knowledge.

GOVERNMENT WEBSITES

Australian Department of Foreign Affairs Ⓦ dfat.gov.au, Ⓦ smartraveller.gov.au.
British Foreign & Commonwealth Office Ⓦ gov.uk.
Canadian Department of Foreign Affairs Ⓦ international.gc.ca.
Irish Department of Foreign Affairs Ⓦ dfa.ie.
New Zealand Ministry of Foreign Affairs Ⓦ mft.govt.nz.
US State Department Ⓦ travel.state.gov.
South African Department of Foreign Affairs Ⓦ dfa.gov.za.

ICELAND ONLINE

Environment Agency Ⓦ ust.is. Some useful practical information for travelers in Iceland's wilder corners.
Explore Iceland Ⓦ exploreiceland.is. What's on around Iceland, plus flight, accommodation and tour bookings, and information on the country.
Iceland Review Ⓦ icelandreview.com. Daily round-up of local news stories in English, all reported with an Icelandic quirkiness – gives a good feel for the country.
Randburg Ⓦ randburg.is. Excellent information and booking service covering just about anything you could do in Iceland.
Reykjavík Grapevine Ⓦ grapevine.is. Website for the irreverent weekly listings magazine, with all upcoming attractions, parties, bands and events, plus archived reviews of accommodation, restaurants, cafés and places to visit around the country.
Visit Iceland Ⓦ visiticeland.com. Icelandic Tourist Board site, with comprehensive regional rundowns, listing the main sights and recommended services – and, of course, their unique "Ask Guðmundur" search engine.
Vatnajökull National Park Ⓦ vjp.is. Background and travel advice for Europe's largest national park.

Travellers with disabilities

Iceland is fairly well prepared for **disabled travellers**. New hotels are required by law to make a percentage of their rooms accessible, while transport – including coastal ferries, airlines and a few public tour buses – can make provisions for wheelchair users if notified in advance.

Your first contact in Iceland is **Sjálfsbjörg**, Reykjavík's Disabled Association, at Hátún 12, 105 Reykjavík (☏ 550 0360, ✉ sjalfsbjorg@sjalfsbjorg.is), whose staff can advise on accessible accommodation and travel around Iceland. Alternatively, contact service operators direct; details are listed throughout the Guide.

Reykjavík

REYKJAVÍK CITYSCAPE

1

Reykjavík

The world's most northerly capital, Reykjavík has a sense of space and calm that comes as a breath of fresh air to travellers accustomed to the bustle of the traffic-clogged streets in Europe's other major cities. Although small for a capital (the population is around 120,000), Reykjavík is a throbbing urban metropolis compared with Iceland's other built-up areas; the Greater Reykjavík area is home to two out of every three Icelanders. If you're planning to visit some of the country's more remote and isolated regions, you should make the most of the atmosphere generated by this bustling port, with its highbrow museums and a buzzing nightlife that has earned the place a reputation for hedonistic revelry.

Split roughly into two halves by the brilliant waters of the large, naturally occurring **Tjörnin** lake, the tiny **city centre** is more a place to amble around and take in the suburban-looking streets and corner cafés than somewhere to hurtle through between attractions. Reykjavík lacks the grand and imposing buildings found in other Nordic capitals, possessing instead apparently ramshackle clusters of houses, either clad in garishly painted corrugated iron or daubed in pebbledash as protection against the ferocious North Atlantic storms. This rather unkempt feel, though, is as much part of the city's charm as the views across the sea to glaciers and the sheer mountains that form the backdrop to the streets. Even in the heart of this capital, nature is always in evidence – there can be few other cities in the world, for example, where greylag geese regularly overfly the busy centre, sending bemused visitors, more accustomed to diminutive pigeons, scurrying for cover.

Amid the essentially residential city centre, it is the **Hallgrímskirkja**, a gargantuan white concrete church towering over the surrounding houses, that is the most enduring image of Reykjavík. Below this, the elegant shops and stylish bars and restaurants that line the main street and commercial thoroughfare of **Laugavegur** are a consumer's heaven. The central core of streets around Laugavegur is where you'll find a range of engaging museums, too. The displays in the Landnámssýningin and the **Saga Museum**, for example, offer an accessible introduction to Iceland's stirring past, while you'll find the outstanding work of sculptors **Ásmundur Sveinsson** and **Einar Jónsson** outdoors in the streets and parks, as well as in two permanent exhibitions.

With time to spare, it's worth venturing outside the city limits into **Greater Reykjavík**, for a taste of the Icelandic provinces – suburban style. Although predominantly an area of dormitory overspill for the capital, the town of **Hafnarfjörður** is large enough to be independent of Reykjavík and has a couple of museums and a busy harbour, though it's perhaps best known for its **Viking feasts**. Alternatively, the flat and treeless island of **Viðey**, barely ten minutes offshore from Reykjavík, is the place to come for magnificent

WHALE WATCHING UNDER THE MIDNIGHT SUN

Highlights

❶ **Landnámssýningin (Settlement Exhibition)** See how the first Icelanders lived in this underground museum, whose centrepiece is the extensive remains of a tenth-century Viking hall – still in its original location. **See p.58**

❷ **Whales of Iceland** Walk among life-size, silicone models of the whales found in Icelandic waters in this informative new museum, and learn all about the giants of the sea. **See p.61**

❸ **Hallgrímskirkja** Ride the lift to the top of the tower of this Reykjavík landmark for one of the most awe-inspiring views in the whole country. **See p.67**

❹ **Swimming in Nauthólsvík geothermal lagoon** Take a dip in the sublime waters of the capital's open-air lagoon and laze on its golden sands before jumping into the hot pot. **See p.69**

❺ **Whale watching** With handy departures from the city harbour, this is one of the most cost-effective ways of seeing whales up close. **See p.74**

❻ **Friday night in Reykjavík** Join the locals on their *rúntur*, a good-natured pub-crawl, and wind your way round some of the city's top bars and clubs. **See p.82**

HIGHLIGHTS ARE MARKED ON THE MAPS ON P.52 & PP.54–55

1

EXCURSIONS FROM REYKJAVÍK

The capital makes a good base for excursions **around Reykjavík**, including to three of Iceland's most popular attractions: the site of the old parliament, **Alþingi**, at Þingvellir (see p.101), the waterspouts and waterfalls of **Geysir** and **Gullfoss** (see p.108 & p.109), and **Skálholt** cathedral (see p.107) – all within simple reach by public transport or, more expensively, on day-long guided tours from the city. Also worthwhile is the **Reykjanes peninsula** (see p.95), a bleak lavafield that's as good an introduction as any to the stark scenery you'll find further into Iceland, and home to the mineral-rich waters of the **Blue Lagoon** (see p.95), the most visited attraction in the country. If you're only in the city for a short break, or flying on to either the US or Europe, Reykjavík is also the place to fix up two of Iceland's most ususual trips: either a tour inside the Langjökull glacier near Húsafell (see box, p.160) or a descent into the extinct volcano at Þríhjúkahellir, southeast of Reykjavík (see p.88).

views of the city and of the surrounding mountains – there are also some enjoyable walking trails here, which lead around the island in a couple of hours.

Brief history

As recounted in the ancient manuscripts *Íslendingabók* and *Landnámábók*, Reykjavík's origins date back to the country's first settler, **Ingólfur Arnarson**, who arrived in 874 AD, brought here by his high seat pillars – emblems of tribal chieftainship, tossed overboard from his boat – and settling, in pagan tradition, wherever they washed up. He named the place "smoky bay" (*reykja* meaning "of smoke", *vík* meaning "bay", cognate with English *wick*), mistakenly thinking that the distant plumes of steam issuing from boiling spring water were smoke caused by fire. It was a poor place to settle, however, as the soil was too infertile to support successful farming, and Reykjavík remained barely inhabited until an early seventeenth-century **sea-fishing** boom brought Danish traders here, after which a small shanty town to house their Icelandic labour force sprang into existence. Later, in the middle of the eighteenth

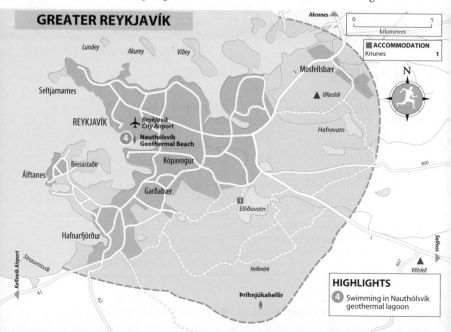

GREATER REYKJAVÍK

Akranes

0   5
kilometres

■ ACCOMMODATION
Kríunes   **1**

N

Lundey   Akurey   Viðey

Mosfellsbær

Seltjarnarnes

▲ Úlfarsfell

REYKJAVÍK   ✈ Reykjavik City Airport

Hafravatn

4 Nauthólsvík Geothermal Beach

Kópavogur

Bessastaðir

360

Álftanes

Garðabær

1 Elliðavatn

Hafnarfjörður

Selfoss

Straumsvík

Heiðmörk

407   ▲ Vífilsfell

Keflavík Airport

41

42

Þríhnjúkahellir

HIGHLIGHTS

4 Swimming in Nauthólsvík geothermal lagoon

century, **Skúli Magnússon**, the official in charge of Reykjavík's administrative affairs (*landfógeti*), a man today regarded as the city's founder, used Reykjavík as a base to establish Icelandic-controlled industries, opening several mills and tanneries and importing foreign craftspeople to pass on their skills. A municipal charter was granted in 1786, when the population totalled a mere 167 – setting the course for Reykjavík's acceptance as Iceland's capital. At the end of the eighteenth century, the city replaced Skálholt as the national seat of religion and gained the Lutheran cathedral, Dómkirkjan; eighty years later, with the opening of the new Alþingi building, it became the base of the national parliament.

Since independence in 1944, **expansion** has been almost continuous. As a fishing harbour, a port for the produce of the fertile farms of the southwest and a centre for a variety of small industries, Reykjavík provides employment for over half the country's population. The city has also pioneered the use of geothermal energy to provide low-cost heating – which is why you have to wait for the cold water instead of the hot when taking a shower, and why tap water always has a whiff of sulphur.

Over recent years there's been a substantial boom, too, in **tourism**. The ever-increasing visitor numbers to Reykjavík are largely due to the greater number of airlines now operating to Iceland, and the collapse of the country's banking system and currency in 2008, which saw prices drop by half virtually overnight for anyone converting money into the formerly overvalued Icelandic króna. Consequently, Iceland has never provided better value for money. The seemingly endless hotel construction boom in Reykjavík is a sure sign that tourism has never been more important and that the Icelandic economy is well and truly back on track.

Central Reykjavík

You'd be hard pushed to find another capital as diminutive as Reykjavík, and a leisurely walk of just an hour or two will take you around almost the entirety of the centre. Such smallness accounts for the city's lack of contrasting and well-defined areas: for convenience, we've covered the northern and western side of **Tjörnin** lake first, then continued with sights on the eastern side. These areas are split neatly by the road, **Lækjargata**, which runs from the lake's eastern border, past Reykjavík's main square, **Lækjartorg**, and down towards the harbour. Even the few things of note further out from the centre can be reached in a few minutes on public transport.

Lækjartorg and Austurstræti

The best place to get your first taste of Reykjavík is the area around **Lækjartorg** and the adjoining pedestrianized **Austurstræti** on its western side – a general meeting place for Reykjavík's urbanites, where people stroll, strut and sit on benches munching cakes, ice creams and burgers bought from the nearby fast-food outlets and supermarket. The square has always been at the heart of Reykjavík life; indeed, it was here that farmers bringing produce to market ended their long journey from the surrounding countryside, and set up camp to sell their goods. Lækjartorg was once overlooked from its western end by the headquarters of the main daily newspaper, *Morgunblaðið*, the implication being that journalists needed only to look through their windows to discover what was happening in the city – which was usually very little. Today, however, the area can be one of the most boisterous in the city. On Friday and Saturday evenings, particularly in summer, hundreds of drunken revellers fill the square when the clubs empty out at 5 or 6am, jostling for prime position – although the noise from the throng can be deafening, the atmosphere is good-hearted and not at all intimidating. By day, the area resumes its busy commercial air as people dash in and out of the post office or pop in to the Eymundsson bookshop

1

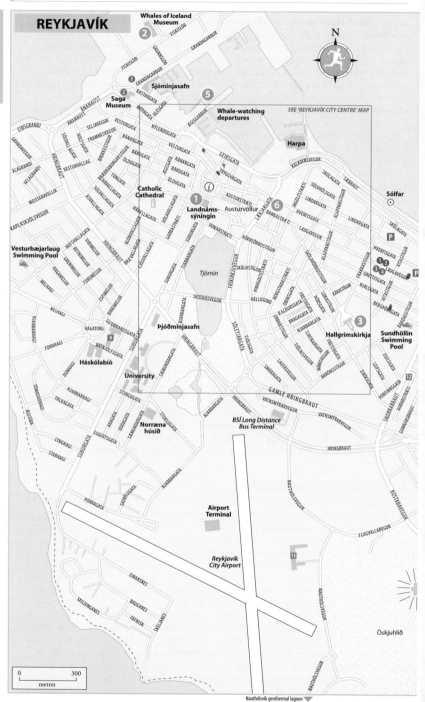

REYKJAVÍK

Whales of Iceland Museum

Saga Museum

Sjóminjasafn

Whale-watching departures

SEE 'REYKJAVÍK CITY CENTRE' MAP

Harpa

Catholic Cathedral

Landnáms-sýningin

Austurvöllur

Sólfar

Vesturbæjarlaug Swimming Pool

Tjörnin

Þjóðminjasafn

Hallgrímskirkja

Sundhöllin Swimming Pool

Háskólabíó

University

Norræna húsið

BSÍ Long Distance Bus Terminal

Airport Terminal

Reykjavík City Airport

Öskjuhlíð

N

0   300
metres

Nauthólsvík geothermal lagoon

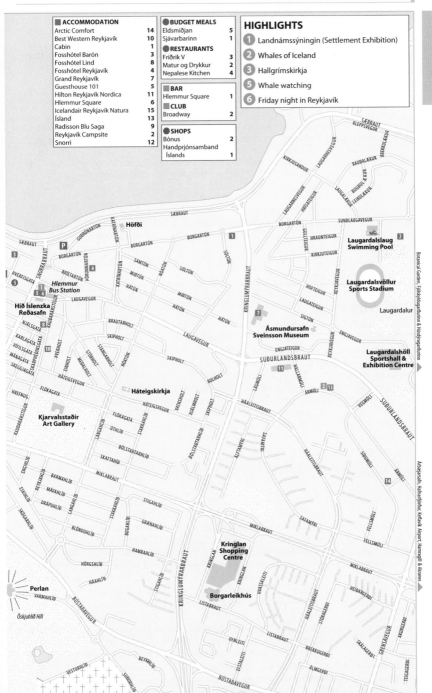

■ ACCOMMODATION

Arctic Comfort	14
Best Western Reykjavík	10
Cabin	1
Fosshótel Barón	3
Fosshótel Lind	8
Fosshótel Reykjavík	4
Grand Reykjavík	7
Guesthouse 101	5
Hilton Reykjavík Nordica	11
Hlemmur Square	6
Icelandair Reykjavík Natura	15
Ísland	13
Radisson Blu Saga	9
Reykjavík Campsite	2
Snorri	12

● BUDGET MEALS

Eldsmiðjan	5
Sjávarbarinn	1

● RESTAURANTS

Friðrik V	3
Matur og Drykkur	2
Nepalese Kitchen	4

■ BAR

Hlemmur Square	1

■ CLUB

Broadway	2

● SHOPS

Bónus	2
Handprjónsamband Íslands	1

HIGHLIGHTS

1 Landnámssýningin (Settlement Exhibition)

2 Whales of Iceland

3 Hallgrímskirkja

5 Whale watching

6 Friday night in Reykjavík

1

ICELANDIC PEOPLE POWER

Every Saturday between mid-October 2008 and late January 2009, thousands of Icelanders gathered in Austurvöllur square to voice their anger over the **collapse** of the Icelandic **banking system** which, it's estimated, left one in five families bankrupt. The protesters began by burning the flag of Landsbanki, though soon also called for heads to roll. The main target of popular discontent was the leader of the Icelandic Central Bank and former long-serving politician, Davíð Oddsson, who was squarely blamed for the economic collapse. The **demonstrators** became more vocal as the lack of decisive action by the government continued. Three and a half months of protests, in Austurvöllur and at various locations around the country, finally convinced Prime Minister Geir Haarde that his administration had no future; to national jubilation, it fell on January 26, 2009. However in 2012 a special court found Haarde not guilty of negligence over the economic meltdown, accusing him merely of failing to hold cabinet meetings when things turned critical. Equally exonerated, Davíð Oddsson is today editor of the country's biggest newspaper, *Morgunblaðið*.

(see p.84). Beyond its junction with Pósthússtræti, Austurstræti gives itself over solely to pleasure, as this is where some of the city's best **bars** and **restaurants** can be found. This is also the location for the *vínbúð* state alcohol store, a futuristic glass-and-steel structure at no. 10a (see p.84), where those who want to drink at home have to come to buy their alcohol supplies.

Austurvöllur

Pósthússtræti, running south from Austurstræti, leads into another small square, **Austurvöllur**, a favourite place for city slickers from nearby offices to catch a few rays during their lunch breaks, stretched out on the grassy lawns edged with flowers. Yet the square's modest proportions and nondescript apartment blocks belie its historical importance. This was the site of Ingólfur Arnarson's farm; it's thought he grew his hay on the land where the square now stands, and it marks the original centre of Reykjavík. Similarly, the square's central, elevated **statue** of the nineteenth-century independence campaigner **Jón Sigurðsson**, entitled *The Pride of Iceland, its Sword and Shield*, faces two of the most important buildings in the country – the Alþingishúsið and the Dómkirkjan – though you'd never realize their status from their appearance.

Alþingishúsið
Austurvöllur square

The **Alþingishúsið** (Parliament House) is ordinary in the extreme, a slight building made of grey basalt quarried from nearby Skólavörðuholt hill, with the date of its completion (1881) etched into its dark frontage – yet this unremarkable structure played a pivotal role in bringing about Icelandic independence. In 1798, the parliament moved to Reykjavík from Þingvellir (see p.101), where it had been operating virtually without interruption since 930 AD. Within just two years, however, it was dissolved as Danish power reached its peak, but with great pride and after much struggle, the Alþingi regained its powers from Copenhagen as a consultative body in 1843, and a constitution was granted in 1874, making Iceland self-governing in domestic affairs. The Act of Union, passed in this building in 1918, made Iceland a sovereign state under the Danish Crown, although the act was open for reconsideration at any time after 1940. By then, however, Denmark was occupied by the Nazis and the Alþingi had assumed the duties normally carried out by the monarch, declaring its intention to dissolve the Act of Union at the end of the war. Today, the modest interior, illuminated by chandeliers, more resembles a town council chamber than the seat of a national parliament.

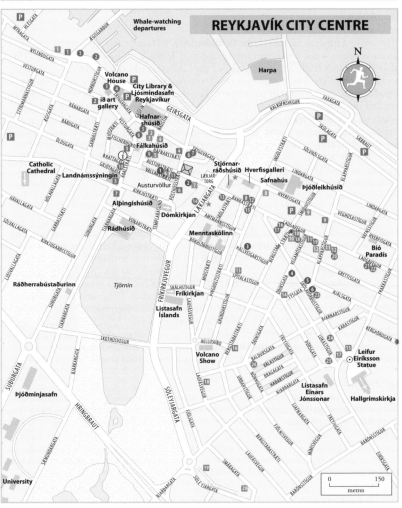

REYKJAVÍK CITY CENTRE

■ ACCOMMODATION		● BUDGET MEALS		● RESTAURANTS		■ BAR AND CLUBS	
Adam	17	Bæjarins Beztu Pylsur	7	Café Loki	25	Bjarni Fell	7
Anna	20	Búllan	1	Einar Ben	9	Bravó	11
Baldursbrá	18	Grillhúsið	5	Fish & More	23	Dolly	5
Borg	6	Icelandic Fish & Chips	4	Fish Market	10	Enski Barinn	6
Frón	12	Krua Thai	3	Gló	19	Frederiksen Ale House	4
Holt	16			Hornið	8	Kaffibarinn	10
Icelandair Reykjavík Marina	1	● CAFÉS		Jómfrúin	14	Kaldi Bar	12
Klöpp	9	Café Paris	11	Kól	24	Mikkeller & Friends	8
Leifur Eiríksson	15	Kaffi Sólon	12	Lækjarbrekka	13	Slippbarinn	1
Luna	13	Kaffitár	15	Restaurant Reykjavík	6		
Óðinsvé	14	Kofi Tómasar Frænda	16	Rosso Pomodoro	22	■ LIVE MUSIC VENUES	
Plaza	3	Mokka	17	Sægreifinn	2	Celtic Cross	9
Radisson Blu 1919	4	Sandholt	21	Scandinavian Smørrebrød	20	Dubliner	3
Reykjavík Centrum	5			Vegamót	18	Gaukurinn	2
Reykjavík Downtown Hostel	2			Þrir Frakkar	26		
Reykjavík Loft Hostel	8					● SHOPS	
Room with a view	11					Bónus	3
Salvation Army Guesthouse	7					Eymundsson	2/6
Skjaldbreið	10					Geysir	4
Travel-Inn	19					Handprjónasamband Íslands	5
						Vínbúð	1

1

Dómkirkjan

Lækjargata 14a • Mon–Fri 10am–4.30pm • Free

Reykjavík's Lutheran cathedral, the **Dómkirkjan**, is a Neoclassical stone structure shrouded against the weather in corrugated iron. It was built between 1787 and 1796 after Christian VII of Denmark scrapped the Catholic bishoprics of Hólar in the north, and Skálholt in the south, in favour of a Lutheran diocese in what was fast growing into Iceland's main centre of population. The church may be plain on the outside, but venture inside and you'll discover a beautiful interior: perfectly designed arched windows punctuate the unadorned white-painted walls at regular intervals, giving an impression of complete architectural harmony. The cathedral is now deemed too small for great gatherings and services of state, and the roomier Hallgrímskirkja is preferred for state funerals and other such well-attended functions, although the opening of parliament is still marked with a service in the Dómkirkjan followed by a short procession along Kirkjustræti to the Alþingishúsið.

Aðalstræti

From the southwestern corner of Austurvöllur, Kirkjustræti runs the short distance to Reykjavík's oldest street, **Aðalstræti**, which follows the route taken in the late ninth century by Ingólfur Arnarson from his farm at the southern end of the street down to the sea. In addition to the remains of a Viking-age farmhouse on display inside the Landnámssýninginin museum, Aðalstræti also holds Reykjavík's **oldest surviving building**, a squat timber structure at no. 10. It dates back to 1752, and was formerly a weaving shed, a bishop's residence and the home of Skúli Magnússon, High Sheriff of Iceland, who encouraged the development of craft industries here. On the opposite side of the street, a few steps north towards the sea outside the present no. 9, is Ingólfur Arnarson's freshwater well, **Ingólfsbrunnur**, discovered by fluke when the city council carried out roadworks here in 1992, and now glassed over for posterity.

Landnámssýningin

Aðalstræti 16 • Daily 9am–8pm • Settlement Exhibition 1400kr; Saga Exhibition 1000kr; both exhibitions 2200kr • ⓦ reykjavik871.is

The **Landnámssýningin** (Settlement Exhibition), whose centrepiece is the extensive ruins of a **Viking-age farmhouse**, is one of Iceland's most remarkable museums. Housed in a purpose-built hall directly beneath Aðalstræti, the structure's oval-shaped stone walls, excavated in 2001, enclose a sizeable living space of 85 square metres with a central hearth as the focal point. Dating the farmhouse has been relatively straightforward, since the layer of volcanic ash which fell across Iceland following a powerful eruption in around 871 AD lies just beneath the building; it's estimated, therefore, that people lived here between 930 and 1000. As you wander around the exhibition, look out for the animal spine, probably that of a horse or cow, buried under part of the farmhouse's western wall as a talisman to ward off evil spirits, a common practice during the Viking period. The exhibition's wall space is given over to panoramic views of forest and scrubland to help give a realistic impression of what Reykjavík would have looked like at the time of the Settlement. Indeed, when the first settlers arrived in the area, the hills were covered in birch woods. However, just one hundred years later, the birch had all but disappeared, felled to make way for grazing land or burnt for charcoal needed for iron smelting. Recent excavation work outside the museum at the corner of Kirkjustræti and Tjarnargata unearthed traces of eight iron-smelting furnaces and a charcoal pit, also from the 870s, where bog iron was used to produce various goods. Artefacts from the dig, including an ornate silver bracelet, are on display in the Settlement Exhibition.

The Saga Exhibition

Housed in a side room to the left of reception, the Saga Exhibition is the place to see some of Iceland's medieval documents. Sadly, there are only five manuscripts on display here (the Book of Icelanders, the Saga of the People of Kjalarnes, the Book of Settlements, Jónsbók and the Deed of Purchase for Reykjavík from 1615), and you're bound to leave with your appetite barely whetted. However, once construction of the Hús íslenskra fræða (House of Icelandic Studies), opposite the national museum, is completed several years hence, this modest display will close and a more comprehensive exhibition will open in its place in the new building which will also house the Árni Magnússon Institute, the keeper of Iceland's medieval manuscripts.

Hafnarstræti

Many of the buildings on the south side of **Hafnarstræti** were formerly owned by Danish merchants during the Trade Monopoly of 1602–1855 (see p.339), and indeed this street, as its name suggests (*hafnar* means "harbour"), once bordered the sea and gave access to the harbour, the city's economic lifeline and means of contact with the outside world. Today, though, Hafnarstræti is several blocks from the ocean after landfill extended the city foreshore. Instead, it's home to some excellent bars and restaurants and, together with Austurstræti to the south and Tryggvagata to the north, makes up a rectangular block of eateries and drinking-holes that are well worthy of exploration.

Fálkahúsið

Corner of Aðalstræti and Hafnarstræti

Opposite the tourist office, and covered in corrugated iron for protection, **Fálkahúsið** is another of Reykjavík's beautifully restored timber buildings, one of three in the city where the King of Denmark once kept his much-prized Icelandic falcons before having them dispatched by ship to the Court in Copenhagen. There was outrage when the building was converted into a restaurant, inevitably subjecting the ancient timbers to the wear and tear of hundreds of stomping feet. Despite this, its turret-like side walls and sheer size still impress, especially when you consider the huge amount of timber that was imported for the job, as Iceland had no trees of its own. Cast an eye to the roof and you'll spot two carved wooden falcons still keeping guard over the building, either side of a garish modern representation of a Viking longboat.

Tryggvagata

Tryggvagata, one block north of the bustle of Hafnarstræti, is remarkable for a few things other than the number of consonants in its name: the imposing multicoloured mosaic **mural by Gerður Helgadóttir** (1928–75) close to its junction with Pósthússtræti, portraying a busy harbour scene complete with fishing trawlers and cranes, and livening up the otherwise frightfully dull **Tollhúsið** (Customs House); **Hafnarhúsið**, part of the **Reykjavík Art Museum; Ljósmindasafn Reykjavíkiur** (Reykjavík Museum of Photography) and the **Volcano House** film show.

Hafnarhúsið

Tryggvagata 17 • Daily 10am–5pm, Thurs till 8pm • 1400kr • Ⓦ artmuseum.is

The large, austere **Hafnarhúsið** (Harbour House) was originally constructed in the 1930s as warehouse storage and office space for the Port of Reykjavík, but has now been converted into six large exhibition halls, connected by a corridor running over a central courtyard. Although there's certainly plenty of space here, the layout is less than obvious since the confusing array of corridors, which once linked the former warehouse's storage areas, twist and turn around the museum's supporting concrete and steel pillars, leaving the visitor quite lost at times. Although the museum plays host to frequently changing displays of contemporary Icelandic and international **art**, the only permanent exhibition is that dedicated to the multicoloured cartoon-like work of Icelandic artist **Erró**.

1

Ljósmyndasafn Reykjavíkur

Tryggvagata 15 • Mon–Thurs noon–7pm, Fri noon–6pm, Sat & Sun 1–5pm • Free • Ⓦ ljosmyndasafnreykjavikur.is

The top floor of the city library building, Grófarhús, is given over to a changing exhibition of contemporary photography. Though the space is modest, the museum holds a collection of around six million photographs which it showcases alongside work from established, visiting photographers. In addition, posters and postcards of some of the museum's collection are available for sale.

Volcano House

Tryggvagata 11 • Daily 10am–10pm • 1990kr • Ⓦ volcanohouse.is

Unless of a serious geological bent, you're unlikely to want to give but the merest of glances to the collection of lumps of pumice, tephra and jasper displayed at the **Volcano House**. Actually more cinema than museum, it's worth visiting for the twenty-minute **films** of the 1973 Westman Islands and 2010 Eyjafjallajökull eruptions which are shown every hour on the hour. Although rather grainy, the **Westman Islands** film is the more interesting of the two, documenting the devastating impact of the eruption on the island community. The **Eyjafjallajökull** film, while outlining the basics of what happened geologically during the eruption, barely mentions the ensuing chaos in the skies across Europe; if you're looking for something altogether more comprehensive on Eyjafjallajökull, check out the National Geographic film shown at the Eldfjallasafn in Stykkishólmur instead (see p.172). The Volcano House is also the location of the *Icelandic Fish and Chips* restaurant (see p.80).

The harbour

North of Geirsgata, the busy main road which runs parallel to the shoreline, Reykjavík **harbour** is built around reclaimed land – the beach where vessels once landed their foreign goods is now well inland from here and long since covered over. Street names around here, such as Ægisgata (ocean street) and Öldugata (wave street), reflect the importance of the sea to the city, and a stroll along the dockside demonstrates Iceland's dependence on the Atlantic, with fishing trawlers being checked over and prepared for their next battle against the waves, and plastic crates of ice-packed cod awaiting transportation to village stores around the country. Keep an eye out, too, for the black **whaling vessels**, each with a red "H" painted on its funnel (*hvalur* is Icelandic for "whale"), which are moored here. Paradoxically, the harbour is also the departure point for **whale-watching tours** (see box, p.74).

Saga Museum

Grandagarður 2 • Daily 10am–6pm • 2000kr • Ⓦ sagamuseum.is

Housed in a former fish storehouse on the western edge of the harbour, the excellent **Saga Museum** is Iceland's answer to Madame Tussaud's. The expertly crafted **wax models** of

---

ICELANDIC POP ART

Erró is Iceland's best-known **pop artist**. His vibrant collages, depicting everything from Viking warriors to space-age superheroes all seemingly caught up in the same explosive battle, are certainly striking, if somewhat eye-blinding and not to everyone's taste. Born Guðmundur Guðmundsson in Ólafsvík on the Snæfellsnes peninsula in 1932, Erró grew up in Kirkjubæjarklaustur before moving abroad to study at the art academies of Oslo, Florence and Ravenna, and finally settling in Paris where he still lives today. In 1982 Erró (nobody knows why he chose this name, although he was forced to change from Ferró to Erró in 1967 after being sued) donated about two thousand of his works, including oil paintings, prints and sculptures, to the City of Reykjavík, a selection of which is on display inside the Hafnarhúsið (see p.59).

characters from the sagas and their reconstructed farms and homes are used to superbly enliven medieval Icelandic life, often a confusing period in the country's history. A visit here will give you a genuine sense of what life must have been like in Iceland centuries ago. All the big names are here: Snorri, who even breathes deeply as he ponders; Eirík the Red; and Leifur Eiríksson and his sister Freyðis, the latter portrayed slicing off her breast as a solitary stand against the natives of Vínland who, after killing one of her compatriots, turned on her – according to the sagas, however, on seeing Freyðis brandish a sword against her breasts, they immediately took flight. An informative audioguide (included in the admission fee) explains a little about each of the characters on display – and the smells of the period which have been synthetically reproduced inside, too.

Sjóminjasafn

Grandagarður 8 • Daily 10am–5pm; daily guided tours of Óðinn at 1pm, 2pm & 3pm • Museum 1400kr; Óðinn tour 1200kr; 2000kr for both • ⓦ maritimemuseum.is

Given Iceland's prominence as a seafaring nation, Reykjavík's Maritime Museum is a disappointment. A ragtag collection of old fishing hooks, dried fish and model boats, this tired exhibition of fisheries through the ages is dull in the extreme. The only saving grace is the former coastguard vessel, *Óðinn*, moored in the dock outside. Built in Denmark in 1959, the ship patrolled Iceland's territorial waters in the North Atlantic until 2006, taking part in all three cod wars with the United Kingdom. The cutters used to slice through the nets of British trawlers are displayed on *Óðinn*'s rear deck.

Whales of Iceland

Fiskislóð 23 • May–Sept daily 9am–9pm; Oct–April daily 9am–6pm • 2900kr • ⓦ whalesoficeland.is

This creative new museum may well have drawn a fair amount of criticism over its inflated entry price, but Whales of Iceland offers a unique opportunity to see whales for what they really are – massive marine mammals whose true bulk is hidden under the surface of the water. Located in a vast purpose-built warehouse, the museum contains no fewer than 23 life-size models of whales, suspended from the ceiling. Walking below and between the models really does give an amazing perspective of just how big these creatures are. The man-made models, complete with steel skeletons and silicone skins, are exceptionally well executed, having been made in China and shipped to Iceland in sections – the model of a blue whale, for example, is as long as a tennis court. The museum contains a model of virtually every species of whale present in Icelandic waters and consequently presents a great opportunity to see what some of the whales you'll become familiar with as you travel around Iceland actually look like: the sperm whale, humpback, minke and even beluga are all here. In addition to the models, there are information panels on each of the species and a few short video presentations.

Harpa

Austurbakki • Daily 8am–midnight • Free • ⓦ harpa.is

A striking new addition to the Reykjavík skyline, on the eastern side of the harbour, the eye-catching **Harpa opera house** had a difficult birth. At the time of the economic crash in 2008, the structure was barely half-built and a tide of politicians and decision-makers called for the scheme to be scrapped: Iceland shouldn't be building an opulent new opera house in the midst of a severe financial crisis. Amid much derision, however, the project went ahead and has produced one of Reykjavík's most memorable buildings. Taking its cue from Iceland's unusual geological forms, Harpa's exterior is composed of hexagonal glass cubes, designed to resemble the basalt columns of lava seen all over the country; during the dark winter months, **light shows** illuminate the glass panels producing ingenious displays of colour and shape. The main feature of the airy interior

1

is the classic shoebox-shaped concert hall, **Eldborg**, with seating for up to 1800. The country's premier venue for concerts and theatre productions, Harpa is also home to the Icelandic symphony orchestra and national opera. Visitors are free to wander around the building at leisure, and the café on the ground floor makes an agreeable place to watch the comings and goings of the harbour through the hexagonal windows.

Tjörnin

From the harbour, Pósthússtræti leads south past the bars and restaurants of Tryggvagata, Hafnarstræti and Austurstræti to Vonarstræti and **Tjörnin**, invariably translated into English as "the lake" or "the pond". *Tjörn* and its genitive form of *tjarnar* are actually old Viking words, still used in northern English and Scottish dialects as "tarn" to denote a mountain lake. Originally formed by a lagoon inside the reef that once occupied the spot where Hafnarstræti now runs, this sizeable body of water, roughly a couple of square kilometres in size, is populated by forty to fifty bird species – including the notorious **arctic tern**, known for its dive-bombing attacks on passers-by, and found at the lake's quieter southern end. The precise numbers of the lake's bird population are charted on noticeboards stationed at several points along the bank.

Ráðhúsið

Tjarnargata 11 • Mon–Fri 8am–7pm, Sat & Sun noon–6pm • Free

Occupying a prime position on the northern edge of Tjörnin is **Ráðhúsið** (City Hall). Opened in 1992, it's a showpiece of Nordic design, a modernistic rectangular structure of steel, glass and chrome that actually appears to sit right on the lake itself. Inside, in addition to the city's administration offices, is a small café and, in one of the small exhibition areas, a fabulous self-standing **topographical model** of Iceland. This gives an excellent idea of the country's unforgiving geography – you can marvel at the sheer size of the Vatnajökull glacier in the southeast (as big as the English county of Yorkshire) and the table mountains of the West Fjords, and gain instant respect for the people who live amid such restricting landscapes.

Ráðherrabústaðurinn

Tjarnargata 32 • Closed to the public

One of Reykjavík's grandest old wooden buildings, **Ráðherrabústaðurinn** (Minister's residence) is an impressive structure. It was first built at Sólbakki in Önundarfjörður in the West Fjords and formerly owned by a rich Norwegian businessman who's said to have either given it or sold it to Iceland's first Home Rule minister, Hannes Hafstein, in 1904 for the princely sum of 1kr; today it's used by the Icelandic government for official receptions. Timber has always been a much prized commodity in Iceland since the country has no forests capable of producing construction-grade wood. The practice of moving wooden houses from one location to another was common in former times, particularly during the nineteenth century when some wooden buildings were even shipped from Norway for reconstruction on site in Iceland.

Suðurgata

One of the best **views** of Reykjavík can be had from **Suðurgata**, a street running parallel to Tjörnin's western shore; to get there from the city hall, walk west along Vonarstræti, crossing Tjarnargata. Suðurgata is lined with tidy little dwellings, but from it you can see across the lake to the suburban houses of the city centre, whose corrugated-iron roofs, ranging in colour from a pallid two-tone green to bright blues and reds, have been carefully maintained by their owners – the familiar picture-postcard view of Reykjavík.

Þjóðminjasafn

Suðurgata 41 • May to mid-Sept daily 10am–5pm; mid-Sept to April Tues–Sun 10am–5pm • 1500kr • ⓦ natmus.is

1

Þjóðminjasafn, the National Museum, offers a comprehensive historical overview of the country's past from the days of the Settlement right up to the birth of the Republic in 1944 and beyond. Having seen the exhibits, it's worth having a quick look at the changing displays of contemporary photography, which are displayed within an undistinguished room known rather pompously as the **National Gallery of Photography**; it's behind the museum shop on the ground floor.

The first floor

The **first floor**, devoted to the period from 800 to 1600, is by far the most engaging part of the museum; the video presentation within the "Origin of Icelanders" exhibition, devoted to the early Viking period and the use of **DNA testing**, is particularly good. Recent genetic research has shown that whereas around eighty percent of today's Icelanders are of Nordic origin, sixty-two percent of the early Viking-era women originated from the British Isles; the conclusion, therefore, is that the first settlers sailed from Scandinavia to Iceland via the British Isles where they took wives. An informative video display shows how DNA testing of the pulp cavity of the teeth of these first settlers is being carried out in an attempt to add scientific credence to the recent genetic research results.

Other prime exhibits include a small human figure, about the size of a thumb and made of bronze, which is thought to be over a thousand years old and to portray either the Norse god Þór or Christ. More spectacular is the **carved church door** from Valþjófsstaður in Fljótsdalur (see p.127), dating from around 1200, and depicting the medieval tale *Le Chevalier au Lion:* it features an ancient warrior on horseback slugging it out with an unruly dragon. The Danish authorities finally gave up the treasure in 1930 and returned the door to Iceland, together with a host of medieval manuscripts. Check out, too, the impressive Romanesque-style carved **Madonna** dating from around 1200, which hails from northern Iceland and is displayed within the "Medieval church" section.

The second floor

The **second floor** of the museum, devoted to the period from 1600 onwards, canters through key events in Icelandic history such as the Trade Monopoly (1602–1787) and the Birth of the Republic. It terminates in a revolving airport-style conveyor belt laden with twentieth-century appliances and knick-knacks, featuring everything from a Björk LP to a milking machine.

Norræna húsið

Sturlugata 5 • Mon–Fri 9am–5pm, Sat & Sun noon–5pm • Free • ⓦ nordice.is

South of the university, **Norræna húsið** (Nordic House), designed by the renowned Finnish architect Alvar Aalto in 1961 and buzzed over by aircraft landing at the nearby city airport, is devoted to Nordic culture, with an extensive library of books written in all the Nordic languages. It holds books on virtually any aspect of Nordic life, from Faroese knitting to Greenlandic seal hunting, as well as the main Nordic newspapers. There are also temporary **exhibitions** (often photographic) in the hall and basement, and frequent evening events, from classical **concerts** to **talks** covering topics from history to politics to music (sometimes in English). Check what's on from the posters inside or at the tourist office (see p.73).

Listasafn Íslands

Fríkirkjuvegur 7 • June–Aug Tues–Sun 10am–5pm; Sept–May Tues–Sun 11am–5pm • 1000kr • ⓦ listasafn.is

A few minutes' walk north from the Nordic House brings you to the Hringbraut highway, from where Sóleyjargata runs along the eastern side of Tjörnin (passing the

1

offices of the Icelandic president at the corner of Skothúsvegur). Here you'll find the **Fríkirkjan** (Free Lutheran Church), a simple wooden structure painted whitish grey. Its best feature is its tall green roof and tower, useful as a landmark to guide you to the neighbouring former ice house, known as Herðubreið. Once a storage place for massive chunks of ice, hewn in winter from the frozen lake and used to preserve fish stocks, the building has been enlarged and completely redesigned, and now houses **Listasafn Íslands** (the National Gallery of Iceland). Icelandic art may lack worldwide recognition, but all the significant names are to be found here, including Erró, Jón Stefánsson, Ásgrímur Jónsson, Guðmundur Þorsteinsson and Einar Hákonarson – though disappointingly, lack of space (there's only three small exhibition rooms containing barely twenty or so paintings each) means that the works can only be shown in strictly rationed portions from the museum's enormous stock of around eleven thousand pieces. You may well leave with your artistic appetite no more than whetted, but you can get an idea of the paintings not on display by glancing through the postcards sold at reception; other works from the gallery's collection are also currently exhibited at the Safnahús (see p.66).

Lækjargata

Northeast of the National Gallery, Lækjartorg leads on to **Lækjargata**, which once marked the eastern boundary of the town; Tjörnin still empties into the sea through a small brook (*lækjar* comes from *lækur*, Icelandic for "brook") which now runs under the road here, and occasionally, when there's an exceptionally high tide, sea water gushes back along the brook, pouring into Tjörnin. The cluster of old timber buildings up on the small hill parallel to the street is known as **Bernhöftsstofan** and, following extensive renovation, they now house a couple of chichi fish restaurants. Named after Tönnies Daniel Bernhöft, a Dane who ran a bakery in nearby Bankastræti, they're flanked by two of Iceland's most important buildings: the elegant old Reykjavík Grammar School, **Menntaskólinn**, built in 1844, which once had to be accessed by a bridge over the brook, and housed the Alþingi before the completion of the current Alþingishúsið in nearby Austurvöllur square (see p.56); and a small unobtrusive white building at the bottom of Bankastræti, which is, in fact, **Stjórnarráðshúsið** (Government House), another of Iceland's very parochial-looking public offices. One of the oldest surviving buildings in the city, built in 1761–71 as a prison, it now houses the cramped offices of the prime minister.

Up on **Arnahóll**, the grassy mound behind the building, a statue of Ingólfur Arnarson, Reykjavík's first settler, surveys his domain; with his back turned on the National Theatre, and the government ministries to his right, he looks out to the ocean that brought him here over eleven centuries ago. Experts believe this is the most likely spot where Ingólfur's high seat pillars finally washed up; according to *Landnámabók* they were found "by Arnarhvál below the heath".

Laugavegur

Beyond Bankastræti and on up the small hill is **Laugavegur** (hot spring road); local washerwomen once walked this way to the springs in Laugardalur. This is Iceland's major commercial artery, holding the main shops and a fair sprinkling of cafés, bars and restaurants. Not surprisingly therefore, on Friday and Saturday evenings in summer it's bumper to bumper with cars, horns blaring and with well-oiled revellers hanging out of the windows. However, before you give yourself over to extensive retail therapy, there are a couple of more cerebral attractions worthy of your time and attention in this part of town.

CLOCKWISE FROM TOP ÖSKJUHLÍÐ (P.68); TJÖRNIN (P.62); VIEW FROM THE HALLGRÍMSKIRKJA (P.67) >

1

Safnahús

Hverfisgata 15 • Daily 10am–5pm • 1200kr • ⓦ culturehouse.is

Sadly, the grand former National Library, now the **Safnahús** (Culture House), has lost its way. Until recently the home of a remarkable exhibition about Iceland's medieval manuscripts, today the museum has been subject to an amateurish makeover and contains nothing more than a savage hotchpotch of seemingly random items from the country's past. While individual items may impress, the overriding impression the muddled exhibition, known as "Points of View", leaves the visitor, is one of disappointment – this could, and should, be so much better.

The ground floor

Though the **ground floor** is predominantly given over to religious art, it also, confusingly, contains more contemporary items such as a photographic portrait of former Icelandic president, Vigdís Finnbogadóttir, plonked alongside an ornate seventeenth-century tapestry and a sculpture of Mary from the church in Vatnsfjörður, dated around 1400–1500. It's a juxtaposition which doesn't work. Elsewhere on the ground floor look out for the various copies, dating from 1281 to 2004, of the ancient legal document of Jónsbók; most impressive is the copy from 1363, replete with ornately decorated initial letters.

The first and second floors

These contain a mishmash of exhibits and, once again, the ad hoc combination of items is quite arbitrary: a magnificent altar piece from the church at Grenjaðarstaður, dating from 1766, for example, uncomfortably rubs shoulders with a garish piece of modern art from 1948, "Big sister and little brother" by Kristján Daviðsson. As you stumble around the museum, do make sure you see the stuffed great auk, hidden away in a small alcove off the main staircase leading to the top floor. Bought at auction in London in 1971, it's thought the bird was killed at Hólmsberg on the Reykjanes peninsula – the last two great auks in the world were bludgeoned to death on June 3, 1844 on the nearby island of Eldey.

MAGNÚSSON'S MANUSCRIPTS

Despite so many of Iceland's sagas and histories being written down by medieval monks for purposes of posterity, there existed no suitable means of protecting them from the country's damp climate, and within a few centuries these unique artefacts were rotting away. Enter **Árni Magnússon** (1663–1730), humanist, antiquarian and professor at the University of Copenhagen, who attempted to ensure the preservation of as many of the manuscripts as possible by sending them to Denmark for safekeeping. Although he completed his task in 1720, eight years later many of them went up in flames in the Great Fire of Copenhagen, and Árni died a heartbroken man fifteen months later, never having accepted his failure to rescue the manuscripts, despite braving the flames himself. As he noted at the time of the blaze, "these are the books which are to be had nowhere in the world"; the original **Íslendingabók**, for example, the most important historical record of the Settlement of Iceland, written on calfskin, was destroyed, though luckily it had been copied by a priest in Iceland before it left the country.

The manuscripts remained apart from their country of origin until long after Icelandic independence in 1944. In 1961, legislation was passed in Denmark decreeing that manuscripts composed or translated by Icelanders should be returned, but it took a further ruling by the Danish Supreme Court, in March 1971, to get things moving, as the Danes were reluctant to see these works of art leave their country. Finally, however, in April that year, a Danish naval frigate carried the first texts, **Konungsbók Eddukvæða** and **Flateyjarbók**, across the Atlantic into Reykjavík, to be met by crowds bearing signs reading "handritin heim" ("the manuscripts are home") and waving Icelandic flags. Even so, the transfer of the manuscripts wasn't completed until 1997. A new building, the Hús islenska fræða (House of Icelandic Studies), is currently under construction near the National Museum on Suðurgata to house the collection.

Hallgrímskirkja

Skólavörðuholt • Daily: June–Aug 9am–9pm; Sept–May 9am–5pm • Free; viewing platform 800kr • ⓦ hallgrimskirkja.is

From the western end of Laugavegur, the tongue-twisting Skólavörðustígur streaks steeply upwards to the largest church in the country, the magnificent **Hallgrímskirkja**. This is a modern concrete structure, whose neatly composed space-shuttle-like form dominates the Reykjavík skyline. Work began on the church – named after the renowned seventeenth-century religious poet Hallgrímur Pétursson – immediately after World War II, but was only finally completed a few years ago, the slow progress due to the task being carried out by a family firm comprising one man and his son. The work of state architect Guðjón Samúelsson, the church's unusual design – not least its 73m phallic steeple – has divided the city over the years, although locals have grown to accept rather than love it since its consecration in 1986. Most people rave about the organ inside, the only decoration in an otherwise completely bare Gothic-style shell; measuring a whopping 15m in height and possessing over five thousand pipes, it really has to be heard to be believed. The cost of installing it called for a major fundraising effort, with people across the country sponsoring a pipe – if you fancy putting money towards one yourself, for which you'll receive a certificate, ask the staff in their office on the right as you enter the church.

The tower has a **viewing platform**, accessed by a lift from just within the main door, giving stunning panoramic views across Reykjavík; it's open to the elements, so bring a warm hat and scarf if you come up here in winter. Incidentally, don't expect the clock at the top of the tower to tell the correct time – the wind up there is so strong that it frequently blows the hands off course. In fact, it's rare for any two public clocks in Reykjavík to tell the same time due to the differing wind conditions throughout the city.

Leifur Eiríksson statue

With his back to the church and his view firmly planted on Vínland, the imposing statue of **Leifur Eiríksson,** Discoverer of America, was donated by the US in 1930 to mark the Icelandic parliament's thousandth birthday. It's a favourite spot for photographs and makes as good a place as any to survey your surroundings – this is one of the highest parts of Reykjavík, and on a clear day there are great **views** out over the surrounding streets of houses adorned with multicoloured corrugated-iron facades.

Listasafn Einars Jónssonar

Eiríksgata • June to mid-Sept Tues–Sun 2–5pm; mid-Sept to Nov & Feb–May Sat & Sun 2–5pm • 1000kr • ⓦ lej.is

The heroic form of the Leifur Eiríksson statue is found in several other statues around the city, many of them the work of **Einar Jónsson** (1874–1954), who is remembered more officially by the pebbledash building to the right of Hallgrímskirkja at the corner of Eiríksgata and Njarðargata, home to the **Einar Jónsson museum**. Einar was Iceland's foremost modern **sculptor**, and this cube-like structure was built by him between 1916 and 1923. He lived here in the upstairs apartment with his Danish wife, Anna, and also worked here in an increasingly reclusive manner until his death in 1954, when the building was given over to displaying more than a hundred of his works, many based on religious themes and Icelandic folklore. A specially constructed group of rooms, connected by slim corridors and a spiral staircase, takes the visitor through a chronological survey of Einar's career – and it's pretty deep stuff. Einar claimed that his self-imposed isolation and total devotion to his work enabled him to achieve mystical states of creativity, and looking at the pieces exhibited here, many of them heavy with religious allegory and all dripping with spiritual energy, it's a claim that doesn't seem far-fetched; look out for his **Vökumaðurinn** (*The Guardian*) from 1902, a ghost keeping watch over a graveyard to make sure the dead receive a decent burial. If the museum is closed, peek into the **garden** at the rear, where several examples of Einar's work are

1

displayed alfresco; his most visible work, the statue of independence leader Jón Sigurðsson, stands in front of the Alþingishúsið in Austurvöllur square (see p.56).

Hið Íslenzka Reðasafn

Laugavegur 116 • Daily 10am–6pm • 1250kr • ⓦ phallus.is

Undoubtedly the most offbeat museum in the whole of Iceland, Reykjavík's **Hið Íslenzka Reðasafn** (Phallological Museum) is easy to spot opposite the bus station at Hlemmur – there's often a group of bemused tourists standing outside the front door not quite believing that this, indeed, is a museum dedicated to the penis. Around three hundred specimens are displayed in jars of formaldehyde and alcohol, from the sizeable member that once belonged to a young male sperm whale (now hollowed out, salted, dried and placed on a wooden plaque) to that of a rogue polar bear found drifting on pack ice off the West Fjords, shot by Icelandic fishermen and then unceremoniously butchered. Until recently, many visitors left disappointed over not being able to size up a human specimen. However, following the death of Akureyri man, **Páll Arason**, at the ripe old age of 95, the museum now has its *pièce de résistance*. In line with Páll's wishes, his frankly rather unimpressive penis, complete with long wisps of old man's white pubic hair, is now on public display for all to see – altogether not for the faint-hearted. But it doesn't stop there: the misshapen foreskin of a 40-year-old Icelander donated by the National Hospital after an emergency circumcision operation and the testicles of an unknown 60-year-old donor are also available for perusal. After all that, you'll be more than ready for the plaster cast and photos of several former museum visitors, which leave little to the imagination.

Kjarvalsstaðir

Flókagata 24 • Daily 10am–5pm • 1400kr • ⓦ artmuseum.is

Despite being surrounded by birch trees and pleasant grassy expanses, the **Kjarvalsstaðir** art gallery is an ugly 1960s-style concrete structure, though inside it's surprisingly bright and airy. Part of the Reykjavík Art Museum, it's devoted to the work of Iceland's most celebrated artist, **Jóhannes Sveinsson Kjarval** (1885–1972). After working on a fishing trawler during his youth, Jóhannes moved abroad to study art, spending time in London, Copenhagen, France and Italy, but it was only after his return to Iceland in 1940 that he travelled widely in his own country, drawing on the raw beauty he saw around him for the quasi-abstract depictions of Icelandic landscapes which made him one of the country's most popular twentieth-century painters. Painted in oils, much of his work is a surreal fusion of colour: his bizarre yet pleasing **Krítik** (*Critique*) from 1946–7, a melee of icy blues, whites and greys measuring a whopping 4m in length and 2m in height, is the centrepiece of the exhibition, portraying a naked man jauntily bending over to expose his testicles while catching a fish, watched over, rather oddly, by a number of Norse warriors. The museum is divided into two halls – the east one shows Jóhannes's work, while the west hall is dedicated to visiting temporary exhibitions. Although it may take a while for his style to grow on you, it's certainly worth dropping by.

Öskjuhlíð

Perlan Lift daily 10am–9pm

If you arrive in Reykjavík from Keflavík airport, it's hard to miss the space-age-looking grey container tanks that sit at the top of the wooded hill, **Öskjuhlíð**, immediately south of Kjarvalsstaðir, across Miklabraut and southeast along Bústaðavegur. Each is capable of holding four thousand litres of water at 80°C for use in the capital's homes, offices and swimming pools; it's also from here that water has traditionally been pumped, via a network of specially constructed pipes, underneath Reykjavík's pavements to keep them ice- and snow-free during winter. The whole thing is topped by a revolving restaurant. The structure is one of Reykjavík's best-known landmarks and is the best place for a 360-degree panoramic **view** of the entire city; simply take the lift to the fourth floor and step outside. On a clear day you can see all the way to the Snæfellsjökull glacier at the tip of the Snæfellsnes peninsula, as well as the entirety of Reykjavík. Before leaving, make sure you see the artificial indoor **geyser simulator** that erupts every few minutes from the basement, shooting a powerful jet of water all the way to the fourth floor: it's a good taste of what's to come if you're heading out to the real thing at Geysir.

Öskjuhlíð itself was also an important landmark in the days when the only mode of long-distance transport was the horse, as it stood out for many kiolometres across the barren surrounding plains – and more recently served as a military base for the British army during World War II. Today, though, it's a popular **recreation area** for Reykjavíkers who, unused to being surrounded by expanses of woodland, flock here by foot and with mountain bikes to explore the **paths** that crisscross its slopes. In fact, Öskjuhlíð has only been wooded since 1950, when an extensive forestation programme began after soil erosion had left the area barren and desolate. Today the western and southern flanks of the hill are covered with birch, spruce, poplar and pine.

Nauthólsvík geothermal lagoon
Nauthólsvegur • Café and changing facilities mid-May to mid-Aug daily 10am–7pm • Free

At the southern end of Öskjuhlíð at **Nauthólsvík**, on Nauthólsvegur road close to the Reykjavík Sailing Club, there's an artificial **beach** of bright yellow sand where it's possible to swim in a sea-water lagoon (the water temperature is generally 18–20°C), thanks to the addition of hundreds of litres of **geothermally heated sea water** into the open-air **pool** next to the beach, where there are also two hot pots (30–35°C), one of which is built into the sand. There are no lockers in the changing rooms, just baskets for your clothes, so don't bring any valuables with you.

Sólfar
Sæbraut

From Öskjuhlíð, it's a twenty-minute walk north along Snorrabraut to the seafront where, three blocks to the left (opposite the northern end of Frakkastígur), the striking **Sólfar** (*Sun Voyager*) **sculpture** is worthy of your attention. This sleek contemporary portrayal of a Viking-age ship, made of shiny silver steel by Jón Gunnar Árnason (1931–89), sits elegantly atop the city shoreline and is fast becoming one of the most photographed of Reykjavík's attractions.

Höfði
Borgartún • Closed to the public

From Sólfar, it's a five-minute stroll back east along Sæbraut to **Höfði**, a stocky white wooden structure built in 1909 in Jugendstil style, which occupies a grassy square beside the shore, between Sæbraut and Borgartún. Originally home of the French consul, the house also played host to Winston Churchill in 1941 when he visited British forces stationed in Iceland.

Although the house is best known as the location for the 1986 snap **summit** between Soviet president Mikhail Gorbachev and US president Ronald Reagan (see box, p.70), Icelanders know it equally well for its resident **ghost**, said to be that of a young girl who poisoned herself after being found guilty of incest with her brother. Between 1938 and 1951 the house was occupied by diplomats, including one who was so troubled by the supernatural presence that one dispatch after another was sent to the Foreign Office in London begging for a transfer until he finally got his way. In recent years, lights have switched themselves on and off, paintings have fallen off walls and door handles have

1

COLD WAR HOT SPOT

Called at the suggestion of the former Soviet president Mikhail Gorbachev, the **Reykjavík superpower summit** held at Höfði (see p.69) in 1986 aimed to discuss peace and disarmament between the United States and the Soviet Union. Although agreement was reached on reducing the number of medium-range and intercontinental missiles in Europe and Asia, the thornier question of America's strategic defence initiative of shooting down missiles in space remained a sticking point. However, the summit achieved one major goal – it brought the world's attention to Iceland, which, in the mid-1980s, was still relatively unknown as a destination for travellers, in effect marking the beginning of the tourist boom that Iceland is still enjoying today.

worked themselves loose. Today – apart from international summitry – the principal purpose of the house is as a centre for the city's municipal functions.

Ásmundursafn

Sigtún • Daily: May–Sept 10am–5pm; Oct–April 1–5pm • 1400kr • ⓦ artmuseumm.is

If sculpture is your thing, you'll want to check out the domed **Ásmundursafn**, dedicated to the work of Ásmundur Sveinsson and part of the Reykjavík Art Museum, a ten-minute dog-leg walk from Höfði; first head east along Borgartún, then south into Kringlumýrarbraut and east again into Sigtún where you'll see the peculiar white igloo shape beyond the trees on your right-hand side. Ásmundur Sveinsson (1893–1982) was one of the pioneers of Icelandic sculpture, and his powerful, often provocative, work was inspired by his country's nature and literature. During the 1920s he studied in both Stockholm and Paris, returning to Iceland to develop his unique sculptural cubism, a style infused with Icelandic myth and legend, which you can view here at his former home that he designed and built with his own hands in 1942–50; he lived where the museum shop and reception are currently located.

The museum is an uncommon shape for Reykjavík because when Ásmundur planned it, he was experimenting with Mediterranean and North African themes, drawing particular inspiration from the domed houses common to Greece. The crescent-shaped building beyond reception contains examples of the sculptor's work, including several busts from his period of Greek influence, though the original of his most famous sculpture from 1926, **Sæmundur á selnum** (*Sæmundur on the Seal*), is not on display here. Instead, it stands outside the main university building on Suðurgata, showing one of the first Icelanders to receive a university education, the priest and historian Sæmundur Sigfússon (1056–1133), astride a seal, psalter in hand. A smaller version of the original now stands in the museum grounds, where you'll also find many of Ásmundur's other soft-edged, gently curved monuments to the ordinary working people of the country.

Laugardalur and around

After rambling through central Reykjavík for a good couple of kilometres, Laugavegur comes to an end at the junction with the main north–south artery, Kringlumýrarbraut (actually Route 40, leading to Hafnarfjörður). Beyond here Suðurlandsbraut marks the southern reaches of **Laugardalur** valley, hemmed in between the low hills of Grensás to the south and the northerly Laugarás, just behind Sundahöfn harbour, whose Þvottalaugarnar springs have been known since the time of the Settlement as a source of hot water for washing. The springs are still here, the spot commemorated by the Ásmundur Sveinsson statue, **Þvottakonan** (*The Washerwoman*), but the area is best known as the site of Iceland's premier **sports ground**, Laugardalsvöllur, as well as the superb Laugardalslaug outdoor **swimming complex** (see box, p.75), a campsite (see p.78) and the

FROM TOP NAUTHÓLSVÍK GEOTHERMAL LAGOON (P.69); HARPA (P.61)>

1

indoor sports hall and concert venue, Laugardalshöll. The green expanses beyond the sports ground contain the country's most impressive **botanical garden** and a **zoo**.

Botanical garden

No set hours • Free

Barely ten minutes on foot from the Ásmundur Sveinsson sculpture museum, reached by walking east along Engjavegur, the **botanical garden** contains an extensive collection of native Icelandic flora, as well as thousands of imported plants and trees. This place is particularly popular with Icelandic families who come here not only to enjoy the surroundings but also to show kids the adjoining family park and zoo.

Húsdýragarðurinn and Fjölskyldugarðurinn

Hafrafell • June–Aug daily 10am–6pm; Sept–May daily 10am–5pm • 800kr • ⓦ mu.is • Buses #2, #15 and #17 run from the city centre; get off at the Laugardalshöll stop

With children in tow, the **Húsdýragarðurinn zoo** makes a pleasant afternoon's visit, home to Icelandic mammals such as seals, foxes, mink and reindeer. There's also a collection of fish caught in local rivers and lakes which will keep younger visitors entertained. Once the attraction of the animals starts to wane, you can check out the surrounding **Fjölskyldugarðurinn family park**, where there's a small duck lake complete with replica Viking longboat, and other activities based loosely on a Viking theme: a fort, an outlaw hideout and even a go-kart track.

Árbæjarsafn

Kistuhylur 4 • June–Aug daily 10am–5pm • 1400kr • ⓦ arbaejarsafn.is • Bus #19 from Hlemmur bus station or the botanical garden

The **Árbæjarsafn Open-Air Museum**, around 8km southeast of the city centre, is a collection of turf-roofed and corrugated-iron buildings on the site of an ancient farm that was first mentioned in the sagas around the mid-1400s. The buildings and their contents record the changes that occurred as Iceland's economy switched from farming to fishing – the industrial revolution being heralded by the arrival of the fishing trawler – and Reykjavík's rapid expansion. The pretty turf church here, dating from 1842, was carefully moved to its present location from Skagafjörður on the north coast in 1960. Next to it, the farmhouse is dominated by an Ásmundur Sveinsson sculpture, *Woman Churning Milk*, illustrating an all-but-lost traditional way of life.

ARRIVAL AND DEPARTURE   REYKJAVÍK

BY PLANE

Keflavík airport (airport code KEF; ☏425 6000, ⓦ kefairport.is) Much the larger of Reykjavík's two airports, 52km west of Reykjavík at the tip of the Reykjanes peninsula, this is where most international flights arrive and depart, and has currency exchange offices and ATMs. Taxi fares into Reykjavík are 13,000–15,400kr, depending on the time of day and worth considering if you're in a group. Two companies operate coaches from immediately outside the terminal into Reykjavík in connection with all arriving flights, and journey time is around 45min: Flybus (1950kr single/3500kr return or 2500kr single/4500kr return for Flybus Plus tickets which include hotel shuttle transfer within Reykjavík; ☏580 5400, ⓦ flybus.is) run to the BSÍ bus terminal (see opposite) from where there are connecting shuttles to all the major hotels in the city, as

well as several guesthouses and the campsite at Laugardalur (see p.78). GrayLine (1914kr single or 2355kr single with hotel shuttle transfer; ☏540 1313; ⓦ grayline .is) operate to much more central Lækjartorg, from where shuttles leave for central accommodation locations.

Reykjavík city airport (airport code RKV; ☏570 3030) Built by the British during their World War II occupation of Iceland and adjacent to Icelandair's *Reykjavík Natura* hotel (see p.77) on the edge of the city centre, this is served by all domestic flights as well as international services from Greenland and the Faroe Islands (seasonal), and is essentially little more than a glorified bus station.

Destinations Akureyri (7 daily; 50min); Bíldudalur (1 daily; 40min); Egilsstaðir (4 daily; 1hr); Gjögur (2 weekly; 50min); Höfn (1–2 daily; 1hr); Húsavík (2 daily Tues, Thurs & Fri; 50min); Ísafjörður (2 daily; 40min); Westman Islands (2 daily; 30min).

BY BUS

The long-distance bus situation in Reykjavík is a mess. Although the city does have a long-distance bus station, the BSÍ terminal on Vatnsmýrarvegur, it is owned by just one company who pettily refuse to allow their competitors to use it. Hence, buses for destinations across Iceland leave from any number of stops across the city. Since these stops (and routes) change frequently, the only way to be absolutely sure of where your bus leaves is to check online. Things are further complicated by the fact that some destinations are served by more than one operator. For an overview, the best website to check is ⓦ publictransport.is. Here you'll find a map and can establish which bus company operates to your chosen destination. The situation with city buses is more straightforward. The bus station at Hlemmur is the main terminal and most services pass through it. Lækjartorg also functions as a smaller hub.

Companies The main operators are Strætó (☎ 540 2700, ⓦ bus.is); Sterna (☎ 550 0700, ⓦ sternatravel.is); Iceland on your own (also known as Reykjavílk Excursions & SBA-Norðurleið; ☎ 580 540 or ☎ 550 0700, ⓦ ioyo.is or ⓦ sba .is); TREX (☎ 587 6000, ⓦ trex.is); and Gray Line (☎ 540 1313, ⓦ grayline.is).

Destinations Akureyri (2 daily; 7hr); Blönduós (2 daily; 5hr); Blue Lagoon (hourly; 45min); Borgarnes (5 daily; 2hr); Búðardalur (1 daily, change at Borganes; 3hr); Gullfoss/Geysir (2–4 daily; 2hr 30min); Höfn (2 daily; 8hr); Hólmavík (1 daily, change at Borgarnes; 4hr); Ísafjörður via Hólmavík (3 weekly; 7hr 30min); Landeyjahöfn (3 daily; 3hr); Ólafsvík (2 daily, change at Borgarnes and Stykkishólmur; 4hr 30min); Sauðárkrókur (2 daily; 5hr 30min); Skaftafell (1 daily; 8hr); Stykkishólmur (2 daily, change at Borgarnes; 3hr 30min); Þingvellir (2–4 daily; 1hr).

INFORMATION

Tourist information Reykjavík's tourist office is at Aðalstræti 2, close to the Parliament in the heart of the old town (June to mid-Sept daily 8.30am–7pm; mid-Sept to May Mon–Fri 9am–6pm, Sat 9am–4pm, Sun 9am–2pm; ☎ 590 1550, ⓦ visitreykjavik.is or ⓦ icetourist.is). It's the best source of up-to-date information on both Reykjavík and the rest of the country, providing untold amounts of brochures and maps. If travelling independently, you can check your itinerary here with the staff before setting off for the more remote regions.

Listings information The tourist office stocks the useful

What's On booklet with complete listings of events throughout the capital. Look out also for *The Reykjavík Grapevine* (ⓦ grapevine.is), a handy free newspaper in English with numerous listings, readily available in most bars and cafés.

Gay information Reykjavík's limited gay scene is in a constant state of flux. Bars and club nights disappear or change seemingly as soon as they open, so for the most up-to-date information it's best to check out ⓦ gayice.is, or, in Reykjavík itself, drop into the gay community centre, Samtökin, in new premises at Suðurgata 3 (Mon–Fri 1–5pm; ⓦ samtokin78.is).

GETTING AROUND

Reykjavík is easy to navigate. The heart of the city is the low-lying quarter between the harbour and the lake, busy with shoppers by day and young revellers by night; most of the sights are within **walking distance** of here.

BY BUS

City buses Known as *Strætó* (☎ 540 2700, bus.is), these depart from the central Lækjartorg and from the city bus station at Hlemmur, at the eastern end of Laugavegur (roughly every 30min by day and hourly in the evenings and at weekends, Mon–Sat 7am–midnight, Sun noon–midnight).

Tickets The flat, single-trip fare is 400kr and it must be paid with exact change; if you're changing buses, ask for a *skiftimiði* ticket, which you then show to the next driver. More economical options include a strip of nine tickets,

called a *farmiðaspjald*, for 3500kr or, better, a series of cards providing unlimited bus travel in the Greater Reykjavík area, which cover the surrounding satellite towns including Hafnarfjörður: the most useful are the 1-day card (1000kr), 3-day card (2500kr) and green card (10,900kr), which is valid for one month. All these tickets are available at the Hlemmur bus station.

Routes Useful routes for getting around the centre are #15, which runs from Hlemmur via Snorrabraut and the BSÍ coach terminal to the city airport; and #5, from Hlemmur via Snorrabraut and the coach terminal to *Hotel Natura* and

THE REYKJAVÍK CITY CARD

The **Reykjavík City Card** gives you unlimited transport on buses within greater Reykjavík, entry to the main museums and galleries, and all swimming pools in the capital, plus a wide range of other discounts across the city. It's available at the tourist office in Aðalstræti (see above), *Reyjavík Campsite* (see p.78) and most major hotels (details at ⓦ visitreykjavik.is/travel /reykjavik-city-card; 3300kr/24hr; 4400kr/48hr; 4900kr/72hr).

1

ACTIVITIES AROUND REKYJAVIK

Reykjavík offers a host of **activities**, everything from swimming to trips for the truly adventurous. **Whale-watching** and **puffin-spotting tours**, and **sea angling** trips, depart from Ægisgarður, the main jetty in Reykjavík harbour, between Geirsgata and Mýrargata. Other activities include **helicopter tours**, **horseriding** and trips out to the southwest's **glaciers** aboard a super-jeep. The latest offering – and it's proving inordinately popular – is a **trip inside the Langjökull glacier**, near Húsafell (see box, p.160). The glacier is about a two-hour journey from Reykjavík. If you're here during the winter months, there are also excursions to see the **Northern Lights**. All prices quoted are per person.

WHALE WATCHING, PUFFIN SPOTTING AND SEA ANGLING

The two main operators are Elding (Whale watching 9000kr; puffin spotting 5500kr; sea angling 12,500kr; ☎519 5000, ⓦ elding.is) and Special Tours (Whale watching 9000kr; puffin spotting 5000kr; sea angling 11,500kr; ☎560 8800, ⓦ specialtours.is), both based at Ægisgarður.
Whale watching Tours leave year-round (up to 12 departures daily depending on season), sailing for Faxaflói bay north of Reykjavík. You're most likely to encounter minke whales, orcas, humpbacks and dolphins, although, occasionally, blue, fin and sei whales also put in an appearance.
Puffin spotting Between mid-May and mid-August (after which the birds head out to sea for the winter months), there are twice-daily tours around the islands of Lundey and Akurey, where puffins gather to breed in the summer. Although it's not possible to go ashore, you'll have a great view of the cliffs and grassy slopes which make up the islands' sides, and the burrows where the puffins live. Remember, though, that puffin numbers have fallen in recent years due to a lack of the birds' main source of food, the sand eel.
Sea angling Between May and August, sea angling tours also depart three times daily from the harbour, giving you a chance to try out your deep-sea skills – you get to keep anything you catch.

HELICOPTER TOURS

Departing from the City Airport, **helicopter tours** of Reykjavík and the surrounding area are fast becoming one of the city's most popular excursions. True, they don't come cheap but the views of the capital and the dramatic scenery of the Reykjanes peninsula and Faxaflói bay are, of course, unsurpassed. Prices start at 24,000kr for a twenty-minute flight over the capital; throw in a landing on top of Mount Esja and you're looking at 29,000kr. Three companies operate from the airport, offering a broadly similar programme of trips; there are full details on the websites: Helicopter Service of Iceland (☎561 6100, ⓦ helo.is); Norðurflug (☎562 2500, ⓦ heli.is); Reykjavík Helicopters (☎589 1000, ⓦ reykjavikhelicopters.com).

GLACIER TOURS

For sheer exhilaration, it's hard to beat a **glacier tour**. The most popular trip is inside the **Langjökull glacier** near Húsafell (see box, p.160), though other options include a glacial ride in a super-jeep, and although the ticket price is high, it's worth splashing out – especially if you're intent on seeing this part of the country without your own transport. The nine-hour tours take in the Langjökull glacier, Iceland's second largest, alongside some of western

---

the Nauthólsvík geothermal pool. If you want to see the city cheaply, bus #15 is excellent – as well as running to the city airport, it also operates in the opposite direction from Hlemmur east via Laugavegur and Suðurlandsbraut, passing close to both the swimming pool (see box above) and the campsite at Laugardalur (see p.78).

BY CAR

Parking Finding a space is relatively straightforward and certainly not the nightmare you might expect in a capital city. Most residential streets, although often full with residents' cars, are unmetered, while the city centre has parking meters and plenty of multistorey car parks, most

conveniently just off Skólavörðustígur; all are marked on the tourist office's Reykjavík map. Although the city's traffic is generally free-flowing, even at rush hours, it can be busy on Fri and Sat nights, when it's wise to avoid Laugavegur, which mutates into a long snaking line of slow-moving cars.
Car rental Avis, Knarrarvogur 2 (☎591 4000, ⓦ avis.is); Bílaleiga Akureyrar/Europcar, Skeifan 9 (☎568 6915, ⓦ holdur.is); Budget, Vatnsmýrarvegur 10 (☎562 6060, ⓦ budget.is); Hertz, Flugvallarvegur 5t (☎522 4420, ⓦ hertz.is); Sixt, Fisklóð 18 (☎540 2220, ⓦ sixt.is).

BY TAXI

Cabs are not as expensive as you might think: 1600–1800kr

Iceland's other attractions. You'll head first for Hvalfjörður fjord, before cutting inland to the Deildartunguhver hot spring and the Hraunfossar waterfalls, and taking the Kaldidalur Interior route towards the glacier, where a super-jeep (the ones with the supersized tyres) takes you to the top of the ice sheet. There's also a stop at Þingvellir before the return to Reykjavík. Try Activity Group (tours daily May–Aug; 35,700kr; ☎580 9900, ☻activity.is).

HORSERIDING

Several companies offer **horseriding** all year round, including Eldhestar Völlum, Hveragerði (☎480 4800, ☻eldhestar.is); Íshestar, Sörlaskeið 26, Hafnarfjörður (☎555 7000, ☻ishestar.is); and Íslenski Hesturinn Surtlugata 3, Reykjavík (☎434 7979, ☻islenskihesturinn.is). Excursions range from a one- or two-hour canter through the countryside to longer excursions around the local lavafields and even trips out to Geysir and Gullfoss; a two-hour tour usually costs around 11,000kr, with most companies offering pickups from Reykjavík.

NORTHERN LIGHTS TOURS

The **Northern Lights**, or Aurora Borealis, are most commonly seen between October and March, and one of the best ways to view them is to take a boat trip from Reykjavík harbour, which allows you to get well away from the city lights. Bear in mind, though, that the sky needs to be clear and free of cloud; on days when it's too windy to put out to sea, the tour transfers to a coach that drives out of the city. Both Special Tours and Elding operate tours and a three-hour trip with Elding costs 9000kr, 8500kr with Special Tours; departure times are generally 9pm or 10pm – details are on the websites (see opposite).

SWIMMING

The **swimming pool** is to Icelanders what the pub is to the British or the coffee shop to Americans. This is the place to come to meet people, catch up on the local gossip and to relax in divine geothermally heated waters. The abundance of natural hot water around the capital means there's a good choice of pools, which are always at a comfortably warm 29°C, often with hot pots at 39–43°C. Opening hours, entrance fees and details on reduced price multi-buy entrance deals are listed at ☻itr.is, under the swimming pools link. Bear in mind that because pool water in Iceland doesn't contain large amounts of chlorine as is common in most other countries, you must shower naked, without a swimming costume, before entering the pools and thoroughly wash the areas of your body marked on the signs by the showers.

Laugardalslaug Sundlaugavegur ☎411 5100; map pp.54–55. Iceland's largest outdoor swimming complex, with a 50m pool, four hot pots, a jacuzzi, steam room, waterslide and masseuse. Entry 650kr. Mon–Fri 6.30am–10pm, Sat & Sun 8am–10pm.

Sundhöllin Barónsstígur 45A ☎411 5350; map pp.54–55. Until construction on a new outdoor pool is complete, the 25m pool here is indoors. However,

there are two outdoor hot pots, plus single-sex nude sunbathing terraces, too – a veritable suntrap on warm days. Entry 650kr. Mon–Thurs 6.30am–10pm, Fri 6.30am–8pm, Sat 8am–4pm, Sun 10am–6pm.

Vesturbæjarlaug Hofsvallagata ☎411 5150; map pp.54–55. A 25m outdoor pool plus three hot pots, a sauna, steam bath and solarium. Entry 650kr. Mon–Thurs 6.30am–10pm, Fri 6.30am–8pm, Sat & Sun 9am–8pm.

should be enough to take you across the city centre. The main ranks are centrally located on Lækjargata, between the junctions with Bankastræti and Amtmannsstígur, as well as opposite Hallgrímskirkja church on Eiríksgata and the Hlemmur bus station. It's also possible to call one of the main operators: Hreyfill (☎588 5522) is best, or try BSR (☎561 0000). Remember that Icelandic taxi drivers don't expect tips.

BY BIKE

Bike rental Central outlets include Borgarhjól, Hverfisgata 50 (Mon–Fri 8am–6pm, Sat 10am–2pm; ☎551 5653, ☻borgarhjol.is); rentals are also available at the campsite in Laugardalur (see p.78); all charge around 4200kr per 24hr.

ACCOMMODATION

Although Reykjavík's **accommodation** options continue to mushroom as the tourist influx increases, pressure on beds in the summer months is always great and it's a good idea to book in advance, especially in June, July and Aug. **Prices** rise by around a third between May and Sept; those given here are for the cheapest double room during the summer months.

1

HOTELS

Without exception, Reykjavík's hotels are heavy on the pocket. While standards are uniformly high, a buffet breakfast is not usually included in the cheaper room rates. If you fancy splashing out for a night or two of luxury, the following are the city's best-value options.

CITY CENTRE

Borg Pósthússtræti 11 ☎ 551 1440, ⓦ hotelborg.is; map p.57. The city's very first hotel, opened in the 1930s and the unofficial home of visiting heads of state ever since. A showcase of sophistication and four-star elegance, each room is individually decorated in Art Deco style with period furniture – and prices to match. **45,000kr**

★ **Frón** Laugarvegur 22A ☎ 511 4666, ⓦ hotelfron .is; map p.57. If you're self-catering, this hotel right in the city centre should be your first choice. In addition to regular double rooms, it offers stylish, modern studios (25,500kr) and larger apartments (28,800kr), each with bath, kitchenette and TV. **24,000kr**

Holt Bergstaðastræti 37 ☎ 552 5700, ⓦ holt.is; map p.57. Over three hundred paintings by Icelandic artists adorn the rooms and public areas of this luxury, centrally located place which first opened its doors in 1965. Rooms are of the Persian-carpet, dark-wood-panelling, red-leather-armchair and chocolate-on-the-pillow variety. **30,000kr**

★ **Icelandair Reykjavík Marina** Mýrargata 2 ☎ 444 4000, ⓦ icelandairhotels.com; map p.57. Bold, bright and refreshingly quirky, this harbourside hotel not only enjoys terrific views of the trawlers in dry dock right outside, but its rooms also have a maritime feel with a twist of chic. **34,500kr**

★ **Klöpp** Klapparstígur 26 ☎ 595 8520, ⓦ center hotels.is; map p.57. Despite its bizarre name, this is one of central Reykjavík's better hotels and a sound choice: modern throughout, with tasteful wooden floors, oak furniture and wall panelling in all rooms. The breakfast room, though, is a little cramped. **25,000kr**

★ **Leifur Eiríksson** Skólavörðustígur 45 ☎ 562 0800, ⓦ hotelleifur.is; map p.57. With a perfect location overlooking Hallgrímskirkja, right in the heart of the city, this is a small, friendly and neatly furnished place; the top-floor rooms, built into the sloping roof, are particularly worthwhile for their excellent views. **27,000kr**

Óðinsvé Þórsgata 1 ☎ 511 6200, ⓦ hotelodinsve.is; map p.57. Long-established place that's stylish, relaxed and within an easy trot of virtually everything. The elegantly decorated

rooms have wooden floors, neutral decor, comfortable Scandinavian-style furniture and feature work by renowned Icelandic photographer, RAX. Unfortunately, recent renovation work has pushed prices upwards. **37,700kr**

Plaza Aðalstræti 4 ☎ 595 8550, ⓦ plaza.is; map p.57. The style in this tastefully renovated old building a stone's throw from Austurstræti is Nordic minimalism meets old-fashioned charm, with the heavy wooden floors, plain white walls and immaculately tiled bathrooms complementing the high-beamed ceilings. **28,700kr**

Radisson Blu 1919 Pósthússtræti 2 ☎ 599 1000, ⓦ radissonblu.com/1919hotel-reykjavik; map p.57. Housed in the elegant former headquarters of the Eimskip shipping line, this Art Deco hotel combines old-fashioned charm with modern chic. Book one month in advance to secure the rate below. The penthouse suites (77,400kr) with elevated sleeping sections and separate dining area are the best Reykjavík has to offer. **39,000kr**

Reykjavík Centrum Aðalstræti 16 ☎ 514 6000, ⓦ hotelcentrum.is; map p.57. Built in traditional early 1900s style, this hotel offers a curious yet pleasing mix of stylish and homely, and is just a stone's throw from the action on Austurstræti. Breakfast is an extra 2200kr. **31,800kr**

Skjaldbreið Laugavegur 16 ☎ 595 8510, ⓦ center hotels.is; map p.57. Though the plain rooms sporting classic Nordic decor may be rather uninspiring, the price for such a central location is extremely competitive. Note, too, that the windows have extra sound-proofing – especially needed on raucous Fri and Sat on Laugavegur. **25,000kr**

OUT OF THE CENTRE

Arctic Comfort Síðumúli 19 ☎ 588 5588, ⓦ arctic comforthotel.is; map pp.54–55. One of the capital's cheapest options, oddly located in a business district a 30min walk from the centre, but perfectly smart and clean, and offering good value for money. Some rooms have self-catering facilities. **22,500kr**

Best Western Reykjavík Rauðarárstígur 37 ☎ 514 7000, ⓦ hotelreykjavik.is; map pp.54–55. Functional and rather uninspiring hotel, roughly 20min walk from the centre. Rooms are plain and simple but clean and presentable, though you might find some disturbingly orange furnishings in them. Book in advance for the best rate quoted here. **32,000kr**

Cabin Borgartún 32 ☎ 511 6030, ⓦ hotelcabin.is; map pp.54–55. The best rooms in this good-value place are at the front, offering great views out over the sea and Mount Esja. There are warm autumn colours throughout, with lots of browns and greys making the decor pleasant and restful. The cheaper double rooms are only ten square metres in size, however, and can feel a little cramped. **20,600kr**

Fosshótel Barón Barónsstígur 2–4 ☎ 562 3204, ⓦ fosshotel.is; map pp.54–55. En-suite doubles and two-person studios with wooden floors, microwaves and showers; most have sea views. The 30-plus apartments vary greatly in

---

TOP 5 PLACES TO STAY

Anna p.77
Icelandair Reykjavík Marina p.76
Leifur Eiríksson p.76
Luna p.77
Reykjavík Loft Hostel p.78

size, so look before you choose. Discounts for stays of three nights and over. Doubles <u>25,300kr</u>, studios <u>30,400kr</u>

Fosshótel Lind Rauðarárstígur 18 ✆ 562 3350, ⓦfosshotel.is; map pp.54–55. Bright, modern and functional hotel offering discounts for stays of three nights or more, and worth considering if other more central places are fully booked. Rooms are plainly decorated and unadventurous, but the location's within easy reach of Hlemmur's buses. <u>24,500kr</u>

Fosshótel Reykjavík Þórunnartún 1 ✆531 9000, ⓦfosshotel.is; map pp.54–55. Sprawling over sixteen floors, the *Fosshótel* chain's jewel in the crown opened for business in the summer of 2015 and is now Iceland's biggest hotel, boasting 320 rooms, all with magnificent views over the city and the waterfront. Rooms are sleek and elegant, there's a spa and a gym, naturally, and even a beer garden. But none of it comes cheap. <u>36,700kr</u>

Grand Reykjavík Sigtún 38 ✆514 8000, ⓦgrand.is; map pp.54–55. The clue's in the name: there's no shortage of opulence here, with marble floors, stylish chrome fittings and wood panels sure to delight, though for the money you may wish to be closer to the centre – it's a good 25min walk from here. <u>35,100kr</u>

Hilton Reykjavík Nordica Suðurlandsbraut 2 ✆444 5000, ⓦreykjavik.nordica.hilton.com; map pp.54–55. The Hilton chain's one and only hotel in Iceland is big on Nordic minimalism: glass, chrome and natural wood are everywhere you look. Rooms at the front of the building enjoy views over the sea to Mount Esja. <u>26,040kr</u>

Icelandair Reykjavík Natura Nauthólsvegur 52 ✆444 4000, ⓦicelandairhotels.com; map pp.54–55. A busy and impersonal hotel stuffed with stopover travellers. The 200-odd rooms here are nice enough, with wooden floors and comfortable modern furnishings throughout, though are on the small side. Free access to the hotel spa. <u>28,240kr</u>

Ísland Ármúli 9 ✆595 7000, ⓦhotelisland.is; map pp.54–55. Although a little too far from the centre (about 2.5km) to be your first choice, the light and airy Scandinavian-designed rooms, with lots of wood panels, glass and chrome, make this worth considering if others are full. <u>29,300kr</u>

Radisson Blu Saga Reykjavik Hagatorg ✆525 9900, ⓦradissonblu.com/sagahotel-reykjavik; map pp.54–55. This large, swanky business hotel, usually packed with conference delegates dashing up to admire the view from the top-floor restaurant, considers itself one of Iceland's finest. The rooms are cosmopolitan in feel and design, and feature bureaux and comfortable armchairs. Book early for the best rates. <u>27,800kr</u>

GUESTHOUSES AND APARTMENTS

Guesthouse prices have rocketed over the past couple of years, and can cost as much as a cheap hotel during July and Aug: reckon on at least 20,000kr for a double, but as guesthouses usually provide kitchens, it's possible to save

money by self-catering. Rooms are always on the simple side, with little to distinguish between them. A central location is as good a reason as any to choose one of the places below over another, though bear in mind that many are fully booked weeks in advance throughout July and Aug.

CITY CENTRE

★**Adam** Skólavörðustígur 42 ✆ 896 0242, ⓦadamhotel .com; map p.57. Although this place likes to think it's a hotel, it's actually an upmarket guesthouse whose smart rooms all boast a kitchenette though some share facilities. Prices rise by about 7000kr for Fri & Sat stays. The price we quote is for Mon–Thurs & Sun, sharing facilities. <u>19,100kr</u>

★**Anna** Smáragata 16 ✆562 1618, ⓦguesthouse anna.is; map p.57. Run by the animated and friendly Anna, who lived in the US for 25 years, this place is located in the elegant former Czechoslovakian embassy building and is definitely one of Reykjavík's friendliest guesthouses with rooms sharing facilities as well as en suite. May–Aug. <u>26,000kr</u>

Baldursbrá Laufásvegur 41 ✆552 6646, ⓦbaldursbra .com; map p.57. Friendly, modern guesthouse with a fantastic location, right in the city centre and overlooking Tjörnin, though with rather narrow beds and unfortunate floral curtains. There's a secluded garden with a Jacuzzi for guests' use. <u>16,900kr</u>

★**Luna** Spítalastígur 1 ✆511 2800, ⓦluna.is; map p.57. If you're looking for beautifully decorated and superbly appointed apartments, this is the place to come. With modern and bright, two-person studios and larger, two-person apartments with top-notch fittings, this is a real home from home. There's also a three-room penthouse for rent. Check in at Baldursgata 36. Studios <u>25,000kr</u>, apartments <u>35,900kr</u>

★**Room with a View** Laugavegur 18 ✆552 7262, ⓦroomwithaview.is; map p.57. A great selection of studios and apartments of various sizes, all located on the sixth floor overlooking the main shopping street, with incredible panoramic views from the shared balcony. Ten percent discount for stays of seven nights or more. Studios <u>25,500kr</u>, apartments <u>29,400kr</u>

Salvation Army Guesthouse Kirkjustræti 2 ✆561 3203, ⓦguesthouse.is; map p.57. The cheapest guesthouse in Reykjavík and often fully booked, despite the narrow rooms with clanking pipes, paper-thin walls and lack of private bathrooms. It's hard to beat if you're on a tight budget, and it's dead central. June–Aug. Dorms <u>15,000kr</u>, sleeping bags <u>4000kr</u>

Travel-Inn Sóleyjargata 31 ✆561 3553, ⓦdalfoss.is; map p.57. One of Reykjavík's top guesthouses, in a tastefully renovated old house with good-sized, comfortable rooms overlooking the southern end of Tjörnin and handy for the BSÍ bus station on Vatnsmýrarvegur. The rooms with shared bathroom are good value. Higher price applies for Thurs–Sun. <u>15,100kr</u>

1

OUT OF THE CENTRE

Guesthouse 101 Laugavegur 101 ☎562 6101, ⓦiceland101.com; map pp.54–55. Reasonably priced but rather soulless place at the eastern end of the city's main shopping street, near Hlemmur, with cheap furniture and cell-like rooms. The location nevertheless makes it worth considering if others are full – it's a 10–15min walk into town. <u>14,700kr</u>

★ **Kríunes** Við Vatnsendur ☎567 2245, ⓦkriunes.is; map p.52. A 15min drive southeast of the city, and a truly fantastic lakeside choice. Surrounded by high trees and with views of the lake, this is a former farmhouse painted in warm Mediterranean colours and sporting nice terracotta floor tiles and wooden floors. <u>23,300kr</u>

Snorri Snorrabraut 61 ☎552 0598, ⓦguesthouse reykjavik.com; map pp.54–55. This pebble-dashed modern block is not one of Reykjavík's most alluring, and the rooms are rather uninspiring, too. But the location is a winner, just a 10–15min walk from the centre, and there's a choice of shared facilities or en suite. <u>17,600kr</u>

CAMPSITE AND HOSTELS

Hlemmur Square Laugavegur 105 ☎415 1600, ⓦhlemmursquare.com; map pp.54–55. Upmarket dorm accommodation (dorms sleep 4–14) with shared facilities is available on the upper floors of this stylish 1930s building located right beside Hlemmur bus station.

Linen and duvets are top-notch and no sleeping bags are allowed. There are also two kitchens on site for guest use. The top floor is given over to eighteen spacious and tastefully appointed double rooms. Dorms <u>4,500kr</u>, doubles <u>35,000kr</u>

Reykjavík Campsite Sundlaugarvegur 32 ☎568 6944, ⓦreykjavikcampsite.is; map pp.54–55. This is the cheapest place to stay in Reykjavík, with cooking and shower facilities on site, plus some rather small two-berth cabins with bunk beds; facilities are shared. The site is perfectly located for Iceland's biggest and best swimming pool, Laugardalslaug. Camping <u>1700kr</u>, cabins <u>12,500kr</u>

★ **Reykjavík Downtown Hostel** Vesturgata 17 ☎553 8120, ⓦhostel.is; map p.57. Swish and stylish, this great, central HI place is more hotel than hostel, with six-berth dorms decorated in subtle pastel colours. A terrific downtown location (just 10min from Lækjartorg) and unbeatable prices. Dorms <u>6150kr</u>, doubles <u>22,700kr</u>

Reykjavík Loft Hostel Bankastræti 7 ☎553 8140, ⓦhostel.is; map p.57. The latest addition to the youth hostel scene in Reykjavík, enjoying an unparalleled location right in the thick of things. There are 6–8-bed dorms as well as private rooms. Both options have a sink but otherwise share facilities, and there's a top-floor café with balcony offering great views over the city centre. Dorms <u>8250kr</u>, doubles <u>26,500kr</u>

EATING

Reykjavík has the best range of **places to eat** in the country, mostly packed into the downtown area around Laugavegur and Austurvöllur square. Restaurant prices tend to be high, though, which may deter you from eating out on a regular basis and draw you towards self-catering, at least during part of your stay.

CAFÉS

★ **Café Paris** Austurstræti 14 ☎551 1020; map p.57. Over the years this French-style café has become a Reykjavík fixture, with outdoor seating overlooking the Alþingi in summer. Daily brunch for 2650kr, as well as excellent pancakes and salads, and coffee and cakes. Daily: May–Aug 8am–1am; Sept–April 9am–1am.

★ **Kaffi Sólon** Bankastræti 7a ☎562 3232; map p.57. One of Reykjavík's most popular cafés, decked out in contemporary Icelandic design and serving a good range of light meals such as beef teriyaki, deep-fried camembert, burgers and salads from 1990kr, as well as more substantial meat and fish mains for around 3990kr. Mon–Thurs 11am–11.30pm, Fri & Sat 11am–1am, Sun 11am–11pm.

Kaffitár Bankastræti 8 ☎420 2732; map p.57. The Icelandic version of *Starbucks*, but with far better coffee, made from expertly blended varieties of beans (available as a brand in supermarkets). The usual run of cakes and

muffins, too, plus good croissants. Mon–Sat 7.30am–6pm, Sun 9am–5pm.

Kofi Tómasar Frænda Laugavegur 2 ☎551 1855; map p.57. Also known simply as *Kofinn*, trendy young Reykjavíkers flock to this chilled place to loll around on the comfortable couches, chat, drink coffee and work on their poetry. Its prime position on Laugavegur is also great for people-watching. Mon–Thurs 10am–1am, Fri & Sat 10am–5am, Sun 10am–midnight.

Mokka Skólavörðustígur 3a ☎552 1174; map p.57. Opened in 1958, this is Reykjavík's oldest café, and was the first in the country to serve espresso and cappuccino to its curious clientele. A changing display of black-and-white photographs adorns the walls, and there's a no-music policy. June–Aug daily 9am–9pm; Sept–May daily 9am–6.30pm.

★ **Sandholt** Laugavegur 36 ☎551 3524; map p.57. The best café-cum-bakery in town with good coffee and excellent strawberry tarts, cinnamon swirls, flans, fresh

1

TOP 5 PLACES TO EAT

Matur og Drykkur p.80
Friðrik V p.81
Icelandic Fish & Chips p.80
Lækjarbrekka p.80
Sandholt p.78

sandwiches and handmade chocolates. Also serves breakfast including fresh croissants, muesli and *skyr*. Mon–Wed & Sun 6.30am–8pm, Thurs–Sat 6.30am–9pm.

BUDGET MEALS

Bæjarins Beztu Pylsur Tryggvagata; map p.57. Down by the harbour, the *Bæjarins* stall is a local institution, serving up the Nordic classic: a *pýlsa* (hot dog; 400kr), with lashings of fried onion and artery-clogging remoulade sauce. Daily 10am–late.

Búllan Geirsgata 1 ☎ 511 1888; map p.57. Little 1950s concrete bunker of a building at the harbour serving a wide variety of burgers (from 1030kr) and nothing else – and doing them very well too, with excellent fries. Expect to queue. Daily 11.30am–9pm.

★**Eldsmiðjan** Laugavegur 81 ☎ 562 3838, ⓦ eldsmidjan.is; map pp.54–55. In a prime location on the main drag, *Eldsmiðjan* serves the best pizzas in Reykjavík, made in a pizza oven that burns Icelandic birchwood. There's also a takeaway service available. A 12-incher starts at 2995kr. Daily 11am–11pm.

Grillhúsið Tryggvagata 20 ☎ 562 3456, ⓦ grillhusid.is; map p.57. Popular and informal grill restaurant decked out to resemble an American diner. The menu runs to steaks, but it's best for its burgers (from 1790kr) or fish and chips (2370kr). Mon–Thurs & Sun 11.30am–10pm, Sat 11am–11pm.

★**Icelandic Fish & Chips** Tryggvagata 11 ☎ 511 1118, ⓦ fishandchips.is; map p.57. Proper sit-down restaurant in the Volcano House serving exactly what you'd expect from the name. The type of fish available varies daily – but whatever you choose, you simply add sides like fries, onion rings or salad, or other garnishes such as delicious home-made dips. Mon–Thurs 11.30am–9.30pm, Fri–Sun 11.30am–10pm.

★**Krua Thai** Tryggvagata 14 ☎ 561 0039, ⓦ kruathai.is; map p.57. This cosy, no-nonsense Thai place offers exceptional value with a huge choice of single-dish meals – green curry, *pad Thai* and the like – for around 1760kr. Portions are generous and prices include a serving of rice. At lunchtime, a portion of three different set dishes with rice goes for a mere 1450kr. Mon–Fri 11.30am–9.30pm, Sat noon–9.30pm, Sun 5–9.30pm.

Sjávarbarinn Grandagarður 9 ☎ 517 3131; map pp.54–55. Handy for the Saga and Maritime museums, this compact little fish place really comes into its own at lunchtime when there's a seafood buffet for just 1790kr,

featuring a good range of fish dishes, a bowl of soup and coffee – it's hard to beat the price. Mon–Fri 9am–9pm, Sat 10am–10pm, Sun 4–10pm.

RESTAURANTS

Since there are restaurants dotted around the whole of Reykjavík's city centre, walking between them can take a fair amount of time and effort. For easy reference, we've listed them in two main areas: Lækjartorg and around; and those located on or near Laugavegur.

LÆKJARTORG AND AROUND

Einar Ben Veltusund 1 ☎ 511 5090, ⓦ einarben.is; map p.57. Named after the poet Einar Benediktsson, this elegant place is brimming with chandeliers and heavy red drapes. The pan-fried salmon with butternut purée (4200kr), and cod fillet with tomato concassé, feta cheese and ginger (also 4200kr) are both superb. An early-bird two-course special is available until 7pm for 3950kr. Tues–Fri 5.30–11pm, Sat & Sun 5–11pm.

Fish Market Aðalstræti 12 ☎ 578 8877, ⓦ fishmarket.is; map p.57. Smart, stylish restaurant heavy on fake greenery, specializing in fish given an Asian twist – try the salted cod with lime (4800kr) or the grilled pork ribs with star anise and cardamom (2800kr). All produce is bought direct from Icelandic fishermen and farmers. Mon–Fri 11.30am–2pm & 6–11.30pm, Sat & Sun 6–11.30pm.

★**Hornið** Hafnarstræti 15 ☎ 551 3340, ⓦ hornid.is; map p.57. Long-time favourite with young Reykjavíkers, who flock here for the excellent pizzas (around 2390kr) and pasta (around 2450kr). They also do a good range of meat and fish dishes, with a daily fish special (3650kr) and a succulent lamb fillet (4990kr). Daily 11am–11.30pm.

★**Jómfrúin** Lækjargata 4 ☎ 551 0100, ⓦ jomfruin.is; map p.57. Popular Danish-influenced place specializing in *smørrebrød* (open rye sandwiches), priced at 1800–3300kr. Pick the fillings from a range including smoked salmon, caviar, shrimps, asparagus, smoked eel and scrambled egg. Fried plaice (2200kr) is the house speciality. Daily 11am–6pm.

★**Lækjarbrekka** Bankastræti 2 ☎ 551 4430, ⓦ laekjarbrekka.is; map p.57. Old wooden building with period furnishings, refined atmosphere and fabulous seafood. The Icelandic feast, for example, includes fermented shark, cured lamb, minke whale, dried fish, lamb, cream of langoustine soup and *skyr* mousse with blueberry sorbet (9500kr). The seafood feast (7900kr) is equally mouthwatering. Daily 11.30am–11pm.

★**Matur og Drykkur** Grandagarður 2 ☎ 571 8877, ⓦ maturogdrykkur.is; map pp.54–55. Inside the Saga Museum building (see p.60), this inventive new restaurant, plainy decorated with a concrete floor and wooden tables, has a truly unusual menu, featuring everything from an entire baked cod's head, complete with throat muscles in batter (3490kr), to cod liver on caraway crackers served with cranberries (1490kr). Mon & Sun 11.30am–5.30pm, Tues–Sat 11.30am–11.30pm.

Restaurant Reykjavík Vesturgata 2 ☎ 552 3030, ⓦ restaurantreykjavik.is; map p.57. Although this restaurant serves a wide and accomplished menu, it's best visited for its justifiably renowned nightly fish buffet (6750kr), which features all manner of smoked, marinated, baked and gratinated fishy treats, plus a wide selection of Icelandic cheeses. Daily 5.30pm–late.

★ **Sægreifinn** Geirsgata 8 ☎ 553 1500, ⓦ saegreifinn .is; map p.57. This harbourside fishmonger-cum-restaurant is a favourite haunt of locals after the superlative lobster soup (1350kr) and fresh halibut. It's also the place to come for minke whale steaks (1850kr), if your conscience allows. Daily 11.30am–11pm.

LAUGAVEGUR AND AROUND

Café Loki Lokastígur 28 ☎ 466 2828, ⓦ loki.is; map p.57. *The* place to come if you're looking to sample traditional, home-made Icelandic fare at reasonable prices: meat soup (1570kr), herring plate (2200kr), sheep head jelly on flatbread (1840kr) and skyr (820kr). Plus, there's great views of Hallgrímskirkja from upstairs. Mon–Sat 9am–9pm, Sun 11am–9pm.

Fish & More Skólavörðustígur 23 ☎ 571 1289; map p.57. Another of Reykjavík's new fish restaurants, though instead of battering and frying, this one dishes up a selection of steamed fish with sides of veggies (2290kr); check the blackboard to see what's fresh in that day. There's usually a deliciously tangy fish soup available, too (1590kr). Daily 10am–9.30pm.

★ **Friðrik V** Laugavegur 60 ☎ 461 5775, ⓦ fridrikv.is; map pp.54–55. Run by the ebullient Friðrik, who trained at London's *River Café*, with a tasting menu that represents new Nordic cooking at its most inventive: Icelandic herbs and flavours blending perfectly with the best of the Mediterranean. Three courses 8400kr, five courses 10,400kr. Tues–Sat 5.30pm–late.

Gló Laugavegur 20B ☎ 553 1111, ⓦ glo.is; map p.57. Unusually decorated with slices of birch trunks, this popular vegetarian place serves up the likes of parsley root soup with hummus (1250kr), and nut stew (1998kr). The emphasis is on fresh produce, much of it served uncooked. Also has a wide range of fresh juices. Mon–Fri 11am–9pm, Sat & Sun 11.30am–9pm.

Kól Skólavörðustígur 40 ☎ 517 7474, ⓦ kolrestaurant.is; map p.57. This classy place is named after the *kól* (charcoal)

they use to cook their steaks over in the oven: the grilled lamb sirloin with polenta, carrots and goat's cheese, for example, is delicious (4890kr). Otherwise, there's a wide selection of Icelandic-meets-Mediterranean dishes such as charred salmon with lemon confit and grilled peppers (4190kr), and fillet of plaice with capers and fennel seeds. Mon–Thurs 11.30am–2pm & 5.30–10pm, Fri 11.30am–2pm & 5.30–11pm, Sat 5.30–11pm, Sun 5.30–10pm.

Nepalese Kitchen Laugavegur 60A ☎ 517 7795, ⓦ nepalesekitchen.is; map pp.54–55. This Nepalese restaurant has a deserved reputation for serving some seriously tasty dishes from the subcontinent: mains, such as Nepalese chicken massala and any number of lamb and vegetarian specialities, start around 2990kr. Ffiteen percent discount for takeaway. Mon–Sat 5.30–11pm, Sun 5.30–10pm.

★ **Rosso Pomodoro** Laugavegur 40 ☎ 561 0500, ⓦ rossopomodoro.is; map p.57. A genuinely good southern Italian restaurant, drawing inspiration from the cuisine of Naples. Pizzas and pasta dishes go for around 2990kr, salads start at 1790kr and grilled chicken with Parma ham, mozzarella and red wine sauce is 4390kr. Mon–Thurs 11.30am–10pm, Fri & Sat 11.30am–11pm, Sun 5–10pm.

Scandinavian Smørrebrød Laugavegur 22A ☎ 578 4888, ⓦ scandinavian.is; map p.57. Under new ownership and, despite its name, this restaurant serves Icelandic rather than Scandinavian specialities such as reindeer pâté, lobster soup and various lamb concoctions. There's a range of open sandwiches, too. Reckon on around 3500kr for a main course. Mon–Thurs 11.30am–1pm, Fri & Sat 11.30am–11pm.

Vegamót Vegamótastígur 4 ☎ 511 3040, ⓦ vegamot .is; map p.57. A favourite hangout for Reykjavík's trendy young things, who come here for the good-value burgers (2590kr), salads (2490kr), Mexican specials (2590kr) and the excellent weekend brunch (Sat & Sun 11am–4pm; from 2390kr). Mon–Thurs & Sun 11.30am–1am, Fri & Sat 11.30am–4am.

★ **Þrir Frakkar** Baldursgata 14 ☎ 552 3939, ⓦ 3frakkar .com; map p.57. Strange name ("Three Overcoats") for this backstreet French-style bistro with definite leanings towards traditional Icelandic game: whale steak in pepper sauce (5190kr), horse tenderloin with mushrooms (5750kr), *plokkfiskur* (fish and potato mash; 3600kr) and smoked guillemot (5190kr). Mon–Thurs 11.30am–2.30pm & 6–10pm, Fri 11.30am–2.30pm & 6–10.30pm, Sat & Sun 6–10.30pm.

DRINKING AND NIGHTLIFE

Thanks to some cunning publicity from the Icelandic Tourist Board, Reykjavík is now deservedly known across Europe and the US for its **nightlife**. Although the scene is actually no bigger than that of any small-sized town in most other countries, what sets it apart is the northerly setting and location for all this revelry – during the light nights of summer, it's very disorientating to have entered a nightclub in the wee small hours with the sun just about to set, only to emerge a couple of hours later into the blinding and unflattering daylight of the Icelandic morning.

1

There's been a strong **rock music** network in Reykjavík for over two decades, represented originally by Björk and the Sugarcubes and more recently by groups such as Sigur Rós, though decent **venues** have always been thin on the ground, with most gigs taking place in the city's bars. Besides the local talent, some British and American acts use Icelandair as a cheap way to cross the Atlantic and they sometimes do a show here on the way.

ESSENTIALS

Drinks For take-away booze, the *vínbúð* alcohol store is at Austurstræti 10a (Mon–Thurs & Sat 11am–6pm, Fri 11am–7pm). Drinking in bars and clubs, you'll need plenty of cash for even a few drinks (a beer in a club costs around 1400kr); and don't be tempted to leave your drink on the bar while you go dancing, as the chances are it'll have been drunk by the time you return.

Dress code Don't expect to get into a club in style-conscious Reykjavík if you turn up in full hiking gear – the dress code is generally smart, and Icelandic men often don a tie to go out clubbing. For foreigners things are more relaxed, but you'll feel more comfortable if you're smart-casual. At some places, jeans and sneakers aren't allowed.

Entry and opening hours Very few people are out much before 10pm, after which time crowds fill the streets and queues develop outside the most popular joints. Things are liveliest on Fri and Sat nights, when most places swing until 4 or 5am; closing time the rest of the week is around 1am. With weekend partying rarely winding up before early morning, it's not uncommon to see hordes of youngsters staggering around Lækjartorg at 4am shivering in the cold air dressed, fashion-consciously, only in their latest T-shirts and jeans – and often in much less. However you're kitted out, don't be surprised if you're approached and chatted up as soon as you've set foot through the door – Reykjavík is a small city and new faces will always draw attention.

Admission fees Prices are not too steep, generally 1000–1500kr if there's live music, otherwise free.

BARS AND CLUBS

Bjarni Fel Austurstræti 20 ☎561 2240; map p.57. Rather small and intimate sports bar (absolutely no music), full of memorabilia and TV with screens angled in all directions; best place to catch the latest football match over a cold beer. Mon–Thurs & Sun noon–1am, Fri & Sat noon–4.30am.

Bravó Laugavegur 22 ☎770 1517; map p.57. In various guises, this spot has been one of Reykjavík's most popular

bars for years, and is a great place to start the evening. Music policy is electro, indie and classic hits. Mon–Thurs & Sun 7pm–1am, Fri & Sat 7pm–4.30am.

Broadway Ármúli 9 ☎533 1100; map pp.54–55. Inside the *Ísland* hotel (see p.77), this is the country's biggest nightspot, with room for over 2000 punters, and is popular with people of all ages, from teenagers to pensioners. It's prone to Vegas-style singing-and-dancing shows. Opening times vary, so call ahead. Usually Fri & Sat evening.

Dolly Hafnarstræti 4 ☎571 9222; map p.57. Cool and rather intimate little lounge bar with battered furniture, playing a range of hip-hop and electronica. It's a popular place with a young crowd who come here to drink (seriously) and dance (unsteadily). Wed & Thurs 8pm–1am, Fri & Sat 8pm–4.30am.

Enski Barinn Austurstræti 12 ☎578 0400, ⓦenskibar inn.is; map p.57. Lager, Guinness and Kilkenny on draught, lots of soccer on TV and weekend live music. There's also the chance to spin the "wheel of fortune", with up to eight free beers as the prize if you win. Mon–Thurs & Sun noon–1am, Fri & Sat noon–5am.

Frederiksen Ale House Hafnarstræti 5 ☎571 0055; map p.57. This well-located pub is always busy at any time of day. There's a decent selection of draught and bottled beers, including Víking classic, Thule and stout. The expert staff are also adept at knocking up wicked cocktails. Mon–Thurs & Sun noon–1am, Fri & Sat noon–5am.

Hlemmur Square Laugavegur 105 ☎415 1600, ⓦhlemmursquare.com/bistro-bar; map pp.54–55. The trendy bar inside the *Hlemmur Square* hostel (see p.78) should be your number one choice for happy hour (4–8pm), with beers priced at an amazing 600kr (there are several Icelandic ones on tap as well as Tuborg), and even cocktails going for just 1000kr. Daily 3–10pm.

Kaffibarinn Bergstaðastræti 1 ☎551 1588; map p.57. With an unmistakable red corrugated-iron frontage emblazoned with the famous London underground logo, this tiny bar fancies itself as an arty hangout and trades on the rumour that Blur's Damon Albarn owns it, however unlikely. Be that as it may, it's still your best chance of a

WRECKED IN REYKJAVÍK

A rite of passage for all young Icelanders, the **rúntur** (literally "round tour") is a drunken pub-crawl that generally takes place between at least half a dozen bars and pubs, whatever the weather. Intent on searching out the place with the hottest action, groups of revellers (already well oiled after downing several generous vodkas before setting out) maraud the city centre, particularly on Friday nights. If you come across them, expect to be engaged in conversation or to see some rather unrestrained behaviour – but then nightlife in Iceland isn't known for its subtleties.

great night out in Reykjavík and is a legend on the scene. Mon–Thurs & Sun 5pm–1am, Fri & Sat 3pm–5am.

Kaldi Bar Laugavegur 20B ☎ 581 2200; map p.57. This is a great place for a beer to start the evening and is always packed as a result. It serves up any number of beers from the Kaldi microbrewery in Árskógssandur near Akureyri. They play low background music, so if you're looking for a place to chat over a beer, it's a sound choice. Mon–Thurs & Sun noon–1am, Fri & Sat noon–3am.

Mikkeller & Friends Hverfisgata 12 ☎ 437 0203; map p.57. With twenty beers on tap, all from microbreweries, this great little top-floor bar is a beer drinker's heaven. It's cosy and snug inside and a really good place to start the evening off with a drink or two. Mon–Thurs & Sun 4pm–midnight, Fri & Sat 2pm–1am.

Slippbarinn Mýrargata 2 ☎ 560 8000; map p.57. This swanky and sophisticated place, inside the *Icelandair Reykjavík Marina* hotel (see p.76), has to be the most novel location for a bar in the whole of town – right beside the slipway where the ships come in to be repainted and repaired. Daily 5pm–late.

LIVE MUSIC VENUES

Celtic Cross Hverfisgata 26 ☎ 571 1033; map p.57. Best of the Brit/Irish pubs in town; the beer is the same (Guinness and lager) but the atmosphere is livelier – especially when rock and R&B bands fire up at weekends. There's some decent pub grub, too. Mon–Thurs & Sun 11.30am–1am, Fri & Sat 11.30am–4am.

Dubliner Naustin 1 ☎ 527 3232, ⓦ dubliner.is; map p.57. Iceland's first-ever Irish pub, and still drawing in the crowds. It's always a good choice for an evening pint, and there's a decent selection of whiskeys, plus live music (often Irish folk and R&B) every night of the week. Mon & Tues 4pm–midnight, Wed 4pm–1am, Thurs 3pm–1am, Fri 3pm–4.30am, Sat 1pm–4.30am, Sun 1pm–midnight.

Gaukurinn Tryggvagata 22 ☎ 781 7273, ⓦ gaukurinn .is; map p.57. Long-established, though recently renovated, live music venue and bar that's been drawing the crowds since even before beer was legalized in 1989. You'll find a mix of live music, karaoke, open mic nights and pub quiz events – details are all on the website. Wed & Thurs 9pm–1am, Fri & Sat 9pm–4.30am.

THEATRE AND CLASSICAL MUSIC

Remarkably, for such a small city, Reykjavík boasts several **theatre** groups, an opera, a symphony orchestra and a dance company. Unfortunately, major theatre productions, and classical concerts by the **Icelandic Symphony Orchestra**, are a rarity in summer, but throughout the rest of the year there are full programmes of both. Events are chiefly held at the National Theatre, and at Harpa, which is home to the Symphony Orchestra and the **Icelandic Opera** (ⓦ opera.is).

Borgarleikhús Listabraut 3 ☎ 568 8000, ⓦ borgar leikhus.is; map pp.54–55. The city playhouse stages all manner of productions, though they are generally always in Icelandic. Note, too, that it's closed during the summer months.

Harpa Austurbakki 2 ☎ 528 5000, ⓦ harpa.is; map p.57.

Performances by the Icelandic Symphony orchestra and other musical events, including those by the Icelandic Opera.

Þjóðleikhúsið Hverfisgata 19 ☎ 551 1200, ⓦ leikhusid .is; map p.57. Classic theatre productions are the name of the game here, though generally only in Icelandic and not during the summer.

ART GALLERIES

With so much art on display in a relatively small city, it can be tempting to purchase a piece of **Icelandic art** while you're in Reykjavík. Should the urge strike, there are two **galleries** worth checking out where you'll find a range of artists and artistic styles represented.

i8 Tryggvagata 18 ☎ 551 3666, ⓦ i8.is; map p.57. A long-established art house working with a group of around twenty artists, Icelandic and international, who produce contemporary fine art. Free entry. Tues–Fri 11am–5pm, Sat 1–5pm.

Hverfisgallerí Hverfisgata 4 ☎ 537 4007,

ⓦ hverfisgalleri.is; map p.57. All bar one of the seventeen artists displayed here are Icelandic and the style is, like nearby i8, also contemporary fine art, though sometimes with 2D work and sculpture on display, too. Exhibitions at both galleries tend to run for around five weeks. Free entry. Tues–Fri 1–5pm, Sat & Sun 2–5pm.

CINEMA

Reykjavík's **cinemas** screen new international releases with Icelandic subtitles; see any of the newspapers (see p.38) or check ⓦ bio.is for full listings.

Bíó Paradís Hverfisgata 54 ☎ 412 7711, ⓦ bioparadis .is; map p.57. One of Reykjavík's oldest cinemas has now moved away from the mainstream to focus on art-house

films and cinema festivals.

Háskólabíó Hagatorg ☎ 591 5145, ⓦ bio.is; map pp.54–55. Mainstream film productions are on offer at this

1

multiplex cinema attached to the university which serves as the city's main picture house.

Volcano Show Hellusund 6A ☎ 845 9548; map p.57. With footage of recent Icelandic eruptions from daringly close quarters filmed largely by the engaging Villi Knudsen, there are two sets of 2hr films in English: during July and Aug, *Villi Knudsen's Volcano Adventures* screens at 11am, 3pm and 8pm, while footage of the Heimaey and Surtsey eruptions follows at noon, 4pm and 9pm. Screenings vary at other times of the year.

SHOPPING

In recent years, Austurstræti, Bankastræti and Skólavörðustígur, in particular, have witnessed a veritable boom in **tourist-oriented shopping outlets** selling everything from oversized cuddly toys in the shape of puffins to woollen blankets and Icelandic sweaters. While the stores are not popular with locals, who consider them to sell poor-quality goods at inflated prices, sooner or later you're bound to find yourself perusing their wares – even if it's only as a respite from the vagaries of the Icelandic weather. There are, however, two stores in particular which stand out from the crowd, which we've listed below.

Bónus Laugavegur 59 & Hallveigarstígur 1 (off Ingólfsstræti) ☎ 527 9000, ⓦ bonus.is; map p.57. Most visitors use one of the two Bónus stores on and around Laugavegur for all their self-catering needs. These two supermarkets are not only the cheapest in town but they are also the most centrally located. Mon–Thurs 11am–6.30pm, Fri 10am–7.30pm, Sat 10am–6pm, Sun noon–6pm.

Eymundsson Austurstræti 18 ☎ 540 2130, ⓦ eymundsson.is; map p.57. The best bookshop in Reykjavík with a good selection of books about Iceland in English as well as videos, postcards and other souvenirs. Mon–Sat 9am–10pm, Sun 10am–10pm.

Geysir Skólavörðustígur 16 ☎ 519 6000, ⓦ geysir.com; map p.57. The only place you should consider buying a pure wool Icelandic blanket. Stocking as they do traditional patterns and designs, prices here are a little higher than in other stores but the quality is far superior. Reckon on around 17,800kr for a woollen blanket. Taxfree shopping available. Daily 9am–10pm.

Handprjónasamband Íslands Skólavörðustígur 19 & Laugavegur 53B ☎ 552 1890, ⓦ handknit.is; map p.57 & map pp.54–55. The Icelandic handknitting association stocks an astounding number of home-made sweaters, scarves, gloves and other woollen goods. Each item has been lovingly produced by a local knitter in the Reykjavík area – something which is evident in the quality of the products for sale. Reckon on around 15,000–20,000kr for a decent sweater. Taxfree shopping available. Skólavörðustígur 19 Mon–Fri 9am–10pm, Sat 9am–6pm, Sun 10am–6pm; Laugavegur 53B Mon–Fri 9am–7pm, Sat 10am–5pm.

Kringlan shopping mall Off Miklabraut, 2km east of the city centre ☎ 517 9000, ⓦ kringlan.is; map pp.54–55. For more main mainstream shopping options, your best bet is this shopping centre. A free shuttle bus operates here from outside the tourist office where you'll find departure times. Alternatively, city buses #1, #3, #4 & #6 all come here. Mon–Wed 10am–6.30pm, Thurs 10am–9pm, Fri 10am–7pm, Sat 10am–6pm, Sun 1–6pm.

DIRECTORY

Currency exchange Landsbankinn, Austurstræti 11 (Mon–Fri 9am–4pm).

Dentist For the duty dentist call ☎ 575 0505. English spoken.

Embassies and consulates Canada, Túngata 14 ☎ 575 6500; India, Skúlagata 17 ☎ 534 9955; UK, Laufásvegur 31 ☎ 550 5100; US, Laufásvegur 21 ☎ 562 9100.

Internet Reykjavík city library (5th floor), Tryggvagata 15 (Mon–Thurs 10am–7pm, Fri 11am–6pm, Sat & Sun 1–5pm).

Pharmacies Lyfja, Lágmúli 5 (daily 8am–midnight; ☎ 533 2300); Lyfja, Laugavegur 16 (Mon–Fri 9am–6pm, Sat 11am–4pm; ☎ 552 4045).

Police Tryggvagata 19 ☎ 444 1000.

Post office Pósthússtræti 5 (Mon–Fri 9am–6pm; ⓦ postur.is).

Vínbúð Austurstræti 10a (Mon–Thurs & Sat 11am–6pm, Fri 11am–7pm; ⓦ vinbud.is).

Around Reykjavík

Home to two out of every three Icelanders, **Greater Reykjavík** is composed of the neighbouring municipalities of Seltjarnarnes, northwest of the city centre, Mosfellsbær to the northeast, and, in the southwest, **Hafnarfjörður**, Garðabær and Kópavogur, the last three of which are passed through by the road into the city centre from Keflavík airport, and all but Hafnarfjörður containing little of interest. Just outside Sundahöfn harbour, to the north of Reykjavík, the island of **Viðey** makes an excellent destination for a short boat trip. It has some enjoyable walking trails and is easily reached on a seven-minute ferry journey from Sundahöfn harbour, northeast of Laugardalur.

Hafnarfjörður

Stealing the limelight from its suburban neighbours thanks to its dramatic setting amid an extensive lavafield, **Hafnarfjörður**, with a population of around 26,000 and just 10km from the capital, is as big as the centre of Reykjavík, although it's not as likeable. There are nevertheless several good reasons to make the 25-minute bus ride out here, the main ones being to sample some real Viking food at the town's Viking village, **Fjörukráin**, and to learn more about the Icelanders' obsession with elves, dwarves and other spiritual beings – Hafnarfjörður is renowned across the country as home to the greatest concentration of **huldufólk** ("hidden people").

Brief history

The town's prosperity stems from its superbly sheltered **harbour** (Hafnarfjörður meaning "the harbour fjord") – the volcano Búrfell, around 5km east of the centre, erupted 7000 years ago, spewing lava out along the northern side of the fjord that is now home to Hafnarfjörður, and creating a protective wall. At the beginning of the fifteenth century the village became a strategic centre for **trade** with England, which was then just starting up, and the harbour was often full of English boats profiting from the then-rich fishing grounds offshore. Seventy-five years later, a dispute broke out between the English and newly arrived German fishermen who challenged, and won, the right to operate out of the burgeoning town. Their victory, however, was short-lived, since Hafnarfjörður fell under the trade monopoly of the Danes in 1602, which lasted until 1787, when the place fell into obscurity.

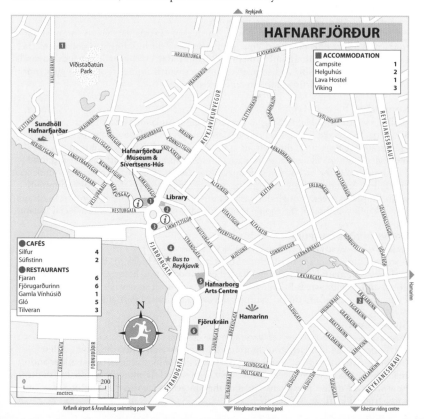

1

> ## MOUNT ESJA
>
> Proudly standing guard over Reykjavík, **Mount Esja** (914m) is a familiar sight to anyone who's spent even a few hours in the capital. At 909m, the mountain appears to change colour – from light purple to deep blue, from light grey to golden – depending on the prevailing weather conditions and the light that reflects on the basalt rock and palagonite minerals which make up the mountain, although locals say it depends on her mood. Several hiking trails wind their way around Mount Esja – a detailed **trail map** is available from the tourist office (see p.73) – but it's best to start out at Mógilsá, beside the Ringroad, where the Icelandic state forestry station has its base. From here an easy path leads up the mountain towards the rocky higher stretches.

Today, Hafnarfjörður is known for its inhabitants, called *hafnies*, the unfortunate subjects of many an Icelandic **joke** – it's said, for example, that local children take ladders when they start at high school, which their parents also use to go shopping with if they hear that prices have gone up. Needless to say, Icelandic humour can be an acquired taste.

The harbour

The **harbour** is the best place to start your wanderings. Home port for many of Iceland's ocean-going trawlers, it's an interesting spot for watching the bustle as fishermen land their catches, wash down their vessels and mend their nets.

Hafnarborg

Strandgata 34 • Mon & Wed–Sun noon–5pm, Thurs noon–9pm • Free

From the harbour, it's a five-minute walk south along Fjarðargata via the roundabout to the arts centre of **Hafnarborg**. In a fit of generosity the building was donated to the town by a local chemist and his wife in 1983 and today exhibits work by local Icelandic artists as well as doubling as a concert venue – it's worth a quick look, but you're more likely to satisfy your artistic appetite in Reykjavík.

Strandgata

Walking south from Hafnarborg and crossing the roundabout into what is now **Strandgata** will take you towards the curious, steeply roofed wooden structure called **Fjörukráin**, set back from the seafront at no. 55. Although a bit of a tourist trap, this self-styled Viking Village is a good place to sample some pretty authentic **Viking food** (see opposite) at the on-site hotel. From *Fjörukráin*, retrace your steps to the roundabout and follow Strandgata back towards the town centre. This is Hafnarfjörður's diminutive main shopping street, though don't expect the stores here to come close to the selection in Reykjavík – although the capital is only just down the road, this is provincial Iceland.

Hafnarfjörður museum

Vesturgata 8 • June–Aug daily 11am–5pm; Sept–May Sat & Sun 11–5pm • Free

A stone's throw from the northern end of Strandgata, one block to the north of the harbour, is **Hafnarfjörður museum**, housed in a wooden warehouse dating from the late 1800s and also known as Pakkhúsið. Inside is a passable if somewhat dull portrayal of Hafnarfjörður's life and times, featuring the likes of a stuffed goat and an old fishing boat.

Sívertsens-Hús

Vesturgata 6 • June–Aug daily 11am–5pm; Sept–May Sat & Sun 11am–5pm • Free

Next door to the Hafnarfjörður museum stands **Sívertsens-Hús**, the town's oldest building, dating from 1803 and once the residence of local trader, boat builder and man-about-town Bjarni Sívertsen. It's now home to a folk museum, stuffed with dreary how-we-used-to-live paraphernalia from the nineteenth century and decorated with some frightfully flowery wallpaper.

Hamarinn cliffs

1

The views from **Hamarinn** cliffs are far more rewarding than Hafnarfjörður's slight attempt at culture. To get there, turn left into Lækjargata from the roundabout just before *Fjörukráin*, then head east along Lækjargata and take the footpath up the hill to the wall of lava; this leads to the viewpoint. The protected wooded natural area up here offers good **views** out over the harbour and the surrounding countryside and is a pleasant place to have a picnic when the weather's good. Incidentally, the ugly red- and white-striped towers you can see from here, which dominate the surrounding flat landscape of lavafields, belong to the vast aluminium smelter at Straumsvík, which imports its raw materials from Australia and uses local geothermal power to produce the metal.

ARRIVAL AND INFORMATION

By bus From Hlemmur and Lækjartorg in Reykjavík city centre, bus #1 runs to Hafnarfjörður (every 30min), passing the tourist information office.

Tourist information office The main office is at Strandgata 6 (Mon–Fri 8am–4pm); there's another inside Hafnarfjörður museum at Vesturgata 8 (Sat & Sun 11am–5pm; ☎ 585 5500, ⓦ visithafnarfjordur.is).

Internet access The library, diagonally opposite the tourist office at Strandgata 1 (Mon–Fri 10am–7pm, plus Sept–May Sat 11am–3pm), has internet access.

HAFNARFJÖRÐUR

Horseriding If you've come to Hafnarfjörður to go horseriding, you'll find Íshestar at Sörlaskeið 26, southeast of the town centre along Kaldárselsvegur (☎ 555 7000, ⓦ ishestar.is). Day tours range from 3–7hr and start at 8400kr per person.

Swimming pool There are two decent indoor swimming pools in Hafnarfjörður, at Ásvellir 2 (Mon–Fri 6.30am–9pm, Sat 8am–6pm, Sun 8am–5pm) and Herjólfsgata 10b (Mon–Fri 6.30am–9pm), while the one at Hringbraut 77 (Mon–Fri 6.30am–9pm, Sat 8am–6pm, Sun 8am–5pm) is outdoor.

ACCOMMODATION

Campsite Hjallabraut 51 ☎ 565 0900, ⓦ lavahostel .is. Located in a quiet part of town within leafy Víðistaðatún park, off Flókagata north of the centre, the town's basic campsite has access to showers and hot and cold running water, though for other facilities campers must use the *Lava Hostel* next door. Mid-May to mid-Sept. **1250kr**

Helguhús Lækjarinn 8 ☎ 555 2842, ⓦ helguhus.is. Family-run guesthouse with just a handful of rather small and plainly decorated rooms; facilities are shared, and there's access to a kitchen. **15,000kr**

Lava Hostel Hjallabraut 51 ☎ 565 0900, ⓦ lavahostel .is. A sound choice housed in a handsome modern timber structure next to the campsite; the compact dorms (sleeping 4–8) and double rooms here share facilities and look out over the park. Dorms **5400kr**, doubles **13,400kr**

Viking Strandgata 55 ☎ 565 1213, ⓦ fjorukrain .is. All 41 rooms here have private facilities and a Viking feel to the decor, with lots of heavy wooden flourishes and Gothic prints hanging on the walls; there are also fourteen new 6-bed cabins. Guests have use of a sauna and hot tub. Doubles **22,700kr**, cabins **30,600kr**

EATING AND DRINKING

Fjaran Strandgata 55 ☎ 565 1213. Cosy, wood-panelled restaurant akin to a British country pub, serving the same

Viking delicacies as *Fjörugarðurinn* (see p.88) though on proper plates rather than wooden platters and offering a

---

THE HIDDEN PEOPLE

The street of Strandgata and neighbouring Austurgata in Hafnarfjörður are, according to Icelandic folklore, home to the town's population of **hidden people** – elves, dwarves and other spirits who live in entire families between the rocks that are dotted around the town centre. Apparently elves are only visible to those with second sight, though a majority of Icelanders are quite prepared to admit they believe in them. In fact, an alarming number of new roads constructed across the country have been subject to minor detours around large rocks after workers attempted to move the boulders only to find that their diggers and earth movers broke down time and again in the process. Should you be keen to try out your second sight, **tours** (Tues & Fri 2.30pm from the tourist office at Strandgata 6; 4500kr; ☎ 694 2785, ⓦ alfar.is) lasting a couple of hours and led by guide and storyteller Sigurbjörg Karlsdóttir weave their way through Hafnarfjörður visiting the homes of the *huldufólk*.

1

TRADITIONAL VIKING FARE: ÞORRABLÓT

The best time to sample some truly weird Viking specialities in Hafnarfjörður is during the old Icelandic month of **Þorri** (from the Friday between Jan 19 & 25 until late Feb) when there are nightly Viking banquets known as *þorrablót* at *Fjörugarðurinn* (see below) This smorgasbord-style feast offers the dubious delight of sampling traditional foods – rotten shark, singed sheep's head and pickled rams' testicles, squashed flat and eaten as a topping to an open sandwich – all washed down with generous quantities of the potent Icelandic schnapps, Black Death.

more fine-dining experience. Daily 6–10pm.

Fjörugarðurinn Strandgata 55 ☎ 565 1213. Designed to resemble a Viking longhouse, this place serves a full Viking dinner (9200kr): seafood soup, shark, dried haddock, lamb shank, and *skyr* for dessert, accompanied by a half-litre of beer and some Black Death schnapps. Daily 6–10pm.

Gamla Vínhúsið Vesturgata 4 ☎ 565 1130. The walls of this wooden-beamed place are lined with old wine bottles, creating a cosy atmosphere to savour baked cod fillet (3450kr), minke whale steak (2800kr), or just a house burger (1800kr). Lunch specials go for 1250kr. Mon–Thurs 11.30am–9.30pm, Fri 11.30am–10.30pm, Sat 6–11.30pm, Sun 6–9.30pm.

Gló Strandgata 34 ☎ 578 1111. A fabulous new restaurant inside the Hafnarborg complex (see p.86) serving the very freshest of ingredients in a variety of complex and mouthwatering salads featuring lots of mint, spinach, pomegranate, mango and sesame oil. Salads 1799kr, soups 1250kr. Mon–Fri 11.30am–9pm, Sat & Sun 11.30am–5pm.

Silfur Fjarðargata 13–15 ☎ 555 6996. Upstairs in the Fjörður shopping centre, this light and airy café enjoys unsurpassed views over the harbour and serves an array of burgers from 1690kr, pasta dishes for around 2290kr plus fish and chips for 1890kr. Mon–Wed 10am–11pm, Thurs–Sat 10am–1am, Sun 11.30am–10pm.

Súfistinn Strandgata 9 ☎ 565 3740. Hafnarfjörður's main coffeehouse, with outdoor seating in good weather, and serving an impressive range of coffees, as well as soup (1240kr), panini (1560kr) and chicken salad (1760kr). It's also a popular place for a beer of an evening. Mon–Thurs 8.15am–11.30pm, Fri 8am–11.30pm, Sat 10am–11.30pm, Sun 11am–11.30pm.

Tilveran Linnetstígur 1 ☎ 565 5250. A justifiably popular seafood restaurant with daily lunch specials including soup, fish of the day and coffee for 2490kr; in the evening you'll pay 2990kr for a succulent fish dish, 4490kr if you prefer something more meaty. Mon–Thurs 11.30am–2pm & 6–9pm, Fri 11.30am–2pm & 6–10pm, Sat 6–10pm.

Þríhnjúkahellir

Tours daily mid-May to Sept 5– 6hr including 40min inside the volcano • 39,000kr including return transport from Reykjavík • ⓦ insidethevolcano.com

About 20km southeast of Reykjavík near the Bláfjöll ski area, **Þríhnjúkahellir** is like nowhere else in Iceland, an accessible, 4000-year-old subterranean magma chamber discovered in the 1970s. There's little to see on the surface – a small volcanic bump amid a landscape covered in thick clumps of moss and grass – but the scale below ground becomes clear as you climb into a safety cage and are lowered by crane into the 120m-deep chamber. Once you've touched down safely at the bottom, you're allowed to wander cautiously over the rough boulders and stones that carpet the floor of Þríhnjúkahellir's 30m-wide chamber; check out the walls, streaked in different colours left by molten minerals, all twisted and spiked by the geological forces. Normally a chamber such as this would fill with magma during an eruption and then solidify, but in Þríhnjúkahellir's case the molten rock drained out through tunnels, still visible at the sides of the cave floor. Note that you should bring warm clothes and tough shoes or boots; there is a 45min walk over rough ground in each direction at the beginning and end of the tour to and from the volcano entrance. The tour ends with hot soup and bus transfer back to Reykjavík.

Viðey

Actually the top of an extinct volcano and measuring barely 1.7 square kilometres, the island of **Viðey** (ⓦ elding.is/videy) boasts a rich historical background. Just 750m outside Sundahöfn harbour, you can see it from the mainland by taking a ten-minute walk

1

THE VIÐEY RESCUE
The greatest **coastal rescue** Iceland has ever seen took place off Viðey's westernmost point in October 1944, after the Canadian destroyer HMCS *Skeena*, with over two hundred men on board, ran aground in heavy seas and blizzard conditions. Although fifteen crew members perished, the remainder were rescued by a team of Icelanders led by Einar Sigurðsson who was later awarded an MBE for his courage and guidance.

north of the Laugardalur area along Dalbraut, which later mutates into Sundagarður. A brisk stroll with views of the ocean and the mainland and a bit of alfresco art thrown in, this is the place to come.

A short walk up the path from the jetty where the ferry deposits you is **Viðeyjarstofa**, once the residence of former royal treasurer and sheriff Skúli Magnússon, now a modest **café**. Designed in simple Rococo style by the architect who worked on the Amalienborg royal palace in Copenhagen, its outer walls are made of basalt and sandstone while the interior is of Danish brick and timber. Standing next to the café is Iceland's second-oldest **church**, consecrated in 1774, and worth a glance inside for its original interior furnishings and Skúli's grave beneath the altar. Walk east of here to the site of the old fort, **Virkið**, of which nothing now remains, to see the Skúli Magnússon **monument** (he died here in 1794) and **Danadys** (Danes' Grave), the final resting place for a number of Danish citizens who lived on the island over the centuries.

The Imagine Peace Tower
To the left of the jetty, in the opposite direction to Viðeyjarstofa and the church, the unusual wishing-well structure you can see is the **Imagine Peace Tower**. Conceived in 2007 by Yoko Ono as a beacon to world peace and inscribed with the words "imagine peace" in 24 languages, the structure emits a powerful tower of light every night between October 9 (John Lennon's birthday) and December 8 (the anniversary of his death), illuminating the Reykjavík sky.

Around the island
There's little else to do on Viðey other than enjoy the spectacular views of the mainland and take a stroll on one of the many **paths** that lead around the island; allow at least two hours to walk all the way round. From Viðeyjarstofa (see above), a road heads right beyond the island's schoolhouse to the easternmost point, from where a path takes over, following the south coast back towards the ferry jetty, skirting a protected area (closed May and June) that's home to thousands of nesting birds. Alternatively, from the easternmost point, a track leads back along the north coast past the café and out to the northwestern part of the island, Vesturey, a peninsula connected to the main island by the small isthmus, Eiði.

While in the western part of the island, keep an eye out for the **Áfangar**, an alfresco exhibit by the American sculptor Richard Serra, consisting of nine pairs of basalt columns (now covered in bird mess) arranged around Vesturey: when viewed from the correct angle, they frame landmarks visible on the mainland.

ARRIVAL AND DEPARTURE   VIÐEY

By ferry Viðey is easily accessible from Sundahöfn harbour, northeast of Laugardalur, itself reached by bus #16 from Hlemmur (see p.73). From the harbour, there's a regular ferry (mid-May to Sept daily every hour, 10.15am–5.15pm; 1100kr return; ⓦ elding.is/videy) that takes just 5min. There's also a twice daily sailing to Viðey from the main harbour in Reykjavík (mid-May to Sept at 11.50am & 2.50pm), which also calls in at Harpa (see p.61) 10min after leaving Reykjavík; the ticket price on this route is also 1100kr.

Southwestern Iceland

SELJALANDSFOSS

Southwestern Iceland

Spread either side of Reykjavík, southwestern Iceland extends barely 200km from end to end, but nowhere else are the country's key elements of history and the land so visibly intertwined. Here you'll see where Iceland's original parliament was founded over a thousand years ago, sites that saw the violence of saga-age dramas played out, and where the country's earliest churches became seats of power and learning. Culture aside, if you're expecting the scenery this close to the capital to be tame, think again: the southwest contains some of Iceland's most iconic – and frequently explosive – landscapes, compelling viewing whether used as a simple backdrop to a day's drive, or as an excuse to spend a week trekking cross-country.

Southwest of Reykjavík, bleak, semi-vegetated lavafields characterize the **Reykjanes Peninsula**, site of the international airport at Keflavík, though the famous Blue Lagoon adds a splash of colour. Due east of Reykjavík, a clutch of essential historical and geological features – including the original parliament site at Þingvellir, Geysir's hot water spouts, and Gullfoss' rainbow-tinged cataracts – are strung out around the **Golden Circle**, an easy route tackled by just about every visitor to the country. Then there's the **central south**, a broad stretch of grassy river plains further southeast again, whose inland regions give way to a blasted landscape surrounding the volcano Hekla and hot springs at Landmannalaugar, itself the starting point for the popular four-day Laugavegur hiking trail. Back on the coast, the rolling farmland of **Njál's Saga country** is dotted with landmarks from this famous tale, not to mention beautiful scenery and further hiking around the glaciated highland valley of Þórsmörk. The **south coast** is decorated with spectacular waterfalls fringing the Eyjafjallajökull and Mýrdalsjökull ice caps, both of which harbour active volcanoes, before the highway runs east out of the region via the attractive coastal hamlet of Vík. Offshore, a short ferry ride from the mainland lands you on Heimaey, the small, intimate core of the **Westman Islands**, alive with birdlife and bearing further recent proof of Iceland's unstable volcanism.

The **climate** in the southwest is relatively mild, despite it being the wettest, windiest part of the country, prone to fog along the coast and potentially heavy snowfalls through the year on higher ground.

HEIMAEY

Highlights

❶ Blue Lagoon Soak outdoors in the steaming waters of Iceland's best-known thermal spa, set among the Reykjanes Peninsula's barren lava flows. **See p.95**

❷ The Golden Circle Circuit three of the country's most famous sights – the rift valley at Þingvellir, Geysir's spurting pools and Gullfoss (the Golden Falls) – on a day-trip from the capital. **See p.101**

❸ Landmannalaugar Soak in hot volcanic springs surrounded by rugged rhyolite mountains, right on the edge of Iceland's Interior. **See p.119**

❹ Laugavegur Follow this four-day hiking trail between Landmannalaugar and Þórsmörk, through some exceptional scenery. **See p.120**

❺ Þórsmörk A beautifully wooded highland valley, surrounded by glaciers, that makes a great spot to camp, hike or just party away the long summer days. **See p.129**

❻ Heimaey Largest of the Westman Islands, this is a wonderful spot to unwind, witness recent volcanic catastrophe and get close-up views of puffins. **See p.139**

HIGHLIGHTS ARE MARKED ON THE MAP ON P.94

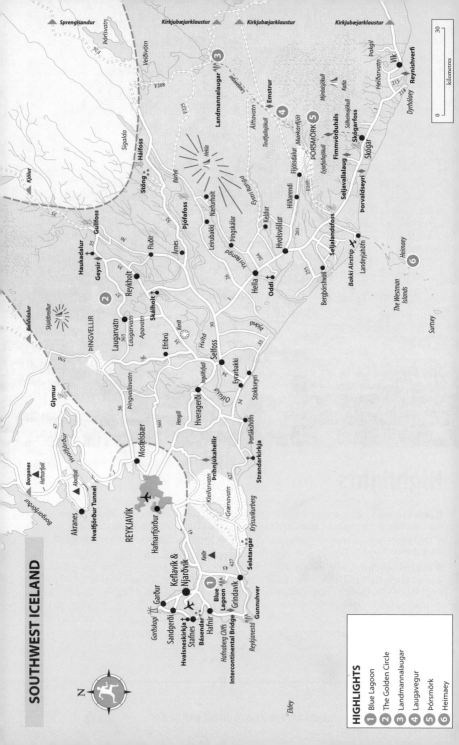

SOUTHWEST ICELAND

HIGHLIGHTS

1 Blue Lagoon
2 The Golden Circle
3 Landmannalaugar
4 Laugavegur
5 Þórsmörk
6 Heimaey

GETTING AROUND   **SOUTHWESTERN ICELAND**

By bus Strætó, Sterna, Reykjavík Excursions and others ply the Golden Circle and coastal Ringroad (Route 1) to Vík throughout the year, with Landmannalaugar and Þórsmörk connected over the summer; services around the Reykjanes Peninsula are more restricted, though you can easily get to the Blue Lagoon or Keflavík.

By car The southwest enjoys good access: most roads – with the exception of a few on the Reykjanes Peninsula, around Hekla, and those to Landmannalaugar and Þórsmörk – are surfaced and generally accessible year-round.

2

The Reykjanes Peninsula

The **Reykjanes Peninsula**, Iceland's southwestern extremity, provides many with their first look at the country as they exit **Keflavík**'s international airport and follow the multi-lane Route 41 east towards Reykjavík. Unfortunately, local vistas are unremittingly barren – rough, contoured piles of lava and distant peaks, the rocks starkly coloured by lichen and mosses – and most people leave Reykjanes behind without a second thought. But if you've a few hours to fill in – before a flight, perhaps – the peninsula has plenty to offer, and is conveniently close to the capital: there's the **Blue Lagoon**, Iceland's most renowned hot spa; a museum at **Grindavík** to that great Icelandic icon, the cod; a **trans-continental bridge** near Hafnir; plus plenty of wild, rocky, surf-streaked coastline with associated birdlife and lonely ruins.

Buses run daily all year from Reyjavík to Keflavík and the airport, and from Reyjavík to the Blue Lagoon and Grindavík; elsewhere you'll need your own vehicle or to arrange a tour from the capital.

The Blue Lagoon

Off Route 43 near Grindavík, around 20km southeast of Keflavík and 45km southwest of Reykjavík • Daily: Jan–May 10am–8pm; June–Aug 8am–10pm; Sept–Dec 10am–8pm • 6500kr for lagoon, with spa, towels, meals packages etc extra; advance booking advised • ⓦ bluelagoon.com

Known in Icelandic as *Bláa lónið*, the **Blue Lagoon** is Iceland's most trumpeted geothermal spa, a surreal splash of colour and warmth amid a bleak satanic wilderness of black lava rubble. It's also a shameless tourist rip-off, though worth the price once for the experience: on cold days, when thick fog swirls over the warm, milky-blue water, your hair, dampened by vapour, freezes solid.

Blue Lagoon is actually artificial, dug into the middle of a flat expanse of black lava blocks and filled by outflow from the nearby **Svartsengi thermal power station**. Svartsengi taps into steam vents fed by sea water seeping down into subterranean hot pots, and by the time it emerges at Blue Lagoon it has cooled to a comfortable 38°C. There are decoratively positioned caves and arches, a sauna, and the famous silvery-grey **silt**, said to cure skin disorders – Icelanders scoop handfuls off the bottom and smear it all over their bodies, and the shop sells beauty products made from it. Whatever the effects on your skin, hair takes a real battering from the lagoon's enriched mineral content; rub conditioner in as protection before bathing.

LAVA TUBE TOURS

Reykjanes is riddled by a subterranean network of **lava tubes**, formed when the sides of a deep lava flow cool and solidify, allowing the still-liquid centre to drain away after the eruption ends. Pick of the local tubes include kilometre-long **Raufarholshellir**; the similarly scaled **Buri Cave**, only discovered in 2005; **Þríhnúkagígur**, though this is actually a drained magma chamber; and **Leiðarendi**, perhaps the most accessible. With the exception of Þríhnjúkagígur (see p.88), you can only visit these as part of a **tour** offered by ⓦ extremeiceland.is (9500–25,000kr/person).

ARRIVAL AND DEPARTURE

BLUE LAGOON

By bus Reykjavik Excursions (@re.is), Gray Line (@grayline.is) and Bus Travel (@bustravel.is) offer return trips and airport transfers from Reykjavík via the Blue Lagoon (3700kr, or 10,500kr including entry); many people make Blue Lagoon their first or final port of call in Iceland. Luggage storage is available.

Destinations Keflavík International Airport (11 daily; 15min); Reykjavík (11 daily; 45min).

ACCOMMODATION AND EATING

Blue Café @420 8800. Sandwiches, sushi and salads served in a glassed-in corner of the lobby, overlooking the lagoon and its steamy surrounds. Expect steep prices – upwards of 1900kr for a sandwich – and unexceptional food, though a coffee won't set you back too much. Daily: June–Aug 11.30am–9pm; Sept–May 11.30am–8.30pm.

Blue Lagoon Health Clinic @426 8650, @bluelagoon.com. Specializing in curing a range of skin ailments, this on-site clinic also provides large, smart rooms with minimalist trim, wooden floors and a charcoal-and-white colour scheme. Price includes breakfast and discounted entry to the Blue Lagoon. **44,000kr**

Northern Light Inn Just off the Blue Lagoon approach road @420 8900, @nli.is. Cosy place, with floral bedspreads and individually shaped rooms that make it feel like a guesthouse, though they're as happy catering to conference groups as they are to couples or families. The restaurant is good, too. Room rate includes buffet breakfast and airport transfers between 5am and 11pm. **35,900kr**

Keflavík

Stretching for 5km along the seafront, **KEFLAVÍK** and its adjoining satellite **Njarðvík** form the Reykjanes Peninsula's biggest centre, with a population of around eleven thousand. Keflavík was a trading port as far back as the sixteenth century, but it was World War II that really established the town, when US defence forces stationed here built an **airstrip** to the west. After Iceland joined **NATO** in 1949, the US used the airstrip as a refuelling **base** for their aircraft, and for over fifty years Keflavík flourished alongside, a service centre for both the US base and the adjacent international airport. But in 2006 the US government closed the facility, and Keflavík lost its major employer. Today the town remains a functional place and, given the frequent fast shuttle buses between Reykjavík and the airport, an unnecessary stopover – with the exception of one excellent museum. Note that Keflavík has no campsite – the nearest is at Garður (see opposite).

Vikingheimar

Víkingabraut 1, Njarðvík; badly signed but the cube of a building is clearly visible about 5km east of Keflavík on the old Reykjavík road • May–Aug daily 9am–6pm • 1500kr • @vikingaheimar.is/en

Vikingheimar (Viking World) fleshes out the stereotypical portrayal of Iceland's founders as a simple bunch of hacking-and-slashing saga heroes. They were also expert craftsmen and sailors, as proved by the centrepiece here, the *Íslendingur*, a full-sized replica **Viking longship** which in 2000 crossed the Atlantic to celebrate Leifur Eiriksson's discovery of "Vinland" (see box, p.335) a thousand years before. You can actually climb aboard; it's broad and surprisingly spacious, though spending months on it crossing the rough Atlantic must have taken courage. The rest of the two-storey building houses archeological evidence for the short-lived settlement in Vinland and locally found Viking remains from Hafnir and Sandgerði (see p.98), plus "Fate of the Gods", a multi-media walk-through exhibition on **Viking myths** with some lively, brilliantly designed graphics.

ARRIVAL AND INFORMATION

KEFLAVÍK

By bus From main-street Hafnargata, Strætó route #55 serves Reykjavík's BSÍ terminal; Route #88 runs to Grindavík (you might have to change en route); and Route #89 runs to Garður.

Destinations Garður (Mon–Fri 10 daily, Sat 4 daily, Sun 3 daily; 20min); Grindavík (Mon–Fri 7 daily, Sat & Sun 4 daily; 35min); Reykjavík (Mon–Fri 9 daily, Sat & Sun 3 daily; 1hr).

By car The Route 41 expressway from Reykjavík divides on the edge of town, with Njarðarbraut and then Hafnargata running west through to the harbour, and Reykjanesbraut forking southwest for 5km to the international airport.

Tourist information There's a friendly but not especially useful office at the free Duushús Museum at the harbour on Hafnargata (Mon–Fri 9am–5pm, Sat noon–5pm; ☎ 421 3796).

Services The main road, Hafnargata, has banks with ATMs, the post office and a Nettó supermarket (Mon–Fri 10am–7pm, Sat 10am–6pm, Sun noon–6pm). Keflavík's excellent swimming pool is a few streets south of Hafnargata at Sunnubraut 31 (Mon–Fri 6.45am–9pm, Sat & Sun 8am–6pm), with outdoor and indoor pools, three hot pots, a sauna and twisting water slide. For taxis, call ☎ 421 4141 or ☎ 421 1515.

2

ACCOMMODATION AND EATING

Alex Aðalgata 60 ☎ 421 2800, ⊕ alex.is. Set on a grassy roadside halfway to the airport on the southern edge of town. The facilities comprise spacious, well-appointed rooms with toilets but shared showers, and self-contained en-suite wooden cabins. Free airport transfers and breakfast. Doubles **17,900kr**, cabins **19,900kr**

FIT Hostel Fitjabraut 6A, Njarðvík ☎ 421 8889, ⊕ fithostel.is. Large building, though a lack of signage makes it hard to spot; it's on the seaward side of the road just as the highway from Reykjavík enters town. A dreary, blocky exterior, but warm and well equipped inside, if starting to show its age in places. There's a laundry, large kitchen and communal area with TV. Sleeping-bag dorm beds only. Sleeping bags **5000kr**

Keilir Hafnargata 37 ☎ 420 9800, ⊕ hotelkeilir.is.

Offering the best value among Keflavík's hotel options, this is a new place with moderately sized rooms decked in slate and pine furnishings, comfortable enough for a night. Breakfast and airport shuttle included. **24,900kr**

Raín Hafnargata 19 ☎ 421 4601. Long-established restaurant-bar with sea views and pizzas, fish dishes and salads (the pan-fried ling is superb). Mains around 4000kr; lobster soup will set you back 2280kr. The bar is a popular watering hole with locals. Mon–Thurs & Sun 11am–1am, Fri & Sat 11am–3am.

Thai Keflavík Hafnargata 39 ☎ 421 8666. There's the usual run of good-value spicy soups, noodles, vegetables, red-cooked meat and deep-fried fish (nothing over 2000kr), though the best deal is their lunchtime buffet for 1490kr. Mon–Fri 11.30am–10pm, Sat & Sun 4–10pm.

Garður

Just 7km from Keflavík at the Reykjanes Peninsula's northwestern tip, **GARÐUR** is a tiny, scattered community whose distinguishing feature is an overpowering smell of rotting seaweed. A grassed-over ridge marks the remains of an old wall, apparently the original eleventh-century estate boundary (*garður*); the discovery of nine **Viking graves** found south of here in the 1860s supports the theory – the bones included humans, dogs and horses. Later associations can be found at the nineteenth-century **Útskálakirkja**, a church dedicated to Iceland's only saint, **Þorlákur Þórhallsson**, bishop at Skálholt in the period 1178–93.

Garðskagi

Reykjanes' northwestern tip, **Garðskagi**, is marked by two lighthouses; the shorter, square, red-striped affair on the seafront was once used to monitor bird migrations. Its base makes a sheltered spot from which to look westwards over the sea – with a pair of binoculars you can spot seals, eider ducks, turnstones, gannets and assorted wading birds – and admire the 11pm summer sunsets.

ARRIVAL AND DEPARTURE   GARÐUR

By bus Strætó route #89 runs between Keflavík and Garður.

Destinations Keflavík (Mon–Fri 10 daily, Sat 4 daily, Sun 3 daily; 20min).

ACCOMMODATION

Campsite Garðskagi. Free campsite on the lawn between the two lighthouses and sheltered from the sea by 2m-high storm walls, but you wouldn't want to be here in bad

weather. There are on-site toilets and washing-up sinks; the nearest shop is about 2km back along the road at the N1 service station.

Stafnes

About 15km south from Garður along Route 45, via the bland regional centre of **Sandgerði** and a huge **arctic tern colony**, the vestigial hamlet of **STAFNES** sits under another lighthouse, orange this time. Views from the seafront take in heavy surf and distant airport buildings, and there's a half-day walking trail south along the coast to Hafnir, which after about 1km passes the site of **Básendar**, the Reykjanes Peninsula's largest trading town until it was totally destroyed by an overnight storm in January 1799 – killing just one person. Very little remains besides nondescript rubble.

Hafnaberg cliffs

Coastal Route 425 heads south past the village of **HAFNIR** over rugged lava terrain, with the 15km **Prestastígur walking trail** to Grindavík crossing it southeast via a line of square-sided **cairns** (drily known locally as "priests", because they point the way to salvation but never go there themselves). A well-signed parking bay on the west side of the road here marks a tiring 3km trail over grey sand to the coastal **Hafnaberg cliffs**, home through the summer to tens of thousands of nesting kittiwakes and fulmars, along with a dusting of shags and no fewer than three species of guillemot, all of which you'll hear (and smell) well before you arrive. Note that loose soil and strong winds make approaching the edge extremely dangerous.

Bridge Between Two Continents

About 2km south from the Hafnaberg car park, the **Bridge Between Two Continents** is a thin steel span in the middle of nowhere, supposedly crossing the rift separating the North American and Eurasian continental plates. The bridge is decked in steel mesh, so you can look down into the shallow ravine below; "contrived" doesn't begin to describe the site, but the idea is fun and it's perked up by "Welcome to America" and "Welcome to Europe" signs at either end.

Reykjanestá

Reykjanestá is the Reykjanes Peninsula's southwestern extremity, an abrupt headland surrounded by solidified lava flows whose seaward face is rapidly disintegrating into the sea. There's a good, 2km-long gravel road in here off Route 425 (marked "Reykjanesviti") past the shiny polished steel curves of **Reykjanesvirkjun**, a 100MW geothermal power station, all pipes and clouds of steam; along the way the track divides to reach either the coastal lighthouse or the Gunnuhver thermal springs.

The lighthouse and Eldey

A tall white **lighthouse**, standing safely inland on a knoll, sits above Reykjanestá's headland (the original fell into the sea during an earthquake). From here, you can look westwards over the waves to the sheer-sided distant platform of **Eldey**, Europe's biggest gannet colony. Eldey island also has the sad distinction of being the place where the last known pair of **great auks** (and their single egg) were destroyed on June 3, 1844; there's a giant bronze auk in the Reykjanestá car park, its beak pointing towards the island.

Gunnuhver thermal springs

The second fork of the gravel road from Route 245 ends at **Gunnuhver thermal springs**, a small area of viciously hissing, malodorous muddy pools into which an eighteenth-century witch is said to have been dragged by a magic rope after she'd killed her landlord. Incredibly, remains of foundations outline where some optimistic farmer attempted to establish a hothouse here in the 1930s, but Gunnuhver proved too unpredictable; the area last blew itself apart in 2005. Stick to the new boardwalks (remains of the old ones can be seen suspended over a steaming void of mashed-up ochre clay).

Grindavík

Located about 30km from Keflavík, and about 60km from Reykjavík, **GRINDAVÍK** is a well-serviced fishing port of two thousand souls down on the Reykjanes Peninsula's south coast, a sizeable town for this part of the country. It has a long history as a trading centre and was important enough to be raided by pirates looking for slaves and plunder in 1627; its harbour still supports a fishing fleet, whose catches are processed at the large factory here. Grindavík is also the closest settlement to the Blue Lagoon – just 5km to the north – and the town's eccentric museum is definitely worth a look.

Kvikan

Hafnargata 12a • Daily 10am–5pm • 1200kr • ⓦ grindavik.is/kvikan

Of the three exhibitions here, by far the best is **Saltfisksetur Íslands** (Icelandic Saltfish Museum), whose motto – *Lífið er saltfiskur*, "Life is saltfish" – kicks off a fine display of models, videos, dioramas and life-sized photos, all laced with the pervasive aroma of **cod**. It's no exaggeration to say that modern Iceland was built on the back of this fish: the country's original coat of arms, ratified by the Alþing in 1593, was a golden cod, filleted and crowned on a red field. Fishing nevertheless started off slowly as a seasonal adjunct to farming, the catch preserved as wind-dried **stockfish** until salt began to be imported in bulk during the nineteenth century. This coincided with the first large, ocean-going vessels being used in Iceland, which increased catches six-fold and sparked a new industry that undermined Iceland's traditional agricultural economy, drawing people off the land to swell coastal settlements. Today, saltfish accounts for sixty percent of Iceland's exports, most of it ending up in Spain, West Africa and South America.

ARRIVAL AND INFORMATION   GRINDAVÍK

By bus Though there are some direct services on bus #88 from Keflavík, you generally have to switch buses to #55 along the way.
Destinations Keflavík (Mon–Fri 7 daily, Sat & Sun 4 daily; 35min).
By car Route 43 drops south into town as Víkurbraut. Ránargata heads 250m down to the harbour from here, and halfway along you cross the intersection with Hafnargata, where many services are located.

Tourist information There's a desk at Kvikan, Hafnargata (daily 10am–5pm; ☎ 420 1190), with brochures and maps of the region.
Services The N1 fuel station and Nettó supermarket are close to each other on Veikurbraut. The swimming pool (Mon–Fri 7am–8pm, Sat & Sun 10am–5pm), with water slide and usual hot pots and sauna, is two streets back near the sports field.

ACCOMMODATION AND EATING

★**Bryggjan** Miðgarði 2 ☎426 7100. Fisherman's hangout in an old warehouse decorated with maritime memorabilia at the harbour – check out the "Sea Kings" plaque, recording which boats landed the biggest catches before the quota system was introduced in 1984. Try coffee and waffles (around 1000kr), or the excellent lobster soup with a hunk of home-made bread (1800kr). Daily 8am–10pm.
Campsite Cnr Hafnargata and Austurvegur, the highway east out of town. Split into bays with a play area, toilets, showers, BBQ area and laundry; it's also sunken, with buildings to seawards, so fairly sheltered. Guests get a

2-for-1 deal at the town museum (see above). 1200kr
Guesthouse Fiskanes Hafnargata 17–19 ☎695 8103, ✉runasz@hotmail.com. Marked only by a sign directly above the doorway, this concrete block of a building offers basic but tidy en-suite studio rooms with small kitchens. June–Aug. Doubles 6500kr, sleeping bags 5000kr
Papa's Hafnargata 7a ☎426 9955. Opposite the museum, this decent-value grill house offers 12" Hawaiian pizza for just 2050kr – though their house topping (seafood, meat, veg etc) costs half as much again, and a fried cod and chips will set you back 2400kr. Daily noon–10pm.

2

Route 427

The recently surfaced **Route 427** heads eastwards from Grindavík along the Reykjanes Peninsula's south coast to Þorlákshöfn, a 60km run across a succession of ancient, mossy lava flows squashed between low coastal ranges and the sea. In good weather there are a few places to get out and explore, though the land here has, disturbingly, been rising over the last few years, perhaps indicating future volcanic activity.

Selatangar

About 12km from Grindavík, a short gravel road south of Route 427 ends at a parking area, from where it's a kilometre on foot along a vague track to the remains of **Selatangar**, a seasonal fishing settlement last used in the 1880s. Lava-block dwellings sit perched above the sea, ranging from buildings the size and shape of a hollow cairn to large, walled-in caves; poke around and you'll soon find a score or more sites. No roofs have survived; these may well have been constructed from driftwood (plenty washes up here) or weatherproofed cloth. With near constant wind howling in from the south, rapidly bringing in and dispersing fog with little warning, Selatangar can be spooky – some say that there's even a resident ghost named **Tanga-Tómas** – and it doesn't take much imagination to conjure up how hard life must have been here when the place was last occupied.

Krýsuvíkurberg

Some 22km from Grindavík, a signpost marked "Krýsuvíkurbjarg" points 4km seawards down a rough gravel road, prone to flooding in places – take care in a normal vehicle, and be prepared to walk if necessary. At the end is **Krýsuvíkurberg**, a long, curved cliff topped by a crust of green grass, packed solid all summer long with nesting **birds**: the cliffs are kittiwake Grand Central, and you might just get lucky and spot a few resident puffins too. The east end is topped by a triangulation point, with wonderful seascapes from the red scoria headland behind.

Strandarkirkja

Off towards the eastern end of Route 427, a short turn-off leads to the coastal hamlet of **STRANDARKIRKJA**. It's named after the pretty, pale-blue **church** here, built around 1900 by thankful sailors who had made it ashore after their ship was wrecked in a storm; climb the sea wall opposite and there's a good chance of spotting seals playing in the tidal lagoons offshore. The excellent free campsite nearby (see below) is a bonus (but watch out for arctic terns if walking between the two).

ACCOMMODATION AND EATING   STRANDARKIRKJA

★**Campsite** At the eastern end of the road. Free site run by a farmer who has installed showers, toilets, sinks and picnic tables. A gently sloping aspect offers perfect pitches on a calm summer night, while a tiny store opposite sells hotdogs and fizzy drinks. There's a donation box if you want to contribute towards the site's upkeep.

T-Bær Café Part-way between the campsite and church ☎ 483 3150. Given that Strandarkirkja comprises only about a dozen buildings, it's nice that one of them is this popular café serving home-made bread and cakes. Mon–Wed & Fri–Sun 10am–10pm, Thurs 2–10pm.

Þorlákshöfn

At the eastern end of Route 427, **ÞORLÁKSHÖFN** is a service town settled by those fleeing the 1973 eruption on Heimay (see p.139). The only reason you're likely to visit is if bad weather has diverted Westman Island ferries from Landeyjahöfn to Þorlákshöfn's port (see p.139). From here, it's a short run east to Eyrarbakki or Hveragerði, or west to Strandarkirkja.

The Golden Circle

The name **Golden Circle** might be a tourist-industry tag, but it's also apt, as this broad circuit east from Reykjavík covers many of Iceland's best-known features and touches on the root of much of its history. The key area is **Þingvellir**, whose dramatic and geologically unstable rift valley marks the place where the Icelandic state sprang into being in Viking times. South from here is the religious centre of **Skálholt**, where Iceland's last Catholic bishop was assassinated in 1550; travelling northeast takes you past the spa town of **Laugarvatn** to **Geysir**, the original hot blowhole that has lent its name to similar vents worldwide, before sealed roads end on the edge of Iceland's barren Interior at **Gullfoss**' thundering twin cataracts.

The tangle of routes connecting all this together runs through beautiful countryside: fertile, flat, framed by distant hills and startlingly green in summer, thanks to one of Iceland's longest rivers, the **Hvítá**. This originates around 140km northeast at Hvítarvatn, an isolated lake below Langjökull on the Kjölur route, and flows swiftly to Gullfoss, where it drops into the plains above Skálholt before running south to the sea.

Wild and romantic though the region is, don't expect to appreciate it in solitude: most of the sights suffer year-round **visitor overload**, with tour buses clogging car parks until well into the evening.

Þingvellir

The land northeast of Reykjavík is scarred by one of the world's great geological boundaries, a **rift valley** marking where the North American and Eurasian continental plates are physically tearing apart. Although this rift stretches right across Iceland, nowhere else is it so expansively evident – a 4km-wide, 40m-deep slash in the landscape, sided in basalt columns and extending for 16km from Iceland's largest lake, **Þingvallavatn**, to the low, rounded cone of the **Skjaldbreiður** volcano in the northeast. It was in this monumental landmark that Iceland's clan chieftains first gathered in the tenth century to formalize their laws and forge a national identity for themselves (see box, p.103).

Þingvellir itself – the "assembly plains" at the southwestern end of the rift – has been protected since 1930 as a national park. The main focus is a surprisingly small area at the southwestern corner of the park where the narrow **Öxará** – the Axe River – flows down to the lake shore past a church and other historic monuments, all

---

TOURING THE GOLDEN CIRCLE

For more than one person, the cheapest way to cover the Golden Circle is to **rent a car** for the day. From Reykjavík, take Route 36 northeast to Þingvellir (watch out for ice in winter), then continue east along the 365 to Laugarvatn, from where routes 37 & 35 run up to Geysir and Gullfoss. On the way back, follow Route 35 southwest to Selfoss, detouring briefly along the way to visit Skálholt and Kerið crater (see p.112). Selfoss itself is on the Ringroad 30km east of Reykjavík (see p.112).

Without your own vehicle, you can pack all this into a nine-hour **Golden Circle tour** offered by Reykjavík Excursions (Ⓦ re.is; 9900kr), Gray Line (Ⓦ grayline.is; 9500kr) and Sterna (Ⓦ sterna.is; 9300kr). All can collect from Reykjavík accommodation and a guide provides commentary in English en route.

Slightly cheaper (8900kr return) are Reykjavík Excursions' daily Þingvellir–Laugarvatn–Geysir–Gullfoss **scheduled buses** from the BSÍ terminal in Reykjavik, which stop long enough at all the sights for you to get a good look; you can, of course, arrange to spread this trip over several days and stay overnight at places along the way. Be aware too that summer buses heading to Akureyri via Kjölur (see p.326) travel the same route (though most skip Þingvellir), so you might not need to make a separate trip to see the Golden Circle.

hemmed in on the west by the 2km-long **Almannagjá**, the valley's most impressive rift wall. While the landscape is imposing and it's hard to overstate Þingvellir's historical importance, there are few specific monuments, and to capture the spirit of the place you need to familiarize yourself with the natural formations around which events were played out.

The Visitor Centre and lookout

Daily: Jan–May & Sept–Dec 9am–5pm; June–Aug 9am–6pm • Free

Coming from Reykjavík, your first stop should be the **Visitor Centre**, just where Route 36 grazes the top of Almannagjá, less for the interactive videos outlining Þingvellir's history (and certainly not for the toilets, which – outrageously for Iceland – you have to pay for), but for the superb **lookout** alongside. You're right on the edge of the **North American continental plate** here: the Alþing site is directly below, with the church over on the far side of the Öxará, which flows south to the lake. Looking northeast up the rift, the massifs of **Ármannsfell** and **Hrafnabjörg** frame the valley, fist-like and solid. Permanence is an illusion, however – the rift is widening by 1.5cm further each year as the continental plates drift apart. As they move, the valley floor sinks, on average, a couple of millimetres annually, though it fell half a metre in 1789 following an earthquake. Away in the distance, Skjaldbreiður's apparently low summit is easily overlooked, though at 1060m it's actually one of the highest peaks in view.

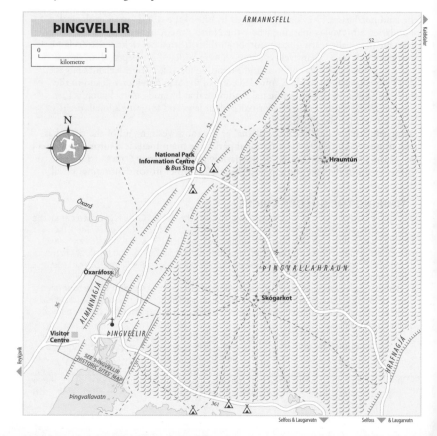

THE ALÞING AT ÞINGVELLIR

With laws shall our land be built up, but with lawlessness laid waste.   Njál's Saga

By the beginning of the tenth century, Iceland's 36 regional chieftains recognized the need for some form of national government. Rejecting the idea of a paramount ruler, Norwegian law was adapted and the first **Alþing**, or General Assembly, was held in the rift valley north of Þingvallavatn in 930 AD, at a place which became known as **Þingvellir**, the Assembly Plains. Though the Alþing's power declined through the ages, Þingvellir remained the seat of Iceland's government for the next eight centuries.

The Alþing was held for two weeks every summer, and attendance for chieftains was mandatory. In fact, almost everyone who could attend did so, setting up their tented camps and coming to watch the courts in action or settle disputes, pick up on gossip, trade, compete at sports and generally socialize. The whole event was coordinated by the **lawspeaker**, while the laws themselves were legislated by the **Law Council**, and dispensed at four regional courts, along with a fifth **supreme court**. Strangely, however, none of these authorities had the power to enforce their verdicts, beyond bringing pressure to bear through public opinion. The adoption of **Christianity** as Iceland's official religion in 1000 AD, was one of the Alþing's major successes, but if litigants refused to accept a court's decision, they had to seek satisfaction privately. *Njál's Saga* (see box, p.123) contains a vivid account of one such event, when a battle between two feuding clans broke out at the Alþing itself around 1011 AD, while *Hrafnkel's Saga* (see box, p.292) shows how people manipulated processes at the Alþing and could, if they wanted, ignore court verdicts.

This lack of real authority undermined the Alþing, creating a power vacuum that ultimately saw Norway and then Denmark assume control of the country. By the late thirteenth century the Alþing was losing its importance, with the lawspeaker's position abolished and the courts stripped of all legislative power. Eventually, while still meeting for a few days every year, the Alþing became a minor affair, and the last assembly was held at Þingvellir in 1798, replaced by a national court and parliament at Reykjavík.

During the mid-nineteenth century Þingvellir became the focus of the **nationalist movement**, with large crowds witnessing various independence debates here – the Danish king even attended Iceland's millennial celebrations at Þingvellir in 1874. The site remained a symbol of national identity through the twentieth century, peaking when half the country turned up at Þingvellir to hear the **declaration of independence** from Denmark and the formation of the Icelandic Republic on June 17, 1944.

Almannagjá

From the Visitor Centre, a boardwalk and gravel track descend through the deep **Almannagjá** canyon, whose vertical basalt walls form the west side of Þingvellir's rift. To one side is a flagpole marking the presumed site of **Lögberg**, the rock where important speeches were made and the lawspeaker recited Iceland's laws to the assembled masses below. Nearby traces of foundations outline the remains of **buðs**, the temporary roofed camps raised by participants during assemblies.

Öxaráfoss

Along the rift wall past the flagpole, the **Öxará** cascades over Almannagjá as the 20m-high **Öxarárfoss**. Rocks in the river are barely worn, suggesting that the Öxará's path is fairly recent: this supports oral accounts of the river's diversion into the rift around 1000 AD to provide water for the sizeable chunk of Iceland's population who descended at each Alþing. After Danish laws were enforced in the sixteenth century, **pools** near the second falls were used to drown women convicted of witchcraft or sexual offences (men were beheaded or burnt at the stake for the same crimes), though the idea of a death penalty was repugnant to Icelanders and few such executions were carried out.

Flosagjá and Peningagjá

East of the church is the splintered wall forming **Flosagjá**, a deep fissure whose southern end has been flooded by underground springs creating **Peningagjá**, an exceedingly clear, deep wishing pool; coins glint silver and electric blue at the bottom. The marshlands between here and the river were once possibly an island where duels at the Alþing were fought, before the practice was banned in the thirteenth century.

Þingvellir church

Þingvellir's **church** was founded in 1018 after the Norwegian king Ólafur Haraldsson supplied timber for the original building. The current white and blue structure, from 1859, is misleadingly unpretentious, as by the eighteenth century the church here owned a huge swathe of farmland stretching right up the valley. A raised area behind is reserved for the tombs of outstanding Icelanders; at present the only two incumbents are the patriotic poets **Einar Benediktsson** and **Jónas Hallgrímsson**. The latter did much to inspire the nineteenth-century independence movement and drew great inspiration from Þingvellir.

The rift valley

Þingvellir's valley is covered in the overgrown nine-thousand-year-old lavafield of **Þingvallahraun**, product of the up-valley Skjaldbreiður (Shield-broad). Though now extinct, this was the first **shield volcano** ever to be classified, a type that spews out high-volume fluid lava in a steady rather than violent eruption, leaving wide, flattened cones. The valley is beautiful in summer and early autumn, carpeted in dense thickets of dwarf forest and heathland plants – as, perhaps, much of Iceland was at the time of Settlement. A web of marked **walking trails** cuts through it all, though note that some of these cross minor rifts and gorges, which might be

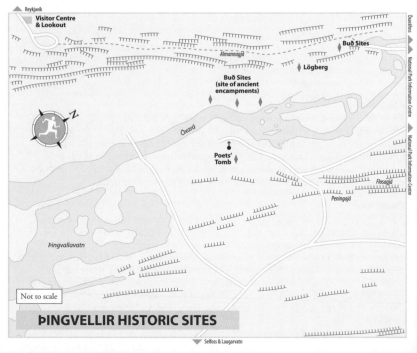

ÞINGVELLIR HISTORIC SITES

ÞINGVELLIR TRAILS

You can make an easy, satisfying 10km circuit of Þingvellir and the rift valley along marked trails in under three hours. Starting at the National Park Information Centre, walk a short way east along the road past the campsite until you see a marker for the 2km footpath to **Hrauntún** through a landscape of mossy rocks, lava pavements and dwarf birch scrub. Hrauntún is the site of an abandoned farm, still ringed by a lava-block wall. There isn't a single tree on the site – clearing them all must have taken some effort.

Turn south and follow a well-used 3km track to **Skógarkot**, a sheep farm abandoned in the 1930s, whose ruined but strongly constructed **stone buildings** occupy a grassy hillock roughly halfway across the valley. It's not a high position, but still elevated enough for you to take in a panorama of distant peaks and rift walls, and feel dwarfed by the scale of the Þingvallahraun lava flow which stretches all the way from the lake to Skalbreiður. From here bear west towards the church at Þingvellir – a further 2km along a decent trail – and then follow Almannagjá for a final 3km back to your starting point.

dangerously concealed if there has been any snow. To venture further, or climb any of the mountains, you'll need at least basic orienteering skills and Landmælingar Islands' *Þingvellir* 1:25,000 **map**.

Þingvallavatn

Immediately south of Þingvellir, **Þingvallavatn** formed nine thousand years ago when fresh lava blocked off a spring and the valley backfilled to form a 14km-long lake. Þingvallavatn and its sole outflow, the **Sog River**, are surrounded by rugged hills and undulating moorland, while the lake itself is dotted with tiny volcanic islands and, on rare windless days, forms a perfect blue mirror to the sky. Surprisingly unobtrusive **hydroelectric stations** at the head of the Sog provide power for the region, while healthy stocks of char and brown trout keep the fly population down and anglers happy – winter fishing is especially popular, when holes have to be cut through the ice (permits are available from Þingvellir's national park office).

You can circuit Þingvallavatn in your own transport along a gravel road which runs around the south side of the lake before meeting up with Route 36 about 25km north of Selfoss.

ARRIVAL AND INFORMATION

ÞINGVELLIR

By bus Golden Circle tours aside, Reykjavík Excursions (w re.is) operate the only scheduled bus service to Þingvellir, stopping at the Visitor Centre/Viewpoint and National Park Information Centre, just where Route 36 descends into the western side of the rift.

Destinations Geysir (1 daily; 1hr); Gullfoss (1 daily; 3hr); Laugarvatn (1 daily; 20min); Reykjavík (1 daily; 30min).

By car Route 36 runs northeast from Reykjavík to Þingvellir, crosses the rift valley, and then follows Þingvallavatn and the Sog River south to Selfoss and the Ringroad. Þingvellir also marks the southern terminus of the Kaldidalur route through from Reykholt (see box, p.163).

Tourist information The National Park Information Centre (June–Aug daily 9am–10pm; ☎ 482 2660, w thingvellir.is), on Route 36 where the road descends into the western side of the rift, has a phone, free hot showers, a basic café, useful orientation maps and regular weather reports.

TOURS AND ACTIVITIES

Tours The Information Centre (see above) offers free hour-long tours of the locality that leave from the church at 10am and 3pm daily throughout summer.

Scuba diving The fever-clear waters of Silfra, a flooded chasm between the lake and Þingvellir, make it one of the world's top freshwater scuba sites, though you're looking at around 39,000kr for diving and 17,000kr to snorkel, with all equipment, guides and transport provided. Divers must be certified, and dry-suit experience is recommended. Operators include Scuba Iceland (☎ 892 1823, w scuba.is) and Dive Iceland (☎ 663 2858, w dive.is).

ACCOMMODATION

Camping Of Þingvellir's five campsites, the main one is right next to the National Park Information Centre, and has toilets, showers, an open-sided shelter shed with sinks and benches, and plenty of flat, grassy space. The three lakeshore sites are tent only (no vehicles) with limited facilities and beautiful views over the water. Pay at the National Park Information Centre. All sites <u>1300kr</u>

Laugarvatn

Around 20km east of Þingvellir on Route 37, roughly halfway to Geysir, the small lakeside village of **LAUGARVATN** sits below the steep heights of Laugarvatnfjall. Home to Iceland's National School for Sports, there's also an excellent natural hot spa, making it a tempting place to break your journey for a couple of hours.

Fontana

Hverabraut 1 • Daily: mid-May to Sept 10am–11pm; Oct to mid-May 11am–9pm • 3400kr • ⓦ fontana.is

Built over a natural hot spring right on the lakeshore (turn at the N1 roadhouse and follow the signs), **Fontana** spa features three steam rooms, a sauna, hot pot, small swimming pool and a long, shallow pool for wallowing around in, perhaps enjoying a low-strength beer from the bar. The views over the lake are fantastic, the modern building innovative (the turf roof is a nice touch), but overall it's expensive for what you get. The steam rooms are nevertheless an experience, what with the hot spring coughing and churning around below the floor, spewing out completely unpredictable quantities of heat and vapour.

ARRIVAL AND INFORMATION

Buses Reykjavík Excursions (ⓦ re.is) from Reykjavík and Strætó (ⓦ straeto.is) from Selfoss run daily buses to Laugarvatn, stopping at the N1 roadhouse and Fontana. Destinations Geysir (1 daily; 35min); Gullfoss (1 daily; 2hr 30min); Reykjavík (1 daily; 1hr 40min); Selfoss (1 daily; 1hr 10min); Þingvellir (1 daily; 20min).

Services The N1 roadhouse, on the main road, has fuel pumps and a Samkaup supermarket (Mon–Fri 9am–10pm, Sat & Sun 10am–10pm). Laugarvatn's swimming pool (Mon–Fri 9am–9pm, Sat & Sun 10am–6pm) is diagonally opposite Fontana Spa, and, while only a fraction of the price, has none of the panache.

ACCOMMODATION AND EATING

Edda IKI Laugarvatn Right on the lakeshore near Fontana ☎ 444 4820, ⓦ hoteledda.is. Smaller and least institutional of Laugarvatn's two summer-only *Edda* hotels. Rooms are all en suite and the restaurant has lake views. Breakfast is an extra 1900kr. <u>22,500kr</u>

★ **Efstidalur** About 15km east towards Geysir along Route 37 ☎ 486 1186, ⓦ efstidalur.is. Easily the finest place to eat in the region, with much of what they serve up home-reared. Try the steak (4600kr) or carpaccio (1950kr), or a pan-fried trout (3800kr). You can stay here too in one of their tidy en-suite doubles, with breakfast included. Restaurant daily 11am–10pm. <u>24,000kr</u>

IYHA Dalsel Dalbraut 10 ☎ 899 5409, ⓦ hostel.is. On the main road near the N1 roadhouse, this newly renovated hostel has everything you'd expect, including dorms, en-suite doubles, a kitchen, laundry, dining room and small bar. At busy times extra guests are housed in alternative buildings. Breakfast is available for 1500kr. Dorms <u>4100kr</u>, doubles <u>13,400kr</u>

Skálholt

The region of small lakes and streams above the middle Hvítá is known as **Biskupstungur** (Bishop's Tongue), a name perhaps related to the church at **SKÁLHOLT**, just east of Route 35 – it's halfway between Selfoss and Geysir, though a bit of a detour on back roads from Laugarvatn. It's easy to overdose on churches in Iceland, but Skálholt's definitely warrants a stop: seat of a bishopric as early as 1056 AD, Skálholt's huge wooden **cathedral** developed into a religious school, and by the early thirteenth century there were two hundred people living here, making it the country's largest settlement. Surviving the Reformation and destruction by fire, Skálholt, along with

Hólar in northern Iceland, became a major seat of learning, which lasted until a catastrophic earthquake in the late eighteenth century. The bishop subsequently shifted to Reykjavík, and Skálholt's ruins were largely abandoned until the cathedral and school were rebuilt and reconsecrated in 1963. Given the scarcity of public transport (see below), it's best to visit Skálholt on a Golden Circle tour (see box, p.101) or in your own vehicle.

The cathedral
Daily 10am–5pm • Free

2

Skálholt's **cathedral** is elegantly underplayed, the sober black-and-white building unusual only for its size and hilltop isolation. Inside, a mitre over the door identifies Skálholt as a bishopric; there are abstract stained-glass windows and a tapestry-like **mosaic** of Christ behind the altar. Reconstruction work in the 1950s uncovered a thirteenth-century stone **sarcophagus** belonging to Bishop Páll Jónsson, a charismatic churchman who added a tower and sumptuous decorations to the original building. A wooden crook carved with a dragon's head was found with his remains (now in the National Museum, Reykjavík), and the sarcophagus itself is on view here in the summer.

The excavations
Ongoing **excavations** alongside the church have revealed the foundations of the original bishop's residence – there's a plan which explains what each area was for, and gravel paths around the site. Some 100m away, a rough-cut stone monument commemorates Iceland's last Catholic bishop, **Jón Arason**, who was executed here in 1550 while attempting to prevent the Danish king from forcing Lutheranism on the country (see p.338).

ARRIVAL AND DEPARTURE SKÁLHOLT

By bus Strætó buses pass by enroute to Selfoss (Mon–Fri 2 daily, Sat & Sun 1 daily; 30min).

ACCOMMODATION AND EATING

Café Attached to the school, just next to the church. Coffee and light meals – lunchtime soup and bread is 1250kr – with a pleasant, sheltered courtyard and indoor terrace covered in vines. Daily 10am–5pm.

Fagrilundur 7km up Route 35 at the tiny hothouse town of Reykholt, just off the roundabout at Skólabraut 1 ☎ 486 8701, ⓦ fagrilundur.is. Family-run B&B inside a large wood-clad chalet, whose comfortable doubles have en-suite or shared bathrooms. 17,500kr

Skálholtsskóli Next to the church ☎ 486 8870, ⓔ skoli@skalholt.is. Skálholt's school offers year-round accommodation, either private doubles (rates include breakfast) or self-contained summerhouse cabins. During school holidays at least, it's a quiet place with plenty of easy walking in the area. Doubles 21,000kr, cabins 18,000kr

Flúðir

FLÚÐIR is simply a knot of services – a bank, supermarket, accommodation and a couple of places to eat – focused around a junction on Route 30, a back road to Gullfoss. The main reason to visit is to soak in the **Secret Lagoon**.

Secret Lagoon
Head north out of town on Route 30, and turn east immediately over the bridge • May–Sept daily 10am–10pm; Oct–April Mon–Thurs & Sun 2–6pm, Fri & Sat 2–8pm • 2500kr • ☎ 555 3351, ⓦ gamlalaugin.is

The Gamla Laugin (Old Hot Pool) at Hverahólmi, is just north of town, where thermal springs in a grassy field have been diverted into a no-frills, open-air pool the size of a village duck pond. Constructed in 1891 but later abandoned, recent renovations have tidied everything up and converted the old hothouses to changing rooms; it's a secret no longer and is incorporated into several tours.

ACCOMMODATION AND EATING FLÚÐIR

Campsite Just on the northern outskirts of Flúðir, west of the highway ☎486 6161, ⦿tjaldmidstod.is. Well located as it is, just a short way from both Gullfoss and Geysir, Flúðir's campsite is one of the largest in Iceland. It's on a huge grassy space above the river, with toilets, showers and washers. 1250kr

★**Minilik** On Route 30 through town, known as Hrunamannavegur ☎846 9798, ⦿minilik.is. Iceland's only Ethiopian restaurant is impossible to miss, boldly striped in green, yellow and red. The food is authentically tangy, sour and spicy and served with traditional *njeera*, fermented dough pancakes; they have vegetarian dishes and their coffee is heart-poundingly strong. Count on 2500kr a head. Opening hours are anyone's guess; call ahead to check.

Geysir

Right beside Route 37, 60km from Selfoss and a bit less than that from Þingvellir

Visible from many kilometres away as a pall of steam rising above the plains, hot springs at the **Geysir thermal area** bubble out over a grassy slope at the foot of **Bjarnfell**, studded with circular pools atop grey, mineral-streaked mounds. The area has been active for thousands of years, but the springs' positions have periodically shifted as geological seams crack open or close down; the current vents appeared following a thirteenth-century earthquake.

Just what makes geysers erupt is subject to speculation, but what nobody doubts is just how hot the springs are: underground temperatures reach 125°C, and even surface water is only just off boiling point – under no circumstances should you wander off marked paths (there are no protective barriers to speak of), step anywhere without looking first, or put any part of your body in the springs or their outlets.

The geysers

The large, deep, clear blue pool of **Geysir** (the Gusher) itself is, of course, what everyone comes to see, and in its heyday it was certainly impressive, regularly spitting its load 70m skywards. After decades of inactivity, an earthquake in 2008 seems to have got things going again, though eruptions are extremely irregular and you'll probably have to be content with the antics of nearby **Strokkur** – the Churn – which fires off a 30m spout every few minutes. A split second before it explodes, Strokkur's pool surface forms a distinct dome, through which the rising waters tear. Lesser spouts in the vicinity include **Blesi**'s twin pools, one clear and colourless, the other opaque blue; the unpredictably tempered **Fata**; and **Litli Geysir**, which does little but slosh around violently.

ARRIVAL AND INFORMATION GEYSIR

By bus Buses stop at the Visitor Centre, and all stop here for up to an hour: long enough to catch an eruption and get a quick feed, but not to ascend Bjarnarfell or get out to Haukadalur.

Destinations Akureyri (2 daily; 11hr); Gullfoss (3 daily; 10min); Hveravellir (2 daily; 7hr 15min); Laugarvatn (1 daily; 20min); Reykjavík (3 daily; 2hr 30min); Selfoss (3 daily; 1hr 30min); Þingvellir (1 daily; 45min).

SHORT WALKS AROUND GEYSIR

From the hot springs area, well-worn **tracks** lead to the summit of **Bjarnarfell** (727m) for views down on Geysir's surrounds. Another option is to follow the signposted 3km gravel vehicle track from Geysir up to a forestry reserve and church at **Haukadalur**. In saga times Haukadalur was an important holding, another famous educational centre that was eventually incorporated into Skálholt's lands. Extensive felling and ensuing erosion put paid to the estate, which was in a sorry condition when turned into a reserve in the 1930s. Since then, the hillsides here have been planted thickly with green pine trees, and thousands of new saplings spread down the valley. Have a quick look at the nineteenth-century **church**, too, whose brass door-ring is said to have belonged to the friendly giant Bergþór, who asked to be buried here.

Tourist information The Visitor Centre, opposite the hot springs (June–Aug daily 10am–10pm), has fuel, brochures, a gift shop and a café and restaurant.

ACCOMMODATION AND EATING

For budget **accommodation**, a late-opening bar and an alternative campsite, head 3km up the road to *Skjól* (see p.110).

Campsite 100m back down the road from the hot springs car park ☎480 6800. Beautiful grassy sites, with free showers and a barbecue area. Check in at the hotel (see below). 1700kr

Geysir Opposite the hot springs ☎480 6800, ⓦgeysircenter.is. Comfortable en-suite studio cabins, with views eastwards over the rural plains, and a small swimming pool with hot pots. They also own an adjacent guesthouse and have plans for considerable expansion. Breakfast 2200kr extra. Restaurant daily 11am–9pm.

Hotel doubles 26,000kr, guesthouse 19,000kr

Restaurant Geysir Glíma At the Visitor Centre. Nordic-chic glass, slate and basalt-block decor plus a photo exhibition of that odd sport *glíma* (Icelandic wrestling) – this was the site of Iceland's first wrestling school. Prices are reasonable enough: quiche and salad for 1790kr, pizza from 1550kr, soup of the day at 1490kr and all manner of cakes and coffee. A separate canteen around the corner has a smaller menu and lower rates. Daily 10am–5pm.

2

Gullfoss

About 6km up the road from Geysir, the young Hvítá River thunders into a 2km-long canyon, dropping as it does into a pair of broad cataracts known as **Gullfoss**, the Golden Falls: the first steps out 10m in full view, then the river twists sharply and falls a further 20m into the gorge's spray-filled shadow. It's most spectacular in early summer, when the Hvítá's feeder glaciers upstream are first melting; the force of the water makes spray and mist balloon up over the canyon, filling it with rainbow fragments – though the sight of this giant spectacle frozen and silent in winter is pretty memorable too.

There are two **viewing areas** for the falls, each providing a completely different take on the river's character. People tend to make a beeline for a flat rocky platform that projects out into the river right above the falls; it's spectacular here among the spray, but note the very Icelandic lack of safety barriers and warning signs – take care. The other viewpoint is up above at the top of the canyon, where you get a broad panorama of Gullfoss and the river and can also appreciate the location, right on the border of Iceland's Interior: snowcapped mountains and glacier caps fill the northern horizon; south is all green farmland.

ARRIVAL AND INFORMATION   GULLFOSS

By bus Buses stop at the Visitor Centre. Gullfoss marks the end of the Golden Circle, though the Kjölur route continues northeast across the Interior from here, and is covered by summer buses.

Destinations Akureyri (2 daily; 10hr 30min); Geysir (3 daily; 15min); Hveravellir (2 daily; 6hr 30min); Laugarvatn

(1 daily; 35min); Reykjavík (3 daily; 2hr 30min); Selfoss (3 daily; 1hr 45min); Þingvellir (1 daily; 1hr).

Tourist information The huge Visitor Centre, right by the car park (daily 9am–9.30pm), has the usual array of brochures, plus expensive brand-name outdoor clothing and woollen jumpers.

AN EARLY CONSERVATIONIST

Gullfoss still exists only because **Sigríður Tómasdóttir**, daughter of the owner of the estate that incorporated the falls, fought first her father and then the government to prevent a hydroelectric dam being built here in the 1920s. Permission to build the dam was granted, but public feeling – fanned by Sigríður – ran so strongly against the project that construction never began. Gullfoss was donated to the Icelandic Nature Conservation Council, and the area became a protected reserve in 1979.

2

ACCOMMODATION AND EATING

Hotel Gullfoss Brattholt Farm, 3km south off the approach road to the falls ☎ 486 8979, ⓦ hotelgullfoss .is. The only hotel close to the falls, featuring a pitched-roof dining area and single-storey hotel. En-suite rooms here are a little on the small side and drably furnished, but staff are friendly and there's an outdoor hot pot. 25,500kr

★ **Skjól** On the main road, halfway between Geysir and Gullfoss ☎ 899 4541, ⓦ skjolcamping.com. Nine dorm rooms in a modern, self-contained block, with shared facilities and a laundry; there's also a huge camping site. The centrepiece is the dark timber lodge-style bar, a convivial place with dartboard, beer and excellent nibbles

and grills – nothing is over 2000kr. The helpful owner can organize horseriding, snowmobile and 4WD tours, and point you towards private hot pools. Restaurant daily from late morning until midnight. Dorms **5000kr**, camping 1200kr

Visitor Centre restaurant Right by the car park. Pricey: a cake and coffee will set you back 1250kr, while the lamb soup – delicious though it is – costs a whopping 1950kr. The setting at the top of the gorge provides great views of the peaks and glaciers to the north, though you can't see the falls themselves. Daily 9am–9.30pm.

The central south

East of Reykjavík on the Ringroad, the hothouse town of **Hveragerði** and nearby transit hub **Selfoss** are the gateway to Iceland's **central south**, a swathe of fertile plains watered by the Hvítá, Rangá and Þjórsá – Iceland's longest river at 230km – and the clutch of bulky glaciers to the east. The inland area here cowers beneath **Hekla**, a destructive volcano whose antics have put paid to regional farming at least twice in recorded history, with tracks past the mountain leading to hot springs and brightly coloured hills at **Landmannalaugar**, right on the edge of Iceland's rugged Interior. If you enjoy the great outdoors, Landmannalaugar's surrounds are worth a trip to Iceland in their own right, not least for the superb four-day **Laugavegur hiking trail**. If you're not that serious, consider less demanding tracks over the hills above Hveragerði, also featuring steaming hot springs.

GETTING AROUND

By bus The Ringroad (Route 1) is the regional artery, running east via Hveragerði and Selfoss and plied year-round by Strætó, Sterna and Reykjavík Excursions from their respective stations in Reykjavík. In summer, there are

also daily services to stages on the Laugavegur trail (see p.120) and past Hekla to Landmannalaugar (p.119), though these are not accessible in a conventional vehicle.

Hveragerði

Following the Ringroad southeast from Reykjavík, you cross various flat, lichen-covered lava flows for 45km before the road twists down off the ranges to the coastal plains and the glowing hothouses of **HVERAGERÐI**, a cluster of low buildings on the Vármá (Warm River), nestled beneath steaming fell slopes. Sitting on the edge of an active geothermal area, a wool mill and hydroelectric dam were already established here when, for the first time in Iceland, subterranean heat was used to grow vegetables in the 1920s; you'll notice the town's drains steaming on cold mornings.

Now Iceland's largest and best-known hothouse town, Hveragerði suffers regular **earthquakes**; in 2008, a new geothermal area opened up in the hills above, while the tourist information centre straddles an older fissure which can be viewed through a glass panel in the floor. Hveragerði's numerous **hothouses** are mostly involved in the propagation and sale of vegetables and exotic plants – both Blómaborg at Breiðumörk 12, and Ingibjörg at Heiðmörk 38, are open to the public.

Hveragerði is laid out either side of the main drag Breiðamörk, which runs north off the highway past fuel stations and a large shopping centre, up through the compact town, and out into the countryside and the start of hiking trails.

Geothermal Park

Hveramörk 13, near the church and behind Kjöt & Kúnst café (see p.112) • Mon–Sat 9am–6pm, Sun 10am–4pm • 250kr, mud bath 750kr

Hveragerði's **Geothermal Park** provides a quick taste of what the Reykjadalur area north of town has to offer. There are steaming vents, bubbling mud pools and a low-spouting geyser (though a much better one, Grýla, stopped erupting after a quake in 2007), all viewed from a small network of paths. You can buy fresh eggs to boil in a spring (using poles with bags on the end, not your hands), buy bread baked in a steam oven, or take a therapeutic mud bath said to revitalize skin and cure all sorts of ailments.

2

ARRIVAL AND DEPARTURE HVERAGERÐI

By bus Hveragerði is a stop for most long-distance buses running to Skaftafell, Landmannalaugar, Þórsmörk and Mývatn via Sprengisandur; and also Strætó buses between Reykjavík and Selfoss. Services pull up at the shopping centre.

Destinations Hella (6 daily; 1hr); Hvolsvöllur (3 daily; 1hr 30min); Kirkjubæjarklaustur (2 daily; 6hr 20min); Landeyjahöfn (port for Heimaey ferry; 2–3 daily; 1hr 30min); Landmannalaugar (2 daily; 4hr); Leirubakki (2 daily; 1hr 50min); Mývatn (2 daily; 11hr); Þórsmörk (2 daily; 3hr); Reykjavík (hourly 8am–7pm; 1hr); Selfoss (hourly 8am–7pm; 20min); Seljalandsfoss (3 daily; 1hr 50min); Skaftafell (2 daily; 7hr 20min); Skógar (3 daily; 2hr 40min); Vík (2 daily; 4hr 40min).

INFORMATION AND TOURS

Tourist information South Iceland Information Centre, inside the shopping centre at the entrance to town (Mon–Fri 9am–6pm, Sat 9am–4pm, Sun 9am–2pm; ☎483 4601, �🌐visitsouthiceland.is), is a helpful outlet whose staff give useful advice, hand out brochures and sell maps and books. Check out the Earthquake Simulator (300kr), which reproduces the 6.6 strength quake the town suffered in 2008.

Services The shopping centre houses toilets, a Bónus supermarket (Mon–Thurs 11am–6.30pm, Fri 10am–7pm, Sat 10am–6pm, Sun noon–6pm), a bank with ATM and a post office. Hveragerði's excellent pool (Mon–Fri 6.30am–8.30pm, Sat & Sun 10am–6.30pm) is up past the campsite on Reykjamörk.

Horseriding Eldhestar, one of Iceland's largest riding stables, is about 2km southeast of Hveragerði at Vellir (☎480 4800, �🌐eldhestar.is), and offers anything from one hour to two weeks in the saddle.

ACCOMMODATION AND EATING

Café Rose Cnr Breiðamörk and Austurmörk ☎483 1100. Cheerful (if overly casual) diner just up from the shopping centre serving crepes, grills, burgers and pizza from around 1500kr; also has beer in the evenings. Daily noon–9pm.

Campsite Reykjamörk, east of and parallel with Breiðamörk ☎483 4605. Well-equipped with sheltered pitches, showers, toilets, laundry and a covered area to wash up and sit in when it's raining. Uniquely in Iceland, the picnic tables have metal plates on them, useful for those with fuel stoves. **1100kr**

HVERAGERÐI HIKES

Reykjadalur, the steamy heights above Hveragerði, is covered in trails and hot springs, its hillsides stained by volcanic salts and heathland plants, and, in fine weather, offering inspiring views coastwards – not to mention the thermal streams, warm enough to bathe in, so take your swimwear. **Maps** of the area, available at the information centre, have all trails and distances marked; on the ground, many routes are staked out with coloured pegs. As always, carry a compass and come prepared for bad weather.

For an easy four-hour circuit, follow Breiðamörk north out of town for about forty minutes to a **bridged stream** at the base of the fells, from where a pegged trail heads uphill. Crossing the muddy top, you descend green boggy slopes into **Reykjadalur** (Steam Valley), named after the hot stream that runs through the middle. You need to wade across this at any convenient point – there's a shallow ford – and then follow the far bank at the base of the forbidding rubble slopes of **Molddalahnúkar**, past a number of dangerous, scalding pools belching vapour and sulphur – stay on the path. At the head of the valley, 3km from the bridge, the stream bends west, with **Ölkelduhnúkur's** solid platform straight ahead and the main trail following the stream west along **Klambragil**, another steamy valley. There are a number of shallow, warm places to soak here – just test the water temperature before getting in.

2

Frost og Funi Hverhamar, out of town off Brieðamörk on the way to the walking trails ☎483 4959, ⓦ frostogfuni.is. Too upmarket for a guesthouse but more intimate than a hotel, the smart, timber-floored en-suite rooms are popular with honeymooners. Riverside hot tubs are a definite bonus. <u>27,000kr</u>

★ **Frumskógar Guesthouse** Frumskógar 3 ☎896 2780, ⓦ frumskogar.is. Three streets west of Breiðamörk, offering cosy doubles with shared facilities upstairs in the main house, and self-contained two-person studio apartments

with spas in a new block behind. It's a spotless, welcoming place, with unlimited use of the hot tub and steam room. Breakfast 1700kr. Doubles <u>16,400kr</u>, studios <u>21,500kr</u>

★ **Kjöt & Kúnst** Up towards the north end of town on Breiðamörk 21 ☎483 5010. Delicious home-cooked food, including *hverabrauð*, rye bread baked in on-site geothermal ovens. They also cook fish in the same way (4190kr), and offer everything from heavy cream cakes and coffee to salads, grills, soup and meatballs. Most mains around 2500kr. Mon–Sat noon–8.30pm.

Selfoss

Some 15km east of Hveragerði, the Ringroad passes the junction of Route 35 north towards the Geysir–Gullfoss area, before crossing a suspension bridge over the fast-flowing Öfulsá and running into the bustling town of **SELFOSS**. Caught between the looming bulk of **Ingólfsfjall** to the north and flat grasslands running to the horizon in all other directions, the town has been the centre of Iceland's **dairy industry** since the 1930s, and now has a population of around four thousand. There are no specific attractions here, but the town's crossroads position means that you'll almost certainly pass through on your way around Iceland. Selfoss is laid out along a 1500m-long stretch of the Ringroad, which runs east–west through town as Austurvegur.

The bridge

The original English-engineered **suspension bridge** is the reason Selfoss came into being. Roads originally ran further south, to where traffic was ferried across the hazardous Öfulsá estuary, but when the bridge opened in 1891 it became an immediate focus for shops and homes that gradually coalesced into the country's **first inland town**. The bridge also gave Selfoss the distinction of hosting the country's first strike, after construction workers downed tools over being given only salmon to eat. The current bridge dates from 1945, built after the original collapsed when two milk trucks crossed it simultaneously.

Kerið

About 15km north of Selfoss up Route 35, photogenic **Kerið crater** is an ancient collapsed scoria cone. The bottom of the 70m-deep, red-gravel crater is flooded and used for farming fish, and there's an easy, fifteen-minute path around the rim, with a view northwest to the similar **Seyðishólar** crater.

ARRIVAL AND DEPARTURE

SELFOSS

By bus The N1 fuel station on Austurvegur at the eastern exit of town is a staging post for long-distance buses and Strætó.

Destinations Eyrarbakki (10 daily; 30min); Hella (6 daily; 1hr); Hveragerði (hourly, 8am–7pm; 20min); Hvolsvöllur (3 daily; 1hr 15min); Kirkjubæjarklaustur (2 daily; 6hr); Landeyjahöfn (port for Heimaey ferry; 2–3 daily; 1hr

15min); Landmannalaugar (2 daily; 4hr); Laugarvatn (1 daily; 1hr 10min); Leirubakki (2 daily; 2hr); Mývatn (2 daily; 11hr); Þórsmörk (2 daily; 3hr); Reykjavík (hourly, 8am–7pm; 1hr 15min); Seljalandsfoss (3 daily; 1hr 30min); Skaftafell (2 daily; 7hr); Skálholt (1–2 daily; 30min); Skógar (3 daily; 2hr 30min); Stokkseyri (10 daily; 30min); Vík (2 daily; 4hr 30min).

INFORMATION

Tourist information Next to *Hótel Selfoss* (see opposite) at the western end of town on Eyravegur (Mon–Fri 8am–8pm, Sat 10am–4pm; ☎899 8663, ⓦ icelandforever .is). They dispense free brochures, maps and advice, sell plush puffin souvenirs and make all bookings.

Services There's a Krónan supermarket (Mon–Fri 10am–8pm, Sat & Sun 10am–7pm) at the western end of town, and a Bónus supermarket (Mon–Fri 10am–8pm, Sat & Sun 10am–7pm) close to the N1 service station on the east side. Banks with ATMs line Austurvegur.

ACCOMMODATION

Gesthús Selfossi Engjavegur 56, two blocks south of parallel Austurvegur ☎ 482 3585, ⓦ gesthus.is. Large, well-managed campsite with a solid, weatherproof building housing bathrooms, laundry, huge kitchen and a dining area. They also have clean but fairly cramped en-suite wooden cabins with kitchenettes sleeping 2–3 people. Camping 1300kr, cabins 14,500kr

IYHA Selfoss Austurvegur 28 ☎ 660 6999, ⓦ hostel.is. Well-appointed, conveniently located hostel in a russet-red house, offering rooms sleeping 1–4 people with shared facilities and the usual kitchen, laundry and social area. Staff are pretty helpful and you can arrange breakfast and packed lunches. There's also a hot tub. Doubles 13,000kr

Selfoss Eyrarvegur 2, close to the bridge ☎ 482 2500,

ⓦ selfosshotel.is. Large conference venue with a range of spacious rooms – check out the suites, whose four-poster beds and carved pine cabinets are about as close as Nordic design gets to Baroque. Facilities include a restaurant and hotel spa. 42,500kr

★**Vatnsholt** Follow signposts 15km southeast of Selfoss via Route 305 ☎ 482 4829, ⓦ hotelvatnsholt.is. Family-run farmstay out on grassy plains towards the coast. There are standard modern doubles, slightly more expensive suites with views and a self-catering house for groups. Horseriding and fishing can be arranged; there are also various unusual pets – a parrot, raven and arctic fox – and a dancing goat. Breakfast included, with a restaurant open in the evenings. Doubles 19,000kr, house 33,100kr

EATING

Kaffi-krús Austurvegur ☎ 482 1266. Cosy place near the Krónan supermarket serving coffee, excellent cakes and light meals, with a sunken outdoor patio screened from the main road. It's not cheap though, at 1820kr for a coconut-seafood soup and 3410kr for a grill and salad. Daily 10am–midnight.

Menam Near Hotél Selfoss at Eyravegur 8 ☎ 482 4099. Filling and tasty Thai dishes such as green chicken curry and Massaman beef, all served with rice. Most mains under 2600kr. Daily 11.30am–2pm & 5–10pm.

Tryggvaskáli Austurvegur 1, on the roundabout by the bridge ☎ 482 1390, ⓦ tryggvaskali.is. Though the food here is good – try cod and kale (3950kr), lobster salad (3100kr) or slow-cooked salmon and barley (4350kr) – it's the atmospheric 1890s timber interior that really impresses, cosy in a way that only those who have to build against sub-Arctic chill can carry off. There are several dining rooms, all different sizes, and the intimate feeling of being inside a private home. Daily 11.30am–11pm.

Stokkseyri

South from Selfoss, Route 34 runs straight to the coast across the **Flói**, a 10km-broad spread of land so flat that halfway across you can see both your starting point and destination. At the far end, the pretty seaside village of **STOKKSEYRI** is a former fishing port set behind a protective storm wall. Over the wall is a windswept, vestigial and unattended **harbour** – though even in its heyday in the 1900s it must have been tough to launch a boat here – and, oddly, a little yellow sand beach nestled among black, weed-strewn rocks. Stokkseyri´s most famous resident was **Thurídur Einarsdottír**, a nineteenth-century woman who worked on commercial fishing boats and is renowned for successfully defending, in court, her then-illegal preference for wearing men's clothing. The **Cultural Centre**, inside the black-and-russet paintwork of the old fish factory at Hafnargata 9, houses (among other things) the workshop of Iceland's only pipe organ maker, Björgvin Tómasson, who has built instruments for many of Iceland's churches.

ARRIVAL AND DEPARTURE   STOKKSEYRI

By bus Stræteó bus #75 runs a Selfoss–Stokkseyri–Eyrarbakki return route.

Destinations Eyrarbakki (Mon–Sat 4–7 daily; 15min); Selfoss (Mon–Sat 4–7 daily; 45min).

ACCOMMODATION AND EATING

Art Hostel On the second floor of the old fish factory, above the galleries at Hafnargata 9 ☎ 854 4510, ⓦ arthostel.is. You wouldn't guess from the battered exterior, but inside this warm hostel has plain but comfortable and well-appointed en-suite doubles, some

with a kitchenette, along with other doubles and dorms with shared facilities. There's even space to crash out on the floor – bring your own sleeping mat. A lounge, communal kitchen and dining area complete the picture. Dorms 5500kr, doubles 14,000kr, floor space 2000kr

★**Fjöruborðið** Eyrarbraut 3a ☎ 483 1550, ⓦ fjorubordid .is. Inside a single-storey wooden shack right against the sea wall, this is probably the most famous lobster restaurant in Iceland; former patrons have included Clint Eastwood, and they dish up fifteen tonnes of lobster a year. It's fair value considering what you get: a set meal of lobster soup, 300g of langoustine tails and a dessert costs 8400kr, but you could always just order the soup (2700kr) or 250g of tails (4700kr) – add 950kr for a side order of potatoes, cucumber salad and extra dips. Booking essential. Daily noon–9pm.

Eyrarbakki

Some 4km west of Stokkseyri, **EYRARBAKKI** is a larger version of its neighbour, and has a greater claim to fame: local boy **Bjarni Herjólfsson** sailed from here in 985 aiming for Greenland, lost his way in a storm, and became the first European to set eyes on North America – though, displaying an incredible lack of curiosity, he failed to land. On reaching Greenland he told his story and sold his ship to Leifur Eiríksson, who retraced Bjarni's route, made landfall, and named the place "Vinland" after his foster-father reported finding grape vines. The details are recounted in *Greenlanders' Saga* and *Eirik the Red's Saga* (see p.353).

Until the early twentieth century, Eyrarbakki's **harbour** was considered one of the best in southern Iceland, though boats had to be launched by dragging them through the surf into deeper water where they could be rowed out. Fishing and a proximity to the Ölfusá estuary ferry ensured Eyrarbakki's prosperity until the Selfoss bridge was completed and the town's harbour was rendered redundant by a safer, man-made effort west across the Ölfusá at Þorlákshöfn. Today, the hamlet's main employer is the local **jail**, one of Iceland's largest. Despite this downturn of fortune, Eyrarbakki sports an attractive core of early twentieth-century houses, an older timber-sided **church**, and the nearby **Húsið** museum complex.

Húsið

Búðarstígur • May–Sept daily 11am–6pm • 1200kr • ⓦ husid.com

Húsið, a Norwegian wooden kit-home dating back to 1765, now incorporates several museum exhibitions. The most interesting is the Maritime Museum, whose centrepiece is a wooden fishing boat of the kind used until the 1930s; a few photos and weather-beaten oilskins complete the display. Outside, climb the **storm wall** for a look seawards at what fishermen were up against as they set off or returned – a difficult entry over a rocky shore.

ARRIVAL AND DEPARTURE   EYRARBAKKI

By bus Stræteó bus #75 runs a Selfoss–Stokkseyri–Eyrarbakki return route.

Destinations Selfoss (Mon–Sat 4–7 daily; 45min); Stokkseyri (Mon–Sat 4–7 daily; 15min).

EATING

★**Rauða húsið** Búðarstíg 4 ☎ 483 3330, ⓦ raudahusid.is. Eyrarbakki's answer to Stokkseyri's *Fjöruborðið* (see above), though the menu is broader: lobster, of course (6650kr), but also daily fish duet (4500kr), glazed lamb fillet (5500kr), or a simple starter platter of smoked and cured salmon (2150kr). Their coffee and warm chocolate cake is the business, too. Book ahead. Mon–Thurs 11.30am–9pm, Fri–Sun 11.30am–10pm.

Þjórsárdalur

Around 45km due east from Selfoss, the powerful Þjórsá – Iceland's longest river – cuts down from Iceland's barren Interior through **Þjórsárdalur**, a once fertile valley laid waste over nine hundred years ago by a particularly violent eruption of **Hekla**, which rises just across the river to the east. Broad and flanked by dismal gravel slopes, all overlooked by the fist-like outcrop of **Búrfell**, Þjórsárdalur is an awesomely sterile place; Route 32 follows the bank of the river and then cuts right across the mouth of the valley, with side-tracks leading to an excavated Viking-age longhouse at **Stöng** and **Þjóðveldisbærinn**, a modern reconstruction.

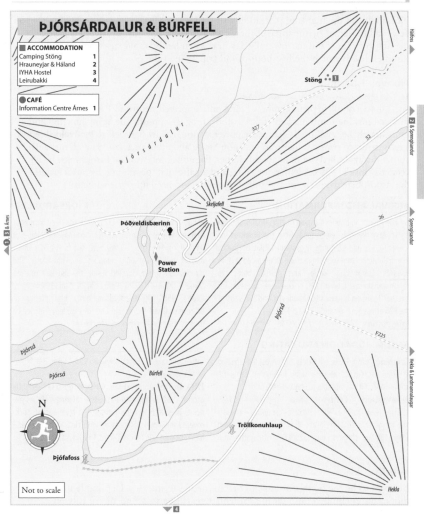

ÞJÓRSÁRDALUR & BÚRFELL

■ ACCOMMODATION
Camping Stöng	1
Hrauneyjar & Háland	2
IYHA Hostel	3
Leirubakki	4

● CAFÉ
Information Centre Árnes	1

Stöng

Þjórsárdalur

327

32

Skeljafell

Þóðveldisbærinn

Power
Station

26

32

Þjórsá

F225

Þjórsá

Þjórsá

Búrfell

Tröllkonuhlaup

N

Þjófafoss

Hekla

Not to scale

Stöng

On Þjórsárdalur's eastern side, a very rough Route 327 heads 7km north to where a red tin roof protects the remains of **Stöng**. This was the home of a chieftain named **Gaukur Trándilsson** until Hekla erupted in 1104, smothering all of Þjórsárdalur under a 20cm-thick layer of ash and pumice. The **Viking homestead** here was excavated in 1939: a longhouse formed the main hall, with a second, smaller hall and two attached outhouses serving as women's quarters, washroom and pens, all built from stone and timber, and sided with turf. Neatly built stone foundations, a central fireplace and post supports provide an outline of the original buildings, and further archeological work in the 1990s revealed the foundations of a contemporary **church** and **smithy** nearby.

Háifoss

From the car park at Stöng it's an 8km hike up the valley on a marked trail to **Háifoss**, Iceland's fourth-highest waterfall at 120m. The falls are an impressive sight, where the

Þjórsá falls off the highland plateau in a single narrow curtain, the deep, narrow canyon below all undercut by the force of the water. A second falls just upstream is joined to the first by a short but narrow gully. It's best when fed by rapid snowmelt in early summer, but is worth the five-hour round trip at any time.

Þjóðveldisbærinn

June–Aug 18 daily 10am–6pm · 600kr · ⓦ thjodveldisbaer.is

For a more complete picture of how Stöng once appeared, return to Route 32 and take the surfaced turning south marked "Búrfellsstöð", roughly opposite the Stöng junction and immediately below Búrfell. Before the power station, follow signs left to **Þjóðveldisbærinn**, a reconstructed period homestead based on Stöng and other sites, roofed with turf and authentically decked out in hand-cut timber, flagstones and woollen furnishings. It's all very cosy inside; indeed, with a fire going and a handful of people and livestock around, the atmosphere would be pretty stuffy – though you'd need it for the winters.

ARRIVAL AND INFORMATION   ÞJÓRSÁRDALUR

By car There's no public transport to Þjórsárdalur, though it's an easy drive on sealed roads from the Ringroad via routes 30, 326 and 32. Route 32 continues 15km northeast to join Route 26; turn south here along an unsealed section towards Leirubakki, Hekla and 4WD routes to Landmannalaugar (see p.119), or continue northeast for another 15km on bitumen to Hrauneyjar and the start of the F26 across Sprengisandur (see p.325).

Information The closest services to Þjórsárdalur are about 25km west on Route 326 at the scattered hamlet of **Árnes**, where there's an N1 roadhouse (Mon–Sat 9am–9pm, Sun 10am–9pm) with fast food and a mini-market selling camping supplies and provisions. The information centre, located inside the big hall marked "Árnes" (Mon–Fri 9am–9pm, Sat & Sun 10am–9pm; ☏ 664 6555, ⓦ arnesferdamenn.is), has plenty of brochures about the region and an excellent film which follows the Þjórsá from glacier to the sea.

ACCOMMODATION AND EATING

Camping Stöng. There are toilets and a washing-up shed at Stöng's car park, and no signs forbidding camping, implying that it's acceptable to stay here overnight.
Information Centre Árnes ☏ 664 6555, ⓦ arnesferdamenn.is. Pleasant café-restaurant – the last one for quite a distance in any direction – serving lamb soup (1800kr), chicken salad (2200kr) or straightforward coffee and cake (1250kr). Mon–Fri 9am–9pm, Sat & Sun 10am–9pm.
IYHA Hostel Árnes ☏ 486 6048, ⓦ hostel.is. Slightly eccentric set-up but with all the self-catering facilities you need. They also run the campsite, a couple of tussock-covered meadows 250m away with cleared patches and basic showers and toilets. Dorms 4550kr, camping 1200kr

Hekla

Believed to be the literal entrance to hell in medieval times – a fact that left the mountain unclimbed until daring students Eggert Olafsson and Bjarni Palsson scrambled up in 1750 – **Hekla** is Iceland's second most active volcano, with at least eighteen eruptions known to have occurred in the last thousand years. Oriented northeast, the mountain forms a 40km snow-covered oval ridge cresting at around 1500m; it should be visible for many kilometres around, but a heavy smudge of cloud usually obscures the peak and gives Hekla (Hooded) its name.

> ### HIKING HEKLA
>
> At the time of writing, **Hekla** was closed to hikers because of worries over potential eruption. Usually, the return **hike** to the top takes around eight hours, involving rough gravel terrain with snow higher up; you need to contact Ferðafélag Íslands, the Icelandic Hiking Association (ⓦ fi.is), for advice about current routes and conditions. Alternatively, Arctic Adventures (ⓦ adventures.is) lead day-hikes to the summit (40,000kr/person).

FROM TOP BLUE LAGOON (P.95); LAVA CLIFFS NEAR LANDMANNALAUGAR (P.119) >

2

Hekla's **earliest recorded eruption** was the one that buried Stöng in 1104. The mountain tends to fire up with little warning, spraying out clouds of fluorine-rich **tephra**, which blankets the landscape, poisons groundwater and kills livestock. Lava follows the ash, welling up along a fissure that splits Hekla's crest lengthways for 5km; during the notorious 1768 eruption – before which the mountain had been dormant for seventy years – flows covered over 65 square kilometres. Eruptions subside equally quickly, followed by months of grumbling – the anguished voices of tormented souls, according to legend.

Hekla has erupted regularly since 1970, the **most recent eruption** occurring on the evening of February 26, 2000. It wasn't much by the mountain's standards but triggered the largest emergency operation in Icelandic history, when over a thousand rubbernecks from Reykjavík needed rescuing after a sudden snowfall trapped them on Hekla's slopes. Fortunately, the lava went the other way.

Leirubakki and the Hekla Centre
Hekla Centre May–Sept daily 10am–10pm • 800kr

About 30km east of Selfoss along the Ringroad, the lonely Vegamót fuel station marks the place where Route 26 points northeast towards Hekla, whose unmistakable snowcapped dome is a beautiful sight on cloudless days. A further 30km up Route 26, where the landscape of lush horse pasture eventually gives way to lava rubble, buses pull in on the mountain's western foothills at **Leirubakki farmstay**, whose **Hekla Centre** offers a history of the mountain from folklore to science, with some spectacular videos of past eruptions.

Þjófafoss
Past Leirubakki, Route 26 continues through a wilderness between the Þjórsá River and Hekla's western slopes, the ground covered in tiny pieces of lightweight yellow **pumice** that are mined hereabouts for export. After about 5km there's a road towards the mountain itself and Næfurholt farm, one of the area's few functioning survivors – though it had to be moved after one eruption – then a roadside ridge blocks in Hekla's foothills while the Búrfell mesa springs up ahead of you. Wheel ruts and guide posts heading off-road towards Búrfell at this point can be followed for 4km to **Þjófafoss**, where the river bends right under Búrfell's southern tip in a wide, low waterfall, a friendly splash of colour among the monochrome landscape.

Tröllkonuhlaup
Route 26 runs right past **Tröllkonuhlaup**, the Troll Woman's Leap, a waterfall named after one of these unpleasant creatures crossed the river in a single bound while chasing a farmer. Bearing east directly opposite is **Route F225**, the four-wheel-drive-only track to Landmannalaugar.

ARRIVAL AND DEPARTURE	HEKLA

Buses Landmannalaugar and Sprengisandur buses stop at *Leirubakki*.

Destinations Hella (3 daily; 45min); Hveragerði (3 daily; 1hr 25min); Landmannalaugar (2 daily; 2hr); Mývatn (1 daily; 9hr); Reykjavík (3 daily; 2hr 20min); Selfoss (3 daily; 1hr 15min).

By car Route 26 is surfaced past Leirubakki, after which it becomes rough gravel for 15km, until the junction with Route 32. Turn west at the junction for Þjórsárdalur (p.114), or continue northeast on a good road to Hrauneyjar and the start of the 4WD-only F26 across Sprengisandur (see p.325). Note that there's a fuel pump at both of the listed accommodation options.

ACCOMMODATION

Hrauneyjar & Háland Route 26, 13.5km northeast of the intersection with Route 32 ☏487 7782, ⓦhrauneyjar.is. Wonderful staging post for expeditions tackling 4WD-only routes to Landmannalaugar or across Sprengisandur, this sprawling, single-storey complex has a warren of bedrooms with and without bathrooms, a huge kitchen, restaurant and bar, a lounge area and extremely helpful management. Breakfast is 1700kr. A separate building offers self-contained suites and apartments. They also rent out 4WDs for local use (12hr maximum; 37,000kr). Doubles **20,700kr**, sleeping bags **8600kr**, suites and apartments **39,000kr**

Leirubakki Route 26 ☎487 8700, ⊛leirubakki.is.

Year-round hotel and restaurant with Hekla's snow-smudged summit as a backdrop. Comfortable but plain doubles with or without bathroom, sleeping-bag accommodation in bunk rooms and a campsite with access to showers and toilets. Guests can also use the outdoor lava-block "Viking Pool", lukewarm but with superlative views of the mountain. Doubles 23,400kr, sleeping bags 6100kr, camping 1100kr

2

Landmannalaugar

Thirty kilometres east of Hekla via the four-wheel-drive F225, **Landmannalaugar** is an astonishing place, a **hot springs** area set in a flat gravel plain between a glacial river and the front of a fifteenth-century lava flow. The rugged landscape oozes grandeur, with sharp-peaked rhyolite mountains, brightly streaked in orange, grey and green, rising to a snowy plateau. Despite its proximity to Hekla, the area has provided summer pasture for sheep since medieval times, and was once a stage on back-country routes to the coast when flooding from Katla had closed the preferred coastal trails. Today, hikers have made Landmannalaugar a popular destination in its own right, not least for its position at the start of the exceptional four-day **Laugavegur trail** down to Þórsmörk, though many campers simply come to enjoy a hot soak among the wild scenery. Note that accommodation (see p.120) should be booked as far in advance as possible, and that the area is closed from September to mid-June.

The hot springs

Your first stop at Landmannalaugar has to be the celebrated **hot springs**, which are in a patch of green at the end of a boardwalk up against the lava front. A scalding stream emerges from underneath the lava and merges with a cold flow; you simply wade up the latter to where they mix, find a spot where the temperature is just right, and sit down up to your neck. You have to keep shifting every time a fellow bather moves, which alters the water currents and temperature, but you couldn't ask for a better place to unwind. Be aware that some unidentified **parasite** in the hot pools has caused paralysis in ducks; the effects on humans are unknown but locals certainly don't care.

Brandsgil and Brennisteinsalda

For a couple of easy **hikes** from the Landmannalaugar campsite, either head south for 2km down **Brandsgil**, a tight, colourful canyon full of shallow streamlets and hot springs in the riverbed, or west past the hut and up onto the obsidian-rich **Laugahraun** lavafield, following the first couple of kilometres of the Laugavegur trail. You end up on a ridge overlooking the flow, near a concentration of steam vents at **Brennisteinsalda**, from where you can circuit back to the campsite via **Grænagil**, a narrow canyon.

Bláhnúkur

On a clear day you really should ascend **Bláhnúkur** (945m), the large, bald peak to the south. There's a straightforward, marked trail up the northeast face from near the campsite; it's steep, but around an hour should see you on the summit enjoying 360-degree views; all around are multicoloured hills, with the campsite edged by moss-covered lava. Off to the northeast is **Tungnaá**, a sprawling area of lakes and intertwined streams at the source of the Skaftá, which empties into the sea near Kirkjubæjarklaustur. For the descent, either retrace your steps or – if you've good boots and little fear – follow the trail along the peak and off down the steep, slippery scree slope covering Bláhnúkur's west face. You end up at the edge of the Laugahraun lavafield (see above), with a choice of paths back to base.

2

FJALLABAK BUSES

Fjallabak is an area covering two **old traffic routes** which ran, quite literally, *fjallabak* – "behind the mountains" north of the Mýrdalsjökull glacier. Today, one of these has been resurrected as the F208, which runs from Landmannalaugar to Kirkjubæjarklaustur (see p.318) via **Eldgjá**, a deep, 40km-long volcanic canyon with a spectacular accompanying waterfall, **Ófærufoss**. From late June until September, daily **Landmannalaugar to Skaftafell buses** (Ⓦ re.is) cover this route in just five hours, though you'll definitely need to stop off along the way at Eldgjá to get the most from the journey.

ARRIVAL AND DEPARTURE   LANDMANNALAUGAR

By bus Landmannalaugar's bus stop is at the hot springs area. Depending on the weather, return services from Reykjavík travel via Hella and Leirubakki daily from mid-June to mid-Sept; there are also onwards connections east from Landmannalaugar to Skaftafell via the Fjallabak route (see above), and north to Mývatn via Sprengisandur (p.325).

Destinations Eldgjá (1 daily; 1hr 15min); Hella (2 daily; 2hr 15min); Hveragerði (2 daily; 3hr); Kirkjubæjarklaustur (1 daily; 3hr 45min); Leirubakki (2 daily; 1hr 45min); Mývatn (1 daily; 10hr); Reykjavík (2 daily; 4hr); Selfoss (2 daily; 3hr 15min); Skaftafell (1 daily; 4hr 45min).

By car The main road to Landmannalaugar is the 4WD-only F225, which turns east off Route 26 just past Tröllkonuhlaup (see p.118) via black ash and lava deposits on Hekla's northern flanks, crosses a couple of rivers and intermittent oases of grassland, and finally reaches a major ford immediately west of Landmannalaugar.

INFORMATION AND TOURS

Tourist information The ranger's office (roughly 8am–10pm; ☎ 568 2533) is at the hot springs area, where you can buy maps of the hiking trails. You need to register here before starting the trail to Þórsmörk; having had to rescue many badly equipped hikers over the years, rangers might check that your clothing and kit are up to scratch before allowing you to head off.

Tours 4WD day tours to Landmannalaugar, Hekla and surrounds are offered by South Coast Travel (☎ 777 0705, Ⓦ isct.is), South Iceland Adventure (Ⓦ siadv.is) and Into the Wild (☎ 866 3301, Ⓦ intothewild.is). See websites for pickup points, and expect to pay upwards of 37,000kr/person.

ACCOMMODATION

Campsite Hot springs area ☎ 568 2533, Ⓦ fi.is. In response to escalating tourist numbers and consequent erosion, plans are afoot to relocate the campsite and restrict numbers, so check before turning up. Ensure your tent is sound: the weather here can be atrocious, with incredibly strong winds. Campers are not allowed to use the hut's kitchen, so bring cooking gear along. **1600kr**

Hiking Hut Hot springs area ☎ 568 2533, Ⓦ fi.is. Ferðafélag Íslands, the Icelandic Hiking Association, runs a large, self-catering lodge at Landmannalaugar sleeping 75 people with toilets, showers and ample kitchen space. Accommodation is in bunk beds (bring your own sleeping bag). **7000kr**

Laugavegur

Laugavegur, the 55km hiking trail between Landmannalaugar and Þórsmörk, is the best of its kind in Iceland, with easy walking and magnificent scenery. Huts with campsites are laid out at roughly 14km intervals, splitting Laugavegur comfortably into **four stages**: five days is an ideal time to spend on the trip, allowing three for the trail and a day at either end, though you could hike the trail in just two days. Once at Þórsmörk, there's also the option of hiking south over the mountains to Skógar (see p.132) or, once the bridge has been built, west to Fljótsdalur (p.127).

Landmannalaugar to Hrafntinnusker

The 12km stretch between Landmannalaugar and the first hut at Hrafntinnusker is mostly uphill. You leave Landmannalaugar via Brennisteinsalda onto the muddy moorland atop the plateau, surrounded by stark, wild hills. About two-thirds of the way along is **Stórihver thermal area**, a steaming gully and rare patch of grass, beyond

2

LAUGAVEGUR HIKING ESSENTIALS

Depending on the weather, the Laugavegur trail should be **open** from early June until mid-September, when **buses** run daily from Reykjavík to the end points at Landmannalaugar and Þórsmörk, and also to Álftavatn, Hvanngil and Emstrur (see below).

Ferðafélag Íslands' **huts** sleep up to seventy people, cost 7000kr a night for sleeping-bag space, have toilets, kitchens and usually showers, and need to be booked well in advance; you can apply for the coming year after the route closes in September. **Campsites** at the huts cost 1600kr, with access to toilets and showers, but not kitchens. Bring everything with you, including food and sleeping bag (you can get water at the huts) and, if camping, a tent, stove and cooking gear.

Weather varies between fair and foul, with gale-force winds a speciality of the region; you need full waterproof gear, warm clothing, solid hiking boots and some old trainers or surf boots for fording the several frigid **rivers**. The trail is well pegged, but at the very least you need to carry Landmælingar Íslands' *Þórsmörk-Landmannalaugar* **map** and a compass. Although the overall **gradients** are the same whichever end you begin, in practice it's easier from the north, where you spend a whole day gradually reaching the trail's apex (around 1120m) between Hrafntinnusker and Álftavatn, instead of doing it in one short, brutal ascent from the south.

which there's a scramble onto a higher **snowfield** which peaks at **Söðull**, the ridge above the huge volcanic crater of **Hrafntinnusker**. "Hrafntin" means **obsidian**, and just about all rocks in the area are made of this black volcanic glass. The Hrafntinnusker **hut** has no shower and the campsite is on bleak scree and very exposed; many people skip staying here altogether and push on to Álftavatn or Hvanngil.

The tightly folded ridges due west conceal Iceland's densest concentration of **hot springs**, with a pegged walking track (about 40min each way) out to where one set rises under the stratified edge of a glacier, hollowing out **ice caves**. Do not enter the caves; people have been killed doing so.

Hrafntinnusker to Álftavatn

It's a further 12km from Hraftinnusker to the second hut at Álftavatn. The first stage continues across the snowy plateau to a rocky outcrop just west of **Háskerðingur**, whose sharp, snow-clad peak makes a good two-hour detour – though views northwest from the base, over worn rhyolite hills, patches of steam from scattered vents, and Laufafell's distinctive black mass, are just as good. The plateau's edge at **Jökultungur** is not much further on, revealing a blast of colour below which is a bit of a shock after the highland's muted tones: Álftavatn sits in a vivid green glacial valley, lined with sharp ridges and abrupt pyramidal hills, with Mýrdalsjökull's outlying glaciers visible to the south.

The subsequent **descent** into the valley is steep but not difficult, and ends with you having to wade a small stream before the trail flattens out near the **two huts** (one owned by Útivist; ☎562 1000, ⊛utivist.is) and campsite on the lakeshore at **Álftavatn**. After getting settled in, hike around Álftavatn's west side and follow the valley for 5km down to **Torfahlaup**, a narrow canyon near where the **Markarfljót River** flows roughly between the green flanks of Stóra-Grænfjall and Illasúla, two steep-sided peaks.

Álftavatn to Botnar-Emstrur

The next stage to Botnar-Emstrur is 16km. Around 5km east from Álftavatn via a couple more streams, **Hvanngil** is a sheltered valley with a Ferðafélag Íslands' **hut** and **campsite**; after here you cross a bridge over **Kaldaklofskvísl**, and have to wade the substantial but fairly shallow **Bláfjallakvísl**. The scenery beyond opens up into a grey-brown gravel **desert**, fringed by the surreally green hills and Mýrdalsjökull's ice cap, as you follow a four-wheel-drive track southwest. Part-way across the desert, there's another bridge over the **Innri-Emstruá**, where this chocolate-brown glacial river hammers over a short waterfall with such force that it sends geyser-like spurts skywards. Then it's back across the gravel, up and over various hillocks, until you find yourself descending bleak slopes to the **hut** at **Botnar-Emstrur**, whose campsite is in a small, surprisingly lush gully. Otherwise, the immediate scenery appears barren, though there's a short walk west to **Markarfljótsgljúfur**, a narrow, 180m-deep gorge on the Markarfljót, and superlative views of **Entujökull**, the nearest of Mýrdalsjökull's glaciers, from clifftops around 3km southeast of the hut.

Botnar-Emstrur to Þórsmörk

The final 15km southwest to Þórsmörk is perhaps the least interesting section of the journey, though there's initially another good view of the glacier, just before the path crosses the Emstruá over a narrow bridge. This is followed by a climb onto a gravelly heath, with the Markafljót flowing through a series of deep canyons to the west – easy enough to investigate, though out of sight of the path. As you follow the ever-widening valley, you'll start to encounter a few shrubs before crossing a further bridge over the **Ljósá** and descending to the gravel beds of the **Þröngá**, the deepest river you have to ford on the trail – don't attempt it if it's more than thigh deep. Once across, you immediately enter birch and juniper **woodland** marking Þórsmörk's boundary at **Hamraskógar**: shady, carpeted in thick grass, and with colourful flowers everywhere. From here, it's a final 2km into Þórsmörk to the huts (see p.131) at either Húsadalur or Skagfjörðsskáli.

ARRIVAL AND DEPARTURE
LAUGAVEGUR

By bus Aside from services to Laugavegur's end points at Landmannalaugar (see p.119) and Þórsmörk (p.129), Reykjavík Excursions (⊕re.is) run a daily Reykjavík– Selfoss–Hella–Álftavatn–Hvanngil–Emstrur bus between late June and late Aug, though the Emstrur drop-off is 5km from the hut. Wardens at the various huts can help book bus seats out if you decide to cut your trek short along the way.

Njál's Saga country

Heading southeast from the Þjórsá on the Ringroad, the first thing you'll notice are disproportionate numbers of four-wheel-drives towing boxes, and a wide, rolling expanse of pasture, positively reeking of **horse**. This is one of Iceland's premier horse-breeding areas, with Oddhóll, the country's biggest stud farm, near the small town of **Hella**. The countryside between here and the distant slopes of **Eyjafjallajökull** to the east comprises the plains of the two-pronged **Rangá** river system, famed for its salmon and the setting for much of the action of Iceland's great medieval epic, *Njál's Saga*.

With the highway towns of Hella or **Hvolsvöllur** as a base, getting out to a handful of the saga sites is straightforward enough in your own vehicle, even if you do find more in the way of associations rather than concrete remains when you arrive. A more tangible draw is **Þórsmörk**, a beautiful highland valley only accessible by four-wheel-drive or hiking in from Landmannalaugar and Skógar; you're also within striking distance of the **ferry to Heimaey** in the Westman Islands. Ringroad **buses** pass through Hella and Hvolsvöllur year-round, as do additional summer services to Þórsmörk and Landmannalaugar.

Hella

A service centre of six hundred inhabitants where the highway crosses the narrow flow of the **Ytri-Rangá** (also known as the **Hólsá**), **HELLA** grew through the twentieth century to serve **Rangárvallahreppur**, the fertile farming district beyond Hekla's southwestern

NJÁL'S SAGA

Speared in the belly, Þorgrim dropped his shield, slipped, and fell off the roof. He walked back to Gizur and the rest. "Is Gunnar at home?", asked Gizur, looking up. Þorgrim replied, "You'll have to find that out for yourself – but his spear certainly is." And then he fell dead.

There's nothing to beat the laconic, hard-bitten delivery of **Njál's Saga**, Iceland's gripping tale of Viking-age clan warfare. The story centres on the life of **Njál Þorgeirsson** and his family, who are casually ensnared in a minor issue that somehow escalates into a frightful, fifty-year feud. Bound by their own personalities, fate and sense of honour, nobody is able to stop the bloodshed, which ends only after the original characters – and many of their descendants – have been killed. But there's far more to *Njál's Saga* than its violence, and the tale paints a vivid picture of Iceland at what was, in some ways, an idyllic time: the power of the Alþing at Þingvellir was at its peak and the country's free settlers lived by their own efforts on farming and freebooting.

The tale splits into three uneven parts, beginning in the late tenth century at a point where the fate of several participants is already intertwined. Gifted with foresight and respected by all, Njál himself is often a background figure, mediating and advising rather than confronting or fighting, but his sons play a far more active role, especially the proud and ferocious **Skarp-héðinn**. Njál's best friend is the heroic **Gunnar Hámundarson** of Hlíðarendi, whose superb martial skills and physical prowess never get in the way of his generosity or sense of justice. Balancing this nobility is the malevolent **Mörð Valgarðsson**, a second cousin of Gunnar's who spends the saga's first third plotting his downfall.

Early on in the tale Gunnar marries "Thief-eyed" **Hallgerð**, a thorny character who provokes a violent feud with Njál's household. Njál and Gunnar remain friends, but Njál's sons are drawn into the fray by the murder of their foster-father, and the cycle of payback killings begins. Mörð sees his chance, and manipulates various disreputable characters into picking fights with Gunnar, who emerges undefeated yet increasingly worn down from each confrontation. After one fight too many, Gunnar is outlawed – exiled from Iceland – but finds himself unable to leave his homeland, and is hunted down to Hlíðarendi by a posse led by Mörð and the upstanding chieftain Gizur the White. When Gunnar's bowstring snaps during the siege, Hallgerð spitefully refuses to give him two locks of her hair to restring the weapon: "To each their own way of earning fame," Gunnar memorably responds, and is cut down.

After an interlude describing Iceland's **conversion to Christianity** in 1000, the violence sparked by Hallgerð thirty years earlier resurfaces when Njál's sons kill their distant relative, the arrogant Þráin Sigfússon. Attempting to placate Þráin's family, Njál adopts his son **Höskuld** and buys him a priesthood, and for a while all seems well. But resentment at this favouritism eats away at Njál's sons, and, encouraged by Mörð – who, now that Gunnar is dead, has shifted his vindictive attentions to Njál – they murder Höskuld. Höskuld's influential father-in-law **Flósi of Svínafell** agrees initially to a cash settlement for the murder, but Njál inadvertently offends him: confrontation is inevitable and the 80-year-old Njál, bowing to fate, retreats with his sons to his homestead **Bergþórshvoll**. Flósi and his men torch the building, killing all but Njál's son-in-law **Kári**.

Public opinion against the burning of Njál runs so high that at the following Alþing Kári is able to confront Flósi and his allies – now known as the **Burners**. Mörð stirs up trouble again and a pitched battle breaks out; in the aftermath, all but Kári accept the Alþing's conditions for peace, which banish Flósi and the Burners from Iceland until tempers have cooled. For his part, Kári swears vengeance, and the action follows his peregrinations around Europe as he hunts down his enemies. Returning to Iceland, Kári's ship is wrecked at Ingólfshöfði off the southeast coast; walking inland through a blizzard, he finds sanctuary at Svínafell and becomes reconciled with Flósi, bringing *Njál's Saga* to an end.

extremities – most of Iceland's potatoes are grown here, and as the climate warms, formerly unknown cash crops such as rapeseed are being experimented with. Other than hosting the annual Landsmót **National Horse Show** in late June, Hella is really only of interest as somewhere to pause before heading on, either to historic sites nearby, or towards Hekla, clearly visible 50km to the northeast.

By bus The bus stop is in a car park close to the Olís fuel station.

Destinations Álftavatn (1 daily; 3hr 20min); Emstrur (1 daily; 5hr 30min); Hvanngil (1 daily; 4hr 50min); Hverageði (6 daily; 55min); Hvolsvöllur (3 daily; 30min); Kirkjubæjarklaustur (1 daily; 3hr 30min); Landeyjahöfn (port for Heimaey ferry; 2–3 daily; 40min); Leirubakki (2 daily; 25min); Mývatn via Sprengisandur (1 daily; 9hr 30min); Reykjavík (6 daily; 1hr 35min); Selfoss (6 daily; 35min); Seljalandsfoss (3 daily; 40min); Skafatfell (1 daily;

6hr 20min); Skógar (2 daily; 2hr 20min); Vík (2 daily; 3hr); Þórsmörk (2 daily; 2hr).

Services There's a Kjaraval supermarket (daily 9am–8pm) next to the Olís fuel station, and a bank with ATM around the corner on riverside Þrúðavegur.

Tours MudShark (w mudshark.is) offer fishing, hiking, 4WD tours and trips to intriguing man-made caves which might well predate Viking settlement of Iceland. For horseriding – anything from 1.5hr to five days in the saddle – contact Hella Horse rental (t 864 5950, w hellahorserental.is).

ACCOMMODATION

Árhús 100m along from the coastwards turn-off at the highway roundabout ☎487 5577, w arhus.is. Large riverside campsite with cabins. Facilities include showers, toilets, a spacious indoor dining area and a self-catering kitchen (including cookers and toasters, but no crockery or pans). Their restaurant has a range of burgers (from 1850kr), pizza and fair-value mains such as fillet of lamb (4900kr). Cabins 17,000kr, camping 2500kr

Hella Þrúðvangur 6 ☎487 4800, w hotelhella.is. Undergoing much-needed renovations at the time of writing, the newly furnished rooms are on the small side but warm and have everything you need, while the management is keen and breakfast is included. 24,000kr

★ **Rangá** 8km east of Hella just south off the Ringroad ☎478 5700, w hotelranga.is. Upmarket fishing lodge, whose lobby features a huge mounted salmon, caught locally (and a stuffed polar bear, from Greenland). The

whole place is designed like a giant log cabin and rooms are cosily panelled in pine; the suites (almost double the price of standard rooms) each have their own theme, with furnishings from each of the seven continents. Fishing licences are available; salmon needs a year's advance notice and a healthy bank balance; char and trout might be available on the day. 51,000kr

Stracta Rangárflatir 4, on the coastal side of the highway ☎851 8010, w stractahotel.is. Large modern complex with a disorienting layout of corridors. The rooms are comfortable Nordic – wooden floors, smart bathrooms and lots of white – and the enormous tubs in the self-contained studio suites (111,000kr) would make for a romantic overnighter. They also have budget beds with shared bathrooms. All guests get use of hot tubs and "barrel" saunas. 20,900kr

Keldur

June 15–Aug 15 daily 9am–5pm • 700kr

Just beyond Hella, Route 264 heads northeast off the Ringroad towards Hekla. Some 20km along, the pretty farm of **Keldur** is named after the "cold springs" (*keldur*) that seep out from under a vegetated lava flow to form a sizeable stream winding off across the plains. There's a modern farmhouse here, but Keldur is mentioned in several of the sagas and an older string of a half-dozen **turf-covered halls** date, in part, right back to the Viking period – incredibly, it was lived in until 1946. The entrance hall is low-ceilinged and flagstoned, leading to a kitchen and store-room; there's a timber stave dated 1641, but a few of the roof beams and doorway panels are incised with simple **line decorations**, typical of the Viking era. To the left, another room has a **concealed tunnel** leading 25m out into the fields; this dates from the twelfth century and was built as an escape route in case of siege. **Snorri Sturlusson**, Iceland's great medieval man of letters, was raised at Keldur by his foster-father Jón Ólafsson (the adoption of children having always been a widespread practice in Iceland; during the Viking era it cemented ties between families); even earlier, Keldur was home to **Ingjald Höskuldsson**, uncle of Njál's illegitimate son, who supported Kári against the Burners.

Once you've looked around inside, take a moment to register Keldur's location, right on the steep front of one of Hekla's flows: the few stone walls defining the fields below were built to limit ash drifts and erosion following periodic eruptions.

FROM TOP ÞÓRSMÖRK (P.129); RAINBOW, SKOGAFOSS (P.132) >

GUNNARSSTEIN

Ask at Keldur for directions to **Gunnarsstein**, a boulder 3km east where Gunnar and his allies were ambushed by a group led by local horseman **Starkað of Þríhyrningur**. The battle that followed contains some of *Njál's Saga*'s most savage imagery; when it was over, Gunnar's side had killed fourteen of their attackers, but at the cost of Gunnar's brother **Hjört** (whose name means "heart"). The tale describes Hjört's burial here afterwards, and in the mid-nineteenth century a mound at the site was indeed found to contain a skeleton and a bracelet engraved with two hearts.

2

Oddi

Not mentioned in *Njál's Saga*, though of a similar vintage, **ODDI**'s couple of houses and prominent, red-roofed **church**, all set on the only hill for many kilometres around, are 5km southwest down the highway from Hella and then the same distance directly south along Route 266. Though you'd hardly credit it today from the modern church's location and plain decor, Oddi was once famous: the French-educated **Sæmundur Sigfússon** became priest here in 1078 and established an ecclesiastical school, whose later alumni included thirteenth-century lawspeaker, historian and diplomat Snorri Sturlusson (see box, p.158) and St Þorlákur Þórhallsson.

Hvolsvöllur

Eleven kilometres southwest down the Ringroad from Hella you reach **HVOLSVÖLLUR**, a few short streets at the edge of the broad **Markarfljót valley**, whose intricately tangled streams flow down from Þórsmörk, over to the east between the Eyjafjallajökull and Mýrdalsjökull ice caps.

Hvolsvöllur makes a good place to get to grips with *Njál's Saga*; you're close to the settings for some of the most important scenes in the tale, and Hvolsvöllur itself – or rather the farm, Völlur, 5km north – was the homestead of Mörð Fiddle, grandfather to the tale's arch-villain, Mörð Valgardsson. On a practical note, the town is also the last place to stock up on **provisions** before heading on to Þórsmörk.

The Saga Centre

Hlíðarvegur 14 • May 15–Sept 15 daily 9am–6pm; Sept 15–May 15 Sat & Sun 10am–5pm • 950kr • ☏ 487 8781

Hvolsvöllur's main attraction is the **Saga Centre**, just off the highway down Route 261; allow an hour for a good look around. The bulk of this museum explores the saga period, with replica clothes and artefacts, and models of Viking houses and ships, maps, dioramas and paintings showing the location of local sites and the extent of Viking travels across the northern hemisphere. At the time of writing, work was also continuing on a 90m-long, Bayeaux-like **tapestry** of *Njal's Saga*, featuring all the major episodes from the tale; hopefully it will be on display when completed.

ARRIVAL AND INFORMATION   HVOLSVÖLLUR

By bus Ringroad buses stop at the N1 roadhouse; you might need to change services here for Þórsmörk.
Destinations Hella (4 daily; 10min); Hveragerði (3 daily; 55min); Kirkjubæjarklaustur (1 daily; 3hr); Landeyjahöfn (port for Heimaey ferry; 2–3 daily; 30min); Reykjavík (3 daily; 1hr 55min); Selfoss (3 daily; 1hr); Seljalandsfoss (4 daily; 35min); Skaftafell (1 daily; 5hr 45min); Skógar (2 daily;

50min); Vík (2 daily; 2hr); Þórsmörk (2 daily; 1hr 25min).
By car Hvolsvöllur is on the Ringroad, where Route 261 kinks east at the N1 fuel station.
Services Hvolsvöllur's bank, post office and Kjaraval supermarket (daily 9am–10pm) are all on the highway near the N1 roadhouse. The modern swimming pool (daily 10am–4pm) is signposted a few streets back on Vallabraut.

ACCOMMODATION AND EATING

★**Asgarður** Hvolstrod ☏ 487 1440, ⓦ asgardurinn.is. Simple but modern chalets set among trees and sleeping

up to four, each with a bathroom and kitchen. Turn off the highway up Route 261 and it's down the red gravel driveway right beside the church. Breakfast is 1400kr extra. Dorms 6600kr, sleeping bags 4900kr

Campsite Off the Ringroad just west from the N1 roadhouse ☎ 487 8043. All facilities, but otherwise a functional spot on the highway and overlooked by the transmission tower. The picturesque Seljalandsfoss campsite, 20km east, is a better bet (see p.128). 1200kr

★ **Eldstó** Austurvegur 2 ☎ 482 1011, ⓦ eldsto.is. Pottery, gallery, café and guesthouse in a comfy, old-style timber and tin building opposite the N1 roadhouse. Rooms are small, bright and homely, all with shared bathroom and use of a kitchenette; the pleasant café serves the likes of Greek salad (2090kr), lamb soup (2100kr) or house burgers (2490kr). A cake and coffee comes in at about 990kr. Restaurant daily 11am–10pm. Doubles (per week) 44,000kr

Hvolsvöllur Hlíðarvegur 7 ☎ 487 8050, ⓦ hotel hvolsvollur.is. Not far off the Ringroad, the building looks as if it were constructed from shipping containers, and the rooms, while cosy, are uninspiringly dated. There's a decent restaurant and good service throughout; breakfast is included. 29,600kr

Fljótshlíð

There's a beautiful 30km run east from Hvollsvöllur up along Route 261 and **Fljótshlíð**, the flat-bottomed, heavily farmed northern border of the Markarfljót valley, with the saga site of **Hlíðarendi** and valley setting at **Fljótsdalur** to draw you out this way. Ahead loom Eyjafjallajökull's black sided, ice-capped heights, and on a clear day the view south extends all the way to the sea. In summer, streams and ponds draining the wetlands in between are alive with birds, especially black-tailed godwits, with their vivid orange and black plumage.

Hlíðarendi

The road follows the base of a long line of green hills heading up the valley, whose slopes contrast strongly with the starker-toned mountains opposite. About 17km from Hvollsvöllur, a side road climbs steeply up to **Hlíðarendi**, where a red-roofed **church** and handful of farm buildings command a splendid view of the area. In the tenth century the site was home to Njál's great friend Gunnar, the most exemplary of all saga characters; unfortunately his fine character always tended to inspire envy rather than admiration, and it was here that he finally met his end (see box, p.123).

Though Hlíðarendi's church is worth a look for its chandelier and **blue-panelled ceiling** inset with golden stars, nothing besides the scenery remains from the saga period. Look on the plains below for the isolated rocky platform of **Stóra-Dímon** (called Rauðuskriður in the saga), where Njál's sons Skarp-héðinn and Helgí ambushed Þráin Sigfússon, who had participated in the murder of their foster-father. Þráin spotted them but Skarp-héðinn slid over the frozen river and killed Þráin before he had time to put on his armour, setting in motion events which were to lead to the burning of Njál.

Fljótsdalur

East of Hlíðarendi, the hills grow steeper as the valley narrows, with a frill of small, ribbon-like **waterfalls** dropping down to the roadside. A track pointing south past Stóra-Dímón to the Ringroad marks the start of the gravel, and then you're running alongside the Markarfljót river system's continually shifting maze of flat, intertwined streams up **Fljótsdalur**, a valley caught between the steep, glaciated slopes of Tindfjöll to the north and Eyjafjöll to the south.

SÆMUNDUR AND THE SEAL

Sæmundur Sigfússon is the subject of several legends, including one in which the devil – disguised as a seal – offered to carry him back to Iceland from France so that Sæmundur could apply for the post at Oddi. When they were within sight of the shore, the resourceful Sæmundur cracked the devil over the head with a psalter, swam to safety, and got the job. Less to his credit, he's also held responsible for causing Hekla's 1104 eruption by tossing a keepsake from a jilted lover – who turned out to be a witch – into the volcano.

About 10km from Hlíðarendi and 27km from Hvolsvöllur, the gravel road crosses a ford and becomes a four-wheel-drive track. There's accommodation here at the tiny, isolated **Fljótsdalur youth hostel** (see below), and any number of **treks** to attempt in the area; plans are also under way to build a **footbridge over the Markarfljót** upstream, which will make Þórsmörk accessible to hikers from here.

ACCOMMODATION FLJÓTSDALUR

★ **IYHA Fljótsdalur** Up on the slope above the end of the all-vehicle road ☎ 487 8498, ⓦ hostel.is. This low-ceilinged timber and turf-roofed hostel sleeps around a dozen people in bunks and matresses on the floor (bring your own sleeping bag); there's a kitchen, a garden to sit out in, and good days provide stunning views of Eyjafjallajökull, which rises up the valley to the east. All facilities are shared and they don't take credit cards. The nearest shops are in Hvolsvöllur. Dorms and sleeping bags **3900kr**

Bergþórshvoll

South of Hvollsvöllur, follow Route 255 coastwards for 20km off the Ringroad and across the flat, waterlogged countryside to **Bergþórshvoll**, where Njál's homestead sat a thousand years ago. Today, a modern farmhouse occupies the low crest 1km from the sea, and there's no visible trace of the original hall, which was besieged by Flósi and his hundred-strong Burners in the autumn of 1011. The two sides met in the open, but, urged by the old man, the defenders retreated into the house, and Flósi – certain that Njál's sons would kill him if they escaped – ordered the building to be set alight. After women, children and servants were allowed to leave, Njál, his wife and sons burned to death; only "lucky" Kári managed to break out. In support of the story, charred remains found here during twentieth-century excavations have been carbon-dated to the saga period.

Seljalandsfoss

Back on the Ringroad heading east from Hvolsvöllur – and passing the turning **to Landeyjahöfn**, the Westman Islands' ferry port – it's around 20km to where Route 249 to Þórsmörk heads inland around the platform of Eyjafjallajökull's western foothills. Not far along is **Seljalandsfoss**, a narrow but powerful waterfall that drops 60m off the undercut fellside into a shallow pool. Paths run behind the curtain – you'll get soaked, but the noise of the falls is impressively magnified – and the lighting is especially atmospheric in the evening, when the low sun makes the waterfall glow gold. There are a couple of smaller falls (one of which is almost enclosed by the cliff-face) up towards the adjacent *Hamragarðar* campsite (see below), the boggy meadow in between thick with a summer crop of cotton grass, kingcups and angelica.

ARRIVAL AND DEPARTURE SELJALANDSFOSS

By Bus Buses along the Ringroad and all Þórsmörk services stop for a while at Seljalandsfoss.
Destinations Hella (4 daily; 45min); Hveragerði (4 daily; 1hr 20min); Hvolsvöllur (4 daily, 35min); Kirkjubæjarklaustur (1 daily; 3hr); Reykjavík (4 daily; 1hr 55min); Selfoss (4 daily; 1hr); Skaftafell (1 daily; 5hr 45min); Skógar (2 daily; 50min); Vík (1 daily; 2hr 25min); Þórsmörk (2 daily; 1hr 25min).

ACCOMMODATION

★ **Hamragarðar campsite** 500m up the Þórsmörk road from the falls ☎ 866 7532 or ☎ 867 3535. Wonderful setting facing west over the Mjarkafljot valley, with acres of thick grass to pitch a tent on. There's a modern indoor kitchen and dining area with cookers and sinks, showers, toilets and washing machines (but no dryers), plus a small on-site café-bar. **1300kr**

Stóra Mörk III 7km up the Þórsmörk road from Seljalandsfoss ☎ 487 8903 or ☎ 698 0824. Historic dairy farm with views up the valley towards Þórsmörk, which featured in *Njál's Saga*; this is as far as you can take a normal vehicle. They offer two modern self-contained cabins sleeping up to ten people each (sheets can be rented for 1000kr/person), with showers, toilets and small kitchens; there's also TV and wi-fi. Excellent value for a group. Cabins **20,000kr**

Þórsmörk

Hidden from the rest of the world by encircling glaciers and mountain wilderness, **Þórsmörk** covers a highland valley north of Eyjafjallajökull, watered by a host of multistreamed glacial rivers that flow west off Mýrdalsjökull's heights and down into the Markarfljót. Green-sloped, covered in dwarf willow, birch and wildflowers, with icy peaks rising above, this is one of Iceland's most beautiful spots and, through the summer months, it's a magnet for everyone from hard-core hikers coming to tackle the numerous trails to equally energetic partygoers here to unwind in a bucolic setting.

Þórsmörk is laid out west–east along the 7km-long **Krossá river valley**, the river splitting the reserve into two distinct sections: the area to the north is **Þórsmörk** proper, while south is **Goðaland**. Aside from local hiking routes described below, Þórsmörk sits at the southern terminus of the multi-day **Laugavegur trail** from Landmannalaugar (see p.120), and at the northern end of the nine-hour trail up over **Fimmvörðuháls** to the Ringroad at Skógar, via lava from the 2010 eruption under Eyjafjallajökull (see p.131).

North of the Krossá

Húsadalur, at Þórsmörk's western end, comprises a **bus stop** and accommodation, but is actually outside the main valley with no views to speak of; best to hike 2km east – either on a direct path or via a steep trail over the summit of knuckle-like **Valahnúkur** – to Ferðafélag Ísland's **Skagfjörðsskáli** hut (see p.131) and ranger station. You'll also wind up here at the end of the hike down from Landmannalaugar, in which case the sudden glut

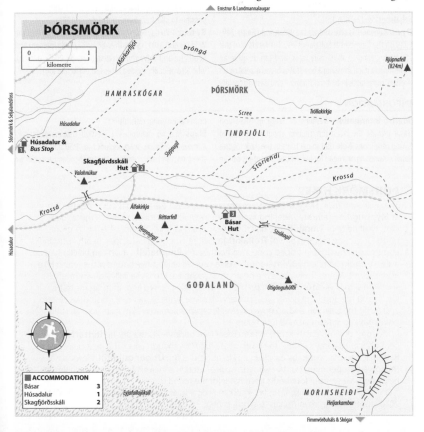

of vegetation and colour is striking. Valahnúkur's summit makes a brilliant place to orient yourself, with views out over the flat riverbed's interlaced streams to where the rough hills opposite, buffed in green, are suddenly terminated by Mýrdalsjökull's blue-white mass.

South of the Krossá

The landscape south of the Krossá is dominated by steep, green, looming slopes ultimately rising to the Eyjafjallajökull ice cap. The first target here is the river-level **Básar** hut (see opposite), ranger station and campsite, reached either by bus (some terminate here) or from Skagfjörðsskáli via a footbridge over the Krossá – though at the time of writing this had washed away, replaced by a mobile pontoon. Note that under no circumstances should you attempt to wade across the river's main channel; people have drowned doing this. Básar marks the start of the **trail to Skógar**, though the warden here has excellent suggestions for shorter hikes within Þórsmörk.

ARRIVAL AND DEPARTURE   ÞÓRSMÖRK

By bus Þórsmörk's main bus stop is on the western edge of the reserve at Húsadalur, but some services continue to Básar – check with the driver.

Destinations Hella (2 daily; 1hr 45min); Hveragerði (2 daily; 2hr 25min); Hvolsvöllur (2 daily; 1hr 35min); Reykjavík (2 daily; 3hr 20min); Selfoss (2 daily; 2hr 15min); Seljalandsfoss (2 daily; 1hr).

By car Þórsmörk is accessed via the 30km-long Route 249/ F249 off the Ringroad at Seljalandsfoss. The last half of this is a high-clearance, 4WD-only track, and can be quite an adventure in itself, crossing a handful of broad glacial rivers – often impassable in bad conditions – and passing rapidly

shrinking Steinsholtsjökull, before reaching the reserve's western end at Húsadalur.

By foot The main hiking trails to Þórsmörk are along Laugavegur from Landmannalaugar (see p.120), and from Skógar via Fimmvörðuháls (see box, p.134). Once the footbridge over the Markarfljót is built, it should also be possible to hike here from Fljótsdalur (p.127).

By tour 4WD day tours to Þórsmörk are offered by Into the Wild (☎ 866 3301, 🖥 intothewild.is; 37,000kr/person) and South Iceland Adventures (🖥 siadv.is; 34,000kr/person), who also offer 8hr guided hikes (38,000kr/person).

INFORMATION

Tourist information Wardens at Skagfjörðsskáli and Básar provide the latest information about weather and hiking conditions. Note that many trails in the park require some scrambling or a head for heights, and wardens can be

rather blasé about difficulties.

Maps Mal og menning's 1:100,000 *Landmannalaugar-Þórsmörk-Fjallabak* map includes a 1:50,000 Þórsmörk sheet on the back; combine this with hiking association

---

ÞÓRSMÖRK HIKES

The main walk from Skagfjörðsskáli (see opposite) starts at the next bay east from the hut at **Slyppugil**, a gradually widening, wooded gully which you follow uphill to the jagged east–west ridge of **Tindfjöll**. The trail then weaves along Tindfjöll's gravel, landslip-prone north face to the solitary spire of **Tröllakirkja**, before emerging onto open heath at Tindfjöll's eastern end: the double-tipped cone 2km northeast is **Rjúpnafell**, which can be climbed up a steep, zigzag path to its 824m summit – give yourself at least five hours for the return hike from the hut. Alternatively, cross the heath to descend back into the valley down Tindfjöll's southern slopes via **Stóriendi**; the path is intermittently pegged and often seems to be leading off the edge, but always reappears, with some fantastic views of Þórsmörk's eastern end along the way. You end up down at river level approximately 2km from your starting point; this circuit takes around four hours.

The most obvious local excursion from Básar (see opposite) is straight up **Réttarfell**, the peak above, via a low saddle – the path is easy to follow though tiring. The next peak east of Réttarfell, and connected by a walkable 5km ridge, is 805m **Útigönguhöfði**. Views from the top are stupendous, but be warned, the final section is incredibly steep, with chains to help you. Give yourself four hours from Básar for the round trip.

One final option is to hike from Þórsmörk to Skógar in around ten hours, via the site of the 2010 eruption at Fimmvörðuháls (see box, p.134).

maps (available from the huts and Húsadalur). The latter are too inaccurate to use alone, but do show the trails – which are only vaguely pegged on the ground.

Supplies The closest shops are at Hvolsvöllur or Vík, so bring everything you need with you.

ACCOMMODATION

Básar ☎ 893 2910, ⓦ utivist.is. Útivist's modern, well-equipped and spacious hut has toilets, showers and a kitchen and dining area, though just the usual sleeping arrangements in bunks or on communal shelves off the floor. The campsite is close to the river with some barbecue areas and picnic benches. Dorms 5000kr, camping 1500kr

Húsadalur ☎ 552 8300, ⓦ volcanohuts.com. A range of cosy bunkhouses and cabins, offering private rooms or shared dorms sleeping four (you need your own sleeping bag); the campsite has an outdoor cooking area and the usual amenities block. There's also an on-site restaurant, the only one at Þórsmörk, open through the day

– otherwise, bring all your own cooking gear. There's also an on-site sauna and spa pool. Dorms 7000kr, cabins 25,000kr, camping 1600kr

Skagfjörðsskáli ☎ 568 2533, ⓦ fi.is. Ferðafélag Íslands's lodge and campsite, beautifully located at river level beneath Valahnúkur – you can sit on the porch and watch vehicles attempting the river crossing (the hut has a photo album of 4WD disasters). Inside there are two kitchens, a dining area, two long dorms and a handful of bunks; the amenities block is separate. Dorms 7000kr, camping 1600kr

The south coast

Southeast from the Þórsmörk junction, the Ringroad finds itself pinched between the coast and the **Eyjafjallajökull** ice cap. Though dwarfed in scale by its big sister **Mýrdalsjökull** immediately to the east, Eyjafjallajökull's 1666m apex is southwestern Iceland's highest point, and the mountain has stamped its personality on the area: an active volcano smoulders away below the ice, responsible for major eruptions in the seventeenth and nineteenth centuries. In 2010 Eyjafjallajökull awoke from dormancy in a fairly small-scale event, but one in which massive **clouds of ash**, swept southwards by high-altitude winds, caused chaos across Europe by grounding aircraft – something that (along with listening to foreign reporters' stumbling efforts to pronounce "Eyjafjallajökull") created a perverse sense of pride in Iceland.

The base for exploring all this is the Ringroad hamlet of **Skógar**, with its magnificent waterfall and superb **hike to Þórsmörk** via a pass between Eyjafjallajökull and Mýrdalsjökull at **Fimmvörðuháls**, site of the 2010 eruption. Moving down the coast, mountain ridges supporting Mýrdalsjökull – and occasional outlying glaciers, such as **Sólheimajökull** – intrude further and further towards the sea, finally reaching it around Iceland's southernmost tip, **Dyrhólaey**, where they form impressively sculpted cliffs, home to innumerable seabirds. Past Dyrhólaey, the sleepy village of Vík has black-sand beaches, more birds and some easy walks, and marks the beginning of the long cross-desert run into southeastern Iceland.

Ringroad **buses** pull up at Skógar and Vík, though you'll need your own transport elsewhere.

Þorvaldseyri

Around 20km east along the Ringroad from the Route 249 junction at Seljalandsfoss, **Þorvaldseyri** is a small tongue of farmland which was nearly devastated by ash from the 2010 eruption. There's a fine museum here to the event, and it's also an easy trip inland to some enjoyable **hot springs**.

Eyjafjallajökull Erupts Visitor Centre

On the Ringroad • Daily: June–Aug 9am–6pm; Sept–May 11am–4pm • Toilet €1 • Film 800kr

Housed in a small, bunker-like building, the **Eyjafjallajökull Erupts Visitor Centre** has an exhibition of photos covering the history of the volcano – at 800,000 years old, one of the longest-active in Iceland – and in particular the events of 2010. The accompanying 20min **documentary of the eruption** runs several times per hour and follows the fortunes of the family at nearby Þorvaldseyri farm, whose fields were buried under ash; the sight of the farmer's face when he first returns home is heartbreaking. There's also close-up footage of the short but fierce spill of lava, and an incredible moment when a shockwave from deep inside the crater visibly blasts out through the ash cloud.

Make sure you cross the road from the centre and look at **Þorvaldseyri farm** itself, the red-roofed building directly inland from the centre, now running as normal – in fact, the ash-fertilized fields gave them a bumper harvest in 2011.

Seljavallalaug

Some 5km east of Þorvaldseyri, or the same distance west of Skógar, the bumpy, gravel Route 242 runs a few kilometres north to a parking area. From here it's a fifteen-minute walk along a small stream to the head of a rocky, steep-sided valley and **Seljavallalaug**, a waist-deep, rectangular swimming pool fed by a hot spring. Though you can't see it, Eyjafjallajökull's icy skirt caps the plateau above and the rubbly slopes are strung with little waterfalls; the pool was choked by ash from the 2010 eruption, but now that it's clear again, having a soak is an intrinsically Icelandic experience.

ACCOMMODATION AND EATING   **ÞORVALDSEYRI**

Edinborg Lambafell, on the Seljavallalaug road ☎487 1212, ⓦwelcome.is. Smart, chalet-like country hotel with a range of en-suite twins and family rooms. There's plenty of timber furnishings and an outdoor hot tub, and wild scenery in every direction – Seljavallalaug is only a short drive away. **36,000kr**

Gamla Fjósið Ringroad about 2km west of the Visitor

Centre ☎487 7788, ⓦgamlafjosid.is. Housed in a low-cielinged former cowshed, this café-restaurant takes pride in serving up fresh local produce: burgers from 2000kr, lobster from the Westman Islands (6920kr), or catch of the day (3990kr). Their beer is pricey, however, at 1000kr for a 300ml bottle. Daily 11am–9pm.

Skógar

SKÓGAR is an insubstantial, scattered collection of buildings set back off the Ringroad beside **Skógarfoss**, the biggest of the local waterfalls and worth a look even if you've otherwise had enough of these things. Other reasons to stop are the entertaining **museum** and a superb **hiking trail** to Þórsmörk via still-steaming lava at Fimmvörðuháls. Skógar has no centre; a 1km road runs inland off the highway, with the waterfall and most buildings to the west, and the museum off the end of the road to the east.

Skógarfoss

Skógarfoss is justifiably famous, looking good from a distance and nothing short of huge, powerful and dramatic close-up, as the curtain of water drops 62m off the plateau. Stand on the flat gravel riverbed in front of the rainbow-tinged plunge pool and the rest of the world vanishes into soaking white mists and noise; in full flood, the outward blast of air caused by the falling water makes it impossible to get within 50m of the falls. A metal staircase climbs to the top, beyond which a muddy trail heads upstream to a much smaller but still violent cataract and brilliant views coastwards and up across mossy moorland towards the distant glacier cap. If you're properly prepared, you can follow the river in this direction right up to Þórsmörk (see box, p.134).

Folk Museum

East end of the access road • Daily: June–Aug 9am–6pm; Sept–May 11am–4pm • 2000kr • ☎487 8845, ⓦskogasafn.is

Skógar was settled by the twelfth century, and you'll find a detailed record of the region's farming and fishing communities at the **Folk Museum**. Various types of

FROM TOP SIGNPOST, HEIMAEY (P.139); VÍK (P.136); EYJAFJALLAJÖKULL (P.131) >

SUNDLAUG

TJALDSVÆÐI

MIÐBÆR

NÁTTÚRUGRIPASAFNIÐ

SKANSINN

traditional **turf-roofed farm buildings** have been relocated to an adjacent field, while inside the main building, the centrepiece is a 10m-long wooden **fishing boat** from 1855, tough enough to survive being dragged regularly over kilometres of sand and gravel to be launched. Pick of the other exhibits includes a Viking **jade cloak pin**, an edition of Iceland's first printed **Bible**, dating from 1584, and a fourteenth-century fragment from the Book of David written in Icelandic on vellum. Ask to be shown (it's easy to overlook otherwise) the **brass ring** found hundreds of years ago, said to have once adorned a chest of gold hidden behind Skógarfoss by the Viking settler Þrasi – legend has it he argued with his children and didn't want them to inherit his wealth.

ARRIVAL AND DEPARTURE   SKÓGAR

By bus The bus stops at Skógar's campsite, in front of the falls (see opposite).
Destinations Hella (2 daily; 1hr 30min); Hveragerði (2 daily; 2hr 10min); Hvolsvöllur (2 daily; 1hr 20min);

Kirkjubæjarklaustur (1 daily; 2hr 50min); Reykjavík (2 daily; 3hr); Selfoss (2 daily; 2hr); Seljalandsfoss (2 daily; 30min); Skaftafell (1 daily; 3hr 50min); Vík (2 daily; 1hr 10min).

INFORMATION AND TOURS

Tourist information There's an information desk at the *Fossbúð* café (see opposite), located off the road to the falls (daily 9am–8pm).
Tours Accompanied Skógar–Þórsmörk treks can be made

with Ferðafelag Íslands (ⓦ fi.is), Útivist (ⓦ utivist.is), Arctic Adventures (ⓦ adventures.is), Extreme Iceland (ⓦ extreme iceland.is) and Mountain Guides (ⓦ mountainguides.is); you're looking at about 30,000kr per person for a 10hr/

THE SKÓGAR–ÞÓRSMÖRK TRAIL

The 25km **hiking trail** from Skógar, over the **Fimmvörðuháls pass** between the Eyjafjallajökull and Mýrdalsjökull ice caps, then down the other side to Þórsmörk, offers spectacular views and traverses **lava** from the 2010 eruption at Eyjafjallajökull. Although it's feasible to do the whole thing in under ten hours, many people spread the trip over two days, overnighting at one of the two mountain **huts** en route, for which bookings are essential. The trail is usually **passable** without equipment from around mid-June to September; outside these times you'll probably need an ice axe to cut steps during the descent to Þórsmörk, and possibly crampons. Whatever the time of year, come prepared for possible rain and snow, poor visibility and cold; the **track** is easy to follow in clear weather, but play safe and carry a compass and Mál og menning's *Landmannalaugar-Þórsmörk-Fjallabak* **map**.

The trail starts by taking the staircase up Skógarfoss, then follows the river uphill over a muddy, shaly **heath** carpeted by thick patches of moss. There are many small **waterfalls** along the way, each of them unique: some twist through contorted gorges, others drop in a single narrow sheet, bore tunnels through obstructive rocks, or rush smoothly over broad, rocky beds. Around 8km along you cross a **bridge** and leave most of the vegetation behind for a dark, rocky plain flanked by the smooth contours of Eyjafjallajökull and Mýrdalsjökull. It's another hour from here, following marker poles across gravel and snowfields, to the recently refurbished *Baldvinsskali* **hut** (ⓦ fi.is; 5000kr). Alternatively, push on for another forty minutes to the larger **second hut**, *Fimmvörðuskáli* (☎ 893 4910, ⓦ utivist.is; 5500kr), actually just west off the main trail.

From here you're halfway along and crossing **Fimmvörðuháls** (1043m), the flat pass in between the two glaciers; there's a pale blue tarn and then a gentle ascent to where the path weaves around and over the rough **lavafields** created in 2010. You end up at the top of a slope with a fantastic vista of Þórsmörk laid out below, Mýrdalsjökull's icy outrunners hemming in the view to the east. The slope is snow-covered well into the summer and the quickest way down is to cautiously slide it on your backside, using your feet as brakes. This brings you to **Heljarkambur**, a narrow, 50m traverse with a vertical rockface rising on one side and a steep snowfield dropping 75m on the other; winds here can be appalling. At the far end is the flat, muddy gravel plateau of **Morinsheiði**: look at where steaming new lava is dispersing the glacier edge in a noisy **waterfall** at the neck with Heljarkambur. Cross the plateau and it's a straightforward descent to Þórsmörk (though the short, knife-edge "Cat's Spine" ridge can be nervous work, despite a helpful chain) and the Básar hut – see p.131.

overnight excursion.

Services There's a small store with biscuits, milk, bread and a few vegetables off the road to the falls at the *Fossbúð* café

(daily 9am–8pm). The nearest fuel is a self-service pump 15km west at tiny Steinar, past the Eyjafjallajökull Erupts Visitor Centre (see p.131). The closest bank and ATM is at Vík.

ACCOMMODATION AND EATING

Campsite 200m in front of the falls ☎ 863 8064. A timber amenities block (including tiny shelter shed with sinks) and a large, flat, grassy area to pitch tents on. Given the location, it can, unsurprisingly, get a bit damp when spray channels outwards. **1100kr**

Edda Just off to the right at the far end of the access road, en route to the museum ☎ 444 4830, ⓦ hoteledda.is. This well-managed budget hotel has plain and functional doubles; the walk-in rate for a mattress on the floor in a common room is good value (available after 5pm only), and includes breakfast. Otherwise, breakfast is 1900kr. All facilities are shared. Doubles **19,000kr**; mattresses **4500kr**

Fossbúð On the road to the falls ☎ 487 8843. Somewhere to take shelter over a coffee in bad weather. Their roadhouse-style menu of burgers, soup, buns and chips won't win any prizes, but the lunchtime special of

pork schnitzel, soup and coffee costs a reasonable 2500kr. Free wi-fi too. Daily 7am–9pm.

IYHA hostel On the road to the falls ☎ 487 8801, ⓦ hostel.is. Recently renovated to include under-floor heating, a massive kitchen in stainless steel and the usual run of bunk-bed dorms, bathrooms and a dining area. Dorms **4100kr**, doubles **10,600kr**

Skógar On the falls road ☎ 487 4880, ⓦ hotelskogar.is. Small hotel with smart Nordic-style rooms featuring pine flooring; there's also an outdoor sauna and hot tubs, and the restaurant features a real fire. **33,400kr**

Skogarfoss Between the *Fossbúð* café and the youth hostel on the falls road ☎ 487 8780, ⓦ hotelskogarfoss. is. Long, low new affair whose seventeen smart en-suite rooms sport Nordic floral decor; some have views towards the falls. Wi-fi reception is poor. **24,900kr**

Mýrdalsjökull

The country's fourth-largest ice cap, **Mýrdalsjökull** weighs down the inland plateau between Skógar and Vík. Like neighbouring Eyjafjallajökull, Mýrdalsjökull harbours a powerful volcano, 1300m **Katla**, whose volcanically induced flash floods (see box, p.317) have devastated the area's farms a dozen or more times since Settlement, washing out the fine black sand which forms the **beaches** hereabouts. Katla last erupted in 1918 and is worryingly overdue for another blast; they occur once every seventy years on average, and a recent spate of **earthquakes** in the region – not to mention the 2010 eruption under Eyjafjallajökull – might be heralding future activity.

Sólheimajökull

Not far east of Skógar, the Ringroad crosses the shallow Jökulsá Fulilækur, a glacial river with origins beneath the ice surrounding Katla. Look upstream from the roadside and you'll see the apparently insignificant, narrow ice tongue of **Sólheimajökull**, one of Mýrdalsjökull's outrunners; gravel Route 221 heads 4km up the broad river valley to a parking area, a fifteen-minute walk from the glacier front. Sólheimajökull is well worth a look, especially if you haven't seen this sort of thing before: the glacier tongue is steep-faced, blackened with melted-out grit and heavily streaked in crevasses.

MÝRDALSJÖKULL ACTIVITIES

Both Mountain Guides (ⓦ mountainguides.is) and Arcanum (ⓦ arcanum.is) run 1–3hr **ice-walking** and climbing excursions (13,000–26,000kr/person) through the summer at Sólheimajökull; contact them in advance for details. You don't need prior experience and they supply crampons and ice axes. Arcanum also offers **snowmobile trips** across the upper heights of Mýrdalsjökull from **Sólheimskáli**, a mountain hut 10km inland off the Ringroad along the rough gravel Route 222 (22,000kr/hr). Call ahead if you need a pickup from anywhere between Reykjavík and Vík, though this will add considerably to the price.

Dyrhólaey

Closed or with restricted access May 8–June 25 for the nesting season • Free

East down the Ringroad from the Sólheimajökull turn-off, Route 218 slides 6km coastwards past a handful of farms and then over a causeway to where the country reaches its southernmost extremes at **Dyrhólaey**. A set of basalt cliffs rising over a long expanse of black sand, Dyrhólaey is a beautiful place just to watch the sea on a sunny day, though it's also a noted **seabird reserve**. Beyond the car park you'll find yourself on a rocky shelf above the sea with the swell hammering into the low cliffs at your feet; there's a surprisingly sheltered bay around to one side, though, where a dense matting of tussocky grass holding the clifftop together is riddled with **puffin burrows** – sit still for long enough and you can get some good photos.

Just west, a dumpy, orange-topped **lighthouse** sits atop a grassy headland: mainland Iceland's southernmost point. Below, the narrow cliff is pierced by a 115m **arch**, tall enough for a yacht to pass beneath – you can see this best from Reynishveri (see below). One of the volcanic stacks just offshore from here is also hollow, the interior reached along a tiny passage from the open water, just large enough for a rowing boat.

ACCOMMODATION   DYRHÓLAEY

Dyrhólaey 5km inland off the Ringroad ☏ 487 1333, ⓦ dyrholaey.is. Perched on a high ridge facing south, so views from the forecourt down over Dyrhólaey are fantastic, despite the hotel being some way from the sea. Rooms are clean, though the decor – floral curtains and angular wooden furniture – could do with modernizing and the dining room is institutional, the tables and chairs arranged in long rows. The friendly staff are a huge bonus. <u>32,000kr</u>

Reynishverfi

As the Ringroad continues east towards Vík, it has to climb over the back of **Reynisfjall**, a ridge that divides the southwest's fertile farmland from the bleak expanses of sand beyond. It also blocks the weather: it's not unknown for it to be snowing on one side, and bright and sunny on the other. Route 215 runs coastwards down the length of Reynisfjall's western side to **Reynishverfi**, a polished pebble shingle where the puffins bob offshore. It's a beautiful spot on a sunny day, perfect for a picnic; there's black sand, a steep cliff faced in twisted basalt columns, and a large cave, **Hálsanefshellir**, around to the left (though beware getting cut off at high tide, and keep well clear of the treacherous **surf**, which can knock you flat and suck you out to sea). The three stacks offshore are the Troll Rocks, better viewed from Vík – which is just around the impassable headland. From the car park, don't miss the brilliant views westwards to Dyrhólaey's arch.

EATING   REYNISHVERFI

Black Beach Café At the Reynishverfi car park ☏ 571 2718, ⓦ blackbeach.is. Surprisingly discreet against the cliffs, this angular basalt block building features a glass front, allowing long views down the coast towards the arch. Despite being aimed squarely at the tourist trade, prices are reasonable: coffee and cake cost 990kr, a hearty lamb soup 1690kr and pan-fried char 3790kr. Toilets and free wi-fi for customers. Daily 11am–10pm; à la carte 6–9pm.

Vík

Despite averaging the highest rainfall in Iceland, **VÍK** – known more fully as Vík-í-Mýrdal – is a pleasant place of three hundred souls nestling on the toe of Reynisfjall's steep eastern slopes, a last haven before taking on the deadening horizons of **Mýrdalssandur** to the east, the desert laid down by Katla's overflows. Iceland's only coastal village without a harbour, Vík got going as a trading station in the late nineteenth century and today serves a few farms and the tourist traffic. The town is laid out either side of a 500m stretch of the Ringroad, with Víkurbraut – where most of the town's services are located – heading south towards the sea.

Brydebúð

Víkurbraut • Summer daily 10am–8pm • Free

Vík's older quarter is south of the highway along the 100m-long main street, Víkurbraut – though the only sight as such is **Brydebúð**, the original nineteenth-century general store. This was actually built in 1831 on the Westman Islands and relocated here in 1895; it now houses Vík's information centre (see below), a restaurant (see below) and a small **museum** of photographs showing village life through the years.

Reynisdrangar

Past Brydebúð, a road and walking track run down to a black beach at Reynisfjall's southern tip. Offshore here are three tall spires known as **Reynisdrangar**, the Troll Rocks, said to be petrified trolls caught by the sun as they were trying to drag a boat ashore. The headland above is a huge, stratified bird colony: lower down are kittiwakes, with puffins nesting on the steep middle slopes and fulmar occupying the rocky cliffs near the top; the sky is full of evening activity as birds return from a day's fishing.

ARRIVAL AND INFORMATION   VÍK

By bus The bus stop is on the eastern side of town at the N1 roadhouse.

Destinations Hella (1 daily; 3hr 30min); Hveragerði (1 daily; 4hr 30min); Hvolsvöllur (1 daily; 3hr); Kirkjubæjarklaustur (1 daily; 1hr); Reykjavík (1 daily; 5hr); Selfoss (1 daily; 4hr); Seljalandsfoss (1 daily; 2hr); Skaftafell (1 daily; 2hr); Skógar (1 daily; 50min).

Tourist information There's a desk at Brydebúð on Víkurbraut (daily 10am–8pm; ☎ 487 1395), where you can

pick up hand-drawn maps marking out several good hiking trails.

Services The well-stocked Kjarval supermarket is on Víkurbraut (daily 9am–10pm), next door to a bank and ATM. The swimming pool is a couple of streets behind the supermarket (daily 10am–7pm). Note that the N1 roadhouse has the only fuel between Kirkjubæjarklaustur and Steinar, 15km west of Skógar. You can rent a horse from Víkufjara, down towards the beach (☎ 787 9605; 5000kr/hr).

ACCOMMODATION

Campsite On the eastern side of town opposite the N1 fuel station ☎ 897 3587. Big grassy space, between the road and a low cliff; it's a little exposed and soggy after rain, but they've put in an embankment for cover. There's also a large covered kitchen and dining area, plus toilets and showers. **1200kr**

Edda Vík In front of the more visible Icelandair (see below) ☎ 444 4840, ⓦ hoteledda.is. Long, modern, sharp-roofed affair in front of the more visible *Icelandair*, with bay windows in the lobby offering views seawards. Rooms are minimalist, with pine flooring, white walls and two-tone bedspreads; the cheaper cabins – actually self-contained chalets for two – feel a bit more welcoming. Breakfast 2280kr extra. Doubles **26,500kr**, cabins **23,300kr**

Icelandair Hotel Immediately behind the Edda (see above) ☎ 487 1480, ⓦ icelandairhotels.com. Brand-new, upmarket concrete-and-glass affair, whose neatly furnished en-suite doubles all have pine flooring and superb feature windows, some of them facing seawards. Breakfast 2280kr. **36,800kr**

★ **IYHA Vík** Suðurvíkurvegur 5 ☎ 487 1106, ⓦ hostel .is. North off the road and up near the church, this spotless

hostel makes a relaxing base for exploring Vík and the nearby coast, with friendly, helpful and organized staff, wonderful views seawards and a modern kitchen. It's almost always full, so book well in advance. **4550kr**

Vík Vikurbraut 26 ☎ 487 1212, ⓦ vikhotel.is. Vík's original hotel, now freshly modernized, has the atmosphere of a homestay. There are two buildings: the inn-like main house has the better-equipped rooms with en-suite doubles, while cheaper rooms are available in the adjacent tin-sided "hostel" with shared bathrooms and self-catering facilities. Main house doubles **28,000kr**; hostel doubles **19,000kr**

★ **Þakgil** About a 30min drive from Vík, turning inland 5km east of Vík at Höfðabrekka and following the rough, twisting gravel Route 214 for 17km ☎ 893 4889, ⓦ thakgil.is. Isolated cul-de-sac of a valley with an exceptional campsite and self-contained cabins with bunks sleeping up to four. There's also a communal dining area inside a large cave, and great hiking trails in the area. Contact in advance to check on access conditions. June–Aug. Camping **1500kr**, cabins **22,000kr**

EATING

Halldórskaffi Víkurbraut ☎ 487 1202. Popular place for a hot drink or light meal inside the snug old wooden building,

Brydebúð (see above). All the usual choices, but most people come for their superb pizzas: a 12" seafood special with

2

shrimps, mussels and tuna costs 2800kr. You can't book, so get here early or be prepared to wait. Daily 11am–8pm.

Strondin Austurvegur 18 ☎487 1230. Lively bistro behind the N1 roadhouse, with sea views and an outdoor terrace. Steer clear of the inevitable fast-food options (or, if you do want them, the N1 roadhouse is cheaper); instead, try chicken pasta with basil and tomatoes (2350kr), lamb stew (2100kr) or – for those without tastebuds – a platter of *hákarl* (fermented shark) with the essential *brennevin* chaser (2200kr). Daily 6–10pm.

Suður-Vík Suðurvíkurvegur 1, up towards the church and hostel ☎487 1515. Another nicely restored old wooden building serving as a café-restaurant. There's an eclectic menu – soup of the day (1300kr), satay pork and rice (2500kr) and pan-fried char (3600kr) – including 12″ pizzas from 1600kr. Daily noon–10pm.

SHOPPING

Víkurprjón Next to the N1 fuel station on the Ringroad. Barn-like outlet for Vík's own wool factory: downstairs has all the designer woolwear, blankets, felt hats and outright tourist tat; upstairs is a collection of less fashionable outdoor wear – fleeces, raincoats, heavy-duty woollen jumpers – at surprisingly reasonable prices. Daily 7.30am–10.30pm.

The Westman Islands

The **Westman Islands** – Vestmannaeyjar – are an archipelago of fifteen or so scattered, mostly minuscule volcanic islands around 10km off the coast south of Hvolsvöllur. The only inhabited one in the group, **Heimaey**, is an easy trip from the mainland on the frequent ferries, and there are two immediate draws: **Eldfell** volcano, still steaming from its 1973 eruption, an event that doubled the width of the island and almost swallowed Heimaey town; and the sadly reduced numbers of seabirds and **puffins** (see box, p.142). You can pack everything the island has to offer into a couple of days, though many visitors simply take a **day-trip** from the mainland, arriving late morning on the first ferry and departing in the evening.

Heimaey aside, the other Westmans are difficult to land on and so only infrequently visited, but you may be very lucky and score a rare trip around **Surtsey**, the group's southernmost outpost and newest island, which sprang from beneath the waves during the 1960s.

Brief history

Geological babies at only 12,000 years old overall, the Westman Islands played a part in the tale of Iceland's official first settlers, Ingólfur Arnarson and his foster-brother Hjörleifur Hróðmarsson. The brothers had British slaves with them who, coming from the lands at the west of the Viking world, were known as **Westmen**; Hjörleifur's slaves rebelled, killing him and fleeing to these islands – hence the name.

The Westmans lay more or less outside the mainstream of Icelandic history until **Algerian pirates** raided Heimaey on July 16, 1627, killing or enslaving several hundred people. It took some time to get over this disaster, but by the twentieth century mechanization and the country's economic shift from farming to fishing saw Heimaey becoming a prosperous little haven, well positioned for taking advantage of the North Atlantic's richest cod and haddock grounds.

Fresh problems lay ahead, however. On January 23, 1973, a 2km-long **volcanic fissure** suddenly opened up eastern Heimaey. Within 24 hours the island had been evacuated and the new volcano, **Eldfell**, was gushing lava in violent spasms; houses were buried beneath the flow or simply collapsed under the weight of accompanying ash. Worse still, the lava threatened to block the harbour mouth until halted by the novel method of pumping sea water onto the front of the flow. When the eruption ceased in June, Heimaey was two square kilometres bigger, had a new mountain and, amazingly, a better harbour – the entrance is narrower now, but more effectively shielded from prevailing easterly winds. Only one person was killed during the eruption.

ARRIVAL AND DEPARTURE   **THE WESTMAN ISLANDS**

The main **port** and **airstrip** for the Westman Islands are at Landeyjahöfn, 15km south off the Ringroad at Seljalandsfoss via Route 254.

By plane You can fly to Heimaey, though weather frequently cancels or delays services. Atlantsflug (☎854 4150, ⓦflightseeing.is) flies from tiny Bakki airstrip at Landeyjahöfn by arrangement (10min; 15,265kr return), while Eagle Air (☎562 2640, ⓦeagleair.is) departs Reykjavík City airport (2 daily; 25min; 19,000kr each way, substantial online discounts available).

By bus Strætó bus #52 runs from the Mjódd terminal in Reykjavík to the Landeyjahöfn ferry terminal via Ringroad towns; the first service originates at BSÍ before heading to Mjódd. Note that if the ferry is cancelled or diverts to Þorlákshöfn

near Hveragerði (see p.110), buses terminate at Hvolsvöllur.

Destinations Hella (2–3 daily; 45min); Hveragerði (2–3 daily; 1hr 35min); Hvolsvöllur (2–3 daily; 30min); Reykjavík (2–3 daily; 2hr 10min); Selfoss (2–3 daily; 1hr 15min).

By ferry The *Herjólfur* car and passenger ferry (☎482 2800, ⓦherjolfur.is) departs from Landeyjahöfn (3–5 daily; 30min; pedestrians 1260kr each way; cars 2660kr plus 1260kr/person). In rough weather ferries might use the old port at Þorlákshöfn near Hveragerði (see p.110), in which case the crossing takes 3hr and there are only two services daily.

2

Heimaey

By far the largest of the Westman Islands, **Heimaey** – Home Island – is only around 6km in length. At its broad top end you'll find **Heimaey town** and the harbour faced by a narrow peninsula of sheer-sided cliffs; east of here, buildings are hemmed in by Eldfell, the fractionally higher slopes of Helgafell, and the rough, grey-brown solidified lavafield, **Kirkjubæjarhraun**, under which a third of the original town vanished in 1973. Moving south, you pass the cross-shaped airstrip, beyond which the island tapers to a narrow isthmus, over which the rounded, grassy hummock of **Stórhöfði** rises as an end point – one of the best places on Heimaey to watch birds.

Heimaey town

HEIMAEY TOWN is an attractive place, quiet and low-key, with puffin-themed signposts directing you towards key sights. The small centre is split by the south-running main street, **Heiðarvegur**, with most services and attractions in the streets east of here between the harbour and Hásteinsvegur. Down at the **harbour**, you'll find a tightly packed fleet of fishing boats, several warehouses processing their catches, and yards piled with kilometres of black and green fishing nets being examined and repaired.

Aquarium and Natural History Museum
Heiðarvegur 12 • May–Sept daily 10am–5pm; Oct–April Sat 1–4pm • 1000kr • ⓦsaeheimar.is

Heimaey's **Aquarium and Natural History Museum** (Sæheimar) is in three parts. Most interesting is the aquarium itself, full of tanks of live fish and some enormous crabs;

SURTSEY

On November 14, 1963, a colossal explosion in the sea 15km southwest of Heimaey, accompanied by towering plumes of steam and ash, heralded the birth of **Surtsey**. Within a week, there was a volcano rising 70m out of the sea; April 1964 saw lava appear for the first time; and when the eruption finished three years later, what was suddenly the Westmans' second-largest island covered almost three square kilometres. Erosion has since shrunk it by half, but Surtsey remains of great interest to scientists, who are using it as a model to study how islands are colonized by plants and animals.

As it's a special reserve, **landing on Surtsey** is prohibited unless you're part of a scientific team. Your only chance of a trip over is with Viking Tours (see p.142), which makes four- to six-hour circuits from Heimaey once or twice each summer, if they get enough people interested and the weather's suitable – you'll get a good look but they don't land.

2

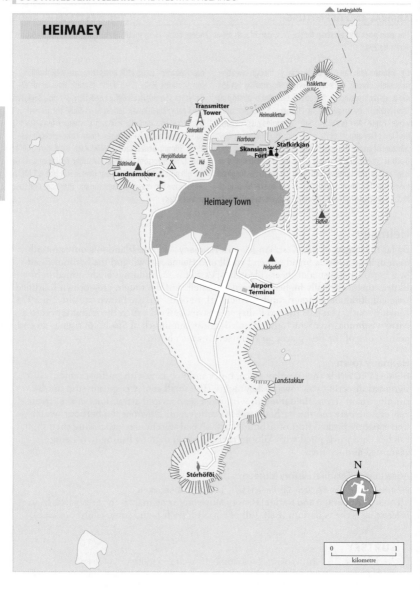

check out the endearingly ugly lumpfish, an important part of the local fishing industry. The remaining sections of the museum are more humdrum: glass cases of stuffed birds, including almost every species that breeds in Iceland, and a similarly thorough display of rocks from all over the country. Ask whether they have any orphaned seabirds that you can handle; there's currently a **tame puffin** and guillemot living at the museum.

Skansinn

Strandvegur

East of the harbour along Strandvegur, the road crosses the edge of Eldfell's 1973 flow and passes the neat lava-block walls of **Skansinn fort**. Only chest-high, this wall is pretty much a token defence, built by English pirates in the thirteenth century and revived after the pirate raid to house Iceland's first and only army. This wasn't the sole occasion that pirates took advantage of the Westmans' isolation: a sixteenth-century rover named Gentleman John once stole Heimaey's church bell.

2

Stafkirkjan

Strandvegur • June–Aug daily 10am–4pm • Free

Just across from Skansinn, the extraordinary **Stafkirkjan** is a Viking-era-style wooden church with a steep, black shingle roof, consecrated in 2000 to celebrate a thousand years of Christianity in Iceland. The building faces the presumed site of the country's first purpose-built church, raised by Gizur the White a few years before he championed the new faith at the Alþing in 1000 AD.

Kirkjubæjarhraun

South of the harbour, you can follow first Kirkjuvegur and then Heimagata and Helgafellsbraut below the two-storey-high, steeply sloping **Kirkjubæjarhraun lava flow** that swallowed up the eastern end of town. Steps from Heimagata take you up on top of the lava, though it's hard to imagine this huge mass of sharp-sided, weirdly shaped rubble moving at all, let alone flowing. Signs map out the original street plan 16m underfoot, while engraved headstones and collections of little stones painted with windows and doors mark where somebody's home lies buried.

Eldheimar

Helgafellsbraut • Daily 11am–6pm • 2600kr including audioguide • ☎ 488 2000, ⦿ eldheimar.is

This modern **museum**, covered in rusting iron cladding, makes an emotive monument to all the islanders who lived through the 1973 eruption. The centrepiece is the surviving lower storey of a **house**, recently excavated and left exactly as it was found: walls buckled by the weight of the ash; the kitchen with unfinished washing-up; glass light fittings dangling from the ceiling; a cracked ornamental plate among the rubble. Photos and footage in the rest of the museum document the awful night when Heimaey's inhabitants were turfed from their beds, crammed into emergency vessels clutching their pets and trinkets, and evacuated to the mainland. Many were so traumatized that they never returned.

Landakirkja

Kirkjuvegur

For a final idea of just what Heimaey's population went through in 1973, follow Kirkjuvegur south from the harbour to black-roofed **Landakirkja**, the island's main

---

WHEN TO VISIT HEIMAEY

If possible, pick a sunny couple of days between May and September to **visit Heimaey**, allowing time for walks, close contact with puffins and thirty other breeding bird species, plus the chance to see whales, orca and seals. If you want to party, join in the August Bank Holiday Weekend **Þjódhátíð**, a festival to commemorate Iceland's first steps towards full independence in 1874, which involves bands, fireworks, a huge bonfire and three days of hard drinking with thousands of other revellers. All accommodation and transport to the island gets booked long in advance.

As to the Westmans' **weather**, temperatures are among the mildest in Iceland, but things can get extremely blustery – the country's highest windspeed, 220km an hour, was recorded here.

2

HEIMAEY'S PUFFINS

Puffins – *lundi* in Icelandic – are, without doubt, the most charismatic of Iceland's seabirds, plump little auks with an upright build and pied plumage, all set off by bright orange feet and a ridiculous sail-shaped bill striped yellow and red. This comical livery is compounded by an aeronautic ineptitude: their method of landing seems to consist simply of putting out their feet and stopping flying – bad enough to watch on water, but painful to see them bounce and skid on land. Puffins also seem to get victimized by just about every other seabird species: when feeding young, they fly back from fishing with their catch carried crosswise in the beak like a moustache, a clear signal for gulls, skuas and even razorbills to chase them, hoping they'll drop their chick's meal.

Until very recently, some two million puffins bred on Heimaey each year, excavating their burrows and raising their chicks – **pufflings** – in huge, dense colonies on the island's grassy cliffs. Each August, all the adult birds depart Heimaey at the same time, and hunger draws the pufflings out for their first flight. Many then become confused by the town's bright lights and fly, dazzled, into buildings; local cats get fat on this easy prey, but residents round up birds and release them.

However, since 2005 the **puffin population** on Heimaey – in common with all colonies across the rest of Europe – has gone into serious decline, most likely because warming sea water has driven away the **sand eels** (herring fry) on which they feed. In some years adults have abandoned the young too early, while in others they haven't even hatched their eggs. For the time being you can still see plenty of puffins here, but unless the situation changes it's likely that they might have almost vanished from Iceland within the next decade.

church. Enter the cemetery opposite through its arched, wrought-iron gates and on the left you'll find the grave of Theódóra Jónsdóttir, whose 2m-high memorial is topped by a statuette of an angel, missing a hand. Ash buried this to the angel's thighs; it took Heimaey's residents over a year after the eruption to dig their town out of the black drifts.

ARRIVAL AND DEPARTURE   HEIMAEY TOWN

By plane The airport is a couple of kilometres south of town; a bus or taxi meets all flights.
Destinations Reykjavík (2 daily; 25min).
By ferry The ferry terminal is at the north end of

Heiðravegur. Ferries usually run to Landeyjahöfn, though in rough weather they might be diverted to Þorlakshöfn.
Destinations Landeyjahöfn (3–5 daily; 30min); Þorlakshöfn (2 daily in rough weather only; 2hr 45min).

INFORMATION AND TOURS

Tourist information There's a friendly but somewhat clueless information office (Mon–Fri 9am–6pm, Sat 10am–4pm, Sun 1–4pm; ⓦ visitwestmanislands.com) east of the port at the corner of Strandvegur and Bárustígur, with brochures, souvenirs and a small café. The website is useful.
Tours Viking Tours (cnr Strandvegur and Heiðarvegur; ☏ 488 4884, ⓦ vikingtours.is) organizes popular daily boat trips around the island (5900kr), with the chance to see whales, birds, orca and seals; they also offer on-demand whale-watching tours, deep-sea fishing and trips to Surtsey (13,900kr). Ribsafari (☏ 661 1810, ⓦ ribsafari.is)

does similar round-island speedboat trips (11,500kr), as well as Surtsey (16,500kr). All are weather-dependent.
Services Banks with ATMs are at the eastern side of town, on or near Vestmannabraut. There are two supermarkets: Vöruval, which looks like a domed tent, on Vesturvegur (Mon–Fri 7.30am–9pm, Sat 10am–9pm, Sun 11am–9pm); and the slightly better-stocked Krónan over on Strandvegur (Mon–Fri 11am–7pm, Sat & Sun 11am–6pm). The large, indoor saltwater pool is a 15min walk southwest of the centre off Illugata (Mon–Fri 6.30am–9pm, Sat & Sun 9am–6pm).

ACCOMMODATION

With tourism to Heimaey booming through the summer, accommodation can be packed; always **book ahead**. You'll be very lucky to find a room for the Þjóðhátíð festival – all are reserved up to a year in advance – so plan to camp.

Árný Illugata 7 ☏ 481 2082, ⓦ arny.is. Charming guesthouse a few minutes' walk west of the centre, with

clean rooms ranging from five-person family rooms to doubles and decent-sized suites. Facilities are shared.

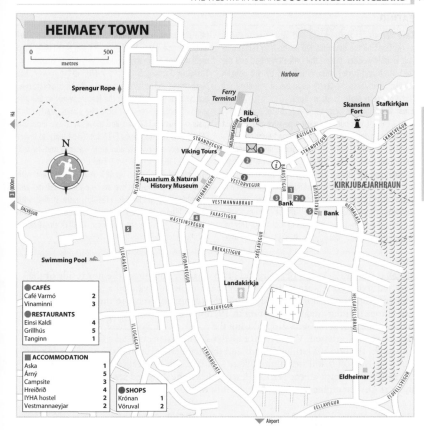

There's a glassed-in terrace, and you're just a short walk from the pool. **15,200kr**

Aska Bárustigur ☏ 662 7266, ⓦ askahostel.is. Bright and helpful hostel with pine-and-slate decor right in the centre of town, sleeping 31 people in dorms, doubles and family rooms. There's a laundry and shared bathrooms, though the "kitchen" is pretty notional. Breakfast 1300kr. Dorms **5900kr**, doubles **14,900kr**

★**Campsite** 1km west of town at Herjólfsdalur ☏ 846 9111. Dramatically located, inside the open bowl of a long-extinct volcano – you'll be lulled to sleep by the mutterings of thousands of fulmars roosting above you. There are showers, toilets, laundry, a shelter-shed for cooking and a BBQ area. Come a few days early for the Aug festivities to find a pitch. **1300kr**

★**Hreiðrið** Cnr Faxastígur and Heiðarvegur ☏ 481 1045, ⓦ tourist.eyjar.is. This long-running budget favourite is the pick of the island's guesthouses, with the friendly, informed owner offering pleasant themed rooms in a family home; it's really self-catering but breakfast can be arranged (1600kr). They won't put strangers together in a double room, and they offer expert hiking info for the island's trickier trails. Shared bathrooms. Doubles **12,500kr**, sleeping bags **4300kr**

IYHA Hostel Vestmannabraut 28 ☏ 481 2900, ⓦ hotelvestmannaeyjar.is. Two-storey affair right behind the *Vestmannaeyjar* (which is where you check in), with plainly furnished doubles and slightly cramped dorms, all with shared bathrooms. The kitchen is very small, but well equipped with fridge, stove and all manner of crockery. Dorms **5000kr**, doubles **11,200kr**

Vestmannaeyjar Vestmannabraut 28 ☏ 481 2900, ⓦ hotelvestmannaeyjar.is. The town's sole real hotel is comfortable, modern and welcoming after a recent facelift; the priciest rooms have got polished wooden floors, leather lounges and a trendy monochrome colour scheme, and you get access to the new hot tub. Good buffet breakfast included. **21,900kr**

EATING

Café Varmó Cnr Herjolfsgata and Strandvegur ☎481 1674. Don't be too downhearted at the frilly tablecloths and wobbly wooden tables; the coffee's not bad and the thick lamb and barley soup with bread costs a bargain 1700kr. Their cakes are pretty good too, if you like thick layers of cream. Mon–Fri 9am–6pm.

Einsi Kaldi In the *Vestmannaeyjar* hotel (see p.143) ☎481 2900. Easily both the most expensive and smartest restaurant in town, with coloured mood lighting and a vaguely volcanic theme to the decor. Recommended choices are the monkfish (3890kr), lamb fillet with thyme (5200kr) and the lobster tails (6190kr). The conscience-impaired could sample their smoked puffin, guillemot and gannet plate (2590kr). Daily 11am–2pm and 5–9pm.

Grillhús Vestmannabraut, across from the *Vestmannaeyjar* hotel (see p.143) ☎482 1000. Tidy red timber diner which does what it says: T-bone steak (4990kr), lobster burgers (2690kr), fish and chips (2190kr) and, of course, pizza. Hard to resist the scent of barbecued meat wafting out in the evening. Daily 11am–10pm.

Tanginn Tangagata ☎414 4420, ⊕tanginn.is. The black ceiling and heavy furniture are all a bit corporate chic, but harbour views through the feature windows and the smell of cooking seafood should lure you in. Start with a plate of mussels (1750kr) and move on to the monkfish (3290kr) or cod and chips (3190kr). Good place to linger over a beer afterwards and stare vacantly out to sea. Mon–Fri 11am–11pm, Sat & Sun 11am–1am.

Vinaminni Barustígur ☎481 2424. Large café with good coffee and just above average meals: salmon and scrambled egg sandwiches (1250kr), pitta stuffed with various fillings (1900kr) and the inevitable pizzas and burgers – which are not bad (from 1700kr). Occasionally gets live bands in. Daily 10am–10pm.

Eldfell

Eldfell is the easiest climb of the island's two adjacent volcanoes: the north side of the dark red scoria cone was washed away by the outflowing lava, and a path leads up the remains from the road to the west – allow thirty minutes to get to the top. One of the first things islanders did on returning in 1973 was to start turfing Eldfell's slopes to stabilize the ash; aerial seed drops during the 1990s also helped, and today about half the cone is well grassed. Views from Eldfell's 205m eastern rim take in the lava flow to the north, the other Westman islands and the mainland's southwestern coast and crisp ice caps. The soil is still steaming up here – in fact, 1m down it's over 500°C. The intrepid can attempt a near-vertical descent down the dark-red scree of the volcano's inner slopes, emerging on the road back into town.

HEIMAEY'S COASTAL TRAILS

Due to the airstrip running over the eastern cliffs, it's not possible to circuit Heimaey completely, though that still leaves you with a decent 12km of **coastal trails** to follow. A clear 6km path heads down the west coast from the golf course, a pleasant couple of hours following the crumbly clifftops south. The little beach at the end is good for ducks and waders, then it's a steep, short climb up grassy **Stórhöfði**, its top capped by a transmitter tower. There's a viewing platform on the northwestern side for watching bird activity, while the south cliffs house a sizeable **puffin colony** and are a good spot to scan the seas for whales and gannets, the latter nesting on the sheer-sided islets to the southwest.

From Stórhöfði, carry on up Heimaey's **east coast** to a steeper, rockier and weedier beach, often with some serious surf – this side of the island catches the prevailing winds – and occasional **seals** dodging in and out of the swell. Tidal pools and a couple of interesting caves might slow you down for a while – if you can get to them – else climb the messy scree behind up onto a ridge and follow this north until it reaches a fence line. A stile here gives access to the high, stumpy **Landstakkur** peninsula, complete with another puffin colony and scenic views. Continuing up the coast, you stay high above the sea with a dramatic drop into the deep blue on one side, and a gentle, grassy backslope on the other. Another stiff stretch uphill and you're at a **beacon** above the airstrip, from where you'll have to cut west across country to the road and so back up to town.

Helgafell

Immediately southwest of Eldfell, **Helgafell** looks similar but is a bit taller (226m) and some five thousand years older. The north and southwest faces present the swiftest routes to the summit, which was used as a lookout post during Heimaey's pirate period; today the crater is almost filled in, a shallow, sterile depression.

Herjólfsdalur

Open access

A kilometre west of town is **Herjólfsdalur**, a dramatically scaled bowl formed from a long-dead, partially collapsed volcano. The setting for the August festival and for the island's **golf course**, it is also home to the remains of **Landnámsbær**, Iceland's oldest known settlement. While only traces of the original buildings survive at the edge of the golf course, you can see from the nearby timber, lava-block and turf **reconstruction** what this Norse-style longhouse looked like, with separate kitchen area, pigsty and outhouses. Carbon dating places parts of Landnámsbær in the seventh century, though Icelandic historical records say that the farm was founded two hundred years later. Either way, it was abandoned around 1100, perhaps due to overgrazing on the island.

The path up Herjólfsdalur's grassy crater slope looks much steeper than it is, and once at the top you'll find yourself on a narrow rim, with a drop down the far side straight into the sea. The peak to the west is Blátindur (273m), scaled by a slippery path, while east is a tricky goat-track along the rim to Há – tackling either is not recommended.

Há

The easiest ascent of **Há** starts from the western side of Heimaey's town harbour on Hliðarvegur, where there's a rope dangling down the rocks for practising **sprengur**, the traditional method for collecting puffins and birds' eggs. Free beginners' sessions are held here in July (ask at the tourist office when to turn up). Walk up the steep grassy hillside behind and you're on Há, from where you can peer down into Herjólfsdalur, or walk north along the rim to opposite the transmitter tower atop **Stóraklif**.

The west coast

SNÆFELLSNES PENINSULA CLIFFS

The west coast

The panorama of the bay of Faxa Fiord is magnificent – with a width of fifty miles from horn to horn, the one running down into a rocky ridge of pumice, the other towering to the height of five thousand feet in a pyramid of eternal snow, while round the intervening semicircle crowd the peaks of a hundred noble mountains.

Letters from High Latitudes, Lord Dufferin

Reykjavík and the Reykjanes peninsula together form the southern edge of Faxaflói, the sweeping bay that dominates Iceland's west coast and any journey north of the capital – the Ringroad clings to its shores as far as the small commercial centre of Borgarnes before striking off inland on its way towards Brú and the north coast. Although the scenery is not Iceland's most dramatic, it provides visitors travelling clockwise around the country with their first taste of small-town Iceland and as such makes a satisfying introduction to the rest of the country. In summer the views of flower meadows dotted with isolated farms sheltering at the foot of cloud-topped mountains are picture-postcard pretty.

Travelling north, the first town you come to is ugly **Akranes**. With its concrete factory and fish-processing plants, it's certainly no beauty, but its museum quarter can make an interesting diversion on the way to **Borgarnes**. Besides having an excellent museum, the town serves as a jumping-off point not only for tours inside Iceland's second-largest glacier, Langjökull, and the country's biggest hot spring, **Deildartunguhver**, both near **Húsafell**, but also the historical riches of **Reykholt**, the setting for **Egill's Saga** and home to the only saga writer known by name, the thirteenth-century politician **Snorri Sturluson**.

The "pyramid of eternal snow" which Dufferin referred to when he sailed his yacht *Foam* to Iceland in 1856 was the glacier, **Snæfellsjökull**, which sits majestically on top of a dormant volcano at the tip of **Snæfellsnes**, a long arm of volcanic and mountainous land jutting out into the sea, which is the highlight of any trip up the west coast. Divided by a jagged mountain ridge, the peninsula not only marks the northern edge of Faxaflói bay but also the southern reaches of the more sheltered **Breiðafjörður**, with its hundreds of islands and skerries, over which lie the table mountains of the West Fjords. On a clear day the snowcap is clearly visible across the water from both Reykjavík and the West Fjords. A gem of a place on the peninsula's north coast, **Stykkishólmur** is not only the main town hereabouts but also one of Iceland's most attractive, with its brightly painted wooden houses nestling by a vibrant

SNÆFELLSJÖKULL FROM ARNARSTAPI

Highlights

❶ Deildartunguhver hot spring, Reykholt
Witness the power of Iceland's geothermal activity at the country's biggest natural hot spring. **See p.159**

❷ Langjökull glacier Take a glacier jeep ride up onto the glacier before walking inside the glacier itself through a network of tunnels – a truly unique experience. **See p.160**

❸ Kaldidalur valley An excellent taster of Iceland's remote landscapes of glaciers and grey-sand deserts. **See p.163**

❹ Eiríksstaðir, Haukadalur valley Stand on the spot from which the Vikings set out to discover Greenland and North America. **See p.165**

❺ Stykkishólmur, Snæfellsnes peninsula The west coast's prettiest town, with a mêlée of brightly coloured wooden houses set against an island-studded coastline. **See p.170**

❻ Flatey, Breiðafjörður A night spent in the hotel on this idyllic farming island is the perfect escape from the beaten track. **See p.176**

HIGHLIGHTS ARE MARKED ON THE MAP ON P.150

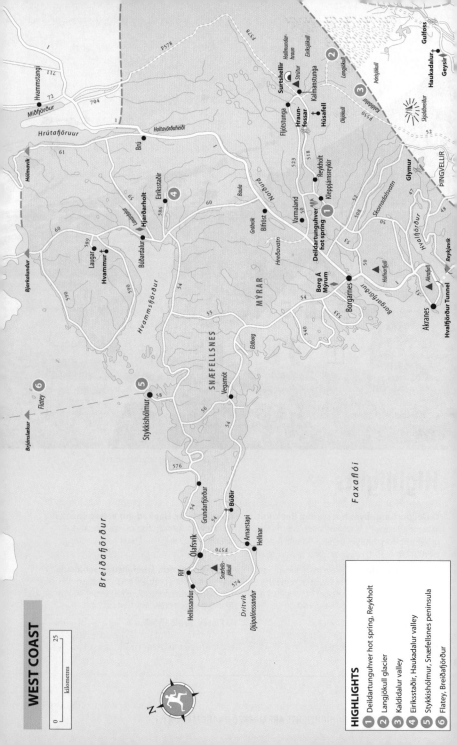

WEST COAST

0   25

kilometres

Faxaflói

Breiðafjörður

SNÆFELLSNES

MÝRAR

Hvammsfjörður

Hrútafjörður

Holtavörðuheiði

HIGHLIGHTS

1. Deildartunguhver hot spring, Reykholt
2. Langjökull glacier
3. Kaldidalur valley
4. Eiríksstaðir, Haukadalur valley
5. Stykkishólmur, Snæfellsnes peninsula
6. Flatey, Breiðafjörður

Hvammstangi
Miðfjörður
Hólmavík
Bjarnarlundur
Bjálfslækur
Flatey ⑥
Stykkishólmur ⑤
Grundarfjörður
Ólafsvík
Rif
Hellissandur
Snæfellsjökull
Dritvík
Djúpalónssandur
Hellnar
Arnarstapi
Búðir
Vegamót
Eldborg
Borg á Mýrum
Borgarnes
Akranes
Hvalfjörður Tunnel
Akrafjall
Hafnarfjall
Hvalfjörður
Reykjavík
Skorradalsvatn
Glymur
ÞINGVELLIR
Gulfoss
Geysir
Haukadalur
Þórisjökull
Langjökull
Eiríksjökull
Hallmundarhraun
Surtshellir
Strútur
Kalmanstunga
Fljótstunga
Húsafell
Hraunfossar
Reykholt
Kleppjárnsreykir
Deildartunguhver hot spring ①
Varmaland
Hreðavatn
Grábrók
Bifröst
Baula
Norðurá
Eiríksstaðir ④
Hjarðarholt
Búðardalur
Laugar
Hvammur
Brú
② ③
N

harbour busy with chugging fishing vessels. It's from here that the ferry sails for the pastoral delights of **Flatey**, the largest island in Breiðafjörður. From **Arnarstapi** on the peninsula's southern coast it's possible to take a snowmobile up onto Snæfellsjökull for some of the most exhilarating driving – and vistas – you'll ever experience. For splendid isolation, nearby **Búðir** can't be beaten, its wide sandy bay home only to an unusually charismatic hotel complete with creaking floorboards and ocean views. Occupying a sheltered spot in the neck of land which links the West Fjords with the rest of the country, **Laugar** in Sælingsdalur has some hot springs and a few cultural diversions, and makes a good place to break the long journey from Reykjavík to the West Fjords.

What the west coast may lack in scenic splendour, it makes up for in historical and cultural significance – landscapes here are steeped in the drama of the sagas. Close to **Búðardalur**, to the north of Snæfellsnes along Route 586, Haukadalur valley was the starting point for **Viking** expansion westwards, which took explorers first to Greenland and later to the shores of North America as heroically recounted in the **Saga of Eirík the Red**. He and his wife lived at **Eiríksstaðir** and, having been outlawed from Iceland, together they pioneered the settlement of Greenland. It's also thought that **Leifur Eiríksson**, the first European to set foot in North America, was born on a farm that has now been expertly reconstructed on the original site. More saga history can be found in Laxárdalur valley, northeast of Búðardalur, where characters from the **Laxdæla Saga** lived out their feud-torn lives.

3

GETTING AROUND   **THE WEST COAST**

By bus The Ringroad (Route 1) cuts right through the region to Brú, covered year-round by Reykjavík–Akureyri buses via Borgarnes. From Borgarnes, Route 54 and more year-round buses head northwest to Snæfellsnes, while for the Búðardalur area you need to turn north off the Ringroad up Route 60 at Bifröst, a route served by buses (all year) heading for Hólmavík in the West Fjords, where connections are available for Ísafjörður (summer only). Note that despite the growing importance of Húsafell (see p.157) as an activities hub, it is not served by buses.

By ferry In some ways it's worth seeing the west coast as a stepping stone to the West Fjords: another point of entry is the regular ferry from Stykkishólmur on Snæfellsnes to Brjánslækur, from where there are bus connections to other West Fjord locations; the Búðardalur bus presses on to Hólmavík in the West Fjords, though you can only travel northeast of here in your own vehicle.

Hvalfjörður

Once beyond Reykjavík and its adjacent overspill town, Mosfellsbær, the Ringroad weaves northwards around the towering form of Mount Esja to **Hvalfjörður** (whale fjord), the biggest in southwest Iceland, named after the large number of whales seen here by the original settlers. During World War II, the fjord's deep anchorages made it one of the most important bases in the North Atlantic, when British and American naval vessels were stationed here, providing a port and safe haven for supply ships travelling between Europe and North America. As the fjord kinks some 30km inland, however, it was something of an obstacle to road travel, until the opening of an impressive 6km submarine **tunnel** in 1998. It was completed despite concerns from the people of Akranes that the shorter distance to the capital (49km through the tunnel compared with a massive 108km round the fjord) would kill off their local shops and services – fortunately their fears have proved unfounded. Twenty-four-hour **tollbooths** are in place at both ends charging 1000kr per car, which is well worth it to save a tedious detour.

Akranes

Just beyond the exit from the Hvalfjörður tunnel, Route 51 strikes off west from the Ringroad for **AKRANES**, the west coast's biggest town with a population of 6700.

Fishing and fish processing account for roughly half the town's income, and there's a busy, commercial air to the place. Akranes is also renowned for its **sporting** prowess – the local football team, Íþróttabandalag Akraness (ÍA), are frequent national champions – and its two sports halls, swimming pools and soccer stadium are of a correspondingly high standard. Yet Akranes is hard to like: it's gritty, entirely without architectural charm and can be a terribly cold spot even in summer, as icy winds straight off the sea howl round street corners sending the hardiest locals scurrying for cover. However, it's a good base from which to do some decent hikes around the heights of easterly Mount Akrafjall or, when the sun is shining, to explore the long sandy beach, **Langisandur**, a fifteen-minute walk from the town centre. Once you've exhausted the beach and the harbour area with the town's lighthouse just beyond, it's best to press on to the **Museum Centre**, where you can get to grips with the history of the 1970s Cod Wars and admire some of Iceland's sporting heroes.

3 Akranesviti

Breiðargata • June–Aug daily 10am–4pm • Free

At the foot of Breiðargata, a ten-minute walk west from what passes as the main square, Akratorg, **Akranes lighthouse** is arguably the most interesting of the town's offerings to visitors. It was built at the end of World War II and still functions today, though it's only recently been opened to the public. A series of 76 steps will take you up to a viewing platform at the top of the 20m-tall structure from where there are panoramic views over the town and back across the bay towards Reykjavík; the lighthouse sits at the exposed, seaward point of the narrow spit of land which is home to central Akranes. Unusually, the interior of the lighthouse is given over to art exhibitions which spread across the five floors the staircase winds its way up through. Concerts have even been held in the lighthouse, using the structure's acoustics to impressive effect.

Langisandur

Behind the sports centre complex off Garðabraut

The 1km stretch of sandy beach known as **Langisandur** is a must when the sun is shining, since the southern aspect of the shore will do wonders for your tan. Bear in mind, though, that although the water can look tempting on a sunny day, it fails the big-toe test by a long way; it's barely 5°C warm at the height of summer.

Museum Centre

Garðar • June–Aug daily 10am–5pm; Sept–May Mon–Fri 1–5pm • 500kr • Ⓦ museum.is

Unusually for a provincial town, Akranes boasts three different museums, all set in the **Museum Centre** off Garðagrund, though only the folk museum will delay you more than a couple of minutes. **Outdoor exhibits** include several antique buildings; a granite monument inscribed in Gaelic and Icelandic commemorating the Irish role in Akranes' history; and the **twin-masted ketch** *Sigurfari*, built on Britain's River Humber in 1885, which carries the honour of having been the last sailing ship in the Icelandic fleet before being sold to the Faroe Islands where, remarkably, it fished until 1970.

Akranes Folk Museum

Indoors, the **Akranes folk museum** is housed in the building between the granite monument and the *Sigurfari*. The most interesting exhibits are the hook-shaped cutters that were used to sever the nets of British trawlers during the Cod Wars of 1972 and 1975. Though quite ordinary to look at, they proved devastatingly effective when dragged across British trawler wires by the Icelandic coastguard.

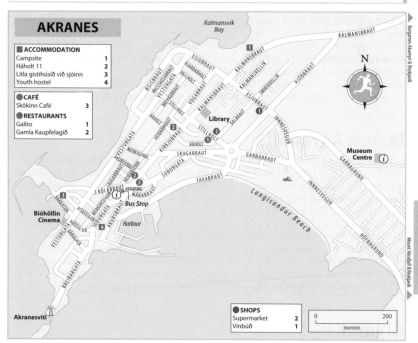

AKRANES

■ ACCOMMODATION	
Campsite	1
Háholt 11	2
Litla gistihúsið við sjóinn	3
Youth hostel	4

● CAFÉ	
Skökinn Café	3

● RESTAURANTS	
Galito	1
Gamla Kaupfelagið	2

● SHOPS	
Supermarket	2
Vínbúð	1

ARRIVAL AND INFORMATION

By bus Buses from Reykjavík arrive and depart from outside Ráðhúsið in Akratorg.

Destinations Reykjavík (Mon–Fri 7 daily, Sat 4 daily, Sun 3 daily; 1hr 15min).

Tourist information There's an office in the main square at Suðurgata 57 (May Mon–Fri 10am–4pm; June–Sept Mon–Fri 10am–4pm, Sat 10am–4pm, Sun noon–4pm; ☎ 433 1065, ⓦ visitakranes.is).

Services There's internet access at the library at Dalbraut 1

AKRANES

(May–Sept Mon–Fri 10am–6pm; Oct–April Mon–Fri 10am–6pm, Sat 11am–2pm). The swimming pool (Mon–Fri 6.15am–9pm, Sat & Sun 9am–6pm; ☎ 433 1100) and sports centre are off Garðabraut at Jaðarsbakkar; the pool's changing rooms have a steam room, and there's an outdoor pool and four hot pots. The supermarket (daily 10am–8pm) is adjacent to the library at Dalbraut 1. The *vínbúð* is located at Þjóðbraut 13 (Mon–Thurs noon–6pm, Fri 11am–7pm, Sat 11am–2pm).

ACCOMMODATION

Campsite Kalmansvík ☎ 894 2500. Located in Kalmansvík bay on the outskirts of town, about 10min from the centre beside Route 509 to Borgarnes, the campsite looks out over the sea and makes a great spot for birdwatching. April–Sept. **750kr**

Háholt 11 Háholt 11 ☎ 431 1408, ⓦ haholt11.com. A delightful homestay run by the endearing Ólína, who has limited English but is extremely friendly. Rooms are small, cosy and welcoming and share facilities. Free wi-fi is also available. Breakfast is 1500kr per person. **7000kr**

Litla gistihúsið við sjóinn Bakkatún 20 ☎ 695 6255,

ⓦ leopold.is/gisting. This winning guesthouse is right by the water and, on a clear day, enjoys uninterrupted views across the sea to Snæfellsnessjökull. The smart rooms are bright and unfussy, sharing bathrooms and a kitchen. **11,000kr**

Youth hostel Suðurgata 32 ☎ 868 3332, ⓦ hostel.is. Located in the town's grand old former pharmacy, the hostel has both private rooms and dorms with shared facilities, as well as two shared kitchens and a spacious lounge. Reception and check-in 8–10am & 5–10pm. Dorms **4550kr**, doubles **12,400kr**

EATING AND DRINKING

Galito Stillholt 16–18 ☎ 430 67675. Akranes's latest culinary offering has a choice of seafood dishes ranging

from salted cod to minke whale steaks, but also Kashmiri chicken, lamb kebab, burgers and pizzas. Count on 3490kr for a fish dish, 1690kr for a burger or around 2400kr for a pizza. Mon–Wed 11.30am–9pm, Thurs & Fri 11.30am–10pm, Sat noon–10pm, Sun 4–9pm.

Gamla Kaupfelagið Kirkjubraut 11 ☎ 431 4343. Decent Mexican food is the best bet at this established town centre bistro: chicken burritos and quesadillas are 1990kr, while burgers go for around 2290kr. Also serves up a range of salads from 1990kr and pasta dishes for 3190kr. Mon–Thurs 11.45am–9pm, Fri & Sat 11.45am–10pm, Sun 5–9pm.

Skökinn Café Kirkjubraut 2 ☎ 431 5100. The town's best café, located in the main square, serves a range of sandwiches and cakes and dishes up a lunch special 11.30am–2pm on weekdays for 1290kr. Mon–Wed, Sat & Sun 11am–6pm, Thurs & Fri 11am–10pm.

Mount Akrafjall

On approaching Akranes from the Ringroad you'll have driven by **Akrafjall** mountain; at 643m, it's 200m higher than Reykjavík's Mount Esja, and dominates the skyline east of town. The mountain offers one of the best panoramas in the west of Iceland, with spectacular **views** not only of Akranes but also, on a clear day, of Reykjavík. On a sunny day you'll find most of the town out here, either climbing the flat-topped mountain itself or picnicking in the lush meadows at its foot – during summer you'll also find copious numbers of **seabirds**, especially kittiwakes, nesting on Akrafjall's craggy sides. Of the mountain's two peaks, the southern one, **Háihnúkur** (555m), is easier to climb thanks to a well-defined **path** leading to the summit from the car park below. The higher northern peak, Geirmundartindur, is split from the other by a river valley, Berjadalur, through which most of Akranes' water supply flows.

Glymur

From Mount Akrafjall, Route 47 winds its way east around the northern shore of Hvalfjörður towards Iceland's highest waterfall, **Glymur**. The falls drop nearly 200m from the boggy ground to the west of **Hvalvatn** lake, but it can be difficult to find a vantage point from where to see the spectacle at its best. A rough **track** leads up through Botnsdalur valley at the head of Hvalfjörður towards the falls – allow about an hour from the road. Incidentally, according to Icelandic folklore, a mythical creature, half-man, half-whale, which once terrified locals from its home in the dark waters of Hvalfjörður, was tricked into swimming out of the fjord, up the river and the Glymur falls, before dying in the waters of Hvalvatn – where, oddly, whale bones have been found.

Borgarnes

North of Akranes, the Ringroad covers a lonely and exposed 38km before reaching **BORGARNES** which, despite comprising little more than a few streets filling a narrow, 1500m-long peninsula, is the principal town of the Borgarfjörður region. Home to barely two thousand people, Borgarnes not only enjoys a spectacular setting on a narrow neck of land stretching out into the fjord but also has excellent views inland to the glaciers of Eiríksjökull and Langjökull. Unlike most of Iceland's coastal settlements, Borgarnes isn't dependent on fishing – powerful tidal currents in the fjord have put paid to that – but is primarily a service centre for the surrounding dairy farmers who rely on the town's slaughterhouse and good roads for their livelihoods. Its main claim to fame is its historical association with the ninth-century settler, Skallagrímur Kveldúlfsson, father of the pirate, thug and poet **Egill Skallagrímsson**, hero of *Egill's Saga* (see box opposite). Their lives and times are explored in a first-rate **museum**, while plenty of Borgarnes' streets recall characters from the saga: Skallagrímsgata, Kveldúlfsgata, Böðvarsgata and Egilsgata, to name but a few.

EGILL'S SAGA

Few characters in literature have been as sharply drawn as the eponymous hero of **Egill's Saga**. The story tells the life of the sullen, brutish and ugly **Egill Skallagrímsson** (c.910–990), whose personality is glimpsed before he even appears in the tale, when both his grandfather and father are revealed as "shape-shifters", or werewolves. From his youth through to his dotage, Egill is depicted as relentlessly mean and trouble-making, though also industrious, clever and a gifted poet, and the final picture of him is of a remarkable and complex individual, who never seeks an easy path through life. The saga was probably written by the thirteenth-century politician **Snorri Sturluson**, and it's no coincidence that its central framework, that of a free man stubbornly defying the might of the Norwegian throne, mirrored the political situation in Iceland at the time of its composition, when Norway was attempting to annex the country.

Egill was born to Norwegian parents who had settled in Iceland to escape the wrath of their king, Harald Fairhair. The most telling event of his youth is when his father **Skallagrímur's** wolfish nature erupts during a ball game, and he tries to kill the 12-year-old. Egill's nurse saves him, but both she and Egill's best friend are killed by Skallagrímur, and Egill's revenge is to murder his father's favourite slave at dinner that night. A few months later, Egill makes the first of many **Viking expeditions**, meeting the man who is to become his arch-enemy: King **Eirik Bloodaxe** of Norway (c.895–954), Harald's son. Re-igniting the family feud, Egill falls out with the king and manages to humiliate him publicly, kill his son and survive an attempt by Queen Gunnhildur to poison him – all in one night. Having lost the respect of his subjects and been shamed out of Norway, King Eirik takes up residence across the North Sea in Viking Jórvík (York), only to receive an unexpected visitor – Egill has been shipwrecked on the Yorkshire coast and decides to settle up with his foe. Although condemned to death, he composes a poem in praise of the king and his life is spared.

After many successful years as a Viking, Egill returns to Iceland around 957 and settles down as a farmer. Then tragedy strikes: his **sons** Böðvar and Gunnar die in accidents and Egill is so distraught he decides to starve himself to death. But his daughter **Þorgerð** tricks him into drinking some milk and composing a **poem** – known as *Sonatorrek*, "Lament for my sons" – and he becomes so caught up in the work that his spirits revive.

According to the Saga Egill lived out his **final years** in Mosfell, just outside Reykjavík. There, taunted by servants as he sits blind and incontinent by the fire, he plans one last act of mischief: to take his hoard of Viking silver to the Alþing, and start a riot by scattering it among the crowds. Frustrated in this by his daughter-in-law, one night Egill vanishes along with his loot and two servants. He's found the next morning, stumbling blindly alone in the fields, and admits to having hidden his treasure and killed the men. He dies later that year, irascible to the last, and is eventually interred – as befits his violent, pagan life – at the boundary of Mosfell's churchyard.

Skallagrímsgarður

Borgarbraut • Open access • Free

The main drag, **Borgarbraut**, runs southwest down the peninsula from the highway to the sea. About halfway along is **Skallagrímsgarður**, a small but pleasant park at the junction with Skallagrímsgata. By the entrance on the left is the **burial mound** of one of Iceland's earliest settlers, **Skallagrímur Kveldúlfsson**, complete with horse, weapons and various other Viking accoutrements. Originally just plain Grímur, he obtained the first part of his name, Skalla ("bald"), because he lost all his hair at an early age. Skallagrímur's son, **Egill**, is portrayed on the accompanying monument carrying home the body of his own son, Böðvar, who drowned in the Hvítá River during a storm: it was in Böðvar's memory that Egill composed his great poem, *Sonatorrek* (see box above).

Landnámssetur Íslands

Brákarbraut 13–15 • Daily 10am–9pm • 1900kr per section, combined ticket 2500kr • ⑩ landnam.is

There are a couple of museums in Borganes, but by far the best is the modern, well-designed **Landnámssetur Íslands** (Settlement Centre of Iceland), down at the far end of Borgarbraut. The museum is in two parts, for each of which you can pay

3

> ### WHEN THE NORTH WIND DOTH BLOW
> The stretch of road from Akranes, particularly around Hafnarfjall, on the southern approach to Borgarnes, is one of the most **hazardous** in the entire country. Totally exposed to the Atlantic, it takes the full brunt of violent **storms** which drive in from the sea; not surprisingly, it closes frequently during the winter months, as cars have been overturned here by the brute force of the wind. In summer things are not quite so severe, but it is still an extremely windy spot.

separately and are given an informative audioguide, complete with superb sound effects, which leads you around the exhibits and accompanying video displays. The **first section** uses interactive models (such as the swaying prow of a Viking longship which you can ride) and audiovisual displays to give an idea of what Iceland's first 400-odd settlers would have found, and where they chose to locate their farms when they arrived to carve up the country between them during the Settlement period (about 870–930). But for sheer gothic atmosphere you can't beat the **second exhibition**, in the basement, which illustrates *Egill's Saga*, with surreal and often nightmarish figurines, woodcarvings and lighting portraying Egill's violent life – look out for his werewolf grandfather lurking in the shadows, and the misshapen skull with Paget's Disease towards the exit – it's thought Egill may have suffered from this abnormal condition which causes bones to become hardened and ridged like a scallop shell.

Hlíðartúnshúsin

Borgarbraut • Open access • Free

The only other sight in Borgarnes is the three turf-roofed houses, known as **Hlíðartúnshúsin**, signposted on the left-hand side, just after the shopping centre, as you drive into the village along Borgarbraut. Built in 1919 and in use until the 1980s, the stone-and-turf structures are a good example of the primitive conditions many Icelanders endured until the 1950s. The buildings, all with their original earth floors and boulders for walls, were, however, used for keeping sheep rather than human habitation.

ARRIVAL AND INFORMATION

By bus All buses pull up in Brúartorg, next to the highway and adjacent to the filling stations.

Destinations Akureyri (2 daily; 5hr); Búðardalur (4 weekly; 1hr 10min); Hólmavík (4 weekly; 2hr 10min); Reykholt (3 weekly; 40min); Reykjavík (Mon–Fri 8 daily, Sat 6 daily, Sun 4 daily; 1hr 20min); Stykkishólmur (2 daily; 1hr 30min).

Tourist information The town's office is at Borgarbraut 58–60 (June–Aug Mon–Fri 9am–6pm, Sat 10am–4pm, Sun noon–4pm; Sept–May Mon–Fri 9am–5pm; ☎437 2214, ⑩westiceland.is), inside the Hyrnutorg shopping centre. Staff here are a mine of information about west Iceland; they also sell maps and books about the region.

Services The Hyrnutorg shopping centre, Borgarbraut 58–60, has an ATM, a supermarket (Mon–Fri 9am–8pm,

BORGARNES

Sat 9am–6pm, Sun noon–6pm), *vínbúð* (June–Aug Mon–Thurs 11am–6pm, Fri 11am–7pm, Sat 11am–4pm; Sept–May Mon–Thurs noon–6pm, Fri 11am–7pm, Sat 11am–2pm), pharmacy (Mon–Fri 10am–6pm, Sat 10am–2pm) and post office (Mon–Fri 9am–4.30pm). Check out the excellent farmers' market, Ljómalind (daily 11am–6pm), too, just next to the post office, selling good-quality handicrafts and woollen sweaters. Borgarnes' excellent open-air swimming pool and sports centre (Mon–Fri 6.30am–10pm, Sat & Sun 9am–6pm; ☎437 1444; 580kr) at Þorsteinsgata 1, a continuation of Skallagrímsgata, is right by the water's edge with great views of the fjord and the surrounding hills; there are also a couple of hot pots here, a waterslide, a steam room and a sauna.

ACCOMMODATION

Bjarg ☎437 1925, ⑩farmholidays.is. Guesthouse accommodation on a working farm a 20min walk out of town along Borgarbraut. There's a rustic, four-person studio apartment with kitchen and private bathroom as well as three double rooms with shared facilities. Doubles **16,250kr**, apartment **26,800kr**

Borgarnes B&B Skúlagata 21 ☎434 1566 and ☎842 5866, ⑩borgarnesbb.is. Excellent guesthouse with beautifully decorated rooms in modern Nordic style, consequently mercifully low on floral flourishes and swirls. Rooms have private or shared facilities, and there's a large sitting room with stupendous sea views. **16,800kr**

Borgarnes campsite Granastaðir ☎ 695 3366. Located beside the Ringroad just outside the town centre and run by the youth hostel, the campsite has showers and toilets and there's the opportunity to have breakfast at the youth hostel. Mid-May to mid-Sept. **1200kr**

Hótel Borgarnes Egilsgata 12–14 ☎ 437 1119, ⓦ hotelborgarnes.is. This comfortable, modern hotel has 90-odd well-appointed rooms with neutral decor, carpeted floors and good views of the snowcapped mountains across the fjord, as well as a number of self-catering, two-person apartments in the building opposite. Feb–Nov. Doubles **26,800kr**, apartments **24,000kr**

Youth hostel Borgarbraut 9 ☎ 695 3366, ⓦ hostel.is. Borgarnes's youth hostel is perfectly located on the main street, and has comfortable dorms as well as double rooms with and without private facilities. Dorms **4550kr**, doubles **12,400kr**

EATING AND DRINKING

Hyrnan Brúartorg 1 ☎ 430 5550. The basic fast-food restaurant attached to the N1 filling station is popular with drivers on the Ringroad as well as coach tours, so can be busy at certain times; the best bet is the filling meat soup (1690kr), though there's also the usual run of pizzas, sandwiches and burgers. Daily 8am–11pm.

Matstofan Brákarbraut 3 ☎ 437 2017. This Filipino-run place dishes up burgers (from 700kr) and a couple of none-too-genuine Asian stir-fries and curries (around 1790kr), and also functions as the town's one and only pub come the evening. Mon–Thurs 6pm–midnight, Fri & Sat 6pm–1am.

Settlement Centre Brákarbraut 13–15 ☎ 437 1600. By far the best choice for something to eat for many kilometres, the recently extended restaurant upstairs at the Settlement Centre serves a good-value lunch buffet till 3pm (2200kr), as well as lasagne (2600kr), grilled lamb (4500kr) and an excellent *plokkfiskur* (2800kr). Daily 10am–9pm.

Borg á Mýrum

2km north of Borgarnes on Route 54 • Open access • Free

Another site mentioned in the sagas, the farm of **Borg á Mýrum**, is easily reached by buses to the Snæfellsnes peninsula. First settled by **Skallagrímur Kveldúlfsson**, Egill's father, Borg á Mýrum is, to Icelanders at least, of double historical significance because of its association with one of Iceland's greatest writers, Snorri Sturluson (see see box, p.158). It's a popular spot with misty-eyed home-grown tourists, though few remain more than ten minutes or so, because the original farmhouse is long gone and there's precious little to see here today other than a small white church, the *borg* (or large rock), after which Skallagrímur's original farm was named, and a sculpture by Ásmundur Sveinsson entitled *Sonatorrek*, after Egill Skallagrímsson's moving poem (see box, p.155). Like so many of Iceland's historical sites, archeological remains are thin on the ground, so you'll have to arm yourself with the facts and let your imagination do the rest.

THE MEN OF BORG

Skallagrímur Kveldúlfsson ended up at Borg á Mýrum very much by chance after falling foul of his king, Harald Fairhair of Norway. Together with his father, **Kveldúlfur** ("Evening Wolf", so-called because he grew violent and supernaturally strong as dusk came on), he fled the wrath of King Harald and set sail westwards for Iceland. However, during the lengthy and stormy voyage, Kveldúlfur fell ill and ordered that, on his death, his coffin be tossed overboard and his grieving family settle wherever it washed up. Following his father's instruction, Skallagrímur first set foot in Iceland in an area rich in bogs, forests and salmon rivers, at Borg á Mýrum (Rock in the Bogs), where he raised his family, naming the surrounding area, accordingly, Borgarfjörður (Rocky Fjord).

The third great man to live at Borg was **Snorri Sturluson**. At the age of 19 Snorri married the only daughter of Father Bersi the Wealthy, of Borg, and moved to the farm following his father-in-law's death in 1202 to run the estate as his heir. However, his marriage was not a happy one and just four or five years later, around 1206, he decided to move inland to Reykholt, leaving his wife behind.

Reykholt

A forty-minute drive from Borgarnes, about 40km east off the Ringroad down Route 50 and then Route 518, the tiny hamlet of **REYKHOLT** is the cultural highlight of any trip up the west coast. Not only does it sit among the wide-open spaces of the fertile Reykholtsdalur valley, enjoying stunning views of dusky mountains and the sleepy Reykjadalsá River, but it also contains tangible memorials to **Snorri Sturluson**. The excellent museum here is far and away the best place to get to grips with Iceland's rich, and at times downright confusing, history of saga events, characters and writing.

Snorrastofa

Below the village church • May–Sept daily 10am–6pm; Oct–April Mon–Fri 10am–5pm • 1200kr • ⓦ snorrastofa.is

The critically acclaimed **Snorrastofa** museum will leave you in no doubt as to Reykholt's importance in Icelandic minds, packed as it is with exhibits relating to Snorri Sturluson and his writings, along with accounts of Reykholt's role as a centre of learning over the centuries. Inside, check out the copy of a page from *Egil's Saga* (thought to have been written in 1250). Alongside this handwritten version, you'll see the same text presented in modern Icelandic and then again in English translation. Look carefully at the old and modern Icelandic versions and you will see they are virtually identical – a remarkable sign of how little Icelandic has changed since medieval times. Look out, too, for the map of Europe, posted up on the wall, which shows the Icelandic names of many an English town, as per *Heimskringla* (the Kings' Saga): Hjartapollur (Hartlepool), Hvítabýr (Whitby); Skarðaborg (Scarborough), Grímsbær (Grimsby) and, naturally, Jórvík (York). The museum's curators are known throughout Iceland for their outspoken views on all things Snorri, and have even done battle with the Icelandic government over the taxation of the Snorri estate, quoting a medieval document penned by the great man himself in their defence. The church itself, with its specially designed acoustic walls, hosts the **Reykholt Music Festival** (ⓦreykholtshatid.is; 3500kr per concert or 9000kr for all four concerts) during the last weekend in July, when visiting singers and musicians gather for a series of classical music concerts open to the public – look out for details posted around the village.

SNORRI STURLUSON

Born at the farm of Hvammur (see p.167) near Búðardalur in 1179, **Snorri Sturluson** was descended from some of the greatest figures in early Icelandic history; on his father's side were influential chieftains, on his mother's, among others, the warrior poet Egill Skallagrímsson. At the age of 2 he was fostered and taken to one of Iceland's leading cultural centres, Oddi (see p.126), where, over the years, he became acquainted not only with historical writing but also the court of Norway – a relationship that would eventually lead to his death. In 1206, following his marriage to a wealthy heiress, he moved to Reykholt and consolidated his grip on power by becoming a chieftain, legislator and respected historian and writer; he also developed a distinct taste for promiscuity, fathering three children to women other than his long-suffering first wife, Herdís.

Snorri Sturluson is the most celebrated figure in Icelandic literature, producing first his *Edda* (an account of Norse mythology) then *Egill's Saga* and *Heimskringla* (a history of the Norwegian kings up to 1177), which from its geographical detail shows that Snorri spent several years living in Norway. During this period he developed a close bond of allegiance to the Norwegian earl who reigned alongside the teenage king, Hákon. However, following a civil war in Norway, which resulted in the earl's death, the Norwegian king declared Snorri a traitor and ordered one of his followers, Gissur Þorvaldsson, to bring the writer back to Norway – dead or alive. On the dark night of September 23, 1241, seventy armed men led by Gissur burst into Snorri's farmhouse in Reykholt, sending him fleeing from his bed unarmed and defenceless, down into the cellar. Five of the thugs pursued Snorri, and there they hacked Iceland's most distinguished man of letters to death.

Snorralaug and Snorri statue

Across the lawn from the Snorrstofa (see opposite)

Located at the foot of a hillock, **Snorri's pool**, the **Snorralaug**, provides a rare visual
example of a piece of medieval Iceland and is even mentioned in the *Landnámabók*
(*Book of Settlements*) and the *Sturlunga Saga*. A 4m-wide geothermally heated pool
ringed with stones, this is thought to have been where Snorri would bathe and receive
visitors, and next to it are the restored remains of the **tunnel** leading to the cellar of
Snorri's farmhouse, where he was assassinated in 1241 (see box opposite). The pool is
fed by an ancient stone aqueduct from the nearby hot spring, Skrifla. Back up the steps
from the pool, the Snorri **statue** which graces the front of the former school was
presented to Iceland by Norway's King Olaf shortly after independence in 1947. It's a
clear reminder of the continuing wrangle between the two Nordic nations over Snorri's
origins; the Norwegians strongly maintain that Snorri is theirs and claim he was born
in Norway. Although the Icelanders have gratefully accepted over three million
Norwegian kroner to help set up the Snorri exhibition hall, the new library and the
Heimskringla museum and research centre, suspicions remain that the Norwegians
haven't yet renounced their claims on Snorri.

ARRIVAL AND INFORMATION   REYKHOLT

By bus Buses to Reykholt run just three a week (Mon, Tues
& Thurs) from Borgarnes, and terminate at the filling
station at the eastern end of the village. Return buses leave
on the same days, and also travel via Varmaland.

Destinations Borgarnes (3 weekly; 40min).

Services There's a small shop at the filling station (daily
10am–9pm) which sells most basics, including food.

ACCOMMODATION

Á Kirkjubóli 2, 10km east of Reykholt ☎ 435 1430,
ⓦ hotela.is. Overlooking the Hvítá glacial river, this stylish
hotel, with a dozen or so doubles (with and without private
facilities), is big on Nordic simplicity. Rooms are plainly
decorated in natural colours and the tasteful bathrooms
feature slate-walled showers. There's also a restaurant;
reckon on around 5000kr for a three-course dinner with
fish. **18,500kr**

Reykholt Adjacent to Snorrastofa ☎ 435 1260,
ⓦ fosshotel.is. Originally built as a boarding school in
1931, and still with an institutionalized feel to it despite
being refitted as a hotel. Rooms are modern and have
fantastic views of the Okjökull and Eiríksjökull glaciers.
There's also a restaurant, priced in line with *Hótel Á*.
29,700kr

Deildartunguhver

5km west of Reykholt on the side of Route 50 • Open access • Free

While in the Reykholt area, it's well worth checking out the biggest **hot spring** in
Europe, **Deildartunguhver**, which lies near the hamlet of Kleppjárnsreykir. Drawing on
the geothermal reserves that lie all around Reykholtsdalur valley, and pumping out a
staggering 180 litres of 97°C water a second, the billowing clouds of steam created by
this mighty fissure are truly impressive, reaching up high into the cool air – in fact it's
water from here that runs via two specially constructed pipelines to heat Borgarnes and
Akranes, 34km and 64km away respectively. As in so many other geothermal areas
around Iceland, water from the spring is also used to speed up the growth of plants and
vegetables by heating up the surrounding **greenhouses**, and during the summer local
farmers often set up stalls here to sell their produce to passing visitors. From the car
park, a footpath leads to the spring.

Húsafell and around

Route 518 runs 25km east from Reykholt to the pastoral hamlet of **HÚSAFELL**, a
favourite activity centre for holidaying Icelanders and a fantastic place to fetch up for a

couple of days of hiking and sightseeing. Though the main draw here was always the vast lavafield **Hallmundarhraun**, things are changing fast in little Húsafell, which has big aspirations thanks to its proximity to Iceland's second-biggest glacier, Langjökull. A stylish new hotel has been built in the village, there are plans to revamp the swimming pool and transform it into a spa, and a new bistro (see p.162) has also opened. Although the locals are coy about all these developments, it's plain to see that they're linked with what's been happening up on the glacier. Húsafell is now the departure point for adventure tours which not only go up onto the ice cap – nothing new there – but, quite extraordinarily, into it, as well (see box below).

Clearly, as thousands upon thousands of tourists flood in to shy and retiring Húsafell, the village is changing and, naturally, opinion is split across Iceland about whether offering tours inside a glacier is the right thing to do. Be that as it may, in Húsafell everyone wants a piece of the cake and more development will surely follow. In addition to tours into Langjökull, Húsafell also makes a good base for some excellent **hiking trails** leading off into the **Húsafellsskógur** forest and, more adventurously, up to two other nearby glaciers, **Eiríksjökull** and **Okjökull**. In summer, you can also push further out from here for a taste of Iceland's Interior, by following the **Kaldidalur route** (Route 550) southwest to Þingvellir. Public buses can get you as far as Reykholt, but from here you really need your own vehicle to explore.

Set amid dwarf birchwoods, the village itself consists of little more than a **church**, originally built in 1170 but today dating only from 1905, and a hundred or so private summer cottages, mostly owned by the trade unions (whose employees use the cottages in rotation) and individual families. Note that there are no street addresses in Húsafell – just head to the hotel (see p.162) and all services are located adjacent to it.

LANGJÖKULL: TOURS INTO THE GLACIER

Just 20km southeast of Húsafell, in an isolated location on the western edges of the Interior, lies Iceland's second largest ice cap, **Langjökull** (Long Glacier). Covering 950 square kilometres, the glacier resembles a narrow protruding finger wedged between the Hallmundarhraun lavafield and Kjölur, and is visible for miles around. It's now the subject of the tour that everyone in Iceland is talking about – a trip **inside a glacier**. Until now, at various locations across the country, it's been possible to take a trip by special vehicle up onto a glacier, but never to go inside a live, moving glacier. In June 2015 that all changed and Húsafell is at the forefront of this ground-breaking development.

Tours (daily at 11am, 1pm & 3.30pm; times are from **base camp**, 30min earlier from the booking office; 17,900kr/person , 2000kr extra for shuttle to base camp; reservations should be made before arrival In Húsafell; T578 2550, Wintotheglacier.is) begin either at the service centre in Húsafell (next to the bistro), or at the so-called base camp where the gravel road up towards the glacier peters out; the exact location changes depending on the extent of the glacier so you should always check when you book where you should meet the tour if you decide to make your own way to the start point. Here, you transfer to a converted mobile rocket launcher, formerly in service with NATO, equipped with huge tyres which can be automatically deflated or inflated depending on the ice conditions. Having trundled up the glacier to a height of 1260m above sea level, you're now at the entrance to the series of tunnels which have been hollowed out from the icecap. It takes roughly an hour to walk through the 600m of **tunnels** which form a circular loop – at the furthest extent you'll be around 200m inside the glacier with 30m of snow and ice above and 300m below you. Since the glacier moves at around 20–30cm per year and the tour is in its infancy, it's not yet known what will happen to the tunnels over time, though it's expected some renovation work will be required to keep them open. In total, the tour lasts around two hours, though the descent by glacial truck back down the glacier is much faster than the ascent.

Should you decide not to take the tour, you can still see Langjökull if you take either the Kjölur or Kaldidalur Interior routes (see p.326 & box, p.163), since both roads pass close to its foothills.

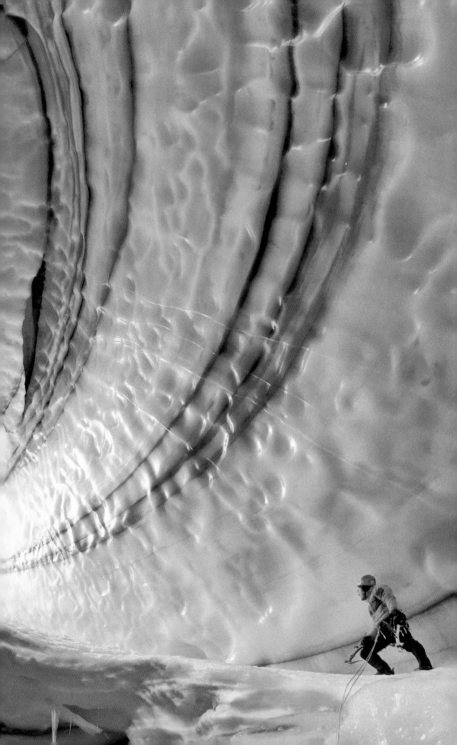

HIKING AROUND HÚSAFELL: OKJÖKULL AND EIRÍKSJÖKULL

One of Iceland's smaller glaciers, **Okjökull** (Ok) is perfect for a **day-hike** from Húsafell. At a height of 1141m, the glacier sits in a dolerite shield volcano and is easily reached from Húsafell by first following the western edge of the Bæjargil ravine up to the Drangsteinabrún ridge. Cross to the eastern side of the small ponds which lie south of the ridge and continue straight up to Ok. On a clear day the **views** from here are truly spectacular – west you can see to the coastline and the town of Borgarnes, while inland there are sweeping vistas of the Interior. Allow five or six hours and take enough food and drink to last for a day.

Immediately east of Húsafell, the peak of **Eiríksjökull** (1675m), on the glacier of the same name, is the highest mountain in western Iceland and the long hike here should only be undertaken by seasoned walkers. Before setting out, get detailed information from the service centre in Húsafell (see below), where you can also get helpful **maps**; the following description, however, should help you to trace your route along them. Head along the hard, dry grass of the northern slope of Strútur mountain, northeast of Kalmanstunga farm, from where there are difficult trails east across Hallmundarhraun (see below) to Hvítárdrög at the foot of the glacier. Begin the climb itself by hiking up the prominent ravine on the western edge of the glacier, remembering your route to help your descent – it can be very disorientating up here. Beyond the ravine, the going gets considerably easier, but watch out for crevasses. Allow a full day and bear in mind that sun-melt can make the hike a lot harder.

Húsafell swimming pool

June–Sept daily 10am–10pm; Oct–April Sat & Sun 1–5pm • 800kr

Beside the new hotel, Húsafell's fantastic geothermally heated outdoor **swimming pool** offers great views of the surrounding hills and glaciers; there are two small pools here, plus two hot pots and a waterslide. The pool, however, is due to be renovated – more hot pots will be added – and entry will be included in the room rate at the hotel (though non-guests will still be able to pay for use).

ARRIVAL AND INFORMATION   HÚSAFELL

By bus There is presently no bus connection to Húsafell; services only operate as far as Reykholt. However, Iceland's bus network is in a constant state of flux and things may change; check ⓦ publictransport.is for the latest details.

Tourist information There's a service centre (June–Aug

daily 10am–6pm; ☏435 1556) in the village which provides basic tourist information and also takes bookings for the campsite (see below).

Services There's a food store and filling station next door to the service centre (daily 11am–9pm).

ACCOMMODATION AND EATING

Campsite In the centre of the village ☏435 1556, ⓦ husafell.is. You can pitch a tent at the campsite in the centre of the village or rent one of the ten simple on-site cabins, which sleep two. There's an on-site kitchen for use by campers and those renting cabins. June–Aug. Camping **1400kr**, cabins **7000kr**

Húsafell Built into the hillside ☏435 1551, ⓦ hotelhusafell.com. Much effort has gone into blending this new four-star hotel into the surrounding countryside: constructed of local stone and fronted with larchwood, the hotel oozes contemporary style and natural harmony

– even the underfloor heating is geothermal. Rooms are decorated with pieces of art fashioned from lava by a local artist. A restaurant is also planned in the hotel serving modern Nordic cuisine. **33,500kr**

Húsafell Bistro Beside the hotel ☏435 1556, ⓦ husafell.is. The best option at this cosy little bistro is to tuck in to the sumptuous lunch buffet featuring a variety of freshly and creatively prepared salads (quite a rarity In Iceland), gourmet pasta dishes, pizza, soup and coffee for just 2450kr. Alternatively, go for the excellent Icelandic meat soup. Daily 11am–9pm.

Hallmundarhraun

Some 14km northeast of Húsafell, the **Hallmundarhraun** lavafield – named after the giant Hallmundur of *Grettir's Saga* – is thought to have been formed at the time of the Settlement when magma poured out from beneath the northwestern edge of the Langjökull and entered the Hvítá River. The road there follows first the 518 and then,

THE KALDIDALUR INTERIOR ROUTE

From Húsafell, Route 550 (Kaldadalsvegur) winds its way southwest through the haunting beauty of the **Kaldidalur** valley on its way to the information centre and campsite at Þingvellir (see p.105), a distance of around 60km. If you're short of time but want a taste of the barren expanses of the Icelandic Interior, this is a good option: you'll come face to face with four **glaciers** – Eiríksjökull, Okjökull, Langjökull and Þórisjökull, a small oval-shaped ice cap rising to a height of 1350m – and pass through a vast grey **desert** where ferocious sandstorms can appear in seconds, transforming what was once a clear vista of majestic ice caps and volcanic sands into an impenetrable cloud of grit and dirt. As the neck of land carrying the road narrows to pass between the Ok and Þórisjökull glaciers, the route climbs and rides along the straight Langihyrggur ridge affording spectacular views of Þórisjökull opposite.

The Kaldidalur route is unsealed and rough, though generally open to conventional vehicles from mid-June until late August – you'll need to check road conditions in advance through Ⓦ vegag.is.

3

via Kalmanstunga farm, the F578 to the northeastern edge of **Strútur** mountain (939m); you can walk on the lava, but it is hard going and requires tough-soled shoes – take care not to twist an ankle. Off the F578 is **Surtshellir**, a 1970m-long cavern thought to have been a hideout of the eighteenth-century outlaw Eyvindur and his friends (see box, p.328). Exercise extreme caution if you decide to go inside, as the uneven floor and darkness can prove disorientating; you'll need to bring a torch with you. Nearby **Stefánshellir**, part of the same cave network, is also worth a quick look but is essentially more of the same – together these cave systems measure a whopping 3.5km in length.

In summer the road to Hallmundarhraun is usually passable for all cars as far as the caves, after which point it deteriorates as it continues past the lavafield towards the Arnarvatnhæðir hills, Route 704 and eventually the Ringroad near Hvammstangi; the total distance of this interior route from Kalmanstunga to Núpsárbrú bridge in Austurárdal valley (Route 704) is 42km.

Hraunfossar and Barnafoss

Six kilometres west of Húsafell on Route 518, the waterfalls of Hraunfossar and Barnafoss are two of the best-known natural features in Iceland. Although both are on the Hvítá, it's **Hraunfossar** (Lava Falls) that make for the best photographs; however, don't expect thundering white torrents – the falls here are gentle cascades of bright, turquoise water, emerging from under the moss-covered lava to tumble down a series of rock steps into the river. From here, a track leads upstream to **Barnafoss** (Children's Falls), which is far more lively – it was here that two children fell to their deaths when crossing a narrow stone arch that once spanned the river. A modern footbridge now affords an excellent view of the water churning violently as it channels through the ravine below.

Varmaland and around

Between Borgarnes and Brú, a distance of 85km along the Ringroad, there is little to detain you. However, if you fancy a spot of **hiking** amid lavafields or lush river valleys, or scaling a couple of extinct **volcanic craters** before hitting the north coast, there are a couple of diversions worthy of your attention. The first is the village of **VARMALAND**, a small and uneventful place northwest of Reykholt popular with holidaying Icelanders. Other than its geothermally heated **swimming pool** and the market-gardening centre, Laugaland, where mushroom production began in Iceland, there's little to the place, but it is the starting point of a decent **hike** to Bifröst (see box, p.164).

HIKING FROM VARMALAND TO BIFRÖST

The 13km **day-hike to Bifröst** follows one of the country's best salmon rivers: the **Norðurá**. Originating high on the moors of Holtavörðuheiði south of Brú, the river flows southwest to meet up with western Iceland's biggest river, the glacial Hvítá, at the head of Borgarfjörður where it finally empties into the sea. From Varmaland, you follow the river upstream: head north along Route 527 to Einifell farm, where the road downgrades into a jeep track as it heads to a T-junction west of Höll farm. From here, head west around the foot of Hallarmúli hill (260m) towards the **Laxfoss waterfalls** in the Norðurá. Continue past the abandoned farm, Veiðilækur, on to the farmstead at Svartagil and the **Glanni waterfalls**. Here you pick up Route 528 and fork left, crossing the Norðurá and Bjarnardalsá rivers, over the **Grábrókarhraun lavafield** (see below) to join the Ringroad a kilometre or so east of Bifröst.

3

ARRIVAL AND DEPARTURE   VARMALAND

By bus Buses from Reykholt to Borgarnes (3 weekly; 30min) pass through the village as they do a loop from Borgarnes.

ACCOMMODATION

Varmaland campsite Stafholtstungur ☎775 1012, ✉varmaland.camping@gmail.com. A small and compact campsite close to the main road, with hot and cold running water and a children's playground. Mid-May to Aug. **1200kr**

Bifröst

Around 30km northeast of Borgarnes, the minuscule settlement of **BIFRÖST** amounts to little more than a filling station on the Ringroad. A couple of kilometres to the south and spread either side of the Ringroad, you'll find the heather-encrusted **Grábrókarhraun** lavafield, formed three thousand years ago when lava spewed from three craters on the north side of the main road: Grábrók, Grábrókafell and a third cone that has now been dug up to provide gravel for road building. Otherwise, the forested shores of **Hreðavatn**, 1km southwest of Bifröst, make for a pleasant stroll and a picnic if the weather's playing along; there's also trout fishing here. Look out for plant fossils in the rocks around the lake.

Northeast of the village, the **Grábrók** crater can be ascended by means of a marked trail, as can the **Baula** rhyolite mountain (934m), 11km from Bifröst and reached along Route 60; if you don't fancy walking from the Ringroad, you can take one of the **buses** heading for Búðardalur (see below). Although the sides of this cone-shaped mountain are steep and scree-covered, there are no particular obstacles to the ascent and once at the summit there's a small shelter made of rocks.

ARRIVAL AND DEPARTURE   BIFRÖST

By bus Buses from Bifröst's filling station head back down to Borgarnes, north via Route 60 to Búðardalur and Hólmavík, and northeast up the Ringroad for Akureyri.

Destinations Akureyri (2 daily; 4hr 30min); Borgarnes (2 daily; 30min); Búðardalur (4 weekly; 40min); Hólmavík (4 weekly; 1hr 40min); Reykjavík (2 daily; 2hr).

ACCOMMODATION

Hraunsnef Norðurárdalur ☎435 0111, ⊕hraunsnef .is. A family-run country hotel located about 3km north up the Ringroad from Bifröst whose smart rooms each have their own private entry from the grounds. Guests have access to the hot tubs by the stream just outside. **24,400kr**

Búðardalur and around

North of the Snæfellsnes peninsula and some 45km from Bifröst, the wide and sheltered **Hvammsfjörður** lies protected from the open sea at its mouth by dozens of small islands. Accessed via Bifröst on Route 60, or from Route 54 along the north coast of the Snæfellsnes peninsula, its main service centre is **BÚÐARDALUR**, an uninspiring place that is best passed over in favour of the rich **saga country** close by. Running northeast from Búðardalur is **Laxárdalur**, the valley around which one of the best-known Viking romances, the **Laxdæla Saga**, was played out. South of here, **Eiríksstaðir**, in Haukadalur, was home to **Eirík the Red**, discoverer of Greenland, and the birthplace of his son, **Leifur**, who went on to discover North America.

Búðardalur itself is home to just 250 people, and provides limited banking, postal and retail services to the surrounding rural districts. It's an unkempt place, consisting of little more than a collection of a dozen or so suburban streets, and the only reason to break your journey here is to pop into the museum en route to the nearby saga sites.

Leifsbúð

Búðarbraut 1 • April–Sept daily 11am–7pm; Oct–March Mon–Fri & Sun 11am–3pm • Free

Búðardalur's one and only attraction is **Leifsbúð**, a modest museum dedicated to Leifur Eiríksson and his voyage to North America from Greenland. Despite such a rich historical theme to draw upon, the museum will barely whet your appetite with its disappointing collection of wooden models and uninspiring photographs.

3

ARRIVAL AND INFORMATION   BÚÐARDALUR

By bus Buses call at the filling station beside the main road in Búðardalur. Since the completion of the new road to Hólmavík, there are now direct services to the West Fjords from here.

Destinations Bifröst (4 weekly; 45min); Borgarnes (4 weekly; 1hr 10min); Hólmavík (4 weekly; 1hr).

Tourist information The tourist office (April–Sept daily 11am–7pm; Oct–March Mon–Fri & Sun 11am–3pm; ☏ 434 1441, ⓦ dalir.is) is housed in the former nineteenth-century warehouse down by the harbour which also contains the *Leifsbúð* café (see below).

Services The *vínbúð* is located on the northern side of the village at Vesturbraut 15 (Mon–Thurs 4–6pm, Fri 1–7pm, Sat noon–2pm).

ACCOMMODATION AND EATING

Campsite Vesturbraut ☏ 430 4700. Located beside the main road near the junction with Miðbraut and (unusually for Iceland) surrounded by trees; pitches are separated by low hedges. Mid-May to Aug. 1000kr

Dalakot Dalbraut 2 ☏ 434 1644, ✉ dalakot@gmail.com. A simple guesthouse in the centre of the village with just a handful of rooms both en-suite and also sharing facilities. Attached to the guesthouse is the only restaurant in town, serving a variety of pizzas (2250kr) and burgers for

around 1600–2100kr, plus some really good lamb chops for a reasonable 1850kr. Restaurant June–Aug daily 8am–10pm; Sept–May Mon–Fri 6–8pm, Sat & Sun 6pm–9pm. 15,500kr

Leifsbúð Búðarbraut 1 ☏ 434 1441. The café at the tourist office and museum serves up a limited menu comprising meat soup (1900kr), home-made sandwiches (800kr) and cakes (600kr). April–Sept daily 11am–7pm; Oct–March Mon–Fri & Sun 11am–3pm.

Eiríksstaðir

June–Aug daily 9am–6pm • 1250kr • ☏ 434 1118, ⓦ leif.is

The country which is called Greenland was discovered and settled from Iceland. Eirík the Red was the name of a man from Breiðafjörður who went out there and took possession of land in the place which has since been called Eiríksfjörður. He named the country Greenland and said it would make people want to go there if the country had a good name.
Extract from *Book of the Icelanders* by Ari the Learned (1067–1148).

Twenty kilometres southeast of Búðardalur and reached by Route 586 (8km from the junction with Route 60) into Haukadalur valley, the former farm of **Eiríksstaðir** is one of the most historically significant locations in Iceland. This was the starting point for all westward expansion by the Vikings, first to Greenland and later to the shores of North America. Following a couple of earlier failed archeological digs, a third attempt was made between 1997 and 2000 to excavate this site, which experts believe to be the most likely home of Eiríkur Þorvaldsson, better known as **Eirík the Red** and father of

3

THE VIKINGS, GREENLAND AND NORTH AMERICA

Although Icelanders don't like to admit it, **Eirík the Red** and his father were actually Norwegian. According to the Book of Settlements, *Landnámabók*, they left Norway to settle in the Hornstrandir region of the West Fjords, where they lived until Eirík's father died. It's believed that Eirík moved to **Haukadalur** from Drangar in Hornstrandir after marrying Þjóðhildur, whose parents already lived at nearby Vatn in Haukadalur. However, he was an unruly man, and, after getting into a row and murdering several of his neighbours, he was driven out of the valley having lived there for ten to twenty years. Eirík then set up home on Suðurey (part of Brokey) and Öxney, two islands east of Stykkishólmur in Breiðafjörður, where he once again fell out with his neighbours and was outlawed as a result – it was then, with a ship full of friends, that he set sail, charting a course south of Snæfellsnes, for new land and adventure. He eventually discovered land in 985 and, according to the sagas, promptly named it **Greenland**, "because it would encourage people to go there if the land had a good name". He settled at Brattahlíð in a fjord he named after himself, Eiríksfjörður, near present-day Narsarsuaq. No doubt inspired by his father, Leifur set out to the west from his new home, Greenland, first reaching barren, rocky land that he named Helluland (Baffin Island), from where he continued south to an area of flat wooded land he named Markland (Labrador), in 1000 AD. After another two days at sea he reached more land, where, the sagas have us believe, grapes grew in abundance. Leifur named this land **Vínland**, which some experts believe could mean "Wineland". However, since two days' sailing from Labrador would only take him as far south as current-day New England, not exactly known for its wines, speculation remains as to where Viking Vínland is.

Leifur, who became the first European to set foot in North America (see box above). During the dig archeologists found the remnants of a 50-square-metre hall dated to 890–980 AD, and, although no timber was unearthed, they did come across doorways, clearly marked out with stone paving.

An evocative reconstruction of Eiríkur's original **longhouse** now stands in front of the ruins and is a must for anyone interested in the Viking period. Its turf walls, 12m long by 4m wide, are huddled around a dirt floor and support a roof made of rafters covered over with twigs atop a layer of turf. Story-telling **guides**, evocatively dressed as Vikings, expertly bring the period to life and will also point out the significant features of the ruins. To the untrained eye they can be hard to find (they're located immediately behind the small statue of Leifur; from the statue take the gravel path to the right up the hillside heading towards the waterfall).

ACCOMMODATION   EIRÍKSSTAÐIR

Stóra Vatnshorn Adjacent to Eiríksstaðir ☎ 434 1342, Ⓦ storavatnshorn.is. Comfortable accommodation in cottages sleeping three people, located on a working farm with fantastic views out over the Haukadalsá River to the summit of Jörfahnúkur (557m). Mid-May to mid-Sept. **19,500kr**

Laxárdalur

The tragedy renowned as one of the great masterpieces of medieval literature, the **Laxdæla Saga** (see box, p.168), unfolded in **Laxárdalur**, the valley northeast of Búðardalur and traversed by Route 59. Although there are few remains of the homes of the characters of the tale, the rolling green landscapes are reminiscent of the most romantic scenes in the epic, and the mere mention to an Icelander of virtually any local place-name will conjure up images of forsaken love; handy information boards recounting the main events of the saga are placed at the key sites involved.

Hjarðarholt

Five kilometres out of Búðardalur just to the north of Route 59 lies the farm of **Hjarðarholt**, established by Ólafur the Peacock and later taken over by his son, Kjartan.

In the saga, Ólafur moves his livestock from **Goddastaðir**, now a couple of kilometres to the northeast off Route 587, to Hjarðarholt and asks a local chieftain, Höskuldur, to watch the procession from his own farm. The first of Ólafur's animals were arriving at Hjarðarholt while the last were still leaving Goddastaðir – a visual demonstration of wealth which can still be appreciated today by standing at Hjarðarholt and looking at the distant hillside to the northeast. Incidentally, Höskuldur lived next door to Ólafur at **Höskuldsstaðir**, directly located on Route 59 and still inhabited today. Route 59 continues east over the lake-studded moors of Laxárdalsheiði to the fjord of Hrútafjörður from where Route 61 heads north to Hólmavík in the West Fjords and south to the tiny settlement of Brú (see p.228).

Hvammur

The other branch of Ólafur the Peacock's feud-torn family lived around 17km north of Búðardalur, at a couple of sites not far off Route 60, tiny **Hvammur** and nearby Laugur (see below). Some 2km west off Route 60 and then north along a minor road just after Skerðingsstaðir farm, Hvammur is one of Iceland's oldest settlements and was first occupied by Auður Djúpúðga (Auður the Deepminded) around the year 895, the only woman recorded in the Book of Settlements. Firm but compassionate, she was the matriarch of a leading family in the saga age, though confusingly, the *Laxdæla Saga* refers to her as Unnuras. Auður, the daughter of Ketill Suðureyjajarl (Earl of the Hebrides) and married to King Ólafur Hvíti of Dublin, first came to Iceland with her children and grandchildren around 890 after one of her sons, Þorsteinn, died in battle in Scotland, and she brought with her a large number of Scots and Irish slaves. The land settled by Auður was long occupied by her descendants, one of whom was Þorfinn Karlsefni, who explored America for three years in an attempt to establish a Viking settlement. There's a small memorial to Auður at Hvammur, erected by the University Women of Iceland, and it remains the hamlet's only tangible sign of the Saga era. She was the first in a long line of prominent Icelanders to live here, the most famous being **Snorri Sturluson** (see box, p.158), who was born here in 1179; a memorial in his honour stands in the churchyard. **Árni Magnússon**, whose greatest achievement was to persuade Denmark to return many of the sagas to Iceland, was also born and raised here.

ARRIVAL AND DEPARTURE   HVAMMUR

By bus The Búðardalur–Hólmavík bus (see p.165) can drop you nearby; Ísafjörður connections via Hólmavík (see p.217).

Laugar and around

A little further up Route 60 from the Hvammur junction and about 2km west, **LAUGAR** in Sælingsdalur valley was the birthplace of Guðrún Ósvifsdóttir. Remains of the **old baths** where she had frequent meetings with Kjartan (see box, p.168) can still be seen at Laugar farm; follow the signs to it along Route 589. This valley is also where her husband Bolli was ambushed and murdered by Kjartan's brothers. In Guðrún's day, the geothermal springs here were an important landmark for travellers on the long journey to and from the West Fjords. Today they feed a wonderful outdoor **swimming pool** (daily 10am–9pm; 600kr) and small steam room which forms part of the *Edda Laugar* **hotel** (see p.168).

From Laugar, Route 60 continues north, following the course of the Svínadalsá River through Svínadalur, which contains the gorge where Kjartan was ambushed and murdered. Past here, the road reaches the bridge over Gilsfjörður, marking the start of the West Fjords.

ARRIVAL AND DEPARTURE   LAUGAR

By bus The Búðardalur–Hólmavík bus (see p.165) can drop you nearby; Ísafjörður connections via Hólmavík (see p.217).

THE LAXDÆLA SAGA

The *Laxdæla Saga* has three main characters – the tall, blond and heroic **Kjartan**; the beautiful **Guðrún Ósvífsdóttir**; and Kjartan's cousin **Bolli**, who lurks in the background to complete a classic love triangle. It takes thirty or so chapters before the three figures are centre stage, but before they have met, a wise man predicts that Guðrún will have four husbands. After seeing Kjartan and Bolli swimming together, he later predicts that one day Bolli will stand over the dead Kjartan, and be killed for his deeds; and thus the inescapable template for the characters' lives is set out to the reader.

Guðrún is married to her first husband against her will and divorces him after two years. She then marries Þord, who incurs the enmity of a family of sorcerers and is drowned as a result. Guðrún then meets Kjartan, and they become close, but Kjartan decides to seek his fortune abroad, and asks Guðrún to wait three years for him, but she refuses.

While in Norway, Kjartan is held hostage, but still finds time to have an affair with the beautiful princess Ingibjorg. Bolli, who has been on Viking expeditions with his cousin during Kjartan's courtship with Ingibjörg, now returns to Iceland and tells Gudrún that Kjartan intends to settle in Norway, whereupon Gudrún's family persuade her to marry Bolli. Kjartan subsequently returns and marries another woman, Hrefna, giving her a priceless **headdress** as a wedding gift, a gift actually bestowed on him by Ingibjorg, who had told him to give it to Gudrún as a wedding present.

There is no love lost between the two neighbouring households, and things only worsen when the headdress is stolen. In revenge, Kjartan lays siege to Guðrún and Bolli and humiliates them by not letting them go to the lavatory for three days. Eventually, Guðrún goads Bolli and his brothers to try to kill Kjartan – Bolli is reluctant but eventually joins the fight, dealing a death blow to a barely injured but exhausted Kjartan, who gives himself to be killed by Bolli and dies in his arms. Guðrún gloats over his death but Bolli is inconsolable. Kjartan's brothers avenge him by eventually killing Bolli – Guðrún is pregnant at the time, and one of the killers wipes his sword on her dress.

Eventually Guðrún gives birth to a son whom she names Bolli, after his father. She decides she won't marry again until her husband is avenged, and makes a promise to Þorgils Hölluson that she will marry no other man in the land than him if he kills her husband's murderer. This he does, at which point Guðrún reveals she is betrothed to another, Þorkel Eyjólfsson, who is abroad. She does indeed marry Þorkel, but he drowns, after which Guðrún becomes a nun. She dies a hermit at Helgafell (see p.174), but before she dies, her son Bolli asks her which man in her life she loved the most, to which she replies "I was worst to him I loved the most" – one of the best-known lines of saga literature.

ACCOMMODATION AND EATING

Edda Laugar Laugar í Sælingsdalur ☎444 4930, ⓦhoteledda.is. Set in a boarding school just a 2min walk from a natural geothermal pool. Half of the rooms have private bathrooms while the others have just a washbasin. There's also a campsite with hot water and showers. The restaurant serves good fish and lamb dishes from 3000kr, and provides breakfast for guests. Restaurant daily 6–10pm. June–Aug. Doubles $\overline{14,800kr}$, camping $\overline{1100kr}$

The Snæfellsnes Peninsula

From Borgarnes, Route 54 branches off west past Borg á Mýrum through the sparsely populated **Mýrar** district, a region of low-lying plains and bogs with a few small lakes, heading for the southern coast of the **Snæfellsnes Peninsula**, a rugged yet beautiful arm of the Icelandic west coast that juts out into the Atlantic between Faxaflói bay and Breiðafjörður. The north and south coasts are divided one from the other by a string of spiky mountains which run down the spine of the peninsula and culminate in the magnificent **Snæfellsjökull**, a glacier at the land's westernmost point. Towns – and regional **buses** – are mostly confined to the north coast, where harbours are good and plentiful, and it's from picturesque **Stykkishólmur**, far and away the best place to base yourself on the peninsula, that boat trips can be made across to the peaceful island haven of **Flatey**. From here a road runs west round the tip of the peninsula via uneventful **Ólafsvík**, though if you're keen to head straight for the glacier, aim for the south-coast township of **Arnarstapi** where **snowmobile tours** of Snæfellsjökull can be arranged. Remember that it's the south coast which more often than not bears the brunt of the moisture-laden low-pressure systems that sweep in from the Atlantic, emptying their load here rather than over the mountains on the north coast.

GETTING AROUND

THE SNÆFELLSNES PENINSULA

By bus Bus services to Snæfellsnes are fairly comprehensive, though none runs all the way along the peninsula's south coast. Services run daily from Borgarnes to Vatnaleið (the junction of route 56 and 54) and on to Stykkishólmur. For the north-coast towns of Grundarfjörður, Ólafsvík and Hellissandur, change at Vatnaleið. A bus also runs from

Stykkishólmur to Arnarstapi via Hellisandur, returning along the same route.

Maps Mál og menning's *Snæfellsnes 1:100,000* is a good map of the region, detailed enough for most purposes, including hiking.

Route 54 from Borgarnes

Heading to Snaefellsnes from the southeast along **Route 54**, the first place of interest is **Fagraskógarfjall** mountain, once the haunt of Grettir of *Grettir's Saga* (see box, p.235). William Morris described it as "a savage and dreadful place" in 1871, though these days it seems much more green and peaceful. North of here, along Route 55, the caves of **Gullborgarhraun** lavafield are a maze of intricate passageways containing coloured stalagmites and stalactites. Seek local advice before exploring them.

Back on Route 54, the road swings past the oval-shaped **Eldborg** crater, which sits conspicuously amid the flat expanse of the **Eldborgarhraun** lavafield, before reaching an unnumbered gravel road pointing north, signed "Rauðamelur" and "Gerðuberg". This leads in a couple of kilometres to the start of the **Gerðuberg basalt columns**, a 2km-long shattered escarpment of grey, 50m-tall hexagonal columns breaking down into scree – the longest such formation in the country.

A further 20km west along the main road, the pit stop of **Vegamót** marks the point where Route 56 (and the bus) branches off across the peninsula towards Stykkishólmur and the north coast. Along the way, the road runs parallel to the narrow Kerlingarskarð, a pass named after a female troll who, legend has it, was caught by the sun and turned to stone while on her way home from a good night's fishing. Locals say she can still be seen with a line of trout over her shoulder on a ridge of the Kerlingarfjall mountain. Stories were also rife of drivers experiencing the eerie presence of an extra passenger in their cars as they drove through the pass – not surprisingly perhaps, Route 56 was shifted some years ago and now runs to the west of the pass.

BOAT TRIPS FROM STYKKISHÓLMUR

Stykkishólmur is an excellent place from which to take a **boat trip** out into the island-studded waters of Breiðafjörður. **Sæferðir**, Smiðjustígur 3 (☎433 2254, ⓦsaeferdir.is), operates a catamaran and offers **nature-watching tours**, known as the Viking Sushi Adventure (1–2 daily all year; 2hr 15min tour 7090kr, 1hr 20min tour 5250kr), which also heads out to the dozens of tiny islands northeast of Stykkishólmur. During the tour the crew fish for shellfish using a small drag net and everyone on board gets a chance to taste the contents. On both tours you'll see plenty of species of birds including puffins, eider ducks, kittiwakes, cormorants and, if you're lucky, the white-tailed eagle, and you'll pass close to the small and now uninhabited **Öxney** island, east of Stykkishólmur, where Eirík the Red and his son, Leifur Eiríksson, lived for several years (see box, p.166). Between mid-May and mid-October, a similar 2.5-hour nature-watching tour also runs and includes a light dinner for a total of 9270kr. Sæferðir also operates the car ferry to Flatey (see p.177) and Brjánslækur in the West Fjords (see p.209).

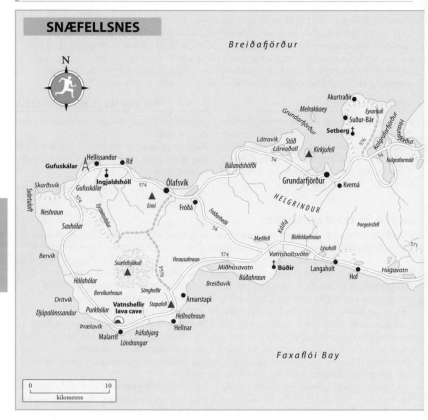

SNÆFELLSNES

Breiðafjörður

N

Akurtraðir
Melrakkaey
Grundarfjörður
Eyrarfjall
Suður-Bár
Setberg
Kolgrafarfjörður
Húnsnes
Látravik
Stöð
Lárvaðall
Kirkjufell
Búlandshöfði
54
Kolgrafarmúli
Hellissandur
Gufuskálar
Rif
576
Grundarfjörður
Kverná
54
Skarðsvík
Gufuskálar
Ingjaldshóll
574
Ólafsvík
H E L G R I N D U R
Svörtuloft
574
Enni
Fróðá
Fróðárheiði
Neshraun
54
Kálfá
Þorgeirsfell
Saxhólar
Mælifell
Bláfeldarhraun
571
Bervík
Snæfellsjökull
Hnausahraun
574
Vatnsholtsvötn
Lýsuhóll
F570
Miðhúsavatn
Búðir
Langaholt
Hof
Hágavatn
Hólahólar
Sönghellir
Búðahraun
Bervíkurhraun
Breiðavík
Dritvík
Purkhólar
Vatnshellir
lava cave
Stapafell
Arnarstapi
Djúpalónssandur
Hellnahraun
Þrælavík
Púfubjarg
Hellnar
Malarrif
Lóndrangar

Faxaflói Bay

0 ——————— 10
kilometres

Stykkishólmur

The first town of note on the north coast, whether you're approaching from Búðardalur or from Borgarnes, is picturesque **STYKKISHÓLMUR**, with its brightly coloured harbourside buildings. The largest and most enjoyable town on Snæfellsnes, with a population of around 1100, it is renowned today for its halibut and scallops landed from the waters of Breiðafjörður, which borders the northern coast of the peninsula and is technically more a sea bay than a fjord, full of skerries and rocky islets.

The Stykkishólmur region was actually one of the first to be settled in Iceland, and the countryside here features in several tales, most notably the **Erbyggja Saga**. This strange story, thick with evil spirits, bloody family vendettas and political intrigue, follows the life of the morally ambivalent Snorri Þórgrímsson, a pagan priest and son of a Viking who finally becomes a champion of Christianity. Easily accessible sites from the period include **Þingvellir**, an assembly ground just south of the town; and the nearby mountain **Helgafell**, the final resting place for Guðrún Ósvifsdóttir, heroine of the *Laxdæla Saga* (see box, p.168). In fact, it was at the foot of Helgafell that the first settler in the region, **Þórólfur Mostraskegg**, found his high-seat pillars; in true Viking seafaring fashion he'd thrown them overboard vowing to settle wherever they washed up. He named the *nes* (or promontory) where he found them after the god of thunder, Þór – hence the name Þórsnes.

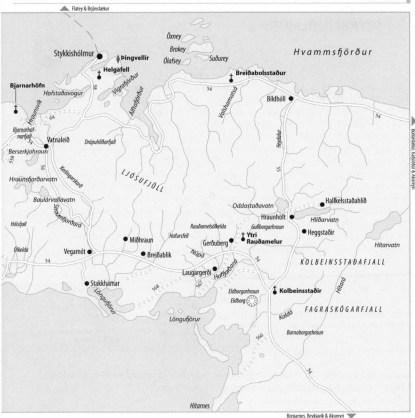

Norska húsið

Hafnargata 5 • Mid-May to Aug daily 11am–6pm • 800kr

It wasn't until the beginning of the nineteenth century that things really got moving in Stykkishólmur, when a man by the name of Árni Thorlacius (1802–91) inherited the town's trading rights from his father and became the town's leading merchant, buying and selling all manner of goods, though predominantly fish. In 1832, he set about building **Norska húsið** (Norwegian House) with coarsely hewn timber from Norway, as was the tradition in the nineteenth century – Iceland then, as now, had little timber of its own. The building is still the town's most impressive today, and houses a **museum** that attempts a potted history of Stykkishólmur; look out for the old black-and-white photographs of Árni and his wife, Anna, with whom he had eleven children, on the second floor, which has been reconstructed as their living room. Rather curiously, Icelanders remember Árni not so much for his commercial success in drawing the town into the modern age but for his pioneering **weather reports** from 1845.

Vatnasafn

Bókhlöðustígur 17 • June–Aug daily 1–6pm; at other times by appointment • 500kr • ⓦ libraryofwater.is

From Norska húsið, it's a short stroll up the hill to the former library, which now houses the intriguing **Vatnasafn** (Library of Water), a constellation of tall, glass columns containing glacial water collected from around Iceland, which is the work of the American artist Roni Horn. As natural light is refracted through the columns, unusual

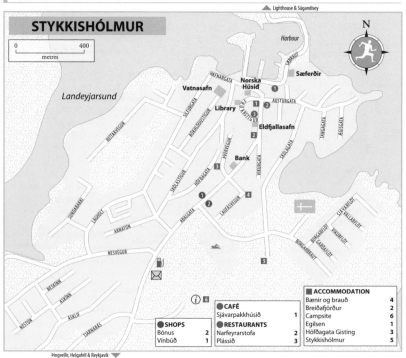

shapes and shadows are created on the floor, which is inscribed with Icelandic and English words that describe the weather or human moods.

Súgandisey

From the harbour, it's worth strolling along on Sæbraut past the Sæferðir shipping office to the set of steps leading up to **Súgandisey**, the rocky island which protects the town from the ravages of the open waters of Breiðafjörður. From the bright orange **lighthouse** that sits amid tussocky grass at the highest point of the island, there are unsurpassed postcard-perfect views of the multicoloured houses of Stykkishólmur, with Helgafell in the distance.

Eldfjallasafn

Aðalgata 6 • May–Sept daily 11am–5pm • 900kr • W eldfjallasafn.is

Stykkishólmur's other main place of interest is the unusual **Eldfjallasafn** (Volcano Museum), a repository of all things volcanic, including an impressive collection of "volcano art", paintings which all portray volcanic eruptions: there's even an original by Andy Warhol from 1985, whose explosive reds and oranges show an erupting Vesuvius. Founded by Iceland's leading volcanologist, local man Haraldur Sigurðsson, the museum also contains samples of the main rocks found in Iceland as well as ancient stone artefacts discovered in Pompeii and Herculaneum. Don't leave without seeing the fascinating English-language **film** (upstairs) which recounts Haraldur's expedition to the Tambora volcano in Indonesia and his discovery of a buried village in the crater. The museum is also the best place in Iceland to get to grips with the impact of the 2010 **Eyjafjallajökull eruption**. A superb hour-long National Geographic film (also shown upstairs) gives a comprehensive and easily understandable account of the volcano's effect on local people as well as international airline flights; it also features an informative interview with Haraldur.

GETTING TO THE WEST FJORDS FROM STYKKISHÓLMUR
If you're heading to the **West Fjords**, you'll cut out a long and tedious detour around the coast by catching the **car ferry** from Stykkishólmur harbour to Brjánslækur (2 daily June–Aug, 1 daily Sept–April; 3hr; 5250kr single, plus 5250kr per car; ☎ 433 2254, ⓦ saeferdir.is).

If you take the early ferry in summer, it's possible to continue by bus (June–Aug daily) from Brjánslækur to Patreksfjörður (see p.211), Rauðasandur and the Látrabjarg bird cliffs (see p.214); two buses leave Brjánslækur after the ferry arrival at 11.45am, one heading for Patreksfjörður, the other for Rauðsasandur where there's a 15min stop before driving back to the main road. At the road junction near Hvalsker you can then change buses and pick up the service from Patreksfjörður to Látrabjarg. Tell the bus driver in advance if you are heading to Hotel Látrabjarg (see p.213). The same journey applies in return, connecting with the late sailing from Brjánslækur to Stykkishólmur. **Times and fares** are at ⓦ wa.is and the bus must be booked in advance. Various fare options are available, including passes which allow travel over several days.

The church

3

Borgarbraut • Daily June–Sept 10am–5pm • Free

The only other sight in town is the space-age-looking **church**, a ten-minute walk from the harbour up on a rocky hill overlooking the town and with good views on a clear day out towards the waters of Breiðafjörður. Although construction began in 1975, the church wasn't consecrated until fifteen years later; its design includes a vast white ladder-like bell-tower rearing up over the doorway and a semicircular domed rear roof. The interior is equally unusual, lit by hundreds of light bulbs suspended from the ceiling.

ARRIVAL AND INFORMATION

STYKKISHÓLMUR

By bus Buses stop at the entrance to town by the filling station at Aðalgata 25, which functions as the town's bus station; from here, it's a 10min walk along Aðalgata into town. For connections to and from towns west of Stykkishólmur on the peninsula, you change buses at Vatnaleið, 15min west of Stykkishólmur.
Destinations Arnarstapi (1 daily; 2hr); Borgarnes (2 daily; 1hr 30min); Grundarfjörður (2 daily; 40min); Hellissandur (2 daily; 1hr 15min); Ólafsvík (2 daily; 1hr).
Tourist information It's expected the tourist information office (June–Aug daily 9am–5pm; ☎ 438 8120, ⓦ stykkisholmur.is) will relocate to the campsite at the entrance to the town – check online for the precise location.

Services Internet facilities are available at the library (June–Aug daily 1–6pm) at Hafnargata 7 down by the harbour. On the way into town from the campsite you'll pass the Bónus supermarket (Mon–Thurs 11am–6.30pm, Fri 10am–7.30pm, Sat 10am–6pm, Sun noon–6pm); an excellent outdoor swimming pool (Mon–Thurs 7am–10pm, Fri 7am–7pm, Sat & Sun 10am–6pm; 700kr), at the corner of Borgarbraut,, with three hot pots and a sports complex; and the state liquor store, the *vínbúð* (Mon–Thurs 2–6pm, Fri 2–7pm, Sat 11am–2pm), is at Aðalgata 24. The post office (Mon–Fri 9am–4.30pm) is on Aðalgata and the bank (with ATM) is a few doors along.

ACCOMMODATION

★**Bænir og brauð** Laufásvegur 1 ☎ 820 5408, ⓦ baenirogbraud.is. Run by the delightful Greta, this cosy guesthouse is a real find: friendly, stylish and mercifully no chintz. Guests can use the hot tub and the barbecue on the outdoor terrace, and the freshly prepared breakfast is a special treat. 17,500kr
Breiðafjörður Aðalgata 8 ☎ 433 2200, ⓦ hotel breidafjordur.is. Right in the heart of the town, this friendly, easy-going hotel has just a dozen or so modern rooms, all with private facilities. There's also a delightful conservatory with good views over the town. Cheaper, more basic rooms sharing facilities are also available. Doubles 9500kr
Campsite Aðalgata 27 ☎ 438 1075. The town's campsite

is located next to the sports field at the entrance to the town, just off the main street. There are plenty of pitches for tents and caravans, plus a service building with showers and toilets. Late May to Aug. 1300kr
★**Egilsen** Aðalgata 2 ☎ 554 7700, ⓦ egilsen.is. Housed in an atmospheric timber building from 1867, Stykkishólmur's new boutique hotel is the best place to stay in town: wood-panelled rooms painted in subtle pastel colours replete with top-quality beds will ensure a sound night's sleep. 30,500kr
Höfðagata Gisting Höfðagata 11 ☎ 694 6569, ⓦ hofdagata.is. A long-established, comfortable and modern guesthouse, handy for the centre of town, though with just four rather small rooms, one with private

facilities. Although there's no kitchen, guests do have access to a fridge and a barbecue. **17,500kr**

Stykkishólmur Borgarbraut 8 ☎430 2100, ✆hring hotels.is. Atop a small hill behind the swimming pool, this eighty-room hotel is the largest of the town's accommodation options. Rooms here are subtly decorated in warm, autumnal colours, and many look out over the green expanses of the golf course. **27,000kr**

EATING AND DRINKING

Narfeyrarstofa Aðalgata 3 ☎438 1119. Cosy brasserie serving a good range of fresh fish dishes for 3950kr, as well as a deliciously different lamb goulash soup at 2450kr and a tasty lamb plate consisting of tenderloin and shank served with birch syrup for 5100kr. Daily noon–10pm.

Plássið Frúarstígur 1 ☎436 1600. This pleasant place specializes in good-quality fish dishes: the pan-fried blue ling with smoked salmon barley and fresh salad (3950kr) is particularly tasty. There's also a range of lighter pasta dishes, including scallops and seafood, from 2400kr. Daily noon–9pm.

Sjávarpakkhúsið Hafnargata 2 ☎438 1800. Housed in the town's former fish-packing factory, this snug little café serves a delicious fish soup (1590kr), though the local blue mussels and fish of the day (both 2990kr) are also excellent. Mon–Thurs & Sun 6pm–midnight, Fri & Sat 6pm–3am.

Þingvellir

A couple of kilometres south of Stykkishólmur, a small track off Route 58 to the east (and running parallel with the Nesvogur inlet) leads to the old local parliament site of **Þingvellir** (not to be confused with the country's principal Þingvellir site in Southwest Iceland; see p.101), right at the water's edge. This became a meeting place for the surrounding area following the death of the region's first settler, Þórólfur Mostraskegg. During his lifetime the parliament was on the nearby promontory of Þórsnes, and it was here that Eirík the Red was outlawed following a spate of murders (see box, p.166). A few ruins can still be seen, including a **sacrificial site** that served as an altar to the god Þór, as recounted in the *Erbyggja Saga* – the only mention in any saga that the Vikings practised human sacrifice.

Helgafell

From Þingvellir, the small mountain you can see to the southwest conspicuous on the flat plain is **Helgafell** (73m), or Holy Mountain, which – like many mountains around Iceland with the same name – was regarded sacred in pagan times when it was believed to be an entrance to Valhalla. Indeed, Þórólfur Mostraskegg considered the mountain so holy that he forbade anyone to relieve themselves within sight of it, a decision that later sparked the *Erbyggja Saga*'s central feud, when a neighbouring clan attending the Þingvellir assembly refused to abide by this law. Much later, a **monastery** moved here from the island of Flatey, and stood at the foot of the mountain from 1184 until the Reformation.

It's possible to climb the mountain: the path on the west side is easy enough, but the eastern descent is steep and rocky and you have to pick your way carefully. The ascent is worth making, though: at the top there are ruins of a tiny thirteenth-century **chapel**, Tótt, and striking **views** over the islands of Breiðafjörður and to the mountains of the West Fjords. Guðrún Ósvifsdóttir, heroine of the *Laxdæla Saga* (see box, p.168), spent the last years of her life at the farm at the southern foot of Helgafell and, over nine hundred years on, people still decorate her grave with wild flowers – it's in the simple churchyard (itself at the foot of the mountain and separate from the chapel), marked by a headstone. Even today, local myth has it that anyone climbing from her grave to the chapel remains on top of the mountain will be granted three wishes, on the condition that they climb in silence and the wishes are pure-hearted, kept totally secret and made while standing beside the remains facing east.

From Stykkishólmur, it's a 4km walk to Helgafell on Route 58: once past the airstrip and the Nesvogur inlet, take the second turning on the left. All buses in and out of Stykkishólmur pass this junction.

FROM TOP STYKKISHÓLMUR (P.170); LANDNÁMSSETUR ÍSLANDS, BORGARNES (P.155) >

Flatey

The largest of the Breiðafjörður islands, **FLATEY** is a tranquil haven of two dozen or so restored wooden cottages set amid fields that are bright yellow with buttercups in summer. If you like the idea of having nothing to do all day but stroll through undisturbed meadows while taking in magnificent vistas of the West Fjord mountains and Snæfellsjökull, then dining by evening on succulent cod caught the same afternoon, this is the place to come. The weather is most dependable in August, but remember if you're coming here out of season the island will be virtually deserted, since most of the houses are only occupied in summer by Reykjavík city slickers; just five people spend the winter on Flatey.

Although low-key in the extreme today, Flatey was once one of Iceland's leading cultural centres, and in 1172 a **monastery** was founded on the island's highest point, a little behind where the present-day church stands, though there's nothing left of it today.

The old village

From the ferry jetty it's a ten-minute walk down the rough track that passes as the island's one and only road to the **old village**, a restored collection of painted houses nestling around a tiny **harbour**. It's from here that Flatey's sheep are painstakingly bundled into boats and taken to surrounding islands for summer grazing – quite a sight if you're around to witness it.

Past the harbour the track bears right, turns into a well-trodden path and climbs a little to the diminutive **Lundaberg** cliffs where you'll find plenty of **black guillemot**, **kittiwakes**, **fulmars** and **puffins** from April onwards; half of all the different species of bird that breed in Iceland are found on the islands of Breiðafjörður.

The church and library
Church open access

Flatey's **church**, with its dramatic roof, is easily reached by a footpath from the village's main street. Inside, you'll see paintings of island life – and puffins – by the Catalan painter **Baltasar Samper**. Quite the entrepreneur, while visiting the island in the 1960s he suggested painting the church in return for free accommodation; his picture behind the altar shows Christ, unconventionally wearing a traditional Icelandic woolly sweater, standing alongside two local sheep farmers. After much hard work, the yellow building behind the church has been restored to its former glory and proudly claims the title of the oldest and smallest library in Iceland, established in 1864.

The rest of the island

Beyond the Lundaberg cliffs, the footpath continues towards the eastern part of the island, which has been declared a **nature reserve**, marked by the odd sign or two and closed to the public during the breeding season (May 15 to July 20); the birds migrate south in late August or early September. Even during the breeding season, however, it's possible to walk *around* the eastern part of the island following the marked wooden

---

FLATEYJARBÓK

Flatey was once home to the **Flateyjarbók**, a collection of illuminated medieval manuscripts written on 113 calfskins. Although the book was written at Víðidalstunga in northern Iceland around 1387, it somehow turned up on the island and remained in the possession of a local farmer's family until they gave it to the Bishop of Skálholt, who in turn sent it by royal request to King Frederik III of Denmark in 1659. The Flateyjarbók finally returned to Iceland in 1971 and is today stored in Reykjavík.

posts, to Flatey's south coast, though the latter is also closed at this time – you can reach it but you cannot walk along it. Here you'll be bombarded by arctic tern, which show no mercy for man or beast – even the island's sheep are subject to regular divebombing raids. If you don't mind this (keeping still seems to deter the birds a little), there are some secluded pebbly coves here, home to the odd wrecked fishing boat, with excellent views on a clear day across to Snæfellsjökull.

ARRIVAL AND DEPARTURE   **FLATEY**

By ferry The car ferry between Stykkishólmur and Brjánslækur calls in at Flatey once daily in each direction from Sept to May and twice daily from June to Aug; schedules are at ⑩ saeferdir.is, and single fares to Flatey are 3580kr from Stykkishólmur and 2985kr from Brjánslækur. Destinations Brjánslækur (1hr 15min); Stykkishólmur (1hr 45min).

ACCOMMODATION

★**Flatey** ⊘ 422 7610, ⑩ hotelflatey.is. Oozing rustic charm, this is one of Iceland's most appealing hotels. Set in two former warehouses which date from the island's heyday in the 1800s, the eleven snug rooms share facilities, and have wood-panelled interiors that perfectly complement the sturdy timber buildings. The restaurant functions as a small café during the day with home-made cakes, a tasty soup of the day for lunch at 2100kr and more substantial evening dishes such as fresh mussels from Breiðafjörður (2900kr). Below the restaurant, the atmospheric *Saltkjallarinn* pub, replete with sturdy stone walls, is a great place for a cold beer after a day's exploring. Restaurant daily noon–9pm; pub daily 6pm–late. June–Aug. **25,500kr**

Berserkjahraun

Just after Vatnaleið (the junction with Route 56), Route 54 crosses **Berserkjahraun**, a 4000-year-old lavafield named after the two **Berserkers** who cleared a route through it in 982 AD. Periodically mentioned in the sagas, Berserkers were formidable warriors, able to go into a trance that made them impervious to wounds; though much valued as fighters, they were given a wide berth socially, since they were considered to be very dangerous. Here, as related in the *Eyrbyggja Saga*, local man Víga-Styr gave the two the odd task of forging a route through the lava because one of the Berserkers had fallen in love with his daughter, and completing this well-nigh impossible task was a condition Víga-Styr had set for their marriage. However, with help from the tale's arch-schemer Snorri Þórgrímsson, he later killed the Berserkers and married his daughter to Snorri. Just east of the junction with Route 56, there's a rough but usually navigable 5km **vehicle track** (Route 558) heading inland off the main road, which loops west across the centre of the lavafield to rejoin Route 54; look carefully and you'll see the path the men cut, known as Berserkjagata, beside which is their burial mound.

Grundarfjörður

Once across the small bridge over Hraunsfjörður, Route 54 swings into **GRUNDARFJÖRÐUR**, 45km west of Stykkishólmur and dominated by the neighbouring **Kirkjufell** mountain. Established in 1786 by the Danish king as one of six commercial centres in Iceland, the place exerted a strong influence on the west coast; in the early 1800s, for example, traders could only operate in the region if they had a branch in Grundarfjörður. From 1800 to 1860, French fishermen also profited from the excellent harbour here and used the town as a base, owning the church, hospital and shipping operations. When they left, they dismantled their buildings and even exhumed their dead, shipping the bodies back to France. Today the village and its 850 inhabitants depend on their position as the commercial centre of western Iceland, and on the local freezing plant, for prosperity.

3

WHALE-WATCHING AND PUFFIN TOURS FROM GRUNDARFJÖRÐUR

Departing from the harbour at the foot of Hrannarstígur, Láki Tours (Norðurgarður; ☎ 546 6808, ⓦ lakitours.com) operate winter **whale-watching tours**, in addition to **puffin-spotting trips** during the summer months when the birds congregate on the Melrakkey islands just offshore, as well as summer fishing trips. During the winter months, killer whales can be seen just offshore, attracted by the plentiful supplies of herring in the surrounding waters. From November to mid-April, tours operate once or twice daily to see the orcas (2–3hr; 9400kr; see website for precise details). For summer whale-watching trips (mid-May to mid-Sept 1 or 2 daily; 3hr; 8900kr), the departure location is nearby Ólafsvík, though you should book in Grundarfjörður at the harbour office. Possible sightings in summer include sperm whales, fin whales, orcas, humpback and minke whales. Tours also operate from Grundarfjörður between June and mid-September to see puffins; sailings are generally twice daily and last around an hour (5000kr). There's also the option to go birdwatching and sea-angling from Grundarfjörður – departures are weather dependent (around 3hr; 7900kr). Full details can be found on the website.

ARRIVAL AND INFORMATION

By bus Buses stop at the filling station on Grundargata, the main road.

Destinations Arnarstapi (1 daily; 1hr 15min); Hellissandur (2 daily; 35min); Ólafsvík (2 daily; 20min); Stykkishólmur (2 daily; 35min).

Tourist information The office inside the heritage centre (mid-May to mid-Sept daily 9am–5pm; ☎ 438 1881, ⓦ grundarfjordur.is) also has internet access and a small café.

Services The local swimming pool (Mon–Fri 7am–9pm,

GRUNDARFJÖRÐUR

Sat & Sun 10am–6pm; 600kr), with an outdoor pool, two hot pots and sauna, is located at the southern end of Borgarbraut. The supermarket (Mon–Sat 9am–8pm, Sun 10am–8pm), with ATM inside, is opposite the heritage centre at the junction of Grundargata and Hrannarstáigur. If you want to buy alcohol, you'll have to time things carefully, since the *vínbúð* at Grundargata 30 has ludicrously short opening hours (May–Aug Mon–Thurs 4–6pm, Fri 1–6pm; Sept–April Mon–Thurs 4–6pm, Fri 2–6pm).

ACCOMMODATION AND EATING

Campsite 1km east of the village at the farm by the Kverná River ☎ 530 8564. This is a very basic campsite with just one shower and one toilet; the ground is rather rocky in parts, too. Pay at the swimming pool. **1100kr**

Framnes Nesvegur 8 ☎ 438 6893, ⓦ hotelframnes.is. Pleasant waterfront hotel originally built as a fisherman's hostel in the 1950s. It's now completely refurbished and looks smart and modern; all rooms have en-suite facilities. There's a hot tub and sauna for guests' use, too. The hotel restaurant offers upmarket dining; the speciality is gourmet seafood, freshly caught and landed in Grundarfjörður. There's usually also a couple of vegetarian dishes on the menu, and mains around 3500kr. Restaurant daily 6.30–9pm. **27,900kr**

Láki Hafnarkaffi Nesvegur 5 ☎ 546 6808. Owned by the nearby hotel, this trendy little harbourside café serves a great range of speciality coffees, panini, cakes and soup.

There are also pizzas on offer for around 2495kr. Perfect for a coffee break before going on a whale-watching tour (they leave from just outside). Daily 9am–9pm.

Rú Ben Grundargata 59 ☎ 436 6446. Named after owners Heiðrun and Ben, this glorified truckers' café-cum-bar serves up a good-value set lunch for 1550kr including coffee, burgers from 1600kr, fish and chips for 3100kr, and a decent pasta dish of chicken, bacon and mushroom for 3000kr. Outside terrace, too. Mon–Thurs 11am–11pm, Fri & Sat 11am–1am, Sun noon–10pm.

Youth hostel Hlíðarvegur 15 ☎ 562 6533, ⓦ hostel.is. Open all year round, the town's hostel has rooms in several locations in Grundarfjörður which come in various sizes, both with and without private facilities. The main building also has a kitchen for guest use. Check-in 3–9pm. Dorms **5000kr**, doubles **11,000kr**

Ólafsvík

The most productive fishing town on Snæfellsnes, **ÓLAFSVÍK** is also Iceland's oldest-established trading town, having been granted its charter in 1687. Squeezed between the sea and the towering Enni peak (415m), it's a quiet working village whose population goes about its daily business seemingly unmoved by the groups of travellers who turn up here in search of **Snæfellsjökull**, the nearby glacier (see box opposite). The **church** on

Kirkjutún is worth a quick look for its three-legged detached bell tower and its sharply pointed spire. Whale-watching tours depart from Ólafsvík in summer (see box opposite).

Gamla Pakkhúsið

Ólafsbraut • June–Aug daily noon–5pm • 500kr

Other than the ice cap, Ólafsvík's main sight is the **Gamla Pakkhúsið**, a solid-looking timber warehouse built in 1844 by the town's leading trading firm which, naturally, dealt in fish. Today it houses a **folk museum**, which has a few good black-and-white photographs of the town and the obligatory exhibitions about fishing.

ARRIVAL AND INFORMATION　　　　　　　　　　　　　　　　　　　ÓLAFSVÍK

By bus Buses arrive at, and depart from, the forecourt of the filling station on the main road, Ólafsvík.

Destinations Arnarstapi (1 daily; 55min); Hellissandur (2 daily; 15min); Grundarfjörður (2 daily; 20min); Stykkishólmur (2 daily; 1hr).

Tourist information There's an office at Kirkjutún 2 (June–Aug Mon–Fri 9am–5pm, Sat & Sun 10am–4pm; ✆ 433 9930, ⓦ westiceland.is).

Services The supermarket is just up from the harbour at Norðurtangi 1 (Mon–Thurs 9am–6pm, Fri 9am–8pm, Sat & Sun 1–5pm); the *vínbúð* is at Ólafsbraut 55 (May–Aug Mon–Thurs 2–6pm, Fri 1–7pm, Sat 11am–2pm; Sept–April Mon–Fri 2–6pm); and the indoor swimming pool is at Ennisbraut 9 (Mon–Fri 7.30am–9pm, Sat & Sun 10am–5pm; 500kr). The post office is at Bæjartún 5 (Mon–Fri 10am–4pm).

ACCOMMODATION AND EATING

Campsite Hvalsá ✆ 433 6929. Easily identifiable by the old fishing boat stranded nearby on the main road by the Hvalsá River, 1km east of the town centre, the site has hot and cold running water and toilets. **500kr**

Grillið Ólafsbraut 19 ✆ 436 1362. Rather charmless grill restaurant-cum-DVD store serving burgers (from 1530kr) and run-of-the-mill pizzas (2340kr); it's best used for a quick dine-and-dash experience. There's a handful of stools

---

SNÆFELLSJÖKULL

Enter the Snæfellsjökull crater, which is kissed by Scatari's shadow before the first of July, adventurous traveller, and thou wilt descend to the centre of the Earth.

Journey to the Centre of the Earth, Jules Verne

Made world famous in the nineteenth century by Jules Verne's *Journey to the Centre of the Earth*, **Snæfellsjökull** stands guard at the very tip of the peninsula to which it gave its name (**Snæfell** means "Snow Mountain"; Snæfellsnes means "Snow Mountain Peninsula"). It is from here that Verne's hero, the German geologist Professor Lidenbrock of Hamburg, descends into a crater in the dormant volcano under the glacier and embarks on a fantastic subterranean journey accompanied by his nephew and an Icelandic guide with the very un-Icelandic name of Hans. The professor has managed to decipher a document written in runic script that leads him to believe that this is the way to the centre of the Earth; rather inexplicably, he finally emerges on the volcanic Mediterranean island of Strómboli. This remote part of Iceland has long been associated with supernatural forces and mystery, and stories like this only strengthen this belief – at one time the glacier even became a point of pilgrimage for New Age travellers, though they're not much in evidence today. The 1446m, three-peaked glacier sits on a dormant volcano marked by a large crater, 1km in diameter, with cliff walls 200m high; three eruptions have occurred under the glacier in the past ten thousand years, the last around 250 AD.

Experienced hikers have a choice of **ascents**, though you'll probably need ice axes and crampons, and should also first talk to the national park office in Malarrif (late May to mid-Sept daily 10am–5pm; ✆ 436 6888, ⓦ snaefellsjokull.is) about the condition of routes and the likely **weather**. There are two **trailheads**: either east off the four-wheel-drive-only Route F570, which clips Snæfell's eastern flank as it runs for 18km between Ólafsvík and Arnarstapi; or at the ice cap's northwestern corner, via a track running east of Neshraun. **Hiking trails** cross between these two starting points via the glacier's apex, Jökulþúfur (1446m), which sits atop three crags on the crater rim – allow at least four hours to make the crossing, not counting the time it takes to reach the trailheads themselves.

inside, should you choose to eat in. Daily 10am–11pm.
Hraun Grundarbraut 2 ☎ 436 1300. Built from imported Lithuanian pine, this cosy restaurant resembles a giant log cabin – and the food is great: the blue mussels with coriander and chilli (3900kr), cod fillet (3900kr) or any of the pizzas (from 1490kr), including one with lobster, are all good bets. There's live music here each weekend, too. Daily noon–10pm.
Ólafsvík Ólafsbraut 20 ☎ 436 1650, ⓦ hringhotels.is. This rather average hotel has rooms both with and without private facilities as well as a number of apartments which include a small seating area as well as a simple kitchen. The

hotel restaurant serves dinner only: 5200kr will buy a three-course meal with fresh fish, whereas 6900kr is the price for three set courses with lamb. Restaurant daily noon–9pm. **20,900kr**
Við Hafið Ólafsbraut 55 ☎ 436 1166, ⓔ vidhafid @hotmail.com. A newly opened guesthouse, right above the *vínbúð* (see p.179) in the centre of Ólafsvík. The interior is decorated throughout in pine and there's dorm accommodation in bunk beds as well as regular double rooms. Guests have access to a kitchen, too, for self-catering. Dorms **5000kr**, doubles **15,000kr**

Hellissandur

From Ólafsvík, Route 574 continues west past the dramatic Harðikambur black-sand beach on its way towards the minuscule fishing hamlet of **Rif**, really nothing more than a well-protected harbour and a few fish-processing plants. Some 2km further on, its marginally bigger neighbour, **HELLISSANDUR**, known locally as just Sandur, is the westernmost settlement on Snæfellsnes and home to most of the fishermen from nearby Rif. It's also the terminus for **buses** from Reykjavík and the starting point and terminus of the clockwise summer service around the peninsula's tip. There's very little to do in Hellissandur other than to pay a quick visit to the Sjómannagarður museum, though the village makes a good base from which to tackle the various **hikes** around western Snæfellsnes (see box, p.183).

Sjómannagarður
June to mid-Aug Tues–Fri 9.30am–noon & 1–6pm, Sat & Sun 1–6pm • 500kr
Beside the main road, Útnesvegur, two old **fishermen's cottages**, complete with turf roofs, make up the **Sjómannagarður** (Maritime Museum). The larger of the two buildings holds an assortment of elderly fishing equipment and the oldest rowing boat in Iceland, dating from 1826.

Western Europe's tallest structure
Just two kilometres west of Hellisandur, at a spot known as Gufuskálar, you'll come across a huge radio mast, anchored down at five levels by wire cables against the brute force of Atlantic storms. At 412m in height, the mast is the tallest structure in the whole of western Europe and is over 100m taller than both London's Shard and the Eiffel Tower in Paris. Originally built in 1963 as part of the now defunct LOPRAN navigation system for aircraft and shipping, the mast now transmits the booming 189kHz long-wave signal for Icelandic national radio, including detailed shipping forecasts which are a lifeline for the many fishing vessels off the Icelandic west coast. Indeed, such is the power radiated from the mast that a fluorescent light bulb will light up if held close to it, and radio reception in nearby Hellissandur is all but nonexistent due to the interference the mast produces. If you're here in windy weather (likely), you'll witness the top of the mast swaying by up to 7m – quite a sight.

ARRIVAL AND INFORMATION   HELLISSANDUR

By bus Buses arrive at, and depart from, the car park at *Hótel Hellisandur* (see p.182).
Destinations Arnarstapi (1 daily; 40min); Grundarfjörður (2 daily; 40min); Ólafsvík (2 daily; 15min); Stykkishólmur

(2 daily; 1hr 15min).
Services Hellissandur's skeletal facilities – most usefully an ATM and fuel station – are located along the main road, Klettsbúð.

OPPOSITE LIGHTHOUSE, SNÆFELLSNES PENINSULA (P.168)>

ACCOMMODATION AND EATING

Campsite Sandahraun ☎433 6929. Hellissandur's grassy campsite is beautifully located by an open meadow on the eastern edge of the village, and has a service building with hot water and showers. Mid-May to Sept. **500kr**

Freezer Hostel Hafnargata 16, Rif ☎865 9432 ⓦthefreezerhostel.com. Housed in a former fish factory in Rif, next to Hellissandur, this place is both hostel and theatre, admittedly a curious mix, but somehow it works. Accommodation is in dorms only with shared facilities in one part of the building, with the theatre and exhibition space right next door. Dorms **4500kr**

Hellissandur Klettsbúð 9 ☎430 8600, ⓦhotel hellissandur.is. Upmarket hotel with just twenty plainly decorated wood-panelled rooms offering agreeable views out towards the glacier. There's a restaurant here, too, serving a range of fresh fish for 1700kr at lunch and 3900kr for dinner. Restaurant daily 6–9pm. **27,900kr**

Kaffi Sif Klettsbúð 3 ☎577 3430. Set in the former doctor's surgery, this compact little café is a real treat: try the home-made fish gratin or *plokkfiskur* for 2700kr, though the delicious crêpes are also tempting. Owner Sif also makes a wicked fish soup (2300kr). Mon–Thurs & Sun 11am–8pm, Fri & Sat 11am–11.30pm.

Dritvík and around

Beyond the radio transmitter at Gufuskálar the landscape becomes increasingly desolate – there's nothing but wilderness between here and **Dritvík** bay, 24km southwest of Hellissandur, first along Route 574 then down the 572 signed for Dritvík and Djúpalónssandur. Once home to sixty fishing boats and one of the most prolific fishing villages on the peninsula, the bay is uninhabited today, and centuries of fishing tradition would have been completely lost if it were not for the continuing presence of four mighty lifting **stones** at nearby **Djúpalónssandur beach**, a short stroll south from the bay, all with individual names: the largest, *fullsterkur* (full strength), weighs in at 155kg, next comes *hálfsterkur* (half strength) at 140kg, then *hálfdrættingur* (weakling) at 49kg and finally *amlóði* (useless), weighing just 23kg. Any fisherman worth his salt had to be able to lift at least the latter two onto a ledge of rock at hip height to prove his strength. The smallest stone is now broken – perhaps after one too many attempts by weakling tourists.

Lóndrangar

The lofty **Lóndrangar** rock pillars are just 5km southeast of the Djúpalón lagoon and easily reached from Route 574 on the unnumbered road signed "Malarrif". The taller of the two is 75m high and known locally as the "Christian pillar", with its smaller neighbour called the "heathen pillar", although nobody seems to know why; both are remnants of a basalt cinder cone. Malarrif will also be the new location of the Snæfellsnes National Park office.

Vatnshellir lava cave

1km before the turn to Malarrif, on the left-hand side of the road • Mid-May to mid-Sept guided walking tours every hour on the hour, 10am–6pm; rest of the year daily at 1pm, 2pm & 3pm; around 45min • 2500kr • ☎665 2818, ⓦvatnshellir.is

The 8000-year-old Vatnshellir cave offers an opportunity to go 35m below ground to follow the course of a former river of lava. Tours involve a descent via a series of staircases to access the cave proper. Once underground, you walk around 200m along the course of the lava flow into the cave. Helmets and torches are provided.

Hellnar

Just like its western neighbour of Dritvík, the tiny settlement of **HELLNAR**, 35km south of Hellissandur, was once one of the peninsula's most prosperous fishing communities. However, the village is better known as the birthplace of one of medieval Iceland's greatest explorers and travellers, **Guðríður Þorbjarnardóttir**, the wife of Þorfinnur Karlsefni. Together they attempted to settle in Viking Vínland in

HIKING IN WESTERN SNÆFELLSNES

Hellissandur (see p.180) makes a good base for exploring the foot of the Snæfellsjökull and the surrounding **lavafields**. A recommended day hike of around 20km leads from the village to Eysteinsdalur valley; take the unmarked secondary road between the campsite and the maritime museum that leads towards the glacier. After around 1km the road becomes a hiking path which strikes out across the **Prestahraun** lavafield, joining up after 4km with the unnumbered road that runs up through the valley. Here, on the south side of the road, a signed path leads up the hill, **Rauðhóll**, to a red scoria crater. An impressive rift in the lava can also been seen to the east of the hill. Continue another 1km along the road towards the glacier and you'll come to a signposted path to the south of the road, which leads to the prominent basalt spur, **Klukka**, and a beautiful waterfall, **Klukkufoss**, where the Móðulækur River flows through a narrow canyon lined with basalt columns. Back on the main road and another 1km towards the glacier, a path to the north of the road leads to the **Blágil** ravine, where the Ljósulækir glacial river thunders through the narrow rugged gorge. To return to Hellissandur, retrace your steps along the main road, beyond the turn for the waterfall, to the hiking path that heads out to the north across the **Væjuhraun** lavafield for Rif. From here, simply head west along the coastal road to Hellissandur. Maps of these routes should be available from the tourist office in Ólafsvík (see p.179) and the hotel in Hellissandur (see opposite).

Another recommended day hike (18km) leads first to the sandy bay of **Skarðsvík**, walled in by cliffs and crags on its northern and western edges. The lava above the cliffs is overgrown with moss and can be a good place to see rare plants. Excellent **fishing** can be had in the bay's protected waters and it's therefore a favourite spot for local boats. To get here, follow Route 574 west out of Hellissandur to its junction with the unnumbered road signed for Skarðsvík; it's at this point that the main road swings inland, heading for the glacier and the turn for Eysteinsdalur valley. Just 2km west of Skarðsvík the road terminates at the peninsula's westernmost point, **Öndverðarnes**, a dramatic and weatherbeaten spot marked only by a lonely lighthouse and a stone well which legend has it is linked to three springs: one of fresh water, one of sea water and one of wine. The promontory is a favourite destination for basking **seals**, which favour the pebbly beach here. South of the cape the **Svörtuloft** cliffs are worth a visit; swarming with **seabirds** in summer, the cliffs provided a major source of eggs and birds for the tables of local villagers until the 1950s, when living standards began to rise. The free-standing crag in the sea here, **Skálasnagi**, was once connected to the mainland by a natural stone bridge until it fell victim to the pounding of Atlantic breakers in 1973. From the cliffs, a path heads east, inland through the **Neshraun** lavafield to an area of small hillocks known as **Neshólar**, before emerging at Skarðsvík.

3

1004, and, indeed, Gúðríður gave birth to the first white child to be born in America, Snorri Þorfinnsson. She eventually settled back in Iceland at Glaumbær, near Sauðárkrókur, where a statue in her memory stands in the churchyard (see p.233). Today, though, Hellnar consists of nothing more than a couple of farm buildings, a hotel and the odd holiday cottage either side of a steep, dead-end road that winds its way down to a picturesque hoof-shaped **harbour** and a tiny pebbly **beach** where the occasional fishing boat is moored. To the left of the harbour, the **Baðstofa** sea cave is known for its rich birdlife as well as its unusual light shades and hues caused by the swell of the sea.

ARRIVAL AND INFORMATION   HELLNAR

By bus Buses arrive at, and depart from, the car park of the *Hellnar* hotel (see p.184).

Destinations Arnarstapi (1 daily; 10min); Hellissandur (1 daily; 30min); Stykkishólmur (1 daily; 1hr 45min).

National park office Known as the *Gestastofa*, the national park office at the entrance to the village (late May

to mid-Sept daily 10am–5pm; ☎436 6888, ⓦ snaefellsjokull.is) has photographs and information boards about the Snæfellsnes glacier, useful if you're planning an ascent. Note that the office is scheduled to move to Malarrif, though no fixed opening date had been decided as we went to press.

ACCOMMODATION AND EATING

★**Fjöruhúsið** Right by the water's edge ☏ 435 6844. Atmospheric café with just six tables in an old salting house, and with an outside terrace, serving home-made cakes (900kr) as well as excellent fish soup (2450kr); the arty interior is lit by a dozen light bulbs suspended on long wire flexes. Late May to late Sept daily 10am–10pm.

Gíslabær On the hill down into Hellnar ☏ 435 6886, ✉ gisting@simnet.is. Rather simple guesthouse accommodation in a house looking out over the sea. Rooms share facilities and breakfast is available on demand. **7000kr**

★**Hellnar** At the entrance to the hamlet ☏ 435 6820, ⓦ hellnar.is. Rooms here enjoy stunning views out over the sea or of the Snæfellsnes mountains and are tastefully decorated in bright colours which perfectly complement the dramatic views outside. The hotel has been awarded a Green Globe certificate for its contribution to ecological sustainability, and its restaurant prides itself on its use of locally sourced fish, such as succulent pan-fried plaice (3950kr), as well as a range of meat and organic vegetarian options. Restaurant May to mid-Oct daily 6–9.30pm. **25,000kr**

Arnarstapi and around

Just east of Hellnar along the main road – or a short walk along a clifftop path – the village of **ARNARSTAPI** sits at the foot of Stapafell (526m). It comprises little more than a few holiday cottages and a **harbour**, reached by following the road through the village down to the sea – but beware of the large number of arctic tern that gather here during summer and take pleasure in divebombing unsuspecting intruders. On entering the village, look out too for the large stone **monument** to the pagan-age figure Barður Snæfellsás who, according to local legend, still lives in Snæfellsjökull and protects the area from evil.

ARRIVAL AND DEPARTURE
ARNARSTAPI

By bus Buses arrive at, and depart from, *Snjófell* cottage (see below).

Destinations Hellissandur (1 daily; 40min); Stykkishólmur (1 daily; 2hr).

ACCOMMODATION AND EATING

Snjófell At the entrance to the village ☏ 435 6783, ⓦ snjofell.is. This red-walled, turf-roofed cottage offers sleeping-bag accommodation as well as regular double rooms in a converted two-storey building. It's also possible to camp here with full facilities. The decent restaurant inside the complex is also the only place to eat in town, serving the likes of soup (1600kr), lamb chops (3900kr) and fresh fish (3300kr). Restaurant daily 11.30am–late. May–Sept. Doubles **14,250kr**, sleeping bags **5000kr**

Búðir

Nineteen kilometres east of Arnarstapi, **BÚÐIR** is a romantic, windswept location, a former fishing village at the head of the sweeping expanse of white sand that backs the Búðavík bay. The settlement, like so many others in this part of the country, was abandoned in the early nineteenth century and today consists of nothing more than a hotel and a church, both situated just a stone's throw from the ocean. Surrounded

---

SNÆFELLSJÖKULL TOURS FROM ARNARSTAPI

Arnarstapi is a starting point for hikes and jeep drives up to Snæfellsjökull via Route F570 (see box, p.179), but is also known for its **snowmobiling** excursions across the glacier. *Snjófell* cottage (see above) organizes 90min trips (Feb to mid-June; 25,000kr/person); speeding along the ice top is an exhilarating experience, and the views of the glacier and the coastline are breathtaking when the weather is good – but don't be tempted to head onto the ice if it's raining because you'll see nothing. If speed isn't your thing, a slower **snowcat**, a sort of open-top truck on caterpillar tracks, also carries groups of twenty or so across the ice (Feb–Aug; 1hr; 10,600kr/person).

LÝSUHÓLL

Five kilometres east of Búðir and 27km west of Vegamót, reached on Route 54, the dot on the map that is the horse farm of **Lýsuhóll** (☎435 6716, ⓦlysuholl.is) is one of the few places on the Snæfellsnes Peninsula with its own source of geothermal mineral water. The spring provides natural algae-rich water for the outdoor **swimming pool** and hot pot (June–Aug Mon–Sat 1.30–8.30pm, Sun 1.30–6pm; 650kr) and offers fantastic views of the surrounding mountains. It's also possible to go **horseriding** from the farm; reckon on 6000kr for the first hour, then 5000kr per hour after that. There's also **accommodation** available here (see below).

by the **Búðahraun lavafield**, rumoured to be home to countless elves, and enjoying unsurpassed views out over the Atlantic, the tiny pitch-black **church** with its three white-framed windows dates from 1703, and cuts an evocative image when viewed from the adjoining graveyard with the majestic Snæfellsnes mountain range as a backdrop. Look out too for the unusual wall, made of lava and topped with turf, that surrounds the churchyard.

3

ACCOMMODATION

BÚÐIR

★**Búðir** ☎435 6700, ⓦbudir.is. Once a favourite haunt of Iceland's Nobel-prize-winning author Halldór Laxness, this wonderful place right by the sea is a perfect blend of modern comfort with a hint of old-world nostalgia and opulence: rooms are individually decorated and sure to please. **36,300kr**

Lýsuhóll 5km east of Búðir ☎435 6716, ⓦlysuholl.is.

Accommodation at this horse farm (see box above) comes in the shape of a cabin or a double room, while the small restaurant serves home-made food: lunch here is 2500kr, while the delicious dinner buffet, featuring any number of fish dishes, is a good-value 3900kr. Restaurant daily 8am–9pm. Doubles **20,000kr**, cabins **25,000kr**

The West Fjords

DYNJANDISVOGUR

The West Fjords

Attached to the mainland by a narrow isthmus of land barely 10km wide, the West Fjords are one of the most breathtakingly beautiful and least-visited corners of Iceland. This peninsula of 8600 square kilometres, stretching out into the icy waters of the Denmark Strait, with dramatic fjords cutting deep into its heart, is the result of intense glaciation. Everything here is extreme – from the table mountains that dominate the landscape, to the ferocious storms that have gnawed the coastline into countless craggy inlets. Life up here, on the edge of the Arctic Circle, is tough – even in summer, temperatures seldom rise above 10°C, and drifting pack ice is never far from the north coast.

Since flat land is at a premium in this rugged part of the country, towns and villages have grown up on the narrow strip of lowland that separates the mountains from the fjords. Geologically all but cut off from the outside world, the inhabitants of the West Fjords have historically turned to the sea for their livelihood, and today the majority of the seven thousand people who still live here are financially dependent on **fishing** and its related industries. However, the traditional way of life is changing, and the effects of rural depopulation are being felt in every village as outlying farms are abandoned and dozens of young people choose the bright lights of Reykjavík over a precarious and uncertain future in the most isolated corner of Iceland.

The unforgiving geography of the West Fjords makes travel here difficult and convoluted. Many roads are surfaced with gravel, and they're always potholed and often circuitous. **Route 61**, for example, wiggles its way exasperatingly round no fewer than seven deeply indented fjords en route to the regional capital, **Ísafjörður**. Benefiting from a spectacular setting on a narrow spit of land jutting out into **Ísafjarðardjúp**, the town makes an excellent base from which to explore this 75km-long arm of the Denmark Strait at the heart of the West Fjords. From here, you can also take in **Drangajökull**, the only glacier in the region, and the outstanding natural beauty of the uninhabited **Hornstrandir** peninsula, which offers some of the wildest and most rewarding hiking in Iceland. From Ísafjörður, Route 60 weaves its way over mountain tops, round several fjords and past a handful of tiny fishing villages on its way to the ferry port of **Brjánslækur**, from where a ferry leaves the West Fjords for Flatey and Stykkishólmur. A brooding, lonely peninsula reaches out into the Atlantic from this point, terminating at **Látrabjarg**, Europe's most westerly point and one of the world's greatest bird cliffs, with large numbers of puffins, razorbills and other seabirds. The peninsula is also home to **Breiðavík**, one of Iceland's most stunning beaches, with mile upon mile of deserted golden sand. Nearby **Patreksfjörður**, the second town of the West Fjords, is the only place in the west of the region with a population big enough for life to go on independently of Ísafjörður.

PUFFIN, LÁTRABJARG CLIFFS

Highlights

❶ **Hiking in Hornstrandir** Experience nature in the raw in this remote and unspoilt national park of lush valleys and rocky plateaux on the very edge of Europe. **See p.200**

❷ **Dynjandi, Arnarfjörður** Meaning "The Thundering One", this mighty triangular-shaped waterfall is West Fjords nature at its most powerful. **See p.208**

❸ **Swimming in Patreksfjörður** Soak and swim in the heated waters of this fjordside pool with unsurpassed views of mountains and sea. **See p.212**

❹ **Breiðavík beach, southwestern peninsula** The white sands and aquamarine water of this idyllic bay make the perfect place to chill out and work on your tan – weather permitting. **See p.214**

❺ **Puffin spotting, Látrabjarg** Seek out Iceland's most endearing bird along this vertiginous cliff face, the westernmost point in Europe. **See p.214**

❻ **Djúpavík, Strandir coast** Get away from it all in this remote corner of the West Fjords, once the region's herring capital. **See p.220**

HIGHLIGHTS ARE MARKED ON THE MAP ON P.190

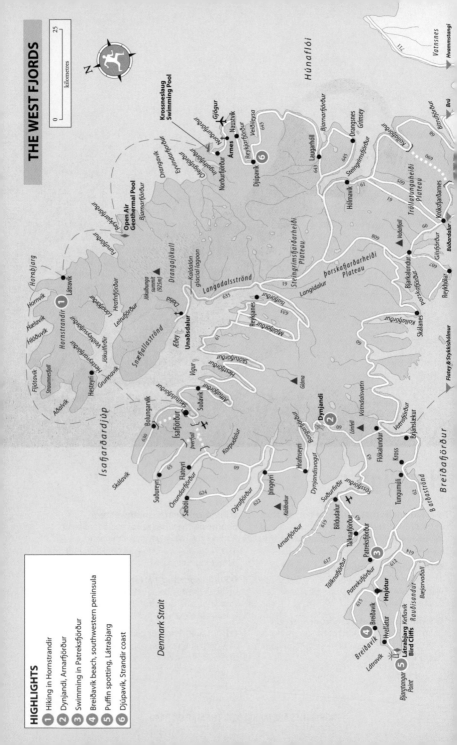

THE WEST FJORDS

HIGHLIGHTS

1. Hiking in Hornstrandir
2. Dynjandi, Arnarfjörður
3. Swimming in Patreksfjörður
4. Breiðavík beach, southwestern peninsula
5. Puffin spotting, Látrabjarg
6. Djúpavík, Strandir coast

0 — 25 kilometres

Denmark Strait

Hornstrandir

Ísafjarðardjúp

Breiðafjörður

Húnaflói

Vatnsnes

Krossneslaug Swimming Pool

Open Air Geothermal Pool

Látrabjarg Bird Cliffs

On the other side of the West Fjords, the eastern Strandir coast, which stretches north from the busy fishing village of **Hólmavík**, is hard to beat for splendid isolation, its few villages hardly visited by tourists, and with some of the most dramatic, forbidding landscapes this corner of the country has to offer, particularly around the former herring port of **Djúpavík**.

GETTING THERE   **THE WEST FJORDS**

By plane The West Fjords' airports are at Bíldudalur, Gjögur and Ísafjörður – all connected to Reykjavík. Details of services are given in the respective accounts of the three towns (p.210, p.221 & below).

By bus Operating all year, buses run four times per week from Borgarnes via the Ringroad village of Bifröst and along Route 61 to Hólmavík, from where there are connections to Ísafjörður; advance booking required (☎ 893 1058; ✆ isafjordur.is). Check the timetable (under the "How to get here and around link") carefully since

connections to Ísafjörður only operate two to three times per week depending on season. Local buses also run between Ísafjörður and Bolungarvík, Flateyri and Suðureyri.

By ferry The most interesting option for reaching the West Fjords is to catch the ferry from Stykkishólmur on the Snæfellsnes peninsula (see box, p.173). This lands at Brjánslækur, from where summer buses leave daily for Rauðasandur and Látrabjarg via Patreksfjörður, and also to Ísafjörður; advance booking required (☎ 456 5006).

Ísafjörður

With a population of around 2600, **ÍSAFJÖRÐUR** is far and away the largest settlement in the West Fjords, and is where most travellers choose to base themselves when exploring the region – not least because this is the only place from which to reach the Hornstrandir peninsula by boat, a major goal for many visitors. All administration for the area is centred here, too, and there's also a significant **fishing industry**. It's hard to imagine a much more dramatic location; built on the L-shaped sandspit, **Eyri**, which stretches out into the narrow waters of **Skutulsfjörður** fjord and provides exceptionally good shelter for ocean-going fishing vessels, the town is surrounded by towering mountains on three sides and by the open waters of **Ísafjarðardjúp** on the fourth.

During the long winter months, locals are forced to battle against the elements to keep open the tiny airport, which very often provides the only point of contact between the entire region and the rest of the country. Should you arrive in Ísafjörður by plane, however, you'll be treated to an unforgettable experience as you bank steeply around the fjord, then skim past the sheer mountainside of Kirkjubólshlíð before dropping onto the landing strip. In fact, during the darkest months of the year (Dec and Jan), the sheer height of the mountains either side of the fjord prevents the low winter sun from shining directly onto the town for a number of weeks, and the sun's reappearance over the mountain tops at the end of January is celebrated with **sólarkaffi**, "sun coffee" (in fact just normal coffee) and pancakes on January 25.

Today, Ísafjörður is a quiet and likeable place where you'd be wise to make the most of the shops and restaurants on offer before venturing out into the wilds beyond. There's very little of note, though, in the town itself – Ísafjörður's pleasures are more to be found in strolling through its streets or watching the fishermen at work in the harbour than in tourist sights. However, Byggðasafn Vestfjarða, the **West Fjords Heritage Museum**, one of the very few museums in the region, is worth visiting for an insight into the extreme conditions that past generations have lived under here. That it's located in one of the country's oldest timber buildings is unusual in itself, when you consider that the climate here is so severe that anything made out of wood tends to be quickly decimated by the elements.

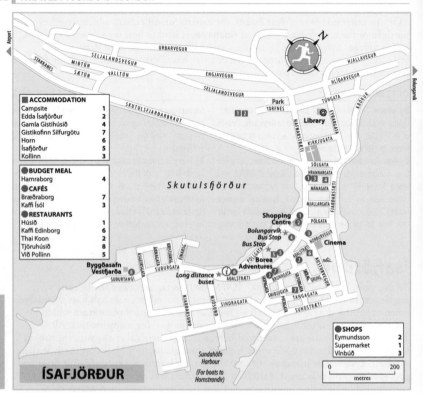

ACCOMMODATION
Campsite	1
Edda Ísafjörður	2
Gamla Gistihúsið	4
Gistikofinn Silfurgötu	7
Horn	6
Ísafjörður	5
Kollinn	3

BUDGET MEAL
Hamraborg	4

CAFÉS
Bræðraborg	7
Kaffi Ísól	3

RESTAURANTS
Húsið	1
Kaffi Edinborg	6
Thai Koon	2
Tjöruhúsið	8
Við Pollinn	5

SHOPS
Eymundsson	2
Supermarket	1
Vínbúð	3

ÍSAFJÖRÐUR

Brief history

According to the *Landnámabók*, a Viking by the name of **Helgi Hrolfsson** was the first person to settle in Skutulsfjörður, building his farm here during the ninth century. However, although the sandspit was inhabited from the time of the Settlement, it took several centuries for Eyri at Skutulsfjörður, as Ísafjörður was then called, to emerge as one of the country's main commercial centres, an enviable status due to the establishment of a trading post here by foreign merchants during the late sixteenth century. It was also around this time that the town's most notorious resident, **Jón Magnússon**, a fundamentalist priest, ordered two men on a neighbouring farm to be burned at the stake for sorcery, which was reputed to be widespread in the West Fjords at the time. Finally, in 1786, with the winding-up of the Danish trade monopoly, the town was granted municipal status and became one of Iceland's six official trading posts. Just over a hundred years later, Eyri finally received city status and celebrated by changing its name to the present Ísafjörður, meaning Ice Fjord.

Byggðasafn Vestfjarða

Suðurtangi • Mid-May to mid-Sept daily 9am–6pm • 900kr • ⓦ nedsti.is

The town's only tourist sight, **Byggðasafn Vestfjarða** (West Fjords Heritage Museum) aims to portray the history of fishing in this remote corner of Iceland from the cutter to the trawler. It's set in one of Iceland's oldest buildings, Turnhús, a rare timber structure dating from the harsh days of the trade monopoly with Denmark in the late eighteenth century. In addition to the neighbouring **Tjöruhús** which holds an agreeable café-cum-restaurant (see p.195), there are two other buildings on the site, though they're not open to the public.

Turnhús

The carefully restored **Turnhús**, with its unusual roof tower, was constructed in Denmark before being moved to Iceland in 1784, where it was used as a warehouse and fish-salting house. As the tallest structure in Ísafjörður, it also served as a lookout from where returning fishing boats were spotted – livelihoods depended on being first to the dockside when the boats came in, it being paramount that the fish were processed as quickly as possible.

On the **ground floor**, an exhibition canters through the key developments in fishing in the West Fjords, notably the installation of engines in fishing vessels in 1902 (Iceland's first motorized fishing boat sailed from Ísafjörður) and the arrival of the trawler, which heralded the beginning of the Icelandic industrial revolution. Alongside a collection of model boats, ropes and floats, there's also information about prawn fishing and processing, which originated in Ísafjarðardjúp. Curiously, the **first floor** has nothing on fishing, and is given over instead to a rather dreary hoard of harmonicas.

Krambúð and Faktorshús

Of the two remaining buildings on the museum site (both closed to the public), the oldest is **Krambuð**, immediately to the right of Turnhús (when standing in front) and dating from 1757. Used as a storehouse until the early 1900s, it was then converted into a private residence. The **Faktorshús** from 1765, to the left of Turnhús, was once home to the site's trading manager, but is now occupied by the Royal Danish Consulate and must surely rank as one the cutest consular representations Denmark has – a sturdy timber structure with a steep pitched roof painted in black with white window frames and door.

Tangagata and Silfurgata

From the Heritage Museum, retrace your steps north along Suðurgata, turning right into Njarðarsund and then left into Sindragata, to reach the oldest part of town, just north of the harbour. Here, the brightly painted timber houses on **Tangagata** (a continuation of Sindragata) and **Silfurgata**, which crosses it, are particularly beautiful, with a stunning mountain backdrop.

The church

Sólgata 1 • Mon–Fri noon–4pm

Ísafjörður's highly unusual **church** resembles nothing short of a folding concertina. Built to replace the former timber church that burned down in 1987, this architectural monster of peach-coloured pebbledash comprises four column-like wedges that seemingly collapse into one another beneath a brilliant metal roof. It has been the source of much local controversy ever since its inception, and to add insult to injury, during its construction thirty graves were unceremoniously cemented over to make way for it; a plaque bearing the names of those buried there now stands beside the statue of Christ inside the unadorned interior. Beside the church, in the tussocky field in front of the library, stands a **sculpture** of two burly Ísafjörður fishermen hauling in a net full of cod, a reminder of the town's dependence on the sea; the poignant inscription reads simply, "in honour of those who disappeared, for luck for those who still put out to sea".

VIGUR ISLAND

From Ísafjörður's Sundahöfn harbour you can take a **boat tour to Vigur** (mid-June to mid-Aug daily 2pm; 3hr; 9800kr), a small, elongated island west of Ísafjörður in Ísafjörðardjúp. The ride over takes about thirty minutes, and you have a couple of hours to explore the grassy, flat island before enjoying refreshments served up by the local farmer and heading back to town. You'll definitely see swarms of puffins, arctic terns and eider ducks, plus Iceland's one and only windmill, making for a great afternoon's trip in good weather. You can **book tours** through Vesturferðir at the tourist office (☎456 5111, ⓦvesturferdir.is).

Ísafjörður park

Opposite the church, the diminutive but well-tended **town park**, sandwiched between the boarding school and Seljalandsvegur, is remarkable for the arching form of a white-painted whale bone marking the entrance. Dedicated to two local characters, Jón Jónsson and Karlinna Jóhannesdóttir, who painstakingly tended and encouraged all greenery here for several decades, the park is a pleasant place to sit and admire the soaring fjordsides surrounded by angelica and flowering pansies – ultimately, a pure West Fjords experience.

ARRIVAL AND DEPARTURE
ÍSAFJÖRÐUR

By plane The airport, connected by daily flights to Reykjavík, is 7km out of town on a narrow stretch of land on the eastern edge of the fjord; a bus into Ísafjörður meets all flights, and taxis (2300kr) are also available. A minibus (1000kr) runs out to the airport from *Hotel Ísafjörður* on Silfurtorg (see opposite), around 45min before flight departures, and returns to town after flight arrivals. If you intend to take it, inform the hotel reception and they'll make sure it comes to get you.

Destinations Reykjavík (2 daily; 40min).

By long-distance bus Long-distance buses terminate outside the tourist information office at Aðalstræti 7. Services to Hólmavík must be pre-booked on ☎893 1058, those to Látrabjarg on ☎456 5006.

Destinations Brjánslækur (June–Aug 1 daily; 2hr 45min); Hólmavík (2–3 weekly; 4hr); Látrabjarg (June–Aug 1 daily; 5hr 30min); Patreksfjörður (June–Aug 1 daily; 3hr 45min).

By local bus Ísafjörður is linked to four neighbouring villages year-round by local buses, which run on weekdays only (350kr single). Services to Bolungarvík depart from the stop outside the *Hamraborg* restaurant off Hafnarstræti (see opposite); those to Flateyri, Suðureyri and Þingeyri leave from the Pollurinn bus stop on Pollgata. Timetables for all services are under the "How to get here and around" link at ⓦisafjordur.is.

By ferry Hornstrandir ferries (see p.203) use Sundahöfn harbour, at the eastern end of Mjósund, which leads down to the harbour from the tourist office.

INFORMATION AND ACTIVITIES

Tourist information There's an office at Aðalstræti 7 (June–Aug Mon–Fri 8am–6pm, Sat 8am–3pm, Sun 10am–3pm; Sept–May Mon–Fri 8am–4pm; ☎450 8060, ⓦwestfjords.is).

Services Most of Ísafjörður's shops and services are within one block of *Hótel Ísafjörður* on the main street, Aðalstræti, including the Eymundsson bookshop (Mon–Fri 9am–6pm, Sat 10am–2/4pm) and the main shopping centre, with a supermarket (Mon–Sat 10am–8pm, Sun noon–8pm), post office (Mon–Fri 9am–4.30pm) and ATM. The *vínbúð* is at Aðalstræti 20 (Mon–Thurs 11am–6pm, Fri 11am–7pm, Sat 11am–4pm). Bike rental is available from Vesturferðir at the tourist office (6000kr/24hr), and there's internet access at the library (Mon–Fri 1–6pm, Sat 1–4pm), which is beside the church. The indoor swimming pool (Mon–Fri 10am–9pm, Sat & Sun 10am–5pm), Austurvegur 9, has a small sauna (men only Mon, Wed, Fri and Sat; women only Tues, Thurs & Sun).

Sea kayaking Adventure tourism leaders Borea Adventures at Aðalstræti 22B (☎456 3322, ⓦborea.is) offer sea kayaking trips, both in the harbour and out in Ísafjarðardjúp, which vary from 2–3hr to several days; prices start at 9500kr. They can book RIB inflatable tours which go whale watching around Ísafjarðardjúp; a 2hr excursion costs 15,000kr. Borea also run a boat service across to Hornstrandir and can arrange organized tours on foot and by kayak around the area.

Yachts to Greenland Between late July and early Sept, Borea Adventures (see above) operates a handful of trips by yacht across to Greenland, with sailing time around 30hr (the same as from Ísafjörður to Reykjavík); tours last eleven days and return by plane at your expense: the one-way cost is 655,000kr per person with all meals and guiding included.

ACCOMMODATION

Campsite Skutulsfjarðarbraut ☎456 4485. Located behind the *Edda Ísafjörður* (see below), the town's small and simple campsite has access to washing and toilet facilities but little else. Mid-June to mid-Aug. **1200kr**

Edda Ísafjörður Skutulsfjarðarbraut ☎444 4960, ⓦhoteledda.is. The forty simple rooms in Ísafjörður's boarding school in the western part of town have both private and shared facilities. Mid-June to mid-Aug. **14,060kr**

Gamla Gistihúsið Mánagata 5 ☎456 4146, ⓦisafjordurhotels.is/gamla. The former hospital building dating from 1896 has fourteen cosy twin-bedded rooms with shared facilities. There's a communal kitchen for self-catering as well as a TV lounge. **14,700kr**

★**Gistikofinn Silfurgötu** Silfurgata 12 ☎862 5669, ⓦfosshestar.is. Run by engaging Icelandic–Finnish couple Árni and Mimmo, this superbly appointed, four-person studio apartment comes with fully fitted kitchen, high-speed internet and underfloor heating, and makes a real home-from-home. **20,000kr**

Horn Austurvegur 2 ☎456 4611, ⓦisafjordurhotels.is /horn. Still with plenty of old-fashioned charm, this corner building on the main drag has had several reincarnations including operating as a school and local council offices. Today, it's a great new hotel, whose airy, generously proportioned rooms have high ceilings and big windows. The breakfast area, though, is a little cramped. **26,000kr**

Ísafjörður Silfurtorg 2 ☎456 4111, ⓦisafjordurhotels .is/torg. Don't be put off by the 1980s grey concrete exterior of this hotel, perfectly located on the town's main square; inside, the doubles are cosy, decor is mercifully plain and simple, and there are good views out over the fjord. **30,600kr**

Kollinn Hrannargata 2 ☎456 5555. This no-nonsense accommodation in five rooms above the *Húsið* restaurant (see below) is great value. Rooms share facilities and there's a sitting room and kitchen on the same floor for guests' use. Doubles **12,000kr**, sleeping bags **5500kr**

EATING

Bræðraborg Aðalstræti 22B ☎456 3322. A compact, homely little café run by Borea Adventures (see opposite), serving sandwiches with side salad, quiches and soups with bread (all 1690kr), as well as tasty home-made cakes and a wide range of fresh coffees. Mon–Fri 9am–7pm, Sat 10am–6pm, Sun 11am–5pm.

Hamraborg Hafnarstræti 7 ☎456 3166. This pizza and burger joint, crammed into the corner of a video store, is Ísafjörður's answer to an American diner and is inordinately popular with the town's teenagers: pizzas from 1890kr, burgers from 1099kr. Takeaway is available. Daily 8am–11.30pm.

Húsið Hrannargata 2 ☎456 5555. In a characterful old building from 1906 with original wooden floorboards, this popular place serves wonderfully juicy fish (1990kr), lamb chops (2990kr) and a delicious rib-eye steak with onions and mushrooms (2990kr); there are pizzas and burgers, too. Mon–Thurs & Sun 11am–1am, Fri & Sat 11am–3am.

★**Kaffi Edinborg** Aðalstræti 7 ☎456 8335. A great Euro-style brasserie housed in a former warehouse from 1907, which once did extensive trade with Edinburgh. There's a large menu featuring pan-fried fresh fish (2990kr), whale burger (2490kr) and pork schnitzel (3090kr). Try the puffin pizza (seasonal), too, which goes for 3350kr. Mon–Thurs 11.30am–1am, Fri

11.30am–3am, Sat & Sun 11.30am–3am.

Kaffi Ísól Austurvegur 1 ☎456 6670. This café-cum-wine bar, housed in one of the town's old haberdashery stores, specializes in pancakes with fresh cream and jam, and also has Greek salad, chicken wraps and quesadillas for 1650–1850kr. Daily: June–Aug 11.30am–1am; Sept–May 3–8pm.

Thai Koon Hafnarstræti 9–13 ☎456 0123. Now run by Macedonians rather than the original Thai owner, this Southeast Asian restaurant is still as good as it always was, serving genuinely tasty chicken, pork and beef dishes with rice for 1790kr or 1990kr depending on the size of the portion. Mon–Fri 11.30am–8pm, Sat noon–8pm, Sun 5–8pm.

★**Tjöruhúsið** Suðurtangi ☎456 4419. A sensational place to eat, located at the Heritage Museum. The menu here changes daily depending on the morning's catch, but chef, Maggi, always cooks the fish to perfection, serving it in a frying pan, including potatoes and salad. Reckon on 2500kr for lunch, 5500kr for the evening fish buffet. Easter to Sept daily noon–10pm.

Við Pollinn Silfurtorg 2. Inside *Hótel Ísafjörður* (see above), this is the place to come for fine dining in elegant surroundings: try the gratinated salted cod (4100kr) or the roast lamb in Madeira sauce with potatoes and peas (5300kr). Daily 11am–9pm.

Bolungarvík

Fifteen kilometres northwest of Ísafjörður along Route 61, the fishing village of **BOLUNGARVÍK**, at the mouth of Ísafjarðardjúp, suffers from one of the most exposed locations in the country. Not only does it receive some of the foulest weather in Iceland, but its position at the foot of three mountains, two of which are close to 700m high, means it's also susceptible to avalanches and landslides. Consequently the road now passes through a new tunnel which ensures that Bolungarvík is no longer cut off when the winter weather takes a turn for the worse.

Although it's one of the larger settlements in the West Fjords, with a population of around 950, Bolungarvík is a workaday place with little to entertain visitors, though it does boast a couple of good **museums**.

Ósvör Maritime Museum

Aðalstræti 21 • June–Aug daily Mon–Fri 9am–5pm, Sat & Sun 10am–5pm • 950kr, or 1550kr with the Natural History Museum • ⓦ osvor.is

At the entrance to town, just before the bridge, the open-air **Ósvör Maritime Museum** is well worth the twenty-minute trip from Ísafjörður. The tiny, turf-roofed huts here, with their thick stone lower walls, are reconstructions of structures that were once used to house fishing-boat crews, a salting house and a rack for drying fish, and give a good idea of how cramped conditions were in the early twentieth century. The museum also has a six-oared rowing boat from the 1940s, built to a traditional local design, on display. The landing stage beyond the huts was used when the weather conditions were too severe for boats to land in more exposed Bolungarvík itself.

Natural History Museum

Vitastígur 3 • Mon–Fri 9am–5pm, plus June to mid-Aug Sat & Sun 10am–5pm • 950kr, or 1550kr with Ósvör Maritime Museum • ⓦ nabo.is

A ten-minute walk from the Maritime Museum, the town's only other attraction is the **Natural History Museum** down by the harbour; to get here, follow the main road into town, Þuríðarbraut, across the Hólsá River, and head straight on into the main street, Aðalstræti, then right into Vitastígur. Inside there's an excellent collection of stuffed seals, arctic fox and various birds – everything from a wigeon to a pink flamingo, which oddly turned up out of the blue in eastern Iceland – you name it, they've got it stuffed. The prize exhibit, though, is the 3-year-old male polar bear (minus penis, which was claimed by the Phallological Museum in Reykjavík; see p.68), found floating on spring pack ice off Hornstrandir a few years ago. The bear was snared by local fishermen who spotted him drifting, exhausted, on the ice, and the fact that its death was most likely caused by dragging the animal to shore, half-hanging over the side of a fishing boat, came in for much public criticism.

ARRIVAL AND INFORMATION   BOLUNGARVÍK

By bus The year-round Ísafjörður–Bolungarvík bus runs twice daily from Ísafjörður, and three times daily from Bolungarvík, terminating at the post office on Aðalstræti.

Services There's a swimming pool at Höfðastígur 1 (June–Aug Mon–Fri 8am–9pm, Sat & Sun 10am–6pm; Sept–May Mon, Tues & Thurs 4–9pm, Wed & Fri 8–10am & 4–9pm, Sat & Sun 10am–6pm; 600kr).

ACCOMMODATION

Campsite Höfðastígur 1 ☎ 456 7381. Located next to the swimming pool and the Hólsá River, where Route 61 from Ísafjörður enters town, the campsite has rudimentary facilities including hot water, toilets and a washing machine. April–Sept. **1000kr**

Einarshús Hafnargata 41 ☎ 456 7901, ⓦ einarshusid .is. Located down by the harbour in an atmospheric old

timber building from 1902, which once served as the village store, there are eight snug, characterful rooms here, each with a washbasin, but otherwise sharing facilities. Breakfast is an extra 1700kr. The delightful restaurant serves fresh fish from 2700kr. Restaurant daily 11.30am–9pm. **16,500kr**

Mánafell Stigahlíð 2–4 ☎ 863 3879, ⓦ orkudisa.com.

This ugly modern block certainly wins no prizes for aesthetics, and the flats inside wouldn't have looked out of place in the Soviet Union – however, they are hard to beat in terms of price, and have kitchens. Doubles 10,000kr; sleeping bags 6000kr

Around Ísafjarðardjúp

The largest and most breathtaking of all the West Fjords, the 75km-long **Ísafjarðardjúp** stretches all the way from the mountains around Bolungarvík at its mouth to the shores of Ísafjörður fjord, the most easterly of the nine smaller fjords that make up the southern coastline of this extended arm of the Denmark Strait. Approaching from the southeast, descending from the Steingrímsfjarðarheiði plateau on Route 61, the views of Ísafjarðardjúp are spectacular: remote, uninhabited, forbidding fjordlands as far as the eye can see. In fact, from the head of Ísafjörður fjord to the regional capital there's just one village along a very lonely road stretching around 200km. Look across the waters of the bay and, on the northern shoreline, you'll see the sheer, snowcapped mountains of **Langadalsströnd** and **Snæfjallaströnd**, themselves divided by the glacial lagoon **Kaldalón**, which is fed by meltwater from the only glacier in the West Fjords, **Drangajökull**. Until just a couple of decades ago these coasts were dotted with isolated farms making an uncertain living from sheep farming and the odd crop; today, most have been deserted, reminders of how difficult life is up here. In addition to working the land, many farmers also eked out an existence as fishermen on Ísafjarðardjúp, where whitefish was once abundant. Nowadays, the bay is better known for the rich shrimping grounds found at its mouth, as the whitefish have moved further out to sea.

Súðavík

Twenty kilometres southeast of Ísafjörður, Route 61 passes through sleepy **SÚÐAVÍK**. This tiny fishing village, with a population of two hundred souls, is your last chance to stock up with essentials before the start of the circuitous negotiation of fjords involved

---

HIKING AROUND SKÁLAVÍK

From the western edge of Bolungarvík, Þjóðólfsvegur (Route 630) continues 12km northwest through the uninhabited Hlíðardalur valley until it reaches the exposed **Skálavík** bay, which takes regular batterings from Atlantic storms as they sweep in mercilessly from the northwest. Although Skálavík is uninhabited today bar a couple of summer houses owned by brave souls who don't seem to mind the weather, at the end of the nineteenth century around one hundred people were living here, eking out an existence from the surrounding barren land. Given the village's vulnerable location between the Deild and Öskubakur mountains, avalanches were always a particular hazard and claimed several lives; perhaps not surprisingly therefore, the last farmer gave up his struggle to keep the village alive in 1964 and left.

There's no public transport to Skálavík, but it is possible to **walk** from Bolungarvík in around two hours – simply follow Þjóðólfsvegur all the way. The bay offers a real chance to commune with nature, and a night spent camping here, battling against the weather, is certainly a memorable experience; bring all the supplies you'll need. There's also some good **hiking** around here; one route (7km) begins at the western edge of the bay and leads west along the shore around Öskubakur to the lonely lighthouse in Keflavík bay, before the Göltur headland. From here, another track (5km) heads inland through the valleys of Norðdalur and Bakkadalur back to Skálavík and the beginning of the track back to Bolungarvík. Details of these routes can be found on the *Vestfirðir & Dalir* **maps**, available from the tourist office in Ísafjörður (see p.194).

> ## THE SÚÐAVÍK AVALANCHE
>
> Spend any time in Súðavík and you'll soon spot that its houses are grouped into two distinct areas. The majority are located in the south of the village, but a handful remain in the northern half, closest to Ísafjörður. In January 1995, this tight-knit community was hit by tragedy when an **avalanche** engulfed the northern part of the village, roaring down from the precipitous slopes of Súðavíkurhlíð, the steep mountain that rears up behind Súðavík, and leaving fourteen people dead. Since then, all new buildings are constructed in the southern part of the village, away from the avalanche risk, while those in the northern half are uninhabited during the winter months. Beside the main road, close to the entrance to the village from Ísafjörður, a stone monument has been raised in memory of those who lost their lives.

in leaving Ísafjörður. There's not much of note in the village, which consists of little more than a main road lined on each side by a few brightly coloured homes, and with a simple wooden **church** (closed to the public) at the Ísafjörður end. Originally built in the now-deserted settlement of Hesteyri (see p.202), across the water on Hornstrandir, the church was dismantled when Hesteyri was abandoned in 1952 and brought to Súðavík, where several families chose to begin their new lives.

Malrakkasetur Íslands

Eyrardalur 4 • June–Aug daily 9am–6pm; other times by appointment • 950kr • ☎ 456 4922, ⓦ arcticfoxcenter.com

The main reason to come to Súðavík is to visit the fascinating **Malrakkasetur Íslands** (Arctic Fox Centre). Don't come here, though, expecting to see dozens of foxes in pens and runs; though you might see an abandoned cub or two during the summer months, which the centre is preparing to release back into the wild, this thoughtful exhibition is more somewhere to learn all about the creatures and their habitat. Over generations, Icelanders have had a love-hate relationship with the arctic fox and many are still killed by farmers who see them as a pest. The centre aims to educate people about the animals through extensive research carried out into their behaviour patterns, in part in Hornstrandir. Displays tackle everything from trapping to breeding, but to gain a real understanding of the animals make sure you see the film shown upstairs, which tracks the arctic fox through the changing seasons.

ARRIVAL AND DEPARTURE   SÚÐAVÍK

By bus The Hólmavík–Ísafjörður bus calls at Súðavík (2–3 weekly), from where it runs on to Ísafjörður airport, handy if you're also using the plane. Timetables can be viewed at ⓦ isafjordur.is under the "How to get here and around" link.

EATING

Amma Habbý Aðalgata 1 ☎ 456 5060. Named after one of Súðavík's best-loved inhabitants, Grandmother Habbý, this roadside café above the harbour serves burgers (1490kr), chicken salad (1790kr), whale steak (2990kr) and a succulent fish of the day (1790kr). June–Aug daily 11am–10pm.

Malrakkasetur Íslands Eyrardalur 4 ☎ 456 4922. The café inside the Arctic Fox Centre is a real treat, serving up wicked home-made cakes and snacks as well as a delicious *plokkfiskur* (1900kr) and vegetable soup (1500kr). The low-ceilinged, creaking wooden house in which it's set is a joy to behold, dating from 1893. June–Aug daily 9am–6pm.

Reykjanes

As Route 61 leaves Súðavík it passes the remains of the **Norwegian whaling station** that provided employment for the village in the early 1900s. The next 150km are remarkable only for their relentlessness – this section is one of the most infuriating in the West Fjords, as you twist around a horde of little fjords that line the foot of Steingrímsfjarðarheiði, repeatedly driving up to 50km, only to make two or three kilometres of actual headway. As you drive, look out for whales, seals and sea eagles because there's a good chance of spotting them in and around Ísafjarðardjúp. A bridge across the mouth of the penultimate fjord, Mjóifjörður, thankfully means one less fjord to negotiate, and leads to the tiny settlement of **REYKJANES**. Set on a geothermal area located on a spit of land at the mouth of Ísafjörður fjord, and looking out onto the open waters of Ísafjarðardjúp, it makes a handy stopover if you want to break the long journey to Ísafjörður.

Iceland's biggest open-air swimming pool

Beside *Hotel Reykjanes* (see below) • Daily 8am–11.30pm • 500kr payable at the hotel reception

Tapping into the ready supply of geothermal water hereabouts, the swimming pool at Reykjanes, built in 1925 beside the hotel and measuring 50.4m long and 12m wide, is a real treat. Nobody seems to know why it is not exactly 50m in length, the Olympic standard, but the extra 40cm are enough to make it bigger than Laugardalslaug in Reykjavík (see see box, p.75), much to the pride of the locals. Not only is it the country's largest swimming pool, but it's also Iceland's biggest hot pot, too, since the water temperature is a balmy 37–39°C. The water is naturally low in sulphur yet especially high in minerals and salt, something you'll notice on your skin if you spend an hour or so in it. Since the pool contains no chlorine, it is especially important to shower in the adjacent changing rooms before swimming. Due to the relatively high temperature of the water, you may find it unpleasant to swim any distance in the pool, though it is slightly cooler at the deep end (3m). The shallow end is just 75cm deep and a bench here runs the entire width of the pool so it can be used as a hot pot. Note that as you approach the shallow end the temperature of the water is not constant and you can come across rather hot flows as the geothermal water enters the pool at 96°C. Only the wind is responsible for reducing the temperature to a more tolerable level.

4

ACCOMMODATION   REYKJANES

Heydalur Mjóifjöður ☎456 4824, ⓦheydalur.is. This horse farm near the head of Mjóifjörður rents out comfortable double rooms in a converted barn and cowshed, and also has camping pitches with electricity, toilets and showers. Kayak rental and horseriding are also available. Doubles <u>15,900kr</u>, camping <u>1200kr</u>

Reykjanes ☎456 4844, ⓦrnes.is. Virtually the only building in Reykjanes, this fjordside hotel has modern and clean double rooms, each with a washbasin though otherwise sharing facilities. It also provides sleeping-bag dorms and has a campsite. There's also a naturally heated outdoor pool. Doubles <u>14,900kr</u>, sleeping bags <u>4950kr</u>, camping <u>2600kr</u>

Kaldalón glacial lagoon

Past Reykjanes, another 15km along Route 61 brings you to a bridge over the Bæjardalsá River, from where it's a straightforward 70km run east to Hólmavík (see p.217). Immediately after the bridge, the unsealed Route 635 turns north up along **Langadalsströnd**, Ísafjarðardjúp's southeastern shore, and it's worth taking the bumpy thirty-minute drive from the junction (there's no public transport) past lush green fields and a few farms scattered up the coast to reach **Kaldalón glacial lagoon**. This is a rare opportunity to see an easily accessible glacial lagoon – most others are hidden in the Interior and hard to reach. As you approach, you'll easily spot the lagoon: it is actually a U-shaped inlet from Ísafjarðardjúp, caught between the cliffs of Snæfjallaströnd to the west and Langadalsströnd to the east. Look out for the unusual-looking trail of brown, muddy meltwater that has come down from the Drangajökull glacier as it merges into the salt water of the bay.

Drangajökull

From the parking area by the low hills at the head of the lagoon it's possible to walk up to the snout of the **Drangajökull glacier** along a **trail**, marked by cairns, in roughly ninety minutes; from the car park head east, following the low hills, to the track leading along the eastern side of the valley up to the glacier. Keep to the eastern side of the cairns and you'll find the going easier, although there are still boulders, stones and streams to negotiate. Note that you shouldn't underestimate the time it'll take to walk to the glacier – the clear air makes the ice appear much closer than it actually is. If you spot the unmarked path leading up the western edge of the snout, past Drangajökull's highest point, **Jökulbunga** (925m), before descending into Furufjörður on the eastern shore of Hornstrandir, don't be tempted to follow it – it's strictly for experienced mountaineers only.

Unaðsdalur

From Kaldalón, Route 635 crosses the glacial river, Mórillá, before continuing northwest for another fifteen minutes' drive to the farming settlement of **UNAÐSDALUR**, where there's a small church right on the shoreline. From here the mountainous coastline of Snæfjallaströnd stretches to the northwest – although it's hard to imagine, this entire region was once inhabited as far as the cliffs at Bjarnarnúpur, which look across to Bolungarvík on the opposite side of the bay. Historically, Unaðsdalur is perhaps best known for the **massacre** of a boatload of Spaniards who were shipwrecked here in 1614 and then beaten to death by farmers when they tried to leave on a "borrowed" vessel the following year. In 1995 the last locals, perhaps unsurprisingly, upped sticks and left this remote, chilly coast – not even in the warmest summer does the snow melt from the mountains here – abandoning Snæfjallaströnd to the elements alone.

4

Hornstrandir

Once you've seen the remote snow-covered hills and cliffs of the Snæfjallaströnd coastline, you'll have an idea of what lies immediately north. A claw-shaped peninsula of land bordered by the Jökulfirðir fjords to the south and the Greenland Sea to the north, and attached to the rest of the West Fjords by a narrow neck of land just 6km

---

HORNSTRANDIR HIKING PRACTICALITIES

Thanks to Hornstrandir's exposed location on the edge of the Greenland Sea, the **weather** is especially unpredictable, and hiking here needs plenty of careful planning. Deep snow often lies on the ground until July and snow showers are not uncommon even in July and August. Fog, too, can be a particular problem. Also, because there are **no functioning settlements** here – those marked on maps are farm buildings, or the remains of farm buildings only – you must be prepared for emergencies if you come to hike. It's essential to bring the following **equipment**: a sturdy tent and warm sleeping bag, waterproof clothing and boots, more food than you'll need in case of unforeseen delays (there are **no shops** or facilities anywhere on the peninsula, except for the guesthouse at Hesteyri; see p.203), a compass and Landmælingar Íslands 1:100,000 *Hornstrandir* **hiking map**.

Although many routes are marked on the map as clearly defined, this is often not the case in reality; in poor weather conditions it can be all too easy to lose the path, so make sure that you can use a compass properly before setting out. Remember, too, that in June and July it doesn't get dark here, which means you can extend your hiking time if needed. You should not count on **mobile phones** working; coverage is improving but is still very patchy, so there are landline phones for use in emergencies in the orange shelters dotted around the coast and marked on maps. Take extra care if you're crossing **tidal flats**, or rounding headlands at low tide, as the going can often be very boggy. There are no footbridges in Hornstrandir, so bring an old pair of running shoes to cross rivers and streams – and be prepared to grit your teeth against the bitingly cold water.

OPPOSITE CROSS-COUNTRY SKIING, HORNSTRANDIR >

HIKING BETWEEN HESTEYRI AND AÐALVÍK

From *Læknishúsið* guesthouse in Hesteyri (see opposite), a good **path** – actually the old road that led west to the now abandoned settlement of Slettá – leads up the hill following the course of a river. At the top, the trail strikes out across an extensive rockfield, which can be hard going in parts; even in July there is a lot of snow left up here. Follow the cairns through the rockfield until the track descends into sandy **Aðalvík**: the bottom of this path is rather boggy. At the foot of the hill you've descended, cross a shallow river to reach the beach and the couple of houses that make up **Látrar**, at the eastern end of Aðalvík bay, or **Sæból** at the western edge, both surrounded by snowy mountains on all sides. To retrace your steps, note that the path to Hesteyri can be found by crossing the river at the rear of the beach and heading for the single house on the river bank. From here head up the hill to the right of the house to reach the rockfield plateau to Hesteyri. Either way this 12km hike takes around four hours to complete.

wide, **Hornstrandir** represents Iceland's very last corner of inhospitable terrain where habitation was at least attempted – the last settlements here were abandoned in the 1950s due to the harsh climate – and its coastline is the most magnificent in the country. The rugged cliffs, precipitous mountainsides and sandy bays backed by meadows of wildflowers make up this official nature reserve on the very edge of the Arctic Circle, and hiking here is an exhilarating experience; it's quite common to walk for an entire day without seeing another person. The highlight of any trip to Hornstrandir is a visit to the majestic **Hornbjarg cliff** (533m) at the eastern end of Hornvík bay and the highest point on the peninsula. The cliff is home to one of the country's greatest **bird colonies** and its many ledges are stuffed full with fulmars, guillemots, kittiwakes, puffins and razorbills. Elsewhere, where farmed sheep once devoured everything edible, there is now wild, lush vegetation of unexpected beauty and the wildlife is free to roam – the arctic fox makes regular appearances – while offshore, seals and whales can be spotted.

Life for settlers on Hornstrandir was always extreme. For starters, the summer is appreciably shorter than elsewhere in the West Fjords and, bar a geothermal spring in remote **Reykjafjörður**, there's no natural hot water source, no waterfall to generate electricity, no natural harbour, and no road or airstrip. In fact, the fertile valleys and inlets throughout this uninhabited wilderness are littered with traces of derelict buildings where hardy farmers and fishermen once attempted to battle against the inhospitable climate. The peninsula's two main settlements, **Hesteyri** and **Aðalvík**, are now almost completely deserted, their abandonment marking the end of yet another Icelandic community.

Hesteyri

Founded in around 1894, **HESTEYRI** depended entirely on a Norwegian whaling station – remains of which can still be seen today at the head of Hesteyrarfjörður fjord – until a drastic decline in stocks led to the station being taken over for the processing of herring. At this time, around eighty people lived permanently in the village, with another hundred temporarily resident at the factory, but a fall in herring stocks led to the closure of the factory in 1940. One by one, farmers and fishermen left, and in 1952 the last families abandoned both Hesteyri and neighbouring Aðalvík.

Today, Hesteyri consists of nothing more than a handful of abandoned cottages, disintegrating skeletons of concrete and timber clothed with bits of corrugated iron, broken stone and blocks of turf, with just one or two being renovated by families whose roots lie here. The **ferry from Ísafjörður** visits almost daily in summer, though the only functioning building is the white and green *Læknishúsið* guesthouse (see opposite).

ARRIVAL AND DEPARTURE

HORNSTRANDIR

By ferry Between June and Aug, ferries from Ísafjörður run daily to Hesteyri, and once or twice a week to other destinations including Hornvík and Aðalvík (though services for the latter two depart mid-June to mid-Aug only). Two companies ply these routes: Vesturferðir, based at Ísafjörður's tourist office (☎456 5111, ⓦwesttours.is) and Borea Adventures, at Aðalstræti 22B (☎456 3322, ⓦborea.is). It costs 9100kr one-way to Hesteyri and 14,200kr to Hornvík, and it's a good idea to book in advance to be sure of a seat. For details of the ferry from Norðurfjörður operated by Strandferðir, see p.221.

ACCOMMODATION

Læknishúsið Hesteyri ☎899 7661, ⓦhesteyri.net. The former village doctor's house from 1901, on the western side of the Hesteyrará River, offers self-catering sleeping-bag accommodation in three rooms. There's also a shared bathroom and a lounge. June–Aug. Sleeping bags 4500kr

The west coast: along Route 60

Passing through some of the most dramatic scenery the West Fjords have to offer, **Route 60** is the access route for the southern and western sections of this region. It's predominantly a mountain road, winding through narrow passes and deep-green valleys as often as it rounds the heads of fjords, past the handful of tiny villages which mark the way down the west coast south of Ísafjörður. It arrives on the south coast at the insubstantial outpost of **Brjánslækur**, where you have the option of continuing south or east and out of the region, or heading down to the West Fjord's southwestern tip at Látrabjarg (see p.214).

Despite Route 60 being one of the West Fjords' main roads, once you're south of the small sleepy fishing villages of **Flateyri** and **Þingeyri**, it's little more than an unsurfaced and badly potholed dirt track, where driving requires slow speeds, much gear changing and even more patience. Things improve after the spectacular climb and descent into minute **Hrafnseyri**, the birthplace of **Jón Sigurðsson**, the man who led Iceland's nineteenth-century independence movement. Beyond here, look out for triangular **Dynjandi** waterfall, at the head of the eponymously named fjord, and a favourite rest break for buses. One of the main entrance points into the West Fjords lies due south of here, the **ferry** terminal at Brjánslækur for connections to the island of Flatey (see p.176) and on to Stykkishólmur (see p.170) on the Snæfellsnes peninsula.

FLATEYRI'S AVALANCHES

Flateyri is known across the country for its **avalanche** problems: the colossal **earth dams** separated by 15m walls on the lower slopes of the omnipresent mountains here are man-made barriers against the snowfalls which occur every year. A memorial stone next to the church, at the entrance to the village, bears the names of the twenty people who died in the most recent devastating avalanche, in October 1995. The tragedy was a painful loss for this closely knit community where the total population is barely over three hundred, not least because the frozen ground and heavy snow prevented the bodies from being buried in the village cemetery; instead, they had to be kept in the morgue in Ísafjörður until the ground thawed and they could be buried in Reykjavík. Extensive rebuilding was necessary after the avalanche, including the erection of the defences which now effectively channel all snow-slides into the sea. From the filling station at the entrance to the village, a short path (10min) leads up to a **viewpoint** on the mountainside giving a superb panorama, not only of Flateyri and Önundarfjörður, but down into the life-saving earth dams.

GETTING AROUND

By bus From June to Aug, a daily long-distance bus service follows Route 60 between Ísafjörður and Brjánslækur, stopping at most settlements along the way (except Flateyri) and connecting with Stykkishólmur ferries. It then continues westwards to Patreksfjörður and Látrabjarg on the southwestern peninsula (see p.214) before retracing its route to Ísafjörður. Timetables are at ⓦ wa.is.

Flateyri

At the southwestern edge of Ísafjörður, Route 60 enters a tunnel to bypass Þverfjall (752m). After 2km, the tunnel divides in two; the right-hand turn, Route 65, leads to the workaday fishing village of **Suðureyri**, while the main tunnel and Route 60 continue for 4km before emerging into Önundarfjörður where there's a junction with Road 64 to the small fishing village of **FLATEYRI**. Just 22km from Ísafjörður, Flateyri was founded as a trading centre in 1792, and was formerly a base for shark and whale hunting. Today a German company is currently operating out of the **fish-processing factory**, one of the largest in Iceland, though its fate seems to constantly hang in the balance. Pleasant though Flateyri may be, it's not a good idea to get stuck here, since there's very little to do other than marvel at the avalanche defences and the open vistas of the surrounding fjord and mountains.

ARRIVAL AND INFORMATION   FLATEYRI

By bus Local buses run all year (three daily) from Ísafjörður, stopping outside Flateyri's post office in Ránargata. Long-distance buses along Route 60 don't call at Flateyri, but can be caught at the junction of Routes 64 and 60, 7km east of town.

Services The swimming pool (Mon–Fri 10am–8pm, Sat & Sun 11am–5pm) is in Tjarnargata, north of the church and close to the mountains.

ACCOMMODATION AND EATING

Campsite Behind the N1 filling station at the entrance to the village ☎450 8460. Flateyri's campsite has toilets and running water, as well as great views of the avalanche defences, which also provide shelter from the wind. June–Aug. **1200kr**

Félagsbær Hafnarstræti 11 ☎456 7710. Run by a couple of local ladies, this simple little café has coffee, a few cakes and sometimes waffles. June–Aug daily 11am–5pm.

Gamla Bókabúðin Hafnarstræti 3 ☎865 5695. Also known as the Eyjólfsson brothers' shop, this former grocery store still features the original shop counter and fittings from 1906 (it now sells books by the kilo) and operates as a cosy summer café complete with period furniture. June–Aug daily 11am–5pm.

Grænhöfði Ólafstún 7 ☎456 7762, ⓦwww .kajaktravel.net. Four good-quality apartments of various sizes, sleeping up to ten, are available for rent by the day or week here. All have a television, fridge and microwave. Kayaks are available for rent. **18,000kr**

Síma Hostel Hafnarstræti ☎897 8700, ⓦicelandwestfjords.com. This new hostel occupies Flateyri's former telephone exchange in the centre of the village. There are eight rooms here, all sharing facilities, plus two kitchens for guests' use. All in all, it's clean and bright, and a sensible choice if you want to stay within striking distance of Ísafjörður. **9800kr**

Vagninn Hafnarstræti 19 ☎456 7751. Locals rave about the expertly prepared dishes on offer at Flateyri's one and only restaurant, claiming it's one of the best in the whole of Iceland. Traditional Icelandic dishes given a modern twist feature heavily on the menu, such as a delicious lamb burger, whale steak and even guillemot. Opening times are a little erratic, so ask around if you find the door locked. Usually June–Aug daily from 6pm, rest of the year Fri–Sun from 6pm.

Önundarfjörður

Flateyri sits on the eastern side of the 40km-long **Önundarfjörður**, which has a couple of scenic spots that are worth checking out. A gravel track opposite the Flateyri turn-off from Route 60 leads southeast down to the **Korpudalur** valley at the neck of the fjord. Surrounded by mountains, it's a great place to hike, kayak or just kick back for a couple of days.

Alternatively, one of the most beautiful **beaches** in the West Fjords, **Ingjaldssandur** (the settlement here is known as **Sæból**, the name used on most maps), is located at the mouth of Önundarfjörður, across the water from Flateyri at the tip of the mountainous finger of land that separates the fjord from its southern neighbour, Dýrafjörður. Bordered to the west and east by tall, craggy mountains and backed by lush green fields, the beach's grassy foreshore is an idyllic place from which to watch the huge Atlantic breakers crash onto the sand and pebbles below. In summer this is a good place to spot arctic tern and various species of waders; oystercatchers are particularly common here. Ingjaldssandur is only accessible with your own transport and entails a circuitous drive of 44km from Flateyri, heading first south down Route 60 towards Þingeyri, before taking the unsurfaced and rough Route 624 back northwest to the Önundarfjörður coast.

ACCOMMODATION   **ÖNUNDARFJÖRÐUR**

Alviðra 20km before Sæból ☏ 895 0080, ✉ alvidra @snerpa.is. This remote working farm, on the shores of Önundarfjörður, is hard to beat for splendid isolation: there's just one studio apartment (sleeping two) with cooking facilities. There are discounts for stays of two nights and more. **16,000kr**

Korpudalur Youth Hostel Kirkjuból ☏ 456 7808, ⓦ korpudalur.is. Located in a converted farmhouse, this hostel has bags of charm, and has a self-catering kitchen, small campsite and bike rental. Mid-May to mid-Sept. Dorms **5000kr**, doubles **13,000kr**

Þingeyri

One of the more attractive settlements in the West Fjords, **ÞINGEYRI**, 48km southwest of Ísafjörður along Route 60, is also one of the oldest. The village takes its name from the ancient *þing* (assembly) mentioned in *Gísla Saga*, and the ruins, nothing more than a couple of grassy mounds, can be seen behind the church in the centre of the village. Over the centuries Þingeyri developed into a significant fishing centre thanks to its sheltered location near the head of Dýrafjörður, and even attracted the interest of the French who applied, unsuccessfully, to establish a base here to service their fishing vessels operating in the region.

Today life is centred on the one main street, **Aðalstræti**, where you'll find all the town's **services**. If you've time to kill, head up Sandafell (367m), which stands guard behind the village. This is a favourite place for locals to watch the sun go down as it offers fantastic views out over the fjord and of the mountain ridge, topped by the highest peak in the West Fjords, Kaldbakur (998m). The latter separates Dyrafjörður from the much larger and multi-fingered Arnarfjörður to the south. Although steep, Sandafell can be climbed from the village – several clear paths lead up the mountainside – and a four-wheel-drive access track heads southwest off Route 60, just 1km south of town.

4

ARRIVAL AND INFORMATION   **ÞINGEYRI**

By bus The filling station on the main road also functions as the terminus for buses. The only year-round service goes to Ísafjörður (for times, see ⓦ isafjordur.is under the "How

to get here and around" link), while from June to Aug the service from Ísafjörður to Látrabjarg calls here (see ⓦ wa.is for times; advance booking required).

ACTIVITIES IN ÞINGEYRI

Þingeyri makes a marvellous place to get out in the great outdoors. Belgian-Danish couple, Wouter and Janne, who run the *Simbahöllin* café at Fjarðargata 5 (☏ 899 6659), rent out top-quality **mountain bikes** (10,000kr/24hr) as well as running **horseriding tours** at 10am and 1pm into neighbouring Sandadalur (9500kr/2hr). If you're stuck for transport to Þingeyri, they can usually arrange to pick you up from Ísafjörður.

Tourist information There's limited information about the town and the surrounding area available at the tourist office in the old, low wooden building on Hafnarstræti opposite the *Sandafell* hotel (June–Aug daily 11am–6pm; ☎ 456 8304, ✉ umthingeyri@snerpa.is).

Services The swimming pool is at Þingeyraroddi (Mon–Fri 8am–9pm, Sat & Sun 10am–6pm; 570kr), while the bank is at the other end of the village at Fjarðargata 2 (Mon–Fri 11.30am–4pm), though there's no ATM.

ACCOMMODATION AND EATING

Campsite Hrunastígur 1 ☎ 450 8470. The town's campsite, with showers, toilets and electricity, is located next to the swimming pool at the western end of the village. Mid-May to mid-Sept. <u>1200kr</u>

Sandafell Hafnarstræti 7 ☎ 456 1600, 🌐 hotelsandafell .com. This bright and airy place overlooking the harbour likes to think of itself as a hotel but it's really a smart guesthouse. Rooms are both en suite and with shared facilities. The restaurant serves *plokkfiskur* for 2600kr, as well as a hearty meat soup (also 2600kr) and a juicy fillet of lamb (3800kr). Look out, too, for the home-made chocolate cake which goes for 1250kr. Restaurant June–Sept daily 8am–10pm. <u>17,600kr</u>

Simbahöllin Fjarðargata 5 ☎ 899 6659. Creative new life has been breathed into the town's creaking old timber

grocery store (dating to 1905): it's now a cute café serving soup, genuine Belgian waffles, home-made cakes and evening suppers such as lamb tajine. Daily: early June & late Aug noon–6pm; mid-June to mid-Aug 10am–1am.

Vera Hlíðargata 22 ☎ 456 8232, ✉ skuli@snerpa.is. Cheery Vera rents out a comfortable, two-person studio with kitchen facilities located in the basement of her own home. It's available all year and there are discounts for longer stays. <u>18,000kr</u>

Við Fjörðinn Aðalstræti 26 ☎ 847 0285, 🌐 vidfjordinn .is. Offering just ten cosy rooms both with and without private facilities, this guesthouse is worth checking out if you're here out of season when the *Sandafell* hotel is closed. <u>15,500kr</u>

Hrafnseyri

The 17km drive south from Þingeyri to minuscule **HRAFNSEYRI** is one of the most dramatic sections of Route 60. Climbing all the while to squeeze through a narrow pass between mountains over 700m high, the road then makes a stunning descent into Hrafnseyri on the shores of **Arnarfjörður**; when viewed from the hamlet below, the road appears to cling precariously to a vertical wall of rock. Named after the fjord's first settler, Örn (meaning "eagle", *arnar* being its genitive case), who lasted just one winter

---

JÓN SIGURÐSSON

To Icelanders, **Jón Sigurðsson** (1811–79) is what Winston Churchill is to the British and George Washington to the Americans. This is the man who, through his tremendous skills of diplomacy, achieved independence from the Danes, who had almost bankrupted Iceland during the time of the Trade Monopoly. Born in Hrafnseyri in 1811, Sigurðsson spent the first 22 years of his life in his native West Fjords, and after completing the entry examination for university study, he left for Copenhagen where he chose history and political science among his subjects. Although a committed student, he never graduated from the university, opting instead to dedicate his life to the **Árni Magnússon Institute**, then a powerful symbol of the struggle for recognition against the Danes; this institute fought a long battle to have many of Iceland's most treasured medieval manuscripts, kept in Copenhagen by the Danish authorities, returned home.

However, it wasn't until 1841 that Sigurðsson began his political activities, publishing a magazine in which he put forward historical arguments for Iceland's right to independence. A prolific writer about Icelandic history, politics and economics, he was later elected to the Icelandic parliament, which regained its powers as a consultative body in 1843 thanks to his agitation. Further reforms followed as a direct consequence of his influence, including the right to free trade in 1854, and eventually, twenty years later, a **constitution** making Iceland self-governing in home affairs. Sadly, Sigurðsson didn't live to see Iceland become a sovereign state under the Danish crown on December 1, 1918, nor Iceland gain full independence from Denmark on June 17, 1944, the anniversary of his birth – he died in Copenhagen in 1879, and his body was returned to Reykjavík for a state funeral.

CLOCKWISE FROM TOP DYNJANDI WATERFALL (P.208); ARCTIC FOX (P.198); HORNSTRANDIR (P.200) >

here, Arnarfjörður is 30km long and up to 10km wide: it forks at its head to form four smaller fjords, including Suðurfirðir, to the southwest, and Borgarfjörður and Dynjandisvogur inlet to the northeast. It's widely, and quite rightly, regarded by locals as the most picturesque of all the West Fjords, enclosed by towering mountains.

Hrafnseyri itself, consisting of a tiny church and a museum, is one of only two settlements on Arnarfjörður (the other is Bíldudalur, 79km away). It was named after one of Iceland's earliest doctors, **Hrafn Sveinbjarnarson**, who died here in 1213, having trained in Europe then returned home to practise. A memorial stone next to the church commemorates his life, and the grass mound nearby is thought to be the site of his boathouse. However, the settlement is best known as the birthplace of **Jón Sigurðsson** (see box, p.206), the man who won independence for Iceland in the nineteenth century. The best time to be in Hrafnseyri is **Icelandic National Day** (June 17), when a special Mass is held in the church and prominent Icelanders from across the country travel to the village to remember their most distinguished champion of freedom. Although it's a serious occasion, there's a mood of optimism and good humour, with plenty of singing and celebration.

Jón Sigurðsson Museum

Adjacent to Hrafnseyri's church • June–Aug daily 11am–6pm • 800kr • ⓦ hrafnseyri.is

The excellent **Jón Sigurðsson Museum** records the man's life, mostly with photographs, some of his letters and contemporary drawings. Particularly evocative is the painting of the meeting of 1851, which Sigurðsson and a number of Icelandic MPs held with representatives of the Danish state in the Grammar School, Menntaskólinn, in Reykjavík, and which helped pave the way for Icelandic independence.

Turf farmhouse

Next to the church

The birthplace of Jón Sigurðsson (and also part of the museum) is the restored **turf farmhouse**, with its three gabled roofs. At the rear of the building, his bedroom, containing the desk from his office in Copenhagen, has been kept in its original state and offers an insight into the ascetic life of one of Iceland's most revered figures.

Dynjandi

Twenty kilometres east of Hrafnseyri, at the point where Route 60 weaves around the northeastern corner of Arnarfjörður, the impressive **Dynjandi** waterfall plunges over a 100m-high clifftop into the fjord at Dynjandisvogur inlet, forming a triangular cascade roughly 30m wide at its top spreading to over 60m at its bottom. Below the main waterfall a series of five smaller chutes carries the waters of the Dynjandisá to the sea. Lit by the low sun, it's an incredibly pretty place to camp out on a summer night, though the waterfall is famously noisy – *dynjandi* means "the thundering one".

All long-distance buses make a ten-minute stop at Dynjandi; and with your own transport, it's possible to reach the head of the falls – continue south along Route 60 for around 5km, and once the road has climbed up onto the Dynjandisheiði plateau, you'll see the Dynjandisá River, which crosses the road; walk west from here, following the course of the river to the falls.

Flókalundur and around

South of Dynjandisheiði, Route 60 continues over a spectacular highland plateau, passing **Lónfell** (725m) and the turn-off onto Route 63 for Patreksfjörður via Bíldudalur (see p.210), before finally descending to the south coast and Route 62 at

FLÓKALUNDUR. Consisting of just a hotel, restaurant and a petrol pump, there's little to note here other than the fact that the Viking **Flóki Vilgerðarson**, who named Iceland, once spent a winter here. He climbed Lónfell, only to be dismayed by the icebergs floating in the fjord and named the land "Ísland", as the inscription on the monument in front of the *Flókalundur* hotel (see below), overlooking Vatnsfjörður, reminds modern-day Icelanders.

Vatnsfjörður Nature Reserve

Staff at the *Flókalundur* hotel can fill you in on the surrounding **Vatnsfjörður Nature Reserve**, which spreads northeast from here and provides endless **hiking** opportunities – one easy trail (8km; 2–3hr) begins at a lake some 5km east along the main road and leads along the eastern shore of **Vatndalsvatn**, a lake known for its rich birdlife and a favourite nesting spot for the dramatically coloured harlequin duck, as well as the red-throated and great northern diver. Don't attempt to cross the Vatnsdalsá at the head of the lake in order to return down the western shore, since the river is very wide and fast flowing; instead, retrace your steps.

ACCOMMODATION   **FLÓKALUNDUR**

Flókalundur ☎ 456 2011, ⊛ flokalundur.is. This hotel excels in terms of views but leaves something to be desired when it comes to rooms – all are functional and a little on the small side. The restaurant is nothing special, but it does serve up burgers from 1790kr, pizzas from 2650kr and fish dishes from 3150kr, and is useful for a break on the long journey in and out of the West Fjords. The adjacent campsite, also run by the hotel, has running water and toilet facilities. Restaurant mid-May to mid-Sept daily 11am–9pm. Doubles <u>20,950kr</u>, camping <u>1200kr</u>

Brjánslækur

Barely 7km west of Flókalundur on Route 62, **BRJÁNSLÆKUR** is essentially just the departure point for **ferries to Stykkishólmur** via Flatey (see below), though there is a snack-bar-cum-ticket-office in the small wooden building on the main road by the jetty.

ARRIVAL AND DEPARTURE   **BRJÁNSLÆKUR**

By bus Long-distance buses connect daily (June–Aug only; advance booking required; ⊛ wa.is) with ferries, then head back along Route 60 to Ísafjörður, or continue westwards to Patreksfjörður and Látrabjarg on the southwestern peninsula.
Destinations Ísafjörður (daily; 2hr 45min); Látrabjarg (daily; 2hr 30min).
By ferry The Seatours ferry (☎ 433 2354, ⊛ seatours.is) sails from Brjánslækur for Flatey (1–2 daily; 1hr 15min; 2985kr one-way) and Stykkishólmur (1–2 daily; 3hr; 5250kr one-way).

The southwestern peninsula

From its mountain-top junction with Route 60 by Lónfell, Route 63 descends towards Trostansfjörður, one of the four baby fjords which make up the **Suðurfirðir**, the southern fjords, forming the southwestern corner of **Arnarfjörður**. This section of the road is in very poor condition and features some alarmingly large potholes and ruts. Unusually for the West Fjords, three fishing villages are found within close proximity to one another here – barely 30km separates the uneventful port of **Bíldudalur** from its neighbours, identical **Tálknafjörður**, and the larger **Patreksfjörður**, a commercial centre for the surrounding farms and smaller villages. However, it's the **Látrabjarg** cliffs, 60km beyond Patreksfjörður to the west, that draw most visitors to this last peninsula of rugged land. Here, in summer, thousands upon thousands of **seabirds** – including guillemots, kittiwakes and puffins – nest in the cliff's nooks and crannies, making for one of the most spectacular sights anywhere in the region; and what's more, the cliffs are easily accessible from nearby **Breiðavík**, an idyllic bay of aquamarine water backed by white sand and dusky mountains.

THE FOSSHEIÐI TRAIL

What Bíldudalur lacks in attractions it more than makes up for with stunning scenery, and there are some lovely hikes in the area, such as the excellent 15km **Fossheiði trail** (4–5hr) up the Fossdalur valley to the tiny settlement of Tungumúli on the Barðaströnd coast (Route 62). It begins at **Foss farm**, 6km south of the airport at the head of Fossfjörður, following the route taken by local postmen in the late 1800s. From the western side of the farm, the track leads up through Fossdalur towards the small lake, Mjósund, beyond which the route forks. Keep right and take the path over the **Fossheiði plateau**, which has fantastic views over the surrounding rocky countryside, until it descends through Arnbylisdalur valley on the western edge of Tungumúlafjall mountain, to the coast and Route 62 at **Tungumúli**. The route is shown on the *Vestfirðir & Dalir* maps available from regional tourist offices. From Kross and Tungumúli, it's possible to link up with the three weekly summer **buses** to Látrabjarg or Brjánslækur – check the schedules first at Ísafjörður's information office (see p.194) or online at ⓦ bsi.is.

GETTING AROUND

By bus From June to Aug, the long-distance bus from Ísafjörður continues on from the Brjánslækur ferry jetty to Patreksfjörður, Rauðasandur, *Hótel Látrabjarg* (see p.213) and Breiðavík, before terminating at Látrabjarg. Around 11hr 15min later, it heads back along the same route to Brjánslækur and then north to Ísafjörður; advance bookings are essential (ⓦ wa.is).

Bíldudalur

4

A thriving fishing port processing vast amounts of local shrimp, workaday **BÍLDUDALUR** sits at the foot of Bíldudalsfjall mountain on the southern shores of Arnarfjörður, and is home to two hundred people. The main thing to do here is visit the town's two museums, though Bíldudalur's nearby **airport** can be useful as a quick way in or out of the West Fjords, avoiding a long and circuitous drive.

Skrímslasetrið
Strandgata 7 • June to mid-Sept daily 10am–6pm • 1000kr • ⓦ skrimsli.is

Tales of sea monsters are always part of the folk culture in maritime nations, and Iceland is no exception. It seems fitting, then, that **Skrímslasetrið** (Sea Monster Museum) has opened in Bíldudalur, since it's off this part of the coast that most sightings and reports of these elusive beasts are made. Inside, multimedia displays double with first-hand accounts from eyewitnesses to re-create a picture of the outlandish creatures that supposedly lurk in the depths offshore. There's also a simple restaurant here (see opposite).

Tónlistarsafn
Tjarnarbraut 5 • No set times, just knock on the door • 500kr

Cobbled together by Bíldudalur's most famous son, singer Jón Kristján Ólafsson (who doesn't speak English), the curious **Tónlistarsafn**, or Memories of Melodies **music museum**, holds a rambling collection of old vinyl records and other Icelandic music memorabilia from the 1940s to the 1960s. While certainly a worthy tribute to Iceland's past musical greats, it's unlikely to grab the attention of foreign visitors since the featured singers and groups were, mercifully, never big abroad.

ARRIVAL AND DEPARTURE   BÍLDUDALUR

By plane Bíldudalur's airport is 7km south of the village at the mouth of Fossfjörður, and is a useful gateway to the southeastern peninsula, with regular connections with Reykjavík cutting out the need for the long and tiring journey from Ísafjörður.

Destinations Reykjavík (Mon–Fri & Sun 1 daily; 50min).
By bus Aside from the June–Aug service from Ísafjörður to Látrabjarg (ⓦ wa.is), year-round buses, departing from outside the post office and bank in the main street, run between Bíldudalur, Tálknafjörður and Patreksfjörður

(Mon–Fri & Sun; exact times at ⓦ nat.is/travelguideeng /bus_schedule_patro_bildud_talknafj.htm). There are also airport services connecting with flights to and from Reykjavík, operated by Eagle Air (ⓦ ernir.is).

ACCOMMODATION AND EATING

Bjarkarholt Stóra Krossholt, Mórudalur ☎ 456 2025, ⓦ bjarkarholt.is. Handy for the southern end of the Tungumúli hike (see box opposite), this little coastal hideaway 15km west of Brjánslækur offers both double rooms and sleeping-bag dorms, or you can even rent an entire cottage. Doubles <u>12,000kr</u>, sleeping bags <u>4000kr</u>, cottage <u>22,500kr</u>

Campsite Hafnarbraut 3 ☎ 894 0809. Bíldudalur's campsite is located beside the sports field on the southern edge of the village. Showers, hot and cold running water, and a washing machine and drier are available. June to mid-Aug. <u>1350kr</u>

Skrímslasetrið Strandgata 7 ☎ 456 6666. The restaurant attached to the Sea Monster Museum (see opposite) serves up a limited range of food during the day: soup (1890kr), a changing dish of the day (2200kr), waffles and cakes are about the run of it. Note, though, that the restaurant is licensed and serves beer and wine to thirsty diners. June to mid-Sept daily 10am–6pm.

Vegamót Tjarnarbraut 2 ☎ 456 2232. The one and only dedicated eating place in Bíldudalur is one of the first things you see on entering town. It's none too special, but does have fish of the day (2950kr), burgers (1350kr) and an excellent fisherman's brunch of fried egg, bacon, fries, sausage and mushrooms (2150kr). June–Aug Mon–Fri 10am–10pm, Sat & Sun 11am–10pm; Sept–May Mon–Fri 11am–8pm, Sat & Sun noon–8pm.

Youth hostel Hafnarbraut 2 ☎ 456 2100, ⓦ hostel.is. This pebble-dash building down by the harbour is perfect for watching the fishing boats coming and going, and comes complete with guests' kitchen; rooms share facilities. Dorms <u>4550kr</u>, doubles <u>12,400kr</u>

Tálknafjörður

Southwest from Bíldudalur, it's 15km along Route 63 to the junction with Route 617, which heads 4km north to the equally tiny **TÁLKNAFJÖRÐUR**, a stop for the year-round Bíldudalur–Patreksfjörður bus. The only real reason to detour here is to ease your muscles at the superb open-air **swimming pool** by the church at Sveinseyri (daily 8am–9pm; 600kr), which comes complete with hot pots and fantastic views over the surrounding mountains. There are also a couple of natural alfresco hot pots fed by water from a spring just behind the church on the western outskirts of the village; follow the gravel road out of town for a couple of kilometres and then turn right at the "Pollurinn" sign.

ARRIVAL AND DEPARTURE

TÁLKNAFJÖRÐUR

By bus Year-round Bíldudalur–Patreksfjörður buses (Mon–Fri & Sun) stop at the filling station on the main road in Tálknafjörður (for timetables, see ⓦ nat.is/travelguideeng /bus_schedule_patro_bildud_talknafj.htm).

ACCOMMODATION AND EATING

Café Dunhagi Sveinseyri ☎ 662 0463. Finally, Tálknafjörður has somewhere decent to eat, housed in a former dance hall next to the swimming pool. Owner Dagný (who lived in the States for years and speaks great English) serves up the freshest of fish from the village fishermen (around 3500kr), local lamb and a divine fish soup. Don't miss the local version of *ruccola* which grows on the beach and appears with most dishes. June to mid-Aug daily 11.30am–10/11pm.

Campsite Sveinseyri ☎ 456 2639. Located in the centre of the village next to the swimming pool, the town's campsite is perfectly located for birdwatching on the fjordside. June–Aug. <u>1300kr</u>

Gistiheimilið Bjarmaland Bugatún 8 ☎ 891 8038, ⓦ guesthousebjarmaland.is. Run by four sisters, this is the better of the town's two guesthouses, though it's unlikely to be the highlight of your stay in Iceland: clean, neat and compact but nothing special. Breakfast is an extra 1,500kr. <u>14,200kr</u>

Patreksfjörður

Located on the shores of the southernmost of all the West Fjords, **PATREKSFJÖRÐUR** (known locally as Patró) is named after **Saint Patrick**, who acted as spiritual adviser to one of the region's first settlers, Örlygur Hrappson. With a population of 770, the village is now large enough to exist independently of Ísafjörður, 172km away, and is the only place in the West Fjords outside the regional capital to boast more than the odd shop and restaurant. Over the years, this tiny place has won a reputation for pioneering excellence: trawler fishing in Iceland began here; a particular style of saltfish now popular in Mediterranean markets was developed here; and, somewhat less notably, the village also dispatched the only Icelandic vessel ever to hunt seal in the Arctic.

Built on two sand spits, Geirseyri and Vatnseyri, Patreksfjörður comprises a main road in and out of the town, **Strandgata**, which runs along the shoreside to the harbour. Several side streets branch off Strandgata's western end, including Eyrargata, while the main shopping street, Aðalstræti, runs parallel to it. There's little to do in town other than amble up and down the parallel streets peering in windows, or take a swim in the open-air **pool**.

Swimming pool

Aðalstræti 55 • Mid-May to mid-Sept Mon–Fri 8am–9.30pm, Sat & Sun 10am–6pm; rest of the year Mon–Fri 7am–8.30pm, Sat & Sun 10am–5pm • 600kr

Patreksfjörður's one real attraction is its spectacularly located open-air **swimming pool**, perched high above the fjord at the western edge of the tiny town centre. As you swim here, you're treated to uninterrupted views across the fjord to the mountain of Vatnsdalsfjall, which rises on Patrekfjörður's sandy southern shore; soaking in the hot pots, drinking in the views, is equally as pleasurable. Though the pool should have been built a little longer (the neighbouring graveyard is in the way), a swim here is one of the most restorative and relaxing activities in the whole of the West Fjords region.

ARRIVAL AND INFORMATION
PATREKSFJÖRÐUR

By bus Both year-round buses between Patreksfjörður, Tálknafjörður and Bíldudalur, and summer services (advance booking required; ⑩wa.is) to Látrabjarg, Brjánslækur and Ísafjorður, depart from the Esso filling station on Strandgata.

Destinations Bíldudalur (1 daily Mon–Fri & Sun; 1hr); Brjánslækur (daily; 45min); Ísafjörður (daily; 3hr 45min); Látrabjarg (daily June–Aug; 1hr 20min); Tálknafjörður (1 daily Mon–Fri & Sun; 30min).

Services The post office (Mon–Fri 10am–4.30pm) is at Bjarkargata 10. For cash withdrawals there's an ATM at the bank (Mon–Fri 9am–4pm) opposite, at Bjarkargata 1. Nearby, at Þórsgata 10, down by the harbour, you'll find the *vínbúð* (Mon–Thurs 2–6pm, Fri 2–7pm; May–Aug also Sat 11am–2pm), while the Albína supermarket and bakery

(Mon–Fri 8am–10pm, Sat & Sun 10am–10pm), Aðalstræti 89, is the most central place for provisions.

Activities Due to the increasing number of tourists now spending the night in Patreksfjörður at the *Fosshótel* (see below), there's now a range of activities available for booking through Westfjords Adventures who are handily located just beyond the hotel at Aðalstræti 62 (☎456 5006, ⑩westfjordsadventures.com/tours/scheduled-bus/). In addition to operating the Ísafjörður–Brjánslækur–Látrabjarg bus service, the company offers seal watching at Rauðasandur, birdwatching excursions (generally at Látrabjarg), photography tours as well as jeep trips to various remote locations in the southern West Fjords. Advance booking is required for all tours (and the bus service).

ACCOMMODATION AND EATING

Fosshótel Westfjords Aðalstræti 100 ☎562 4000, ⑩fosshotel.is. Opened in June 2013, the brand-new Patreksfjörður *Fosshótel* has forty rooms and far outstrips any other accommodation in town. Rooms may have the usual chain feel, but are bright, airy and comfortable and have great views over the fjord. The restaurant serves a limited menu of one fish and one meat dish for 3990kr each. Restaurant daily 6–9pm. **31,700kr**

Heimsendi Eyrargata 5 ☎456 5150. Nicely located down by the harbour and with an outside terrace, this new café rustles up a momentous mountain lamb sandwich with

mushrooms, onions, fries and salad for 1990kr. Otherwise, there's a choice of fish dishes as well as burgers and salads. Mon–Fri 4–10.30pm, Sat 4pm–1am, Sun 4–10.30pm.

Ráðagerði Aðalstræti 31 ☎456 0181, ⑩radagerdi .com. A new hotel, owned and run by a designer and architect couple. Clever use of bold colours enlivens the white interiors to great effect: bright, airy and very stylish. April–Sept. **16,200kr**

Stekkaból Stekkar 19 ☎864 9675, ⑩stekkabol.is. Located behind the church off Aðalstræti, this simple guesthouse offers a choice of plain double rooms or

4

sleeping-bag dorms; breakfast is 1700kr. Doubles **14,400kr**, sleeping bags **4500kr**
Stúkúhúsið Aðalstræti 50 ☎ 456 1404. Engaging owner Steinunn has done an amazing job at renovating this old wooden building, which dates back to 1925. With elegant wallpaper and walls painted a delicate egg-shell blue, this winning bistro is perfect for fillet of lamb, quiche, seafood soup or even chicken satay salad. The coffees are expertly prepared and the home-made chocolates to die for. June–Aug daily 11am–11pm; Sept–May Wed–Sat noon–4pm.

Hnjótur

Route 62 runs southeast from Patreksfjörður down to the south coast. Around 12km from town, the unsealed **Route 612** branches westwards to run along the underside of yet another fjord, passing a beached shipwreck and the town's now disused airport at Sandoddi. After 25km, the road reaches the hamlet of **Hnjótur**, diagonally across the bay from Patreksfjörður, and little more than a couple of houses. Its poignant semicircular stone monument is dedicated to the sailors who lost their lives off the treacherous shores of the southwestern peninsula during the early twentieth century – all bar one were from the British ports of Grimsby and Hull.

Folk Museum

May to mid-Sept daily 10am–6pm • 1000kr

The settlement's main attraction is the **Folk Museum**, where you can check out a short film about the rescue of the British trawler, *Sargon*, and the items which were saved from the ship, and the *Dhoon* (see box, p.216). Upstairs, there's a small display dedicated to the life of Gísli Gíslason (1907–86), a hermit who lived all of his 79 years in remote Selárdalur at the mouth of Arnarfjörður and only once ventured to his nearest village, Bíldudalur. On the few occasions he spoke, even Icelanders found his bleating speech virtually incomprehensible, and there was general disbelief that such an existence was still possible in modern times. Otherwise, the museum contains a jumble of old maritime items such as fishing boats, nets, ropes and hooks – look out for the whale bones which were once used in roof construction.

Incidentally, the American DC3 that you can see adjacent to the museum once served at the American NATO base at Keflavík and took part in the evacuation of Heimaey during the eruption of 1973. In the hangar behind, there's also an Aeroflot Antonov biplane that landed in Iceland after running out of fuel, having been turned back to Russia from the US, where it was refused permission to land. Due to a long-running local dispute, these planes are not part of the Folk Museum and belong to a local man whose father founded the museum.

ARRIVAL AND DEPARTURE   **HNJÓTUR**

By bus Between June and Aug you can reach Hnjótur by bus from Brjánslækur, Patreksfjörður and Ísafjörður; timetables are at ⓦwa.is; advance reservation necessary.

Destinations Brjánslækur (1 daily; 1hr 40min); Ísafjörður (1 daily; 4hr 40min); Patreksfjörður (1 daily; 1hr 10min).

ACCOMMODATION

Hótel Látrabjarg Route 615, Örlygshöfn ☎ 456 1500 or ☎ 825 0025, ⓦlatrabjarg.com. It's hard to find a more picture-perfect location for a hotel than this. Sitting high above the vast sandy beach, Örlygshöfn, with sweeping views across the fjord to Patreksfjörður and the mountains beyond, you're virtually guaranteed a great night's rest at this remote former boarding school turned stylish hotel. Three-course dinners are available for 6900kr. To get here, turn right onto Route 615 just after the Hnjótur museum, and pass the farms of Efri Tunga and Neðri Tunga. The Látrabjarg bus will also call in on request. Mid-May to mid-Sept. **21,800kr**

Breiðavík

Beyond Hnjótur, Route 612 will bring you, after 10km or so, to a **church** and handful of buildings comprising the settlement at idyllic **Breiðavík bay**, with open views westwards over white sand to the aquamarine waters of the Atlantic. This exquisite **beach**, without a doubt one of Iceland's finest, is irresistible, and when the sun shines the sands are seen to their best advantage: kilometres of empty, unsullied white strands, punctuated solely by trickling mountain streams finally reaching the ocean, flocks of squawking seabirds and the odd piece of whitewashed driftwood, which can provide welcome shelter from the wind if you're intent on catching the rays.

ACCOMMODATION   **BREIÐAVÍK**

Breiðavík Right next to the beach ☎456 1575, ⓦbreidavik.is. This former fox farm and boarding school has been extensively renovated and offers camping pitches, sleeping-bag accommodation in double rooms, and regular double rooms with private facilities, though all rooms are a little cramped. The home-cooked meals are legendary – a three-course dinner with fish costs around 6900kr. Mid-May to mid-Sept. Doubles <u>**19,400kr**</u>, sleeping bags <u>**10,500kr**</u>, camping <u>**2000kr**</u>

Látrabjarg

Beyond Breiðavík, Route 612 climbs up and over a plateau (there's an extremely rough 12km gravel road off here to Keflavík) and then steeply down to the coast again before expiring a few kilometres further on, below the **lighthouse at Bjargtangar**, the westernmost point in Europe. The Ísafjörður–Brjánslækur–Patreksfjörður **bus** spends about two-and-a-half hours here before heading back – don't miss it unless you can afford to wait for the next one; there is nothing there.

The lighthouse also marks the start of **Látrabjarg cliffs**, which rise up to 441m above the churning sea as they run 14km east from here to the small inlet of **Keflavík**. A footpath leads along the clifftops, with excellent views of the thousands of **seabirds** that come here to nest on the countless ledges below. For centuries, locals would abseil down the cliffs to collect their eggs and trap the birds for food – it's estimated that around 35,000 birds were caught here every year until the late 1950s – and, occasionally, they still do.

ARRIVAL AND DEPARTURE   **LÁTRABJARG**

By bus Between June and Aug it's possible to get to Látrabjarg by bus from both Brjánslækur and Ísafjörður; timetables are at ⓦwa.is; advance reservation is necessary.

Destinations Brjánslækur (1 daily; 2hr); Ísafjörður (1 daily; 5hr); Patreksfjörður (1 daily; 1hr 30min).

Rauðasandur

East of Látrabjarg, the clifftop path rounds Keflavík bay and, after around 20km, finally descends to the serene red-orange sands at **Rauðasandur** bay (also known as Rauðisandur), where a couple of farming families still live. The lush, open fields that slowly give way to the vast expanse of sand that forms this part of the Breiðafjörður's shore have been cultivated for centuries, and today flocks of hardy sheep wander from field to shore in search of patches of grass. It's also possible to reach Rauðasandur along Route 614 which

---

LÁTRABJARG'S BIRDS

Although the **guillemot** is the most common bird at Látrabjarg, it's the thousands of **puffins** that most people come here to see. The high ground of the clifftops is riddled with their burrows, often up to 2m in length, since they nest in locations well away from the pounding surf, ideally surrounded by lush grass and thick soil. They return to the same burrows they occupied the year before, almost always during the third week of April, where they remain until August or September. The cliffs are also home to the largest colony of **razorbills** in the world, as well as to thousands of other screeching breeds of seabird including **cormorants**, **fulmars** and **kittiwakes**; the din here can be quite overpowering, as can the stench from the piles of guano on the cliff face.

OPPOSITE LÁTRABJARG CLIFFS >

> ### THE LÁTRABJARG RESCUE
> One of Iceland's most daring **sea-rescue operations** occurred at Látrabjarg in December 1947, when farmers from Hvallátur set out to rescue the crew of a British trawler, the *Dhoon*, which had been wrecked off the rocky shoreline during a severe snowstorm. After sliding down the ice-covered cliffs by rope, the Icelanders pulled the sailors to safety using a rescue line they fired across to the stricken vessel – although it took two separate attempts to hoist all the men up the treacherous cliff face, from where they were taken by horseback to nearby farms to recover. A year later, a film crew arrived in Hvallátur to make a documentary about the accident, in which several locals were to re-enact the rescue – however, while they were filming, another British trawler, *Sargon*, became stranded in nearby Patreksfjörður, giving the film-makers a chance to catch a drama on film for real.

heads south 12km from its junction with Route 612, a few kilometres before the disused airport at Sandoddi and Hnjótur, all the way to the beach and the **Bæjarvaðall** lagoon.

ARRIVAL AND DEPARTURE RAUÐASANDUR

By bus Between June and Aug a daily bus heads to the beach from Patreksfjörður; see ⓦ wa.is for details.

The south coast

East from Brjánslækur and Flókalundur, the south coast of the West Fjords is all but uninhabited. As Route 60 rounds the head of Vatnsfjörður east of Flókalundur, it's well over 100km before civilization reappears at **Bjarkalundur**, itself little more than a hotel and a filling station. Although still dramatic, the mountains along this stretch of road are less rugged and angular than those along the northern and western coasts, and the coastline is dominated by small bays separated by high bluffs, with wide areas of heavily vegetated flatland gently sloping down to the shores of Breiðafjörður. However, things become considerably wilder between Djúpifjörður and Þorskafjörður, just west of Reykhólar, around an area known as Hjallahals. Here, Route 60, now a mere gravel track potholed beyond belief, gingerly negotiates a number of steep ascents and descents around the tightest of hairpin bends, affording some truly spectacular views – altogether classic West Fjords.

Bjarkalundur

Hiking is just about all there is to do at the small service centre of **BJARKALUNDUR**, 126km east of Flókalundur, nothing more than a restaurant and a modern and uninspiring **hotel**. Roughly 1km east of the hotel, a four-wheel-drive track marks the beginning of a **trail** (7km) leading to the twin peaks of **Vaðalfjall**, an extinct volcano whose outer layers have eroded away, leaving just a bare chimney from where there are fantastic views out over the fjords and islands of Breiðafjörður. To return to Bjarkalundur, head southwest from the mountains to the old road that leads down to Kinnarstaðir farm, from where it's a couple of kilometres east along Route 60 to the hotel.

ACCOMMODATION BJARKALUNDUR

Bjarkalundur ☎434 7762, ⓦbjarkalundur.is. Roadside hotel offering comfortable wood-panelled accommodation, best used to break a long journey rather than as a destination in itself. The clean but plain double rooms have shared or private bathrooms, and there's also a campsite with toilet and shower facilities. Doubles 19,900kr, camping 1300kr

Djúpidalur 35km before Bjarkalundur ☎434 7853, ✉djupadal@simnet.is. This remote place, at the head of narrow Djúpifjörður, has great views out over the water and is a real country retreat. There are just five snug double rooms and a geothermal swimming pool – nothing else. Doubles 12,000kr, sleeping bags 4000kr

Reykhólar

From Bjarkalundur, Route 607 runs 15km southwest to **REYKHÓLAR**, a farming settlement home to just 120 people with attractive views out over Breiðafjörður to the Reykjanes peninsula. Although Reykhólar's history can be traced back to the time of the sagas, there's little reminder today of the village's wealthy past, when it was considered to have some of the best farmland in all of Iceland; the village once made a handsome profit from selling the wheat grown on the three hundred or so offshore islands hereabouts and the surrounding areas on the mainland. It is one of the few places in the West Fjords to have a ready supply of **geothermal energy**, which today has been harnessed and provides the village with its main source of activity – the ugly Þörungaverksmiðja algae plant, located a couple of kilometres south of the village, that extracts minerals from seaweed to make toothpaste, soap and handcream. There's little to do in the village except enjoy a relaxing dip in the warm waters of the outdoor **swimming pool** (Mon–Fri 1–9pm, Sat & Sun 11am–9pm; 500kr), which also has two hot pots.

INFORMATION
REYKHÓLAR

Tourist information There's an office, on Maríutröð, at the entrance to the village (June–Aug daily 11am–5pm; ☎434 7830). In the same building you'll find the frightfully poor Boat and Gift of Nature Exhibition (same opening times), which contains a handful of stuffed birds, seals and a fishing boat – save your 750kr entrance fee and give it a miss.

ACCOMMODATION

Campsite Reykjabraut 12 ☎434 7738. The town's campsite can be found at the opposite end of the village to the guesthouse, next to the swimming pool, and has toilets, running water and showers. June–Aug. 1600kr

Hólmavík and the Strandir coast

From Brú in the south to Norðurfjörður in the north, the lonely 220km of the **Strandir coast** form the West Fjords' easternmost extremities and one of the least-visited corners of Iceland – if you're looking to get off the beaten track, this is the place to come. The main entry point, and the region's only substantial settlement, is **Hólmavík**, accessed along Route 61 from either Ísafjörður or the Ringroad at Brú. North of here, the land is rugged, with snowcapped mountains and deeply indented fjords, the setting for some of the country's most isolated communities, dependent on fishing and sheep farming for their existence. The only thoroughfare, the 80km **Route 643**, is always in poor condition, prone to landslips and impassable from autumn's first snows until road maintenance crews break through again in late spring. There's **no public transport**, but it's worth making every effort to drive this earth road to really experience the wild and pioneering spirit of Iceland, notably at **Djúpavík**, a former herring-fishing village that's now all but abandoned, and is home to one of the West Fjords' most welcoming hotels. Beyond here, the road battles on north towards Iceland's most remote airport, **Gjögur**, handy for reaching this forgotten corner of the country, and end-of-the-road **Norðurfjörður**, where it finally expires, marking the jumping-off point for ambitious overland treks north towards the uninhabited wilds of Hornstrandir.

Hólmavík

A thriving fishing village on the southern shore of Steingrímsfjörður with a population of around 390, **HÓLMAVÍK** was granted municipal status in 1890 but only really began to grow during the twentieth century. Today life is centred around the natural **harbour** at the northern edge of the village, home to around a dozen fishing boats and the shrimp-processing plant, Rækjuvinnsla, that potent symbol of economic independence in rural Iceland, of which locals are justifiably proud.

Other than the West Fjords' most offbeat exhibition, the Museum of Sorcery and Witchcraft, there are no sights to speak of, though sooner or later you'll undoubtedly come across the oldest building in the village, **Riishús**, on the main street, Hafnarbraut, which runs parallel to the fjord. Built by and named after local merchant Richard Peter Riis, the two-storey wooden structure dates from 1897 and is now home to one of the town's restaurants (see opposite).

Galdrasýning á Ströndum

Höfðagata 8–10 • Daily 9am–9pm • 900kr • ⓦ galdrasyning.is

Located in the turf-roofed building behind the shrimp plant, the **Galdrasýning á Ströndum** (Museum of Sorcery and Witchcraft) should be your first port of call in town. An English audio commentary guides you through the various exhibits, which recount the occurrence of witchcraft and sorcery in this part of the country during the seventeenth century. The Strandir region, always one of Iceland's most remote, seems to have hung onto Viking superstitions longer than elsewhere, and even today is reputed as the home of cunning. During the late 1600s, twenty men and one woman were burnt at the stake in the West Fjords for sorcery, which included the practice of wearing *nábrók* ("**necropants**"), a supernatural means of getting rich quick; having gained the permission of a living man to dig up his body after death, the sorcerer would skin the body from the waist down and step into the skin, which would become one with his own. On placing a coin in the dead man's scrotum, the coin would continually draw money from other living people. A copy of a pair is on display in the museum, alongside other items such as a tree trunk with shackles and birch twigs for whipping offenders. Look out, too, for the eerie **stone bowl**, kept in a glass cabinet off reception, which is thought to have been used for sacrifices. Discovered at nearby Góðadalur in 2003, the bowl appears to show traces of human blood from heathen sacrificial rituals.

Strandakúnst

Höfðagata • June–Aug daily 1–5pm; at other times call ☎ 694 3306 or ask at the Museum of Sorcery and Witchcraft

Located next door to the museum, Strandakúnst is a not-for-profit handicrafts store selling any number of high-quality gifts which make perfect souvenirs. There's seemingly everything from hand-carved wooden seabirds to hand-knitted woollen sweaters. What's more, the prices are considerably less than you would shell out in Reykjavík. The money you pay for any item purchased in the store goes directly to the person who made it.

ARRIVAL AND INFORMATION   HÓLMAVÍK

By bus Buses from the N1 filling station at the entrance to the village link Hólmavík with Ísafjörður – a full 223km away – and with Borgarnes, offering connections for Akureyri at Bifröst.
Destinations Ísafjörður (2–3 daily; 3hr 40min); Borgarnes (4 weekly; 2hr 10min).
Tourist information The office is located in the witchcraft museum at Höfðagata 8–10 (daily 9am–9pm; ☎ 897 6525, ⓦ holmavik.is/info), and also has free internet access.
Services Hólmavík functions as a service centre for the

surrounding sheep farms and boasts a large supermarket at Höfðatún 4 (daily 9am–10.30pm) and a *vínbúð* next door (May–Aug Mon–Thurs 4–6pm, Fri 1–7pm, Sat noon–2pm; Sept–April Mon–Thurs 4–6pm, Fri 2–6pm). The post office and bank with ATM are together at Hafnarbraut 19 (both Mon–Fri 9am–4.30pm), while the outdoor swimming pool with two hot pots (June–Aug daily 9am–9pm; Sept–April Mon & Tues 3–9pm, Wed & Thurs 9am–9pm, Fri 9am–4pm, Sat & Sun 2–6pm; 520kr) is at the entrance to the village off Hólmavíkurvegur.

ACCOMMODATION AND EATING

Broddanes Youth Hostel Broddanesskóli, Kollafjörður ☎ 618 1830, ⓦ broddanes.is. Located on the eastern

shore of Kollafjörður, 35km south of Hólmavík along Route 68 towards Brú, this is the closest hostel to Hólmavík.

Accommodation is available in both dorms and double rooms and there are two kitchens on site for self-catering. Mid-May to mid-Sept; reception 8–10am & 5–10pm. Dorms 4750kr, doubles 16,000kr

Campsite Jakobínutún, off Hólmavíkurvegur ☎451 3560. Located at the entrance to the village next to the swimming pool; showers and toilets are available in the building adjacent to the pool. 1000kr

★ **Café Riis** Hafnarbraut 39 ☎451 3567. Accomplished food is served up at this wood-beamed old place, whose interior is full of black-and-white photographs of Holmavík's fishing past: succulent cod chins (3290kr), roast breast of chicken (3290kr) and pan-fried puffin breast (3590kr) are all winners. There are pizzas, too, from 1540kr. June–Aug Mon–Fri & Sun 11.30am–10pm, Sat 11.30am–3am.

Finna Hótel Borgabraut 4 ☎451 3136, �🌐finnahotel

.is. A sound self-catering choice, overlooking the harbour and the snow-covered mountains on the opposite side of the fjord and offering newly renovated rooms both with and without private facilities. 17,000kr

Restaurant Galdur Höfðagata 8–10. This little café inside the Sorcery and Witchcraft Museum, run by knowledgeable curator Siggi, serves local mussels from the fjord – deliciously fresh and juicy (2600kr), fresh fish, usually ling (2300kr) and seafood sop (1400kr). You can also get beer, wine, coffee and cakes. Daily 9am–9pm.

★ **Steinhúsið** Höfðagata 1 ☎856 1911, �🌐steinhusid .is. Hólmavík's first-ever concrete house, erected in 1911 down by the harbour, offers comfortable self-catering rooms with creaking wooden floors, steep steps and period furniture. There's also two apartments for rent next door. Doubles 13,500kr, apartments 20,600kr

Laugarhóll

Eleven kilometres north of Hólmavík, **Route 643** begins its journey along the Strandir coast. After some 15km, it passes through the hamlet of **LAUGARHÓLL**, consisting of little more than a couple of farms grouped around a source of geothermal water, which feeds an **outdoor pool** and a natural **hot pot**. Even if you're just driving by, stop and have a look at the unusual turf-roofed **Kotbýli Kuklarans**, or sorcerer's cottage (mid-June to mid-Aug daily 10am–6pm; free). Just to the left of the hotel, it's a simple peasant dwelling, with stretched sheep's stomachs for windows, where it's believed witchcraft was practised during the seventeenth century.

ACCOMMODATION   **LAUGARHÓLL**

Laugarhóll Bjarnarfjöður ☎451 3380, �🌐laugarholl.is. The main reason to stay at this country hotel is for easy access to the natural hot pot and outdoor pool right outside, though it does have inspiring views of the gentle

Hólsfjall mountains, which form a serene backdrop to the tiny village. Rooms, both with and without private facilities, can be a little on the small side but are comfortable enough. 18,200kr

Drangsnes

From Laugarhóll, it's 20km southeast on Route 645 to **DRANGSNES**, a tiny fishing village at the mouth of Steingrímsfjörður overlooking the island of **Grímsey**, home to the second-largest **puffin colony** in the world; twice-daily boat trips out to the island operate between mid-June and August (☎461 4345 or 853 6520, ✉malarhorn @simnet.is; 7000kr/person, minimum 4 people). The puffins generally leave Grímsey on August 10.

INFORMATION   **DRANGSNES**

Services Drangsnes has a petrol pump and a village shop (Mon–Thurs 9am–noon & 1–6pm, Fri 9am–noon & 1–7pm, Sat 11am–3pm). The new open-air swimming pool (June–Aug daily 11am–6pm; rest of the year Tues, Wed & Fri 3–6pm, Sat & Sun 1–5pm) is next to the

Malarhorn guesthouse on Grundargata (see p.220), while there are three seafront hot pots as you enter the village on the right hand side, adjacent to the church, with showers on the roadside opposite.

ACCOMMODATION

Campsite Aðalbraut ☎844 8701, ✉drangsnes @snerpa.is. Beside Baldur Community Centre above

Drangsnes' harbour, with washing and toilet facilities in the community centre next door, this tiny campsite is rather

exposed to the wind. April–Sept. **1100kr**
Malarhorn Grundargata 17 ☎ 451 3237, ⓦ malarhorn
.is. This place offers a range of accommodation: as well as
regular double rooms, whose interiors resemble traditional
wooden cabins, there's an entire cottage sleeping eight,

and a separate apartment. The on-site restaurant serves
tasty fish mains from 3190kr. Restaurant June to mid-
Sept daily 11am–9pm. Doubles **16,500kr**, cottage
34,000kr, apartment **29,900kr**

Djúpavík

North of Laugarhóll, Route 643 cuts into one of the most remote corners of Europe,
where towering rock buttresses plunge precipitously into the icy sea and the coastline is
strewn with vast expanses of **driftwood** that originated on the other side of the Arctic
Ocean, in Russian Siberia. Tourist facilities here are virtually nonexistent, but the
region is stunningly beautiful and somewhere to really experience Iceland's rawness
close up. The road is in shocking condition (particularly around Veiðileysa, the fjord
south of Djúpavík), however, with huge potholes and some alarming narrow stretches,
while the wind on this exposed coast is ferocious at best, hurling rocks and scree down
from the mountain slopes onto the road below and blowing cars from one side of the
road to the other.

Life in these remote parts has never been easy, and the village of **DJÚPAVÍK**, 70km
from Hólmavík (count on a journey time of 1hr 30min) close to the head of shadowy
Reykjarfjörður, is testimony to this hardship, dominated by the huge carcass of its old
herring factory and the rusting hull of the 100-year-old former passenger and cargo
ship *Suðurland*, another victim of the West Fjords weather. Despite the evident failure
of the herring adventure (see below), there's an endearing air to diminutive Djúpavík,
consisting of just seven houses and one of Iceland's most charming **hotels**, the *Djúpavík*
(see below), located beneath a braided waterfall.

The old herring factory

Tours June–Aug daily 10am & 2pm • 1000kr **Steypa exhibition** June–Aug daily 9am–6pm • Free • ⓦ djupavik.com/steypa

When the herring industry was at its height in the mid-1940s, several hundred people
lived in Djúpavík, women salting the fish, men turning the remains into animal meal
and oil. The herring factory became unprofitable in 1955 following a disastrous
collapse in fish catches, but the enormous costs involved in demolishing the building
– once the largest concrete structure in Europe – mean that its hulking hollow shell
remains, reminiscent of a Hollywood film set; Icelandic band Sigur Rós saw its
potential in 2006 and even played a concert in it, attracting over three hundred people,
a veritable throng in these parts.

The *Djúpavík* hotel (see below) now owns the herring plant and runs **tours** inside,
which take in the **Sögusýning Djúpavíkur** (Historical Exhibition of Djúpavík), a
collection of evocative black-and-white photographs from the herring years. Check out,
too, the international photography exhibition, Steypa, which is held every summer in
the old factory. The one key link between all the photographs on display is that they
have all been taken in Iceland.

ARRIVAL AND DEPARTURE   DJÚPAVÍK

By plane Other than driving, the only way to reach
Djúpavík is to fly to Gjögur (see opposite), though there

are only one or two departures per week depending on
season.

ACCOMMODATION

Hótel Djúpavík ☎ 451 4037, ⓦ djupavik.com. Originally
built as a hostel for the women who worked on the dockside
and in the factory, this remote retreat has rooms (all with
shared facilities) in the main building, and an adjacent

annexe where the simpler rooms offer sleeping-bag
accommodation and share a kitchen. Breakfast is 1800kr;
dinner is also available (7–9pm) and costs from 2750kr.
Doubles **12,500kr**, sleeping bags **3800kr**

THE FERRY TO HORNSTRANDIR

Every Friday and Sunday, between mid-June and mid-August, a **boat** sails from the harbour in **Norðurfjörður** to **Reykjarfjörður** (9500kr) and Látravík (14,500kr), providing access to the remote east coast of Hornstrandir. From both destinations it is then possible to hike west to meet up with the boats which sail across to Ísafjörður from Hesteyri among other places (see p.203). Schedules and further information are available at ⓦ strandferdir.is.

Norðurfjörður

Fifteen kilometres up the coast from Djúpavík, you pass tiny **Gjögur airport**, from where it's a further 13km to the end of the road at **NORÐURFJÖRÐUR**, one of Iceland's most remote places (a 45min drive from Djúpavík and – at a distance of 104km – a 2hr drive from Hólmavík), with a population of just twelve people. Occupying a stunning position amid fertile farmland at the head of the fjord of the same name, the village is dominated by the Krossnesfjall mountain (646m) to the east.

Krossneslaug

4km northeast of Norðurfjörður, north of the farm at Krossnes • No fixed times • 450kr

One of the country's most dramatically situated swimming pools, **Krossneslaug** boasts natural springs which provide a continuous source of hot water to feed the **open-air pool** and hot pot down on the grey pebble beach. The pool's walls are barely a couple of metres from the icy waters of the Atlantic; a swim here is one of the most memorable experiences Iceland has to offer.

ARRIVAL AND INFORMATION

By plane Norðurfjörður is linked to Reykjavík via the nearby Gjögur airport. There are one or two flights per week operated by Eagle Air (or Ernir in Icelandic; ⓦ ernir.is). Destinations Reykjavík (1–2 weekly; 50min).

NORÐURFJÖRÐUR

Services Down at Norðurfjörður's harbour, there's a small food store (June–Aug 9am–noon & 1–6pm; Sept–May Mon, Tues, Thurs & Fri 1–5pm) selling a limited range of fruit and vegetables, and a petrol pump.

ACCOMMODATION AND EATING

Bergistangi At the harbour ☏ 451 4003, ⓔ gunnsteinn@simnet.is. Just two doubles (sleeping bag only) are available at this simple guesthouse, though the same people have three more rooms (also sleeping bag only) for rent in the converted meat-freezing plant next door. **5000kr**

Kaffi Norðurfjörður On the first floor of the building opposite the food store ☏ 862 3944. This airy harbourside café has fish soup (1850kr) as well as the catch of the day (3250kr), lamb steaks (4650kr), burgers (1850kr) and sandwiches with fries (1250kr). June–Aug daily 8am–late.

Urðartindur At the entrance to Norðurfjörður at the foot of Urðartindur peak ☏ 843 8110, ⓦ urdartindur.is. Two wooden cabins (each sleeping up to four people with a kitchen), plus four double rooms with private facilities in a converted barn, and a campsite. Doubles **18,000kr**, cabins **22,500kr**, camping **1000kr**

Valgeirsstaðir hostel Trékyllisvík ☏ 451 4017 or ☏ 568 2533, ⓦ fi.is. Run by Ferðafélag Ísland, with an adjoining tiny campsite, this snug little hostel is located a kilometre or two before Norðurfjörður itself and has twenty dorm beds and a shared kitchen. Dorms **6500kr**, camping **1600kr**

4

Northwest Iceland

EYJAFJÖRÐUR

5

Northwest Iceland

Compared with the neighbouring West Fjords, the scenery of Northwest Iceland is much gentler and less forbidding – undulating meadows dotted with isolated barns and farmhouses are the norm here, rather than twisting fjords, though there are still plenty of impressive mountains to provide a satisfying backdrop to the coastline. However, what makes this section of the country stand out is the location of two of Iceland's great historical sites, most notably Þingeyrar, once the site of an ancient assembly and monastery where some of Iceland's most outstanding pieces of medieval literature were compiled.

As the Ringroad heads northeast from Þingeyrar on its way to Akureyri, the best place to break the long journey is likeable **Sauðárkrókur**, enlivened by stunning sea views out over Skagafjörður and **Drangey** island, once home to saga hero **Grettir**, who bathed here in the nearby natural hot pool now named after him. Just half an hour's drive away is the north's second great historical site, **Hólar í Hjaltadal**, which functioned as the ecumenical and educational centre of the north of the country between the twelfth century and the Reformation. A further detour up Route 76, via the Vesturfarasetrið (Icelandic Emigration Centre) at **Hofsós**, brings you to the pretty fishing village of **Siglufjörður**.

Slicing deep into the coastline of this part of northern Iceland, **Eyjafjörður** is the country's longest fjord and was for centuries **Akureyri**'s window on the world as ships sailed its length to deliver their goods to the largest market in northern Iceland. Today, though, fisheries have taken over as the town's economic mainstay, profiting from the rich fishing grounds found offshore. With a population of fifteen thousand making it the largest town outside the Reykjavík area, not only does Akureyri boast a stunning setting at the head of Eyjafjörður, but it's also blessed with some of the warmest and most stable weather anywhere in the country.

Though the sleepy villages of **Dalvík**, with ferry connections across to Hrísey, and **Ólafsfjörður** both make excellent day-trips once you've exhausted Akureyri, it's more fun to head out to the beautiful island of **Grímsey**, where the cliffs and skies are alive with around sixty different species of screeching birds, many of which consider you an unwelcome intruder.

GETTING AROUND   **NORTHWEST ICELAND**

By bus Buses between Reykjavík and Akureyri run through the region year-round along the Ringroad; if you're arriving from the West Fjords, you'll need to change buses at Bifröst. There are also local bus routes from the Ringroad town of Varmahlíð to Sauðárkrókur, as well as from Akureyri northwest to Dalvík, Ólafsfjörður and Siglufjörður (year-round).

By car You can also enter the Northwest direct from Gullfoss in southwestern Iceland along the Kjölur route through the Interior, which lands you on the Ringroad around halfway between Brú and Akureyri. This summer-only road is open to conventional cars (with extreme care) and is covered by daily buses; see p.326 for more about the route.

Highlights

❶ **Seal watching, Ósar** Get close to a rare seal-breeding colony on the Vatnsnes peninsula. **See p.229**

❷ **Þingeyrakirkja, Þingeyrar** One of Iceland's most spectacular church interiors, with an intricate wooden pulpit from the late 1600s. **See p.229**

❸ **Skagi peninsula, Skagafjörður** Witness the austere beauty of one of Iceland's most exposed coastlines. **See p.231**

❹ **Herring museum, Siglufjörður** Get to grips with Icelanders' fascination with fish in this excellent museum. **See p.239**

❺ **Ptarmigan spotting, Hrísey** In summer dozens of these plump game birds waddle

through Hrísey's main village with their offspring in tow. **See p.243**

❻ **Botanical Garden, Akureyri** Seemingly defying the northerly latitude, this delightful garden is awash with colour during the short summer months. **See p.248**

❼ **Hiking in Í Fjörðum** Hike through uninhabited valleys and mountain passes, all within easy striking distance of Akureyri. **See p.255**

❽ **The Arctic Circle, Grímsey** Crossing the magic line gives a real sense of achievement, and Grímsey is one of the best places to see the Midnight Sun. **See p.255**

HIGHLIGHTS ARE MARKED ON THE MAP ON PP.226–227

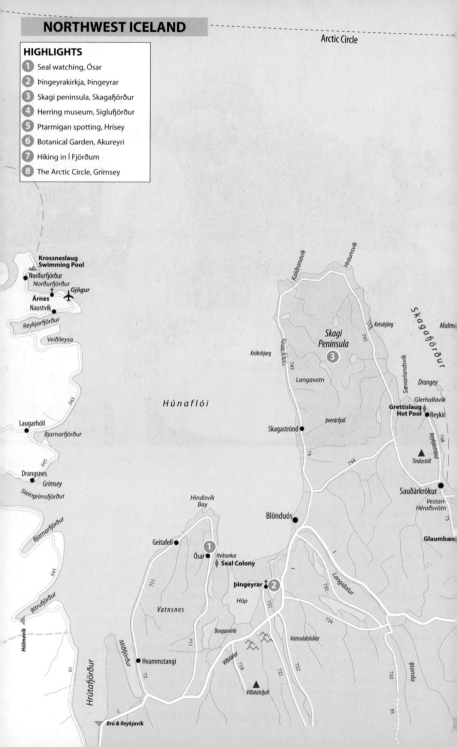

NORTHWEST ICELAND

HIGHLIGHTS

1. Seal watching, Ósar
2. Þingeyrakirkja, Þingeyrar
3. Skagi peninsula, Skagafjörður
4. Herring museum, Siglufjörður
5. Ptarmigan spotting, Hrísey
6. Botanical Garden, Akureyri
7. Hiking in Í Fjörðum
8. The Arctic Circle, Grímsey

Arctic Circle

Krossneslaug
Swimming Pool
Norðurfjörður
Norðurfjörður
Gjögur
Árnes
Naustvík
Reykjarfjörður
Veiðileysa

Laugarhóll
Bjarnarfjörður

Drangsnes
Grímsey
Steingrímsfjörður

Bjarnarfjörður

Bitrufjörður

Hólmavík

Hrútafjörður

Brú & Reykjavík

Húnaflói

Hindisvík
Bay

Geitafell
Ósar
Hvitserkur
Seal Colony

1

Vatnsnes

Borgarvirki

Miðfjörður

Hvammstangi

Víðidalur

Víðidalsfjall

Þingeyrar

2

Hóp

Blönduós

Kaldranavík

Hraunsvík

Ketubjörg

Skagi
Peninsula

3

Langavatn

Króksbjarg

Skagaströnd

Langidalur

þverárfjall

Skagafjörður

Malmé

Sævarlandsvík

Drangey

Glerhallavík

Grettislaug
Hot Pool
Reykir

Tindastóll

Sauðárkrókur

Vestari-
Héraðsvötn

Glaumbær

Vatnsdalshólar

Blanda

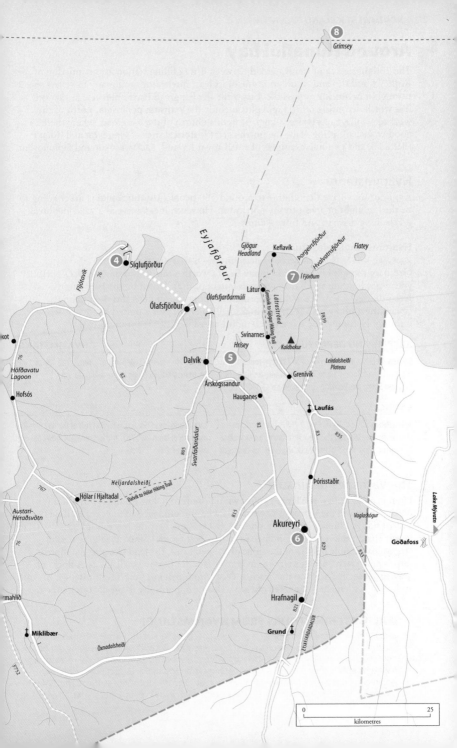

5

Around Húnaflói bay

The 230km stretch of the Ringroad between **Brú** (a filling station at the junction of Routes 1 and 61) and Akureyri is one of its least interesting, and many travellers speed through it as quickly as possible. But while the Ringroad itself holds few attractions, it is worth detouring off it: highlights include the **Vatnsnes peninsula**, north of the workaday village of Hvammstangi, 5km or so north of the Ringroad, where there's a good chance of seeing seals; the north's great historical sites of **Þingeyrar** and **Hólar í Hjaltadal**; and two fine examples of small-town Iceland, **Sauðárkrókur** and **Siglufjörður**.

Hvammstangi

A humdrum village that's home to around 580 people, **Hvammstangi** is never going to be the highlight of a visit to the northwest. However, it can serve as a welcome break on the long drive to and from Akureyri.

Hvammstangi Selasetur

Strandgata 1 • May & Sept daily 9am–4pm; June–Aug daily 9am–7pm • 950kr • ☎ 451 2345, Ⓦ selasetur.is

Ordinary though Hvammstangi may be, it's worth a quick stop on your way north if you're not heading to Ósar to see seals (see opposite). Down by the harbour, the Icelandic Seal Centre contains information about the animals and their habitat (including a film which is shown in a small cinema), plus a potted history of seal hunting. Naturally, there is also a handful of stuffed seals for your perusal.

ARRIVAL AND DEPARTURE   HVAMMSTANGI

By bus All buses on the Reykjavík to Akureyri route stop at the junction of Routes 1 and 72, from where a shuttle bus (4 daily; 5min; pre-booking is required on ☎ 540 2700 at least 2hr before departure) runs the 6km into Hvammstangi, stopping at the filling station.

EATING

Sjávarborg Strandgata 1 ☎ 869 7992. Upstairs from the seal centre (see above), this new restaurant, an airy place of concrete and huge glass windows, does an excellent burger and fries (1990kr) as well as fish of the day (3450kr) and rack of lamb (4800kr), and has pleasant views out over Miðfjörður. Daily 11am–10pm.

The Vatnsnes peninsula

From Hvammstangi, you'll need your own transport to follow Route 711 as it heads northeast around the **Vatnsnes peninsula**, a wild and uninhabited finger of land on the eastern side of Húnaflói known for its superb views out over the bay towards the needle-sharp peaks of the Strandir coast in the West Fjords. While ascending tiers of craggy, inaccessible hills form the spine of the peninsula, the land closer to the shore is surprisingly green and is given over to grazing land for horses; you'll also spot flocks of **greylag geese**, and seals on the beach at **Ósar**. Around 30km from Hvammstangi, the café at the tiny settlement of **Geitafell** offers a welcome opportunity to break your journey.

SEAL-WATCHING TOURS FROM HVAMMSTANGI

From the harbour outside the seal centre (see above), the handsome former fishing boat, *Brimill*, sails across to the sands on the southwestern shores of Miðfjörður, a favourite resting spot for seals; as there is no road access to the area, the boat trip provides the only opportunity to **watch seals** in their natural environment from Hvammstangi and sightings are virtually guaranteed. Trips are run by Selasigling, Höfðabraut 13 (mid-May to Sept at 10am, 1pm & 4pm; 1hr 45min; 7900kr includes entrance to Selasetur; minimum two people per trip; ☎ 897 9900, Ⓦ sealwatching.is).

Ósar

On the promontory's more sheltered eastern coast, 29km north of the Ringroad along Route 711 and 18km east of Geitafell, there's a **seal-breeding ground** at the farm-cum-youth hostel, **Ósar**, where adult seals and their young can be spotted lolling idly on the black volcanic sands during June and July – a rare opportunity to see these appealing creatures at close quarters. A short path leads down to the sands from the friendly youth hostel. Ósar is also the location of the 15m-high **Hvítserkur** rock formation, a striking landmark just offshore. Sculpted by the tremendous force of the sea, this craggy rock looks like a forbidding sea monster rearing up from the waves.

ACCOMMODATION AND EATING   **VATNSNES PENINSULA**

Geitafell Café Geitafell ☎861 2503. Just around the head of the promontory from Ósar in Geitafell, this winning café is set in a converted barn and run by Sigrún and Róbert, who grow their own produce and serve a hearty seafood soup (2700kr), a filling bean soup (2000kr), and a range of home-made cakes, including one made of *skyr*. Daily June–Aug 11am–10pm.

★**Ósar Youth Hostel** Ósar ☎862 2778, ⓦhostel.is. A self-catering hostel run by the delightful Knútur set in the peaceful surroundings of a dairy farm. There are snug log cabins sleeping up to six as well as regular dorms; both enjoy undisturbed views of the rugged coastline of the Skagi peninsula. Breakfast is 1800kr. May–Oct. Dorms __4500kr__, cabins __30,400kr__

Viðidalur

As it heads southwards down the eastern shore of Vatnsnes, Route 711 rejoins the Ringroad in **Viðidalur**. One of the area's most populated valleys, it's dotted with some beautifully located farms, most notably **Auðunarstaðir** (between the junctions of Routes 711 and 716 with the Ringroad), named after the evidently well-endowed settler Auðun Skökull (Auðun the horse penis), to whom the British royals can apparently trace their family line. The breathtaking backdrop of the brown and green hues of Víðidalsfjall mountain (993m) forms the eastern side of the valley through which one of the northwest's best salmon rivers, the lengthy Víðidalsá, flows from its source at Stórisandur in the Interior.

Þingeyrar

Just 6km north of the Ringroad along Route 721, the ancient site of **Þingeyrar** is worth a stopoff on your journey to Akureyri. If you don't have your own transport, you'll find that it's a straightforward walk from the Ringroad. This was originally the site of a **legislative assembly** during the Icelandic Commonwealth (p.335), and the first Bishop of Hólar, Jón Ögmundarson, pledged to build a church and an associated farm here if God were to relieve a severe local famine. When the land began to regain its productivity, the bishop took things one step further and established Iceland's **first monastery**, Þingeyraklaustur, here in 1133, which remained in existence until the Reformation in 1550. The monks went on to copy and transcribe some of the country's most outstanding pieces of medieval literature, and it was on this spot that many of the **sagas** were first written down for posterity.

Þingeyrakirkja

July–Sept daily 10am–6pm; at other times call in at the adjacent horse farm, Þingeyrar, where the keys are kept • Free

There's nothing left of the monastery, but a superb nineteenth-century church, **Þingeyrakirkja**, now stands adjacent to where the monks once lived and worked. Constructed of large blocks of basalt, brought here on sledges dragged across the nearby frozen lagoon of Hóp, the church was the first building on the site to be made of stone – all previous structures had been of turf – and it brought much admiration from local worthies. Although its grey mass is indeed an impressive sight, clearly visible from many kilometres around, it's the **interior** that really makes a trip here worthwhile,

5

with stark white walls setting off the blue ceiling, painted with a thousand golden stars, and the simple green pews. The wooden pulpit dates from 1696 and is thought to come from Denmark or Holland, whereas the altarpiece, inset with religious figures made of alabaster, dates from the fifteenth century and was originally made in the English town of Nottingham for the monastery there.

Blönduós

From the Þingeyrar junction, it's a further 19km along the Ringroad to **BLÖNDUÓS**, the focal point of Húnaflói bay, with a huge hospital and its modern, multicoloured houses grouped on either side of one of Iceland's longest rivers, the glacial Blanda. Without a good harbour, the town is merely a service centre for the locality, pasteurizing milk from the surrounding farms. Consisting of a handful of uneventful streets and the odd shop, the centre of town straddles both banks of the river, accessed from the Ringroad by the roads of Blöndubyggð on the southern side and Húnabraut on the northern shore. There's little reason to stop here, other than to pop quickly into the town's only attraction, the **Hafíssetrið** exhibition on sea ice.

Hafíssetrið

Ólafsbyggð • June–Aug daily 11am–5pm • 500kr

Just off Blöndubyggð and down by the river near Aðalgata, the informative **Hafíssetrið** (Sea Ice Centre) is housed in Hillebrandtshús, one of Iceland's oldest wooden buildings, dating from 1733. Húnaflói is generally the first bay in Iceland to encounter **sea ice** during the winter months, and the museum displays explain how this phenomenon occurs – and covers the **polar bears** that sometimes ride the ice as it floats from Greenland to Iceland. Indeed, the exhausted and half-starved polar bear which came ashore near Skagaströnd in July 2008, now stuffed, is on display here. Check out, too, the twenty-minute documentary featuring candid interviews with local fishermen and farmers voicing their concerns about the effects of global warming on the sea ice – and their livelihoods.

ARRIVAL AND INFORMATION
BLÖNDUÓS

By bus All buses on the Reykjavík to Akureyri route stop at the N1 filling station.

Departures Akureyri (2 daily; 2hr 15min); Reykjavík (2 daily; 4hr 15min); Sauðárkrókur (2 daily; 40min).

Tourist information There's an office opposite the filling station, down by the river on Brautarhvammur (early June to late Aug Mon–Fri 8am–8pm, Sat & Sun 4–7pm; ☎820 1300, ⊕northwest.is).

Services The swimming pool (Mon–Fri 8am–9pm, Sat & Sun 10am–8pm; 600kr) and the supermarket (Mon–Fri 10am–7pm, Sat 10am–6pm, Sun 1–5pm) are opposite each other on Melarbraut, below and behind the church, while the *vínbúð* (May–Aug Mon–Thurs 2–6pm, Fri 1–7pm, Sat 11am–2pm; Sept–April Mon–Thurs 2–6pm, Fri 2–7pm) and the bank with ATM (Mon–Fri 9am–noon & 1–4pm) are next door to each other at Húnabraut 5.

ACCOMMODATION

Blönduós Aðalgata 6 ☎452 4205, ⊕hotelblonduos.is. Overlooking the sea, the *Blönduós* offers en-suite rooms

decorated in bold reds and pinks, and inclusive breakfast, in its main building; the annexe next door has more neutrally

---

VATNSDALSHÓLAR

Clustered around the turn-off to Route 721 for Þingeyrar and Route 722, the extensive area of small hillocks known as **Vatnsdalshólar** is in fact leftover debris from a massive landslide from the Vatnsdalsfjall mountains west of the Hóp lagoon. These conical-shaped hills cover a total area of around four square kilometres and are so numerous that they have become one of Iceland's three "uncountables": the other two are the islands of Breiðafjörður and the lakes of Arnarvatnsheiði moors near Húsafell. One of the hillocks, **Þrístapar**, has gone down in history as the location for Iceland's last beheading, when a couple were executed on it in 1830 for a double murder.

decorated, cheaper rooms sharing facilities, and breakfast is extra. Hotel <u>22,000kr</u>, annexe <u>15,000kr</u>
Campsite Brautarhvammur ☎820 1300. Located next to the tourist information office, the site is right beside the Ringroad and can be noisy. Hot showers and toilet facilities are available in the on-site service building. May to mid-Sept. <u>1000kr</u>
Glaðheimar Brautarhvammur ☎820 1300, ⓦgladheimar.is. Good-value wooden cabins next to the tourist office and overlooking the river, though close to the

Ringroad traffic, too; each sleeps up to eight, is complete with kitchen and shower, and most also have their own outdoor jacuzzi on the terrace. <u>13,000kr</u>
Kiljan Aðalgata 2 ☎452 4500, ⓦkiljanguesthouse .com. Just nine wood-panelled rooms, all sharing facilities, are available at this friendly new guesthouse overlooking the sea, which makes a much better bet than the anonymous hotel next door. New tastefully appointed, two-person apartments also available. Doubles <u>10,500kr</u>, apartments <u>15,000kr</u>

EATING AND DRINKING

Kiljan Aðalgata 2 ☎452 4500. Polish-run café serving a couple of central European classics such as Wiener schnitzel (2800kr) and a tasty lobster soup (1900kr) as well as the usual range of Icelandic staples such as salmon, trout and cod (2950kr). Daily 7–9pm.
Ömmukaffi Húnarbraut 2 ☎452 4678. Homely café-bar which serves up grilled panini with various toppings (900kr), bagels (1100kr) and soup and fresh bread

(1300kr). However, it's the weekend brunch that's arguably the best choice – a spread of salads and fish dishes for 1500kr. Daily 9am–11pm.
Potturinn Norðurlandsvegur 4 ☎453 5060. Bright and airy place beside the main road and the filling station, offering fish of the day (3295kr), tandoori chicken breast (3995kr) and lamb steak (3995kr). Lunch specials, generally fish, are around 1500kr. Daily 11am–10pm.

The Skagi peninsula

Barely a kilometre outside Blönduós, where the Ringroad swings sharply inland to follow the course of Langidalur valley towards Varmahlíð, Route 74 strikes off north for 23km towards the **Skagi peninsula**, a lonely, uninhabited landscape of desolate rocky moors and tussocky grassland studded with tarns. Beyond the peninsula's one and only town, **Skagaströnd**, the unsurfaced Route 745 begins its tour of the peninsula proper.

Skagaströnd

SKAGASTRÖND is a rather ugly place dominated by a hulking fish factory down by the harbour and the brooding heights of the **Spákonufell** (646m) mountain, which bears down on the settlement from across the main road. Although trading began here centuries ago, there's precious little to show for it, since most buildings date from a tasteless expansion during the 1940s herring boom.

Spákonuhof

Oddagata 6 • June–Sept Tues–Sun 1–6pm • 900kr; fortune-telling 4000kr extra • ☎861 5089

Skagaströnd's new museum focuses on the life and times of the area's first named inhabitant, Þórdís the fortune-teller (c.932–75), who lived on nearby Spákonufell in the late tenth century. On entering the museum you'll come face to face with a wax model of Þórdís (even though there's actually no description of what she looked like), a couple of stuffed ravens and a mock-up of a wooden shack with a thatched roof – an approximation of the hut she might have lived in. Other than a tapestry portraying the key events in her life, notably efforts to raise Iceland's first Christian missionary, there's little else here to detain you.

EATING   SKAGASTRÖND

Borgin Hólanesvegur 11 ☎452 2829. Housed in an enormous log cabin, Skagafförður's only restaurant serves up unusual fare such as horsemeat (4300kr), whale steaks (4500kr) and fried guillemot (4500kr) as well as more

mainstream burgers and fries (from 1950kr), and pizzas (2000kr). Mon–Thurs & Sun 11.30am–10pm, Fri & Sat 11.30am–1am.

5

Around the Skagi peninsula

From Skagaströnd, Route 745 follows the eastern shoreline of Húnaflói bay as it heads north up the peninsula. Roughly 15km north of Skagaströnd, the 10km-long cliffs at **Króksbjarg** and the glittering **waterfall** where the Fossá River tumbles down the cliff-face into the sea are an essential first stop. Beyond Króksbjarg, the road passes several deserted farms before reaching the sweeping bay of **Kaldranavík**, at the tip of the peninsula, which offers some truly magnificent ocean vistas. Having weaved past the remote farm of Hraun, at Hraunsvík on the northeastern extremity of the peninsula, the road finally veers south following the coastline of **Skagafjörður** fjord for the rugged sheer sea cliff **Ketubjörg** (signed from the road), actually the remains of an old volcano, and the accompanying rock pillar, **Kerling**, just off the shore to the northeast. From here it's an uneventful and easy drive on towards Sauðárkrókur (see opposite).

Varmahlíð and around

East from Blönduós along the Ringroad, it's 25km to where Route 732 heads south to join the **Kjölur Route** (Route 35) across the Interior to Gullfoss (see p.326). About the same distance again along the Ringroad, the minuscule settlement of **VARMAHLÍÐ** is of interest only as the junction with Route 75 heading north up to Sauðárkrókur via **Glaumbær farm**, and for one of Iceland's best activity centres specializing in **whitewater rafting** (see box below).

Glaumbær

Late May to late Sept daily 9am–6pm • 1200kr • ⓦ glaumbaer.is • Buses between Varmahlíð and Sauðárkrókur stop outside Glaumbær

About 14km from Varmahlíð up Route 75 is the immaculately preserved historical farm, **Glaumbær**. Though founded in Settlement times, Glaumbær's current row of wood-fronted turf-walled and turf-roofed dwellings dates from 1750 to 1879, and was inhabited up until 1947. With their lop-sided, hobbit-like construction (such as wooden-frame windows set into the grassy walls), the buildings are both charmingly rustic and a powerful reminder of the impoverished lifestyle many people led in Iceland during the eighteenth and nineteenth centuries.

Adjacent to the cottages, a timber building houses the Skagafjörður **folk museum**, with a collection of rustic implements once used on the farm, from spinning wheels to brightly painted clothes chests. Not only does the farm demonstrate centuries-old Icelandic building techniques, it's also where **Snorri Þorfinsson**, the first American born of European parents (in 1003), is buried; Snorri came to Iceland with his parents and lived out his life on the farm here.

ARRIVAL AND DEPARTURE   VARMAHLÍÐ AND AROUND

By bus All Ringroad buses between Reykjavík and Akureyri, plus the Kjölur service, call at the filling station in Varmahlíð.

Destinations Akureyri (2 daily; 1hr 10min); Reykjavík (2 daily; 5hr 15min); Sauðárkrókur (2 daily; 20min).

WHITEWATER RAFTING NEAR VARMAHLÍÐ

Established in 1983 and located at Hafgrímsstaðir, 15km south of Varmahlíð along Route 752, **Arctic Rafting** (☏571 2200, ⓦ rafting.is) operates rafting tours (mid-May to mid-Sept 2–3 daily) of varying degrees of difficulty on the nearby rivers, **Vestari Jökulsá** and **Austari Jökulsá**. Trips range from four hours of relatively easy rafting (9900kr) to three days of serious rapids-shooting (69,900kr); pickups from Reykjavík and Akureyri are available for certain tours for an extra fee.

Sauðárkrókur and around

Set at the base of the broad, north-facing Skagafjörður, 25km north of Varmahlíð,
SAUÐÁRKRÓKUR is the second-largest town on the northern Icelandic coast, with a
population of 2600. It's a likeable spot, occupying a triangle of suburban streets
bordered by fjordside Strandvegur, Hegrabraut and Skagfirðingabraut. Sauðárkrókur's
brightly painted houses and wide-open spaces, with views of the bustling harbour on the
edge of its centre, lend a pioneering edge to the town, and wandering around the streets
is a pleasant enough way to pass an hour or two, popping in at the fascinating fish skin
tannery on the way. The main attractions, though, are the boat trips to the nearby island
of **Drangey** and a dip in **Grettislaug hot pool**, both connected to Iceland's classic outlaw
tale, *Grettir's Saga*, and **horseriding** tours out into the surrounding countryside.

Minjahús

Aðalgata 16B • Mid-June to Aug daily noon–7pm • 1200kr

Sauðárkrókur's **Minjahús** (museum) will not set your pulse racing. It's safe to ignore the
frankly rather poor collection of local art and home in instead on the only other
exhibit: the story of an errant **polar bear**, shot just 15km from the town centre in June
2008 and now stuffed for posterity. The hungry bear had swum over from Greenland
before roaming the hills above Sauðárkrókur looking for food; check out the alarming
photograph of the foolhardy cameraman and local farmer, who came within 20m of
the bear – both are lucky to be alive today.

Gestastofa Sútarans

Borgarmýri 5 • Mid-May to mid-Sept Mon–Fri 9am–6pm, Sat & Sun 11am–3pm; rest of the year Wed & Fri 1–4pm; 45min tour Mon–Fri
10am & 2pm • 500kr • ☎ 512 8025, ⓦ sutarinn.is

The captivating **Gestastofa Sútarans** (fish skin tannery) is definitely worth checking out
while you're in Sauðárkrókur. The tour reveals how the skins (mostly from fish caught
in Icelandic waters, though some larger varieties are imported from Africa) are tanned,
dyed and shaped. The finished product is remarkably similar to leather, yet is thinner
and more workable, and is used for the production of everything from Gucci shoes to
Dior handbags, mostly for the Italian and French fashion markets. At the end of the
tour there's a chance to buy finished skins in the tannery shop.

The harbour

Before leaving town make sure you walk down past the shrimp processing plant to the
harbour, where there's a vast collection of **dried fish racks**. Row upon row of wooden
frames have been erected and draped in several hundred thousand fish heads and
bodies – all awaiting export to Nigeria, where wind-dried Icelandic fish is considered
a delicacy and is used to make soup; the stench, though, can be quite overpowering.

ARRIVAL AND INFORMATION

By bus Buses operate all year, stopping at the filling
station at Aðalgata 22. For times see ⓦ bus.is.
Destinations Akureyri (2 daily; 1hr 30min); Blönduós
(2 daily; 40min); Borgarnes (2 daily; 3hr 30min); Reykjavík
(2 daily; 5hr).
Services The swimming pool (June–Aug Mon–Fri
7am–9pm, Sat & Sun 10am–5pm; Sept–May Mon–Thurs
7am–8.30pm, Fri 7am–8pm, Sat & Sun 10am–4pm) is at
Skagfirðingabraut 20 in the town centre, while the main

supermarket (Mon–Fri 9am–7pm, Sat 10am–4pm) and
the post office (Mon–Fri 9am–4.30pm) are a little south of
the centre at Ártorg, next to the N1 filling station. The
vínbúð is close by at Smáragrund 2 (May–Aug Mon–Thurs
11am–6pm, Fri 11am–7pm, Sat 11am–4pm; Sept–April
Mon–Thurs noon–6pm, Fri 11am–7pm, Sat 11am–2pm).
Bike rental is available at *Hótel Mikligarður*,
Skagafirðingabraut 21 (2500kr/2hr).

5

ACCOMMODATION

Campsite Skagfirðingabraut 20 ☎ 899 3231. Next to the swimming pool, at the southern end of town, this campsite now boasts a new service building with hot showers and toilets. Mid-May to mid-Sept. **1200kr**

Mikligarður Skagfirðingabraut 21 ☎ 453 6330, ⦿ arctichotels.is. There are 65 fresh, bright and nicely appointed rooms at this summer-only hotel housed in the town's local boarding school. With a top-notch restaurant now in the same building (see below), this is a sound choice to spend the night. There's also sleeping-bag accommodation in double rooms. June–Aug. Doubles **23,000kr**, sleeping bags **6000kr**

Mikligarður Kirkjutorg 3 ☎ 453 6880, ⦿ arctichotels .is. A pretty guesthouse with a balcony opposite the church

in the centre of town, offering small but perfectly adequate rooms, with and without bathrooms, and decorated in restful natural greens, plus a superbly appointed guest kitchen upstairs. **17,000kr**

★ **Tindastóll** Lindargata 3 ☎ 453 5002, ⦿ arctichotels .is. An elegant 1820s listed timber building that oozes old-fashioned charm at every turn. Marlene Dietrich stayed here during World War II while entertaining British troops stationed in the area, and the room she stayed in – the *Guðríður Þorbjarnardóttir* suite – is reputedly haunted. There are also nine more modern rooms, with private facilities, in the annexe next door. Hotel **30,300kr**, annexe **27,000kr**

EATING AND DRINKING

Drangey Skagafirðingabraut 21 ☎ 453 6330. Inside the town's boarding school, which is also home to *Hótel Mikligarður* (see above), this new restaurant is a real find. It serves expertly prepared dishes (the chef is a TV celebrity) using traditional Icelandic ingredients such as cured wild goose, roast lamb and horse tenderloin. Mains 4990kr, starters 2890kr. June–Aug daily 6–11pm.

Hard Wok Café Aðalstræti 8 ☎ 453 5355. Southeast Asian stir-fries have found a new home in Sauðárkrókur: the pork in Penang curry sauce for 2790kr is a winner. Otherwise, there's the garlic fried chicken for 2990kr, burgers from 1690kr or pizzas from 1850kr. Great pancakes, too, from 450kr. Daily noon–9.30pm.

Kaffi Krókur Aðalgata 16 ☎ 453 6299. A modern, airy bistro serving burgers (from 1690kr), pasta (from 2290kr) and several puffin dishes, including an Oriental-style curry

(from 1690kr). It's equally popular as a place to drink and is especially busy on Fri and Sat evenings. June–Aug Mon–Wed & Sun 11.30am–11pm, Thurs 11.30am–1am, Fri & Sat 11.30am–3am.

Micro Bar Aðalgata 19 ☎ 467 3133. This funky, brand-new little bar marks a departure for Sauðárkrókur and is long overdue. Serving a selection of bottled Icelandic beers, it's a great place for a drink, though be sure to double-check the opening times before venturing there. Wed & Thurs 6–11.30pm, Fri 4pm–2.30am, Sat 6pm–2.30am.

★ **Ólafshús** Aðalgata 15 ☎ 453 6454. Don't miss this bright blue wooden building on the main street, renowned as a fine dining establishment, with top-notch fish and meat dishes – try the excellent lamb chops (3070kr) or go for the amazingly good-value lunch buffet (1650kr). Daily 11am–1pm.

Reykir and around

To revive himself after the swim to Drangey, the hero of *Grettir's Saga* (see box opposite) jumped into a hot pool now known as **Grettislaug** (no set hours; 750kr), located at the tiny settlement of **REYKIR** and reachable via the unmade 20km Route 748 from the harbour in Sauðárkrókur. Although stone slabs now act as seats and the area around it has been paved with blocks of basalt, you can still do as Grettir did and step into the hot water (around 39°C) and steam to your heart's content (there are now two pools), admiring the 20km-long, snow-splashed mountainface of Tindastóll (989m) on one side, the open ocean and views of Drangey on the other – a quintessentially Icelandic experience. Hot showers and changing facilities, located next to the pools, are included in the bathing fee.

From Grettislaug, you can walk along the beach and around the foot of Tindastóll to the enchanting **Glerhallavík** bay, where the sight of thousands and thousands of shining quartz stones on the beach, buffed by the pounding surf, is quite breathtaking. Note that it's forbidden to remove them from the bay.

ACCOMMODATION

Reykir Cabin Right beside the Grettislaug hot pots ☎ 821 0090, ⦿ drangey.net. This two-storey log cabin has snug double rooms upstairs sharing facilities, as well as sleeping-bag accommodation. It's also possible to rent the

whole house by the night. There's a simple campsite here, too, with toilet facilities. Doubles **15,000kr**, sleeping bags **4800kr**, whole house **35,000kr**, camping **100kr**

DRANGEY AND GRETTIR THE STRONG

Iceland's great outlaw story, **Grettir's Saga**, centres on a man who is born out of his time: Grettir has the wild spirit of a Viking, but lives a generation after the country's conversion to Christianity. Outlawed for three years in his youth for killing a man, Grettir spends the rest of his life performing great deeds – often for the benefit of others – yet something bad always seems to result from his actions, isolating him from his fellow men and eventually forcing him into perpetual banditry. In the end, he and his brother **Illugi** settle on Drangey, living off sheep left here by local farmers. Yet even as he is granted a pardon at the Alþing for his past crimes, Grettir is hunted down by his enemies and finally killed after three years on the island.

The stretch of bitterly cold sea between Drangey and the farm at Reykir on the mainland opposite is known as **Grettir's Swim**, which the outlaw reputedly swam across to fetch the glowing embers he'd spotted on the mainland after his own fire had gone out; its 7.5km are still sometimes swum for sport, despite the fact that the water temperature in summer barely rises above 9°C. However, if the bawdy humour of the sagas is anything to go by, this feat certainly takes its toll, even on Viking superheroes; according to *Grettir's Saga* two young women, finding Grettir lying naked on the ground numb after his swim through the freezing waters, declare, "He is certainly big enough in the chest but it seems very odd how small he is farther down. That part of him isn't up to the rest of him," to which Grettir retorts, "The wench has complained that my penis is small and the boastful slut may well be right. But a small one can grow and I'm still a young man, so wait until I get into action, my lass."

Drangey

Boat tours (operated by Drangey Tours) June to mid-Aug daily 11am • 9900kr • 453 6310, drangey.net

Located in the mouth of Skagafjörður, equidistant between Reykir on the fjord's west coast and the headland, Þórðarhöfði, on the eastern shore, the island of Drangey makes a great day-trip from Sauðárkrókur. Now a bird sanctuary where kittiwakes, puffins and guillemots can be seen in abundance, the steep-sided, flat-topped island of **Drangey**, roughly 5km northeast of Reykir and resembling an arrow pointing north, is best visited on the four-hour **boat tours**, which leave from the harbour at Reykir (see opposite). Offering an unbeatable combination of birdlife and history, the tour is easily one of the best on offer in northern Iceland – although it's not for the faint-hearted, given the steep climb required once ashore and the dizzying drops as you ascend.

From the boat moorings, a narrow winding path streaks steeply up rocky cliffs to the grassy meadow at the summit of Drangey's 180m-high plug of palagonite rock. The deep hollow in the turf here, where the bedrock shows through, was once the hideout of Grettir the Strong (or **Grettir Ásmundarson**), hero of **Grettir's Saga** (see box above). The island's **northern summit** is accessible only by climbing a rusty ladder, erected by local bird hunters, which overhangs an area of crumbling rock – definitely not one to attempt if you're afraid of heights. Incidentally, for fresh water Grettir depended on a spring virtually hidden under a steep rock overhang on the island's southern cliff. Even today, the only way to reach the source is to clamber hand over hand down a knotted rope, trying not to look at the 500m sheer drop beneath.

Eastern Skagafjörður

From Sauðárkrókur, it's a 100km run along routes 75 and 76 up the eastern side of Skagafjörður to **Siglufjörður**. It's worth making the short detour off Route 76 to **Hólar í Hjaltadal**, which was northern Iceland's ecumenical and educational centre until the Reformation. Today, this tranquil place in the foothills of Hjaltadalur valley consists solely of a cathedral and an agricultural college, and is a remote and peaceful spot that's worth seeking out – particularly if you fancy **hiking**, since a trail leads from here over to Dalvík (see p.241). Beyond Hólar, Route 76 leads north to **Hofsós**, another diminutive settlement, best known as a study centre for North Americans of

5

Icelandic origin keen to trace their roots, before rounding the headland and pressing on to Siglufjörður.

Hólar í Hjaltadal

Lying 12km down Route 767, which runs east off Route 76 about thirty minutes from Sauðárkrókur, the hamlet of **HÓLAR Í HJALTADAL**, or simply Hólar, was very much the cultural capital of the north from the twelfth until the eighteenth century: monks studied here, manuscripts were transcribed and Catholicism flourished until the Reformation. Now home to just sixty-odd people, most of whom work at the agricultural college – this and the cathedral are the only buildings remaining – it was the site of the country's **first printing press** in 1530, set up by Iceland's last Catholic bishop, Jón Arason (who was beheaded twenty years later at Skálholt for his resistance to the spread of the Reformation from the south).

The cathedral

June–Aug daily 10am–6pm; if the door is locked, ask at the college next door • Free

A church has stood on this spot since Arason's time, but the present **cathedral** was built in 1759–63 in late Baroque style, using local red sandstone from the mountain Hólabyrða, and is the second-oldest stone building in the country. Inside, the fifteenth-century alabaster altarpiece over the cathedral's south door is similar in design to that in the church at Þingeyrar (see p.229), and was likewise made in Nottingham, England. The main altarpiece, with its ornate carvings of biblical figures, originated in Germany around 1500 and was given to the cathedral by its most famous bishop. Arason's memory is honoured in the adjacent bell tower: a mosaic of tiny tiles, by Icelandic artist **Erró** (see see box, p.60), marks a small chapel and headstone, under which the bishop's bones are buried.

ACCOMMODATION   **HÓLAR Í HJALTADAL**

Hólaskóli Agricultural College Hólar ☏ 455 6300, ⓦ holar.is. During the summer, Hólar's agricultural college offers a choice of two-person apartments with bedroom and living room or smaller, two-person cottages, both with and without private bathrooms. There's a swimming pool, hot pot and a campsite attached to the college. The on-site restaurant (daily 8am–9pm) serves a variety of dishes, often including locally reared arctic char, for 2500kr. June–Aug. Cottages 16,700kr, apartments 21,300kr

Hofsós

Seventeen kilometres up Route 76 from the Hólar junction, **HOFSÓS** is a tiny, nondescript village on the eastern shores of Skagafjörður, consisting of one street and a tiny harbour, with a population of around two hundred. Nonetheless, it does have two good reasons to stop: a visit to the **Vesturfarasetrið** offers a fascinating insight into Icelandic emigration to North America; and a swim in one of the country's most beautifully located **outdoor pools**.

Vesturfarasetrið

Suðurbraut 8 • June–Aug daily 11am–6pm; other times by arrangement • 700kr for one exhibition; 1500kr for all three • ☏ 453 7935, ⓦ hofsos.is

Hofsós is primarily a base for the hundreds of Americans and Canadians of Icelandic descent who come here to visit the **Vesturfarasetrið**, or Icelandic Emigration Centre, housed in several buildings beautifully set on the seafront by the harbour. The centre's **genealogy** and information service is located in a red-roofed building furthest from the harbour, Gamla Kaupfélagshúsið, which is where you'll find the main exhibition of the migration story, "New Land, New

CLOCKWISE FROM TOP LEFT ICELANDIC HORSES (P.40); PTARMIGAN, HRÍSEY; SALT COD DRYING IN THE WIND (P.221); AURORA BOREALIS (P.330) >

5

BOAT TRIPS FROM HOFSÓS

Sailing from the harbour down by the emigration centre, Hafogland (☎ 849 2409, ⓦ hafogland.is) operate **boat tours** out into Skagafjörður. A two-hour excursion (minimum four passengers; 7500kr/person), perfect for birdwatching, will take you out to Malmey island as well as to the curiously shaped Þórðarhöfði headland which extends into the fjord north of Hofsós via a narrow, pebbly spit of land. Another option is a **sea-angling tour** (from 19,500kr/hr) including all equipment. The boat is also available for private rent with prices dependent on the itinerary decided.

Life", detailing the living conditions of Icelanders who moved to America at the end of the nineteenth century and where they settled. Next door, in the Frændgarður building, the Silent Flashes **exhibition** of around 400 photographs, taken in America between 1870 and 1920, traces the lives of some of the 20,000 Icelanders who emigrated west over the sea. Finally, in the Konungsverslunarhúsið, before the footbridge across to the main exhibitions, there's a moving display of black-and-white photographs, known as the "Prairies Wide and Free" exhibition, recounting the lives of children who emigrated to North Dakota.

Hofsós swimming pool
Suðurbraut • Daily 9am–9pm • 600kr

Designed by the same architect responsible for the Blue Lagoon on the Reykjanes Peninsula (see p.95), the new **swimming pool** in Hofsós is quite simply magnificent. It may not be Olympic size, but because it has been built into the hillside above the sea, the views over to Drangey are breathtaking. It's not strictly an infinity pool, but the impression you get as you swim in the geothermal waters is that you're right next to the sea's edge. The pool was donated to the town just before the economic crash by two bankers' wives, frustrated by the fact they had nowhere to swim.

ARRIVAL AND INFORMATION   HOFSÓS

By bus The service to and from Sauðárkrókur calls in at Hofsós, stopping outside the supermarket on Skólagata. Destinations Sauðárkrókur (2 weekly; 50min; advance booking required on ☎ 540 2700 at least 2hr before departure).

Services The village supermarket (Mon–Fri 9.30am–9.30pm, Sat 10am–8pm, Sun 11am–8pm), complete with ATM in the entrance, is located at the junction of Suðurbraut and Skólagata, opposite the *Sunnuberg* guesthouse.

ACCOMMODATION AND EATING

Sunnuberg Suðurbraut 8 ☎ 861 3474 or ☎ 893 0220, ✉ gisting@hofsos.is. There are comfortable en-suite rooms with sea views available here, but to be honest, Hofsós is not really somewhere you're likely to want to spend the night unless you're researching your ancestry at the Vesturfarasetrið. **15,500kr**

Sólvík Kvósin ☎ 453 7930. Opposite the Emigration Centre, and with a delightful wooden terrace with sea views, this is the only place to eat in town and offers burgers (1580kr), soup (1250kr) and fresh fish dishes (around 3100kr). June to mid-Sept daily 10am–10pm.

Siglufjörður

Having wound northeast around the convoluted coast for 60km from Hofsós, Route 76 cuts through an unpleasantly dark and narrow single-lane tunnel to land you at the enjoyably remote fishing port of **SIGLUFJÖRÐUR** (known locally as Sigló), a highlight of any trip to the northwest. The country's most northerly town, Siglufjörður clings precariously to the foot of steep mountain walls which enclose an isolated narrow fjord on the very edge of Iceland: the **Arctic Circle** is barely 40km away and you're as far

5

SIGLUFJÖRÐUR'S SILVER OF THE SEA

From 1900 to 1970, Siglufjörður was the **herring** capital of the North Atlantic. Hundreds of fishing boats would crowd into the tiny fjord to unload their catches onto the rickety piers that once stretched out from the quayside, where **herring girls**, as they were known, would gut and salt them. During a good season, casual labour and the number of fishermen (who were, in the early part of the century at any rate, primarily Norwegian) could swell the town's population threefold, to over ten thousand.

north here as Canada's Baffin Island and central Alaska. Winters can be particularly severe, though in summer Siglufjörður makes an excellent base from which to **hike** across the surrounding mountains.

Today, Siglufjörður's heyday as a herring-fishing town is long gone and the place is considerably quieter, with a population of just thirteen hundred people. It's a pleasant spot, consisting of a handful of parallel streets with unkempt multicoloured homes grouped around the main street, **Túngata**, which turns into **Snorragata** as it approaches the **harbour**, busy with the goings-on of a low-key fishing port. Here, you'll see fishermen mending their nets in the shipyard and fish hanging out to dry – the town still produces kippers (smoked herring) from a factory down by the harbour. Once you've seen the **herring museum** there's some excellent **hiking** to be had along the trails that lead up out of the fjord (see box, p.240).

Síldarminjasafn Íslands

Snorragata 15 • Daily: June–Aug 10am–6pm; April, May & Sept 1–5pm • 1400kr • ⓦ sild.is/en

Divided into three sections, **Síldarminjasafn Íslands** (the Herring Era Museum) expertly brings Siglufjörður's past to life. The best idea is to start in the **Bátahúsið** and then work your way on to the old herring factory, **Grána**, before finishing in **Róaldsbrakki**, the building which was once home to the herring girls.

Bátahúsið

Home to a collection of ten ships, the **Bátahúsið** (boathouse) offers a fine introduction to some of the vessels that operated out of Siglufjörður during the herring era. The ships are dry-moored around a mock-up of a quayside as it would have looked in the 1950s, and you can even clamber on board two of them; the largest boat in the museum is the *Týr SK33*, made of oak, which operated until 1988, when more modern steel vessels made its design obsolete.

Grána

Next door to the boathouse, you can peep inside **Grána**, the reconstructed herring factory. A whole host of machines help to give an idea of how Siglufjörður once produced vast amounts of fish meal and oil for the European market; the oil was used, for example, to light towns and cities across the continent as well as in the production of Brylcreem, Nivea face cream and Lux soap.

Róaldsbrakki

The herring girls' story is brought to life in photographs and exhibits inside the **Róaldsbrakki** building, alongside Grána. This old salting station once housed around fifty **herring girls** – you can still see graffiti, daubed in nail varnish, on the walls of the second-floor room where they once slept, alongside faded black-and-white photographs of heart-throb Cary Grant. There's usually a couple of atmospheric old films showing, too, which give an idea of the conditions of the time and the work that the herring girls carried out.

5

HIKING AROUND SIGLUFJÖRÐUR

Several excellent day **hikes** can easily be undertaken from Siglufjörður. The trails described below are shown on the hiking **map** of Siglufjörður available at the herring museum (see p.239).

The best of the shorter routes (5–7hr), forming a clockwise circle around the town, begins at the southern edge of Siglufjörður, where the road veers left around the head of the fjord. Follow the walking path up **Eyrafjall**, heading towards the Dalaskarð pass, then over the mountain tops and up **Hafnarfjall**, from where there's an excellent view over the fjord, the surrounding peaks and even Grímsey. From here it's an easy climb up **Hafnarhyrna** (687m), the highest point on Hafnarfjall and the starting point for the easy descent towards the bowl-shaped hollow of **Hvanneyrarskál**, a well-known lovers' haunt during the herring boom. From this hollow, a road leads back down into town.

A second, longer, trail (10–14hr) begins beyond the disused airport on the eastern side of the fjord (follow the main road through the village to get there) and leads southeast up the valley of **Kálfsdalur**, which begins just above the lighthouse beyond the airport, past **Kálfsvatn** lake, over the **Kálfsskarð** pass (450m) before descending into Nesdalur valley on the other side of the ridge. The trail then leads north through the valley to the coast and the deserted farm, **Reyðará**. From the farm, the trail leads west along the steep slopes of Nesnúpur (595m), passing a lighthouse and several abandoned huts, built by the American military during World War II as a radar station. Once back on the eastern side of the fjord, the path trail continues along the shoreline, towards the disused airport and Siglufjörður.

ARRIVAL AND INFORMATION
SIGLUFJÖRÐUR

By bus Buses run to Ólafsfjörður and on to Akureyri from the Olís fiilling station at the eastern end of Aðalgata; information is available from ⓦ bus.is.

Destinations Akureyri (Mon–Fri 3 daily, Sun 1 daily; 1hr 20min); Dalvík (Mon–Fri 3 daily, Sun 1 daily; 30min); Ólafsfjörður (Mon–Fri 3 daily, Sun 1 daily; 15min).

Services There's a *vínbúð* (May–Aug Mon–Thurs 2–6pm, Fri 1–7pm, Sat 11am–2pm; Sept–April Mon–Thurs 2–6pm, Fri 2–7pm) at Eyrargata 25, and the supermarket (Mon–Fri 10am–7pm, Sat 11am–7pm, Sun 1–5pm) is at Suðurgata 2–4. The library, Gránugata 24 (Mon–Fri 1.30–5pm), has internet access, and the post office is at Aðalgata 24 (Mon–Fri 10am–4pm). For the swimming pool (Mon–Thurs 6.30am–7.45pm, Fri 6.30am–7pm, Sat & Sun 2–6pm; 600kr) you'll need to head up to Hvanneyrarbraut 52.

ACCOMMODATION

Campsite Snorragata ☏ 464 9100. Located right in the centre of town between the harbour and the museum, the town's campsite has a small service building with water and toilets. **1000kr**

Gistiheimilið Hvanneyri Aðalgata 1 ☏ 467 1506, ⓦ hvanneyri.com. Siglufjörður's youth hostel is a monument to bad taste: plastic flowers, garish drapes and multicoloured swirls of paint daubed over the staircase. That said, rooms here, sharing facilities, are clean and comfortable and there's a well-equipped kitchen for self-caterers. Dorms **4400kr**, doubles **17,000kr**

Sigló Snorragata 3 ☏ 461 7730, ⓦ siglohotel.is. Totally dominating the harbour area, this new hotel has not been without its critics, who claim it's far too big for little Sigufjörður. Be that as it may, rooms are comfortable and modern with wooden floors, wall panels and neutral decor throughout. Guests have access to the sauna and hot pots. **30,100kr**

Sigló Harbour Hostel & Apartments Tjarnargata 14 ☏ 987 1394, ⓦ sigloharbourhostel.is. The upper floor of this newly converted hostel once housed many of the herring girls, while the ground floor was used to store barrels of herring awaiting export. Accommodation comes in the form of tasteful double rooms with shared facilities (there's a kitchen for guest use) as well as fully appointed, two-person apartments. Doubles **12,500kr**, apartments **26,500kr**

EATING

Hannes Boy Gránugata 23 ☏ 461 7730. Named after a characterful local fisherman, this is the place to come for fine dining from a regularly updated menu: salted cod costs 3990kr, grilled salmon 4190kr and fillet of lamb 4890kr. June–Aug daily 6–11pm.

Harbour House Café Gránugata 5B ☏ 659 4809. Enjoying an enviable position right by the harbourside, this little café, decked out in maritime colours, is a great place for fresh fish: arctic char for 3550kr or a fantastic fish soup for 1500kr. June–Aug daily 11am–late.

Kaffi Rauðka Gránugata 19 ☎461 7733. At last, Siglufjörður has a café-bar which is open all year, set in a snug and solid timber structure down by the harbour and serving a daily lunch special for 1690kr, excellent salads (1590kr), panini (1390kr) and a wicked coconut chicken fillet with fries (2490kr). Mon–Thurs & Sun 11am–8pm, Fri & Sat 11am–1am.

Torgið Aðalgata 30 ☎467 2323. Serves up a range of decent 12-inch pizzas from 1980kr plus a selection of fish dishes for 2600kr and the usual choice of burgers, which go for around 1600kr. Mon–Fri 11am–late, Sat & Sun noon–late.

Western Eyjafjörður

Running up Eyjafjörður's western flank from Akureyri, Route 82 affords stunning views over icy waters to the glacier-formed **mountains** which serve as a protective wall all around the fjord. If you have time, it's well worth making the trip from Akureyri to see not only the mountains but also the rich **farmland** hereabouts, which is heavily grazed during the summer by cattle and sheep. The long hours of daylight in this part of Iceland, coupled with mild temperatures, make excellent growing conditions for various crops, and the small white dots you'll see in the fields are barrel-shaped bundles of hay, neatly packaged in white plastic, to provide the animals with much-needed food during the long months of winter. Noted for its hundreds of wild ptarmigan, the highlight of any trip up the fjord is the island of **Hrísey**, near the mouth of Eyjafjörður and overlooked by the fishing village of **Dalvík**, itself the starting point for some excellent hiking and whale-watching tours. Beyond here, a dark tunnel slices through the exposed headland, Ólafsfjarðarmúli, to reach the isolated village of **Ólafsfjörður**, another notable place from which to see whales. Two new tunnels link the village with Siglufjörður, now just 17km away, making it possible to continue your journey via the north coast south to Varmahlíð and the Ringroad.

Dalvík

A nondescript fishing village 42km north of Akureyri with just 1400 inhabitants, **DALVÍK** enjoys a superbly sheltered location on the western shores of Eyjafjörður overlooking the island of Hrísey. Paradoxically, though, its poor natural harbour hampered the growth of the fishing industry here until a new harbour was built in 1939 to remedy matters, today used as the departure point for the **ferry to Grímsey**. A major shipbuilding and fish-curing centre early in the twentieth century, today Dalvík has lost its buzz, and its quiet **harbour** front, lined by the main road, **Hafnarbraut**, stands guard over the familiar cluster of uniformly shaped modern homes that are so prevalent in the country's smaller communities. Dalvík's lack of older buildings is due to a devastating **earthquake** in 1934, measuring 7.2 on the Richter Scale, which demolished half the structures in the village and caused serious damage to the ones that did survive – two thousand people lost their homes.

HIKING FROM DALVÍK TO HÓLAR

From Dalvík a **long-distance hike**, lasting three or four days, leads over the Heljardalsheiði plateau to the episcopal seat at **Hólar í Hjaltadal** (see p.236). It threads up through Svarfaðardalsá valley, just south of town, passing the wedge-shaped **Stóll**, a mountain which divides the valley in two. Continuing southwest past a couple of farms, the route then passes through some of Iceland's best mountain scenery, heading up over the flat-topped mountains of the Tröllaskagi peninsula, which separates Eyjafjörður from its western neighbour, Skagafjörður, heading for Hólar. It should take two or three days to reach this point, but you'll need another half-day to reach the main road, Route 76, itself reached along Route 767 from here. From June to September, buses run daily except Saturday along Route 76 between Siglufjörður and Sauðárkrókur (see p.233).

5

Byggðasafnið Hvoll

Karlsrauðatorg 7 • June–Aug daily 11am–6pm; Sept–May Sat 2–5pm • 700kr

Most people only pitch up here en route to Grímsey or to go whale watching (see below), but should you find yourself with time to kill, take a quick look inside the folklore museum, **Byggðasafnið Hvoll**, one block back from the harbour. Of the four small sections, it's the collection of photographs and personal belongings of Iceland's tallest man, **Jóhann Kristinn Pétursson**, born in nearby Svarfaðardalur valley in 1913, that catches the eye. Measuring a whopping 2.34m in height (7ft 7in), Jóhann the Giant, as he was known locally, spent most of his life performing in circuses in Europe and America before retiring to Dalvík, where he died in 1984.

ARRIVAL AND DEPARTURE DALVÍK

By bus Buses to and from Akureyri and Ólafsfjörður stop at the filling station on the main road, Hafnarbraut.
Destinations Akureyri (Mon–Fri 3 daily, Sun 1 daily; 50min); Árskógssandur (Mon–Fri 3 daily, Sun 1 daily; 10min); Ólafsfjörður (Mon–Fri 3 daily, Sun 1 daily; 20min).

By ferry The Sæfari ferry (☎458 8970, ⓦland flutningar.is/saefari/english; 9660kr return) runs year-round three times a week (Mon, Wed & Fri) from Dalvík to Grímsey.
Destinations Grímsey (3 weekly; 3hr 30min).

INFORMATION AND TOURS

Tourist information The desk within the Berg cultural centre on Goðabraut (Mon–Thurs 8am–6pm, Fri 1–5pm; ☎460 4000) has limited tourist information, otherwise check online at ⓦdalvik.is.
Services The library in the Berg building (same times as tourist information) has internet access, while the supermarket is opposite the harbour at Hafnartorg (Mon–Fri 10am–7pm, Sat 10am–6pm, Sun 1–5pm). On Hafnarbraut, the post office is at No. 26 (Mon–Fri 10am–4pm), and the *vínbúð* at no. 7 (Mon–Thurs

11am–6pm, Fri 11am–7pm, Sat 11am–2pm). The excellent outdoor swimming pool (Mon–Thurs 6.15am–8pm, Fri 6.15am–7pm, Sat & Sun 9am–5pm; 550kr) has a couple of hot pots and a mixed steam room; it's at Svarfaðarbraut 34, which runs roughly parallel with Hafnarbraut.
Whale watching From Dalvík harbour, Arctic Sea Tours (☎771 7600, ⓦarcticseatours.is) operates up to four daily tours year-round (3hr; 9000kr) out in Eyjafjörður to see humpback and minke whales as well as dolphins and harbour porpoises. Warm clothes are provided.

ACCOMMODATION AND EATING

Campsite Svarfaðarbraut ☎460 4940. Dalvík's campsite is nicely situated just 100m from the swimming pool and has a service building with hot water, showers and toilet facilities. April–Sept. **1700kr**
Fosshotel Dalvík Skíðabraut 18 ☎466 3395, ⓦfosshotel.is. This rambling hotel just off the main road is located in the local boarding school and offers thirty-odd rather institutionalized rooms with shared or private facilities. May–Sept. **11,000kr**
Gísli Eiríkur Helgi Grundargata 1 ☎666 3399. The best place to eat in Dalvík, this new and somewhat rustic little café is named after three rather simple brothers who feature in Icelandic folkore. The café serves a spectacular fish soup, served fresh throughout the day (2200kr) with home-baked bread and coffee, as well as cakes and sandwiches (750kr). It also has a selection of hand-knitted woollen sweaters for sale. June–Aug daily 10am–10pm;

Sept–May daily 1–6pm.
Gregor's Pub Goðabraut 3 ☎847 8846. Opposite the Berg cultural centre and complete with billiards table, this is Dalvík's popular drinking establishment. It also serves fish soup (1500kr), fresh cod or trout (3200kr) and an alternating lamb dish (4200kr). Daily 6–11pm.
Kondó-Bar Hafnarbraut 5 ☎466 2040. This waterside restaurant has a pleasant outside terrace overlooking the harbour, and serves a weekday lunch buffet (noon–2pm) for 1390kr as well as 12-inch pizzas from 1600kr and burgers for 1595kr. Mon–Fri noon–1am, Sat & Sun 6–9pm.
Youth Hostel Hafnarbraut 4 ☎466 1060, ⓦhostel.is. Situated above the harbour, this grand old stone structure is easily Dalvík's most imposing building. Inside, there are four three-bed dorms, one five-bed, one double and one single room, plus a fully equipped shared kitchen. Dorms **4450kr**, doubles **12,400kr**

Hrísey

No trip to the north coast of Iceland is complete without seeing the hundreds of **ptarmigan** on **HRÍSEY**, a flat, teardrop-shaped island at the mouth of Eyjafjörður, reached by ferry from Árskógssandur, about 10km southeast of Dalvík. At 7.5km long

5

HRÍSEY'S BIRDLIFE

Hrísey is home to more **ptarmigan** than anywhere else in Iceland – they're protected by law here and there are no natural predators such as mink or foxes. As a result, the birds are very tame and roam the entire island, and you'll spot them in the village, laying their eggs in people's gardens or, particularly in August after the breeding season, strolling down the main street with a string of fluffy chicks in tow.

Unfortunately for visitors, Hrísey also has the largest breeding colony of **arctic tern** in Europe, and should you come too close to the young birds, adults will readily dive-bomb you from on high – which means you'll pretty much need a hard hat if you get too close to their nesting sites. The island is also a good place to spot **golden plover** and **eider ducks**, which have a significant breeding colony in the northern part of Hrísey, though it's out of bounds to visitors.

and 2.5km wide, it's the country's second-largest island (Heimaey in the Westman Islands is the biggest; see p.139), but it's home to barely two hundred people.

As you might expect, Hrísey's history is tied to fishing. Its population peaked at 340 in the mid-twentieth century, when fishing boats from across the country landed their catches in the tiny harbour, making it the second-largest **herring port** on the north coast, after Siglufjörður. Since then, things have declined: the fish-processing factory down at the harbour was Hrísey's main source of employment until it closed in 1999, and over thirty people left the island to look for work in Akureyri and Reykjavík. Today, it's the Icelandic National Quarantine Centre, established here in 1974 (so that stocks of Galloway cattle could be imported from Scotland), that keeps many islanders in employment. **Reforestation** has also begun in a couple of areas, in an attempt to protect the thin layer of soil, atop the basalt rock of which Hrísey is formed, from further erosion.

Hrísey village

Hrísey's picturesque **village** is tiny, consisting of two or three parallel streets perched on a small hill above the walled **harbour**. Brightly painted houses, unfortunately all of them modern and block-like, look out over the fjord and the handful of small boats that bob up and down in the tiny port. Otherwise, there's a minuscule outdoor **swimming pool** (Mon–Fri 10.30am–7pm, Sat & Sun 10.30am–5pm; 600kr) on the main street, Norðurvegur, at the eastern end of the village; at just 12.5m in length, it's heated by geothermal water from Hrísey's very own borehole, on the island's west coast.

The rest of the island

There's some wonderful **walking** to be had along tracks that head around the southeastern corner of the island; all three colour-coded paths (green 2.3km; yellow 4.5km; and red 5km) begin just ten minutes' walk from the village near the island's southernmost tip, beyond the couple of colourful private summer cottages that look out over the fjord. The **green route** traces a circular route up to the hills of Háaborð, dropping towards Beinalág and returning to the village; the **red path** heads further north along the coast, while the **yellow track** follows essentially the same routing though further inland; both routes turn south again at the Borgarbrík cliffs.

ARRIVAL AND INFORMATION   HRÍSEY

By ferry The ferry to Hrísey (March–Oct every 2hr, 7.20am–11.30pm; rest of the year see website for details; 15min; 1500kr return; ⓦhrisey.net) departs from tiny Árskógssandur, which is just off Route 82 some 10km southeast of Dalvík, and is reachable by bus from Akureyri (Mon–Fri 3 daily, Sun 1 daily; 30min); Dalvík (Mon–Fri 3 daily, Sun 1 daily; 10min); Ólafsfjörður (Mon–Fri 3 daily,

Sun 1 daily; 25min); and Siglufjörður (Mon–Fri 3 daily, Sun 1 daily; 40min).

Services There's a grocery store at Sjávargata 2 (Mon–Fri 11am–6pm, Sat 11am–5pm, Sun noon–5pm), which also serves coffee and light meals, and a bank (Mon–Fri noon–4pm) with an ATM on Skólavegur.

5

ACCOMMODATION

Brekka Brekkugata 5 ☎466 1751, ⓦbrekkahrisey.is. This yellow-painted wooden building up on the hill behind the harbour has just three doubles with shared facilities, but if these are full the owners will endeavour to find a room in a private house somewhere in the village. Lunch in the restaurant, which overlooks the sea and the jagged mountains of the western shore of Eyjafjörður, is truly excellent; try the salted cod in coconut with a pineapple sauce (3250kr). <u>**10,000kr**</u>

Ólafsfjörður

From Dalvík, Route 82 winds its way north for 17km to the fishing village of **ÓLAFSFJÖRÐUR**, clinging all the way to the steep slopes of the mountains that plunge into the steely waters of Eyjafjörður, and with superb views of the snowy peaks of the uninhabited Látraströnd coastline on the opposite shore. On a clear day it's easily possible to spot Grímsey island, northeast of the fjord's mouth. The road enters Ólafsfjörður by means of a single-lane, claustrophobic, 3.4km **tunnel** through the Ólafsfjarðarmúli headland.

Although both the drive to Ólafsfjörður and its setting are breathtaking, the village, unfortunately, isn't: this is an unattractive, workaday place of a thousand people, set behind the working **harbour** on Sjávargata, one block northeast of the main road, Aðalgata.

ARRIVAL AND INFORMATION   ÓLAFSFJÖRÐUR

By bus Buses to and from Ólafsfjörður stop at the *Hótel Brimnes* on Bylgjubyggð (see below).
Destinations Akureyri (Mon–Fri 3 daily, Sun 1 daily; 1hr); Árskógssandur (Mon–Fri 3 daily, Sun 1 daily; 25min); Dalvík (Mon–Fri 3 daily, Sun 1 daily; 15min); Siglufjörður (Mon–Fri 3 daily, Sun 1 daily; 15min).
Services The swimming pool (Mon–Thurs 6.30am–7.45pm,

Fri 6.30am–6.45pm, Sat & Sun 10am–6pm; 600kr) is at Ólafsvegur 4, just off Hornbrekkuvegur, which heads south from Aðalgata. There's a supermarket (Mon–Fri 9am–7pm, Sat 11am–6pm, Sun 1–5pm) at the corner of Strandgata and Aðalgata, next to the harbour, and a post office and a bank with ATM at Aðalgata 14 (both Mon–Fri 9am–noon & 1–4pm).

ACCOMMODATION AND EATING

Brimnes Hotel & Cabins Bylgjubyggð 2 ☎466 2400, ⓦbrimnes.is. The plain doubles here are best passed over in favour of the their Finnish-built log cabins overlooking the lake opposite the hotel, all with shower and bathroom, and sleeping between four and eight. The hotel restaurant serves tasty fish meals (3300kr), as well as pasta (1650kr) and lamb (3900kr), and can also rustle up lighter meals such as burgers with fries and salad for 1450kr. Restaurant daily noon–late. Doubles <u>**8000kr**</u>, cabins <u>**23,400kr**</u>
Höllinn Hafnargata 16 ☎466 4000. Located near the harbour, this simple little restaurant is popular with local fishermen and is the best bet in town, with decent pizzas for 1600kr, burgers at 1400kr or grilled salmon at 3000kr. Mon–Fri 6–9pm, Sat 4–10pm, Sun 4–9pm.

Akureyri

AKUREYRI sits on the Ringroad pretty much halfway along the country's northern coastline, 385km from Reykjavík; 285km from Egilsstaðir and a whopping 555km from Ísafjörður. The largest town in the country outside of Reykjavík, it has a population of around eighteen thousand and is a transport hub and commercial centre for the whole of northern Iceland. If you're doing much touring, you're almost certain to find yourself in Akureyri sooner or later, as the town makes an excellent base from which to explore nearby Lake Mývatn, Húsavík and the Jökulsárgljúfur National Park (all covered in Chapter 6); Akureyri can also be useful as a departure point for tours into the Interior. The town is divided into two distinct areas: the centre, harbour and commercial district north of **Kaupvangsstræti**, and the suburban areas to its south, where the distinctive **Akureyrarkirkja** church, **museums** and the superb **botanical garden** can all be found. As far as entertainment goes, Akureyri is a decent enough place to relax in for a day or two, with an excellent open-air swimming pool and enough cafés and restaurants to keep you well fed and watered. That most un-Icelandic thing, the **forest**, makes a welcome appearance just south of Akureyri in the form of **Kjarnaskógur**, easily accessible on foot from the town centre and a popular destination for locals at weekends, who come here to walk the many trails that crisscross the forest and to picnic.

Brief history

According to *Landnámabók*, the first Viking ships sailed into Eyjafjörður fjord, its mouth barely 40km south of the Arctic Circle, around 890, fifteen years after the Settlement began. The first intrepid pioneers to set foot in the hitherto uninhabited north, **Helgi**

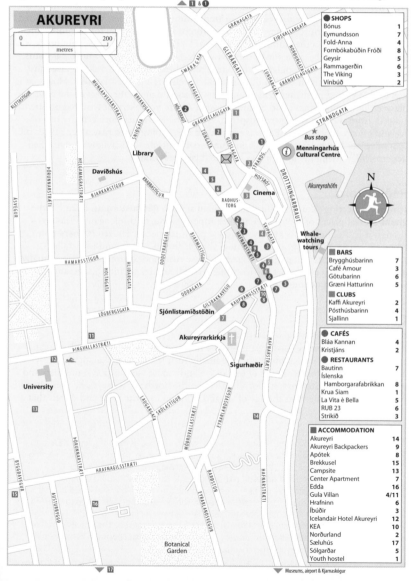

AKUREYRI

0 — 200
metres

● SHOPS	
Bónus	1
Eymundsson	7
Fold-Anna	4
Fornbókabúðin Fróði	8
Geysir	5
Rammagerðin	6
The Viking	3
Vínbúð	2

■ BARS	
Brygghúsbarinn	7
Café Amour	3
Götubarinn	6
Græni Hatturinn	5

■ CLUBS	
Kaffi Akureyri	2
Pósthúsbarinn	4
Sjallinn	1

● CAFÉS	
Bláa Kannan	4
Kristjáns	2

● RESTAURANTS	
Bautinn	7
Íslenska Hamborgarafabrikkan	8
Krua Siam	1
La Vita è Bella	5
RUB 23	6
Strikið	3

■ ACCOMMODATION	
Akureyri	14
Akureyri Backpackers	9
Apótek	8
Brekkusel	15
Campsite	13
Center Apartment	7
Edda	16
Gula Villan	4/11
Hrafninn	6
Íbúðir	3
Icelandair Hotel Akureyri	12
KEA	10
Norðurland	2
Sæluhús	17
Sólgarðar	5
Youth hostel	1

Library

Davíðshús

Bus stop

Menningarhús Cultural Centre

Akureyrahöfn

N

Cinema

RÁÐHÚS-TORG

Whale-watching tours

Sjónlistamiðstöðin

Akureyrarkirkja

Sigurhæðir

University

Botanical Garden

Museums, airport & Kjarnaskógur

5

Magri (Helgi the Lean) and Þórunn Hyrna, made landfall at Kristnes, 9km south of where Akureyri presently stands, believing that Þór had guided them into Eyjafjörður. Their faith seems, however, to have been in a state of confusion since they curiously chose to bestow an unqualified Christian name (Christ's Point) on their new home. Although little more is known about this early period of Akureyri's history, it is thought that Helgi suffered from a nutritional disease he developed as a child in the Hebrides, where he lived with his Irish mother and Swedish father before coming to Iceland.

Several centuries passed with little mention of "the cornfield on the sand spit", as Akureyri's name translates in English, until 1602, when the town became a **trading post**, with the establishment of the commercial monopoly which gave Danish merchants the exclusive right to trade with Iceland. Curiously, though, the traders were not permitted to take up permanent residence in the town, forced instead to leave for Denmark after closing their stores in the autumn. It wasn't until 1787 that this punitive monopoly was lifted and Akureyri became one of six towns in Iceland to be granted **municipal status**, despite the fact that its population then numbered little more than a dozen and most trade remained firmly in the hands of Danish merchants and their families. However, it was to the sea and its sheltered harbour, today located right in the heart of the town between Drottningarbraut and Strandgata, that Akureyri looked for renewed prosperity. Indeed, from then on the town prospered, and in the late nineteenth century one of Iceland's first cooperatives, **KEA**, was established here, going on to play a key role in the economy (see box below). Iceland's only **university** outside Reykjavík was established here in 1987, giving the town a much-needed youthful boost.

Ráðhústorg

If you're expecting Akureyri's diminutive main square, **Ráðhústorg**, to resemble the grand central places of towns in central Europe, it's time to think again. Pleasant though it is, Ráðhústorg is mainly an access point for pedestrianized **Hafnarstræti**, Akureyri's main shopping street, no more than 150m in length, and its parallel neighbour to the east, **Skipagata**. Together, these two modest streets contain virtually all the shops and services that the town has to offer and it's within this rectangle that you'll spend much of your time.

Davíðshús

Bjarkarstígur 6 • June–Aug Mon–Fri 1–5pm • 1200kr • ⓦ akmus.is

From Ráðhústorg, head northwest up to the library, then south onto Oddeyrargata, take the first right into Krabbastígur and finally turn left into Bjarkarstígur to reach the austere **Davíðshús**, former home of one of Iceland's most famous poets, novelists and playwrights, **Davíð Stefánsson**. Born in 1895 to the north of Akureyri, he published his first anthology of poems at the age of 24 and went on to write verse and novels that

---

KEA NOT IKEA

Spend any time in and around Akureyri and you can't fail to notice the ubiquitous **KEA** logo, plastered on hotels, fishing boats and even Kaffibrensla Akureyrar, the town's coffee-roasting plant. It's said locally that KEA, the Kaupfélag Eyfirðinga Akureyri (Cooperative Society of Eyjafjörður and Akureyri) and no relation to Sweden's IKEA, owns everything except the church – and while that's not strictly true, KEA does have fingers in many pies. Established in June 1886 by local farmers keen to win a better price for the live export of their sheep to England, the society opened its first co-op store ten years later and never looked back. Still with headquarters on the main street in Akureyri, and still operating despite the economic downturn, KEA now owns shares in virtually any local business you choose to mention, concentrating on the food and merchandise sectors.

AKUREYRI MUSEUM DISCOUNTS

Five museums in and around Akureyri have clubbed together to offer **reduced admission fees** to anyone visiting more than one of them. While Minjasafnið á Akureyri, Davíðshús, Nonnahús, Sigurhæðir and Laufás (see p.254) each charge 1200kr per admission, they also sell a day ticket for 2000kr and a ticket valid for a maximum one year for 3000kr, both of which are valid for all five museums (and the latter useful if spreading museum visits over several days). Clearly, you only need to visit at least two of these museums to start saving money.

were often critical of the state. It was only after his death in 1964 that Davíð was finally taken into Icelanders' hearts, and he is now regarded as one of the country's greatest writers. Inside, in addition to his numerous books that adorn the walls, are many of his personal effects, including his piano and writing desk as he left them.

Akureyri swimming pool

Þingvallastræti 21 • Pool Mon–Fri 6.45am–9pm, Sat & Sun 8am–7.30pm; sauna women only Tues & Thurs 3–9pm; men only Wed 3–9pm, Fri 2–9pm • 600kr; 850kr with sauna

From the top of Bjarkarstígur, the long, straight Helgamagrastræti (named after Helgi Magri, the first settler in the Eyjafjörður region) leads south to Þingvallastræti and the town's excellent outdoor **swimming pool**. With two large pools, several hot pots, a steam room and a sauna, it's an absolute treat, especially when the sun is shining.

Sjónlistamiðstöðin

Kaupvangsstræti 12 • June–Aug daily 10am–5pm; Sept–May Tues–Sun noon–5pm • Free • ⓦ listasafn.akureyri.is

Head east down Þingvallastræti and you'll come to the frankly rather uninspiring **Sjónlistamiðstöðin** (Centre for Visual Arts). Inside, there's a collection of temporary exhibitions of work by local artists as well as a number of studios, known as Listagilið, where workshops are occasionally held.

The harbour

It's worth venturing east of the commercial centre of town to explore the harbourside, best reached along the main road, Drottningarbraut, running parallel to Skipagata. Although the small southern **harbour**, Akureyrarhöfn, is close to the junction of Drottningarbraut and Kaupvangsstræti, it's really along Strandgata, which runs along the harbour's northern edge, that the industrial face of Akureyri becomes more prominent. The shipyard and freighter terminal here make up the largest **commercial port** outside Reykjavík, a bustling part of town where the clanking of cranes accompanies the seemingly endless unloading and loading of ocean-going vessels at the dockside. In summer it's not uncommon for gargantuan cruise liners to be moored here, too, at the eastern end of Strandgata.

Akureyrarkirkja

Eyrarlandsvegur • Mon–Fri 10am–4pm • Free • ⓦ akirkja.is

Although Akureyri is far from ostentatious, you can't miss the dramatic **Akureyrarkirkja**, whose twin towers loom over the town from its hilltop perch. Comparisons with Hallgrímskirkja in Reykjavík are unavoidable, as both churches were designed by the same architect, Guðjón Samúelsson, and both are modelled on basalt columns. Inside, there are some dazzling **stained-glass windows**, the central panes of which are originally from the old Coventry cathedral in Britain – removed, with remarkable foresight, at the start of World War II before it was demolished

5

WHALE-WATCHING TOURS FROM AKUREYRI

Departing from the quay at the foot of Kaupvangsstræti, year-round **whale-watching tours** courtesy of Ambassador (Torfunefsbryggja jetty; ☎462 6800, ⓦambassador.is) head for the waters around the mouth of Eyjafjörður in order to spot whales. Sailings depend on the season, though generally there are two to three daily, lasting around three hours and costing 10,990kr per person. The company boasts that there's a 95 percent chance of spotting whales – if, however, you're unlucky, your next trip is free.

during bombing raids, and sold to an Icelandic dealer who came across them in an antiques shop in London. The church's other stained-glass windows (also made in England, during the 1970s) depict famous Icelanders, while the **model ship** hanging from the ceiling commemorates a former bishop.

Sigurhæðir

Eyrarlandsvegur 3 • June–Aug Mon–Fri 1–5pm • 1200kr

A pathway from the Akureyrarkirkja leads round to **Sigurhæðir** (House of Triumph), the former home of **Matthías Jochumsson** (1835–1920), the distinguished poet and author of the stirring Icelandic national anthem. Built in 1902, the house was Jochumsson's home until his death in 1920, and now holds a museum containing a small and unexceptional collection of his furnishings and a few portraits – unless you have a burning desire to immerse yourself in obscure Icelandic poetry, it's not of great interest.

Lystigarður

Eyrarlandsvegur • June–Sept Mon–Fri 8am–10pm, Sat & Sun 9am–10pm • Free

At the southern end of Eyrarlandsvegur, the glorious **Lystigarður** (Botanical Garden) was established in 1912 by Margrethe Schiöth, a Danish woman who lived in Akureyri, and offers a rich display of plant life enclosed by that Icelandic rarity, fully grown trees. Besides virtually every Icelandic species, there's an astonishing number of **subtropical plants** from South America and Africa – seemingly defying nature by existing at all in these high latitudes, the annual mean temperature for Akureyri being barely 3.4°C. In summer, when the fragrance of hundreds of flowers hangs in the air, the gardens, with undisturbed views out over the fjord, are a real haven of peace and tranquillity.

Friðbjarnarhús

Aðalstræti 46 • June–Aug daily 1–5pm; Sept–May Sat 2–4pm • 800kr

Below the gardens is the oldest part of Akureyri, where many of its wooden buildings, including several along Aðalstræti, to the southeast, have been preserved and turned into museums. The first of these, the **Friðbjarnarhús** (Good Templars Museum), is the least interesting. The Icelandic Good Templars Order was founded here in 1884, and the occasion is recorded inside with singularly uninteresting documents and photos on the upper floor, while elsewhere you'll find a rather dreary collection of old toys, prams and dolls. The Friðbjarnarhús is named after a local book merchant, Friðbjörn Steinsson, who once lived here.

Nonnahús

Aðalstræti 54 • June–Aug daily 10am–5pm • 1200kr • ⓦnonni.is

Past Friðbjarnarhús, the black wooden house with white window frames is **Nonnahús** (Nonni's House), the childhood home of Jón Sveinsson, the Jesuit priest and author of

5

the **Nonni children's books** – Nonni is the diminutive form of Jón in Icelandic. Based on his experiences of growing up in northern Iceland, the stories are little known to English-speaking audiences but are inordinately popular in Germanic countries – most were written in German – and are translated into around forty other languages. Nonni lived here until he was 12, when, following his father's death, he moved first to Denmark, where he converted to Catholicism, then to France and then, in 1914, to Austria, where he wrote his first book, before settling in Germany. Inside the house, **illustrations** from his stories decorate the walls and numerous translations of his dozen books are displayed. Dating from 1850, the house itself is one of the oldest in the town and still has its original furniture, giving a good indication of the living conditions at the time of construction; note the low ceilings and narrow doorways, which were designed to keep the heat in. Incidentally, when Nonni lived here the fjord stretched right up to his front door – the area east of the house, where the main road now runs, is all reclaimed land.

Minjasafnið á Akureyri

Aðalstræti 58 • June to mid-Sept daily 10am–5pm, rest of the year daily 1–4pm • 1200kr • ⓦ akmus.is

A few strides past Nonnahús is the **Minjasafnið á Akureyri** (Akureyri Museum), set back a little from the street behind a well-tended garden. The upper floor is generally given over to changing exhibitions; however, one exhibition which will be on display for the next few years is dedicated to the fascinating, if highly inaccurate, portrayal of Iceland on medieval maps and charts. All the maps on show were produced in Europe (the oldest dates from 1547) yet show the gaping lack of knowledge and misunderstanding which was commonplace in southern Europe about the far north: sea monsters appear in several productions; archipelagos which never existed are given pride of place; and on one fantastical map produced in Italy in 1566, the Icelanders are shown residing in grand castles and palaces rather than the stone and turf huts which prevailed at that time. **Downstairs**, an exhibition entitled "Akureyri, the town by the bay", detailing how the town has developed from the 1700s to the present day, contains a glorious jumble of household items including a mangle, cash till and even a sleigh.

Mótorhjólasafn Íslands

Krókeyri 2 • June–Aug daily 10am–5pm; Sept–May Sat 2–4pm • 1000kr • ⓦ motorhjolasafn.is

With over one hundred motorbikes on display, Akureyri's new Mótorhjólasafn, close to the airport, is a biker's dream. It was founded in memory of Iceland's best-known biker, Heiðar Jóhansson, who died in a crash in 2006; indeed, a small memorial room off the entrance contains all the man's machines. The museum's prime exhibit is a magnificent Henderson from 1918 which was originally found on a scrapyard and then restored. Have a poke around the collection and you'll come across some really classic motorbikes from the 1970s: a Triumph Trident; a Harley Davidson Heritage Softail; even a Piaggio Vespa. Incidentally, the fastest machine in the museum is a super-dynamic Suzuki CCR 100.

Flugsafn Íslands

Akureyri Airport • June–Aug daily 11am–5pm; Sept–May Sat 1–5pm • 1000kr • ⓦ flugsafn.is

For your aeroplane fix, look no further than the hangar with the nose of a DC6 freighter plane seemingly sticking out through the wall: this is the Icelandic Aviation Museum, located to the right of the airport terminal, where you'll find a collection of twenty planes and gliders. Pride of place goes to the ageing DC3 (kept outside in summer) which flew domestically in Iceland from 1943 to 1980 – it was even used to ferry sheep along the south coast in the 50s before the arrival of the Ringroad. Inside

5

you'll also see a Fokker F27 from 1978 which belonged to the Icelandic Coastguard, alongside other vintage exhibits such as a pre-war German aircraft, a Klemm 25, and the gyrocopter which holds the Icelandic record for the most crash landings. Check out, too, the mannequins of flight attendants in uniform – all from various Icelandic airlines, many of which have long disappeared.

Kjarnaskógur

Around 7km south of the town • Open access

Not content with the trees that line most of Akureyri's streets, locals have now planted an entire **forest** on former farmland, the first stage in a much more ambitious plan to encircle Akureyri with woodland. An easy one-hour walk south of the museums along Drottningarbraut and past the airport, **Kjarnaskógur** is a favourite recreational spot at weekends and on summer evenings, when the air is heavy with the scent of pine. Although birch and larch predominate, there are over fifty species of shrubs and trees here, some of which have grown to over 12m in height, quite a feat for a country where trees rarely reach little more than shoulder height – hence the long-standing Icelandic joke about what to do when you get lost in an Icelandic forest (answer: you stand up). Within the forest there are easy walking paths complete with picnic sites, a jogging track that doubles as a skiing trail in winter, plus a children's play area. Camping is not permitted here.

ARRIVAL AND DEPARTURE   AKUREYRI

By plane The airport is stunningly located on a spit of land in the middle of the fjord, 3km south of town. It's possible to walk in from here to the centre in around 30min following the highway, Drottningarbraut, northwards as it runs parallel to the fjord; alternatively, taxis (2000kr) are available outside the terminal building. Note that there are no buses to and from the airport.
Destinations Grímsey (3–7 weekly; 25min); Þórshöfn (5 weekly; 40min); Reykjavík (7 daily; 50min); Vopnafjörður (5 weekly; 45min).

By bus Long-distance buses terminate in the car park outside the Menningarhús on Strandgata.
Destinations Árskógssandur (Mon–Fri 3 daily, Sun 1 daily; 30min); Blönduós (2 daily; 2hr 15min); Borgarnes (2 daily; 5hr); Dalvík (Mon–Fri 3 daily, Sun 1 daily; 35min); Egilsstaðir (1 daily; 5hr 30min); Húsavík (Mon–Fri 3 daily, Sat 1 daily, Sun 2 daily; 1hr 15min); Mývatn (2 daily; 1hr 30min); Ólafsfjörður (Mon–Fri 3 daily, Sun 1 daily; 55min); Reykjavík (2 daily; 6hr 30min); Sauðárkrókur (2 daily; 1hr 35min); Siglufjörður (Mon–Fri 3 daily, Sun 1 daily; 1hr 10min).

INFORMATION AND TOURS

Tourist information The office is in the Menningarhús cultural centre at Strandgata 12 (mid-May to late May & mid-Sept to late Sept Mon–Fri 8am–5pm, Sat 8am–4pm; early June to mid-June daily 8am–5pm; mid-June to mid-Sept daily 8am–6.30pm; Oct to mid-May Mon–Fri 8am–4pm, Sat 11am–3pm; ☎ 450 1050, ⓦ visitakureyri.is).
Services There's free wi-fi at the tourist office and at the library, which is a veritable haven on rainy afternoons with numerous books in English about Iceland.
Horseriding tours Riding tours are a great way to

explore the countryside around Akureyri. Several companies offer excursions from their bases close to the town; the closest is Hestaleigan Kátur at Kaupangsbakkar, a 5min drive south of the centre along Route 829 (☎ 695 7218, ⓦ hestaleiga.is; 7000kr/1hr, 10,000kr/2hr, evening rides 20,000kr). Further afield, and charging similar prices, are Skjaldarvík, about 5km north of Akureyri off the Ringroad at Skjaldarvík (☎ 552 5200, ⓦ skjaldarvik.is); and Pólar Hestar, Grýtubakki 11, just south of Greinivík on Route 83 (☎ 463 3179, ⓦ polarhestar.is).

GETTING AROUND

By bus Though city-centre buses are free to use in Akureyri, they are of limited use since everywhere can be easily reached on foot.
Car rental Locally based companies include Budget, at

the airport (☎ 562 6060, ⓦ budget.is); Hertz, opposite the airport on Drottningarbraut (☎ 522 4440, ⓦ hertz.is); or Europcar, Tryggvabraut 12 (☎ 461 6000, ⓦ holdur.is).
Taxis For a taxi, you can call BSO on ☎ 461 1010.

5

ACCOMMODATION

Given the continuing increase in tourist numbers to Iceland and Akureyri's position as a key destination, it's wise to book **accommodation** in advance in summer; at other times of the year, it's not necessary. Breakfast is not always included in the price for hotels and guesthouses.

HOTELS, GUESTHOUSES AND APARTMENTS

Akureyri Hafnarstræti 67 ☎ 462 5600, ⓦ hotelakureyri .is. Located in a black-and-white-painted house virtually opposite the bus station, this smart hotel is decorated in Nordic minimalist style. Rooms are plain and tasteful, all with wooden floors and private facilities; those with views of the fjords cost just 2,200kr more. 16,600kr

Apótek Hafnarstræti 104 ☎ 469 4104, ⓦ apotek guesthouse.is. Under new ownership, this winning guesthouse is bang in the city centre, with small but comfy rooms, both with and without facilities. There's also a fabulous top-floor penthouse for rent with outside terrace (37,900kr). 19,900kr

Brekkusel Byggðavegur 97 ☎ 461 2660, ⓦ brekkusel .is. A pleasant suburban guesthouse, handy for the swimming pool, with its own garden and outdoor hot pot. The clean rooms are simple in style, though only some have private facilities; cheaper sleeping-bag doubles are also available. Doubles 13,900kr, sleeping bags 9900kr

Center Apartment Brekkugata 1 ☎ 571 7201, ⓦ centerapartmenthotel.is. Offering both double rooms and 1- to 3-bedroom apartments just off the main square, this a sound choice if you're looking for stylish self-catering accommodation. Tastefully decorated in neutral colours and with wooden floors throughout, it has the edge over *Hotel Íbúðir* (see below). Doubles 25,900kr, apartments 30,000kr

★ **Edda** Þórunnarstræti ☎ 444 4900, ⓦ hoteledda .is. Rooms in this stylish structure, which functions as university accommodation during term time, offer great value for money; some have private facilities. Mid-June to mid-Aug. 25,200kr

Gula Villan Brekkugata 8 & Þingvallastræti 14 ☎ 896 8464, ⓦ gulavillan.is. A total of nineteen identical double rooms in two buildings, most with shared facilities, kitchen and TV; sleeping-bag accommodation is also available. Check-in for both buildings is at Brekkugata 8, and breakfast is 2000kr. Doubles 14,700kr, sleeping bags 12,700kr

Hrafninn Brekkugata 4 ☎ 661 9050, ⓦ hrafninn.is. This long-established guesthouse close to the main square has just five doubles but is a sound choice, with elegantly decorated en-suite rooms. Dark wooden floors and headboards add a nice touch of class. 23,900kr

Íbúðir Geislagata 10 ☎ 462 3727 or ☎ 892 9838, ⓦ hotelibudir.is. Pleasant studios, as well as two- and three-bedroom apartments with sitting room and a fully fitted kitchen, usefully located within a 2min walk of Ráðhústorg. Studios 24,000kr, apartments 37,600kr

Icelandair Hotel Akureyri Þingvallastræti 23 ☎ 518 1000, ⓦ icelandairhotels.com. Icelandair's presence in Akureyri is confirmed with the opening of this new luxury hotel, opposite the swimming pool and with commanding views of the fjord. Room decor is Nordic in style with plenty of soft natural colours. Breakfast is an overpriced 2280kr. 31,600kr

KEA Hafnarstræti 87–89 ☎ 460 2000, ⓦ hotelkea.is. Located in a couple of adjoining buildings, this is the largest and most luxurious hotel in Akureyri, with modern, en-suite rooms kitted out with satellite TV and a minibar, though in recent years it has upped its prices out of all proportion to its status. 38,000kr

Norðurland Geislagata 7 ☎ 462 2600, ⓦ hotelkea.is. A good location for this modern KEA-owned hotel, within easy striking distance of the main square, whose thirty-odd carpeted en-suite rooms are decorated in soft autumnal colours and offer considerably better value than the *KEA* (see above). 30,300kr

Sæluhús Sunnutröð 2 ☎ 618 2800, ⓦ saeluhus.is. Superb studio apartments sleeping up to four people, overlooking the fjord and with their own kitchenette and private veranda. There's also access to a communal laundry and hot tubs. Reckon on a 20min walk into the town centre. 18,000kr

Sólgarðar Brekkugata 6 ☎ 461 1133, ⓔ solgardar @simnet.is. Three highly agreeable, bright and spacious rooms with TV and access to a kitchen, just one minute from the main square. Breakfast is 2000kr extra. Doubles 14,000kr, sleeping bags 11,800kr

HOSTELS AND CAMPSITE

Akureyri Backpackers Hafnarstræti 98 ☎ 571 9050, ⓦ akureyribackpackers.com. With more than a hundred beds over three floors right on Hafnarstræti, this winning new hostel couldn't be more central. Accommodation is in dorms which sleep four (also available as doubles), six or eight and share bathrooms; there's a kitchen, laundry, sauna and barbecue area, too. Dorms 4500kr, doubles 18,000kr

Campsite Þórunnarstræti ☎ 843 0002. Akureyri's campsite is located next to the university and has good toilet and shower facilities on the other side of the street in the school building, plus an on-site playground for kids. June to mid-Sept. 1200kr

Youth hostel Stórholt 1 ☎ 462 3657, ⓦ hostel.is. The 65 beds at this hostel, 1.5km out of town back towards Reykjavík along Glerárgata, fill quickly thanks to the low price – the green, leafy location is an added bonus. There are some doubles as well as dorms. Mid-Jan to mid-Dec. Dorms 4550kr, doubles 12,400kr

EATING AND DRINKING

Unless you've arrived directly from Reykjavík, you'll feel quite dizzy at the wide choice of places to eat in Akureyri. Thanks to the town's small university and its role as a commercial centre for the entire north of the country, there's a fair choice of **cafés** and **restaurants**, so indulge yourself before moving on.

CAFÉS

Bláa Kannan Hafnarstræti 96 ☎461 4600. Housed in an old wooden building on the main street, this atmospheric place with grand, antique chandeliers serves the best coffee in Akureyri, and is popular with local shoppers. They also do great cakes, bagels and panini. Mon–Fri 9am–11.30pm, Sat & Sun 10am–11.30pm.

Kristjáns Hafnarstræti 108 ☎460 5930. At lunchtime, look no further than this bakery on the main street which serves a no-nonsense, inexpensive set lunch dish for just 1500kr (1800kr on Fri). There's also a decent salad bar, pizza by the slice and soup of the day. Mon–Fri 8am–5.30pm, Sat 10am–4pm.

RESTAURANTS

Bautinn Hafnarstræti 92 ☎462 1818. Always busy with both locals and visitors, this is essentially a cheap and cheerful dine-and-dash type of place, and is best for a quick burger and chips (from 1850kr), or fish-and-something from 3820kr. Daily 9am–11pm.

Íslenska Hamborgarafabrikkan Hafnarstræti 87–9 ☎575 7575. Below the *KEA* hotel (see opposite), this new hamburger restaurant has a mega-choice of burgers, both beef and chicken, all cooked medium rare, and costing 1765–2495kr. The bestseller is the delicious Morthens, a burger with bacon, mushrooms, garlic, lettuce, tomatoes and Bernaise sauce (2075kr). Mon–Thurs & Sun 11.30am–9.30pm, Fri & Sat 11.30am–11pm.

Krua Siam Strandgata 13 ☎466 3800. Thai restaurant serving reasonable if not overly authentic dishes. The weekday lunch buffet for 1750kr including a drink is good value; otherwise mains, such as pad Thai, are 1499–1700kr. Vegetarian options available. Mon–Fri 11.30am–1.30pm & 5–9.30pm, Sat & Sun 5–9.30pm.

La Vita è Bella Hafnarstræti 92 ☎461 5858. The most authentic Italian restaurant in town, with pizzas from 2470kr and pasta dishes from 2940kr. There's also a choice of good meat and fish mains, such as grilled salmon, from 4370kr. Daily 6pm–late.

RUB23 Kaupvangsstræti 6 ☎462 2223. A stylish sushi restaurant offering a wide variety of fish, all rubbed in a secret blend of spices, seeds and herbs. Fourteen pieces cost 4290kr, or try a mixed seafood platter for 4990kr. Mon–Thurs 11.30am–2pm & 5.30–10pm, Fri 11.30am–2pm, Sat 5.30–11pm, Sun 5.30–10pm.

Strikið Skipagata 14 ☎462 7100. Following a change of direction this once-popular top-floor brasserie with open-air terrace has lost its way. With every dish on the menu costing 4800–5200k (roast leg of lamb; langoustine; spotted wolffish) you'll certainly need to dig deep in your pocket to enjoy the food and the views from up here. Daily 11.30am–11pm.

NIGHTLIFE

Though still lagging behind Reykjavík, the number of **bars** in Akureyri has mushroomed in recent years. It's fair to assume that as tourism continues to increase, so, too, will the number of drinking establishments.

BARS

Brygghúsbarinn Kaupvangsstræti 23 ☎662 7011. Snug and compact bar which serves all five of the different beers made by the Kaldi microbrewery in nearby Dalvík. It's a great place to strike up a conversation and is the nearest thing Akureyri has to a British pub. Wed & Thurs 8pm–1am, Fri & Sat 8pm–3am.

Café Amour Ráðhústorg 9 ☎461 3030. Check out the ceiling here – decorated with naked modern-day male and female cherubs, flitting around in heaven. After a beer or three, drinkers don't seem to notice the offbeat murals and concentrate on the serious business of boozing instead. Mon–Thurs & Sun 11am–1am, Fri & Sat 11am–4am.

Götubarinn Hafnarstræti 96 ☎462 4747. Akureyri's smartest and trendiest bar, perfectly located on the main shopping street, and now with an outdoor beer garden at the rear. Small it certainly is, but that doesn't stop crowds of people squeezing in between the chunky wooden walls for a beer. Thurs–Sat 5pm–4am.

Græni Hatturinn Hafnarstræti 96 ☎461 4646. A popular, evenings-only pub in the basement of the *Bláa Kannan* (see above), and good for a beer or three. Entrance is down the steps in the small lane off Hafnarstræti. Daily 6pm–late.

CLUBS

Kaffi Akureyri Strandgata 7 ☎461 3999. This popular bar mutates into a club (with occasional live music) at weekends, and starts to fill up from mid-evening onwards. Thurs & Sun 3pm–1am, Fri & Sat 3pm–4am.

Pósthúsbarinn Skipagata 10 ☎866 6186. A new nightclub and lounge bar housed in Akureyri's former post office and attracting a young crowd of twenty- and thirty-somethings. The music's usually a mix of 1980s and 90s classic hits which the crowd thrills to. Thurs–Sun 11pm–late.

5

Sjallinn Geislagata 14 ☎ 462 2770. Dance club where you'll find virtually every young person in Akureyri on weekend evenings grooving to the latest tunes or to live music. Thurs–Sun 11pm–late.

DIRECTORY

Bookshops Eymundsson, Hafnarstræti 91–93 (Mon–Fri 9am–10pm, Sat 10am–10pm, Sun noon–10pm), is good for maps and guidebooks. For secondhand English paperbacks, try Fornbókabúðin Fróði, Kaupvangsstræti 19 (Mon–Fri 2–6pm).
Cinema Sambíóin Akureyri, Ráðhústorg 8 ☎ 575 8900.
Hospital The hospital on Eyrarlandsvegur has a 24hr A&E ward ☎ 463 0100.
Laundry Þvottahúsið Höfði, Hafnarstræti 34 ☎ 462 2580.
Library Brekkugata 17 ☎ 462 4141 (Mon–Fri 10am–7pm, also mid-Sept to mid-April Sat 11am–4pm).
Pharmacy Apótekarinn, Hafnarstræti 95 (Mon–Fri 9am–5.30pm).
Police Þórunnarstræti 138 ☎ 112.

Post office Strandgata 3 (Mon–Fri 9am–6pm).
Supermarket Bónus, Langholt 1, just off the Ringroad past the Youth Hostel, heading towards Reykjavík (Mon–Thurs 11am–6.30pm, Fri 10am–7.30pm, Sat 10am–6pm, Sun noon–6pm).
Vínbúð Hólabraut 16 (Mon–Thurs 11am–6pm, Fri 11am–7pm, Sat 11am–6pm).
Woollen goods Fold-Anna, Hafnarstræti 100 (Mon–Fri 9am–7pm, Sat & Sun 10am–5pm; ☎ 461 4120); Geysir, Hafnarstræti 98 (daily 10am–10pm; ☎ 519 6040); Rammagerðin, Hafnarstræti 94 (daily 9am–10pm; ☎ 535 6695); The Viking, Hafnarstræti 104 (daily 8am–10pm; ☎ 461 5551).

Eastern Eyjafjörður

The eastern shore of Eyjafjörður, covered in part by the Ringroad and then Route 83, offers something quite rare in Iceland: remote, uninhabited wilderness that is relatively accessible from a major town. North of the small village of **Grenivík**, now the only centre of population on the eastern side of the fjord, the perpetually snowcapped **Látraströnd** coastline is made up of some of the most rugged mountains in the north of Iceland, including the peak of **Kaldbakur** (1167m), which dominates any view of the eastern shore. Excellent and challenging **hiking** routes lead through the wilderness to abandoned farms which, until World War II, made up some of the country's most remote and desolate communities, where life in this area of unforgiving Arctic fjordland, known as Í Fjörðum, was a constant struggle against the elements. The region's other attraction, however, is not nearly so remote: the unusual five-gabled turf farmhouse and church at **Laufás**, 10km south of Grenivík and close to the Ringroad.

GETTING AROUND

By bus It's 40km from Akureyri to Grenivík and, though no public transport runs this far, buses heading east from Akureyri to Mývatn or Húsavík can drop you at the start of Route 83, some 20km from town – you'll have to rely on your own car, your legs or passing motorists beyond this point.

Laufás

Mid-May to mid-Sept Mon–Wed & Fri–Sun 9am–6pm, Thurs 9am–10pm • 1200kr

Thirty kilometres north of Akureyri up Route 83, **Laufás** is a superb example of a traditional turf farmhouse. Dating from 1866, the building is timber-fronted and has five gabled roofs, all made of turf, giving the impression that it's composed of several separate cottages all joined under one roof. The most remarkable feature, however, is the fabulous **herringbone** arrangement of turf pieces used to make up part of the front wall. Don't miss the unusual **carved eider duck** that sits on one of the gable ends, serving as a reminder of the local nesting area belonging to the property; the eider down once brought the owners a considerable income. Inside, sadly, is the usual array of mind-numbing how-we-used-to-live paraphernalia, showing household and farm life from the days when the house was used as a manor farm and a parsonage for the next-door **church**, which itself dates from 1865 and contains a pulpit with wood carvings from 1698; the local priest shared the building with his labourers.

5

HIKING FROM GRENIVÍK TO GJÖGUR

A circular four- to five-day **hike** leads from Grenivík via the Látraströnd coast to the Gjögur headland, which guards the eastern entrance to Eyjafjörður, and then east through the coastal Í Fjörðum region to Hvalvatnsfjörður and the beginning of Route F839, which then returns towards Grenivík.

From Grenivík, follow the unnumbered road northwest from the village to the deserted **Svínarnes** farm, where the road ends and a track continues along the Látraströnd shoreline, passing several more abandoned farms, including **Látur**, which has been empty since 1942. The path then swings inland through the **Uxaskarð pass** (in order to avoid the Gjögur headland) and drops down through Keflavíkurdalur to reach the shore at **Keflavík**, one of Iceland's remotest locations, a deserted farm that was regularly cut off from the rest of the country for months in the wintertime. At the beginning of the eighteenth century, people on the farm here were taken ill and died one by one as the harsh winter weather set in – all except for an 11-year-old girl, who remained alone here for ten weeks until people from the nearest farmstead finally managed to dig their way through the heavy snowdrifts to rescue her. Passing Þorgeirsfjörður, the path heads southwest for the next fjord, Hvalvatnsfjörður, and the beginning of the F839 mountain road back over the hills up to the Leirdalsheiði plateau and finally down into Grenivík; there can often be snow along this route until the middle of July.

Grenivík

Ten kilometres northwest of Laufás, **GRENIVÍK** is a modern fjordside village, which only began life in 1910. Although improvements to the tiny **harbour**, around which the village is situated, brought about a slight increase in trade and thus population, there are still only around 250 people who call the place home. Its principal use is as a starting and finishing point for **hikes** along the fjord to **Látraströnd** and the **Í Fjörðum** region of the north coast (see box above).

ACCOMMODATION   GRENIVÍK

Hótel Nátur Around 20km south of Grenivík and 14km north of Akureyri at Þórisstaðir on Route 1 ☎ 467 1070, ⓦ hotelnatur.com. With 36 en-suite rooms in a converted barn and machine shed, this family-run place also serves locally sourced food (evening buffet costs 6000kr) and is a veritable haven of peace and tranquillity. Breakfast included. **26,700kr**

Grímsey

Forty kilometres north of the mainland, the five-square-kilometre chunk of craggy basalt that defiantly rears up out of the Atlantic is the island of **Grímsey**, straddled by the **Arctic Circle**, where Iceland ends and the Arctic begins. First settled by the Viking **Vestfjarða-Grímur Sigurðsson**, and named after him ("Grímsey" means Grímur's Island), the island supports one tiny settlement, scruffy **Sandvík**, on its southwest coast. While many come here to cross that magical geographical line, Grímsey also hosts some amazing birdlife, including **puffins**, **razorbills** and **guillemots**, which are resident on the island's cliffs for most of the year – some 36 species breed here. Take special care when walking around the island since you're likely to be attacked by **arctic tern**, in particular, which will stop at nothing to protect their eggs – they are present on Grímsey from early May to early September.

There's just one **road** on Grímsey, which runs the length of the west coast from the lighthouse at its southernmost point, Flesjar, past the indoor **swimming pool** (which opens if three or more people want to swim – enquire at the store) at the southern end of the airport runway through the village to the airport at Básar – a total length of 3km. Landing here in the Air Iceland Twin Otter plane that links the island with Akureyri can be quite an experience, as it's often forced to buzz over the runway on

5

the initial approach to clear the hundreds of potentially dangerous birds that gather on it before coming in a second time to land. Taking off is no less hazardous – although one of Grímsey's few cars is driven up and down the runway to achieve the same result.

Just past the airport, the **Arctic Circle** is marked not by a line but by a **signpost** – there's a picnic bench beneath it, and you can read the signpost to find out how far you are from home.

Sandvík

SANDVÍK, home to 85 people, is essentially nothing more than twenty or so houses grouped around a harbour, which is where the ferry from Dalvík docks. Southeast of the harbour, the road leads to the community centre, **Múli** (ask at the village shop for the key), where every year on November 11 the birthday of the island's benefactor, nineteenth-century American chess champion **Daniel Willard Fiske** (see box below), is celebrated with coffee, cakes and a day off work.

A few steps beyond the community centre, the whitewashed walls of the village **church**, which was originally built of driftwood in 1867, cut a sharp image against the heavy skies. It seems to be thanks to one former vicar that this isolated community still exists: in 1793, Grímsey came close to being abandoned when a plague swept through the island, killing almost all the men. The six healthiest sailed to the mainland to seek help, but were drowned when their boat capsized, leaving the priest the only able-bodied man on Grímsey.

The rest of the island

Setting out from the airport it's possible to **hike round the island** following a rough sheep track all the way. It's wise to use the clifftops as a guide, as the track soon gets lost amid the many springy tussocks that mark this part of the island, as it heads up the hillside to the east coast. This is by far the most dramatic aspect of the island, with sheer cliffs plunging down into the foam and the roaring waves of the Arctic Ocean. Stretching out to the north, the promontory you can see from here, **Eyjarfótur**, is a good place to watch the birds since it affords views both out over the sea and back over the low fields around the guesthouse and airport where so many species congregate. However, there is no area of the island devoid of birds and simply walking around Grímsey, be it on the cliffs or in the village, will bring you into contact with various varieties. Heading south from the headland following the shoreline, the path climbs a little as it goes over **Handfestuhóll**, from where you can see the rock fissures **Almannagjá** and **Handfestargjá** in the cliff face. Beyond the small islet, **Flatasker**, the coast swings south heading for the lighthouse at Grímsey's southeastern point, **Flesjar**.

Across Grenivík bay from Flesjar, on the southwestern point, Borgarhöfði, a series of **basalt columns** forms a mini-version of Northern Ireland's famous Giant's Causeway.

ANYONE FOR CHESS?

A prominent journalist during the nineteenth century, and a leading scholar on things Icelandic, **Daniel Willard Fiske** left the islanders of Grímsey US$12,000 upon his death and gave instructions for a school and library to be built. Oddly, Fiske had never once set foot on Grímsey, but it seems the islanders' reputation as the greatest **chess** players in the whole of Iceland (chess was introduced to Grímsey by the Vikings) furthered his own love of the game; he also donated eleven marble chess sets to the island. The last remaining set can be seen, alongside Fiske's portrait, in the library inside the Múli community centre, which stands on the original site of the school he financed. Today, the island's children learn to play chess at school and there's even an open-air table opposite the shop if you fancy a game.

5

THE TROLLS OF GRÍMSEY

According to legend, Grímsey was formed when three **night trolls** tried to separate the West Fjords from the rest of Iceland by digging a channel from Húnaflói bay all the way to Breiðafjörður. As the sun rose, the trolls in the west ran east but were turned to stone in Kollafjörður, whereas the troll in the north jumped over Streingrímsfjörður, landing on a rocky peninsula where she had left her ox. In anger she threw down her shovel, breaking off part of the cliff and creating Grímsey. Locals maintain she, too, was turned to stone, and indeed, a tall rock stack known as **Kerling** (The Old Woman) stands down by the sea in the tiny mainland village of Drangsnes (see p.219), between the swimming pool and *Malarhorn* cottage, looking out at her island and ox.

From here the road continues along the west coast into the village and back to the harbour. The headland opposite the church, which you'll pass heading back to the village, is one of the most easily accessible places to spot **puffins**. Quite remarkably, during the course of just one night (usually around August 10), every puffin heads off out to sea for the winter.

ARRIVAL AND DEPARTURE   GRÍMSEY

By plane You can fly to Grímsey from Akureyri (3 weekly; 25min); one-way fares start at 9700kr.

By ferry The Sæfari ferry (☎458 8970, ⊚land flutningar.is/saefari/english; 3hr; 9660kr return) runs three times a week between Árskógssandur (see p.242), just south of Dalvík, and Grímsey; buses from Akureyri to Árskógssandur connect with services and take about an hour.

ACCOMMODATION AND EATING

Accommodation on Grímsey is limited, so be sure to book ahead if you plan to stay overnight. Though there is no formal site here, **camping** is permitted anywhere on the island away from the village.

★**Básar** Opposite the airport building ☎467 3103, ⊚gistiheimilidbasar.is. This simple guesthouse overlooks the island's tiny runway and the sea. Rooms all share facilities and it's a great place to watch the Twin Otter from Akureyri make its approach to the island. Lunch and dinner are available. Doubles 16,000kr, sleeping bags 6000kr

Krían Above the harbour ☎467 3112. This very basic café serves run-of-the-mill burgers and chips (around 2000kr). Other than the guesthouse, it's the only place to eat on the island. Daily noon–8.30pm.

Mývatn and the northeast

HÚSAVÍK

Mývatn and the northeast

Northeast Iceland forms a thinly populated, open expanse between Akureyri and the East Fjords. Tourists, along with most of Iceland's wildfowl population, flock to Mývatn, an attractive lake just over an hour's drive from Akureyri, whose surrounds are thick with hot springs and volcanic formations – many of them still visibly active – as well as a sublime geothermal spa that is the northeast's answer to the Blue Lagoon. North of here, the pleasant town of Húsavík offers summer whale-watching excursions, and is just a short jaunt from Jökulsárgljúfur, where one of the region's glacial rivers thunders through a series of gorges and waterfalls – a superb place to spend a few days hiking or camping.

The eastern half of the region has far less obvious attractions; indeed, the only real access to this mix of mountains, lava desert and boggy lowlands is along the coastal road between Húsavík and **Vopnafjörður**. However, it's a great area for unhurried travel, bringing you close to some wild countryside, breezy coastal walks, and small, isolated communities – plus the chance to reach the mainland's northernmost tip, which lies fractionally outside the Arctic Circle.

Away from Mývatn and Húsavík, services are thinly spread, though most settlements have a bank, a supermarket and somewhere to stay; elsewhere, there are farmstays, a few hostels, and limitless camping opportunities. The northeast's **weather** is much drier and often sunnier than southern Iceland's – and this far north it barely gets dark for three months of the year – though winters are bitterly cold, with heavy snowfalls throughout.

GETTING AROUND   MÝVATN AND THE NORTHEAST

By bus SBA-Norðurleið (ⓦ sba.is) operates a year-round Akureyri–Mývatn–Egilsstaðir route along the Ringroad, adding separate routes to Dettifoss and Ásbyrgi in summer. Strætó (ⓦ straeto.is) also runs year-round from Akureyri to Þórshöfn, via Húsavík and Raufarhöfn. Reykjavík Excursions (ⓦ re.is) runs summer-only buses between Reykjavík and Mývatn via Sprengisandur (see p.325) or Landmannalaugar (see p.119).

By car There are few fuel stations between towns and it's best to top up the tank whenever you can. Main roads are sound, though not always surfaced and sometimes closed at short notice by snow. Minor roads might require 4WD and be open for only a month or two in summer.

By tour Fjallasýn (☎ 464 3941, ⓦ fjallasyn.is) offer tours of the entire region, including Mývatn, Dettifoss, Melrakkaslétta and Langanes.

Mývatn

Around 100km east of Akureyri on the Ringroad, **Mývatn**'s placid, shallow spread of water belies its status as one of the country's most touristed locations. Admittedly, Mývatn has had its detractors ever since the Middle Ages – when the lake and its steaming surrounds were fearfully dismissed as a pool of the devil's piss – though the only annoyance nowadays is summertime swarms of tiny black **flies** (Mývatn means "Midge Lake"). These provide an abundant food source for both fish and the hundreds

Mývatn's ducks p.263
Whale watching in Húsavík p.274

The Ásbyrgi to Dettifoss hike p.277
Hvalreki! p.278

DETTIFOSS

Highlights

① Lake Mývatn Craters, steaming rocks, boiling mud pools and the nesting grounds for most of Iceland's duck species. **See p.260**

② Jarðböðin Nature Baths Glorious thermal spa, where you can soak in warm water while admiring the view down over Lake Mývatn. **See p.269**

③ Krafla and Leirhnjúkur Spend a half-day hiking around this volcano crater and rugged lava flow, still steaming after an eruption in the 1980s. **See p.270**

④ Húsavík Iceland's premier whale-watching venue, where you're almost guaranteed sightings through the summer. **See p.272**

⑤ Ásbyrgi This huge, horseshoe-shaped cliff face is said to be a hoofprint made by the Norse god Oðinn's eight-legged horse. **See p.276**

⑥ Dettifoss Europe's most powerful waterfall is spectacular at the start of summer, when glacial melt upstream turns the river into a furious brown torrent. **See p.278**

⑦ Langanes Peninsula Understated "goose-neck" peninsula jutting northeast towards the Arctic, home to a huge gannet colony and some remote, easy hikes. **See p.281**

HIGHLIGHTS ARE MARKED ON THE MAP ON P.262

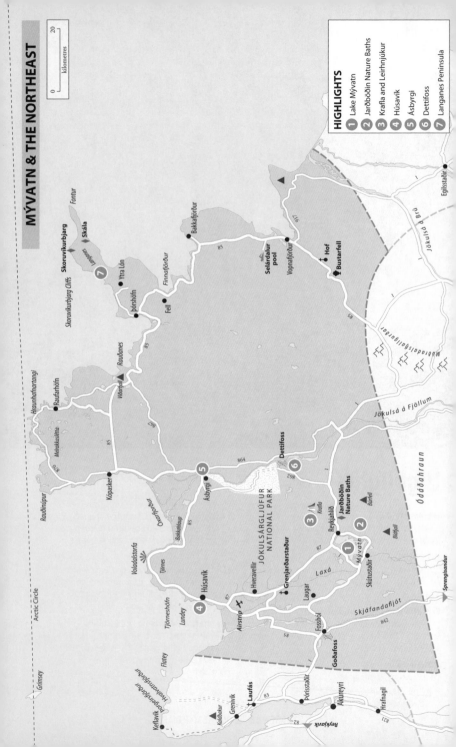

MÝVATN & THE NORTHEAST

Grímsey

Arctic Circle

Fontur

Skoruvíkurbjarg
Skála
Ytra Lón
Langanes
Skoruvíkurbjarg Cliffs
7
Þórshöfn
Fell
Finnafjörður
Bakkafjörður

85

Selárdalur pool
Vopnafjörður
Hof
Bustarfell

917

Raufarhöfn
Raudinúpur
Melrakkaslétta
Hraunhafnartangi
Viðarfjall
Rauðanes

85

85

85

Kópasker

Öxarfjörður

0,38

Bakkahlaup
Ásbyrgi

864

5

Dettifoss

6
862

JÖKULSÁRGLJÚFUR
NATIONAL PARK

Jökulsá á Brú

Egilsstaðir

58

Möðrudalsfjallgarður

Jökulsá á Fjöllum

ÓÐÁÐAHRAUN

Voladalstorfa
Tjörnes
Lundey
Flatey
Tjörneshöfn

Húsavík
4

Hveravellir

Grenjaðarstaður

87

Laxá

Laugar

3
Krafla
Reykjahlíð
Mývatn
1
Jarðböðin
Nature Baths
2
Skútustaðir
Búrfell
Bláfjall

Sprengisandur

Airstrip
Fosshól

85

Skjálfandafljót

842

Goðafoss

Þórisstaðir

Hrafnhagil

Akureyri

821

Reykjavík

82

Laufás
Grenivík
Kaldbakur

Þorgeirsfjörður
Hvalvatnsfjörður
Gjögrafjörður

Keflavík
83

0 ━━━ 20
kilometres

of thousands of **wildfowl** which descend on the lake each year to raise their young: all of Iceland's duck species breed either here or on the **Laxá**, Mývatn's fast-flowing, salmon-rich outlet, and one – **Barrow's goldeneye** – nests nowhere else in Europe.

Most people base themselves at **Reykjahlíð**, a small service centre on the northern side of the lake, though a few alternatives are dotted elsewhere around the shore – especially at southerly **Skútustaðir**. A good **road** circuits Mývatn, with tracks and footpaths elsewhere, and two busy days are enough to take in the main sights. Mývatn looks its best in summer, but can get very crowded then: it's a toss-up to decide whether there are more tourists, insects or ducks. As for the flies: a few bite, but most just buzz irritatingly around your face – keep them off by buying a hat with attached netting. Alternatively, come in winter for watching the Northern Lights; or hit a few good days in late spring and, while you'll miss out on the bird life, there are no flies and you'll have the place to yourself – though facilities are limited out of season.

6

Reykjahlíð

Given the number of visitors who invade each summer, **REYKJAHLÍÐ** is surprisingly insubstantial – just a church and nearby airstrip, a cluster of services surrounding the N1 fuel station, and a handful of quiet residential streets. But most of Mývatn's **accommodation** is here (if Reykjahlíð is full, there's nevertheless further accommodation at Vógar and Skútustaðir), there are **hiking trails** around the east shore to Hverfell, and the setting is grand, right where the low volcanic plateau slopes down to the lakeshore, with views south right across the lake. Birders shouldn't miss the **Slavonian grebes** that nest on the lakeshore directly in front of the *Reynihlíð* hotel (see p.265).

MÝVATN'S DUCKS

In summer, plentiful food and nesting space make Mývatn the best place in northern Europe to see **wild ducks** – it's possible to clock up eighteen species during your stay. Their favourite **nesting area** is in spongy heathland on the northwest side of the lake, though more accessible places to spy on them include Mývatn's southeastern corner (especially good for Barrow's goldeneye); the Laxá outflow on the western side of the lake (for harlequin ducks); and even the shore at Reykjahlíð (anything). Female ducks tend to be drably coloured, to blend in with vegetation while incubating their eggs, and unless otherwise stated, the following descriptions are of breeding drakes.

Several types of duck at Mývatn have a black head with a black and white body. The most celebrated is **Barrow's goldeneye**, resident year-round and easily identified by a characteristic white comma-shaped patch between the manic golden eye and bill. Keep an eye open too for their black-and-white-striped chicks. Barrow's goldeneye are most likely to be confused with either the similar-looking **tufted duck** or **scaup**, though neither shares its "comma" – tufted ducks also have a droopy back-swept crest, while the scaup has a grey, not white, back.

Mývatn's other speciality is the **harlequin duck**, here from May until July, which sports unmistakable chestnut, white and blue plumage. As indicated by the Icelandic name – *straumönd*, stream duck – harlequins are most often seen bobbing in and out of rough water on the Laxá. Other marine ducks spending their summers at Mývatn include the **scoter**, a uniquely all-black diving duck, which in Iceland breeds only at Mývatn, and the **long-tailed** or **old squaw**, another strikingly patterned bird with a summer plumage including a black neck and crown and very long, pointed tail (the similar **pintail** has a white throat, though so does the long-tail in winter).

Otherwise, you'll be fairly familiar with most of Mývatn's ducks, which are primarily freshwater species. Some of the more plentiful include the **mallard**; the red-headed **pochard**; the long-beaked **merganser** and **goosander**; and the wide-beaked **shoveler**; **wigeon**, with their coppery heads and vertical blond streak between the eyes; the uniformly nondescript **gadwall**; and **teals**, which sport a glossy red head and green eyepatch.

The church

At the western edge of town

Standing tall, Reykjahlíð's **church** is a neat white structure whose green spire is topped by an incongruous neon crucifix. The obvious **lava flows** either side date from August 1729, when fast-flowing magma descended from Leirhnjúkur and covered three nearby farms, but was mysteriously deflected around the low-lying church – some say by the cemetery wall, others (in keeping with similar cases elsewhere in Iceland) by prayer. A carving on the pulpit depicts the church of the time under threat, and check out the lava, too: there are some good stretches of rope-lava pavements, and plenty of fissures caused by escaping gases.

Stóragjá

On a cold day vapour rises from cracks in the ground all around Reykjahlíð (the name means "steamy slopes"); for a closer look walk 250m east of the N1 fuel station to the Ringroad intersection, where the rough scrub conceals **Stóragjá**, the most accessible of Mývatn's sunken hot springs. A ladder and rope reach down into the 2m-wide cleft from ground level, and it was a popular bathing hole until it cooled during the 1990s (it's now around 25°C), allowing harmful bacteria to flourish. Some people do still swim here, but at the risk of getting any cuts or grazes infected – best stick to the swimming pool.

ARRIVAL AND DEPARTURE   REYKJAHLÍÐ

By bus Buses pull in at the N1 fuel station, next to the visitor centre. SBA buses run year-round to Akureyri and Egilsstaðir along the Ringroad, with summer services to Höfn, Húsavík, Krafla and Dettifoss. From late June until late Aug, Reykjavík Excursions also head from Mývatn across Sprengisandur to Landmannalaugar or Reykjavík.

Destinations Akureyri (1 daily; 2hr 45min); Dettifoss (1 daily; 1hr 30min); Egilsstaðir (1 daily; 2hr 5min); Goðafoss (1 daily; 40min); Höfn (1 daily; 9hr 30min); Húsavík (2 daily; 45min); Krafla (2 daily; 15min); Landmannalaugar (1 daily; 10hr); Reykjavík via Sprengisandur (1 daily; 11hr 35min).

INFORMATION

Tourist information Mývatnsstofa visitor centre (daily 9am–4pm, National Parks counter daily 9am–noon; ☎464 4390, ⓦ visitmyvatn.is) has internet and a small environmental museum. Staff can provide free maps of the Mývatn area, and there's a rack of brochures by the door; the National Parks counter is where to ask about hiking from Dettifoss to Ásbyrgi (see box, p.277).
Services The N1 fuel station also houses toilets and a well-stocked Samkaup/STRAX supermarket (daily: summer

9am–8pm; winter 10am–6pm); note that there's no fuel available east on the Ringroad between Mývatn and Egilsstaðir (165km). The post office (Mon–Fri 9am–4pm) and bank ATM are directly across the street behind the fuel station. Reykjahlíð's shallow swimming pool (daily 10am–9pm) is 700m away at the end of Hlíðavegur. Hike & Bike, in front of *Reykjahlíð* (June–Aug daily 9am–10pm; ☎899 4845, ⓦ hikeandbike.is), rents out sturdy mountain bikes for 4000kr per day.

TOURS

Geotravel ☎864 7080, ⓦ geotravel.is. Super-jeep trips to Askja and Dettifoss – and, if conditions permit, the new lavafield at Holuhraun (see p.330) – plus seasonal hiking and cross-country skiing tours.
Mýflug Air ☎464 4400, ⓦ myflug.is. This Reykjahlíð-based outfit can take you for a short spin over Mývatn and Krafla (20min; 15,500kr), or out to Askja and Dettifoss (2hr; 50,000kr).
Mývatn Tours ☎464 1920, ⓦ askjatours.is. Lengthy day-trips in a 4WD bus to Askja from late June until Sept (19,000kr); you'll get a good look at the Interior, including

views of Herðubreið and a swim in Víti's lukewarm water (see p.330).
Saga Travel ☎558 8888, ⓦ sagatravel.is. Super-jeeps on demand to Askja (38,000kr/person) and Lofthellir Ice Caves (19,000kr/person); minimum numbers needed.
SBA ⓦ sba.is. From mid-June until early Sept, there are two buses daily to Krafla (1620kr each way), one of which continues to Dettifoss (3420kr each way) from where you can connect with buses to Ásbyrgi (see p.276).

ACCOMMODATION

★ **Bjarg** Overlooking the lake opposite the fuel station ☎ 464 4240, ✉ ferdabjarg@simnet.is. Friendly campsite with laundry and kitchen facilities on a gently sloping lakeside lawn, and two comfortable, good-value double rooms in the main house. Camping **1400kr**, doubles **13,000kr**

Eldá Helluhraun 15 ☎ 464 4220, ⓦ elda.is. Family-run business offering single, double and triple rooms in three houses around Reykjahlíð. Rates include a large breakfast. Sleeping-bag accommodation is available in low season only. Doubles **12,000kr**, sleeping bags **5500kr**

★ **Hlíð** Off the airstrip road and behind the church ☎ 464 4103, ⓦ myvatnaccommodation.is. Spacious campsite, with views of the lake and distant highlands. The roomy, self-catering bunkhouse is favoured by tour groups and has around a dozen four-person dorms, plus a large kitchen and dining area; there's also self-catering, two-person cabins and a B&B option. Camping **1500kr**, sleeping bags **4700kr**, cabins **13,200kr**

Reykjahlíð Right on the lakeshore and overlooking the water ☎ 464 4142, ⓦ icelandairhotels.is. Pleasantly low-key hotel, though its exact future isn't certain; it was recently taken over by Icelandair, and there are plans to perhaps increase the number of rooms. **33,500kr**

Reynihlíð Next to the church ☎ 464 4170, ⓦ myvatnhotel.is. A modern, relatively upmarket affair whose well-furnished rooms are bright (most are carpeted, too), with plenty of Nordic pine trim and bathrooms tiled in shades of white. **32,200kr**

6

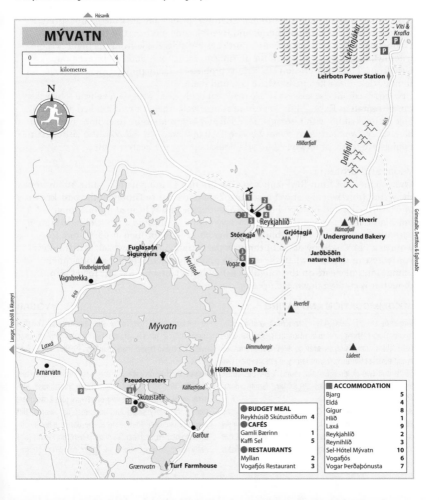

MÝVATN

0 — 4 kilometres

N

Húsavík

Víti & Krafla

Leirbotn Power Station

Hlíðarfjall

Dalfjall

Reykjahlíð

Stóragjá

Grjótagjá

Hverir

Námafjall Underground Bakery

Jarðböðin nature baths

Fuglasafn Sigurgeirs

Vindbelgjarfjall

Vagnbrekka

Nestland

Vogar

Hverfell

Mývatn

Laxá

Dimmuborgir

Lúdent

Arnarvatn

Pseudocraters

Höfði Nature Park

Kálfaströnd

Skútustaðir

Garður

Grænvatn

Turf Farmhouse

Laugar, Fosshóll & Akureyri

Grímsstaðir, Dettifoss & Egilsstaðir

■ ACCOMMODATION
Bjarg	5
Eldá	4
Gígur	8
Hlíð	1
Laxá	9
Reykjahlíð	2
Reynihlíð	3
Sel-Hótel Mývatn	10
Vogafjós	6
Vogar Þerðaþónusta	7

● BUDGET MEAL
Reykhúsið Skútustöðum	4

● CAFÉS
Gamli Bærinn	1
Kaffi Sel	5

■ RESTAURANTS
Myllan	2
Vogafjós Restaurant	3

EATING

For food, make sure you try locally **smoked fish**, along with *hverabrauð* – steam bread baked in the underground ovens east at Bjarnaflag – both of which are usually available at the supermarket.

Gamli Bærinn Next to the *Reynihlíð* hotel (see p.265) ☎464 4270. This cosy café-bar in a converted farmhouse tends to get packed solid around noon when tour buses pass through. There's a broad selection of sandwiches (1000kr), lamb soup (1900kr), burgers (2300kr) and grilled fish with garlic (3500kr), plus cakes, coffee and beer. Daily 10am–10pm.

Myllan In the *Reynihlíð* hotel (see p.265) ☎464 4170. Splash out at this plain but smart restaurant, where much of the food is sourced locally: try the "Country Bliss" (a starter plate of herring, salmon, char, smoked lamb, steam bread and flatbread; 2100kr pp) or the saddle of lamb (3550kr). Daily 6.30–9pm.

The lakeshore

The road curves clockwise around the lakeshore from Reykjahlíð, via the hamlets of **Vogar** and **Skútustaðir**, to where the Laxá drains westwards; from here, the Ringroad crosses the river and heads up the west shore and back to town. This circuit is about 35km long, with several places to make detours: principally at **Grótagjá** hot springs; the rough lavafield at **Dimmuborgir** and **Hverfell** cone, both east of the lake; and **Vindbelgjarfjall**, a peak on Mývatn's northwestern side. Aside from the highly visible wildfowl, keep your eyes peeled for ptarmigan, arctic foxes and maybe even rare **gyrfalcons**. Note that **erosion** is a serious problem at many popular sites and that you should stick to marked paths where you find them.

No tours circuit the lake, so to see it all you really need your own **vehicle** – bicycles can be **rented** in Reykjahlíð. You can of course **walk**; there's a well-marked 8km **trail** linking Reykjahlíð with Grótagjá, Hverfell and Dimmuborgir. To explore away from here, carry *Landmælingar Íslands* Mývatn 1:50,000 map – the Reykjahlíð visitor centre might have these, otherwise Akureyri's bookshops are the nearest source.

Vogar and Grótagjá

Only about 2km from Reykjahlíð, **VOGAR** is a tiny farming hamlet some 500m from the water, from where a gravel road runs 2km northeast to **Grótagjá**, the best-known of Mývatn's flooded fissures. From the outside, the lava is heaped up in a long, 5m-high ridge; entering through a crack, you find yourself in a low-ceilinged tunnel harbouring a couple of clear blue, steaming pools (one for men at 48°C, one for women at 44°C), lit by daylight through the entrance. The drawback is that unless you're here in winter – when the women's pool is just about bearable for a quick immersion (take care on the rough rocks) – Grótagjá is a bit too hot to get into, though it is cooling down each year.

ACCOMMODATION AND EATING   VOGAR

Vogafjós On the lake side of the road ☎464 4303, ⓦvogafjos.is. Three long rows of comfortable pine-and-slate cabins, comprising en-suite doubles neatly furnished in a minimalist Nordic way, plus family rooms sleeping two adults and two children (for the room). Generous buffet breakfast included. Doubles <u>29,500kr</u>, family rooms <u>45,000kr</u>

★ **Vogafjós Restaurant** On the lake side of the road ☎464 4303. Built onto the back of a cowshed, with a view of the animals through a glass panel in the gift shop, this pleasant timber café has large windows overlooking fields to the lake. Aside from coffee and cake, try the "Vogafjós speciality", a platter of smoked lamb, smoked char, *hverabrauð* and home-made relishes (4950kr). June–Aug 7.30am–10pm.

Vogar Þerðaþónusta On the east side of the road ☎464 4399, ⓦvogahraun.is. Simple guesthouse with made-up doubles and sleeping-bag twins, plus a campsite; rooms are pretty small and amenities are shared, but there's a fair-sized lounge area. The dorms have a self-catering kitchen, and there's a pizzeria here too. Restaurant daily noon–11pm. Doubles <u>14,700kr</u>, camping <u>1500kr</u>

Hverfell

Hverfell (also known as Hverfjall) is Mývatn's most easily identified landmark, looking just how a volcano should: broad, conical and strewn with black rubble and rocks, it's a classic **tephra cone**, made of consolidated ash and pumice. At 2500 years old, Hverfell is also a bit younger than the lake, and its rim (400m) presents a satisfying, straightforward climb from the **parking area** 1.5km east off the highway along a gravel track. Two hours is ample time for a slow ascent and circuit of the kilometre-wide caldera, which is a great way to orient yourself: immediately west lie the lake's flat blue waters, its scattering of islands and convoluted shore; views north take in Reykjahlíð, the steaming thermal areas, and the plateau harbouring Krafla; southeast lurks Lúdent, beyond which lava stretches out to the distant string of impressively solid table-top formations of Búrfell, Heilagsdalsfjall and Bláfjall.

6

Dimmuborgir

On the lake road 1km or so south of the Hverfell junction, where the access road runs 1500m east to a car park • Café June–Aug daily 9am–10pm • ☎ 464 1144, ⓦ kaffiborgir.is

Dimmuborgir is a collection of crumbled and contorted lava towers set among birch scrub. Examine the rocks' unexpected and indescribable shapes, none of them very tall but every centimetre differently textured, all finished in tiny twists and spires. The highlight is **Kirkja**, the Church, a giant burst bubble of lava into which around twenty people could comfortably squeeze. Next to the car park, there's a café and a **viewing area** where you can take in Dimmuborgir's weird formations from above.

Höfði

2km south past Dimmuborgir on the lake road • Open access

The private nature park of **Höfði** marks the first specific lakeside stop after Dimmuborgir. Stack-like formations and tiny islets in the crystal-clear waters here attract birds in some numbers, while the redwing-infested birch woodland along the shore offers good cover for watching them. One rarity which nests in the vicinity is the **great northern diver** (known as "loon" in North America); with luck you'll also see the less plentiful red-throated variety, along with scoters and countless Barrow's goldeneyes – this area is their main hangout.

Grænvatn

Rounding Mývatn's southeastern corner, you pass where the lake's **springs** well up from below the surface; they're undetectable except in winter, when their warmth stops the water here from freezing. A kilometre further on, the tiny hamlet of **GARÐUR** marks a 2km road south to **Grænvatn**, a much smaller satellite lake of Mývatn. The lake isn't that interesting but the **turf-roofed farmhouse** here is: built in the late nineteenth century and now one of the oldest buildings in the region, it's still lived in.

Skútustaðir

Three kilometres west of Garður, **SKÚTUSTAÐIR** is a small knot of buildings right by the water comprising a huge roadside parking bay, a church, a **fuel pump** and more flies than anywhere else around the lake. It's known chiefly for its dozen or so closely packed **pseudocraters**, resembling grassy bonsai volcano cones down at the lakeshore, which take an hour to walk around on paths and boardwalks. Pseudocraters form when lava pours over marshland, boiling the water beneath, which bursts through the solidifying crust to form a cone. They occur in clutches around the lake shore, though most of Mývatn's islands are also pseudocraters, including the largest, **Geitey** – a mere 30m high.

ACCOMMODATION AND EATING   **SKÚTUSTAÐIR**

Gígur On the lake side of the road ☎ 460 2000, ⓦ keahotels.is. Rooms are well appointed but surprisingly few overlook the lake (#109 is the best), though superb views from the restaurant certainly compensate. **35,800kr**

6

Kaffi Sel Next to the fuel pump on the south side of the road. Gift shop and café with limited seating, serving a roadhouse menu of lamb soup (1750kr), sandwiches (1050kr) and *pýlsur* (450kr), plus self-service coffee and tea. Daily 8am–10pm.

★ **Laxá** 2km clockwise around the lake from Skútustaðir ☎ 464 1900, ⓦ hotellaxa.is. New complex with Bauhaus-style lines and a retro-Nordic interior whose doubles boast superb feature windows and enormous bathrooms. It's not right at the lake, but there are mountain panoramas in every direction and the hillside location means fewer flies. 38,280kr

Reykhúsíð Skútustöðum Just off the road in front of the church. This family-run smokehouse sells locally caught smoked char, salmon and lamb. As elsewhere in Iceland, where timber is in short supply, they use peat made from compacted sheep dung for smoking, and the results might be coarser than you'd expect. No set opening hours; if there's nobody in, use the intercom provided.

Sel-Hótel Mývatn South of road beside fuel pump ☎ 464 4164, ⓦ myvatn.is. Recently revamped with a smart new wing added, bringing capacity to 58 rooms. The modern en-suite doubles feature Italian-designed furniture; some have vistas of the pseudocraters. 33,500kr

The Laxá

About 4km west from Skútustaðir, the **Laxá** drains quickly out of Mývatn through a collection of low, marshy islands and starts its journey northwest towards the sea at Húsavík. The Ringroad continues west towards Fosshóll and Akureyri, but for the western side of the lake, turn over the **bridge** here onto Route 1. Immediately across the Laxá there's a rough parking area, from where a walking track follows the river's rapids upstream for about 1km – before they head seawards in late June, you'll almost certainly see big groups of **harlequin ducks** here, along with geese, red-necked phalaropes and whooper swans.

Vindbelgjarfjall

From the bridge, Route 1 continues north for 12km along Mývatn's western shore, passing small, black-sand beaches. Beyond rises the unmistakably tall **Vindbelgjarfjall** (529m); there's a parking bay on the main road at a very sharp bend just before Vagnbrekka farm. From here it's a twenty-minute walk along the base of the mountain to where white pegs mark the trail up to the summit; once through lowland heather thickets, it's scree all the way – quite slippery and steep – but the scramble to the cairn marking the summit only takes around thirty minutes, from where there are dramatic **views** of the mountain's steep east face and over the lake.

Neslönd

Between Vindbelgjarfjall and the Reykjahlíð junction, Route 1 clips more **pseudocraters** – less visited and more tightly packed than Skútustaðir's – before passing a track eastwards into **Neslönd**, a marshy, scrubby bird-breeding area. Access is restricted to the track in summer, though you can see plenty of birds on nearby ponds, including divers and grebes.

Fuglasafn Sigurgeirs

At the end of the Neslönd road • Daily 9am–6pm • 1000kr • ☎ 464 4477, ⓦ fuglasafn.is

The **Fuglasafn Sigurgeirs** (Sigurgeir's Bird Museum) is an intelligently presented and informative collection of stuffed birds, covering just about every species that it's possible to see in Iceland, grouped according to habitat – lake, mountain, seashore etc. Captions are bilingual and they've set up telescopes pointing lakewards in the tiny café here, so you can clock up sightings over waffles and rhubarb jam.

Northeast of Mývatn

While Mývatn's immediate surrounds appear fairly stable, the plateau rising just outside Reykjahlíð at **Bjarnarflag** and extending northeast is anything but serene, the barren, pock-marked landscape pouring out lively quantities of steam and – when the mood takes it – lava. This being Iceland, you can see not only how destructive such events have been, but also how their energy has been harnessed. Alongside power stations and even an underground "bakery", there are the **Jarðböðin nature baths**, building on the centuries-old tradition of using the area's plentiful geothermal water for bathing. Beyond here, still on the Ringroad, the bubbling mud pools at **Hverir** are definitely worth a stop en route to the **Krafla volcano**, reached by a detour north along a sealed track. The mountain and the neighbouring plains at **Leirhnjúkur**, still dangerously hot after a particularly violent session during the 1980s, are Mývatn's most geologically active region.

6

Jarðböðin Nature Baths

4km east of Reykjahlíð • Daily: June–Aug 9am–midnight; Sept–May noon–10pm • Summer 3700kr; winter 3000kr • ⓦ jardbodin.is

Bjarnarflag is a thermal zone on the lower slopes of Dalfjall, a long, faulted ridge pushed up by subterranean pressures that runs northeast to Krafla itself. Bjarnarflag has a small geothermal power station (Iceland's first, built in 1969), whose outflow has been harnessed to create the **Jarðböðin Nature Baths**, the local version of Reykjavík's Blue Lagoon. It's an exceptional setting – fractured orange hills rise behind and the poolside overlooks Mývatn itself – where you can loll to your heart's content in milky-blue waters heated to 38–40°C. Just remove any copper or silver jewellery before entering the water, since the high sulphur content of the water can cause discoloration. In addition to the pool, there's a café, hot pot and a couple of steam saunas.

The underground bakery

Near the turno-ff to the nature baths

A brickworks makes a good landmark for locating Bjarnarflag's **underground bakery**. This sounds much more technical that it really is; the "bakery" is simply several small pits dug into the superheated, steaming soil between the road and brickworks, each covered with weighted dustbin lids or sheets of scrap metal. Rye dough is mixed with yeast and molasses in a cardboard milk carton and left underground for a day, where it transforms into neat, rectangular loaves of heavy **hverabrauð** – "steam bread" – which is especially delicious eaten hot with butter. This isn't the only such bakery in Iceland, but it is one of the largest; what isn't made for private consumption is sold through various outlets in Reykjahlíð. Locals will get irate if they catch you lifting the lids, so please leave the ovens alone.

Námafjall

The Ringroad east of Bjarnarflag twists up and over Dalfjall; on the way, look for a big split in the ridges north, marking the line of the Mývatn rift. The high point south of the road's crest is **Námafjall**, streaked in grey gypsum and yellow **sulphur deposits** – these were once mined and exported for use in gunpowder – and there's an easy twenty-minute track to follow from the roadside parking bay through soft mud to the summit's stony outcrop. The whole Mývatn area is spread below; in particular, look for Hrossaberg to the southwest, a large exploded vent with ragged edges simmering quietly away between here and Hverfell.

Hverir

Around 8km from Mývatn

Below Námafjall's steep eastern face you'll find **Hverir**, a large field of **solfataras**: evil-smelling, blue-grey belching mud pools. These are caused by groundwater percolating downwards for over a kilometre to magma levels; heating then forces it back to the surface, where it exits through the sticky red soil at 200°C. It's essential to follow boardwalks and guide ropes here; people have been seriously injured after sinking knee-deep into the scalding pools. These, however, are docile compared with the accompanying **steam vents**, where rocks, gravel and earth have been burst upwards like a bubble to form waist-high, perforated mounds through which vapour screams out ferociously.

Krafla and Viti

Up in the hills north of Hverir, the area around the Krafla volcano has been intermittently erupting for the last three thousand years and shows no signs of cooling down yet. The 7km access road runs north off the Ringroad opposite Hverir, passing right under piping from **Leirbotn** geothermal power station. **Krafla** itself (818m) was last active in the 1720s during a period known as the **Mývatn Fires**, which began when the west side of Krafla exploded in 1724, forming a new crater named **Viti** (Hell). The road ends at a car park in front of Viti, now a deep, aquamarine crater lake on Krafla's steep brown gravel slopes; a slippery track runs around the rim through atmospheric low cloud and plenty of real steam hissing out of bulging vents.

Leirhnjúkur

West of Krafla is **Leirhnjúkur**, a black, compellingly grotesque lavafield whose eighteenth-century eruptions nearly destroyed Reykjahlíð's church. A similar event between 1977 and 1984 reopened the fissures in what came to be called the **Krafla Fires**, and this mass of still-steaming lava rubble is testament to the lasting power of molten rock: thirty years on, and the ground here remains, in places, too hot to touch. Pegged tracks from the parking area mark out relatively safe **trails** around the field, crossing older, vegetated lava before climbing onto the darker, rougher new material, splotches of red or purple marking iron and potash deposits, white or yellow patches indicating live steam vents to be avoided – not least for their intensely unpleasant smell. From the high points you can look north towards where the main area of activity was during the 1980s at **Gjástykki**, a black, steaming swathe between light green hills. As usual, apply common sense to any explorations.

Northwest of Mývatn

There are a couple of historic sites worth a brief stop northwest of Mývatn, on your way between the lake and either Akureyri or Húsavík: **Goðafoss** is an impressive waterfall right beside the Ringroad, while the turf-roofed farm at **Grenjaðarstaður** dates back to the Middle Ages.

Fosshól and Goðafoss

Around halfway between Mývatn and Akureyri along the Ringroad, tiny **FOSSHÓLL** comprises little more than a couple of houses and a fuel pump marking where the Sprengisandur route (see p.325) emerges from Iceland's Interior, and warrants a stop to see where the ice-blue Skjálfandafljöt River tears through horseshoe-shaped basalt canyons in a pair of powerful cataracts. The largest of these, **Goðafoss** (Waterfall of the Gods), is where Þorgeir Ljósvetningagoði – the lawspeaker who decided that Christianity should be Iceland's official religion at the historic Alþing in 1000 – destroyed his pagan statues by pushing them over the falls.

CLOCKWISE FROM TOP LEFT LEIRHNJÚKUR LAVAFIELD; KRAFLA; LAKE MÝVATN (P.260) >

ARRIVAL AND DEPARTURE

FOSSHÓL

By bus Most long-distance services pull in at Fosshól for a few minutes to look at Goðafoss.

Destinations Akureyri (1 daily; 1hr); Egilsstaðir (1 daily; 2hr 55min); Landmannalaugar (1 daily; 10hr); Mývatn (1 daily; 45min); Reykjavík via Sprengisandur (1 daily; 10hr).

ACCOMMODATION

Fosshóll Guesthouse Right by the falls ☎ 464 3108, ⓦ fossholl.is. A cheerful place with a bright yellow exterior and brightly lit interior (though the pink feature wall is probably a mistake). Most of their rooms are simple with shared bathrooms, though they also have slightly cosier and more expensive en-suite doubles. There's a restaurant and bar here too. **19,950kr**

Grenjaðarstaður

Around halfway between Mývatn and Húsavík off Route 87 • June–Aug 10am–6pm • 600kr

Sitting exposed to the prevailing icy winds in a broad valley, **Grenjaðarstaður** is a nineteenth-century church and block of well-insulated turf-roofed farmhouses, now a **museum**. The estate was founded in medieval times (a contemporary altar cloth from the original church is now in the Paris Louvre) when it counted as one of the best holdings in all Iceland, and now comprises the largest collection of period buildings in the country. Most of the rooms are kept as they were when last lived in, full of household items and farming implements from days gone by, though one building has been taken back to its original state, with beaten earth floors and central stone fireplace and kitchen.

Húsavík

HÚSAVÍK is a small, likeable town of 2500 inhabitants hunkered below Húsavíkurfjall on a rare dip in the coastline, the blue-green bay out front patched by cloud shadows and a couple of islands. The ninth-century Swedish rover **Garðar Svavarsson** wintered here while making the first recorded circumnavigation of Iceland; the shelters he built gave Húsavík (House Bay) its name. It's also said that two of his slaves decamped during his stay and established a farm, though later historians – looking for nobler lineages than this – tend to ignore the possibility that they were the mainland's first permanent residents.

The area's economy focused on sheep farming until hit by the nationwide **depression** of the late nineteenth century – caused in part by the 1875 eruption of Viti in Askja (see p.330) – when many switched to fishing or emigrated to Canada or the US. Nowadays, Húsavík has become Iceland's premier centre for **whale watching**; the town is now so dependent on this summer income that Húsavík led criticism within Iceland of the government's decision to resume commercial whaling in late 2006.

The harbour

Húsavík's **harbour**, where international cruise ships sometimes dock, is the place to book and board a whale-watching cruise; over the road, the town's landmark wood-and-tin **church**, with complex eaves and a green painted roof, dates from 1907 (though a large, fifteenth-century crucifix from an earlier structure is now in the National Museum in Reykjavík). Views west across wide **Skjálfandi bay** take in the heights of the peninsula opposite, inhabited until its mountainous terrain prevented roads and power being supplied in the early 1960s, after which its scattered farms were abandoned. Look north up the coast and you may be able to spot **Lundey**, a small, flat-topped island inhabited through the summer by 150,000 puffins.

Whale Museum

By the harbour • April, May & Sept daily 9am–4pm; June–Aug daily 8.30am–6.30pm; Oct–March Mon–Fri 10am–noon & 1–3.30pm • 1400kr • ⓦ whalemuseum.is

Húsavík's excellent **Whale Museum** is housed in an old slaughterhouse. Inside, an informative collection of models, photos, relics and even ten full-size **skeletons** unnervingly suspended above you – all taken from beached or drowned whales – along with several continually playing videos, fill you in on cetacean biology, the history of whaling in Iceland and today's environmental threats caused by pollution. Pick of the exhibits are pieces of tremendously hairy **baleen plates**, with which filter-feeding species strain their nourishing plankton diet like slurping soup through a moustache.

6

Húsavík library and museum

Back from the harbour along Stórigarður • June–Aug daily 10am–6pm; Sept–May Mon–Fri 10am–4pm • 600kr

Pick of the exhibits in Húsavík's **library** and **museum** are bits of medieval **weapons** found near the town, the impressive **family tree** of a local woman born in 1904 showing her descendants back to the time of the Settlement, and a stuffed **polar bear**, this one killed in 1969 on Grímsey after drifting over from Greenland on an ice floe. Downstairs is devoted to maritime history and includes full-sized rowing and fishing boats, but don't miss the eccentric collection of one hundred thousand **beer bottle labels**, zealously put together by a local man who, oddly, was teetotal; the labels are kept in folders by the entrance to the maritime section.

ARRIVAL AND DEPARTURE   HÚSAVÍK

By plane Húsavík airport is 10km southwest of town. Flights are operated by Eagle Air (ⓣ 562 4200, ⓦ eagleair .is).

Destinations Reykjavík (10 weekly; 45min).
By bus Buses stop at the N1 fuel station on Garðarsbraut. From mid-June until the end of Aug SBA (ⓦ sba.is)

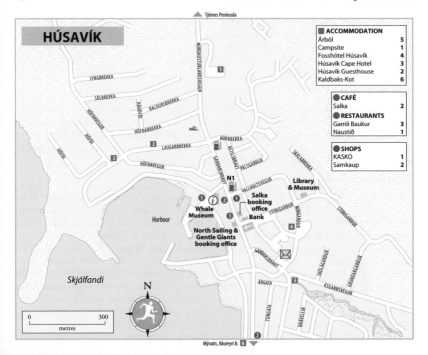

6

WHALE WATCHING IN HÚSAVÍK

The whale-watching industry in Húsavík started after whalers hit by a 1989 moratorium realized that there was still good money to be made by taking tourists out to find the creatures. Despite the resumption of commercial whaling in 2006, whale stocks off Húsavík remain high, and the chances of seeing some are good. Dolphins, porpoises and medium-sized **minke whales** are encountered most frequently, with much larger **humpback whales** runners-up; these are identified by lengthy flippers and their habit of "breaching" – making spectacular, crashing leaps out of the water. Similar-looking **fin whales** are the next most likely candidates, with rarer sightings of colossal **blue whales**, **orca** and square-headed **sperm whales** (for some reason, only males of the last species are seen in Iceland's waters).

Cruises generally head directly across the bay from Húsavík – this can be rough in a northerly wind – where you'll come across puffins and other seabirds fishing; the whales obviously move around a lot but boat crews are expert at locating them. Most of the time you'll see little more than an animal's back, fluke or tail breaking the surface in the middle distance, and perhaps jets of water vapour as they breathe; if you're lucky, whales swim right under the boats, lie on their sides looking up at you, or breach. And you might, of course, see nothing at all.

Whale-watching **trips** run at least daily from May until September, and cost about 10,000kr for three hours, or 16,000kr including puffin-watching around Lundey. Húsavík's three **operators** are Gentle Giants (T 464 1500, W gentlegiants.is), North Sailing (T 464 7272, W northsailing.is) and Salka (T 464 3999, W salkawhalewatching.is); **ticket booths** are at the top of the harbour and it's best to buy in advance. There's little to choose between the operators: all use wooden whaling ships seating around forty people – North Sailing's rigged sailship is the most attractive – and provide essential full waterproof gear, hot drinks and biscuits. Bring binoculars and plenty of warm clothing.

opearate a twice-daily Húsavík–Mývatn bus, and a daily Akureyri–Húsavík–Ásbyrgi–Vesturdalur–Dettifoss service. At Dettifoss, you can connect with buses to Mývatn. Strætó bus #79 (T 540 2700, W straeto.is) runs year-round on an Akureyri–Húsavík–Ásbyrgi–Kópasker-Raufarhöfn–Þórshöfn route, but you need to call the day before to check on times. Note that there's no onwards service in this direction to Vopnafjörður and Egilsstaðir.

Destinations Akureyri (3 daily; 1hr); Ásbyrgi (2 daily; 1hr 15min); Dettifoss (1 daily; 2hr 45min); Kópasker (6 weekly; 1hr 25min); Þórshöfn (6 weekly; 3hr 30min); Raufarhöfn (6 weekly; 2hr 15min); Reykjahlíð (2 daily; 45min); Vesturdalur (1 daily; 2hr 35min).

By car Húsavík is 90km northeast from Akureyri along Route 85, and 55km northwest from Mývatn via Route 87.

INFORMATION

Tourist information The helpful tourist office is inside the whale museum by the harbour (daily May & Sept 10am–5pm; June–Aug 9am–7pm; T 464 4300, W visithusavik.is).

Services Banks with ATMs, two fuel stations, the KASKO supermarket (Mon–Sat 10am–6pm) and swimming pool (Mon–Fri 6.45am–9pm, Sat & Sun 10am–6pm) are all on Garðarsbraut. There's a better-stocked but pricier Samkaup supermarket (Mon–Sat 10am–7pm, Sun noon–7pm) on the main road west of town.

ACCOMMODATION

★**Árból** Ásgarðsvegur 2 T 464 2220, W arbol.is. Warmly hospitable guesthouse in an early twentieth-century wooden building, with bright doubles, triples and quads; room rates include breakfast. Dorms are available out of season only; contact them for prices. Advance booking essential. **19,000kr**

Campsite Alongside the main road at the northern side of town T 464 4300. This big sloping field has toilets and showers, a laundry, a kitchen/diner with cookers and a small children's playground. **1200kr**

Fosshótel Húsavík Ketilsbraut 22 T 464 1220, W fosshotel.is. Welcoming place with seventy cosy rooms, a conference centre and an in-house restaurant. Try for rooms 304, 320–329 or 404, which all have balconies and reasonable views seawards. The imitation shingle flooring is a mistake, though. **30,000kr**

Húsavík Cape Hotel Höfði 24 T 463 3399, W husavikhotels.com. This newly renovated 1950s building overlooks the harbour and features smallish, motel-style bedrooms with tiled floors and firm beds. They also operate a hostel in town, though you check in here. Breakfast included for both locations. Hostel dorms **5000kr**, hotel doubles **31,000kr**

Húsavík Guesthouse Laugarbrekka 16 T 463 3399,

@husavikhotels.com. Bland and box-like from the outside, but a beautifully converted 1947 house inside, with polished wooden floors and period furniture in the dining room and double rooms. Rate includes breakfast. **18,500kr**

Kaldbaks-Kot Kaldbakur, some 3km south of Húsavík

via the main road ☎464 1504, @cottages.is. Set on a rise overlooking the sea and town, these self-contained pine cabins (sleeping 2–8) have TV, kitchenette and bathroom. The geothermal heating is a plus in winter; there's also a hot tub, barbecue area and free fishing on a nearby pond. **21,000kr**

EATING

Gamli Baukur Hafnarstétt ☎464 2442. Wood-panelled, mid-range place at the harbour, where top marks go to the fried saltfish with mash and red-onion sauce (3450kr), and arctic char with barley (3390kr). They sometimes get live bands in, too. Daily 11.30am–9pm.

★**Naustið** Hafnarstétt ☎464 1520. Family-run restaurant inside a long, yellow, corrugated-iron shed at the harbour, best for the simple, filling seafood. Try the langoustine (4500kr) or the famous seafood soup, thick with fish, prawns and veggies (1750kr) – perfect for thawing out after a whale-watching trip. Daily noon–10pm.

Salka Garðarsbraut ☎464 2551. Old warehouse behind the Whale Museum on the harbourside, now converted into a spacious café-bar. Lunchtime mains are reasonable value considering the portion size, especially the cod (3750kr), huge Salka burger (1990kr) and shellfish soup (1890kr). Their pizzas are popular too. Daily 11.30am–10pm.

Tjörnes

North of Húsavík along Route 85, **Tjörnes** is a rather broad, stubby peninsula with brilliant sea views. A few kilometres from town in this direction there's a roadside monument to the locally born patriotic poet **Einar Benediktsson**, one of the key figures of Iceland's early twentieth-century nationalist movement. Past here, now 5km from Húsavík, the headland drops to a low **beach**, reached along vehicle tracks from the road, where you should find the usual melange of **seabirds**, including purple sandpipers, puffins, black guillemots and gannets; in spring, look out for marine ducks and divers (loons) heading to Mývatn. Walking along the beach, it's not unusual to find yourself being followed offshore by **seals**.

Tjörneshöfn

Around 10km from Húsavík, beside some sheer cliffs, a track off the main road descends to **Tjörneshöfn**, a tiny boatshed and harbour looking straight out to puffin-infested Lundey. A shingle beach stretches in both directions below the cliffs, though a small river to the north may stop you heading that way; south there's plenty of seaweed and Pleistocene-period **fossilized shells** in the headland's layered, vertical faces.

Öxarfjörður

Back on Route 85, Tjörnes' northern tip is marked by the **Voladalstorfa lighthouse**, past which there's a roadside viewpoint with vistas out over the staggeringly blue waters of **Öxarfjörður** to Kópasker (see p.280). Puffins and fulmars nest on the grass-topped cliffs right beside the viewpoint; on a clear day it's possible to pick out a very remote Grímsey to the northwest, and **Mánárayjar**, a couple of closer volcanic islets that haven't experienced any stirrings for over a century.

Jökulsárgljúfur National Park

Cutting into the northeast's rocky inland plains, **Jökulsárgljúfur National Park** – an isolated fragment of the enormous Vatnajökull National Park (see p.309) – encloses a 35km stretch of the **Jökulsá á Fjöllum**, Iceland's second-longest river. Originating

6

almost 200km south at Vatnajökull, for much of its journey through the park the river flows through the mighty **Jökulsárgljúfur**, a canyon which is 120m deep and 500m wide in places, forming several exceptional waterfalls and an endless array of rock formations. There are two key sights: the horseshoe-shaped **Ásbyrgi** canyon in the north of the park, an hour's drive from Húsavík; and **Dettifoss**, Europe's most powerful waterfall, at the park's southern boundary near Mývatn. In between, the silt-laden river cuts its way between stark grey gorge walls, all set against an unusually fertile backdrop: over half of the country's **native plant** species are found here, and in summer the heathland above the gorge is lush and splashed pink and white with flowers.

Ásbyrgi and Dettifoss are connected by hiking trails and two **roads** either side of the gorge: westerly **Route 862**, which is rough gravel except for the final 24km stretch between Dettifoss and the Ringroad (there's long been talk of surfacing the entire thing); and easterly **Route 864**, which is gravel the whole way. Note that both roads are closed through winter.

Map captions:
- Húsavík
- Kópasker
- Jökulsárgljúfur National Park Visitor Centre
- N1 Roadhouse
- Ásholði
- N
- Ásbyrgi
- 862
- 85
- 864
- Rauðhólar
- Hljóðaklettar
- Jökulsá á Fjöllum
- Hólmatungur
- Vigabjarg
- 0 2 kilometres
- Hafragilsfoss
- **ACCOMMODATION**
  - Ásbyrgi campsite — 1
  - Dettifoss campsite — 3
  - Vesturdalur campsite — 2
- P Dettifoss
- Grímsstaðir
- Selfoss
- **JÖKULSÁRGLJÚFUR NATIONAL PARK**
- Ring Road & Mývatn

Ásbyrgi

The northern end of the national park is marked by an N1 **roadhouse** in the middle of nowhere on Route 85, behind which you'll find a golf course, the National Parks Visitor Centre and the park's main campsite. Here the gorge is very broad and waterless, the river having shifted course long ago leaving a flat grassland between low walls. You can get a good view of this from **Eyjar**, a long, flat-topped island of rock near the campsite which can be scaled easily enough from its northern end.

Better, though, is **Ásbyrgi**, where the road dead-ends 5km south at a pond fringed in birch and pine woods, beyond which rises a vertical, 90m-high amphitheatre of dark rock patched in orange lichens, home to a colony of gurgling fulmars. Legend has it that this is the hoofprint of the Norse god Óðinn's eight-legged steed **Sleipnir**, though geologists believe that the formation was carved by a series of titanic *jökulhlaups*, volcanically induced flash floods that exploded out from underneath Vatnajökull. Just avoid it in the late afternoon, when the sun catches the cliffs: it looks fantastic, but half of Iceland descends to watch. The view from the top is spectacular, too, though to get up here you need to follow the first few kilometres of the Dettifoss trail (see box opposite).

ARRIVAL AND DEPARTURE

By bus Buses pull up at the roadhouse. From mid-June until the end of Aug SBA (ⓦsba.is) opearate a daily Akureyri–Húsavík–Ásbyrgi–Vesturdalur–Dettifoss service; at Dettifoss, you can connect with buses to Mývatn. Strætó bus #79 (ⓣ540 2700, ⓦstraeto.is) stops year-round on its Akureyri–Húsavík–Ásbyrgi–Kópasker-Raufarhöfn–

Þórshöfn route; call the day before to check on times.

Destinations Akureyri (2 daily; 2hr 10min), Dettifoss (1 daily; 1hr 30min); Húsavík (2 daily; 45min); Kópasker (6 weekly; 35min); Raufarhöfn (6 weekly; 1hr); Vesturdalur (1 daily; 20min); Þórshöfn (6 weekly; 2hr 15min).

By car Ásbyrgi is 60km from Húsavík on Route 85.

ÁSBYRGI

INFORMATION

National Parks Visitor Centre The informative office at Ásbyrgi (daily: May & Sept 10am–4pm; June–Aug 9am–7pm; ⓣ470 7100, ⓦvjp.is) organizes camping permits and has general park information.

Maps The Visitor Centre sells a national park map (300kr), marked with hiking trails; Mál og menning's Akureyri-Mývatn-Dettifoss sheet also has a detailed section for Jökulsárgljúfur.

Activities Active North (ⓣ858 7080, ⓦactivenorth.is) offers horseriding and mountain biking around Ásbyrgi through the summer.

Services The N1 roadhouse (daily 9am–6pm) – run by a Thai family – sells fuel, fast food and a good range of camping-oriented supplies: groceries, refrigerated barbecue meat packs, bread, milk, camping gas and other essentials.

6

THE ÁSBYRGI TO DETTIFOSS HIKE

It takes around two days to hike the straightforward 35km route from Ásbyrgi down the west side of the gorge to Dettifoss, with an overnight stop along the way at **Vesturdalur** (alternatively, the day-return hike to Vesturdalur makes a good trip in itself). Take a tent, cooking gear and all supplies with you; in summer, SBA (ⓦsba.is) runs a daily Akureyri–Húsavík–Ásbyrgi–Vesturdalur–Dettifoss bus, with a connecting Dettifoss–Mývatn service, so you could arrange a drop-off or pick-up along the way.

The **trailhead** is signposted behind Ásbyrgi's National Parks Visitor Centre, soon climbing along the clifftop to exit tight birch scrub onto open heathland. Not far along, the path divides: continuing along the gorge for 3.8km will find you looking north from the rounded rocks atop Ásbyrgi, while bearing east through open scrub and woodland brings you to the brink of the gorge, where jutting rocks offer a good perch for looking down at the grey river rushing smoothly across a shingle bed. The trail now follows the gorge south, via intermittent sections of green heath and ashy basalt, joining up with the path from Ásbyrgi and then entering a slow section of ashy sand. Once through this, a side track makes the short climb to **Rauðhólar**, the remains of a scoria cone whose vivid red, yellow and black gravel is a shock after the recently monochrome backdrop. Past here you descend to **Hjóðaklettar**, where the noise of the river funnelling violently through a constriction is distorted by hexagonal-columned hollows in huge, shattered cliffs. A couple of kilometres away, and some 14km from the Vistior Centre depending on your route, the **Vesturdalur campsite** (June 6–Sept 15; 1200kr) occupies a slightly boggy meadow with toilets and sinks for washing up; there are no showers or cooking facilities.

Over the next 8km, the trail moves above the river and then down to the marshy **Hólmatungur**, where underground springs pool up to create three short rivers which flow quickly into the Jökulsá through some thick vegetation. The trail crosses the largest of these tributaries, the **Hólmá**, on a bridge just above where it tumbles into the main river. Upstream from here on the Jökulsá's east bank, the prominent face of **Vígabjarg** marks where the formerly mighty Vígarbjargfoss ripped through a narrow gorge, before a change in the river's course dried it to a trickle. From here it's another 8km to the 27m-high **Hafragilsfoss**, an aesthetically pleasing set of falls whose path through a row of volcanic craters has exposed more springs, which mix their clear waters with the Jökulsá's muddier glacial flood (there's a particularly good view of Hafragilsfoss off Route 864, on the eastern side of the gorge).

A final tricky couple of kilometres of scrambling brings you to Dettifoss and the sealed road south to the Ringroad; if you're not catching the bus straight away, there's a basic **campsite** nearby – see p.278.

6

ACCOMMODATION

Ásbyrgi campsite Close to the visitor centre and N1 fuel station. The national park's main campsite. The facilities include a laundry with drying cupboards, barbecue and tables, payphone, children's play area and shelter (showers are extra). Mid-May to Sept. **1500kr**

Dettifoss

Some 30km south of Ásbyrgi on the park's southern border

Dettifoss waterfall marks where the violent, dirty-white Jökulsá á Fjöllum River rips across a twisted basalt bed before dropping 45m with enough force to send spray billowing hundreds of metres skywards. There are **lookouts** on both sides of the river, but the best – and closest – vantages are from the east, where you can stand right at the top of the falls and look into the outflow canyon, which is obscured by the overhanging cliff edge on the western side. It's also worth continuing a further kilometre upstream to **Selfoss**, where a diagonal fault across the river has created a broad, 10m-high cataract.

ARRIVAL AND DEPARTURE   DETTIFOSS

By bus Scheduled SBA buses between Akureyri, Húsavík, Ásbergi, Vesturdalur and Dettifoss, and the separate Mývatn–Dettifoss bus, all use Route 862.
Destinations Akureyri (1 daily; 5hr); Ásbyrgi (1 daily; 4hr); Húsavík (1 daily; 3hr 45min); Reykjahlíð (1 daily; 1hr); Vesturdalur (1 daily; 1hr).
By car Dettifoss is most easily reached by taking the Ringroad east from Mývatn for 26km and then turning north along a sealed 24km stretch of Route 862 to a car park, from where it's a 500m walk on rough trails to the west side of the falls. Route 862 continues as a gravel road to Ásbyrgi and Route 85 from here. Alternatively, Route 864 runs down between Route 85 and the Ringroad via the east side of the falls, but is gravel all the way.

ACCOMMODATION

Dettifoss campsite This free campsite, with no facilities, is intended for hikers only. There's a toilet nearby at the Dettifoss car park. Permits and exact directions are available from park offices at Ásbyrgi and Mývatn. **Free**

The northeast

Iceland's extreme **northeast** corner lacks any great sights and Route 85 between Ásbyrgi and the town of **Vopnafjörður** traverses a barren, underpopulated countryside (most people left in the late nineteenth century after the volcanic activity at Askja had sterilized the region). Having said this, if you want to escape Iceland's busier tourist trails, this is where to come: the scattering of small fishing towns and an understated landscape of moorland and small beaches have their own quiet appeal, while the **Langanes peninsula**'s hiking potential is virtually untapped. Don't forget that you're almost inside the **Arctic Circle** here, and summer nights are virtually nonexistent, the

HVALREKI!

The northeast's score of little black-sand and shingle beaches are strewn with two valuable commodities: huge quantities of **driftwood**, mostly pine trunks floated over from Siberia on the currents; and a disproportionate number of **stranded whales**. The latter were once something of a windfall for local landowners (the term *hvalreki*, literally "whale wreck", is used nowadays for "jackpot"), providing meat, oil, bone and various tradeable bits, such as sperm-whale teeth. In saga times, people would actually fight for possession of these riches, but today a whale stranding is a bit of a burden, as the law demands that the landowner is responsible for disposing of the carcass – not an easy matter in the case of a thirty-tonne sperm whale.

CLOCKWISE FROM TOP MALE HARLEQUIN DUCK (P.263); JARÐBÖÐIN NATURE BATHS (P.269); ÞÓRGEIRSDYS LIGHTHOUSE, HRAUNHAFNARTANGI (P.280)>

sun just dipping below the horizon at midnight – conversely, winter days are only a couple of hours long. As for **public transport**, Strætó buses run year-round along Route 85 as far as Þórshöfn, but you'll need your own transport to reach Vopnafjörður.

Melrakkaslétta

Lying fractionally outside the Arctic Circle, **Melrakkaslétta** (Arctic Fox Plain) forms Iceland's northernmost peninsula. The empty tundra might not look that inspiring, but Melrakkaslétta has nearly as much birdlife as Mývatn: a coastline of shingle and sand beaches pulls in plenty of waders, while the tundra and an associated mass of small, fragmented lakes attract big ground-nesting colonies of eider ducks and arctic terns, as well as whimbrel and the rare **grey phalarope**, as well as other shore birds (roadsides are dotted with orange warning signs marked *Fuglar á vegi*, "Birds on road"). To cap all this, Melrakkaslétta is a pit stop for barnacle geese, arctic redpoll and knot (red-breasted sandpiper) in transit between Europe and Greenland or Canada – they pass through in late April and early May, and return with young in September.

Melrakkaslétta has two tiny settlements, **Kópasker** and **Raufarhöfn**, both much reduced in circumstance from former glory days of fishing. The main road across Melrakkaslétta, **Route 85**, manages to skip both while providing fantastic views of the tussocky tundra inland, but it's worth sticking to coastal Route 870, which takes you as far north as you can possibly get on the mainland.

Kópasker

Part-way up Melrakkaslétta's west coast, the port of **KÓPASKER** (Seal-pup Skerry) looks small at a distance, but is actually minute, with an outlying church marking a short side road off the highway into a simple square of streets beside the harbour. The church is next to a Settlement-era **assembly site**, giving Kópasker a surprisingly venerable historical anchor, but otherwise the town is best known for suffering a severe force-eight **earthquake** in January 1976, thanks to activity at Krafla (see p.270) – the eastern side of the village was almost totally destroyed.

ARRIVAL AND INORMATION   KÓPASKER

By bus Strætó (☎ 540 2700, ⊛ straeto.is) stop at the harbour. Call in advance to check the schedule.
Destinations Akureyri (6 weekly; 3hr 25min); Ásbyrgi (6 weekly; 30min); Húsavík (6 weekly; 1hr 15min); Þórshöfn

(6 weekly; 1hr 55min); Raufarhöfn (6 weekly; 50min).
Services Kópasker's bank with ATM, post office, supermarket/café (Mon–Fri 10am–9pm, Sat noon–9pm, Sun noon–6pm) and fuel station are clustered together at the harbour.

ACCOMMODATION AND EATING

Campsite On the left just as you enter town over the cattle grid. This tiny free campsite is moderately sheltered, with picnic tables, washing-up area, and a single block of toilets and showers. **Free**
Youth Hostel Akurgerði 7 ☎ 465 2314, ⊛ hostel.is. A

warm, homely place with a helpful owner who can advise on hiking and generally exploring the area. There's a good kitchen, shared bathrooms, a library and large CD collection to browse through. Despite Kópasker's relative isolation, it can get busy in season. Dorms **4550kr**, doubles **12,400kr**

Hraunhafnartangi and the Arctic Circle

From Kópasker, Route 870 cuts between a string of early nineteenth-century cinder cones before heading 40km up to mainland Iceland's northernmost extremity at **Hraunhafnartangi** – a mere 2.5km outside the **Arctic Circle**. It's marked by the square-sided **Þórgeirsdys lighthouse**; to reach it, leave the road on the very sharp turning and take a rocky path that follows the bay's shoreline, heading for the "No Entry" vehicle sign ahead of you. The anchorage here, beside the lighthouse, was first used during the Middle Ages when pack ice regularly closed the harbour in nearby Raufarhöfn; climb the loosely piled stone sea wall to see the grey-blue Arctic Ocean pounding the far side.

According to *Frostbræðingasaga*, the **cairn** beside the lighthouse is the final resting place of the warrior after whom the lighthouse is named, one Þorgeir Hávarsson; he once slew fourteen men in defence of this place.

Raufarhöfn

Iceland's northernmost town, **RAUFARHÖFN** sits on the Melrakkaslétta's eastern coast some 54km from Kópasker and 10km beyond Hraunhafnartangi. In the 1960s, Raufarhöfn was at the core of Iceland's herring industry and the town's salting plant provided seasonal work that attracted a floating population of thousands. Times have changed, however: the 1990s saw Raufarhöfn's prosperity ebb away as demand for herring dried up, and today the plant limps on by freezing fish for export. Ongoing construction of the **Arctic Henge** – a contrived Nordic version of a megalithic stone circle, easily visible on a rise above town – is an attempt to lure back visitors, and rock-bottom property prices have lured a few bohemian escapees away from Reykjavík, but there's little sign here of the tourist-led recovery that's sweeping the rest of the country.

6

ARRIVAL AND INFORMATION   RAUFARHÖFN

By bus Strætó (☎540 2700, ⓦstraeto.is) stop along the main street. Call in advance to check the schedule.
Destinations Akureyri (6 weekly; 4hr 10min); Ásbyrgi (6 weekly; 1hr 15min); Húsavík (6 weekly; 2hr 10min); Kópasker (6 weekly; 45min); Þórshöfn (6 weekly; 1hr 15min).

Services Raufarhöfn's bank, fuel station and general store are all on the 150m-long main road as it runs through town. There's also a new, well-signposted swimming pool near the campsite.

ACCOMMODATION

Campsite Skólabraut ☎465 1144. Free site at Raufarhöfn's south exit with the usual no-frills, basic facilities: an encircling storm wall, level ground, showers and toilets, sink for washing up and electricity hook-ups for campervans. **Free**
Hreiðrið (The Nest) Aðalbraut 16 ☎472 9930, ⓦnesthouse.is. Even more spartan exterior than the competition, but equally sound once you're through the door. Doubles and triples have shared bathrooms and use

of a small kitchen; the studio apartment is self-contained. Doubles **13,500kr**, studio **22,000kr**
Norðurljós Aðalbraut 2 ☎465 1233, ⓦhotelnordurljos .is. This bleak, stormproof box of a building overlooks the harbour, but it's surprisingly warm and comfortable inside and the charming owners have done their best to make it a welcoming place to stay. Rooms are plain but clean, and there's a lookout deck from the restaurant-bar – the only place to eat in town. **21,000kr**

Rauðanes

About halfway along the 60km coastal strip between Raufarhöfn and Þórshöfn, at Melrakkaslétta's southeastern corner, an attractive headland named **Rauðanes** pokes out to sea, and is a great spot to stretch your legs for a few hours. There's a parking bay 1km up a bumpy gravel road off Route 85, from where an easy 7km marked **footpath** takes you to tall, layered cliffs, caves, a couple of beaches and plenty of surf and birdlife – including a puffin colony on the northernmost skerry.

Þórshöfn

Likeable **ÞÓRSHÖFN** is a compact, busy place, though it's nothing more than a knot of essential services grouped around a T-junction, just north of Route 85. Despite the harbour and fish factory being pretty inactive nowadays, Þórshöfn has the only fuel and well-stocked supermarket for a fair way in any direction; the town is also set at the base of the goose-necked **Langanes peninsula**, offering hikes across grassy fells and moorland out to an uninhabited coast.

The Langanes peninsula

A 35km-long fog-bound prong dividing the Arctic Ocean from a warmer North Atlantic, the **Langanes peninsula** juts northeast from Þórshöfn. Most of the farms here have been abandoned, but gravel **Route 869** runs part of the way up – pretty risky in a normal car, even with extreme care – though you'll have to hike the final 20km to the Fontur lighthouse at Langanes' tip. A major target along the way is **Skoruvíkurbjarg** on the peninsula's northernmost edge, a grassy clifftop with views down on a busy **gannet colony** occupying an offshore rock stack 50m below – bring a camera. Across from here on the south coast, scattered ruins at **Skálar** are all that remains of a once busy hamlet that, until the 1930s, was a seasonal trading post for Faroese fishermen.

6

ARRIVAL AND INFORMATION

By bus Strætó (☎ 540 2700, ⓦ straeto.is) terminate here on their almost-daily run from Akureyri. Call in advance to check the schedule.

Destinations Akureyri (6 weekly; 5hr 10min); Ásbyrgi (6 weekly; 2hr 35min); Húsavík (6 weekly; 3hr 20min); Kópasker (6 weekly; 1hr 45min); Raufarhöfn (6 weekly; 1hr).

Services The road enters Þórshöfn from the south, and runs past the bank (ATM) and N1 fuel station (which has the last fuel for at least 80km) to an intersection. Turn right here, and the road heads uphill towards Langanes past the Samkaup supermarket (Mon–Fri 9.30am–6pm, Sat 10am–2pm) and excellent swimming pool (Mon–Thurs 8am–8pm, Fri 8am–7pm, Sat 10am–2pm).

ACCOMMODATION AND EATING

Báran Eyrarvegur 3; turn seawards at the N1 ☎ 468 1250. The town's café, restaurant and bar in one, serving snacks and light meals (lamb soup, Thai curry, fishballs, spaghetti) for under 2000kr a dish. Comfy sofas for the TV, and candles for the marble table tops. Gets very busy in the evenings and at weekends. Mon–Fri 11am–1am, Sat 5pm–3am, Sun 5pm–10pm.

Campsite Up near the church. Free site on a flat, grassy area; there's a toilet and sink, but you'll need to head to the town's swimming pool (see above) for a shower. <u>Free</u>

★**Ytra Lón** 15km northeast of Þórshöfn along the Langanes road ☎ 846 6448, ⓦ hostel.is. This snug and friendly self-catering IYHA youth hostel is located on a working sheep farm, and makes a great base for exploring the area. They have four-bed dorms and doubles (both with shared bathroom), and self-contained apartments in a newer wing. They'll collect from Þórshöfn with advance notice. Year-round. Dorms <u>4500kr</u>, doubles <u>10,500kr</u>, apartments <u>15,500kr</u>

Bakkafjörður

Some 40km southeast from Þórshöfn along Route 85, **BAKKAFJÖRÐUR** is an isolated cliff-top community of rich, reclusive fishermen, some 5km off the main road. As the region's smallest village, it endures much "butt of the world"-type humour, and in truth there's not much here beyond the obligatory salting plant, a self-service **fuel pump** and a tiny **store**, located at the end of the one and only main road overlooking the sea. But Bakkafjörður is also the most distant settlement from Reykjavík, and if that appeals, you might want to pitch a tent here (see below) and spend a day hiking over the humpy **Digranes headland** and around a rocky coastline to the Svartnes lighthouse.

ACCOMMODATION

Campsite Through town on the right ☎ 468 1515. Free site on a huge grassy expanse; there's an amenities block

with toilet, shower and washing-up sink, though little protection from the weather. <u>Free</u>

Vopnafjörður

Set at the base of a broad inlet on Route 85, **VOPNAFJÖRÐUR** is a relatively sizeable town of two parallel streets arrayed along the narrow, rocky finger of the Kolbeinstangi peninsula, and is famed for its warm weather and salmon fishing. The surrounding area featured in several interconnected Settlement-era tales of clan feuding known as the **Vopnafjörð sagas** – appropriately enough, Vopnafjörður means "Weapons Fjord". Today, Vopnafjörður is really just somewhere to pause where routes to Egilsstaðir, Mývatn and the northeast meet, though there's an interesting folk museum at nearby **Bustarfell** (see opposite) and the region's only thermal pool at **Selárdalur**.

East Iceland Emigration Centre

Kaupvangur 2 • June to mid-Aug Mon & Thurs 12.30–5.30pm, or on request • Donation • ☎ 473 1200, Ⓦ vesturfarinn.is

After the lands southwest of Vopnafjörður were sterilized by the 1875 eruption of Viti in Askja (see p.330), the town became an **emigration point** to the US and Canada for around two thousand impoverished farmers and their families. Canada, which at the time had a "populate or perish" policy, offered subsidized passages for anyone wanting to migrate, and sent ships to take them. The **East Iceland Emigration Centre**, in a restored, yellow-painted corrugated-iron warehouse next to the fish factory, has extensive records and a small photo exhibition on this slice of Vopnafjörður's history, along with a few cases of stuffed birds.

6

Selárdalur pool

About 7km north of Vopnafjörður • Pool daily 7am–11pm • 500kr

From Route 85, a good side road (signed "Selárdalslaug") leads 3km northwest through the Selár valley down to the salmon-rich **Selá** river, where a small **swimming pool** by the water, complete with basic changing rooms and showers, utilizes the northeast coast's only economically viable hot spring.

ARRIVAL AND INFORMATION · VOPNAFJÖRÐUR

By car There is no public transport to Vopnafjörður. To the north, Route 85 runs 65km to Þórshöfn; east is the direct 80km Route 917 to Egilsstaðir (see p.286), though this mountainous gravel road can be closed by snow even in summer; Route 85 continues southwest to join the Ringroad 60km west of Egilsstaðir and 75km east of Mývatn.

Tourist information There's a tourist office inside the Emigration Centre (summer daily 10am–6pm; ☎ 473 1331). **Services** The bank and post office are near the church on Lónabraut; Kauptún supermarket (Mon–Fri 9.30am–6pm, Sat noon–4pm) is beside the Emigration Centre.

ACCOMMODATION AND EATING

Campsite Hamrahlíð 15 ☎ 473 300. Hedges and rocky outcrops create a windbreak; there's a toilet, shower and washing-up sink. Find the brightly coloured school, and it's just uphill across the road. Camping per person **350kr**, plus tent **700kr**

Tangi Hafnarbyggd 17 ☎ 473 1203, Ⓦ hoteltangi.com. The comfortable but characterless modern interior is greatly enhanced by the hospitable staff, with a choice of either shared-bath or en-suite doubles. Their restaurant has a decent range of lamb, fish, chicken, pasta and pizza dishes from about 2000kr. Restaurant daily for lunch and dinner. **19,500kr**

Bustarfell

About 18km south of Vopnafjörður along Route 85 • June 10 to Sept 10 daily 10am–6pm • 700kr • ☎ 471 2211

Bustarfell is an open-air **museum** featuring six well-preserved, turf-gabled farm buildings. The farm was founded in 1770 and has been restored and furnished to reflect what it was like when last occupied in 1966: sepia-toned photos, farm equipment, lamps fuelled by shark or seal oil, and pantries full of wooden storage tubs. Various events through the year bring the place back to life, with people dressing in period costumes – call in advance for dates.

Eastern and southeast Iceland

JÖKULSÁRLÓN

Eastern and southeast Iceland

The 550km strip covering eastern and southeast Iceland a takes in a quarter of the country's coastal fringe, plus some rugged highlands and a good chunk of Europe's largest ice cap. Set on the Ringroad halfway around the country from Reykjavík, Egilsstaðir makes a good base for excursions around Lögurinn lake, where you'll find some saga history, waterfalls and unusually extensive woodlands; or even for an assault on the highlands around Kárahnjúkar and Snæfell, the latter eastern Iceland's tallest peak. The East Fjords feature a sprinkling of picturesque communities – including the port of Seyðisfjörður, with its weekly international ferry – though the main focus is the steep-sided hills and blue waters of the fjords themselves.

7

Below the East Fjords, **southeast Iceland** is dominated by the vastness of Vatnajökull, whose icy cap and host of outrunning glaciers sprawl west of the town of **Höfn**. With a largely infertile terrain of highland moors and coastal gravel deserts known as **sandurs** to contend with – not to mention a fair share of catastrophic volcanic events – the population centres here are few and far between, though you can explore the glacial fringes at the wild **Lónsöræfi reserve**, and at **Skaftafell National Park**, where there are plenty of marked tracks. Further west, the tiny settlement of **Kirkjubæjarklaustur** is the jumping-off point for several trips inland, the best of which takes you through the fallout from one of Iceland's most disastrous eruptions.

GETTING AROUND	EASTERN AND SOUTHEAST ICELAND
By plane Egilsstaðir and Höfn (Hornafjörður) are served by regular flights from Reykjavík.	from Akureyri to Egilsstaðir, and from Höfn to Reykjavík. The East Fjords are mostly covered by individual local services from Egilsstaðir. Note that from mid-Sept until mid-May, there are no buses between Djúpivogur and Breiðdalsvík.
By bus Between mid-May and mid-Sept, Reykjavík Excursions (⊛ re.is) and Sterna (⊛ sternatravel.com) cover all Ringroad destinations, while Strætó (⊛ straeto.is) run	

Egilsstaðir

Whichever direction you've come from, arrival at **EGILSSTAÐIR** is a bit of an anticlimax. This crossroads town dates only to the late 1940s, when a supermarket, a vet, a hospital and a telephone exchange chose to set up shop on a narrow strip of moorland between the glacier-fed **Lagarfljöt River** and the back of the East Fjord fells, bringing the first services into this remote corner of the country. Today Egilsstaðir has grown to fill a couple of dozen streets but remains an unadorned service and supply centre, important to the regional economy but containing neither a proper centre nor much in the way of essential viewing.

TURF-ROOFED HOUSE, BORGAFJÖRÐUR EYSTRI

Highlights

❶ Borgarfjörður Eystri The most isolated and picturesque of the East Fjord towns, famed for its puffins, shattered mountains and stiff hiking trails. **See p.297**

❷ Lónsöræfi You need five days to tackle one of Iceland's most adventurous hikes, through the wild and remote rhyolite highlands between Staffafell and Snæfell. **See p.310**

❸ Vatnajökull Spend an hour skidding across the massive outrunning glaciers of Europe's largest ice cap by 4WD or snowmobile. **See p.312**

❹ Jökulsárlón Watch powder-blue icebergs breaking off the front of a glacier and drifting downstream to the sea – where they wash up, crystal clear, on the black-sand beach. **See p.314**

❺ Skaftafell Occupying a plateau between two glaciers, this national park has hot springs, wind-scoured peaks, a famous waterfall and easy walking across heathland. **See p.315**

❻ Lakagígar This remote string of volcanic craters, accessible on summer-only tours, was the site of Iceland's most destructive recorded eruption. **See p.319**

HIGHLIGHTS ARE MARKED ON THE MAP ON P.288

Egilsstaðir is, however, a major **transportation** hub; the airport has flights to Reykjavík, the international port of **Seyðisfjörður** is nearby, and anyone travelling by bus has to stop here for at least as long as it takes to change services. It's also a springboard to the estuarine grasslands of **Héraðsflói**, as well as the adjacent Lögurinn lake and highland plateau around Snæfell and Kárahnjúkar, and the northern East Fjords.

Minjasafn Austurlands

Tjarnarbraut • June–Aug Mon–Fri 11.30am–7pm, Sat & Sun 10.30am–6pm • 1000kr

Egilsstaðir's main distraction is the **Minjasafn Austurlands**, a museum whose single-room exhibition provides a potted history of the region via battered farming implements, saggy woollen clothes and old riding saddles. The highlight is a relocated traditional **turf house** – minus the turf – whose cramped, wood-framed interior would definitely have become too cosy during the long winter nights. Every year there's a differently themed **exhibition** too; previous displays have been about Viking graves, reindeer and the vanished monastery at Skriðuklaustur (see p.293).

EASTERN AND SOUTHEAST ICELAND

HIGHLIGHTS
1. Borgarfjörður Eystri
2. Lónsöræfi
3. Vatnajökull
4. Jökulsárlón
5. Skaftafell
6. Lakagígar

N

0 — 50
kilometres

ARRIVAL AND DEPARTURE

By plane The airport (ⓦ airiceland.is) is off the Ringroad 1km north of town, with year-round services to Reykjavík. There's much talk of using the airport's international status to lure tourist custom away from southern Iceland, but so far no international services land here.
Destinations Reykjavík (1 daily; 1hr).

By bus Reykjavík Excursions and Sterna stop at the town's campsite (see below); Strætó terminate beside the Visitor Centre (see below), as do the various East Fjord buses – see individual town accounts for operator contact details. Note that Akureyri and East Fjords services operate year-round, but buses to Höfn only run between

EGILSSTAÐIR

mid-May and mid-Sept.
Destinations Akureyri (3 daily; 4hr); Berunes (1 daily; 2hr); Breiðdalsvík (1 daily; 1hr 30min); Djúpivogur (2 daily; 2hr 30min); Eskifjörður (1 daily; 50min); Fáskrúðsfjörður (1 daily; 40min); Goðafoss (1 daily; 3hr 10min); Höfn (2 daily; 3hr); Neskaupstaður (1 daily; 1hr 15min); Reykjahlíð (Mývatn; 3 daily; 2hr 15min); Reyðarfjörður (1 daily; 20min); Seyðisfjörður (1–3 daily; 40min); Stöðvarfjörður (1 daily; 1hr 10min).

By car Budget (ⓦ budget.is), Hertz (ⓦ hertz.is) and Europcar (ⓦ europcar.com) have outlets at the airport; book in advance as rental stocks are small.

INFORMATION AND TOURS

Tourist information The main Visitor Centre, across from the N1 fuel station on Fagradalsbraut (Mon–Fri 8.30am–6pm, Sat 10am–4pm, Sun 9am–5pm; ☎ 471 2320, ⓦ east.is), is well stocked with brochures; staff can make accommodation bookings for the region. There's also an information office at the town's campsite on Kaupvangur (daily 7am–11pm).

Services Most services lie just off the highway, close to the N1 fuel station. The well-stocked Nettó supermarket (Mon–Fri 9am–8pm, Sat 9am–6pm, Sun noon–6pm) is directly behind the N1, with a slightly cheaper Bónus store (Mon–Thurs 11am–6.30pm, Fri 10am–7.30pm, Sat 10am–6pm, Sun noon–6pm) 250m north along the highway. There's an ATM around the side of the Visitor Centre (see above), and at the bank behind the N1 fuel station on Kaupvangur. The

post office is up the hill on Fagradalsbraut. Egilsstaðir's pool is past the museum on Tjarnabraut (Mon–Fri 6.30am–9.30pm, Sat & Sun 10am–6pm) with children's play area, hot pot and lap lanes.

Tours For regional hiking tours and advice, contact Wild Boys (ⓦ wildboys.is), Flótsdalshérað Touring Club (☎ 863 5813, ⓦ fljotsdalsherad.is/ferdafelag) or Ferðaskrifstofa Austurlands, Kaupvangur 6 (☎ 471 2000, ⓦ fatravel.is). Day-trips into the highlands west of town, including around Kárahnjúkur and Snæfell, are offered by Jeep Tours (☎ 898 2798, ⓦ jeeptours.is) and Super Jeep Tours (☎ 699 3673, ⓦ easthighlanders.is). Hikers needing transfers to or from Snæfell (see p.296) should contact Wild Boys or Tanni Travel, based down the coast in Eskifjörður (☎ 476 1399, ⓦ tannitravel.is).

ACCOMMODATION

Accommodation fills up fast in summer, particularly mid-week, when the ferry docks at Seyðisfjördur. For **homestays** with sleeping-bag accommodation, contact the Visitor Centre (see above).

Campsite Kaupvangur ☎ 470 0750. Flat, grassy area behind the N1 fuel station, though you need a river stone to drive pegs into the stony soil. There's a laundry (expensive), toilets, showers and attached information office. Long-distance buses stop here. **1400kr**

Edda Tjarnarbraut 25 ☎ 444 4880, ⓦ hoteledda.is. Summer-only option across from the pool, offering clean and functional en-suite doubles and family rooms, plus conference facilities and a good restaurant. Breakfast is 1900kr extra. **23,300kr**

★ **Gistihús Olgu & Birtu** Tjarnarbraut ☎ 860 2999, ⓦ gistihusolgu.com, ⓦ gistihusbirtu.com. Two adjacent period houses set back from the road, with welcoming management and cute, bright if somewhat plain furnishings, shared bathrooms and wooden floors

throughout. **15,000kr**

Guesthouse Egilsstaðir Just back from the lakeshore 500m west from town ☎ 471 1114, ⓦ lakehotel.is. Recent extensions have expanded this solid stone, nineteenth-century farmhouse to the point where it's more a hotel than a guesthouse, though the intimate atmosphere remains. The en-suite rooms have a smart, homely feel, and there's also a spa and views right up the lake. **32,000kr**

Hérað Miðvangur 5–7 ☎ 471 1500, ⓦ icelandairhotels .com. Icelandair's smart, Nordic-style hotel with aluminium-panelled exterior, reindeer-themed lobby, decent-sized rooms that are all lines and pale colours, and a full range of business facilities. Huge breakfast 2280kr extra. **31,600kr**

EATING AND DRINKING

Kaffi Egilsstaðir Kaupvangur ☎ 470 0200. Located at the bus stop and campsite, this café, restaurant and bar needs an

injection of atmosphere – it's usually empty until Friday night – though the 12" pizzas from 1800kr are fair value.

Café and restaurant daily 11.30am–10pm; bar Fri & Sat 10pm–3am.

★**Restaurant Nielsen** Tjarnarbraut 1 ☎471 2626. Cosy wooden building, with an outdoor terrace and beer, lobster soup (2800kr), pan-fried cod (3950kr) and – if finances allow – reindeer with wild game sauce and blueberries (7200kr). Their lunch-time buffet is very good value (1950kr). Mon–Fri 2–10pm, Sat & Sun 1–10pm.

★**SALT** Miðvangur 2–4 ☎471 1700. Bright and busy bistro, serving good coffee and cakes, salads, fish and chips and the like; the charcoal grill turns out above-average burgers, pizzas and tandoori chicken (mains all around 2250kr). Free wi-fi for customers. Mon–Sat 10am–10pm, Sun noon–10pm.

Héraðsflói

North of Egilsstaðir, a broad, waterlogged valley contains the last stages of the silt-laden Lagarfljót and Jökulsá á Brú as they wind their final 50km to the coast at **Héraðsflói**, an equally wide bay. The spread of ponds and heathlands along the way is strewn with wildflowers and liberally populated by wading birds, ducks, swans, geese, skuas and – through winter – reindeer. With so much game, the area was settled early on in Iceland's history; recent forensic tests on a local Viking-age grave suggested that the young woman buried here had been born in Britain around 900 AD. You'll pass through this way en route to Borgafjörður Eystri (see p.297), but if you fancy a few days among it – plus the chance to see **seals** and indulge in some **horseriding** – head for the beautifully isolated farmstead of **Húsey**, right up near the shore at the mouth of the Lagarfljöt.

★ **Húsey** Take Route 925/926 off the Ringroad about 25km northwest of Egilsstaðir; the hostel is 60km from town ☎ 471 3010, ⓦ husey.de. Self-catering IYHA hostel in an old timber and iron farmhouse, surrounded by summer wildflower meadows. The farm breeds horses and organizes riding packages; there's plenty of wildlife nearby too, including seals. Pickups from the Ringroad are available by arrangement, as is breakfast (1775kr). Dorms **5200kr**, sleeping bags **3850kr**

Lögurinn

Stretching 30km southwest from Egilsstaðir, **Lögurinn** is a long, narrow lake on the mid-reaches of the **Largarfljót River** – which itself originates up in the highlands at Vatnajökull's northeastern edge, near Snæfell (see p.296). Unusually for Iceland, the eastern shore is fairly well **wooded**; there's also saga lore and medieval remains to take in, along with an impressive waterfall. Deep and green, the lake itself is said to be home to the **Lagarfljótsormur**, a monster of the Scottish Loch Ness and Swedish Storsjön clans. First recorded in 1345, it's proved so elusive since that nobody is even very sure what it looks like – keep up to date with the latest sightings (and videos) at ⓦ ormur.com.

7

Lögurinn and its sights take an easy few hours to circuit in your own vehicle (there's no public transport); the two bridges across are both down towards the southern end of the lake. You'll also need to pass by en route to Kárahnjúkar and Snæfell (see p.296), as the road runs off Lögurinn's southwestern shore.

Hallormsstaður

About 25km from Egilsstaðir along Route 931 you'll find yourself between the solitary fuel-pump township of **HALLORMSSTAÐUR** and lakeside camping grounds at **Atlavík**, among the thick **woodland** lining Lögurinn's eastern shore. From the time of Settlement, Iceland's forests were cleared intensively for pasture, ship-building and grazing, and by the twentieth century large swathes of the country were suffering serious erosion problems. Since 1900 considerable effort has been put into expanding the country's tree cover, and the 18km-long stretch of forest around Hallormsstaður is Iceland's most extensive. The woodland here is predominantly birch (distinguished by its smooth red or silver bark), though mature plantations of much larger ash, spruce and larch are wildly popular with Icelanders, who are struck by the novelty of seeing vegetation that is taller than they are. Visitors from lusher climates may feel that the area, pleasant though it is, doesn't warrant so much excitement.

Hallormsstaður arboretum

Just north of Hallormsstaður • Open access • Free

Signposted on the roadside, the **Hallormsstaður arboretum** was established in 1903, but it was large-scale experiments with larch during the 1950s that proved for the first time that commercial timber plantations were viable in Iceland. Marked trails provide a half-hour stroll around a labelled collection of century-old native and imported tree species, including the country's tallest specimen, a pine which towers 22m overhead.

★ **Atlavík campsite** 2km south of Hallormsstaður ☎ 470 2070. Beautiful lakeshore location among birch woodland and just back from the gravel shingle of Atlavík bay. There are toilets, showers, picnic tables and plenty of space for tents, though it gets crowded at weekends. No open fires permitted. **1400kr**

Hafursá Signed east off the road just north of the arboretum ❶893 1428, ✉annagerdur@gmail.com. Two cottages with views across the forest and lake, plus two apartments in the farmhouse, sleeping 3–7 people each. Cottage/apartment <u>24,200kr</u>

Höfðavík campsite Just north of Hallormsstaður ❶470 2070. Set on a sloping lawn amid a fringe of trees above the lake. There are showers, toilets and washing-up sinks, and it's worth considering if *Atlavík* is too busy for you. <u>1300kr</u>

Hallormsstaður Inland off the main road from the fuel pump ❶471 2400, ⊕hotel701.is. Deep in the forest at the foot of the hills, with smart hotel rooms as well as a self-contained guesthouse, cabins, spa, sauna and jacuzzi. Room rate includes breakfast, and horseriding can be arranged. Hotel <u>33,000kr</u>, guesthouse <u>21,000kr</u>, cabins <u>30,000kr</u>

Hrafnkelsstaðir

Around 8km south of Hallormsstaður, out of the woods and on the old gravel road around the lake, is **Hrafnkelsstaðir**, the farm that features in the latter stages of **Hrafnkel's Saga** (see box below). Though there's no trace of saga times in the current buildings, it remains an atmospheric, brooding location, with views across to the steep slopes above Lögurinn's opposite shore, bald and shelved along their length like a very broad flight of steps.

Strútsfoss

Down beyond Hrafnkelsstaðir, past the southernmost bridge, Route 935 slides southwest through Suðurdalur's farms in a blaze of gravel (watch out for free-roaming horses and sheep). Around 15 minutes should bring you to a parking bay at the start

HRAFNKEL'S SAGA

Lögurinn and the lands to the west form the stage for **Hrafnkel's Saga**, a short but strikingly ambiguous story set before the country converted to Christianity in 1000 AD. It tells of the landowner **Hrafnkel**, a hard-working but headstrong devotee of the pagan fertility god Freyr, who settled **Hrafnkelsdalur**, a highland valley 35km west of Lögurinn. Here he built the farm **Aðalból**, and dedicated a shrine and half his livestock to the god – including his favourite stallion, the dark-maned **Freyfaxi**, which he forbade anyone but himself to ride on pain of death.

Inevitably, somebody did. Hrafnkel's shepherd, **Einar**, borrowed Freyfaxi to track down some errant ewes and, caught in the act, was duly felled by Hrafnkel's axe. Looking for legal help, Einar's father enlisted his sharp-witted nephew **Sámur**, who took the case to court at the next Alþing at Þingvellir (see box, p.103). But nobody wanted to support a dispute against such a dangerous character as Hrafnkel, until a large party of men from the suitably distant West Fjords offered their services. As Sámur presented his case, his allies crowded around the gathering and Hrafnkel, unable to get close enough to mount a defence, was **outlawed**.

Disgusted, Hrafnkel returned home where he ignored his sentence, but Sámur and the West Fjorders descended on his homestead early one morning, dragged him out of bed, and told him to choose between death or giving his property to Sámur. He took the latter option, leaving Aðalból and moving east over the Lagarfljót to **Hrafnkelsstaðir**, a dilapidated farm that he was forced to buy on credit.

Over the next six years Hrafnkel built up his new property and, his former arrogance deflated, became a respected figure. Meanwhile, Sámur's brother **Eyvind** returned from a long overseas trip and decided to visit Sámur at Aðalból. Stupidly riding past Hrafnkelsstaðir, Eyvind was cut down by Hrafnkel and his men, who then launched a raid on Aðalból, capturing Sámur and giving him the same choices that Sámur had given him: to die or hand over the farm. Like Hrafnkel, Sámur chose to live and retired unhappily to his former estate. For his part, Hrafnkel regained his former power and influence and stayed at Aðalból until his death.

of a two-hour circuit walk to **Strútsfoss**, a two-tier, 120m-high waterfall tumbling over banded cliffs. The falls themselves are similar to Hengifoss across the lake (see p.294), but the walk up the open valley – not to mention the lack of sightseers – is far more attractive. Strútsfoss looks best from a distance, and be aware that to reach the very foot of the falls you'll have to ford the potentially dangerous river as it flows out through the gorge.

Valþjófsstaður

Over on the west side of the lake, near where the river descends from the highlands and flows into Lögurinn, **Valþjófsstaður** is another historic farm, this one founded by the influential twelfth-century chieftain Þorvarður Þórarinsson. The **church**, built in 1966, replaced a structure from Þorvarður's time whose original carved **wooden door** – now in Reykjavík's National Museum – depicts the medieval romance "The Knight and the Lion". Modern replicas on the back of the church's inner entrance show two roundels deeply carved with intertwined dragons, lions and knights on horseback; the runes translate as "Behold the Mighty King Here Buried who Slew the Dragon".

Skriðuklaustur

Towards the lower end of Lögurinn's southwestern shore, **Skriðuklaustur** was founded as a monastery in medieval times, now comprising a pleasant cobble-block homestead built in the 1930s by novelist **Gunnar Gunnarsson**, the recently excavated **monastery site**, and the **Snæfellsstofa Visitor Centre**, well worth a visit if you're planning on ascending the nearby Route 910 to the highlands.

Gunnar Gunnarsson's house

On the lake side of the road • May & Sept daily noon–5pm; June–Aug daily 10am–6pm; Oct–April on request • 1000kr • ☎ 471 2990, ⓦ skriduklaustur.is

Despite being born and raised in the Skriðuklaustur area, poet and novelist **Gunnar Gunnarsson** (1889–1975) was educated in Denmark and wrote mostly in Danish; the opening volume of his farming epic *Guest the One-eyed* became the first feature film made in Iceland. He returned to his homeland in 1939, building the house at Skriðuklaustur before his wife's ill-health forced a permanent move to Reykjavík.

Upstairs are two **exhibitions**: one on Gunnar's life, with rooms restored to their 1930s appearance; the other covering the **history of the monastery**, including plans and video reconstructions of the site, human bones from the cemetery and religious artefacts recovered from nearby farms – including a large wooden Madonna and child statue. Downstairs is the popular *Klausturkaffi* restaurant, the only one at the lake (see p.294).

Monastery site

At the foot of the low slope between Gunnarsson's house and the lake • Daily June–Aug 10am–6pm • Free to look around on your own; guided tours for groups of ten or more 500kr/person

In recent years Skriðuklaustur's original **monastery site**, covering some 1500 square metres, has been located and excavated. Founded in 1493 by the Augustinians, the cloisters were destroyed just sixty years later during the Reformation, though a church remained here until 1792. Bones from the hospital cemetery (on display at Gunnarsson's house) have yielded surprising details – it seems that syphilis was present in Iceland much earlier than previously believed – while fragments of stained glass indicate unexpected elegance for this relatively small religious centre. Dry-stone walls

7

mark out former building foundations, but there's no interpretation offered, so take a guided tour or visit the exhibition up at the house first.

Snæfellsstofa Visitor Centre

150m north of Gunnar Gunnarsson's home • Daily: May & Sept 10am–4pm; June–Aug 9am–6pm • Free • ☎ 470 0840, Ⓦ vjp.is

The modern concrete, steel and glass building is a little out of place in such an otherwise rural valley, but there's informative digital, video and display board coverage of the highland ecology and geology around Snæfell, just an hour's drive away up Route 910. The shop also sells birch sap, tapped from the forests across the lake.

EATING   SKRIÐUKLAUSTUR

★ **Klausturkaffi** In the basement of Gunnar Gunnarsson's house (see p.293) ☎ 471 2992. Excellent café-restaurant with lakeside views and a generous lunch buffet – meatballs, stew, quiche, salads, cake, fruit and coffee for just 2950kr. Alternatives include a rich fish soup (1990kr), reindeer pie (3590kr) or afternoon cake buffet (1950kr). Daily May & Sept noon–5pm; June–Aug 10am–6pm.

Hengifoss

Around 7km north of Skriðuklaustur and near the junction with Route 910 to Kárahnjúkar, a good-sized parking bay and a noticeboard marks the start of an hour-long return walk up to **Hengifoss**, Iceland's third-highest falls. The path isn't especially steep but is unformed in places, crossing a couple of boggy patches around lesser **Litlifoss**, whose narrow spray is fringed in wild rock formations of basalt columns, bent in all directions. Hengifoss itself drops off the top of the plateau over a cliff-face layered in distinct black and red bands, composed of compressed ash from separate volcanic eruptions. The path proper ends at a viewpoint well back from the base of the falls, though with care you can follow rougher trails to within 250m of the water.

The highlands

The **highlands** southwest of Egilsstaðir form a huge, wild and impressively bleak expanse of moorland around the edges of the Vatnajökull ice cap. Overlooking everything is the permanently snowcapped, sharply ridged peak of **Snæfell** which, at 1833m, is the highest freestanding mountain in Iceland, formed from the eroded core of a long-extinct stratovolcano. While climbing Snæfell needs experience and equipment, you can approach the base on the way to the **Kárahnjúkar hydro dam**, built to provide power for an aluminium smelter down on the coast in Reyðarfjörður (see p.301). You'll also pass by Snæfell if you're hiking the increasingly popular five-day route through Lónsöræfi (see box, p.310). Either way, keep eyes peeled for **reindeer**, geese and whooper swans, all of which breed and feed up here in large numbers.

GETTING AROUND   THE HIGHLANDS

By car Route 910 provides a 60km surfaced road from near Hengifoss on Lögurinn lake to Kárahnjúkar; in summer it's accessible to conventional vehicles. If you've got a 4WD, note that there are also several tracks off Route 910 to Snæfell, Vatnajökull and beyond.

Tours There is no public transport into the region, though operators in Egilsstaðir visit on day tours (see p.289), and *Laugarfell* hostel runs overnight packages including pickup (see below).

Maps Mál og menning maps cover the region between here and Lónsöræfi in two 1:100,000 sheets, which include a 1:50,000 detail of the Snæfell area.

FROM TOP REINDEER, LÓNSÖRÆFI (P.309); ARCTIC TERN AT JÖKULSÁRLÓN (P.314) >

Snæfell

On clear days **Snæfell** looks stunning, the black-streaked flanks rising above desolate moorland to a brilliant, snowy pyramidal tip; sadly, the usual vista is of the lower base vanishing into cloud. There's a sealed road running south off Route 910 which ends up at a viewpoint above the little **Kelduá reservoir**, just 5km east of Snæfell; the white glow south from here is Vatnajökull, and the 15km-long valley in between is **Eyjabakkar**, annual nesting grounds for upwards of three thousand pairs of pink-footed geese. Original plans to flood this valley for hydro power caused such widespread protests from environmentalists that the site was shifted to Kárahnjúkar.

The main road to Snæfell's base is the four-wheel-drive-only **F909**, which winds out via several river crossings to the mountain's west side. Once there, a 30km hiking track **circuits Snæfell**, which is also at the start of the long hike **south to Lónsöræfi** (see box, p.310).

ACCOMMODATION

SNÆFELL

★**Laugarfell** Signed off Route 910 ☎773 7723, ⓦhighlandhostel.is. Brand-new, tin-sided lodge with pine interior; there are dorms and doubles with shared bathrooms, an exposed campsite, a barbecue area with picnic tables, an excellent café serving hearty dinners and two 38°C hot pools to soak in just outside. The management can point you along various hiking trails too, including a pegged route all the way up from Egilsstaðir. Breakfast 1900kr. June–Sept. Dorms 5500kr, doubles 16,000kr, camping 1500kr

Snæfellsstófa On Snæfell's western foothills ☎842 4367, ⓔsnaefellsstofa@vjp.is. This timber-clad hiking organization hut sleeps fifty people in bunks, and has toilets, water and showers, plus a warden for information. You can camp here too. Advance booking essential. Dorms 5500kr, camping 1500kr

Kárahnjúkar

60km from near Hengifoss on Lögurinn lake • Guide on-site Wed & Sat afternoons through summer

Kárahnjúkar, a highland area on the headwaters of the Jökulsá á Dal at the northeastern edge of the Vatnajökull ice cap, is the site of a 690-megawatts **hydroelectric dam** which produces a quarter of all the electricity generated in Iceland. Route 910 crosses over the 200m-high **dam wall** to a viewing area, from where you can look along the length of the **Dimmugljúfur canyon**, a narrow, jagged tear in the landscape clearly caused by a single, violent earthquake: you have to ponder the wisdom of building a dam on what is patently a highly unstable area. Views south take in a huge artificial lake, **Hálslón**, which extends 45km down to Vatnajökull itself. Also note the dam's **spillway**; in late summer, melting ice around Vatnajökull fills Hálslón beyond capacity, and the overflow creates an artificial waterfall here known as **Kárahnjúkafoss**.

The East Fjords

The **East Fjords** cover a 120km stretch of eastern Iceland's twisted coastline between **Borgarfjörður Eystri** in the north and southern **Berufjörður**, with many of the fjords – none of which is particularly large – sporting small villages, mostly given over to fishing. The fjord scenery can be vivid, particularly in summer, with the villages sitting between flat blue sea and steep, steel-grey mountains, their peaks dusted in snow and lower slopes covered in greenery and flowers. Aside from scenery and **puffins** at tiny Borgarfjörður Eystri, highlights include **Seyðisfjörður**, for its Norwegian-style wooden houses and international ferry, and, right at the fjords' southern end, the tiny island of **Papey**, which can be visited on a day-trip from **Djúpivogur**.

GETTING AROUND THE EAST FJORDS

By bus There isn't a continuous road linking the fjords, or a single bus service running out to them, so any thorough exploration of the region requires a bit of backtracking and advance planning. Borgarfjörður Eystri, Seyðisfjörður, the Fjarðabyggð fjords (Reyðarfjörður, Eskifjörður and Neskaupstaður), plus Fáskrúðfjörður and Stöðvarfjörður,

are each on separate roads and separate bus services from Egilsstaðir. The southern fjords of Breiðalsvík and Djúpivogur, lying along the Ringroad, are covered by long-distance summer buses between Egilsstaðir and Höfn. Specific services are detailed in the individual accounts.

Borgarfjörður Eystri

BORGARFJÖRÐUR EYSTRI, also known as **Bakkagerði**, is a diminutive community of farmers and fishermen at the end of the mostly gravel Route 94, some 70km from Egilsstaðir. The journey here on Route 94 crosses Héraðsflói (see p.290), negotiates a steep mountain pass and then descends to the coast and some dangerously loose cliffs, a hazard attributed to the malevolent local spirit **Naddi**. Despite being pushed into the sea by a farmer during the fourteenth century, Naddi remains active, judging by the state of the road; keep an eye out for a protective **cross** by the roadside with the Latin inscription *Effigiem Christi qui transis pronus honora* ("You who hurry past, honour Christ's image"). But once arrived, Borgarfjörður is a charming location, steeped in local lore, with a wide fjord to the front and a backdrop of steep, colourful mountainsides. The core of

7

HIKES FROM BORGARFJÖRÐUR EYSTRI

Borgarfjörður Eystri is quite a hiking haven, with a good number of **marked trails** heading up the valley from town. However, the possibility of dense fogs and atrocious weather with heavy snow on higher ground makes it essential to ensure you're properly equipped, and to seek local advice before setting out. To book hut space along the way, contact the local hiking organization (☎863 5813, ✉ferdafelag@egilsstadir.is; 4500kr).

Prominent behind Borgarfjörður Eystri, **Dyrfjöll**, the "Door Mountain", gets its name from the gap in its sharp-peaked, 1136m-high basalt crest. This is another abode of local spirits, mischievous imps that emerge around Christmas to tie cows' tails together. A round-trip from town would be a major hike, though you could arrange a lift up to the top of the pass at **Geldingafjall** on the Egilsstaðir road, from where there's a marked track around the upper reaches of the mountain, and then down to the end of the valley south of town – a full day's walk.

A good introduction to the area is to hike 4km or so west to the next bay of **Brúnavík**, whose steeply sloping valley was farmed until being abandoned in the 1940s. This is a story typical of the northern East Fjords; as the herring industry fizzled out after World War II, and roads and services began to bypass the region, farms founded in Viking times were given up as people moved on. There's a small shelter shed here today, and a further rough trail over loose-sided fells to **Breiðavík**, where there's a hiking **hut** and campsite with water and toilets and a 7km **jeep track** northwest back to town – the round-trip via Brúnavík and Breiðavík takes about fourteen hours.

It's also possible to spend a few days **hiking to Seyðisfjörður**, initially following another jeep track south down the valley from Borgarfjörður Eystri. One of the highlights is about 10km along where you cross a saddle below **Hvítserkur**, a pink rhyolite mountain, wonderfully streaked with darker bands and stripes. The next valley over sports lush meadows which once supported four farms; at **Húsavík** bay here, there's the remains of a church and another hiking **hut**. You then cross over a steep hillside to the next fjord, **Lóðmundarfjörður**, most of whose population clung on into the 1970s. A partly restored church remains, built in 1891, along with a final, brand-new hut. Lóðmundarfjörður marks the end of the jeep track, but hikers can follow a rough trail through a pass over **Hjálmárdalsheiði** and then down to Seyðisfjörður.

the village surrounds its old **harbour**, while a new harbour, 5km up the coast, is home to a large **puffin colony**.

Borgarfjörður church

Isolated in a field on the edge of town, Borgarfjörður's **church** is a standard nineteenth-century wood and corrugated-iron affair, though the unusual altarpiece is a sunset-hued affair painted in 1914 by **Jóhannes Kjarval** (see p.68). Typically incorporating a local landscape into the work, Kjarval depicted the Sermon on the Mount delivered atop of **Álfaborg**, the rocky hillock behind the church; Álfaborg means "elf-town" and, according to folklore, is home to Iceland's fairy queen.

Hafnarholm

A grassy headland above **Hafnarholm**, 5km around the bay from town at Borgarfjörður Eystri's tiny fishing harbour, is home through the summer to hundreds of nesting seabirds. Wooden steps lead up to an **observation platform** with views out over the headland and an adjacent outcrop of rock. Although there are plenty of fulmars and kittiwakes here – and an eider duck nesting ground from which locals collect valuable eider down – **puffins** are the real draw; they're unusually indifferent to people and show little fear at all of the camera lenses pointed in their direction. Incidentally, it's worth checking at the harbour itself to see if any of the bizarre-looking **Greenland shark** (source of the notorious speciality *hákarl*; see p.36) have been landed.

ARRIVAL AND INFORMATION   **BORGARFJÖRÐUR EYSTRI**

By bus The Egilsstaðir–Borgarfjörður minibus (☎472 9805 or ☎894 8305; 2000kr; 1hr) departs Mon–Fri at 8am from Borgarfjörður Eystri's campsite, and at noon from outside the Visitor Centre at Egilsstaðir.

Tourist information There's useful info at ⓦborgarfjordureystri.is (click on the "English" tab at the top right corner); local accommodation is also a good bet.

Services In the centre of the village, there's a small Samkaup/TRAX store (June–Aug Mon–Fri 10am–6pm, Sat & Sun noon–4pm) and a fuel pump.

Tours *Álfheimar Country Hotel* (see below) specializes in guided hikes of the area. *Borg* guesthouse (see below) can also arrange drop-off/pickups for hiking trails, and 4WD tours (6000kr/hr).

ACCOMMODATION AND EATING

Álfa Café Seawards from the church ☎472 9900. Cosy café whose tabletops are irregular, polished granite slabs – they sell stone jewellery too, and once had an outlet in Reykjavík. Fish soup, thick with seafood, is their most expensive dish (1900kr); there's also sandwiches, waffles, and cakes and coffee. June–Aug daily 10am–10pm.

Álfheimar Country Hotel By the roadside into town ☎861 3677, ⓦalfheimar.com. Slightly bland row of modern wooden cabins, but the thirty en-suite doubles are comfortable and the owners extremely helpful. Wi-fi and breakfast included, and there's also a restaurant. **24,000kr**

★**Blábjörg Guesthouse** Behind the supermarket ☎861 1792, ⓦblabjorg.is. Located in the aluminium-clad former fishworks, where the self-contained studio apartment and doubles with shared bathrooms are Nordic-plain but spotless. There are sea views, a kitchen and hot tubs (open to the public daily 4–10pm), and the owner is a

mine of information about birdwatching and hiking trails. **17,000kr**

Borg Road through the village ☎472 9870 or ☎894 4470. Functional but well-presented rooms and shared bathrooms in three houses around town, all on the road through the village. Contact in advance to arrange breakfast or lunch packages. **14,000kr**

Campsite Behind the church ☎857 2005. Campsite with plenty of spongy grass stretching in all directions, plus a new wooden building housing toilets, showers, kitchen, laundry with dryer and an indoor dining area. **1100kr**

Fjarðarborg Across from the fuel pump ☎472 9920. Grey, pebble-dash block whose bare and basic decor harks back to the 1960s. The menu is straightforward burgers (1500–1900kr), but as the town's sole bar things can get lively in here at the weekends. Nightly in summer.

Seyðisfjörður

Twenty-five kilometres east of Egilsstaðir over a good mountain road (Route 93), **SEYÐISFJÖRÐUR** is an attractive town set at the base of a long, tight fjord. It has a strong Norwegian heritage: first settled by a tenth-century Norwegian named Bjólf, Seyðisfjörður was established as a herring port a thousand years later by entrepreneurs from Norway, who also imported the town's wooden buildings. During its herring heyday, Seyðisfjörður looked set to become Iceland's largest port, but geography limited its expansion. Used as a US naval base during World War II, the town remains an active fishing and fish-processing centre, with a continuing Nordic link embodied by the Faroese-operated **ferry** *Norröna*, which calls in every Thursday on its Iceland–Faroes–Denmark route.

Scattered along a 1km crescent of road, Seyðisfjörður is split by the small mouth of the shallow **Fjarðará** as it empties into the fjord – marked by a short bridge – with the pastel-blue **church** and surrounding older buildings to the north, and the ferry terminal and most amenities to the south. The town's summer rhythms follow the ferry schedule and it's generally busy only on Wednesdays, when there's an afternoon craft **market** and evening classical concert in the church.

7

ARRIVAL AND INFORMATION   SEYÐISFJÖRÐUR

By bus Egilsstaðir–Seyðisfjörður buses (☎472 1515) run year-round Mon–Fri; in summer there's a weekend service too and extra buses on Thurs to cope with passengers using the *Norröna* ferry. The bus stop is at the ferry terminal.

Destinations Egilsstaðir (1–3 daily; 25min).
By ferry The large, blue ferry terminal is at the harbour, offering fresh arrivals car rental, tourist information (Mon–Fri 8am–4pm) and buses to Egilsstaðir. Buy ferry tickets at the separate Smyril office (Mon–Fri 8am–noon & 1–5pm;

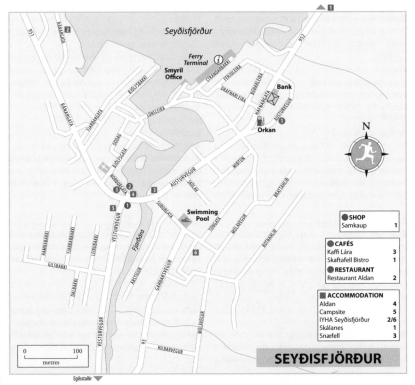

SEYÐISFJÖRÐUR

● SHOP	
Samkaup	1

● CAFÉS	
Kaffi Lára	3
Skaftafell Bistro	1
● RESTAURANT	
Restaurant Aldan	2

■ ACCOMMODATION	
Aldan	4
Campsite	5
IYHA Seyðisfjörður	2/6
Skálanes	1
Snæfell	3

0   100
metres

Egilsstaðir ▼

SEYÐISFJÖRÐUR HIKES

One popular walk from Seyðisfjörður starts by following the road along the north side of the fjord for a couple of kilometres to the **Vestdalsá**, the first real river you'll encounter on the way. Just before you reach it, a trail heads uphill along **Vestadalur**, a valley leading up into the hills to a small lake, Vestdalsvatn, past several pretty waterfalls; allow five hours to make the return hike from town.

In the opposite direction, follow the road through town and out along the south side of the fjord for 8km to the site of **Þórarinsstaðir**, a former farm where archeologists unearthed the foundations of a church dating from the eleventh century, believed to be the oldest such remains in the country. Not much further on, **Eyrar** is yet another abandoned farm, though here the ruins are far more substantial; it's hard to believe now, but this was once one of the region's busiest settlements. Experienced hikers can spend an extra half-day walking south across mountains from here to **Mjóifjörður**, the next fjord south (see opposite).

7

☎472 1111, ⓦsmyril-line.com). The *Norröna* ferry operates year-round but the schedules vary; check the Smyril website for the current timetable.
Destinations Hirtshals, Denmark (2 days); Tórshavn, Faroe Islands (16hr).
Services The Samkaup supermarket (Mon–Fri 9am–6pm,

Sat 11am–4pm) is at the edge of town by the bridge, just on the Egilsstaðir road. The bank (with ATM), post office and ORKAN fuel pump are opposite the ferry terminal on Hafnargata. The swimming pool (June–Aug Mon–Fri 6.30–9am & 3–8pm, Sat 1–4pm) is around the corner from the supermarket on Suðurgata.

ACCOMMODATION

★**Aldan** Norðurgata 2 ☎472 1277, ⓦhotelaldan .com. A heritage-listed gem, one of Seyðisfjörður's original Norwegian wooden kit-homes that housed the town's bank for almost a century and oozes stylish old-fashioned charm, though the interior has been thoroughly updated. **27,900kr**
Campsite Ranargata ☎472 1521. A new amenities block has greatly improved this formerly spartan site, providing a kitchen and dining area, showers, toilets, laundry (far cheaper than Egilsstaðir's) and free wi-fi. **1250kr**
★**IYHA Seyðisfjörður** Suðurgata 8 ☎611 4410, ⓦhostel.is. In two locations: the reception and main building is in town inside a wing of the old hospital, with spacious common areas, kitchen and dining room, plus dorms, en-suite doubles and family rooms. The other building, a single-storey timber home, overlooks the sea

and harbour just north of town along the fjord, a quiet location with similar facilities. Dorms **4400kr**, doubles **17,300kr**
★**Skálanes** About 15km east of town along the south side of the fjord ☎690 6966, ⓦskalanes.com. This private nature reserve makes a great weekend escape. The modernized 1920s farmhouse has doubles with shared facilities right by the sea, surrounded by open fellsides, cliffs and wild landscape. Breakfast is included, and they can collect from town for an extra fee (the road in crosses several rivers, fordable in 4WD only). **21,000kr**
Snæfell Austurvegur 3 ☎472 1277, ⓦhotelaldan .com. Run by the *Aldan* management, this is another nice old wooden building close to the water, which once served as the local post office. Rooms are spacious and clean, and recently renovated with polished wooden floors. Rate includes breakfast. **20,900kr**

EATING

Kaffi Lára Norðurgata 3 ☎472 1277. Resurrected after burning down in 2012, this cosy, wood-panelled café-bar serves as Seyðisfjörður's main watering hole, hung with period photos and a large TV screen. Try out the local El Grillo beer, coffee and heavy cakes, or their burgers, cod and lamb grills (around 2300kr). Mon–Thurs 11am–1.30am, Fri & Sat 11am–3.30am, Sun 2pm–1.30am.
Restaurant Aldan Diagonally across from the supermarket at the hotel of the same name (see above) ☎472 1277. Set in an old open-plan kit-house, with a

terrace out the front, this is an unexpectedly sophisticated café-restaurant. Among the usual seafood and lamb grills are seasonal game meats; mains start around 3500kr. Restaurant daily noon–2pm & 6–9pm; café daily 7.30am–5pm.
Skaftafell Bistro South from the ferry terminal on Austurvegur ☎692 8711. Arty café, gallery and backup bar for the town, this makes a friendly place to relax over a beer or coffee, use the wi-fi and tuck into their cod with mash (2350kr) or home-made pizzas (from 1850kr). Daily noon–9pm.

Mjóifjörður

Reached 45km southeast from Egilsstaðir via Route 953, an abysmally steep, twisting gravel road, it's hard to believe that the tiny hamlet of **MJÓIFJÖRÐUR** once hosted the world's largest whaling station, employing two hundred people. Nowadays the cluster of buildings halfway along the fjord's eider-infested north shore overlooks a few fish farms, and is home to perhaps five families. The road continues a further 20km past the church through gorgeous coastal scenery to **Dalatangi**, a lighthouse at the headland between here and Seyðisfjörður, the fjord immediately north.

ARRIVAL AND DEPARTURE   MJÓIFJÖRÐUR

By car/hike There's no bus service to Mjóifjörður, but aside from the road – about as rough as you'd want to risk a rental car on – you can also hike here over the ridges from Seyðisfjörður (see p.299), though it's quite a tough trail.

By ferry At the time of writing it seemed as if a summertime ferry service to Neskaupstaður, in the next fjord south, might be starting up (see p.303).

ACCOMMODATION

Sólbrekka On the hill, above the church ☎ 476 0007 or ☎ 894 9014, ⓦ mjoifjordur.weebly.com. Summer-only cabin and guesthouse accommodation on a working farm, with kitchen, dining room, laundry, bathroom and hot tub at your disposal. You can camp here too. They've marked out local hiking trails and can supply maps. Breakfast is by arrangement (1600kr); there's also a small café. Cabins June–Sept, guesthouse July & Aug. Doubles ~~12,000kr~~, sleeping bags ~~4000kr~~, camping ~~1200kr~~

Fjarðabyggð

The East Fjords' middle reaches, collectively known as **Fjarðabyggð**, comprise the three relatively large fishing villages of **Reyðarfjörður**, **Eskifjörður** and **Neskaupstaður**, linked by the 60km Route 92 from Egilsstaðir, which dead-ends at Neskaupstaður. There's a scattering of museums, some hiking trails and the most attractive scenery in the East Fjords; a regular bus link from Egilsstaðir runs through the summer.

GETTING AROUND   FJARÐABYGGÐ

By bus The East Iceland Bus Company (☎ 477 1713, ⓦ austfjardaleid.is) runs an Egilsstaðir–Reyðarfjörður– Eskifjörður–Norðfjörður service; there are two buses in each direction Mon–Fri, and one on Sat.

Reyðarfjörður

REYÐARFJÖRÐUR is a functional port surrounded by imposing, flat-topped mountains. Around 4km east on the main road, the kilometre-long **Fjarðaal aluminium smelter** – powered by the controversial hydro dam at Kárahnjúkar (see p.296) – has brought employment, a huge sports centre and an upbeat air to town, once crippled by the fishing industry's downturn. The town has also recently been the unlikely beneficiary of some screen glamour courtesy of Nordic Noir TV drama, *Fortitude*, which used Reyðarfjörður's bleak winter backdrop as the setting for much of its action.

Route 92 runs through Reyðarfjörður as the town's 700m main street; the western half is called Búðareyri, and the eastern end Austurvegur. The church marks where short Hafnargata runs to the sea.

Stríðsárasafnið

Off Hæðargerði • June–Aug daily 1–5pm • 1000kr

Overlooking Reyðarfjörður from its uppermost street, **Stríðsárasafnið** (the Icelandic Wartime Museum) is housed in long, red concrete huts built as a hospital by US forces in 1943. There are vintage jeeps and trucks, a potted history of the site and a collection of photos and mannequins in period clothes, but no explanation as to why such a remote location was chosen for a medical installation.

Grænafell

Grænafell, the mountain ridge north of Reyðarfjörður, isn't particularly high at 581m, but is accessible along a two-hour track (marked from near the museum) that climbs up through a narrow gorge to reveal a broad fjord panorama from the top. Along the way, signposts lead to the grave of **Völva**, which according to local tales was a supernatural being who watches over the town – the name is applied throughout Nordic countries to a range of benevolent female spirits.

ARRIVAL AND INFORMATION   **REYÐARFJÖRÐUR**

By bus The bus stop is on Austurvegur.
Destinations Egilsstaðir (11 weekly; 30min); Eskifjörður (11 weekly; 15min); Neskaupstaður (11 weekly; 35min).
By car Aside from the Egilsstaðir–Neskaupstaður road, there's also a tunnel through the mountains south of town

to Route 96 and Fáskrúðsfjörður.
Services Most of the town's services are along Búðareyri, including fuel stations, post office, supermarket and bank (with ATM).

ACCOMMODATION AND EATING

Campsite North from the roundabout at Reyðarfjörður's western boundary ☎ 470 9000. Set in a pleasant location right next to a "duck pond" (actually a small lake), with toilets, showers and mountain views. __1300kr__
★ **IYHA Hjá Marlín** Vallargerð 9 and 14 ☎ 892 0336, ⓦ hostel.is. Three clean, recently restored older buildings featuring a choice of hostel, guesthouse and hotel accommodation. Management are extremely helpful and facilities include a kitchen, barbecue area, lounge and

sauna; rooms have shared or private bathrooms. Sleeping bags __5500kr__, doubles __12,400kr__
★ **Tærgesen** Hafnargata ☎ 470 5555, ⓦ taergesen.is. Hotel, motel and busy grill restaurant, down past the church near the water in a former dockside storehouse, built in 1870. The whole building is wood; timber panelling and low ceilings mean rooms are cosy, if on the small side. Newer rooms are en suite and rates include a hearty breakfast. There are plans to start running sea-fishing trips too. __21,000kr__

Eskifjörður

Set in its own mini-fjord 15km east of Reyðarfjörður, **ESKIFJÖRÐUR** reeks of fish and revels in fishing, managing to maintain a busy fleet despite the fact that most other East Fjord towns have fallen on hard times. Road junctions are marked by huge propellers and anchors salvaged from trawlers; the fishing fleet is either clogging up the harbour or out on business somewhere between Finland and Ireland; and the town's centre is focused around a huge **fish-freezing plant**, whose walls are covered in bright piscatorially themed murals.

Eskifjörður's centre is compact, with most services along waterfront Strandgata, whose eastern end winds uphill and out of town as Norðfjarðavegur.

Sjóminjasafn

Strandgata 39 • June–Aug daily 1–5pm • 1100kr

Across from the freezing plant you'll find **Sjóminjasafn**, the East Iceland Maritime Museum, atmospherically housed in an early nineteenth-century warehouse made of dark, creosoted timber. Along with a diorama of the town a century ago, it's full of photos and seafaring memorabilia – a skiff, models of bigger boats (including a Viking longship), nets, and bits and pieces from the sea.

ARRIVAL AND INFORMATION   **ESKIFJÖRÐUR**

By bus The bus stop is on Strandgata.
Destinations Egilsstaðir (11 weekly; 45min); Neskaupstaður (11 weekly; 25min); Reyðarfjörður (11 weekly; 15min).
Services The post office, bank and supermarket (Mon–Fri

9am–6pm, Sat 10am–2pm) lie either side of the old freezing plant on Strandgata. The swimming pool (Mon–Fri 6am–9pm, Sat & Sun 10am–6pm) is at the western entrance to town, and has a waterslide and sauna.

Tours Tanni Travel, Strandgata 14 (☎476 1399, ⓦtannitravel.is), offers various day tours around the locality, taking in the Maritime Museum, fishing villages, and waterfalls, plus a taster of fermented shark with a *brennevin* shot to calm you down afterwards. They can also arrange transfers to/from Snæfell (see p.296).

ACCOMMODATION AND EATING

Campsite Strandgata 2 ☎470 9000. On the western side of town, near the church and screened by bushes, there's not really much to the site, though it has the usual amenities and a small children's playground, and is only a short walk from the town swimming pool (see opposite). **1200kr**

Eskifjörður Strandgata 47 ☎476 0099, ⓦpuffinhotel.is. Brand-new place with warm, slightly functional rooms, some equipped with huge bathrooms – good value for the price. Breakfast 1500kr. **19,500kr**

Guesthouse Askja Strandgata ☎477 1247, ⓦhotelaskja.is. Low, long aluminium-clad building on the waterfront at the eastern end of town. There's an open-plan, pine-floored lounge and TV room upstairs, kitchen and dining room downstairs. Rooms are straightforward and bathrooms are shared; breakfast is 1700kr. Dorms **7800kr**, doubles **17,100kr**

Kaffihúsið Strandgata 10 ☎476 1150, ⓦkaffihusid.is. Guesthouse whose comfortable, no-frills doubles all have shared amenities. The attached café-bar offers grills and cream-laden cakes, and half the town seems to gravitate here after dark. Restaurant Tues–Thurs 6–11pm, Fri 6pm–3am, Sat noon–3am, Sun noon–11pm. **13,700kr**

★**Mjóeyri** Strandgata 120 ☎477 1247, ⓦmjoeyri.is. East out of town along the seafront and on its own private sand spit, this guesthouse features dorms, self-catering doubles with shared bathrooms and a row of stylish wooden cabins sleeping 4–7. Their *Randulf* seafood restaurant is rated as one of the best in the region. Dorms **7800kr**, doubles **17,100kr**, cabins **28,100kr**

Neskaupstaður

At the end of Route 92, **NESKAUPSTAÐUR** curls around the northern side of **Norðfjörður** – which is also another name for the town itself. It's Iceland's easternmost town and the East Fjords' largest settlement, but a stretched and insubstantial one. Neskaupstaður's setting is splendid, however, backed by tall, avalanche-prone fells all around, and facing across the fjord to **Rauðubjörg's** red cliffs; judging by the number of antlers hung over front doors, there's also a healthy reindeer population up in the hills.

The museums

Egilsbraut • June-Aug Mon–Sat 1–5pm • 1100kr

Not to be outdone by its neighbours, Neskaupstaður sports two museums, housed together in a large russet building (marked "Safnahús"). The **Museum of Natural History** includes a rock collection and various stuffed and mounted fauna, while the **Maritime Museum** covers the history of the town's seafaring traditions with fading black-and-white photographs and assorted nautical bits and bobs – plus a reconstructed smithy and working boatbuilding exhibition.

ARRIVAL AND INFORMATION

NESKAUPSTAÐUR

By bus The bus stop is on the main street, Egilsbraut. Destinations Egilsstaðir (11 weekly; 1hr 10min); Eskifjörður (11 weekly; 25min); Reyðarfjörður (11 weekly; 35min).

Services The bank and ATM, Olís fuel station and Samkaup supermarket (Mon–Fri 9am–6pm, Sat 10am–2pm) are close to each other on Egilsbraut and Miðstræti. Also on Miðstræti, the pool (Mon–Fri 6am–8pm, Sat & Sun 10am–6pm) has a small waterslide, a sauna, hot pots and a gym.

Tours Plans are afoot to run cruises around the fjord in a renovated wooden trawler looking for birds, whales and

NORÐFJÖRÐUR HIKES

Several hiking trails begin at Neskaupstaður's campsite (see p.304). The easiest follows the coast for 1.5km to **Páskahellir** – Easter Cave – from where it's said you can see the sun dancing on Easter morning. A much tougher proposition is the full-day, marked trail north over the mountains into Mjóifjörður (see p.301); or the 10km return hike up along the ridgetop to **Flesjartangi**, right at the mouth of Mjóifjörður.

fish; the ferry service to Mjóifjörður (see p.301) might also resume. For current information, contact Freysteinn (☎896

9989, ✉freysteinn@tmumbod.is) or the *Hildibrand* hotel (see below).

ACCOMMODATION AND EATING

Campsite At the very top of town, above the *Edda* hotel (see below) ☎470 9000. Located underneath the avalanche defences, this site is pretty exposed, but there are toilets, showers, hiking trails and a great view of Norðfjorður. **1200kr**

Capitano Hafnarbraut 50 ☎477 1800 or ☎861 4747, ⊛hotelcapitano.is. Large corrugated-iron hotel, painted an unmissable deep blue. The century-old interior has been modernized, and the fairly bland rooms perked up with bright artwork by Tryggvi Ólafsson. **21,000kr**

Edda Nesgata 40 ☎444 4860, ⊛hoteledda.is. Views across the fjord from all but one room in this hotel at the eastern end of town. The en-suite rooms are bright if institutional; a generous breakfast buffet costs an extra

1900kr, and they can organize packed lunches for hikers. Summer only (check website for up-to-date details). **23,300kr**

Hildibrand Hafnarbraut 2 ☎477 1950, ⊛hildibrand .com. Doubles and self-contained apartments sleeping 2–4, attached to a restaurant, deli and microbrewery; try the seafood selection for two (5200kr pp) or lobster soup (2690kr). Restaurant daily 11am–10pm. Doubles **25,500kr**, apartments **33,000kr**

★**Nesbær** Hafnarbraut 22 ☎477 1115. Café and bakery with check tablecloths and a menu featuring soups and crêpes (1690kr) alongside fresh bagels or panini with various fillings (700kr) and, of course, coffee and cakes. Mon–Thurs 9am–6pm, Fri 9am–10.30pm, Sat 10am–6pm.

Fáskrúðsfjörður

Until the early twentieth century, the elongated hamlet of **FÁSKRÚÐSFJÖRÐUR** was a busy seasonal base for fishing fleets from northern **France**, and the French even established stores, a hospital and consulate here. Today, other than French headstones in the cemetery, the connection is most tangible during the **Franskir dagir festival** in late July, which celebrates all things Gallic with four days of singing, dancing and, naturally, feasting.

Fransmenn á Íslandi

Inside the Fosshotel on Hafnargata • June–Sept daily 10am–6pm • 1300kr

Housed in an underground tunnel linking the two hotel buildings, **Fransmenn á Íslandi** (French in Iceland museum) features an atmospherically claustrophobic re-creation of a trawler cabin, creatively displayed digital archives, records and artefacts, plus a memorial to sailors who perished over the years. A French film of the town from 1935 is visual proof that there were once an incredible five thousand people in Fáskrúdsfjörður during the fishing season.

ARRIVAL AND INFORMATION   FÁSKRÚÐSFJÖRÐUR

By bus The East Iceland Bus Company (☎477 1713, ⊛austfjardaleid.is) operates a Egilsstaðir–Reyðafjörður–Fáskrúðsfjörður–Stöðvarfjörður–Breiðdalsvík service year-round; Sterna (⊛sterna.is) and Reykjavík Excursions (⊛re .is) follow the same route daily (June–Sept only) on their Egilsstaðir–Höfn runs.
Destinations Breiðdalsvík (5 weekly–2 daily; 50min);

Egilsstaðir (5 weekly–2 daily; 1hr 10min); Stöðvarfjörður (5 weekly–2 daily; 30min).

By car Fáskrúðsfjörður is on Route 96 between Reyðarfjörður and Stöðvarfjörður; there's also the longer, slower Route 955 along the coast to Reyðarfjörður.

Services The bank, post office, pool and supermarket are all on kilometre-long Búðavegur.

ACCOMMODATION AND EATING

Bjarg Skólavegur 49 ☎475 1466, ⊛hotelbjarg.is. You'd never guess from the storm-battered exterior, but rooms are clean, comfortable and smart, if not lavishly decorated, and have shared or private bathrooms. The owner is quietly helpful and organizes boat trips to wind-scoured islands offshore. Breakfast included. **17,500kr**

Café Súmarlina Búðavegur 59 ☎845 8008. Lovely building overlooking the harbour, but the menu is the familiar run of burgers, pizza and sandwiches served up in every roadhouse around the country. Still, prices aren't bad: a large burger, chips and notional salad is 1700kr. Daily 11am–9pm.

Campsite Hafnargata 12 ☎475 1220. Nice spot at the

western edge of town with a meadow and stream, plus a growing screen of trees to reduce the near-constant winds. Toilet but no shower; head to the pool 15min away on Búðavegur. **1000kr**

★**Fosshotel** Hafnargata 11–14 ☎470 4070, ⓦ fosshotel.is. Splendidly located in two fully restored wooden period buildings down on the waterfront, with splendid views over the fjord from the restaurant and outdoor terrace. Original panelling and beams lend historical ambience, but the spacious rooms are essentially modern, comfortable and cosy. Restaurant mains around 4500kr. Restaurant daily 6–11pm. **31,000kr**

Stöðvarfjörður

STÖÐVARFJÖRÐUR is a diminutive harbour town, whose main street – Route 96, here called **Fjarðarbraut** – is barely 300m long. If you're here in spring, you're likely to see snow-white ptarmigans fearlessly eating ornamental berries in people's front gardens; otherwise, a couple of art galleries might tempt you to stop.

Gallerí Snærós

Fjarðarbraut 40 • Daily 10am–5pm • ⓦ gallerisnaeros.is

Gallerí Snærós displays graphic work and ceramics by local artists Sólrún Friðriksdóttir and Ríkhardur Vattingoyer, who are often at work in their studio; there's also a mix of designer clay miniatures and textiles by their daughter Rósa.

Petra Steinasafn

Near the western exit to town • May–Sept daily 9am–6pm • 1000kr • ⓦ steinapetra.is

Petra Steinasafn is an extraordinary private collection of thousands of rocks and mineral samples from all over the place, accumulated over a lifetime of fossicking by elderly Petra Sveinsdóttir, who doesn't speak any English. They're arranged around a terrace and "stone garden", planted with ferns and colourful blooms, and look best on a sunny day.

Hafnarnes

Some 8km north of Stöðvarfjörður along Route 96, **Hafnarnes** comprises a lighthouse and remains of a nineteenth-century fishing village which was deserted after World War II. The outlines of foundations and bits and pieces from buildings are all that's left; it makes you wonder about the future of many East Fjord settlements that are no bigger today than Hafnarnes was.

ARRIVAL AND INFORMATION   **STÖÐVARFJÖRÐUR**

By bus The East Iceland Bus Company (☎477 1713, ⓦ austfjardaleid.is) operates a Egilsstaðir–Reyðafjörður–Fáskrúðsfjörður–Stöðvarfjörður–Breiðdalsvík service year-round; Sterna (ⓦ sterna.is) and Reykjavík Excursions (ⓦ re.is) follow the same route daily (June–Sept only) on their Egilsstaðir–Höfn runs. The bus stop is on Fjarðarbraut.

Destinations Breiðdalsvík (5 weekly–2 daily; 20min); Egilsstaðir (5 weekly–2 daily; 1hr 40min); Fáskrúðsfjörður (5 weekly–2 daily; 30min).

Services There's an N1 fuel pump but no supermarket in town, though the *Brekkan* café (see below) has a tiny store selling basic provisions.

ACCOMMODATION AND EATING

Brekkan Fjarðarbraut 44 ☎475 8939. This no-nonsense diner with tubular metal chairs and plastic tablecloths serves hearty sandwiches, soup, fry-ups and fish dishes from 700kr upwards. Daily 10am–9pm.

Campsite On the main road east of town ☎470 9040. Not much more than flat ground, picnic tables and a toilet; a screen of hedges cuts the wind down a little. **1000kr**

Kirkjubær Fjarðarbraut 37A ☎892 3319, ⓦ simnet.is/birgiral. Up on a small hill, this blue-painted wooden church was moved to its current location in 1925 and has been converted into a comfortable, self-catering lodge capable of sleeping ten, though you pay by the bed. They also rent fishing gear and boats. Dorms **6000kr**, sleeping bags **4500kr**

Saxa Fjarðarbraut ☎511 3055, ⓦ saxa.is. Unmissible yellow building opposite *Brekkan*, with well-appointed en-suite doubles and an open-plan common room with TV; upstairs rooms are brighter. Breakfast 1700kr; other meals by arrangement. There's a nice café here too, serving snacks and home-made cakes. **19,000kr**

Breiðdalsvík

Just off the main coastal road and overlooking the sea, **BREIÐDALSVÍK** marks where Route 96 through the East Fjords joins the Ringroad from Egilsstaðir. The town sits on a border of sorts between the tighter, steeper, more dramatic fjord scenery to the north; and the flatter, broader landscapes to the south. Breiðdalsvík itself barely comprises two streets and there's not much reason to stop here unless you need to change buses.

ARRIVAL AND INFORMATION   BREIÐDALSVÍK

By bus The East Iceland Bus Company (☎477 1713, ☯austfjardaleid.is) operates a Egilsstaðir–Reyðafjörður–Fáskrúðsfjörður–Stöðvarfjörður–Breiðdalsvík service year-round; Sterna (☯sterna.is) and Reykjavík Excursions (☯re.is) follow the same route daily (June–Sept only) on their Egilsstaðir–Höfn runs. In winter, there's no bus between Breiðdalsvík and Dúpivogur, the only stretch of the

Ringroad not covered year-round by public transport.
Destinations Djúpivogur (2 daily; 1hr); Egilsstaðir (2 daily; 2hr); Fáskrúðsfjörður (2 daily; 50min); Höfn (2 daily; 2hr 15min); Stöðvarfjörður (2 daily; 20min).
Services The little N1 fuel station has a small range of meat, vegetables and canned food.

ACCOMMODATION AND EATING

Café Margret About 3km from town on Route 96 ☎475 6625. This chalet-like building has just four rooms, two of which overlook the fjord. The café makes a great place to break a long drive and stare out of the windows over a coffee and home-made German cake. **22,500kr**
Bláfell Sólvellir 14 ☎475 6770, ☯hotelblafell.is. Trusty standby with a "log cabin" exterior; inside, the comfortable en-suite rooms are pine-panelled with chintzy bedcovers

and curtains. Breakfast, wi-fi and use of the sauna included. **26,000kr**
Kaupfélagið Café Sólvellir. Spacious café near to the hotel, with internet, ice cream, cakes and fast food, including lunchtime soup specials, burgers, onion rings and chips – a 16" pizza with the works costs 3500kr. Mon–Thurs & Sun 10.30am–5pm, Fri & Sat 10.30am–9pm.

Berufjörður

Berufjörður, the inlet south of Breiðdalsvík, is narrow but long; Djúpivogur looks close enough to touch across its mouth, but is actually a 30min drive away via the head of the fjord. Part-way along Berufjörður's north side, **Gautavík** is the bay where the fiery Norwegian evangelist Þangbrand (see p.309) landed in Iceland in the late tenth century to convert the country to Christianity.

ARRIVAL AND DEPARTURE   BERUFJÖRÐUR

By bus Sterna (☯sterna.is) and Reykjavík Excursions (☯re.is) stop off at *Berunes* hostel in Berufjörður on their summer-only services between Egilsstaðir and Höfn.
Destinations Breiðdalsvík (2 daily; 30min); Djúpivogur

(2 daily; 30min); Egilsstaðir (2 daily; 1hr 30min); Fáskrúðsfjörður (2 daily; 1hr 20min); Höfn (2 daily; 2hr); Reyðarfjörður (2 daily; 1hr 40min); Stöðvarfjörður (2 daily; 50min).

ACCOMMODATION

★**Berunes IYHA hostel** ☎869 7227, ☯hostel.is. Hospitable operation on former farm, with a wind-screened campsite as well as dorms and doubles with shared bathrooms; the best rooms are in the old wooden

farmstead, clean and cosy and with original fittings. There are also self-catering kitchens plus a café. Breakfast buffet with pancakes is 1750kr. Dorms **5000kr**, doubles **14,500kr**, camping **1350kr**

Djúpivogur

Set slightly off the main road, at the southern tip of Berufjörður, **DJÚPIVOGUR** is the southernmost of the East Fjord settlements. Though Djúpivogur is little more than a couple of streets between the church and harbour, the area has signs of long occupation: one of Iceland's few known **Roman coins** was found over the headland at Hamarsfjörður, while offshore **Papey** – Monks' Island – is believed to have been a retreat for Christian fathers in pre-Viking times. Djúpivogur itself was founded by German traders in 1589, and the tiny, pretty harbourside village is worth a stopover for the half-day trip over to Papey.

Langabúð

By the harbour • Café Mon–Thurs & Sun 10am–6pm, Fri & Sat 10am–6pm & 9pm–late • Museum 800kr • ☎ 478 8220

A long, wooden building, **Langabúð** has variously served as a store, warehouse, slaughterhouse, managers' residence and meeting hall since its construction in 1850. It currently houses a café and unexciting **folk museum** featuring household goods, stuffed birds, a mineral collection and a section devoted to local sculptor **Ríkarður Jónsson** (1888–1977).

Papey

Boats from Djúpivogur June to mid-Sept daily at 1pm; 4hr • 9000kr • ☎ 478 8119 or ☎ 854 4438

Green, hummocky and somewhat boggy, the island of **Papey** covers just two square kilometres, its 58m apex topped by a lighthouse. What makes the four-hour excursion worthwhile is the certainty of seeing **seals** on the bracing voyage over and – while the **seabird population** has diminished over the past decade – incredible numbers of cliff-nesting puffins, razorbills and guillemots on arrival.

According to tradition, Papey was first settled by monks fleeing the ninth-century Viking expansion, and excavations during the early twentieth century uncovered three ancient **crosses**. The island was lived on until the 1950s, with a wooden **church** built in 1807 – said to be Iceland's smallest – still standing, and chained down against fierce winter winds. Papey's only present tenants are a few sheep, ferried over each year in summer.

ARRIVAL AND INFORMATION   DJÚPIVOGUR

By bus Sterna (ⓦ sterna.is) and Reykjavík Excursions (ⓦ re.is) stop at Djúpivogur harbour on their summer-only run between Egilsstaðir and Höfn. On Mon, Wed–Fri and Sun there's also a year-round bus from Djúpivogur to Hornafjörður airport (Höfn); contact the *Framtíð* hotel (see below) for bookings.
Destinations Berunes (2 daily; 30min); Breiðdalsvík (2 daily; 1hr); Egilsstaðir (2 daily; 2hr 20min); Fáskrúðsfjörður (2 daily; 1hr 50min); Höfn (2 daily; 1hr 30min); Reyðarfjörður (2 daily; 2hr 10min); Stöðvarfjörður (2 daily; 1hr 20min).
Services Djúpivogur's services are all within a brief walk of the harbour and comprise a post office, bank with ATM, fuel pump, pool and small Samkaup supermarket (Mon–Fri 10am–6pm, Sat 10am–4pm, Sun noon–4pm).

ACCOMMODATION AND EATING

Campsite On the hill behind the harbour ☎ 478 8887. Run by the *Framtíð* hotel (see below), with sink, shelter shed, toilet and showers, and plenty of space to pitch your tent. Being set in a hollow gives some protection from the wind. 1350kr
Framtíð Vogaland 4 ☎ 478 8887, ⓦ hotelframtid.com. The hotel's main building is a charmingly restored wooden structure from 1906 with en-suite doubles; they also run an alienatingly scaled hostel, albeit good for groups. The restaurant specializes in seafood. Restaurant daily noon–2pm and 6–9pm. Dorms 6600kr, doubles 27,900kr
★ **Klif** Kambi 1, under the radio mast ☎ 478 8802, ⓦ klifhostel.is. Small family-run affair finished in wood and tiles, with comfortable rooms (all with shared bathrooms), a kitchen and warmly hospitable owner. Dorms 5000kr, doubles 16,000kr
Við Voginn On the harbourfont ☎ 478 8860. Diner serving inexpensive burgers, sandwiches, *pýlsur* and chips in various guises from about 1200kr. Mon–Fri 9am–8pm, Sat & Sun 11am–8pm.

The southeast

South of Djúpivogur, the fjords recede into the background and you enter the altogether different world of **southeastern Iceland**, a coastal band between the East Fjords and Vík which is dominated by Europe's largest ice cap, **Vatnajökull**. Covering eight thousand square kilometres, almost 150km wide and up to 1km thick,

Vatnajökull's vast size gradually sinks in as it floats inland for hour after hour as you drive past, its glacier tongues flowing in slow motion from the heights to sea level, grinding out a black gravelly coastline as they go. **Vatnajökull National Park** (🖤 vjp.is) covers 12,000 square kilometres of this unspoiled wilderness – an extraordinary eleven percent of Iceland's total landmass – accessible by hiking, four-wheel-driving or even by snowmobile. Flying is perhaps the only way to absorb Vatnajökull's full immensity: glaring ice sheets shadowed in lilac; pale blue tarns; and grey, needle-sharp *nunataks* – mountain peaks – poking through the ice.

Given Vatnajökull's proximity, Iceland's "mini ice-age" between 1200 and 1900 hit the southeast especially hard – not to mention the devastating **jökulhlaups** (see box, p.317) that flood out from beneath Vatnajökull's icy skirt from time to time – and it remains a thinly settled area, even though all glaciers here are **retreating** as the climate warms once more. Vatnajökull's eastern flank is accessed at **Lónsöræfi**, a private reserve managed by **Stafafell farm**, close to the regional hub of **Höfn**. There's the stunning sight of icebergs floating on the lagoon at **Jökulsárlón**; and the ice cap's southern glaciers and adjacent heaths to explore at **Skaftafell National Park** and **Skeiðarársandur**, a huge glacier-induced wilderness between Vatnajökull and the sea. Moving away from Vatnajökull, **Kirkjubæjarklaustur** is the southeast's second settlement, near where lava-fields and craters at **Lakagígar** stand testament to one of Iceland's most violent volcanic events. Note that almost the only **shops** and **banks** in the entire region are at Höfn and Kirkjubæjarklaustur, which are 200km apart.

7

GETTING AROUND   **THE SOUTHEAST**

By plane Hornafjörður airport, at Höfn, has regular flights to Reykjavík.

By bus Reykjavík Excursions (🖤 re.is), Strætó (🖤 straeto .is) and Sterna (🖤 sterna.is) operate year-round Reykjavík–Höfn buses along the Ringroad; Sterna and RE also have summer-only services through the East Fjords to Egilsstaðir; while RE offers an exciting alternative between Reykjavík and Kirkjubæjarklaustur along the Fjallabak route via Landmannalaugar (see p.119).

Lón

Lón is a glacial river valley whose 30km-wide estuary is framed by **Eystrahorn** and **Vestrahorn**, two prominent spikes of granite to the east and west. The central **Jökulsá í Lóni** is a typical glacial flow, its broad gravel bed crisscrossed by intertwined streams that are crystal clear and shallow in winter but flow murky and fast with increased snowmelt in summer. A sandbar across the mouth of the bay has silted the estuary up into lagoons – *lón* in Icelandic – with good trout fishing, thousands of whooper swans nesting on the eastern side, and reindeer herds descending from the upper fells in winter.

Stafafell

Halfway across Lón and just east of the river, a short road off the Ringroad heads inland to **Stafafell**, comprising a couple of farm buildings, a hostel and an unassuming **church**, surrounded by birch trees. The site was consecrated a generation after the tenth-century Norwegian missionary Þangbrand – armed with a sword and a crucifix instead of a shield – killed Stafafell's pagan owner in a duel and went on to spread the Christian message across Iceland, surviving attacks by sorcery and a berserker in the process. His activities divided the country and finally forced the Alþing to restore unity by accepting Christianity as the national religion in 1000.

Lónsöræfi

The highlands inland from Stafafell are known as **Lónsöræfi**, the Wilderness of Lón, an unspoiled area of streams, moor and fractured rhyolite hills, capped by Vatnajökull's eastern edge (though this is invisible from the main road). Now

HIKING THROUGH LÓNSÖRÆFI

A dozen or so demanding **hiking trails** run north through Lónsöræfi and right up to Snæfell (see p.296). This is a remote area: don't hike alone, and bring everything you'll need with you – warm clothing, food, water and a tent – as weather or navigation errors can see even one-day walks accidentally extended. You'll also want Mál og menning's *Lónsöræfi* 1:100,000 **map**. Note that the reserve's waterways are all glacier-fed, making for unpredictable flow rates in summer. **Hiking huts** along the way – which you need to book in advance – are operated by Ferðafélag Austur-Skaftfellinga (❶868 7624, ❷ferdafelag@gonguferdir.is) and Vatnajökull National Park (❿vjp.is).

GRÁKINN

A short, easy hike (5hr return) follows erratic **marker pegs** uphill behind Stafafell Farm hostel (see below) onto the moor, above but away from the east side of the Jökulsá í Lóni River. It's slightly boggy heathland, with spongy cushions of moss, low birch thickets and hummocks of gravel; there's a tight grouping of fells looming to the northeast, while the west is more open. Following a general northwest bearing, after a couple of hours you'll find yourself above the shattered, orange and grey rhyolite sides of the **Grákinn valley**; scramble west down the scree and then crisscross the stream to where the valley appears to dead-end in a wall of dark cliffs. Push through a short canyon and exit to the Jökulsá í Lóni, which you follow southeast downstream along a dull jeep track to the highway and the farm.

LÓNSÖRÆFI TO SNÆFELL

The hike from Stafafell to **Snæfell** takes at least four days. Contact the farm to arrange a lift in a vehicle across the Jökulsá í Lóni at the start of the hike; at the other end there is no public transport from Snæfell to Egilsstaðir, so you'll need to risk finding somebody to hitch with, or contact Tanni Travel (❿tannitravel.is), who can arrange pickups. There's one short glacier traverse along the way, requiring a little experience; otherwise you just need to be fit.

Once over the multi-streamed Jökulsá í Lóni, there's a hut and campsite at **Eskifell**. From here, you follow an ever-tightening gorge due north to another hut and campsite at **Illikambur**, around 25km from Stafafell, from where there are several day-walks along side-gorges and up nearby peaks, including a route west up to Rauðhamar for views down onto Öxarfellsjökull, Vatnajökull's easternmost extension.

Back on the main track, around 10km north of Illikambur is **Víðidalur**, an attractive valley with a campsite to the south and lakeside hut 2km to the northwest at **Kollumúlvatn**, where there are further glacial views and trails northwest to a collection of wind-scoured outcrops known as **Tröllakrókar**, "troll spires". The next 17km follows Vatnajökull's northeastern edge to the **Geldingafell** hut; from here, the final stage to Snæfell is a lengthy 35km (avoiding unfordable rivers), first westwards over the tip of **Eyjabakkajökull**, then bearing north at Litla-Snæfell to the hut (see p.296) on Snæfell's west side.

incorporated into a private **reserve** accessed through Stafafell farm, Lónsöræfi is beautiful **hiking** country, where you could spend anything from a few hours to several days on remote tracks – or even hike north through to Snæfell, near Egilsstaðir (see box above).

ACCOMMODATION

LÓNSÖRÆFI

Stafafell Farm ❶478 1717, ❿stafafell.is. Hostel inside an old, two-storey wooden house near the church, with warm dorms and doubles (with shared bathrooms), showers, kitchen and dining room. You can also pitch a tent in the field outside. Bring all your own supplies; they don't serve meals and the nearest shops are 20km away in Höfn. They specialize in information about Lónsöræfi hikes and other tours. Höfn–Egilsstaðir transport will drop off and collect from the Ringroad. Doubles <u>11,000kr</u>, sleeping bags <u>3750kr</u>, camping <u>1200kr</u>

Höfn

The staging post for the southeast, **HÖFN** is a small town perched on a narrow neck of land, with a prime view inland of four glacial tongues descending Vatnajökull – at least on days when the pernicious fogs abate. The bay here, **Hornafjörður**, was settled in Viking times by **Hrollaugur Rögnvaldsson**, distant ancestor of saga writer Snorri Sturluson (see box, p.158), though the town itself began life as late as 1897 as a trading post, unimaginatively named Höfn (Harbour) after the bay's deep anchorage. Expansion followed the 1950s fishing boom and the establishment of a fish-freezing plant, which remains the largest local employer; Höfn is famed for its fine **lobster**.

Höfn's main street is Hafnarbraut, which runs for about 1.5km south through the town, with most services in a loose cluster towards or around the harbour.

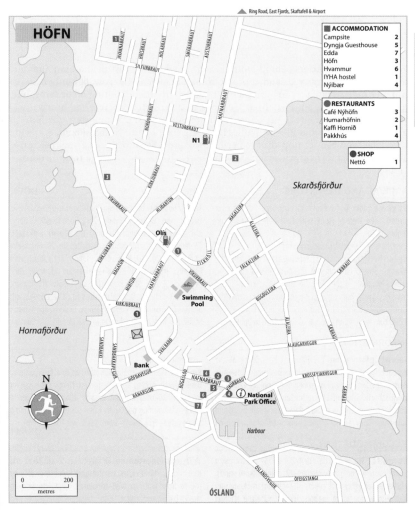

Ring Road, East Fjords, Skaftafell & Airport

HÖFN

7

■ **ACCOMMODATION**
Campsite	2
Dyngja Guesthouse	5
Edda	7
Höfn	3
Hvammur	6
IYHA hostel	1
Nýibær	4

● **RESTAURANTS**
Café Nýhöfn	3
Humarhöfnin	2
Kaffi Hornið	1
Pakkhús	4

● **SHOP**
Nettó	1

Skarðsfjörður

Olís

Hornafjörður

Swimming Pool

Bank

National Park Office

Harbour

N

0   200
metres

ÓSLAND

TOURS FROM HÖFN

From Höfn, Glacier Jeeps (☎478 1000, ⓦglacierjeeps.is) focus on trips to one of the nearby **glaciers** descending Vatnajökull. Base camp is the snowline at **Jöklasel** hut, some 45km west of town along the Ringroad and then 16km up the four-wheel-drive-only Route F985. From here you mount a skidoo and drive out onto the glacier, tearing across a frozen, empty horizon at upwards of 40km an hour. The usual destination is **Brókarbotnstindur**, a sharp-edged *nunatak* with great views west across a deep valley to more tall peaks and ice. Warm clothing, crash helmet and full instruction are provided (bringing sunglasses is a good idea); one hour costs 19,500kr, or 40,000kr for two.

For a different take on glaciers contact Ice Guide (☎661 0900, ⓦiceguide.is), who offer two hours' kayaking on a glacial lagoon (from 15,900kr) and, in winter only, ice cave exploration (19,900kr); Glacier Trips (ⓦglaciertrips.is) take you out on full-day glacier hikes (from 12,500kr). Finally, Fallastakkur (☎478 1517, ⓦfallastakkur.is) make four-wheel-drive trips into Lónsöræfi (see p.309) – contact them for prices.

7

Ósland

For views of the **glaciers** behind Höfn, head through town, past the harbour and out to the seafront at grassy **Ósland**, a protected nature reserve. Don't walk out here in summer unless you fancy being attacked by several thousand nesting **arctic terns**, but in a car you can reach a small hillock capped by an abstract concrete and bronze sculpture, where it's safe to get out and admire the scenery. Looking west, the four glaciers are Hoffellsjökull, Fláajökull, Heinabergsjökull and Skálafellsjökull, and with binoculars you can see how they've been scored and scarred with crevasses; the clear atmosphere plays tricks with your eyes and makes it difficult to judge their distance and scale.

ARRIVAL AND DEPARTURE   HÖFN

By plane Eagle Air (ⓦeagleair.is) connects Hornafjörður airport, 6km west of Höfn, with Reykjavík; there are no flights on Sat.
Destination Reykjavík (8 weekly; 1hr).
By bus Reykjavík Excursions (stopping at the N1 roadhouse; ⓦre.is), Strætó (stopping at the pool; ⓦstraeto.is) and Sterna (stopping at the campsite and YHA; ⓦsterna.is) all have Reykjavík–Höfn services. Sterna and RE also cover the East Fjords to Egilsstaðir in summer. The airport bus (☎478 1250) runs year-round (Mon, Wed–Fri & Sun) to Djúpivogur.

There is no winter bus between Djúpivogur and Breiðdalsvík.
Destinations Berunes (2 daily; 2hr); Breiðdalsvík (2 daily; 2hr 30min); Djúpivogur (2 daily; 1hr 30min); Egilsstaðir (2 daily; 4hr); Fáskrúðsfjörður (2 daily; 3hr 20min); Hella (3 daily; 3hr 10min); Hvolsvöllur (3 daily; 7hr); Jökulsárlón (3 daily; 1hr 30min); Kirkjubæjarklaustur (3 daily; 3hr); Reykjavík (3 daily; 9hr); Reyðarfjörður (1 daily; 3hr 40min); Selfoss (3 daily; 8hr); Seljalandsfoss (3 daily; 6hr 40min); Skaftafell (3 daily; 2hr 40min); Skógar (3 daily; 5hr 45min); Stöðvarfjörður (2 daily; 2hr 50min); Vík (3 daily; 3hr 50min).

INFORMATION

Tourist information The National Park Office at the harbour (daily: May & Sept 10am–6pm; June–Aug 8am–8pm; Oct–April 10am–noon & 4–6pm; ☎470 8330, ⓦvjp.is) grudgingly gives out brochures and practical info about the town, Lónsöræfi and glaciers, and sells maps and souvenirs. They're also a good source of information on

accommodation.
Services Main street Hafnarbraut has two fuel stations, banks (with ATMs), a well-stocked Nettó supermarket (Mon–Fri 10am–7pm, Sat & Sun 10am–6pm) and a modern swimming pool with water slides, hot pots and a sauna (Mon–Fri 6.45am–9pm, Sat & Sun 10am–7pm).

ACCOMMODATION

Campsite Hafnarbraut ☎478 1606, ⓔcamping @simnet.is. Large grassy pitches with shelter from winds, plus attached office with toilets, showers, internet, laundry and somewhere to sit indoors. It's opposite the N1 fuel station, about a 10min walk from the harbour. **1200kr**

★**Dyngja Guesthouse** Hafnarbraut 1 ☎846 0161, ⓦdyngja.com. Friendly, comfortable homestay close by the harbour with six well-appointed rooms (most with shared bathroom), coffee on tap, pleasant lounge area and self-service Nordic-style breakfast. Often booked out months in advance. <u>19,500kr</u>

Edda Ránarslóð 3 ☎ 444 4850, ⓦ hoteledda.is. Hotel with fabulous views over glaciers and the harbour from the lounge (and some of the 36 en-suite rooms). There's no restaurant, but they can provide breakfast (1900kr). Summer-only (check website for up-to-date details). <u>31,000kr</u>

Höfn Víkurbraut, off Hafnarbraut at Ólís fuel station ☎ 478 1240, ⓦ hotelhofn.is. Modern business hotel overlooking the shorefront and glaciers. Standard rooms are in an older complex; those in the spiffier new building, just above on a rise, have sea views. Rates include breakfast. Hotel <u>35,000kr</u>, new building <u>45,000kr</u>

Hvammur Ránarslóð 2 ☎ 478 1544, ⓦ hofninn.is. Warm and weatherproof house close to the harbour. Rooms are on the small side with shared bathrooms, but are also

bright and decently equipped with TV and views of the sea or glaciers. Rate includes breakfast. <u>28,500kr</u>

IYHA hostel Hvannarbraut; turn off Hafnarbraut at the N1 fuel station and then first right ☎ 478 1736, ⓦ hostel.is. Smoothly run budget option inside a former retirement home; there's a large living space, big kitchen and dining room, BBQ area and clean, functional dorms. A separate house has doubles and a kitchen. The disadvantage in bad weather is the 1500m walk to town. Dorms <u>4550kr</u>, doubles <u>12,500kr</u>

Nýibær Hafnarbraut ☎ 478 2670, ⓦ nyjibaerguest house@simnet.is. Guesthouse whose helpful management, large bedrooms (some en suite) and generous breakfast compensate for slightly plain furnishings and the lack of a kitchen. <u>22,400kr</u>

EATING AND DRINKING

Café Nýhöfn Hafnabraut ☎ 478 1818, ⓦ nyhofn.is. The latest of Höfn's characterful period buildings to be co-opted as a seafood restaurant, featuring pan-fried scallops (3200kr) and langoustine focaccia (3200kr). Best of all, however, are their organic barley burgers (3500kr) and the sumptuous carrot cake (1200kr). Daily 11am–10pm.

Humarhöfnin Hafnabraut ☎ 478 1200, ⓦ humar hofnin.is. Smart but laidback lobster restaurant with an unmistakable bright orange facade takes advantage of Höfn's most famous seafood. The langoustine bisque (2100kr) isn't huge but comes packed with seafood; or blow out on 300g of langoustine tails (6800kr).

March–Sept daily noon–10pm.

Kaffi Hornið Hafnabraut 42 ☎ 478 2600. The menu is no big surprise – lobster, burgers and grills (from 2500kr) – but reasonable prices, decent portions and the roomy timber building are a big plus. It can take ages to get seated, however. Daily 11am–10pm.

★ **Pakkhús** Höfn harbour ☎ 692 5624. Set in a 1930s warehouse, all dark beams and plank flooring, with just a bit more warmth and character than the competition. Prices are marginally cheaper too, and the food no less good: langoustine at 5990kr and salt cod for 3950kr. May–Sept daily noon–10pm.

Hoffell valley

Some 15km west of Höfn via the Ringroad and Route 984, the **Hoffell valley** has two big draws: a set of small hot tubs, and a glacier tongue complete with lagoon, similar to the over-touristed Jökulsárlón. Just note that you'll need your own transport, and those in conventional vehicles might have to walk the last few kilometres to the glacier.

Hoffell hot tubs

At the end of Route 984 • Daily 7am–11pm • 600kr

Out on a gravel tongue in the middle of nowhere, a set of five sunken fibreglass **hot tubs** makes the most of a natural thermal spring. There are changing huts, but otherwise you're out in the wilds; check that the water is safe before getting in as the temperature can fluctuate. It's best on a wet, cold day, or even in winter – when (atmospheric conditions allowing) it would be an incredible place to witness the Northern Lights.

Hoffellsjökull

The easiest to reach of several nearby glacier tongues, **Hoffellsjökull** lies 4km beyond the hot tubs at the end of a decent gravel road, though a small glacial stream along the way might prove too deep for low-slung cars. The track ends atop of a vegetated moraine ridge at the head of the valley, where a stunning view greets you at the crest: the distance bleached out by an immense icefield sprawling out between two fells, and a lake full of broken-up ice floes at your feet. Take care if you explore the rockfields either side; landslides are common.

ACCOMMODATION HOFFELL VALLEY

Hoffell Guesthouse Close to the hot tubs at the top of Route 984 ☎478 1514, ⓦglacierworld.is. Set in converted farm buildings, rooms – with or without private bathrooms and kitchenettes – are modern and full of clean lines, tones of white, and pine flooring. Breakfast and use of the hot tubs included. **19,900kr**

Jökulsárlón

On the Ringroad 75km west of Höfn and 55km east of Skaftafell, **Jökulsárlón** is a large, deep-blue lagoon between the nose of **Breiðamerkurjökull** and the sea. Formed after the glacier began shrinking rapidly in the 1940s, the lagoon is chock-full of smallish, powder-blue **icebergs** which have calved off Breiðamerkurjökull's front and float idly in the lake as if performing some slow ballet. A large gravel hill has been created as a lookout point on the lakeshore; check iceberg ledges for basking **seals**.

Once you've seen the lagoon, cross the road and walk down to the black-sand **beach**. The seafront here is littered with transparent ice boulders, the remains of the icebergs which have washed down the 1km-long Jökulsá (Iceland's shortest river) and into the sea – their weird, incredibly sculpted shapes are a striking sight on such a desolate shore.

ARRIVAL AND INFORMATION JÖKULSÁRLÓN

By bus All buses stop at Jökulsárlón long enough for a good look at the lagoon.

Destinations Hella (3 daily; 5hr); Hvolsvöllur (3 daily; 4hr 50min); Höfn (3 daily; 1hr); Kirkjubæjarklaustur (3 daily; 2hr); Reykjavík (3 daily; 7hr); Seljalandsfoss (3 daily; 4hr 30min); Selfoss (3 daily; 6hr); Skaftafell (3 daily; 1hr); Skógar (3 daily; 4hr); Vík (3 daily; 3hr 15min).

Information and tours In a shed beside the lagoon, the often overwhelmed information centre (daily 9am–7pm mid-May to mid-Sept; ⓦjokulsarlon.is) sells souvenirs, sandwiches (850kr) and is the place to book boat tours: 1hr zipping between the icebergs in an inflatable dingy (7500kr); or 30min exploring the shore and lagoon in an amphibious vehicle (4500kr).

Ingólfshöfði

Tractor tours May 1–Aug 25 Mon–Sat • 6900kr • ☎478 1682, ⓦoraefaferdir.is

Jutting 10km out to sea at the extreme eastern edge of Skeiðarársandur (see p.317), the flat prong of **Ingólfshöfði** is reputedly where Iceland's first official settler, **Ingólfur Arnarson**, landed. Tipped by a lighthouse, Ingólfshöfði's soft, grassy turf and low cliffs attract summer colonies of razorbills, guillemots, greater skua and – especially – **puffins**; bring a camera. There's a memorial stone to Ingólfur at the top, and views stretching westwards along the coast over the massive, black-sand desert, with Vatnajökull rising inland. You can't get out here in any sort of conventional vehicle, but Öræfaferðir runs **tractor tours** from the Ringroad (at Hofsnes farm) in summer; just give it a miss if the weather's bad, as there's nowhere to shelter from the rain along the way.

Öræfajökull

Hikes to Hvannadalshnúkur summit 39,900kr/person • ⓦmountainguides.is

Inland from Ingólfshöfði, the Ringroad bends sharply round the base of **Öræfajökull**, an ice cap covering the **Öræfi volcano**, whose devastating eruption in 1362 covered the whole region in tephra and caused its abandonment. Öræfi's protruding peak, **Hvannadalshnúkur**, is the highest point in Iceland at 2199m; you need to be fit and well equipped for the 23km, twelve-hour return hike up through snowfields to the summit. The route doesn't require technical climbing skills, but you definitely need an experienced guide – do not attempt the ascent without one.

Skaftafell National Park

Bordered by Öræfajökull to the east and Skeiðarárjökull to the west, **Skaftafell National Park** covers 1700 square kilometres of barren lowland *sandurs*, highland slopes brimming with wildflowers, sharp mountain ridges and, of course, glaciers. The two major sights here are **Svartifoss waterfall** and the icy tongue of **Skaftafellsjökull**, and the park is also one of Iceland's premier **hiking** venues, featuring paths that offer anything from an hour's stroll to a demanding full-day trek. Aim first for the **Visitor Centre** (see p.317), just north off the Ringroad on Route 998, to get advice and maps.

Skaftafellsjökull

One of Skaftafell's shortest walks runs from the Visitor Centre to the front of **Skaftafellsjökull** itself, an easy thirty minutes through low scrub around the base of yellow cliffs. The woods end at a pool and stream formed from glacial meltwater, beyond which stretch ice-shattered shingle and the glacier's 4m-high front, streaked with mud and grit and surprisingly unattractive. Look seawards to appreciate how much the glacier has retreated in recent times, leaving behind gravel hillocks known as moraines. Don't climb onto the glacier: crevasses and general instability make this extremely dangerous.

Svartifoss

A half-hour walk uphill from the Visitor Centre onto the plateau brings you to **Svartifoss**, the 20m-high Black Falls. Though the curtain isn't especially high or broad, it drops to a small plunge pool over an impressive amphitheatre of dark,

---

SKAFTAFELLSHEIÐI PLATEAU CIRCUIT

A rewarding, 6hr trail circuits the moors atop the **Skaftafellsheiði** plateau. Note that cloud, rain and fog can move in quickly, and you'll need Mál og mennings' 1:100,000 *Skaftafell* **map**, which has a 1:50,000 detail covering the Skaftafellsheiði area.

Beginning at Svartifoss, aim for **Sjónarsker**, a stony 310m ridge where the upper trail to Morsárdalur diverges – it makes a good general orientation point, as you can see from the coast right up to Vatnajökull from here. Heading due north, the path weaves through knee-high birch thickets, silent except for bird calls, towards **Skerhóll**'s steep front, and then climbs the gently sloping rear of this platform. Next comes a short ascent up to **Nyrðrihnaukur**, a long, grassy crest from which you can spy down on Morsárdalur's spread of crumbly grey cliffs, flat valley floor with intertwined streams, and encroaching glaciers.

By now you're about two hours from Svartifoss, right at the foot of **Kristínatindar**, a scree-covered peak rising 1125m to a jagged set of pinnacles. One trail heads eastwards around its south side, but you can also follow unmarked trails over Kristínatindar itself, starting from where the main path curves into a "bowl" between the two main peaks – the ascent is nowhere near as hard as it looks, though tiring enough. You emerge onto an icy saddle, the wind tearing into your face, with the main peak on your left and the minor summit to the right. The mountain is surrounded on three sides by ice, its wedge-like spine splitting Vatnajökull's outflow into the two glaciers which run either side of it – eastern Skaftafellsjökull is closer, a broad, white ribbon, crinkled and ribbed by the vast pressures squeezing it forward. The trail heads down towards it – you have to cast around to find the steep, indistinct track – landing you at **Gláma**, at the top of the sheer-sided valley filled by Skaftafellsjökull, where the trail meets the marked track around Kristínatindar. From here, you follow the stony cliff edge for an hour or so south to **Sjónarnípa**, a vantage above the glacier's front, where the path continues along the edge back to the campsite via birch scrub at **Austurbrekka**.

7

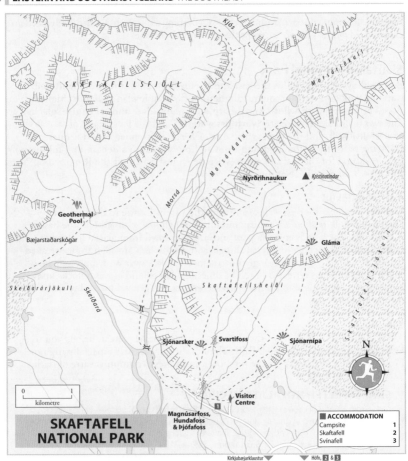

SKAFTAFELL
NATIONAL PARK

ACCOMMODATION	
Campsite	1
Skaftafell	2
Svínafell	3

underhanging hexagonal basalt columns – natural formations which inspired the architecture of Reykjavík's National Theatre. Many of the park's hiking trails begin at the falls.

Morsárdalur

Morsárdalur is the 10km-long, flat-bottomed glacial valley west of the Skaftafellsheiði plateau; you can get here either by following trails from Svartifoss, or along a flatter path direct from the Visitor Centre. The main target here is **Bæjarstaðarskógar**, a small wood of willows and birches, close to a sublime **geothermal pool** just big enough for two people. To extend the hike, continue up Morsárdalur and then bear west in front of little Morsárjökull glacier for **Kjós**, a strikingly beautiful canyon of bare, fractured boulders and sharp yellow crests.

ARRIVAL AND DEPARTURE   SKAFTAFELL NATIONAL PARK

By bus Ringroad buses all stop at Skaftafell; from mid-June until early Sept, they also travel inland via Eldgjá to Landmannalaugar (p.119). Through July and Aug there are return day-trips from Skaftafell, via Kirkjubæjarklaustur, to Lakagígar (see p.319).

Destinations Eldgjá (1 daily; 2hr 30min); Hella (3 daily; 4hr); Hvolsvöllur (3 daily; 3hr 50min); Höfn (3 daily; 2hr 40min); Jökulsárlón (3 daily; 1hr); Kirkjubæjarklaustur (3 daily; 1hr); Landmannalaugar (1 daily; 5hr); Reykjavík (3 daily; 5hr 50min); Selfoss (3 daily; 4hr 50min); Seljalandsfoss (3 daily; 3hr 30min); Skógar (3 daily; 2hr 55min); Vík (3 daily; 2hr 15min).

INFORMATION AND TOURS

Visitor Centre Off the Ringroad on Route 998, right at the foot of the Skaftafellsheiði plateau, the centre (June–Sept daily 9am–7pm; w vatnajokulsthjodgardur.is) provides insight into local geology and natural history via maps, models and information boards; there are also wardens on hand for current weather reports and hiking info. The shop sells maps and souvenirs.

Services Freysnes Roadhouse, 5km east along the Ringroad from Skaftafell, has fuel, a basic mini-mart and fair-value fast food.

Tours Mountain Guides (w mountainguides.is) and Glacier Guides (w glacierguides.is) have offices next to the Visitor Centre and offer glacier walks (from 9000kr), ice climbing (19,900kr) and hard-core ascents of Hvannadalshnúkur (see p.314). To see everything from the air, Atlantsflug (t 854 4105, w flightseeing.is) departs Reykjavík City Airport or Bakki airstrip for 9hr round-flights over Skaftafell and Jökulsárlón (96,000kr).

ACCOMMODATION

Campsite Close to the Visitor Centre t 470 8300. Facilities include toilets, showers, laundry and space on a grassy flat at the foot of the fells for 400 tents, but no shelter sheds or retreat from the weather. You pay at the Visitor Centre. Avoid the rip-off "Glacier Goodies" food cart. **1500kr**
Skaftafell Freysnes t 478 1945, w hotelskaftafell.is. 5km east from Skaftafell along the Ringroad at the no-horse hamlet of Freysnes. Recent renovations have perked up the formerly tired decor; twenty of their tidy and warm, if uninspiring, en-suite rooms have glacier views. Breakfast is included. **35,000kr**
Svínafell t 478 1765, w svinafell.com. Historic farm at the foot of Öræfajökull which featured in Njál's Saga, with a spacious campsite, rather basic cabins where you bring your own bedding and pay per bed, and fantastic glacier scenery. Amenities include showers, toilets, kitchen and an indoor dining area. It's 7km east along the Ringroad. Camping **1400kr**, sleeping bags **4900kr**

7

Skeiðarársandur

A bleak, 60km-wide gravel desert west of Skaftafell, **Skeiðarársandur** is the product of titanic outflows from **Grímsvötn**, a volcano buried inland underneath the Vatnajökull ice cap (see box below). Flowing down off the heights is **Skeiðarárjökull**, Iceland's most mobile glacier, whose 20km-wide front is so vast that it somehow manages to turn a 1000m drop off the top of Vatnajökull into an apparently gentle descent. The complex network of turbulent, ever-shifting glacial rivers flowing out from underneath Skeiðarárjökull was such an obstacle to road building that it was only with the construction of a series of bridges here in 1975 that the Ringroad around Iceland was completed – prior to which, anyone living to the east had to travel to Reykjavík via inland roads or Akureyri.

GRÍMSVÖTN AND JÖKULHLAUPS

Jökulhlaups are massive, volcanically induced flash floods that regularly burst out from under Vatnajökull, carrying untold tonnes of debris and water before them. One cause of these floods is **Grímsvötn**, a smouldering volcano buried 400m under the ice cap inland from Skeiðarársandur. The volcano's last major **eruption** was in 2011, but the biggest event of recent times occurred in October 1996 after a 6km-long vent opened up under the ice. For ten days the volcano blew steam, ash and smoke 6km into the sky; then, at 8am on November 5, the melted ice suddenly drained out underneath Skeiðarárjökull, sending three billion litres of water spewing across Skeiðarársandur in a 5m-high wave, sweeping away 7km of road and – despite design precautions – demolishing several bridges. Fourteen hours later the flood rate was peaking at 45,000 cubic metres per second, and when the waters subsided a day later, the *sandur* was dotted with house-sized chunks of ice ripped off the front of Skeiðarárjökull. Aside from the barren scenery, there's very little evidence for any of this today – the ice has long gone and the bridges are repaired – though look for the twisted remains of **Skeiðarárbrú**, one of the Ringroad bridges destroyed by the event, which are on display by the roadside west of Skaftafell.

Skeiðarársandur is also the largest European nesting ground for **great skuas** – best watched from a distance, as they take exception to being disturbed while raising their young. Keep an eye open, too, for **arctic foxes**, which feed on the birds.

Núpsstaður

Right where the Ringroad meets Skeiðarársandur's western edge, **Núpsstaður** is a neat line of **turf-covered buildings** including an eighteenth-century stone farmhouse and an even older church. This was once considered the most remote place in all Iceland: before Höfn existed, the closest ports were at Djúpivogur and Eyrarbakki near Selfoss, only accessible from here via a packhorse trail inland through the Fjallabak region. The buildings themselves are fairly unremarkable, but the stark location evokes the hardships of farm life in Iceland a century ago.

Kirkjubæjarklaustur

7

KIRKJUBÆJARKLAUSTUR – a tongue-twisting name that even locals often abbreviate to "Klaustur" – is only a single street, Klausturvegur, which stretches 500m west from a highway roundabout. However, as it's the sole settlement of any size in the 300km between Höfn and Vík, it's almost inevitable that you'll stop here. The village sits at the foot of an escarpment on the **Skaftá**, whose circuitous path originates on the western side of Vatnajökull, and is flanked by lavafields from eruptions by **Lakagígar** in 1783, centred some 75km to the northwest (see opposite).

The church

Kirkjubæjarklaustur's modern **church** is sided in granite slabs and has a facade resembling a ski lodge. A **Benedictine convent** was established here in 1186, though two of its nuns had the misfortune to be burned at the stake for heresy. But it was during the Lakagígar eruptions that the church here achieved national fame: as lava flows edged into the town, the pastor, **Jón Steingrímsson**, delivered what became known as the "Fire Sermon", and the lava halted. It's possible to climb the escarpment behind the church by means of a chain, and from the top there's a fine view of the diverted flow, and also of Landbrot, a collection of a thousand-odd **pseudocraters** (see p.267) formed during another eruption in 950.

ARRIVAL AND INFORMATION

KIRKJUBÆJARKLAUSTUR

By bus All Ringroad buses stop at Kirkjubæjarklaustur, as do summer Fjallabak services travelling inland via Eldgjá and Landmannalaugar. From late June until late Sept, Reykjavík Excursions (⊛re.is) also runs Skaftafell–Kirkjubæjarklaustur–Lakagígar day-trips. Buses stop at the N1 fuel station.

Destinations Eldgjá (1 daily; 1hr 30min); Hella (3 daily; 3hr); Hvolsvöllur (3 daily; 2hr 50min); Höfn (3 daily; 4hr 45min); Jökulsárlón (3 daily; 2hr); Landmannalaugar (1 daily; 4hr); Reykjavík (3 daily; 4hr 50min); Selfoss (3 daily; 3hr 50min); Seljalandsfoss (3 daily; 2hr 30min); Skaftafell

(3 daily; 1hr 5min); Skógar (3 daily; 1hr 55min); Vík (3 daily; 1hr 15min).

Tourist information The tourist office at Klausturvegur 15 (June–Sept daily 8.30am–6.30pm; ☎487 4620, ⊛klaustur.is) has toilets, brochures, a looped documentary about Lakagígar and also sells maps.

Services Klausturvegur has an N1 fuel station and roadhouse, a bank with ATM, a supermarket (Mon–Sat 9am–9pm) and small swimming pool with children's slide and hot tub (daily 9.30am–9pm).

ACCOMMODATION AND EATING

Campsite Kirkjubær II farm ☎894 4495, ⊛kirkjubaer .com. Grassy space behind the shopping complex sheltered by trees, with a kitchen, small indoor dining area, bathroom

and laundry. They also have self-contained cottages with bunks, sleeping up to four. Camping **1300kr**, cottages **20,000kr**

Klaustur Klausturvegur 6 ☎487 4900, ⌨iceland airhotels.is. Curiously upmarket business hotel for such an insubstantial, isolated town. The decor is Nordic – antiseptic white rooms with clinical lines – and there are no fewer than four conference rooms. Breakfast is 2800kr. <u>**35,000kr**</u>

Laki Efri-Vík, about 6km southeast of town on Route 204 ☎487 4694. Family-run complex featuring well-furnished hotel rooms with bathrooms (some with lake views), and a grid of small but comfy pine-panelled cabins. An on-site 4WD company offers private tours to Lakagígar. <u>**32,000kr**</u>

Systrakaffi Klausturvegur ☎487 4848. Set in Klaustur's small shopping complex, this spacious café offers a broad menu, including fish stew with rye bread (2300kr) or grilled lamb (4600kr) – plus the usual complement of grills, burgers and pizza. Daily noon–10pm.

Lakagígar

Some 50km northwest of Kirkjubæjarklaustur via a rugged jeep track, **Lakagígar** – the Laki Craters – are evidence of the most catastrophic volcanic event in Iceland's recorded history. In June 1783, the earth here split into a 25km-long **fissure** that, over the next seven months, poured out a continuous thick blanket of poisonous ash and smoke, and enough lava to cover six hundred square kilometres. So thick were the ash clouds that they reached as far as northern Europe, where they caused poor harvests; in Iceland, however, there were no harvests at all, and livestock dropped dead, poisoned by eating fluorine-tainted grass. Over the next three years Iceland's population plummeted by a quarter – through starvation, earthquakes and an outbreak of smallpox – to just 38,000 people, at which point the Danish government considered evacuating the survivors to Jutland.

Over two hundred years later, Lakagígar forms a succession of low, black craters surrounded by a still-sterile landscape, though the flows themselves are largely covered in a carpet of thick, spongy green moss. Pick of the scenery is on the journey in at **Fagrifoss**, the Beautiful Falls, and the view from atop Laki itself (818m), which takes in the incomprehensible expanse of lava.

ARRIVAL AND DEPARTURE   **LAKAGÍGAR**

By bus Reykjavík Excursions (⌨re.is) runs full-day tours to Lakagígar daily from July 1 to September 16. These take in Skaftafell, Kirkjubæjarklaustur and Lakagígar, spend four hours exploring the craters, then retrace the route in reverse. Return fare from Skaftafell is 15,500kr, or 12,000kr from Kirkjubæjarklaustur.

Super-jeep tours Hola Sport, based at *Hotél Laki* (☎660 1151, ⌨holasport.is), offers 9hr super-jeep day-trips to Lakagígar on demand between June and Oct; they need a minimum of two and charge 32,500kr/person.

The Interior

HVERAVELLIR HOT SPRINGS

The Interior

Nothing you might see elsewhere in Iceland prepares you for the desolate, raw beauty of the barren upland plateau that is the Interior – known in Icelandic as *hálendið* or "highlands" – Europe's last true wilderness. The violence of the elements here means that Iceland's heart is a desolate and uninhabited place, with no towns or villages, just cinematic vistas of seemingly infinite grey gravel plains, glacial rivers and lavafields punctuated by ice caps, volcanoes and jagged mountains. Sheep are virtually the only living things that survive here, but pasture and vegetation comprise only scattered clumps of ragged grass, and it's a daunting task for the farmers who venture out every autumn to round up their livestock.

Historically, routes through the Interior were forged in Viking times as a short cut for those making the journey on horseback to the annual law-making sessions at Þingvellir, though the region later provided refuge – if you can call it that – for **outlaws**, who are said to have been pardoned in the unlikely event that they managed to survive here for twenty years. Today, with the advent of the Ringroad and internal flights, the need to traverse this area has long gone, and there are **no sealed roads**, just tracks marked by stakes, and hardly any bridges across the rivers, causing some hairy moments when they are forded.

The Interior's **weather** is Iceland at its most elemental. Not only can fierce winds whip up the surface layer of loose grit in a matter of seconds, turning a beautiful sunny spell into a blinding haze of sand and dirt, but snowstorms are common even in July and August. The summer here is very short indeed, barely a matter of weeks, the winter long and severe, when the tracks are blocked by deep snowdrifts and closed to traffic.

The mainstay of **accommodation** in the Interior is the network of huts, or *sæluhús*, run by Iceland's hiking associations. The better ones have self-catering facilities and running water, though all sleeping space is in dorms and you'll need to bring your own sleeping bag. The huts are very busy during summer, and it's essential to book in advance; see accounts for contact details. If you're **camping**, you need a high-quality tent with enough pegs to anchor it down in the ferocious winds that can howl uninterrupted across the Interior. See Basics for more information.

Of all the various tracks, only two **routes** across the Interior actually traverse the whole way between north and south Iceland. The most dramatically barren of these is **Sprengisandur** (Route F26), which crosses between the Hekla area in the south and Lake Mývatn in the north. The alternative is **Kjölur** (Route 35), from Gullfoss to near Blönduós, which has less dramatic scenery but is the only route on which you might be able to use normal cars.

Other routes lead into the Interior but don't offer a complete traverse. The western **Kaldidalur** route (Route 550) runs between Borgafjörður and Þingvellir (see p.101); east of Lake Mývatn, the F88 follows the course of the mighty Jökulsá á Fjöllum south to the **Askja caldera**, from near where the F902 continues towards **Kverkfjöll**; heading inland from Egilsstaðir, Route 910 heads towards **Snæfell** (en route to Karahnjúkar,

The Kjölurvegur trek p.327   Eyvindur and Halla p.328

HERÐUBREIÐ

Highlights

❶ Sprengisandur The classic Interior trip, across an unremittingly bleak and barren desert stretching to a horizon tipped with ice caps. Not surprisingly, outlaws were once banished here. **See p.325**

❷ Kjölur Unusually for a road across Iceland's hostile Interior, in summer you can generally tackle this rough, stony track in a conventional car. **See p.326**

❸ Hveravellir This steam vent provides a splash of green and a hot spring in the middle of the wilderness, somewhere to break an Interior traverse for a relaxing thermal soak. **See p.327**

❹ Herðubreið This ice-capped "Queen of Icelandic Mountains" forms an isolated, flat-topped platform rising above the middle of a black gravel desert. **See p.328**

❺ Askja Massive caldera rimmed by rough, snowy peaks, where you can swim in a crater flooded with lukewarm water, the remnants of a colossal eruption in 1875. **See p.328**

❻ Kverkfjöll Extremely remote and difficult-to-reach ice caves, hollowed out by hot springs welling up under the northwestern edge of the mighty Vatnajökull ice cap. **See p.331**

HIGHLIGHTS ARE MARKED ON THE MAP ON P.324

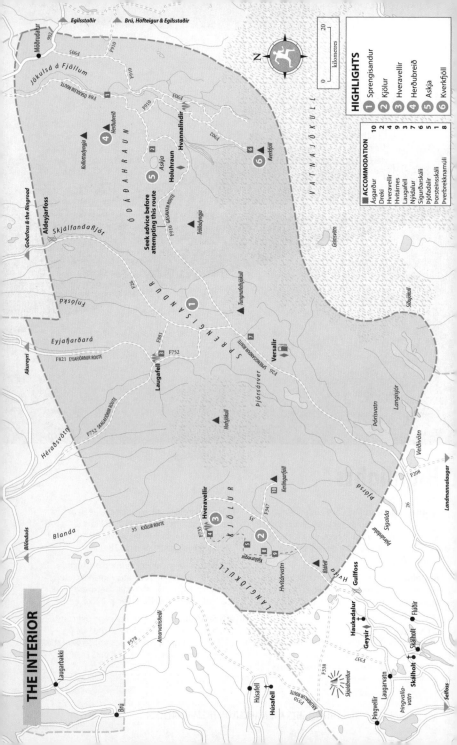

THE INTERIOR

HIGHLIGHTS

1. Sprengisandur
2. Kjölur
3. Hveravellir
4. Herðubreið
5. Askja
6. Kverkfjöll

ACCOMMODATION

Ásgarður	10
Dreki	2
Hveravellir	4
Hvítárnes	9
Laugafell	3
Nýidalur	7
Sigurðarskáli	6
Þorsteinsskáli	5
Þjófadalir	1
Þverbrekknamúli	8

Seek advice before
attempting this route

N

0   20
kilometres

see p.296), before becoming the F910 and kinking northwest to join the F88, while the **Fjallabak route** (F208) runs behind the south coast's ice caps (see box, p.120).

GETTING AROUND

The majority of Interior routes – any prefaced by an "F", as in "F26" – are accessible only by **4WD vehicles, and even then only through the summer; opening dates depend on the weather** (see box, p.31). Several routes are covered by bus tours through the summer, but any self-driving, cycling or hiking trip must be carefully planned. Never underestimate the **extreme conditions**, climatic and geological, which you may encounter en route; you'll also need some previous experience of tackling **glacial river crossings**. Read the relevant sections in Basics (p.32), and take everything you'll need with you, including a recent map plus sat-nav or a compass – at times it can be difficult to determine a route where several sets of car tracks meet.

By bus Scheduled tours through the Interior don't necessarily run every day; see the relevant accounts. Note that it's possible to hop off the buses at any of their stops – there's at least one hut and campsite on each route – and rejoin the service another day.

By car Essential equipment includes a tow rope, shovel, basic spare parts, and you should have enough mechanical knowledge to change a tube and fix most common engine problems. Travel in groups of two or more vehicles, and carry plenty of fuel, as consumption in low-range gears can be half as much again as on well-surfaced roads. Note that off-track driving is illegal in order to minimize erosion, and

carries substantial fines. Rental vehicles are not allowed into the Interior (even along the relatively good Kjölur track); in addition, no vehicle, 4WD or otherwise, is insured for accidents or breakdowns encountered when crossing a river.

Cycling and hiking The only Interior route that cyclists and hikers can tackle unaided is the Kjölur track, whose major rivers are bridged. If you're planning on using other routes, you'll have to hitch rides over the more difficult rivers with passing transport, so will probably spend longer on your journey than you intended – making it all the more vital that you carry surplus food and water.

8

Sprengisandur: Route F26

Featuring the most desolate terrain found in Iceland, **Sprengisandur** is the bleak highland desert east between **Hofsjökull** – the rounded ice cap marking Iceland's geographical centre – and Vatnajökull's northwestern front. Although providing something of a corridor in Viking times between Iceland's northeastern settlements and the summer parliament at Þingvellir, crossing Sprengisandur was always a tough journey, the desert flooded in spring with melting snow and ice, yet too dry in summer to provide any grazing for horses. Indeed, most travellers preferred to take much longer coastal roads, and Sprengisandur was eventually abandoned as a route during the thirteenth century.

Traversed today by the **F26**, which begins northeast of Hekla and runs some 244km across the desolate, icy plateau between Hofsjökull and Vatnajökull to the Ringroad at Goðafoss, the Sprengisandur route remains a challenging one, whose unbridged rivers and stark scenery provide an insight into medieval Iceland's harsh living conditions. The enduring image here is of nothingness: the glaciers and mountains that fringe the horizon seem a long way off, and the space in between is filled with mile after mile of grey sand, stones and rocks that have lain untouched for thousands of years.

Nýidalur

Around 100km northeast along the F26 from Hrauneyjar (see p.118) and almost bang in the centre of Iceland, **Nýidalur**, site of a campsite and hut, occupies a lonely, cold and windswept spot at the base of **Tungnafellsjökull**'s ice cap. The Nýidalur valley leads southeast around the glacier from here towards Vatnajökull, only 20km distant, while well away to the west below Hofsjökull are the **Þjórsárver** wetlands, breeding grounds for a healthy population of pink-footed geese.

Just north of Nýidalur, the F910 to Askja (see p.328) weaves its way across some quite appalling terrain close to Vatnajökull's northwestern flanks, including a number of dangerous rivers. Get local advice if you're thinking of side-tracking along this route, and only travel in convoy.

Laugafell hot springs

Some 30km from the F26 junction • No set hours • Free

The grey waters of **Fjórðungsvatn**, a small lake on the F26 some 15km north of Nýidalur, mark the junction with **Route F752**, which runs northwest to the Ringroad at Varmáhlið (see p.232). The main feature along the way is **Laugafell hot springs**, a geothermal area with a hot bathing pool said to have been first used by a household who fled to this desolate spot during a medieval outbreak of plague. There are huts here offering bunk space in summer (see below).

Aldeyjarfoss

Up at the northern end of the F26 – and only some 40km south of the Ringroad at Goðafoss, near Mývatn (see p.270) – **Aldeyjarfoss** is a lively waterfall framed by a blaze of twisted basalt columns. Despite being close to the green slopes and scattered farms of the relatively fertile Bárðardalur valley, the sand and lava terrain surrounding the falls is bleak in the extreme, with the water providing the landscape's sole source of movement and colour.

ARRIVAL AND DEPARTURE   SPRENGISANDUR

By bus Reykjavík Excursions (W re.is) cross Sprengisandur between Reykjavík and Mývatn daily in each direction between late June and late Aug (11hr 30min; 19,800kr). A connecting service from Landmannalaugar links with Reykjavík–Mývatn buses at Hrauneyjar; Landmannalaugar–

Mývatn (10hr; 15,000kr).
By car Allow at least eight hours if you're driving the F26 yourself – which is nothing compared with the week it took for the first car to traverse it in 1933.

ACCOMMODATION

Laugafell At the hot pools ☎ 822 5192, W ffa.is. These two huts sleep 35 people in bunks (sleeping bag only); one dates to the 1940s and is a bit primitive, but the newer one has toilets and a basic kitchen. There's also a campsite with showers but no kitchen. June–Aug. Sleeping bags 6500kr, camping 1500kr

Nýidalur ☎ 860 3334, W fi.is. Two hostels sleeping 120 people in bunks, with kitchen, showers and toilets. The campsite has shelter sheds for cooking and eating. Rangers here can fill you in on hiking trails around the Tungnafellsjökull ice cap. June–Aug. Sleeping bags 7000kr, camping 1500kr

Kjölur: Route 35

Running between Gullfoss in the south and the Ringroad near Varmahlíð, at 200km long **Kjölur** is the shorter of the two inland routes across Iceland. Pioneered by the earliest settlers and recorded in the *Book of Settlements*, Kjölur was always considered a safer route than Sprengisandur, though it passes between the Hofsjökull and **Langjökull** ice caps and was abandoned after the death of a large party in 1780. Today it qualifies as a highway – if any Interior route can claim to be one – with buses, coaches, four-wheel-drives and even ordinary family sedans bouncing along it during the summer months. All the rivers have been bridged, but be aware that Kjölur's rough gravel track is still capable of shredding tyres, tearing off exhausts and puncturing sumps: keep your speed down, especially if driving conventional, low-slung vehicles. Note that ordinary rental vehicles are not allowed along this route.

Kerlingarfjöll

Around 80km northeast of Gullfoss, the F347 heads east off Route 35 towards where the rumpled peaks of **Kerlingarfjöll** rise out of the landscape, the 1477m summit lightly dusted with year-round snow and ice. There are some excellent **hiking trails** here, including a three-day, 50km circuit of the peaks, for which the privately run mountain huts at **Ásgarður** make a good base (see below).

Hveravellir

Around 100km from either end of Route 35 • ⓦ hveravellir.is

Route 35's midpoint is marked by a short detour west to a grassy depression at **Hveravellir hot springs**, where you'll find a campsite and well-appointed overnight huts. The only **pool** cool enough for a soak is a small, waist-deep affair next to one of the huts, above which boardwalks head up a calcified slope; encrusted with sulphur, the hotter springs here bubble, belch and occasionally erupt violently. One of these is named **Eyvindarhver**, after the outlaw Eyvindur (see box, p.328) who lived at Hveravellir for two years and used the spring to boil up sheep for his dinner. In summer, the springs can get busy, so try to time your dip to avoid scheduled daily bus arrivals in the early afternoon – or stay overnight and have the waters almost to yourself.

ARRIVAL AND DEPARTURE　　　　　　　　　　　　　　　　　　KJÖLUR

By bus SBA (ⓦ sba.is) crosses Kjölur between Reykjavík and Akureyri daily each way, with sightseeing stops at Geysir and Gullfoss (late June to early Sept; 10hr 30min; 13,950kr).

By car The unsealed section of the Kjölur Route, between the Ringroad near Blönduós south through to Gullfoss, is around 200km; if driving yourself, allow at least five hours.

8

ACCOMMODATION

Ásgarður Kerlingarfjöll ☎ 664 7878, ⓦ kerlingarfjoll .is. Large campsite with toilets, and a range of accommodation in basic dorms, or double rooms in huts with made-up beds (which include breakfast). It's largely self-catering, though there is a basic restaurant. Restaurant mid-June to mid-Aug. Early June to mid-Sept. Camping 1500kr, dorms 5000kr, doubles 25,000kr

Hveravellir At the Hveravellir hot springs ☎ 894 1293, ⓦ hveravellir.is. Sleeping-bag accommodation for around fifty people in two huts with toilets and showers; there are also some private rooms. Check in advance to see if the restaurant is open. Breakfast 1500kr. Camping 1200kr, sleeping bags 6000kr, doubles 19,000kr

---

THE KJÖLURVEGUR TREK

The **Kjölurvegur** trek is an excellent two- to three-day hike from Hveravellir to the glacial lake of Hvítárvatn, following the original Kjölur route that ran west of the present Route 35, hugging the slopes of **Langjökull**: it's punctuated by basic huts (book in advance through ⓦ fi.is), roughly four to six hours' walk apart.
From the springs, follow the F735 west towards the glacier for roughly 14km to the tiny **Þjófadalir** hut (4500kr). Here the jeep track peters out into a walking path as it swings southeast, around the tiny Hrútfell glacier, to another hut at **Þverbrekknamúli** (5000kr). From here, it's a further straightforward hike of around four to six hours to reach the half-turfed **Hvítárnes** hut (5000kr), an idyllic if somewhat lonely place to break the journey – the hut is supposedly haunted by a young woman who lived hereabouts when the area was farmed, though only men who sleep in a certain bed in the hut will see her.
From the hut, it's an easy 8km walk back to Route 35 and the bus to either Reykjavík or Akureyri, passing the beautiful **Hvítárvatn** glacial lake, at the foot of Langjökull, on the way.

EYVINDUR AND HALLA

Iceland's most famous **outlaws** were the eighteenth-century **Eyvindur** and his harsh-tempered wife, **Halla**. They are the only Icelandic outlaws to have managed twenty years on the run, thus earning themselves a pardon; many places around Iceland are named after Eyvindur, showing just how much he had to keep moving.

Originally from the West Fjords, Eyvindur and Halla set up at Hveravellir, robbing travellers and stealing sheep from nearby properties. Eventually chased on by a vengeful posse, they shifted south to the Þjórsá (west of Hekla) for a few years – the easiest time of his outlawry, so Eyvindur later said – then to remoter pastures on the Sprengisandur, which at that time hadn't been crossed for many years. Caught after stealing a horse, Eyvindur and Halla were held at Mývatn's church, from where Eyvindur managed to escape by asking to be untied so that he could pray. As luck would have it, a thick fog came down and he was able to hide nearby until people had given up looking for him, thinking him far away. He then stole another horse and rode it south to Herðubreiðarlindir (see below), where he somehow survived an appalling winter in a "cave" he built into the lava here. Later on, he met Halla again and they drifted around the country, always just managing to evade capture but forced by hunger or pursuit to kill their infant children. Tradition has it that after being pardoned they returned to their farm, where they died in the 1780s.

The F88 to Askja

The F88 drops down from the Ringroad east of Mývatn towards two of the Interior's most stunning landmarks: the isolated, ice-bound platform of **Herðubreið**; and the enormous **Askja** caldera, with its twinned crater lakes. Though most people visit on day-tours, there's excellent **hiking** in the region and several convenient huts if you plan to stay longer – check out the "Askja Trail" tab at ⊕ ffa.is/en.

Herðubreiðarlindir

Right on Route F88, the Þorsteinsskáli mountain hut (see p.330) marks **Herðubreiðarlindir**, an oasis of poor grass and hot springs between the glacial **Jökulsá á Fjöllum** and Herðubreið, barely 5km away to the west. On the edge of the encircling lava, a small stream wells out through a wall of lava blocks that conceal **Eyvindur's cave**, said to have been inhabited by this resourceful outlaw during the harsh winter of 1774–75. During this time he survived on dried horsemeat and the bitter roots of angelica plants, which grow in profusion nearby – he always considered this the worst experience of his entire twenty years on the run (see box above).

Herðubreið

Just off Route 88 between Mývatn and the Askja caldera, the crown-like formation of **Herðubreið** towers 1682m over the featureless lavafield of **Ódáðahraun** (Desert of Misdeeds). Herðubreið's brown, snow-streaked platform is so remote that it remained unconquered until 1908, and an ascent to the summit still requires basic mountaineering skills and equipment.

Askja

Off the end of Route F88 in the heart of the dismal Ódáðahraun, **Askja** is an 8km-wide volcanic depression, formed from a collapsed subterranean magma chamber. In the centre is a 217m-deep lake, **Öskuvatn**, its steel-grey waters doing nothing to brighten the setting among a colossal lavafield which drained out of Askja in prehistoric times. More recent events have included the appalling eruption at **Viti** in 1875 (see p.330);

FROM TOP THERMAL POOL; KVERKFJÖLL ICE CAVES (P.331) >

another big outflow of lava in the 1960s, which you traverse en route to the caldera's rim; and, in 2014, a new event at **Holuhraun** (see below), off to the south.

Viti

There's an unexpected blob of colour at **Viti**, a deep crater full of pale blue water at Askja's northern side. A vent here was described by one nineteenth-century traveller as "a complete Devil's cauldron from which all living things fly; horses quake with mortal fear and can hardly stand when taken to the brink." The animals' fears were well founded: in 1875, the vent exploded with such colossal force that two cubic kilometres of rock were vaporized and the debris blown as far away as Denmark. Farmland between here and the coast at Vopnafjörður was buried under drifts of yellow pumice, which poisoned the soil and sterilized the region – some two thousand local farmers emigrated to Canada as a result. It's more docile today; you can scramble down its steep sides, dotted with sulphur springs, to bathe in the opaque blue-white waters, which can be a little tepid sometimes but are perfect for a quick dip.

ARRIVAL AND DEPARTURE   THE F88 TO ASKJA

By bus Mývatn Tours (⊛myvatntours.is) run return trips to Askja from Mývatn (4 weekly during last week of June; daily July to early Sept; 12hr; 19,000kr return). SBA also visit Askja on their Kverkfjöll trip (see opposite).
By car Route F88 passes close to Herðubreið. There's a 5km hiking track from the F88 at Herðubreiðarlindir, and a very

rough vehicle track to Herðubreið's southwest corner off the F88 closer to Askja. Askja itself sits at the end of the F88 south from Mývatn, and the F910 east from Nýidalur on the Sprengisandur route – though note that the F910 should only be driven in convoy and after seeking local advice.

ACCOMMODATION

Dreki Drekagil ☎853 2541, ⊛ffa.is. On Route F88 at Askja's eastern edge, around 9km from Öskuvatn by road, this hut sits at the mouth of a small canyon among the rumpled landscape surrounding Askja. There are two basic huts with dorm bunks sleeping sixty, plus a campsite. Wardens here can advise on local hiking routes to Askja and Herðubreið. Dorms ~~7000kr~~, camping ~~1500kr~~

Þorsteinsskáli Herðubreiðarlindir ☎854 9301, ⊛ffa.is. Dorm accommodation for thirty in this elderly building, with toilets, showers and a basic kitchen; the rangers here can provide information about hiking trails, via Herðubreið, to Askja. There's also a campsite. Dorms ~~6500kr~~, camping ~~1500kr~~

Holuhraun

In late August 2014, a spate of earthquakes opened up a 1.5km-long volcanic fissure in the highlands southwest of Askja at **Holuhraun**, which began spraying out molten rock in a spectacular display that only escaped worldwide attention because the area was so remote. Not that this stopped Icelanders in super-jeeps from braving the journey to have their photographs taken against a backdrop of crimson, flaming fountains, until the government – remembering the massive rescue operation which had to be mounted during Hekla's eruption in 2000 (see p.116) – put **armed police** on the roads to turn back sightseers. When activity subsided in February 2015, Holuhraun's outflow had covered eighty-five square kilometres – the largest lava spill since the Laki eruptions in 1783 (see p.319).

At the time of writing, the region was still closed, but Holuhraun is slated to be included as part of SBA's tour of Kverkfjöll (see p.331), and it's likely that **hiking trails** will be established from Askja (contact Ferðafelag Íslands at ⊛fi.is for the latest information). The nearest **road** to Holuhraun is the F910 between Sprengisandur and Askja.

Kverkfjöll

Set amid a maze of ash hills, **Kverkfjöll** is an active thermal zone right up against the icy skirt of Vatnajökull's northern edge. Low white clouds hover overhead during the long hard slog up the dormant volcano, which erupted to devastating effect in the fifteenth century, and once at the top these are revealed to be steam issuing from deep fissures in the ice. Nearby **sulphur springs**, hissing like boiling kettles, prevent ice from forming in their immediate area, and the bare yellow earth is in stark contrast to the surroundings. The outstanding **views** north from the glacier take in the entire expanse of Ódáðahraun lavafield, the Dyngjufjöll mountains, Herðubreið mountains, and even the jagged peaks that mark the distant northern coast.

Kverkfjöll ice caves

The Jökulsá á Fjöllum rises at Kverkfjöll from hot springs under Vatnajökull, its heat forming an **ice cave** before the water flows north to the sea via Jökulsárgljúfur National Park (see p.275). Some daylight penetrates a few metres into the cave, but visibility rapidly diminishes in the thick, damp fog that fills it. The walls and roof are sculpted by constantly dripping water, and the debris embedded in the ice gives a marbled effect. Be warned, however, that entering ice caves is always **dangerous**, due to the possibility of cave-ins.

Hvannalindir

8

Another set of hot springs, **Hvannalindir**, forms an oasis halfway between Kverkfjöll and Askja, where the outlaw Eyvindur fashioned a rough shelter using lava blocks around a hollow on the edge of the lavafield. He also built a sheep pen with a covered passageway to the nearby stream, so the animals could drink without being spotted and hence not give away his location. Both can still be found but are well concealed, as Eyvindur intended.

ARRIVAL AND DEPARTURE
KVERKFJÖLL

By bus From late July until mid-Aug SBA (⚙ sba.is) offers three-day Akureyri–Mývatn–Askja–Holuhraun–Kverkfjöll return trips, departing Mon. Tours cost 45,000kr, excluding meals and accommodation, and include lengthy hikes.

By car Kverkfjöll sits at the southern end of the F903 and F902, accessed off the F910 from near Askja.

ACCOMMODATION

Sigurðarskáli ☎ 863 9236, ⚙ fljotsdalsherad.is. Bunk accommodation for 85 in two large buildings with toilets, showers and kitchen; there's also an attached campsite. Wardens here act as guides for daily hikes onto the glacier, to the caves and Hvannalindir. Dorms <u>6500kr</u>, camping <u>1500kr</u>

SIXTEENTH-CENTURY MAP OF ICELAND

Contexts

History

Iceland is not only one of the more geologically recent places on Earth, it was also among the last to be colonized. European seafarers may have known that something lay out beyond Scotland as far back as 300 BC, when the historian Pytheas of Marseille wrote about "Ultima Thule" – possibly Iceland – a northern land on the edge of a frozen ocean, where it never became dark in summer.

It wasn't until considerably later, however, that Iceland was regularly visited by outsiders, let alone settled, and it's still unclear who might have been the first to try. Whoever they were, the first arrivals would have found the country much the same as it appears today (though well forested with dwarf willow and birch), and with no large animals.

Discovery

Much of the uncertainty in deciding who discovered Iceland, and when it happened, is down to the lack of archeological and written records. **Roman** coins from around 300 AD, found at several sites along Iceland's south coast, provide the earliest evidence of visitors, and suggest that ships from Britain – which was then a Roman colony and just a week's sail away – made landfall here from time to time. These coins could have been brought in at a later date, however, and no other Roman artefacts or camps have been found. Similarly, the age of a **Norse** homestead on Heimaey in the Westman Islands is disputed; archeologists date it to the seventh century, but medieval Icelandic historians – accurate enough in other matters – state that it was founded two hundred years later. It is also believed that by the late eighth century **Irish** monks, having already colonized the Faroes, were visiting Iceland regularly, seeking solitude and, according to contemporary accounts, believing that they had rediscovered Pytheas' Ultima Thule. Oral tradition and place names link them to certain spots around the country – such as Papey, "Monks' Island", in the east – but they left no hard evidence behind them and were driven out over the next century by new invaders, the **Vikings**.

Vikings were Scandinavian adventurers, armed with the fastest ships of the time and forced by politics and a land shortage at home to seek their fortune overseas through war and piracy. They had already exploded into Britain and Ireland in the 790s, which is why Irish monks had sought out Iceland as a more peaceful place to live. According to tradition, the Vikings came across Iceland by accident when a certain mid-ninth-century freebooter named **Naddoddur** lost his way to the Faroes and landed on the eastern coast of what he called **Snæland**, or Snowland. He didn't stay long, but his reports of this new country were followed up by the Swede **Garðar Svavarsson**, who circumnavigated Iceland in around 860, wintering at modern-day Húsavík in the northeast, where two of his slaves escaped and are thought to have settled. At about the same time, **Flóki Vilgerðarson** left his home in Norway intending to colonize Snæland,

860	c.860	874	930
Swedish Viking Garðar Svavarsson sails round Iceland	Flóki Vilgerðarson spends the winter in Iceland, but later leaves	Ingólfur Arnarson builds his homestead at modern-day Reykjavík	The population of Iceland reaches an estimated 60,000

VIKING RELIGION

Though a few Vikings may have been Christian, the majority believed in the **Norse gods**, the Æsir, which included **Óðinn**, the creator of mankind; his wild and adventurous hammer-wielding son **Þór**; and **Freyr**, the god of fertility and farming. The Æsir themselves were children of the first beings, the Giants, who had also created dwarfs and elves; they lived above the world in **Ásgarður**, where the great hall Valhalla housed the souls of Champions, men killed in warfare. The Champions awaited Ragnarok, when they would join the Æsir in a final massive battle against the Frost Giants, in which the world would be totally destroyed. Fearsome in battle, honour was everything to the Vikings, and the faintest slur could start a century-long blood feud between families.

---

which he was led to by following his pet ravens – hence his other name, Hrafna-Flóki, Raven-Flóki. But a hard winter in the northwest killed all his livestock; climbing a mountain, he saw a fjord on the other side choked with ice and, frustrated, he renamed the country **Ísland**, Iceland, and returned to Norway.

Settlement

Despite Flóki's experiences, the idea of so much free space proved tempting to two other Norwegians, **Ingólfur Arnarson** and his brother-in-law **Hjörleifur Hróðmarsson**, who had lost their own lands in Norway as compensation for killing the son of a local earl. Around 870 they set sail with their households and possessions for Iceland, intending to settle there permanently. When they came within sight of land, Ingólfur dedicated his wooden **seat-posts** – the cherished symbol of his being head of a household – to his gods and threw them overboard, vowing to found his new home at the spot where they washed up. While his slaves searched for them, Ingólfur spent three years exploring Iceland's southern coast, wintering first at Ingólfshöfði (near Skaftafell), Hjörleifshöfði (just east of Vík), and then at Ingólfsfjall (Selfoss). The posts were duly found in a southwestern bay and there Ingólfur built his homestead in 874, naming the place **Reykjavík** ("Smoky Bay") after the steam rising off nearby hot springs, and becoming Iceland's first official resident.

Although Hjörleifur had meanwhile been murdered by his own Irish slaves, things went well for Ingólfur and this attracted other migrants to Iceland, who spent the next sixty years snapping up vacant land in what has become known as the **Settlement**, or Landnám. These first Icelanders, who were mostly Norwegian, were primarily **farmers**, importing their pagan beliefs along with sheep, horses, and crops such as barley, while also clearing forests to create pasture and provide timber for buildings and ships. While it was available, a man could take as much land as he could light fires around in one day, while a woman could have the area she could lead a heifer around in the same time. Landowners became local **chieftains**, whose religious responsibilities earned them the title of *goðar*, or priests, and who sorted out their differences through negotiations at regional **assemblies** (*þing*) – or if these failed, by fighting. Conditions must have been very favourable compared to those in Norway, however, as by 930, when the last areas of the country were claimed, an estimated sixty thousand people already lived in Iceland – a figure not exceeded until the nineteenth century.

930	980	1000	1056	1104
The Icelandic Commonwealth is established by the country's chieftains	Erik the Red is outlawed and sails for Greenland	Iceland becomes Christian	Iceland's first bishop, Ísleifur, is appointed	Violent eruption of Hekla

The Commonwealth: 930–1262 AD

By the early tenth century, Iceland was firmly occupied and had begun to see itself as an independent nation in need of national government. The chieftains rejected the idea of a paramount leader, and instead decided, in 930, on a **Commonwealth** governed by a national assembly, or **Alþing**, which came to be held for two weeks every summer at Þingvellir in southwestern Iceland. Here laws were recited publicly by a **lawspeaker**, and disputes settled by four regional courts, with a supreme court formed early in the eleventh century. Legal settlement typically involved payment to the injured party or their family; the highest punishment was not death but being declared an **outlaw**, thus being exiled from Iceland. Courts had no power to enforce decisions, however, only make recommendations, and though they held great public authority, in practice their decisions could be ignored – something which was to undermine the Commonwealth in later years.

The first century of the Commonwealth was very much a golden era, however: the country was united, resources were rich, and farming profitable. This was the **Saga Age**, the time when the first generations of Icelanders were carving out great names for themselves in events that passed into oral lore and would later be written down.

The coming of Christianity

The late tenth century had seen Norway convert to **Catholicism** under the fiery king **Ólafur Tryggvason**. Ólafur then sent the missionary Þangbrand to evangelize Iceland, where – despite having to physically battle strong resistance from pagan stalwarts – he baptized several influential chieftains. Back in Norway, Þangbrand's unfavourable reports infuriated Ólafur, who was only prevented from executing all Icelanders in the country by the Icelandic chieftain **Gizur the White**, who promised to champion the new religion at home. Gizur mustered his forces and rode to the Alþing in 1000, where civil war was only averted by the lawspeaker Þorgeir, who – having made pagan and Christian alike swear to accept his decision – chose Christianity as Iceland's official religion, though pagans were initially allowed to maintain their beliefs in private. Gizur the White's son Ísleifur became Iceland's first **bishop** in 1056, and his homestead at

THE DISCOVERY OF NORTH AMERICA

In the same way that Iceland itself was discovered, Icelandic seafarers also came across their own new worlds. In 980, Eiríkur Þorvaldsson (better known in English as **Erik the Red**) was outlawed for killing his neighbour and sailed from the West Fjords to follow up earlier reports of land to the northwest. He found a barren, treeless coastline, then returned to Iceland to whip up support for colonizing what he called **Greenland** – a deliberately misleading name, chosen to arouse interest. Enough people were hooked to emigrate along with Eiríkur, and two settlements were founded in Western Greenland which lasted until the sixteenth century. And it was from Greenland that Eiríkur's son **Leifur Eiríksson** heard that land had been sighted even further west, and set sail around the year 1000 to discover Baffin Island, Labrador, and "**Vínland**", an as-yet unidentified area of the north American coast. A couple of attempts made by others to colonize these distant lands came to nothing, however, and America was then forgotten about by Europeans until Columbus rediscovered it.

1106	1117	1130	1220	1262
The diocese of Hólar í Hjaltadalur is established	First laws written down	Ári the Learned compiles the *Íslendingabók* on Iceland's people	Sturlung Age of Icelandic clans begins	Treaty signed giving Norwegian king power over Iceland

Skálholt near Þingvellir was made the bishop's seat, with a second, northern, diocese founded in 1106 at **Hólar**.

The new religion brought gradual changes with it, notably the introduction in 1097 of **tithes** – property taxes – to fund churches. As their wealth increased, churches founded **monasteries** and **schools**, bringing education and the beginnings of **literature**: Iceland's laws were first written down in 1117; and in 1130 the Church commissioned Ari the Learned to compile the **Íslendingabók**, a compendium of the Icelandic people and their lineages. Importantly, Ari wrote not in Latin, the usual language of education and the Church at the time, but in Icelandic, an expression of national identity that was followed by almost all later Icelandic writers.

Collapse of the Commonwealth

Despite these benefits, several factors were beginning to undermine the Alþing's authority. During the twelfth century, for instance, life in Iceland became much tougher. The country's unstable geology made itself felt for the first time with the 1104 **eruption** of the Hekla volcano in southern Iceland, which buried around twenty farms. **Tree felling** had also become so extensive that there was no longer enough timber for shipbuilding; the effects of subsequent **erosion** were compounded by overgrazing and the beginnings of a "**mini ice age**", which was to last until the nineteenth century and caused Iceland's glaciers to expand over previously settled areas – all of which reduced available farmland and made the country dependent on **imports**.

Meanwhile, the tithes were dividing Iceland's formerly egalitarian society. With its taxes, the Church became rich and politically powerful, as did chieftains who owned Church lands or had become priests, and so took a share of the tithes. These chieftains formed a new elite group of **aristocrats**, who bought out their poorer neighbours and so concentrated land ownership, wealth and inherent political power in the hands of just a few clans. At the same time, in 1152 the Icelandic Church came under the jurisdiction of the **Archbishop of Nidaros** in Norway (modern-day Trondheim), giving the expansionist Norwegian throne a lever to start pressuring Iceland to accept its authority. Backed by the Archbishop and **Þorlákur Þórhallsson**, bishop at Skálholt from 1179 and later beatified as Iceland's first saint, the Church began to demand freedom from secular laws.

The Alþing's lack of effective power now became clear, as it proved unable to deal with the Church's demands, or the fighting that was breaking out between the six biggest clans as they battled for political supremacy. The period from 1220 is known as the **Sturlung Age** after the most powerful of these clans, led by the historian, lawspeaker and wily politician **Snorri Sturluson**. Travelling to Norway in 1218, Snorri became a retainer of King Hákon Hákonarson, and returned to Iceland in 1220 to promote Norwegian interests. But his methods were slow, and in 1235 the king sent Snorri's nephew, **Sturla Sighvatsson**, to win Iceland over for Norway, by force if necessary. In the ensuing **civil war**, forces led in part by **Gissur Þorvaldsson**, head of the Haukadalur clan, killed Sturla and virtually wiped out the Sturlungs at the battle of **Örlygsstaðir** in 1238. Snorri escaped by being in Norway at the time, but was killed by Gissur after his return.

Amid this violence, Iceland was also experiencing a literary flowering: Snorri Sturluson wrote the **Prose Eddas**, containing much of what is known about Norse

1280	1362	1397	1402	1420s
The Jónsbók book of laws is compiled	Volcano under Öræfajökull erupts, covering the country in ash	The Kalmar Union places Iceland under Danish control	Plague arrives in Iceland	English bishop is appointed in Hólar í Hjaltadalur

mythology; his relative Sturla Þordarson compiled the **Book of Settlements Expanded**, accounts of the original landowners and their lives; and it was during this period that the **sagas** were composed, romanticizing the nobler events of the early Commonwealth. Meanwhile the war continued, and by 1246 only two chieftains were left standing: Gissur Þorvaldsson, who held the south of the country; and Sturla's brother **Þordur**, who controlled the north. Rather than fight, they let King Hákon decide who should govern; the king chose Þordur, who ruled Iceland until 1250, sharing power with the two bishops – also Norwegian appointees. In the end, the bishop at Hólar denounced Þordur for putting his own interests before Norway's, and the king replaced him with Gissur who, after a further decade of skirmishes, finally persuaded Icelanders that the only way to obtain lasting peace was by accepting **Norwegian sovereignty**. In 1262, Iceland's chieftains signed the *Gamli sáttmáli* or **Old Treaty**, which allowed Iceland to keep its laws and promised that the Norwegian king would maintain order, in exchange for taxes and replacing the chieftainships with government officials. While the treaty didn't give Norway absolute control of the country, and demanded a return for Icelandic obedience, it marked the beginnings of seven centuries of foreign rule.

Decline, the English Century and the Reformation

With the Alþing discredited by over forty years of conflict, Iceland turned to Norway to help draft a new constitution. The **Jónsbók** of 1280 was the result, a set of laws that were to remain partly in force until the nineteenth century. The country was to be overseen by a **governor**, with twelve regional **sheriffs** acting as local administrators; all officials would be Icelanders, though appointed by Norway. The Alþing would still meet as a national court, retaining some legislative power, but its decisions would have to be approved by the king.

The new system should have brought a much-needed period of stability to Iceland, but it was not always administered as planned – officials often abused their position, leading to several **revolts**, such as when the brutal governor Smiður Andrésson was killed by farmers in 1361. Meanwhile, the Danish "lady king" **Margrete I** had absorbed the Norwegian throne under the **Kalmar Union** of 1397, thereby placing Iceland in Denmark's hands.

The English Century

While all this was going on, the underlying struggles between landowners, the Church and the king were escalating, typified by events during what is known as the **English Century**. At the time there was growing demand in Europe for dried **cod**, which after 1400 became a major Icelandic export, exchanged for linen, wine and grain. **Fishing** – formerly a secondary income – boomed, providing a new source of funds for coastal landowners. Soon English and German vessels were vying for trade with Iceland and even beginning to fish themselves; the English gained the ascendancy after setting up a base on the Westman Islands (where they also indulged in kidnapping and piracy), and managing to get an English bishop – **John Craxton** – appointed to Hólar in the 1420s. Denmark, alarmed at England's rising influence and the taxes it was losing through uncontrolled trade, appointed its own **Jón Gerreksson** as bishop at Skálholt, although

1532	1602	1661	1783
The English lose influence in Iceland after battle in Grindavík	The Danish Trade Monopoly puts stranglehold on commerce with Iceland	The Danish king, Frederick III, declares absolute rule over Iceland	Laki eruptions devastate the country; the population falls to 38,000

NATURAL DISASTERS

The fourteenth century heralded a further succession of **natural disasters** in Iceland: severe winters wiped out crops and livestock; Hekla became active again; and the volcano under Öræfajökull in the southeast exploded in 1362, covering a third of the country in ash. But most devastating was the **Plague** or Black Death, which had ravaged Europe in the 1350s and arrived in Iceland in 1402, killing half of the population over the following two years.

this violent man – who had his own military and spent his time levying illegal taxes and harassing his neighbours – ended up being murdered in 1433.

Trying to restore order, Denmark passed laws stopping the Church from raising illegal taxes and banning the English from Iceland. The English response was to murder the Icelandic governor in 1467, so the Danish king encouraged the German **Hanseatic League** to establish trading bases in the country – a popular move, as the League had better goods than the English and gave better prices. The English returned with cannons, a forceful stance that after 1490 gained them the right to fish Icelandic waters as long as they paid tolls to Denmark. All went well until 1532, when trouble flared between German and English vessels at the trading post at **Grindavík** on the southwestern Reykjanes Peninsula, culminating in the death of the English leader. English involvement in Iceland dropped off sharply after this, leaving Icelandic trade in the hands of Danish and German interests.

The Reformation and its effects

The Church, which by now had complete jurisdiction over Iceland's lands, and profitable stakes in farming and fishing, became even more powerful in 1533 when the two bishops – **Jón Arason** and **Ögmundur Pálsson** – were appointed as joint governors of the country. But outside Iceland, a new Christian view first proposed by the German Martin Luther in 1517 had been gaining ground. **Lutherism** revolted against what was seen as the Catholic Church's growing obsession with material rather than spiritual profits, and encouraged a break with Rome as the head of the Church – a suggestion that European monarchs realized would therefore place the Church's riches and influence in their hands.

During the 1530s, all Scandinavia became Lutheran, and converts were already making headway in Iceland, though threatened with excommunication by the bishops. In 1539, the Danish king **Christian III** ordered the Icelandic governor to appropriate Church lands, which led to the murder of one of his sheriffs and a subsequent military expedition to Iceland to force conversion to Lutherism. This was headed by former protégé of Ögmundur (and covert Lutheran) **Gissur Einarsson**, who replaced Ögmundur as bishop at Skálholt in 1542. A skilful diplomat, he encouraged Lutherism without, by and large, antagonizing Catholics. His appointment left Jón Arason at Hólar as the last Catholic bishop in Scandinavia, and on Gissur's death in 1548, Arason unsuccessfully pushed his own Catholic candidate for Skálholt, an act that got him declared an outlaw. Gathering a band of supporters, Arason marched south and captured Skálholt, but was subsequently defeated and executed along with two of his sons on November 7, 1550, allowing Lutherism to be imposed across the entire country.

1787	1843	1852	1871
The Free Trade Charter replaces the Trade Monopoly	The Danish king allows reconstitution of Icelandic parliament	Bill to incorporate Iceland into Denmark defeated	Denmark annexes Iceland

The consequences of the **Reformation** were severe, with the new faith forced on an initially unwilling population, who – in common with many other countries at the time – may have disagreed with Catholic abuses of power but not with Catholicism itself. The Danish king acquired all Church holdings and their revenues, profits from which had previously stayed in Iceland; monasteries were abolished and, deprived of funds, the Church found it hard to sponsor education – though it did manage to publish a translation of the Bible in 1584, the first book printed in Icelandic.

Politically, too, the Church was now an instrument of the king, and the Danish crown gained a far more direct hold on the country. Technically, however, Iceland remained an independent state through its treaty with Norway, but in 1661 King **Frederick III** declared his rule absolute over all Danish lands, and the following year sent an armed ambassador to Iceland to make its people swear allegiance. During an assembly at **Bessastaðir**, near Reykjavík, the Alþing's lawspeaker and Skálholt's bishop were forced to submit, removing their final vestiges of authority and handing complete control of the country to the Danish crown.

In the meantime, Iceland's economy – still based on farming and fishing – suffered a severe blow through the **Trade Monopoly** of 1602. This restricted all trade between Iceland and the outside world to a select few Danish merchants, who charged steeply for their goods, while giving poor prices for Icelandic products. By 1700, the monopoly had ruined the country, creating a poor, dispirited population of tenant farmers and landless labourers. Fishing was also on the wane, partly because a shortage of timber meant that Iceland's vessels were basic and small, and easily out-competed by foreign boats. Aside from a fruitless attempt to introduce **reindeer** as livestock, the only concrete action taken to redress trade imbalances was made by the bailiff **Skúli Magnússon**, who in 1752 founded a company at Reykjavík – still just a small farming settlement at the time – to improve agricultural practices and modernize the wool and fishing industries. Though the company was only moderately successful, its warehouses became the core of Reykjavík town, soon to become Iceland's largest settlement and de facto capital.

Unfortunately, a fresh wave of disasters now swept the country, the worst of which was the catastrophic **Laki eruptions** of 1783–84 in the southeast. Poisonous fallout from Laki wrecked farming over the entire country, and the ensuing **famine** reduced the population to just 38,000. Denmark briefly considered evacuating the survivors to Jutland, but in the end settled for easing the economy by replacing the Trade Monopoly with a **Free Trade Charter** in 1787, which allowed Iceland to do business with a greater range of Danish merchants. Another effect of the eruptions was accompanying **earthquakes**, which knocked over the church at Skálholt and caused subsidence at the Alþing site; the bishopric was moved to Reykjavík, and the Alþing – which by now only met irregularly to discuss minor matters – was finally dissolved.

Nationalism

European political upheavals during the early nineteenth-century Napoleonic Wars had little effect on Iceland, though there was brief excitement in 1809 when opportunistic Danish interpreter **Jörgen Jörgensen** deposed the governor and ran the country for the summer. However, the increasingly liberal political climate that

1896	1904	1915	1918	1940
Iceland's territorial waters are set to three nautical miles	Home Rule comes into force	Women gain the right to vote	Iceland becomes an independent state under the Danish king	British troops occupy Iceland

followed the war encouraged **nationalism** throughout Europe and was championed in Iceland by the romantic poet **Jónas Hallgrímsson** and historian **Jón Sigurðsson**, a descendant of Snorri Sturluson, who pushed for free trade and autonomy from Denmark. Bowing to popular demand, the Danish king reconstituted the Alþing at Reykjavík in 1843, which met every other year and had twenty elected regional members of parliament and six representatives of the king. Jón Sigurðsson was among the first members elected.

Even greater changes were on the way, sparked by the French Revolution of 1789, after which Europe's other royal families began to cede real power in order to avoid a similar fate. Following uprisings in Denmark, the **monarchy** there became constitutional in 1848, allowing Jón Sigurðsson to point out that Iceland's 1662 oath of allegiance to the king as an absolute ruler was therefore no longer valid, and that the Old Treaty was now back in force. This didn't make him popular with the king, a situation exacerbated when he led the defeat of a bill at the Alþing, in 1851, that would have legally incorporated Iceland into Denmark. Sigurðsson also managed to have remaining trade restrictions finally lifted four years later, an act which did more than anything else to improve life in Iceland by bringing in modern farm implements and wood for boats at affordable prices, while allowing the profitable export of livestock, wool and fish.

In 1871 Denmark politically **annexed** Iceland, an event that, though not accepted by Icelanders, gave them a favourable **new constitution**. Broadly speaking, this returned full legislative powers to the Alþing and was ratified by King Christian IX himself, while attending celebrations at Þingvellir in 1874 to mark a thousand years since Settlement. Home control of lawmaking saw further benefits to living conditions: the tithe system was abolished; infrastructure improved; schooling was made compulsory; improvements in boats and fishing equipment caused the growth of port towns; and farmers formed the first Icelandic co-operatives to deal directly with foreign suppliers. There followed a sizeable population boom, despite heavy **emigration** to Canada and the US during the late nineteenth century following another spate of harsh weather, the eruption of Viti in the Askja caldera in northeastern Iceland (see p.330), disease and livestock problems.

Home Rule, Union and Independence

The concept of total political autonomy from Denmark grew from ideas planted by Jón Sigurðsson before his death in 1879. By 1900, differences in the way this could be achieved led to the formation of **political parties**, which in 1904 pressured the king into granting Home Rule under the **Home Rule Party** led by **Hannes Hafstein**. Hafstein's decade in office saw the start of trends that were to continue throughout the century: an emerging middle class led a gradual **population shift** from the land to towns, communications picked up with the introduction of telephones in 1906, and new technologies were adopted for farming and fishing, which boosted output. Workers also founded the first unions, and women were granted rights to an equal education and allowed to vote in 1915.

Hafstein's biggest defeat came in 1908 when the Alþing rejected the **Draft Constitution**, a proposal to make Iceland an independent state under the Danish king.

1940	1941	1944	1949
Iceland declares independence as Denmark is occupied by Nazis	British forces are replaced by Americans, with approval of parliament	Iceland becomes an independent state	Iceland joins NATO

Yet a decade later, a referendum found ninety percent of voters approved of the idea, and in December 1918, Iceland entered into the **Act of Union** with Denmark, where it received recognition as an independent state while still accepting the Danish king as monarch.

World War I itself bypassed Iceland, though during the war the country profited from the high export prices paid for fish, meat, and **wool** (in great demand in Europe for military uniforms). As **World War II** loomed, however, Iceland – dependent on trade with both Britain and Germany – decided to stay neutral, but after the outbreak of hostilities in 1939, the country's strategic North Atlantic location meant that, neutral or not, it was simply a matter of time before either Germany or Britain invaded. The **British** were first, landing unopposed in May 1940, so gaining a vital supply point for the Allies' North Atlantic operations. The following year **US forces** replaced the British with the approval of the Alþing, on condition that they respected Icelandic sovereignty and left once hostilities were over.

Though fighting never came to Iceland itself, World War II was to trigger the end of foreign rule. When Germany invaded Denmark in 1940 the Alþing decided that, as the king could no longer govern, the Act of Union should be dissolved and Iceland should declare its full **independence**. The formal ratification took some time, however, as the government was in disarray, with none of the four political parties holding a parliamentary majority. In the end, acting regent **Sveinn Björnsson** founded an apolitical government, which finally proclaimed independence from Denmark on June 17, 1944, with Björnsson elected as the first president of the **Icelandic Republic**.

The Cold War and Cod Wars

One of the biggest challenges for the new republic came immediately after the war. US troops departed in 1946 as requested, but as the **Cold War** between the Soviet and Western powers began to take shape Iceland felt uncertain about its lack of defence. With neither the population nor desire to form its own military, in 1949 the Alþing voted that Iceland should instead join the US, Britain and others as part of NATO, the North Atlantic Treaty Organization, and in 1951 agreed to have US forces operate an airforce base at Keflavík, using facilities the US had already built during World War II. Though the need for defence was widely accepted, the idea of having foreign influence back in Iceland after having only just got rid of it for the first time in seven hundred years was not popular, and the decision to join NATO caused a riot in Reykjavík.

In addition to the Cold War, the 1950s saw Iceland facing a rather different defence matter: that of preserving its fish stocks – and hence most of its export earnings – in the face of foreign competition. Iceland's territorial waters – the area from which it could exclude foreign vessels – had been set as extending three nautical miles from land in 1896, but as commercial fishing picked up after World War II and fish stocks through the Atlantic declined, most countries increased their territorial limits. In 1958, Iceland declared a twelve-mile limit which Britain protested, sending in naval boats to protect its trawlers fishing in these new Icelandic waters in the first act of the **Cod Wars** (see box, p.342).

1951	1958	1973	1974	1975
A US airbase is established at Keflavík	Start of the Cod Wars with Britain	Volcano on Heimaey erupts	Ringroad completed around the country	Iceland declares a 200-mile territorial limit around its shores

THE COD WARS

Kicking off in the late 1950s, the **Cod Wars** flared on and off for thirty years, with Iceland continuing to expand its claims as fish stocks continued to dwindle, and employing its coastguard to cut the cables of any foreign trawlers that were caught poaching. Things came to a head in 1975, when Iceland declared a two-hundred-mile limit around its shores, at which point Britain broke off diplomatic relations and ordered its Navy to ram Icelandic coastguard boats. The situation was only resolved in 1985, when international laws justified Iceland's position by granting the two-hundred-mile limit to all countries involved in the dispute.

Boom... and bust

Despite victory in the Cod Wars, fishing as the main source of export earnings created a very sensitive economy, while a reliance on imports led to high prices, with many people needing more than one job in order to make ends meet. During the late 1990s, Iceland sought to diversify the economy by investing in **banking**, which initially created incredibly high profits: suddenly a few mega-wealthy Icelanders were buying up everything from English soccer clubs to European supermarkets; and foreign investors, tempted by the fifteen percent interest rates, began pouring in money. But this only accelerated inflation and interest-rates hikes, until national debts were valued at ten times Iceland's actual economy: when the bubble burst in 2008 the economy imploded, leaving one in five households **bankrupt**.

After the crash, a left-wing administration under **Jóhanna Sigurðardóttir** oversaw the first stage of the recovery, but her austerity measures proved unpopular and saw her replaced in 2013 by the Progressives, led by Sigmundur Davíð Gunnlaugsson. Part of the problem was that wages had been kept low since 2008, and many ordinary Icelanders were again having trouble coping with rising costs caused by tourism-driven inflation. Yet the new government proved even less sympathetic to the problem, and in 2015 unions called for nationwide strikes to force the issue. Although these never materialized, popular discontent has seen the independent **Pirate Party** becoming the most popular political group in Iceland, despite its lack of any concrete policy.

Iceland today

Despite this discontent, there's no question that by 2012 the nation's fortunes were on the rebound – partly due to the banks simply writing off much of their debts, and partly through a devalued króna making Icelandic exports more attractive. But it was the eruption of the Eyjafjallajökull volcano which really accelerated the nation's recovery, after the tourist industry cleverly used international attention caused by the event to pitch Iceland as a wild and exciting yet accessible destination. So successful was the campaign that tourism has now overtaken fishing as the nation's primary source of income, with visitor numbers for 2015 approaching one million – three times the Icelandic population. This has brought its own concerns, not least in the visible damage that the sheer number of sightseers has caused at many popular destinations.

Domestically, Iceland is now predominantly **urban**, with two-thirds of the population living in the Greater Reykjavík area, and just 24,000 remaining on the

1975	1985	1994	2008
Britain breaks off diplomatic relations and the Cod Wars intensify	The Cod Wars are resolved, and the 200-mile limit agreed by international law	Iceland joins European Economic Area	Iceland's banking system collapses

land as farmers. Around nine percent of Icelanders now comprise **immigrant** families – often Southeast Asian refugees – rather than traditional Nordic stock. Response to these newcomers has proved tolerant, and despite the events of 2008, standards of living are equal to any European country – in fact, with little industry and low pollution levels, Icelanders are in some ways better off. Virtually all Icelanders are literate and well educated, communications are as good as they can be, given the natural conditions, and Iceland's per-capita usage of computers and the internet is one of the world's highest. New technologies, such as the harnessing of hydro and geothermal energy for electricity, heating and growing hothouse foods, have also been enthusiastically embraced.

2009	2010	2012	2014
New left-wing government appointed under Jóhanna Sigurðardóttir	Eyjafjallajökull eruption causes flight chaos across Europe	Beginnings of tourism boom and economic recovery	Holuhraun eruption creates a vast new lavafield in the Interior

Landscape and geology

Iceland's lunar landscapes are one of the country's prime attractions, but its apparently ancient facade is in fact an illusion. Geologically, Iceland is very young, with its oldest rocks dating back a mere fourteen million years, to a time in the Earth's history when the dinosaurs had long gone and humans were yet to evolve.

Iceland's landscape appears so raw because it sits on a geological hot spot on the mid-Atlantic ridge, where the **Eurasian** and **American continental plates** are drifting east and west apart from each other. As they do so, Iceland is continually tearing down the middle, allowing **magma** (molten rock from the Earth's core) to well upward towards the surface. When the surface cracks – in an earthquake, for instance – magma erupts through as a volcano, and when groundwater seeps down to magma levels it boils and returns to the surface as a **thermal spring** or, more dramatically, a **geyser**.

Almost all such geological activity in Iceland is located over this mid-Atlantic tear, which stretches northeast in a wide band across the country, taking in everything between the Reykjanes Peninsula, the Westman Islands and Mýrdalsjökull in the southwest, and Mývatn and Þórshöfn in the northeast. As this band is where volcanoes are creating all the new land, it's here that you'll find the most recent rocks; conversely, the oldest, most geologically stable parts of the country are around Ísafjörður in the West Fjords and Gerpir cliffs in Iceland's extreme east.

Iceland is also close enough to the Arctic for its higher mountains and plateaux – most of which are in the south of the country – to have become permanently ice-capped, forming extensive **glaciers**. Melt from around their edges contributes to many of Iceland's **rivers**, which are further fed by **underground springs** – also the source of the country's largest **lakes**. Cold, dry air formed by sub-zero temperatures over the ice caps is also responsible for some of the weird **atmospheric effects** you'll encounter here, while the **Aurora Borealis** or Northern Lights are caused by solar wind, or streams of particles charged by the sun, hitting the atmosphere.

Volcanoes

Though Iceland's volcanoes share a common origin, they form many different types, based on the chemical composition of their magma, which flows out of the volcano as **lava**. Where the lava is very fluid and the eruption is slow and continuous, the lava builds up to form a wide, flattened cone known as a **shield volcano**, a type that takes its name from the Skjaldbreiður (Shield-broad) volcano at Þingvellir. Where an eruption is violent, the lava is thrown out as a fine spray, cooling in mid-air and forming cones of ash or **tephra**, a cover-all name for volcanic ejecta; typical examples of tephra cones are found at Mývatn's Hverfjall, and Eldfell on Heimaey in the Westman Islands. Relatively rare in Iceland, **strato volcanoes** are tall, regular cones built from very long-term lava and tephra accumulations; westerly Snæfellsjökull is a good example, though the country's most consistently active volcano, Hekla, has formed in a similar manner but along a line of craters rather than a single vent.

Crater rows are one of the country's most common volcanic formations, caused when lava erupts at points along a lengthy **fissure**, such as occurred at Holuhraun in 2015, Leirhnjukur north of Mývatn in the 1970s, and Lakagígar in southeast Iceland during the 1780s. These eruptions produced a string of low, multiple cones and large quantities of lava – in Lakagígar's case, flows covered six hundred square kilometres. **Submarine eruptions** also occur off Iceland and are how the Westman Islands originally formed, as demonstrated by the creation of the new island of Surtsey in the 1960s. Looking like mini-volcanoes but actually nothing of the sort, aptly named **pseudocraters** – like those at Mývatn and Kirkjubæjarklaustur – form when lava flows over damp ground, vaporizing the water beneath, which explodes through the soft rock as a giant blister.

Most **rocks** in Iceland were created in volcanic eruptions, and two common forms are easily identifiable. **Basalt** forms fluid lava solidifying into dark rock, weathered expanses of which cover the Reykjanes Peninsula and elsewhere. Where basaltic lavas cool rapidly – by flowing into a river or the sea, for instance – they form characteristic **hexagonal pillars**, with excellent examples at Svartifoss in Skaftafell National Park and Hjálparfoss at Þórsárdalur. In contrast, **rhyolite** forms a very thick lava, which often builds up into dome-like volcanoes such as Mælifell on the Snæfellsnes Peninsula. Cooled, it normally produces distinctively crumbly, grey, yellow and pink rocks, typified by the peaks of the central Landmannalaugar region, though in some cases rhyolite solidifies into black, glass-like **obsidian** (best seen at Hrafntinnusker, on the Laugavegur hiking trail). Types of tephra to look for include black or red, gravel-like **scoria**; solidified lava foam or **pumice**, which is light enough to float on water; and **bombs**, spherical or elongated twists of rock formed when semi-congealed lava is thrown high into the air and hardens as it spins – they can be as big as a football but are usually fist-sized.

Aside from their cones and lavafields, volcanoes affect the landscape in other ways. Historically, dense clouds of tephra have destroyed farms and farmland on a number of occasions – such as the twelfth-century eruption of Hekla that buried Stöng in Þórsárdalur, or the 1875 explosion of Viti, at Askja. Volcanic activity under ice caps can also cause catastrophic flash floods known as **jökulhlaups**, the most recent being at Grímsvotn in 1996. On the other hand, extinct volcano craters often become flooded themselves and form lakes, or **maars**; one of the biggest is Öskjuvatn in the Askja caldera, but there are also smaller examples at Grænvatn on the Reykjanes Peninsula and Kerið crater near Selfoss.

Thermal springs and geysers

Thermal springs are found all over Iceland, sometimes emerging at ground level literally as a hot-water spring – such as at Hveragerði – or flooding natural depressions or crevasses to form hot pools, which can be found at Mývatn and Landmannalaugar. In some cases the water emerges from the ground as steam through a vent; where this mixes with clay, boiling mud pits or **solfataras** are formed, of which the most extensive are those at Hverarönd, east of Mývatn. Natural steam is harnessed in Iceland to drive turbines and generate **geothermal power**, and also as heating for homes and hothouses.

While geysers tap into the same subterranean hot water as thermal springs, nobody is quite sure exactly why they erupt – it's either a gradual build-up of water pressure or a subterranean hiccup. Since the Krísuvík geyser blew itself to pieces in 1999, Iceland's only example of note is at Geysir, northeast of Selfoss.

Glaciers, rivers and lakes

Glaciers can be thought of as giant, frozen rivers or waterfalls that move downhill under their own colossal weight. Usually movement is slow – maybe a few centimetres a year – though some can shift a metre or more annually. In Iceland, they're all associated with ice caps, the biggest of which, **Vatnajökull** (which more or less means Glacial Sea), spreads over 150km across the country's southeast. These caps sit atop plateaux, with a few isolated rocky peaks or **nunataks** poking through the ice, off which scores of glaciers descend to lower levels.

Deeper glacial ice is often distinctly blue, caused by the air being squeezed out from between the ice crystals by the weight of the ice above. However, glaciers are also full of debris, either from falls of volcanic ash, or simply from the way they grind down the rocks underneath them into fine gravel or sand. As this dark grit nears the surface of the glacier it warms up in the sunlight, causing surrounding ice to melt, exposing the gravel and thereby making the front of most Icelandic glaciers appear very "dirty". The debris ultimately is carried away from the glacier by streams or rivers which are also the product of glacial friction, and deposited as desert-like **sandurs**, such as those that occupy much of Iceland's southeastern coastline.

It's also possible to see the effects that the glaciers themselves leave on the landscape, as both ice caps and glaciers were formerly far more extensive than they appear today. During previous ice ages – the last of which ended around 12,000 years ago – much of the country was beneath the ice, but there has been considerable fluctuation in glacier limits even in recorded times, and at present most are **shrinking**. The intricate inlets of the East Fjords and West Fjords were carved by vanished glaciers, as were the characteristically flat-topped mountains known as **móbergs**, southeast of Mývatn. Former glacial valleys – typically broad and rounded – can be seen along the Ringroad southwest of Akureyri; and Iceland's most mobile glacier, Skeiðarárjökull in Skaftafell National Park, has been retreating over the last eighty years, leaving raised **moraine** gravel ridges in its wake.

The majority of Iceland's **rivers** are fairly short, glacial-fed affairs, though two of the largest – the **Hvíta** in the southwest, and northeastern **Jökulsá á Fjöllum** – each exceed a respectable 200km in length. Both have quite spectacular stretches where they have carved **canyons** and **waterfalls** out of the landscape: at Gullfoss on the Hvíta; and Dettifoss and Ásbergi along the Jökulsá. Icelandic **lakes** are not especially large and tend to be caused – as with Mývatn or Þingvallavatn – when lava walls dam a spring-fed outflow, causing it to back-flood.

Atmospheric phenomena

One of the strangest features of being in Iceland during the summer is the extremely **long days**. The northernmost part of the mainland is actually just outside the Arctic Circle, and so the sun does set (briefly) even on the longest day of the year, though you can cross over to the little island of Grímsey, whose northern tip is inside the Arctic and so enjoys midnight sun for a few days of the year. Conversely, winter days are correspondingly short, with the sun barely getting above the horizon for three months of the year.

One consequence of Iceland's often cold, dry atmosphere is that – on sunny days at least – it can play serious tricks on your sense of scale. Massive objects such as mountains and glaciers seem to stay the same size, or even shrink, the closer you come to them, and sometimes phantom hills or peaks appear on the horizon. Another effect – best viewed on cold, clear nights – is the **Northern Lights**, or **Aurora Borealis**, which form huge, shifting sheets of green or red in the winter skies. They're caused by the solar wind bringing electrically charged particles into contact with the Earth's atmosphere, and you'll have to be in luck to catch a really good show – they improve the further north you travel.

Wildlife and the environment

Iceland's first settlers found a land whose coastal fringe, compared with today, was relatively well wooded; there were virtually no land mammals, but birdlife and fish stocks were abundant and the volcanic soil was reasonably fertile. Over a thousand years of farming has brought great changes: big trees are a rare sight, fish stocks have plummeted, and introduced mammals have contributed to erosion and other problems, but a growing regard for Iceland's environment is beginning to redress the imbalance, and the country's natural history remains very much alive.

Flora

Though fossils indicate that around twelve million years ago Iceland had stands of maples and other broad-leaved trees, dawn redwood and even giant sequoias, subsequent ice ages had wiped these out long before humans ever landed here. It's likely that the Vikings found woods mostly comprising **dwarf birch** and **willow** that you still see here today. Both can grow up to 10m or so in height, but generally form shrub-like thickets – original forests, however, would have been fairly extensive, reaching from the coast up into highland valleys. Clearances for timber and pasture have reduced Iceland's tree cover to just one percent of the land, though since 1994 over four million trees – including commercial stands of **pine** – have been planted in an attempt to restore levels to pre-Settlement estimates.

The most widespread flora – **mosses** and **lichens** – tend to get overlooked, but they cover almost every lava flow and cliff in the country and provide a colourful mosaic of greens, greys and oranges, especially after rain has darkened the surrounding rocks. **Flowering plants** are most obvious in midsummer, and include the very common, blue vertical spikes of **arctic lupins**, introduced from North America to help reduce erosion; the tiny magenta flowers and spongy green clumps of **arctic river beauty** and **thyme** (which you can also identify from its smell); fluffy **cottongrass** growing in boggy areas; the cauliflower-shaped, yellow-green flower heads of **angelica**, often covered in flies; blue **harebells**; and yellow **kingcups** and **dandelions**. In early autumn, **berries** are also plentiful, and many people collect them to eat.

Mammals

The **arctic fox**, which feeds almost exclusively on birds, was the only land mammal in Iceland when the first settlers arrived. Common throughout Iceland, they're chubbier than European foxes, with short, rounded ears, bushy tail, and a brown coat that turns white in winter. **Polar bears** have never flourished here, though every decade one or two

---

THE NATURE FEE DEBATE

The **right to roam** freely across the country is deeply embedded in the Icelandic psyche, which is why almost all natural sights around the country are open access and **free to enter**. A massive increase in tourist numbers in recent years, however, has caused visible wear and tear at the most popular places. To help fund improvements such as erosion-resistant paths – or, say some cynics, simply to cash in – landowners at Mývatn and Geysir began charging entry fees until the courts ruled it illegal in 2015. As debates over the issue continue, it is possible that some form of nationwide **Nature Fee** may be introduced in the near future.

float over on ice floes from Greenland (which is probably how foxes first arrived too), only to be shot as a dangerous pest by the first person who sees them.

Domestic animals arrived with the Vikings. The **Icelandic horse** is a unique breed descended from medieval Norwegian stock, as none has been imported since the tenth century. Cattle numbers are fairly low, but **sheep** outnumber the human population by four to one. **Reindeer** were introduced from Norway and Finland in the late seventeenth century for hunting purposes – today they're restricted to eastern Iceland, where they stick to high-altitude pasture in summer, descending to coastal areas in winter. Iceland's cold climate has limited the spread of smaller vermin such as **rats** and **mice**, which were unintentionally brought in on boats and only occur around human habitations; escaped **rabbits** have recently established themselves around Reykjavík and on Heimaey, however. **Minks** have also broken out of fur farms and seem to be surviving in the wild, much to the detriment of native birdlife.

Offshore, Iceland has a number of **whale** species. Traditionally, their valuable meat, bones and teeth were most frequently obtained from washed-up corpses, and – as described in *Eyrbyggja Saga* (see p.353) – battles were even fought over the rights to their carcasses. **Commercial whaling** began in the nineteenth century, and resumed after a fifteen-year-long moratorium ended in 2006, though numbers remain high and you've a good chance of seeing some if you put to sea. Most common are a couple of species of **dolphin** and the 5m-long **pilot whale**, but there are also substantial numbers of far larger **fin whales**, **sei whales** and **minke whales**, all of which feed by straining plankton from sea water through moustache-like baleen plates inside their mouths. Far less common are **orca** (also known as killer whales), square-headed **sperm whales**, and **blue whales**, which reach 30m in length and are the largest known animal ever to have lived.

Grey and harbour **seals** are found in Iceland, with the biggest numbers seen around the north coast and off the Westman Islands. Both species are also hunted, despite being depicted as almost human in Icelandic folktales, appearing as "were-seals" who have human families on land and seal families in the sea. According to these stories, if you walk along a beach and find a seal following you out from shore, it may be looking to see if you're one of its children.

Birds

Iceland has some three hundred recorded bird species, of which around eighty breed regularly. The **gyrfalcon**, a large bird of prey with grey-white plumage, is a national icon, once appearing on the Icelandic coat of arms and exported for hunting purposes until the nineteenth century. They're not common, but occur throughout mountainous country; in folklore the gyrfalcon is said to be brother to the ptarmigan, its main source of food. Another spectacular bird of prey is the huge **white-tailed sea eagle**, whose numbers have recently rebounded following a low point in the 1980s, when birds took poison baits intended for escaped minks. Around forty pairs breed annually in the West Fjords, though juveniles travel quite widely over the country.

The **ptarmigan** is a plump game bird with a rattling call, plentiful across Iceland wherever there is low scrub or trees. They're well camouflaged, patterned a mottled brown to blend with summer vegetation, and changing – with the exception of black tail feathers and a red wattle around the eye – to snow-white plumage in winter. Aside from being preyed upon year-round by foxes and gyrfalcons, ptarmigan are also a traditional Christmas food, eaten instead of turkey. Their population goes through boom-and-bust cycles, and in bad years Christmas ptarmigan have to be brought in from Scotland, allowing Icelanders to bemoan the flavour of imported birds.

Other common heathland birds include the **golden plover**, a migrant whose mournful piping is eagerly awaited in Iceland as the harbinger of summer;

long-legged **redshank, whimbrel** and **godwit**; and **snipe**, identified by their long beaks, zigzag flight, and strange "buzzing" noise made by two stiffened tail feathers which protrude at right angles to its body. In fields and estuaries you'll see **greylag geese**, the most common of Iceland's wildfowl species, with **whooper swans** resident even in downtown Reykjavík. Similarly widespread are **raven**, held by some Icelanders to be highly intelligent, though often associated in tales with portents of doom. Norse mythology describes Óðinn as having two ravens called Huginn (Mind) and Muninn (Memory), which report to him on the state of the world; and folklore holds that the congregations of ravens commonly seen in autumn are dividing up Iceland's farms between them, so that each pair will have a home over winter.

Many of Iceland's **ducks** (see box, p.263) are coastal, though you can see almost all recorded species either on or around Mývatn, a lake in the northeast. **Eider** are probably

ICELANDIC BIRD GLOSSARY

Below is a partial list of **Icelandic birds**, with English and Icelandic names (US names are given in brackets where they differ substantially from British usage). You won't have to be an ardent twitcher to clock up most of these, though a couple of less widespread species are also included.

Arctic skua	Kjói	**Merlin**	Smyrill
Arctic tern	Kría	**Oystercatcher**	Tjaldur
Barnacle goose	Helsingi	**Pink-footed goose**	Heiðagæs
Barrow's goldeneye	Húsönd	**Pintail**	Grafönd
Black guillemot	Teista	**Ptarmigan**	Rjúpa
Black-headed gull	Hettumáfur	**Puffin**	Lundi
Black-tailed godwit	Jaðrakan	**Purple sandpiper**	Sendlingur
Black-throated diver (Loon)	Himbrimi	**Raven**	Hrafn
		Razorbill	Álka
Brünnich's guillemot (Thick-billed murre)	Stuttnefja	**Red-necked (Northern) phalarope**	Óðinshani
Cormorant	Dílaskarfur	**Red-throated diver**	Lómur
Dunlin	Lóuþræll	**Redpoll**	Auðnutittlingur
Eider	Æðarfugl	**Redshank**	Stelkur
Fulmar	Fýll	**Redwing**	Skógarþröstur
Gannet	Súla	**Ringed plover**	Sandlóa
Golden plover	Heiðlóa	**Scaup**	Duggönd
Goosander	Gulönd	**Scoter**	Hrafnsönd
Great auk*	Geirfugl	**Shag**	Toppskarfur
Great skua	Skúmur	**Short-eared owl**	Brandugla
Greater black-backed gull	Svartbakur	**Slavonian grebe**	Flórgoði
		Snipe	Hrossagaukur
Greylag goose	Grágæs	**Snow bunting**	Snjótittlingur
Guillemot (Murre)	Langvía	**Starling**	Stari
Gyrfalcon	Fálki	**Storm petrel**	Stormsvala
Harlequin duck	Straumönd	**Teal**	Urtönd
Herring gull	Silfurmáfur	**Tufted duck**	Skúfönd
Iceland gull	Bjartmáfur	**Turnstone**	Tildra
Kittiwake	Rita	**Wheatear**	Steindepill
Lesser black-backed gull	Sílamáfur	**White wagtail**	Maríuerla
		White-tailed sea eagle	Haförn
Little auk (Dovekie)	Haftyrðill	**Whooper swan**	Álft
Longtail duck (Old squaw)	Hávella	**Wigeon**	Rauðhöfðaönd
Mallard	Stokkönd	**Wren**	Músarrindill
Meadow pipit	Þúfutittlingur		
Merganser	Toppönd	*Extinct	

the most famous Icelandic duck, known for their warm down, but birders will want to clock up **harlequin** and **Barrow's goldeneye**, which occur nowhere else in Europe.

Seabirds

Of all the country's birdlife, it's the huge, noisy, teeming **seabird colonies** which really stick in the mind. There are several types of gull – including the uniformly pale **Iceland gull**, and slight, graceful **kittiwake** – but far more common are narrow-winged, stumpy **fulmars**, which look gull-like but are actually related to albatrosses. They nest in half-burrows or overhangs on steep slopes and cliffs, and are relatively fearless, often allowing you to approach fairly close – come too near, however, and they spit a foul-smelling oil from their double-chambered beak.

In summer, flat, open places around the coast are utilized by colossal numbers of ground-nesting **arctic terns**, small, white birds with narrow wings, trailing tails, black caps and bright red beaks. It's interesting to watch the activity in a tern colony, but keep your distance, as the birds relentlessly attack anything that threatens their nests. **Skuas** are heavily built, brown birds with nasty tempers and a piratic lifestyle – they chase and harass weaker seabirds into dropping their catches. Like terns, they also nest on the ground in vast colonies across the southeastern coastal *sandurs*, and are equally defensive of their territory.

Iceland's equivalent to penguins are the similar-looking **auks**, a family that includes **guillemot** (murre), **razorbill** and **puffin**. Like penguins, these hunt fish, live in huge seaside colonies, and have black and white plumage. Unlike penguins, however, they can also fly. Auks' **beaks** are distinctively specialized: long and pointed in guillemots; mid-length and broad in razorbills; and colourfully striped, sail-shaped in puffins – all aids to their specific fishing techniques. The best place to see puffins is on Heimaey in the Westman Islands (see box, p.142) but you'll find other auks anywhere around Iceland where there are suitable nesting cliffs. One exception is the Arctic-dwelling **little auk**, or dovekie, now seen only rarely on Grímsey, Iceland's northernmost outpost.

Books and sagas

With a population of barely over a quarter of a million, Iceland boasts more writers per capita than any other country in the world. The long dark winter months are said to be the reason so many folk put pen to paper, and native-language books on all matters Icelandic can be found in shops across the country. Conversely, as the Icelandic-language market is so small, prices can be inordinately high – specialist publications cost the equivalent of hundreds of dollars, and even a popular-fiction paperback comes in at around 4000kr.

On the other hand, the **sagas** and associated literature have been widely translated into English – Penguin Books, Everyman and Oxford University Press publish a good range of the longer sagas and their own compilations of the shorter tales, some of which are reviewed below (with the publisher of specific compilations indicated in brackets). Icelandic Review also publishes a series of collections of folk tales, lesser sagas, and mythologies, available in bookshops across Iceland.

There's an increasing amount of **contemporary fiction** available in English, too, though it's not always easy to find outside of Iceland. Foreign books about Iceland remain, unfortunately, remarkably scant, and often lapse into "land of fire and ice"-style clichés.

HISTORY AND CULTURE

Þráinn Bertelsson *My Self & I*. Fine autobiography by one of Iceland's most respected film directors and writers, focusing on growing up in 1950s Reykjavík as Iceland was rediscovering itself in the wake of new-found independence.

Johannes Brøndsted *The Vikings*. Solid overview of the causes and motivation of the Viking explosion through Europe, focusing mostly on Scandinavia rather than Iceland but giving heaps of details – backed up by archeology – about religion, customs and daily life.

Jesse Byock *Viking Age Iceland*. A bit academic in character, but helpfully fills in background on the environment, politics and peoples of Iceland's "Viking republic".

Victoria Clark *The Far Farers*. Lively, if slightly shallow, account of Clark's attempt to footstep the route that took an Icelander named Thorvald to Jerusalem, reinforcing how worldly and well travelled many Vikings were.

★**Hugleikur Dagsson** *Avoid Us* (aka *Should You Be Laughing at This?*). Dagsson's cartoon strips of stick-figures engaged in outrageous activities have made him a national icon in Iceland; on publication in English, The *Irish Sun* tabloid clamoured "Ban This Sick Book". Not for the easily offended.

David Roberts *Iceland: Land of the Sagas*. Beautiful glossy pictures by photographer Jon Krakauer accompany the rich text in this coffee-table book of Iceland.

★**Anna Yates** *Leifur Eiríksson and Vínland the Good*. An excellent and readable account of the discovery of North America by Icelandic Vikings. A thorough argument of where exactly Vínland is accompanies debate on why the Norse settlements in North America died out.

MODERN FICTION

★**Frans G. Bengtsson** *The Long Ships*. Buckle your swash for this lusty novel of Viking times, as the irrepressible hero Orm hacks and pillages his way across northern Europe. Though not set in Iceland, it evokes the period with historical accuracy while never letting up on the rollicking, good-humoured pace.

Einar Már Guðmundsson *Angels of the Universe*. A sad, challenging story of a young Icelandic man's descent into schizophrenia and the way society treats him, based on the life of the author's brother. Difficult reading at times but never patronizing or pointlessly grim.

Hallgrímur Helgason *101 Reykjavík*. A wry look at the undemanding values of a modern urban existence, centring on the self-inflicted crisis-ridden life of Reykjavík resident Hlynur Björn, a 30-year-old slacker living at home with his mother. It's also been made into a film that catches the book's humour superbly.

★**Arnaldur Indriðason** *Jar City* (aka *Tainted Blood*). Known in Icelandic as *Mýrin*, this gritty thriller with a uniquely Icelandic twist to the plot introduced the misanthropic Reykjavík detective Erlendur and launched Indriðason's massive success as a crime writer. Others in the series include *Silence of the Grave*, *The Draining Lake* and *Arctic Chill*.

Einar Kárason *Devil's Island*. First in a trilogy of novels set in 1950s Reykjavík, seen through the eyes of an eccentric family housed in an abandoned US army barracks. Lively, satirical and sharp, it has also been made into a film.

Halldór Laxness *Independent People*. Nobel Prize-winning novel about the toils and troubles of the dirt-poor but comically stubborn sheep farmer Bjartur to live free and unbeholden to any man. A potentially downbeat tale

of haves and have-nots, lifted by humorous undercurrents, a lack of bitterness, and real humanity.

Yrsa Sigurðardóttir *Last Rituals*. Well-above-average murder mystery set in modern Reykjavík but descending into a dark world of witchcraft and folklore. Inevitably living in the shadow of Arnaldur Indriðason's novels, but coping well.

Sjón *The Blue Fox*. Lyrical poem written by one-time Björk collaborator about two apparently unconnected events taking place during a nineteenth-century winter's day, and ultimately exploring Icelandic folklore and relationships with the land.

TRAVEL AND WILDLIFE

W.H. Auden and Louis MacNeice *Letters from Iceland*. Amusing and unorthodox travelogue, the result of a summer journey the young poets undertook through Iceland in 1936. Especially enjoyable are the irreverent comments about local people, politicians and literature.

Sigurður Ægisson *Icelandic Whales*. Slim, pocket-sized guide to the 23 species recorded from Icelandic waters, well illustrated and with entertaining, informative text.

Mark Cawardine *Iceland Nature's Meeting Place*. Plenty of colour photos and maps in this wildlife guide, which provides useful information for the amateur naturalist. Advice, too, on where to go to see individual species of birds.

Rob Hume *RSPB Birds of Britain & Europe*. A mine of

superlative photographs covering most of the birds you're likely to encounter in Iceland; invaluable for accurate identification in the field or just handy for some background reading.

★ **Mark Kurlansky** *Cod*. Entertaining and offbeat account of the cod in history, and a trade in it which reached from Iceland to the US and Spain. A good number of recipes too, if you want to see what all the fuss was about.

Tim Moore *Frost on my Moustache*. Highly enjoyable account of the author's attempts to follow in the footsteps of adventurer Lord Dufferin, who sailed to Iceland in 1856. A critical and well-observed account of the Icelandic nation makes this a must-read.

Sagas and classics

Icelanders will tell you that the greatest of the **sagas** contain everything you need to know about life, and getting acquainted with them certainly reveals something of the culture and history of Iceland. No other ancient literature matches them for their hard-boiled style, laconic but gripping delivery, or their trademark theme of individuals caught in inexorable, often terrible, fates.

The word *saga* itself simply means "thing told", and they cover a range of subjects. They were written anonymously between the twelfth and fifteenth centuries, often long after the events they describe; Snorri Sturluson – the thirteenth-century historian and politician – is the only known **author** of any of the sagas, with the *Heimskringla* and *Egil's Saga* attributed to him. All this leaves scholars to debate whether the sagas are historically accurate, or historical novels written to extol the virtues of an earlier age. But none of this really matters – what makes the sagas great is that, even today, they feel immediate and believable.

The most characteristic group of sagas are the so-called "Sagas of Icelanders", which deal mostly with the events of Settlement and the early Commonwealth (around 870–1050). They read like histories, being set in real places (many of which still bear the same name today), and usually begin with a series of genealogies establishing the "historical" origins of the main characters. Some are biographies of individuals, such as in **Egil's Saga** (see box, p.155) or **Grettir's Saga**. Many tell of long-running feuds, from origin to conclusion; **Njal's Saga** (see box, p.123) is the greatest of these, but **Eyrbyggja Saga** and the short but impressive **Hrafnkel's Saga** (see box, p.292) are other good examples. There are also a few that focus on a particular area – most famous is the tragic love story recounted in **Laxdæla Saga** (see box, p.168).

THE GREAT COLLECTOR

The saga manuscripts were first recognized for what they were and collected together by just one man, **Árni Magnusson** (1663–1730). As the Icelanders became increasingly poor under Danish rule, many manuscripts could be found stuffing holes in farmhouse walls, and Árni Magnusson made it his mission to save them and take them to Copenhagen for storage. Once there, however, many were destroyed in a fire, though Árni managed to save some himself. Following Iceland's independence in 1944, a strong political movement arose to return the manuscripts from Copenhagen and an institute was established to receive them. Such was the political importance attached to these priceless artefacts that some were brought back by gunboat.

Other sagas range widely in theme, from chivalric stories of knights in armour and outright romances (often influenced by contemporary foreign literature, or even Homer), to folklore, lives of the saints and Icelandic bishops, and far more historical works such as the **Vinland Sagas**, the massive saga of the Sturlung age (**Sturlunga Saga**), or Snorri Sturluson's **Heimskringla**, the history of the Norse Kings.

Egil's Saga A powerful and lucid narrative, unmatched for the vivid presence of the central figure, Egil, a mean, mischief-making, murdering poet and grandson of a reputed werewolf, whose last wish in old age is to cause a violent riot at the Alþing by publicly scattering his hoarded cash.

Eirík the Red and other Iceland Sagas (Oxford University Press). The tale of one of Iceland's most notorious Viking heroes, whose son went on to discover North America, plus some shorter period pieces – *Hrafnkel's* and the *Vopnafjörd* sagas are the most coherent.

Eyrbyggja Saga A strange and often unsettling story, mixing historical events with tales of ghosts, Viking ceremony and family intrigue, while mapping out the shadowy life of Snorri Þórgrimsson, who advocated the introduction of Christianity in 1000. Uneven, but with some great set pieces and character sketches.

Laxdæla Saga One of the world's great tragic love stories, following the lives of the families sharing a river valley, and the consequences of Gudrún Ósvifsdottir's forced marriage to her lover's best friend.

Njal's Saga The longest of all the sagas, this is a compelling, visceral account of the schemings and personalities involved in a fifty-year medieval feud, full of bloodshed, pride and falls, and laconic humour.

The Sagas of Icelanders (Allen Lane Penguin). Hefty compendium of a dozen key sagas, including *Laxdæla*, *Egil's*, *Hrafnkel's* and the *Vinland Sagas* but strangely omitting that of *Njál*. Comprehensive explanatory text and a few less well-known short stories flesh out the era – and the tale of Auðun and his bear is a gem.

Saga of the Volsungs (Penguin). Said to have inspired Tolkien's *Lord of the Rings* and Wagner's *Ring* cycle, this epic delves deep into Norse mythology and the eternal pitfalls of human nature as it follows the adventures of Sigurd the Dragon Slayer.

Sagas of Warrior-Poets (Penguin). Being a poet brought respect in Viking times, but poets typically suffered from thorny temperaments, often bringing unhappy fates. The most famous is portrayed in *Egil's Saga*, but this collection of shorter tales also emphasizes the poet's lot – the best here is the wonderfully named saga of *Gunnlaug Serpent-tongue*.

Seven Viking Romances (Penguin). Unlike the moral, realistic sagas, these contemporary tales stretch belief a bit and have fun along the way, as warriors outwit gods, overcome monsters and vast armies, and get up to all sorts of bawdy mischief. Tellingly, this always happens away from Iceland – and reliable witnesses.

Snorri Sturluson *King Harald's Saga* (Penguin). Part of the *Heimskringla*, recording the turbulent life of King Harald of Norway, felled in battle at Stamford Bridge in Yorkshire, when invading England in 1066, just three weeks before the Battle of Hastings – had he won, English history might have been very different.

Snorri Sturluson The *Prose Edda*. The *Prose Edda* contain almost all of what is known about Norse mythology, so for the details on everything from the creation of the Æsir to the events leading to Ragnarok, read this book. The other source of Norse myths is the difficult *Poetic Edda*, an earlier compilation of even older poetry fragments.

The Vinland Sagas Two versions of the Viking discovery of Greenland and North America ("Vinland"), recounted in *Saga of the Greenlanders* and *Eirik the Red's Saga*.

Icelandic

Icelandic is an oddly archaic language, heavy with declensions, genders and cases, not to mention Norse peculiarities. Whereas the other principal members of the North Germanic group of languages, Danish, Norwegian and Swedish, lost much of their grammar over time, Icelandic has proudly maintained features that make even the most polyglottal language student cough and splutter. It is also one of the most linguistically pure languages in Europe in terms of vocabulary, and a campaign to rid the language of foreign (mostly English) words has led to the coining of many new, purely Icelandic words and phrases, devised by a committee of linguistic experts. Modern inventions especially have been given names from existing Icelandic words, such as *sími* for telephone (literally "long thread"), hence *farsími* ("travelling long thread") for "mobile phone", and *tölva* ("number prophetess") for computer; and even *fara á puttanu* ("to travel on the thumb") for "to hitchhike". Perhaps worryingly there's no Icelandic word for "interesting", the closest term being *gaman* – "fun". Icelandic has also maintained many old names for European cities that were in use at the time of the Settlement, such as Dyflinni (Dublin), Jórvík (York, in Britain, hence Nýa Jórvík for New York) and Lundúnir (London).

Anyone learning Icelandic will also have to grapple with a mind-blowing use of **grammatical cases** for the most straightforward of activities: "to open a door", for instance, requires the accusative case (*opna dyrnar*), while "to close a door" takes the dative case (*loka dyrunum*). Not only that, but "door" is plural in Icelandic, as is the word for Christmas, *jólin*, hence *jólin eru í desember*, literally "Christmasses are in December" (as opposed to the English "Christmas is in December"). Thankfully, there are no dialects anywhere in the country.

Basic grammar

There are 32 **letters** in the Icelandic alphabet. Accented á, é, í, ó, ú and ý count as separate letters. Letters Þ/þ, Æ/æ and Ö/ö come at the end of the alphabet in that order, while Ð/ð comes after d. Hence a dictionary entry for *mögulegur* comes after *morgunn*.

Verbs come in many classes and are either strong and characterized by a vowel change (*tek, tók, tekinn*: "take", "took", "taken") or weak (*tala, talaði*: "speak", "spoke"), without a vowel shift. Verb endings agree with **pronouns**, which are as follows: *ég* ("I"), *þú* ("you", singular), *hann* ("he"), *hún* ("she"), *það* ("it"), *við* ("we"), *þið* ("you", plural), *þeir* ("you", masculine plural), *þaer* ("you", feminine plural), *þau* ("you", neuter or mixed gender plural).

Icelandic **nouns** can have one of three genders (masculine, feminine or neuter) and can appear in any one of four different grammatical cases (nominative, accusative, genitive and dative). For example, the masculine word *fjörður*, meaning "a fjord", is *fjörður* in the nominative case, *fjörð* in the accusative case, *fjarðar* in the genitive and *firði* in the dative case. The case of a noun is determined by many factors, including the use of a preceding preposition, for instance, *í Reykjavík* ("in Reykjavík") but *til Reykjavíkur* ("to Reykjavík").

Vowels also have an unnerving ability to shift – for example, *hér er amma* ("here is grandma") but *ég sé ömmu* ("I see grandma"); this also happens with proper nouns. There is no **indefinite article** in Icelandic, with the result that *fjörður* can mean both "fjord" and "a fjord". The **definite article**, as in the other Scandinavian languages, is suffixed to the noun; for example, *maður* means "a man", but *maðurinn* means "the man". The definite article is declined according to the gender and number of the noun.

Adjectives generally precede the noun they qualify and are inflected according to the gender and case gender of the noun. The strong declension is used with indefinite nouns, as in *góður maður* – "a good man". Definite nouns (those with the definite article or other determinatives) require the weak declension, so *góði maðurinn*, "the good man".

Names and numbers

Icelanders take the forename of their father as the first part of their own **surname**, plus the Icelandic word for son (*son*) or daughter (*dóttir*). For example, the son of a man whose forename is Jón will have Jónsson as a surname; a daughter of the same man will have Jónsdóttir as a surname. A family of four in Iceland can therefore have four different surnames, which can certainly throw things into confusion when they travel abroad. When asking someone's surname, Icelanders will enquire "*hvers son er Kristbjörn?*" ("Whose son is Kristbjörn?") for example, to which the reply might be "*hann er Egils son*" ("He's Egil's son"). Formally or informally, Icelanders are always addressed by their forename and are listed accordingly in the telephone directory.

When giving their **addresses**, Icelanders put their street names in the dative case but their town and country in the nominative case. They decline their own names, for instance, *ég tala við Önnu* – "I'm speaking to Anna" (*Önnu* is the accusative, genitive and dative form of "*Anna*") and *bókin er eftir Ingibjörgu Sigurðardóttur* – "the book is by Ingibjörg Sigurðardóttir".

When **counting**, the nominative masculine form of the numerals is used, i.e. *einn, tveir, þrír, fjórir*. However, **street numbers** and the **time** are given in the neuter form.

Learning Icelandic

In theory, the Germanic roots of English and Icelandic, coupled with over two centuries of Norse influence in England during the Viking era, should make **Icelandic** a fairly easy language for English-speakers to learn. It doesn't – and any foreigner who has mastered even a smattering of the language will find Icelandic jaws dropping at his every turn. Conversely, most Icelanders speak excellent English, and young people in particular are only too keen to try out turns of phrase on you.

If you want to teach yourself Icelandic, however, your best bet is the widely available and excellent *Colloquial Icelandic* by Daisy L. Neijmann, a thoroughly contemporary and well-constructed beginners' course accompanied by a couple of CDs. There is only one Icelandic reference work in English on the subject of **grammar**, *Icelandic Grammar, Texts and Glossary*, by Stefán Einarsson. Originally published in 1945 and still printed today in paperback, it offers a very thorough if somewhat stodgy analysis of the language.

Dictionaries and phrasebooks

Dictionaries are exceptionally thin on the ground outside Iceland, but the pocket-sized *Icelandic–English, English–Icelandic Dictionary*, published by Hippocrene Books, New York, is good for basic reference and is fairly easy to get hold of. Larger dictionaries are best bought in Iceland, where they are much less expensive.

Of the **phrasebooks**, most useful is Berlitz's *Scandinavian Phrase Book and Dictionary*, which includes a hundred-page section on Icelandic.

Pronunciation

Stress in Icelandic is always on the first syllable. Below is a guide to the pronunciation of Icelandic vowels and consonants – some have no equivalent in English, but the nearest sound has been given to facilitate pronunciation.

VOWELS

a	as in father	ó	as in sow
á	as in cow	u	like u in cute
e	as in get or air, depending	ú	as in fool
	on whether long or short	y	see "i", above
é	as in yeah	ý	see "í" above
i	as in hit	æ	as in eye
í	as in lean	au	as in French feuille
ö	as in fur	ei	as in hay

CONSONANTS

As in English except:

j	as in yet	f before l or n	pronounced **b**, eg Keflavík
ll and rl	like the Welsh ll, or dl pronounced together in English as in saddle	rn	pronounced as **dn**

Note that Icelandic Þ/þ is the same as English "th" in thing. And Icelandic Ð/ð is the same as English "th" in this.

Useful words and phrases

BASIC PHRASES

Yes	Já	Where/when?	Hvar/hvenær?
No	Nei	What/why?	Hvað/hvers vegna?
Hello	Halló/hæ	Who/how?	Hver/hvernig?
How are you?	Hvað segirðu?	How much?	Hvað mikið?
Fine, thanks	Allt fínt, takk	I don't know	Ég veit ekki
Goodbye	Bless/bæ	Do you know (a fact)?	Veistu…?
Good morning/ afternoon	Góðan dag	Is there/are there…?	Er/eru…?
		With/without	Með/án
Good night	Góða nótt	And/not	Og/ekki
Today/tomorrow	Í dag/á morgun	Something/nothing	Eitthvað/ekkert
Tonight	Í kvöld	Here/there	Hér/þar
Please	Afsakið	Near/far	Nálægt/fjarlægt
Thank you	Takk fyrir	This/that	Þetta/það
I'd like…	Ég ætla að fá	Now/later	Núna/seinna
Excuse me	Fyrirgefðu	More/less	Meiri/minni
Here you are	Gerið svo vel (plural)/ gerðu svo vel (singular)	Big/little	Stór/lítill/smár
		Open/closed	Opið/lokað
Don't mention it	Ekkert að þakka	Men/women	Karlmenn/kvenmenn
Sorry? (as in "what did you say?")	Ha?/hvað sagðir þú?	Toilet	Snyrting
		Gentlemen/ladies	Herrar/konur
		Bank	Banki

Post office	Pósthús	What's your name?	Hvað heitirðu?
Stamp(s)	Frímerki	My name is…	Ég heiti…
Where are you from?	Hvaðan ertu?	How do you say…	Hvernig segir maður …
I'm from…	Ég er frá	in Icelandic?	á íslensku?
…America	…Bandaríkjunum	Do you speak English?	Talarðu ensku?
…Australia	…Ástralíu	I don't understand	Ég skil ekki
…Britain	…Bretlandi	Could you speak	Gætirðu talað
…Canada	…Kanada	more slowly?	hægar?
…England	…Englandi	How much is it?	Hvað kostar þetta?
…Ireland	…Írlandi	Can I pay, please?	Ég ætla að borga?
…New Zealand	…Nyja Sjálandi	The bill/check,	Reikninginn, takk
…Scotland	…Skotlandi	please	
…Wales	…Wales		

GETTING AROUND

How do I get to…?	Hvernig kemst ég til …?	Can you let me know	Gætirðu sagt mér
Left/right	Vinstri/hægri	when we get to…?	þegar við komum til…?
Straight ahead/back	Beint áfram/tilbaka	Is anyone sitting here?	Er þetta sæti laust?
Bus (in towns)	Strætó	Is this the road to…?	Er þetta leiðin til…?
Bus (long distance)	Rúta	Where are you going?	Hvert ertu að fara?
Where is the bus station?	Hvar er biðstöðin?	I'm going to…	Ég er að fara til…
Where is the bus stop?	Hvar er strætóstöðin?	Here's great, thanks	Hérna er ágætt, takk
Does this bus go to…?	Fer þessi rúta (strætó) til …??	Stop here, please	Stansaðu hérna, takk
		Single ticket to…	Einn miða, aðra leiðina til…
What time does it leave?	Hvenær fer hún?		
What time does it arrive?	Hvenær kemur hún til?	Return ticket to…	Einn miða, báðar leiðir til…
When is the next bus to…?	Hvenær fer næsta rúta (strætó) til…?		

ACCOMMODATION

Where's the youth hostel?	Hvar er farfuglaheimilið?	I'll take it	Ég ætla að taka það
Is there a hotel/ guesthouse round here?	Er hótel/gistiheimili hér nálægt?	How much is it a night?	Hvað kostar nóttin?
		It's too expensive	Það er of dýrt
I'd like a single/ double room…	Gæti ég fengið einsmanns herbergi/tveggjamanna herbergi…	Do you have anything cheaper?	Áttu eitthvað ódýrara?
		Can I leave the bags here until…?	Má ég geyma farangurinn hérna þangað til…?
…with a bath/shower	…með baði/sturtu		
Bed	Rúm		
Can I see it?	Má ég sjá það?	Can I camp here?	Má ég tjalda hérna?

DAYS AND MONTHS

Days and months are never capitalized. Days are declinable but months are not.

Monday	mánudagur	April	apríl
Tuesday	þriðjudagur	May	maí
Wednesday	miðvikudagur	June	júní
Thursday	fimmtudagur	July	júlí
Friday	föstudagur	August	ágúst
Saturday	laugardagur	September	september
Sunday	sunnudagur	October	október
January	janúar	November	nóvember
February	febrúar	December	desember
March	mars		

NUMBERS

1	einn	20	tuttugu
2	tveir	21	tuttugu og einn
3	þrír	22	tuttugu og tveir
4	fjórir	30	þrjátíu
5	fimm	31	þrjátíu og einn
6	sex	40	fjörutíu
7	sjö	50	fimmtíu
8	átta	60	sextíu
9	níu	70	sjötíu
10	tíu	80	áttatíu
11	ellefu	90	níutíu
12	tólf	100	hundrað
13	þrettán	101	hundrað og einn
14	fjórtán	120	hundrað og tuttugu
15	fimmtán	200	tvö hundruð
16	sextán	500	fimm hundruð
17	sautján	1000	þúsund
18	átján	1,000,000	milljón
19	nítján		

Glossary

Á river
Áætlun timetable
Ás small hill
Bær farm
Bíll car
Bjarg cliff, rock
Blindhæðir blind summit
Brú bridge
Dalur valley
Djúp deep inlet, long fjord
Drangur rock column
Einbreið brú single-lane bridge
Ey island
Eyri sand spit
Fell/fjall mountain
Ferja ferry
Fjörður fjord
Fljót large river
Flói bay
Flugvöllur airport
Foss waterfall
Gata street
Gil ravine, gill (ghyll)
Gisting accommodation

Gjá ravine
Heiði heath
Herbergi room
Hnjúkur peak
Höfði headland
Hraðbanki cash machine (ATM)
Hraun lava
Hver hot spring
Jökull glacier
Kirkja church
Laug warm pool
Lón lagoon
Reykur smoke
Rúta long-distance coach
Staður place
Strætó city bus
Tjörn lake, pond
Trachyte igneous rock, usually light grey and with a rough surface
Vatn lake
Vegur road
Vík bay
Völlur plain, flat land

Small print and index

A ROUGH GUIDE TO ROUGH GUIDES

Published in 1982, the first Rough Guide – to Greece – was a student scheme that became a publishing phenomenon. Mark Ellingham, a recent graduate in English from Bristol University, had been travelling in Greece the previous summer and couldn't find the right guidebook. With a small group of friends he wrote his own guide, combining a highly contemporary, journalistic style with a thoroughly practical approach to travellers' needs.

The immediate success of the book spawned a series that rapidly covered dozens of destinations. And, in addition to impecunious backpackers, Rough Guides soon acquired a much broader readership that relished the guides' wit and inquisitiveness as much as their enthusiastic, critical approach and value-for-money ethos.

These days, Rough Guides include recommendations from budget to luxury and cover more than 120 destinations around the globe, as well as producing an ever-growing range of ebooks.

Visit **roughguides.com** to find all our latest books, read articles, get inspired and share travel tips with the Rough Guides community.

Rough Guide credits

Editor: Brendon Griffin
Layout: Jessica Subramanian
Cartography: Katie Bennett
Picture editor: Lisa Jacobs
Proofreader: Jan McCann
Managing editor: Monica Woods
Assistant editor: Payal Sharotri
Production: Jimmy Lao

Cover photo research: Nicole Newman
Photographer: David Leffman
Editorial assistant: Freya Godfrey
Senior pre-press designer: Dan May
Programme manager: Gareth Lowe
Publisher: Keith Drew
Publishing director: Georgina Dee

Publishing information

This sixth edition published April 2016 by
Rough Guides Ltd,
80 Strand, London WC2R 0RL
11, Community Centre, Panchsheel Park,
New Delhi 110017, India
Distributed by Penguin Random House
Penguin Books Ltd, 80 Strand, London WC2R 0RL
Penguin Group (USA), 345 Hudson Street, NY 10014, USA
Penguin Group (Australia), 250 Camberwell Road,
Camberwell, Victoria 3124, Australia
Penguin Group (NZ), 67 Apollo Drive, Mairangi Bay,
Auckland 1310, New Zealand
Penguin Group (South Africa), Block D, Rosebank Office
Park, 181 Jan Smuts Avenue, Parktown North, Gauteng,
South Africa 2193
Rough Guides is represented in Canada by DK Canada, 320
Front Street West, Suite 1400,Toronto, Ontario M5V 3B6
Printed in Singapore
© David Leffman and James Proctor, 2016
Maps © Rough Guides

368pp includes index
A catalogue record for this book is available from the
British Library
ISBN: 978-0-24123-664-2
The publishers and authors have done their best to
ensure the accuracy and currency of all the information in
The Rough Guide to Iceland, however, they can accept
no responsibility for any loss, injury, or inconvenience
sustained by any traveller as a result of information or
advice contained in the guide.
1 3 5 7 9 8 6 4 2

Help us update

We've gone to a lot of effort to ensure that the sixth edition of **The Rough Guide to Iceland** is accurate and up-to-date. However, things change – places get "discovered", opening hours are notoriously fickle, restaurants and rooms raise prices or lower standards. If you feel we've got it wrong or left something out, we'd like to know, and if you can remember the address, the price, the hours, the phone number, so much the better.

Please send your comments with the subject line "**Rough Guide Iceland Update**" to mail@uk.roughguides.com. We'll credit all contributions and send a copy of the next edition (or any other Rough Guide if you prefer) for the very best emails.

Find more travel information, connect with fellow travellers and plan your trip on ⓦroughguides.com.

ABOUT THE AUTHORS

David Leffman was born and raised in the UK, spent twenty years in Australia, then relocated back to Britain in 2009. Since 1992 he has authored and co-authored guides to Australia, China, Indonesia, Iceland and Hong Kong for Rough Guides, Dorling Kindersley and others, ghost written a Chinese cookbook and contributed articles for various publications on subjects ranging from crime to martial arts and history. If he had spare time he'd go scuba diving.

James Proctor has been with Rough Guides since 1995 and is the company's original Nanook of the North. Co-author of the Rough Guides to Iceland, Sweden and Finland, James has also written the only English-language guides to the Faroe Islands and Lapland. One of his more obscure talents is speaking several Nordic languages – something which never fails to impress and bemuse most Icelanders (and most other people) he meets. Having lived and worked in the Nordic countries in the mid-1990s as the BBC's Scandinavia correspondent, James willingly travels north at any opportunity – clearly a Viking in a past life.

Acknowledgements

David Leffman: Thanks to Narrell, Njóla, Álfrun and Ármann.
James Proctor: James would like to thank the many people he met on the road who helped him on his way and answered his numerous queries. However, above all, special thanks are owed to Ólafur and Kristbjörn in Reykjavík, whose kindness and friendship remain constant. Thanks guys – and see you in Yorkshire!

Readers' updates

Thanks to all the readers who have taken the time to write in with comments and suggestions (and apologies if we've inadvertently omitted or misspelt anyone's name):

Lindsay Dannatt; Eleonora Delvecchio; David Reiner; Lisa Romano; Bart Schouten

Photo credits

All photos © Rough Guides except the following:
(Key: b-bottom; c-centre; l-left; r-right; t-top)

p.1 Robert Harding Picture Library/Lee Frost (t)
p.2 Getty Images
p.4 Travel Pictures Ltd/Tom Mackie Images Ltd
p.5 Arctic Adventure/Ⓦwellithor.com
p.9 Naturepl.com/Erlend Haarberg (t); Corbis/Arctic Images (b)
p.10 Robert Harding Picture Library/Heimir Haroar (bc)
p.11 Corbis/Dave G. Houser (tl); Corbis/Radius Images (tr); Getty Images/Patrick Dieudonne (b)
p.13 Alamy Images/Guy Brown (tr); Robert Harding Picture Library/Michael Nolan (br)
p.14 Corbis/Atlantide Phototravel
p.15 Alamy Images/Jean-François Hagenmuller (tl); Getty Images/Johnathan Ampersand Esper (b)
p.16 Getty Images/Bruno Morandi (t); ipaimages/Sigurdur Jokull Olafsson (b)
p.17 Getty Images/Baldur Pan Photography (t); Corbis/Barry Lewis/In Pictures (c); Getty Images/Holger Leue (b)
p.18 Alamy Images/Henk Meijer (t); Alamy Images/blickwinkel (b)
p.20 Courtesy of Reykjavík City Museum (t); Arctic Adventure/Ⓦellithor.com (b)
p.21 Corbis/Arctic Images (t); Alamy Images/Ken Cavanagh (b)
p.22 Ⓦphallus.is/Melkorka Magnúsdóttir (t); Corbis/Robert Harding Specialist Stock (c); Arctic Adventure/Ⓦellithor.com (b)
p.23 ⓌiStockphoto.com (t); Getty Images/Sven Zacek (b)
p.24 Corbis/Kevin Schafer
p.26 AA Photolibrary/James Tims
p.48 Getty Images/Arctic Images
p.51 Ⓦiceland.is/Ragnar Th Sigurdsson
p.65 Corbis/Arctic Images (t); Getty Images/Alessandro Grussu (bl); Alamy/imagebroker (br)
p.71 SuperStock/Bjarki Reyr (t); Harpa/Nic Lehoux (b)
p.79 Corbis/Layne Kennedy (tl); Getty Images/Magnus Hjorleifsson (tr); Morten Anderson/Creative Commons (b)
pp.90–91 Corbis/Peter Adams
p.93 Corbis/Guido Cozzi
p.117 Getty Images/AWL Images (t); Corbis/Patrick Dieudonne (b)
p.125 Getty Images/Jeremy Walker (b)

p.133 Photoshot/Ashley Cooper (tl); Corbis/Patrick Dieudonne (tr); Hans Strand (b)
pp.146–147 Alamy/Arctic Images
p.149 Corbis/Arctic Images
p.161 Getty Images/Tyler Stableford
p.175 ⓌiStockphoto.com (t)
p.181 Alamy Images/Alexey Stiop
pp.186–187 Alamy/Kevin Ebi
p.201 4Corners/Francesco Tremolada
p.207 Photoshot/Ashley Cooper (tl); Corbis/Franz Christoph Robiller (tr); Corbis/Olaf Krüger (b)
p.215 Alamy Images/Patrick Dieudonne
pp.222–223 Getty Images/Michele Falzone
p.225 The Herring Era Museum/Örlygur Kristfinnsson
p.237 Getty Images/Arctic Images (tl); Alamy Images/Franz Christoph Robiller (tr); Corbis/Arctic Images (bl); Alamy Images/INSADCO Photography (br)
p.251 Alamy Images/Christian Handl (tl); Getty Images/Win Initiative (tr); Ⓦflickr.com/letavua (b)
pp.258–259 Getty Images/Pearl Bucknell
p.261 Corbis/Arctic Images
p.271 Corbis/Arctic Images (tl); Getty Images/Olga Perdiguero (tr); Corbis/Sandro Santioli (b)
p.279 Alamy Images (t); Alamy/Rafael Angel Irusta Machin (bl); Myvatn Nature Baths (br)
pp.284–285 Getty Images/Sven Zacek
p.287 Alamy Images/eye35
p.295 SuperStock (t); Corbis/Arctic Images (b)
p.305 Getty Images/Patrick Dieudonne (tl); Getty Images/Arctic Images (tr); Travel Pictures Ltd/Travel Pictures Ltd (b)
pp.320–321 Alamy Images/imagebroker
p.323 Alamy Images/imagebroker (t)
p.329 Nordic Photos (t); Getty Images/Environment Images/UIG (b)
p.332 Getty Images/De Agostini

Front cover and spine Aerial view of Seljalandsfoss © AWL Images/Peter Adams
Back cover Skógafoss © Alamy Images/RGB Ventures (t); arctic fox © Robert Harding Picture Library/C. Huetter (bl); church, Vik © iStockphoto.com (br)

Index

Maps are marked in grey.
Words starting with Icelandic letters Þ/þ and Ö/ö come at the end of the alphabet.

Map symbols

The symbols below are used on maps throughout the book

═══	Paved road	⟋	Rift	⟋⟋⟋	Cliff	ⓘ	Information office
╌╌╌	Unpaved road	♦	Place of interest	)(	Bridge	@	Internet access
┄┄┄	4WD	⛳	Golf course	⋀	Campsite	⛽	Petrol station
═══	Pedestrian road	♖	Fort	⚓	Swimming pool		Building
╌╌╌	Footpath	♣	Museum	⋔	Lighthouse	✚	Church (town)
──	Ferry route	⚲	Church (regional)	⌂	Hut	◯	Stadium
⌃⌃	Mountains	⚑	Transmitter tower	✈	Airport		Park
▲	Mountain peak	⋙	Viewpont	✕	Airstrip		Beach
⫽	Volcano	⊙	Statue	★	Bus stop		Glacier
⟳	Crater	∴	Ruins	Ⓟ	Parking		Lava flow
⫽⫽	Hill	♨	Waterfall	✉	Post office		Cemetery
⌒	Cave	♨	Hot spring				

Listings key

■ Accommodation

● Cafés/budget meals/restaurants

■ Bars/clubs/live music venues

● Shops